Fashion Accessories

First published in France in 2008 by
Groupe Eyrolles as Accessoires de mode
61, bd Saint-Germain
75240 Paris Cedex 05
HYPERLINK "http://www.editions-eyrolles.com" www.editions-eyrolles.com

English language edition first published in Great Britain 2009
by A&C Black Publishers
36 Soho Square
London W1D 3QY
www.acblack.com

ISBN 978 1 408 11058 4

A CIP catalogue record for this book is available from the British Library.

Ouvrage publie avec l'aide du Ministeere francais charge de la
Culture – Central National du Livre

Translation by Sasha Wardell
Cover design by Sutchinda Thompson

Printed and bound in China

studies in fashion

Fashion Accessories

Olivier Gerval

A & C Black London

Contents

CHAPTER 4
CRAFTSMANSHIP AND MANUFACTURE

CHAPTER V
STEP-BY-STEP

CHAPTER 6
SALES AND PROMOTION

ANNEXES

Preface

Le parfum de l'émotion, l'amour du travail et la perfection de la coupe sont pour moi la ponctuation

The scent of emotions, a love of work and the perfection of the cut are, for me, the factors which punctuate, and inform, style. My inspiration is drawn from words, scents, images, daily sounds and, by putting them down on a blank page, they serve as the starting point for my work. But it is the sensuality of touch which determines my vision for a new season. My accessories, which reinforce a silhouette, can be objects of desire or even dreams come true which, after having been worn, become the next generation of treasured souvenirs.

The fascination I hold for women's accessories has led me to concentrate on two important themes, both of which are re-invented each season: the ballet pump and pearls. Pursuing my day-dream I am once again transported into the world of my eternal source of inspiration, Jeanne Lanvin.

Here there is a burst of plastic and metal, created into huge sparkling items of jewellery which accentuate the wrist, or the incredible 'Himalayan' sandals in fuchsia pink worn by the 2007 winter season woman as she walks towards the future. Last season is now redundant, the giant orchids which either floated on the shoulders of a dress or were pinned onto a lapel, have been left behind. As have my shoes, even, with their vibrant colours ....

In this current book Olivier Gerval recounts the influence of the accessory. He describes how a belt can accentuate the waist by refining or lowering it, how the body can be lengthened or shortened, or how a shoe alters the small of the back or the curve of the leg, all of which have an effect on the proportions of a garment. He also illustrates how an over-sized brooch can obscure a collar, how multiple strings of pearls can decorate a plunging neck line, or even how a bejewelled handbag, hanging from the crook of an arm and brushing against the hip, can balance up the body.

Accessories can dress a silhouette up or down, either accentuating, or detracting, from its style and, being the designer's signature and personality, they can sometimes complement or contradict a garment.

Fashion Accessories is aimed at anyone interested in the fashion world whether they be aspiring students, fashion enthusiasts, amateurs or professionals, window shoppers or even those who simply seek the adrenalin-rush of the catwalk.

Alber Elbaz

Foreword

Fashion Accessories, the second book in the *Studies in Fashion* series, reveals the secrets of a flagship product of the textile industry – the accessory. It evokes the notion of being superfluous when, in reality, it is essential to fashion. The accessory, in fact, 'makes' the style, placing it firmly in position in the world of designer labels, being more representative of a style than an era.

Originally, couturiers did not design their accessories. This was done by accessory companies for the fashion houses, as is still the case in fact with the boot-maker Massaro for Chanel. The conception of an accessory, as we see throughout this publication is, in effect, closely linked to its manufacturing specifications relying on traditional skills, often regionally-based. An example of this is found in the Isère region which has long-remained the international capital of women's footwear.

France has successfully developed the art of the accessory. The designs of Gripoix, Roger Scemana, and Robert Goessens, fine garment specialists to the fashion industry have become museum pieces today. Remembering also that in the 20th century women's footwear was French in origin with designers such as Roger Vivier, Charles Jourdan and his prestigious brand Séducta, or with Carel and Durer.

The Swiss also govern a large segment of this industry with their monopoly on luxury clocks and watches by manufacturers such as Jaeger-Lecoultre and Omega to name but a couple. Swatch perpetuated this tradition in the 1980s by creating more affordable limited-edition pieces and targeting new markets. During the following decades, with the boom in the sports-leisure industry, Tag Heuer, renowned for his waterproof diving watches, enlisted the photographer Peter Lindberg, with his artistic advertising campaigns, and thus elevated the perception of his products. More recently, Hamilton, the American GI's watch brand, chose a Swiss mechanism in an attempt to adapt to market trends and thereby offer a high-quality product.

The Swiss are a very good example of how to successfully adapt exceptional skills of luxury-goods manufacturing to those of mass-production.

We are also aware that Morocco is famous for its leather goods, that silver and metal work are an important part of Asian heritage, that bone and precious stones date back to pre-Colombian civilisations and that pearls come from Japan. One only has to travel the world to discover the abundance of material available for accessories originating from a variety of lands. This notion of travel, dear to the heart of the famous suitcase/briefcase maker Louis Vuitton, is just one of the characteristics of the accessory.

Nowadays, every label offers a 'total look' with clothes and their accessories forming a coherent whole. The fashion house, Dior, which was created in 1947, illustrates this evolution by demonstrating the important role that the accessory played in its collections. More surprising, perhaps, is the fact that accessory labels find themselves in ready-to-wear collections. Gucci, for example, was initially an accessory label around which Tom Ford created a whole world and capitalised upon – the idea being, of course, to cover every market. Prada has just recently launched a range of trainers which incorporates street-wear into their luxury ranges thus underlining the importance the accessory holds today at the luxury-end of the market.

This book aims to illustrate these facts by presenting a brief history of the accessory, a tour of the footwear world, including some distinctive designers as well as the most representative products in this sector. The different skills and techniques required for scarf, jewellery and shoe manufacture are explained, as are the colour choices, pattern designs and step-by-step production stages of a variety of handbags. All of which conclude in a section dedicated to the promotion of these various products.

The presence and choice of an accessory is never without effect. If the famous painting of *Olympia* in 1865 by the impressionist painter Edouard Manet (1832-83) attracted criticism, it was mainly because the subject was not entirely nude: she wears a black scarf around her neck, a large flower in her hair and a golden bracelet. Also, she exudes a certain arrogance. The presence of these accessories contributes to the distancing from the traditionally accepted representation of the nude. This underlines feminine provocation, as well as a lack of morals, both of which were particularly disturbing for that period. All of this is part of the courtesan world – completely different from that of the chaste and unadorned Venus upon which the painting is modelled.

If the archetype of the 19th century 'kept-woman' is to be replaced (evident in Catherine Deneuve's portrayal of a high-class prostitute in Louis Bunuel's film *Belle de Jour*, amongst others), one notices that the use of the accessory defines a certain era. Accessories also accompany economic and social evolutions as well as a change in moral values, each possessing their own history. This is well-documented in museum collections depicting their progression through the ages. A revival of the accessory allows us to understand the concept of the fashion house. For example, Didier Ludot has invented a new metier – that of vintage fashion. In his boutique at the Palais-Royal, he breathes new life into the accessory with the *Lady Di* handbag by Dior, the *Kelly* by Hermès or *Audrey's* glasses by Pierre Marly – all of which have subsequently become cult products.

Apart from the luxury image that it evokes, Louis Vuitton's monogrammed luggage is full of nostalgia, reminiscent of the great transatlantic voyages and the lifestyle which accompanied them. Likewise with Hermès, and his traditional equestrian imagery, we are plunged into the novels of Maupassant and 19th

Chapter 1 - Introduction

century Paris. The skills associated with these accessories represent 'old' Europe. Emerging countries, with their new-found wealth, dream vicariously of adopting this lifestyle by looking towards the West. It is also the wish of the middle-classes, from Asia in particular, who possess a large amount of disposable income and who strive to be different from their parent's generation. Faced with the global infatuation for designer labels, we notice the creation of distribution lines which have become a major development in our world. This phenomenon is evident when we look at the luxury fashions in the Louis Vuitton stores on the Champs-Elysées in Paris, on the Avenue Omotesando in Tokyo or on Fifth Avenue in New York. These are the ambassadors of luxury and French craftsmanship where limited edition and mass-production jostle side by side.

Today, the accessory is closely linked to particular cultural movements. Punks with their body-piercing demonstrated a form of 'confrontational' accessory opposed to established ethical codes. In the middle of the 1980s Madonna gave another meaning to the rosary by adopting subversive undertones. At the same time, Alain Mikly made spectacles attractive – gone are the days when a pair of glasses conjured up a staidness and seriousness synonymous with secretaries and teachers. Glasses are now colourful, giving a new style to the face, allowing people to express another side of their personality.

This chapter illustrates these developments and the eternal reinventing of fashion, drawing from the past the concepts of tomorrow. The origins of these products are presented through different designers and labels, museum visits and a world tour of the shoe. Lanvin, Louis Vuitton, Loulou de la Falaise, Yazbukey, Sonia Rykiel, Christian Louboutin and Eléna Cantacuzène also reveal their ideas and skills.

The History of Louis Vuitton

1

2

A Vocation – Travel

For more than 150 years the House of Louis Vuitton has epitomised French tradition and craftsmanship. Right from the beginning, it knew how to combine skill with creativity, history with modernity and tradition with innovation. In 1835, Louis Vuitton arrived in Paris and became an apprentice packager making trunks and luggage connected with travel. In 1853 he became the favourite packager of Empress Eugénie and a year later created his own insignia which his successors have developed into a luxury fashion and leather goods brand.

The second half of the 19th century coincided with the introduction into Europe of Japanese art and fashion. Georges Vuitton, Louis' son, was inspired by the traditional Japanese motifs to such an extent that he created the now world-famous Louis Vuitton canvas monogram in 1896 in response to this. This period was also synonymous with the great transatlantic voyages and, from the outset, this brand was linked to the spirit of travel: the steamer bag, designed in 1901, bears witness to this as a cult object. This completely new product predates the 'holdall' with its concept of a cylindrical travel bag which can subsequently be stored flat when empty.

An International Reputation

By the beginning of the 20th century, Louis Vuitton had become established in London and New York forging an international reputation for himself. Today his luxury brand is found in more than 350 shops worldwide. His luggage has been linked to illustrious Hollywood

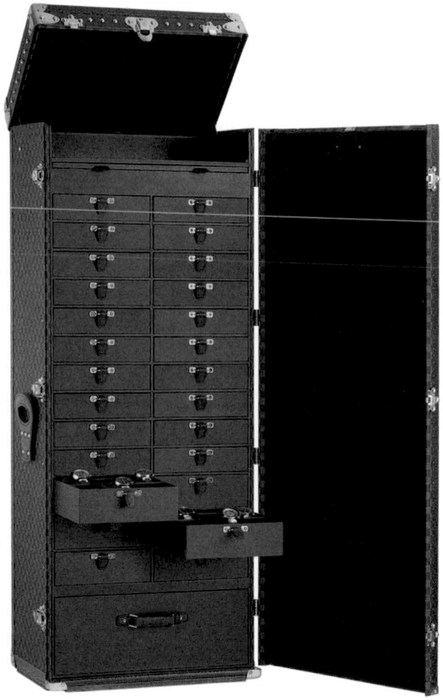

3

4

stars from Cary Grant to Jennifer Lopez, including Marlene Dietrich and Sharon Stone. In 1987 Louis Vuitton merged with Moet-Hennessy to form the LMVH group – the worldwide number one of luxury travel-goods with special commissions giving the brand its originality. Each year the Asnières studio makes some 450 travel trunks, dog carriers, portable leather mini-bars etc.

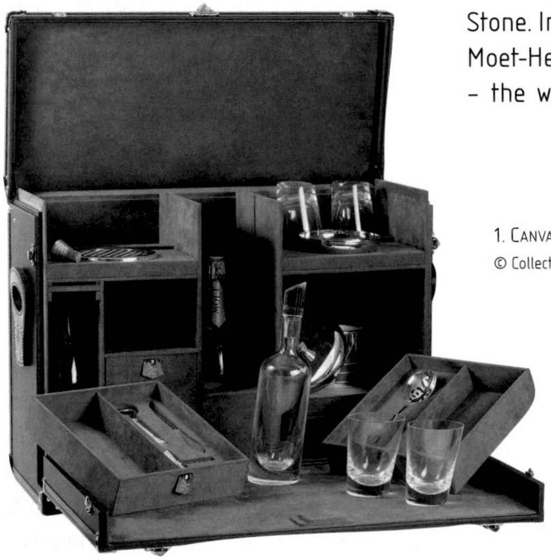

5

1. Canvas steamer bag, forerunner of the soft bag.
© Collection Louis Vuitton/Laurent Bremaud/Lb Productions.

2. Detail of the canvas monogram 'destined for all items of luggage such as suitcases, briefcases' confirming authentication of the Louis Vuitton trademark,which was registered at the National Office of Industrial Property on March 21st 1905.
© Louis Vuitton Archives.

3. Canvas check case designed to transport 100 watches, 2004
© Phillipe Jumin/Lb Productions.

4. Red leather jewellery case with red Moroccan lining, comprising several drawers lined with red silk-velvet. It even has a secret compartment for private correspondance. This piece was created in 2005 to celebrate the year of France in China, as a homage to China's prosperous millenium. It was exhibited in Shanghai in the 'Creative Audacity' show organised by the Comité Colbert – an association which promotes luxury French houses.
© Lb Productions

5. Mini-bar in slate-coloured Taiga leather with a dark grey interior equipped with a bottle of champagne and flutes.
© Collection Louis Vuitton/Philippe Jumin/Lb Productions.

Louis Vuitton's Travel Museum

1

2

3

A family museum

Since 1854, all the traditions, innovations and fundamental values belonging to the Louis Vuitton brand have been housed under one roof in the Louis Vuitton Travel Museum at Asnières. For more than a century now, Louis and his descendants have lived in this house, only a stone's throw away from the production studio which was opened in 1859. It is here where craftsmen still produce high quality, bespoke examples of hat-boxes, travelling wardrobes or vanity cases. The museum is private however, with visits reserved for special guests and employees of Louis Vuitton only.

Another travel history

The museum is organised around the four great travel themes: sea, air, rail and road. This reflects the evolution of the different means of transport which accompanied the Industrial Revolution of the 19th century. These trunks, and their accessories, which have crossed oceans and continents are, in their own right, classic luxury objects evoking a timeless aura implicitly combining aesthetics and function. One can also admire the striped canvas trunk-bed, the leather tea-case and even the car-trunk - the *Excelski* and *Excelsior* predate modern car-boots (trunks). To complete the celebration of these pieces which is entirely dedicated to travel and travellers, one wing of the museum houses the personal collection of Gaston Louis Vuitton, the founder's grandson. This contains some several thousand trunks, cases and travel items from different eras - some of which date from the end of the 14th century.

1. *Excelsior* car-trunk in Vuittonite canvas, 1923. Perfectly shaped to fit into a car.
© Louis Vuitton collection.

2. *Ideale* case in natural calf skin, 1905. Also called the 'Parfaite', this case can hold 5 men's suits, an overcoat, 18 shirts, underwear, 4 pairs of shoes, a hat, 3 walking sticks and an umbrella.
© Louis Vuitton/Antoine Jarrier collection.

3. *Wardrobe 110* in monogrammed canvas, 1930. Made since 1875, these cases mean the traveller never has to unpack.
© Louis Vuitton collection.

4. Travelling tea-case in textured leather, 1926. Made especially for the Maharajah of Baroda, contains everything required for a cup of tea. The hot-plate, teapot and water pot break down into a dozen pieces which fit snugly into one another.
© Louis Vuitton/ Antoine Jarrier collection.

5. Striped canvas trunk-bed, around 1878. Identical model to that of Pierre Savorgnan de Brazza (1852 - 1905) the French explorer who undertook many African expeditions, notably in the Congo where he founded the town of Brazzaville in 1880.
© Louis Vuitton/Antoine Jarrier collection.

4

5

The history of the shoe

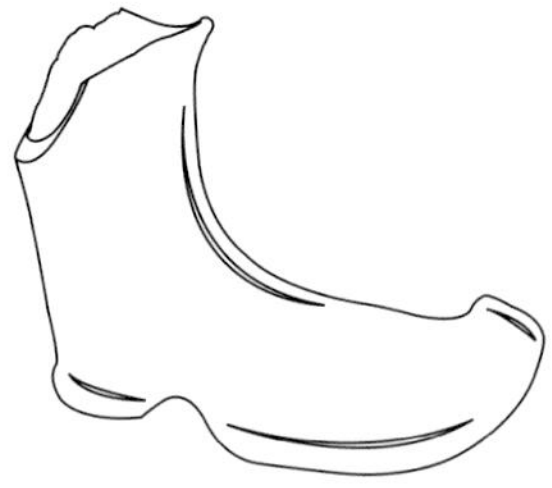

1

2

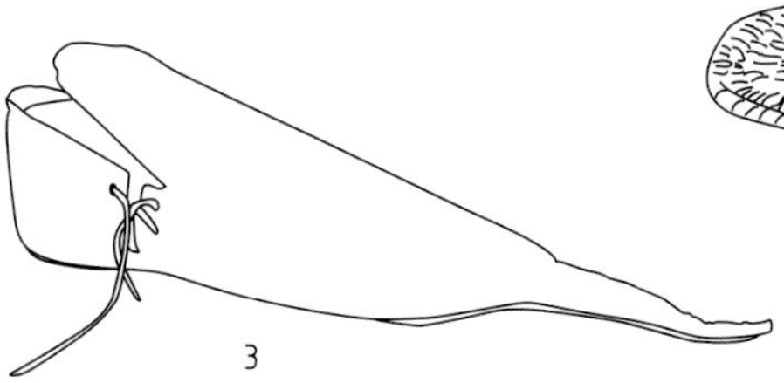

3

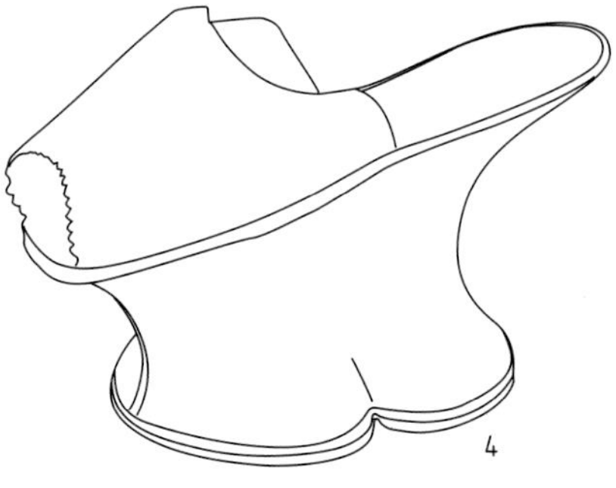

4

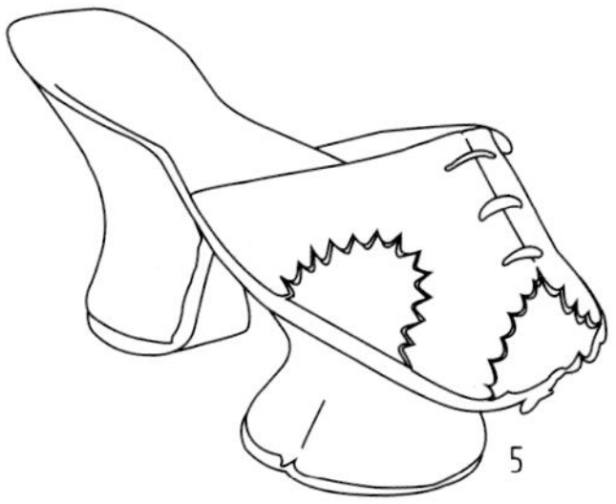

5

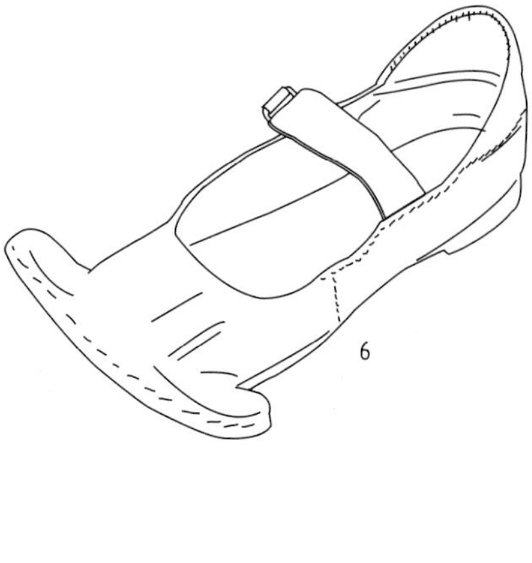

6

Functions and uses

A product is usually made for a specific function with its development often reflecting the cultural and economical evolution of the society from which it has originated. This development is particularly noticeable in the case of the shoe. For example, simple sandals with leather thongs have become real footwear nowadays. So much so that they are indispensable leisure accessories allowing a certain level of sporting performance.

Sport and leisure have become important sources of inspiration and are used more and more in shoe design with an emphasis being placed on unisex accessories, such as the trainer or riding boot. However, it must be noted that unisex shoes have existed since the Middle Ages with the *poulaine,* or pointed shoe (fig. 3) – both men and women wore it to great adversity for it was regarded as obscene due to the length of its point.

The socio-cultural character of the shoe very quickly adopted an entirely protective function. The fact that shoes were placed alongside jewellery and other belongings in ancient burials, indicates the great reverence in which these accessories were held. The aesthetic role of the shoe, which could alter the shape of a silhouette, was very evident in sophisticated Italian courts: footwear of the Middle Ages became more refined shoes, the heels were embellished becoming higher and the fabrics more sought-after. This aesthetic quest occasionally led to extravagant models as with the example (figs 16/17) which shows a mule with a *Cromwell or Himalayan* heel from the beginning of the 20th century. This type of heel still has a place on today's catwalk.

Fashion and historical models

Shape, fabric and manufacturing methods are all specific characteristics which determine the model of a shoe. The colours used in the past were essentially natural tones, however, progress in the textile industry completely over-turned this permitting a much wider colour range, as well as the possibility of imitating expensive materials with synthetic ones. Equally the invention of zips and elastic, allowing for better fitting around the calf for calf-length and ankle boots, contributed to the advent of new designs.

Past models, notably those which used rare or precious fabrics such as damask, or brocade embroidered with golden threads, have been a constant source of inspiration. For example, applied to an Egyptian sandal (fig. 2*)* or a Venetian chopine (figs 4 and 5*)*, today's techniques and materials allow them to be revisited and made into contemporary accessories.

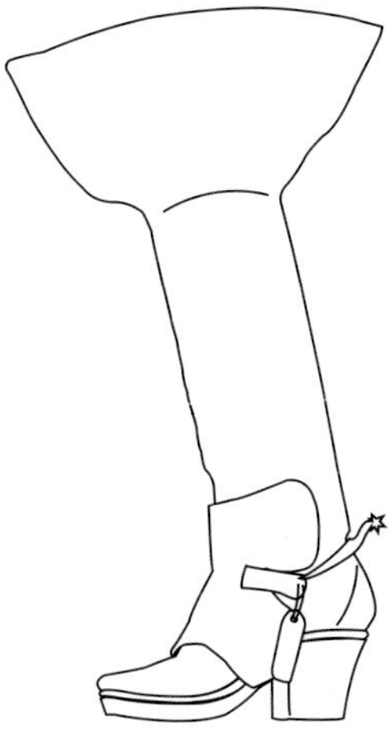

7

8

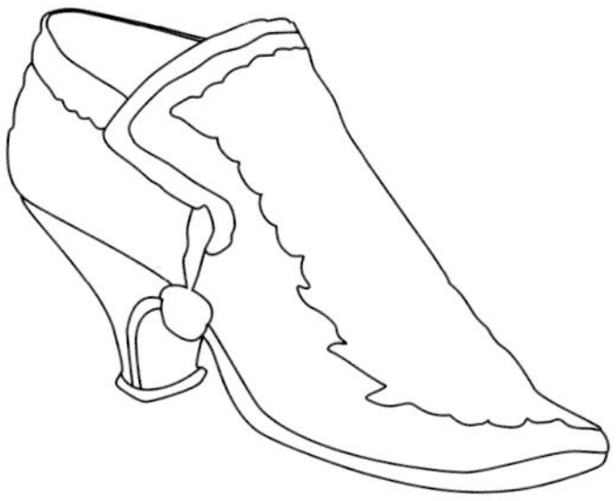

9

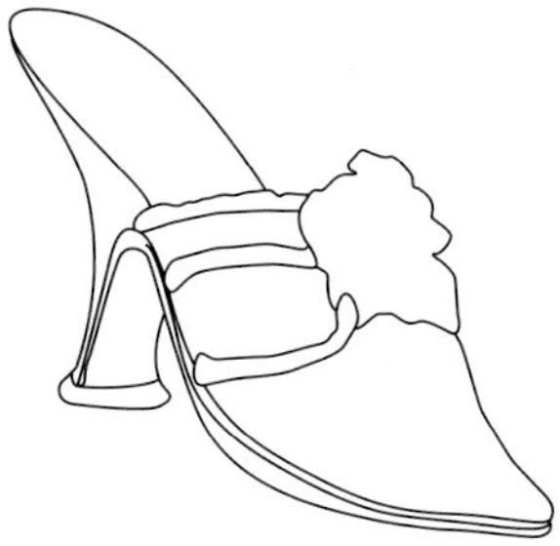

10

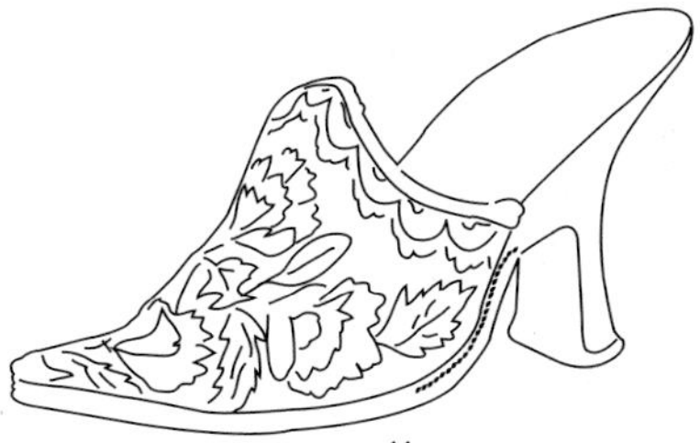

11

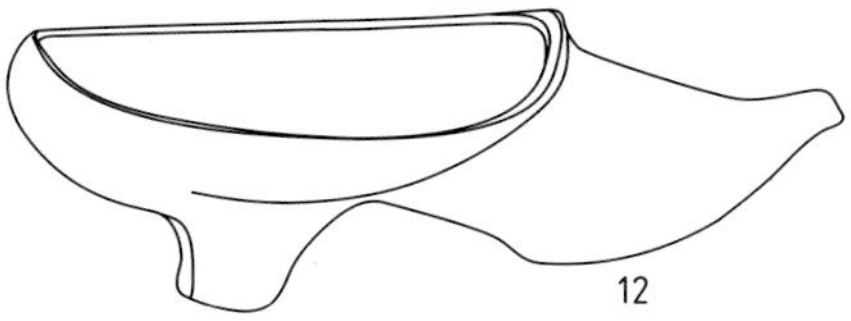

12

1. Clay shoe, Azerbaidjan, 12th and 13th century BC.

2. Egyptian sandal made from vegetable fibres.

3. Leather poulaine or pointed shoe, late Middle Ages.

4. Chopine, Venice, 16th century.

5. Chopine, Venice – around 1600s.

6. Man's shoe - around 1530s-1540s.

7. Musketeer's boot, France, 17th century.

8. Woman's shoe, Italy 17th century.

9. Woman's shoe, France, 17th century.

10. Woman's mule, France - around 1720–1730.

11. Embroidered mule, France between 1700 and 1750.

12. Wooden clog, France, 18th century.

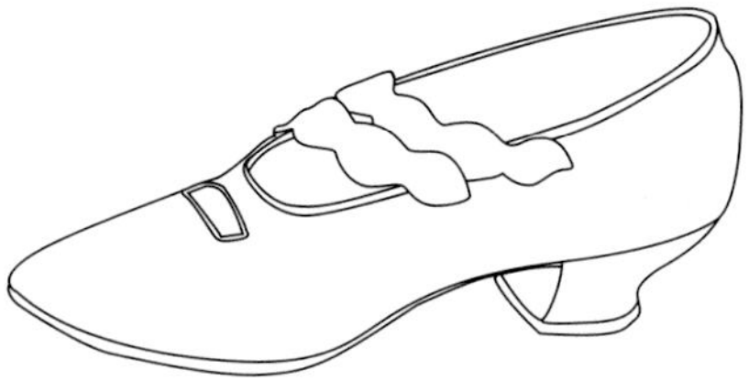

13

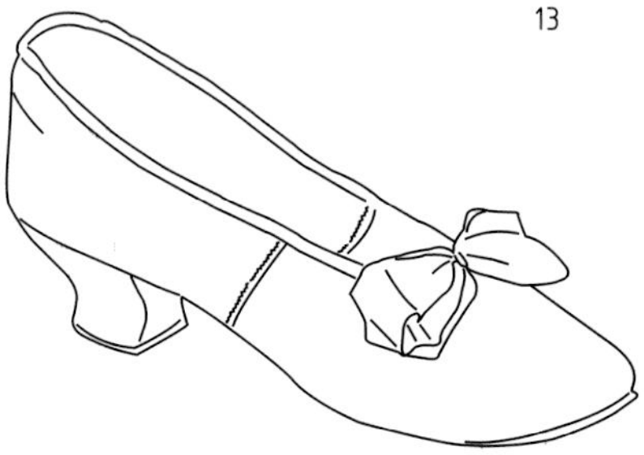

14

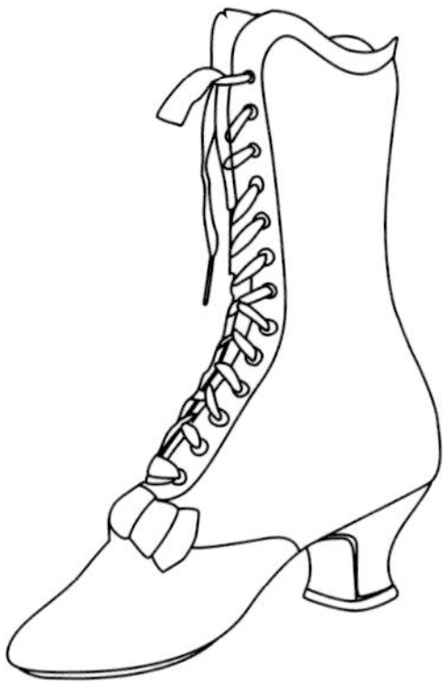

15

16

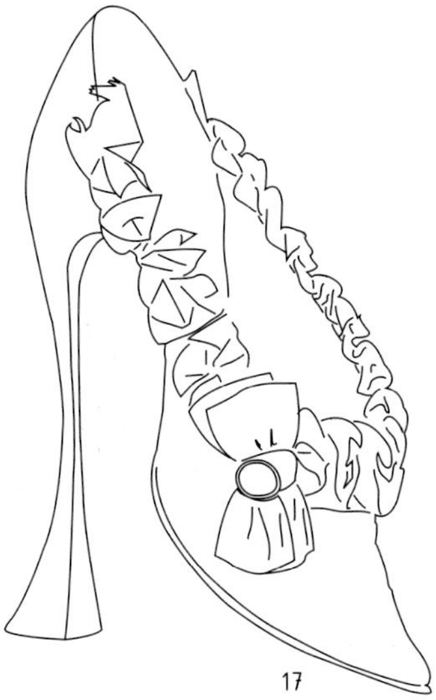

17

Certain models, however, transcend history to become 'classics' - this being the case with the ankle boot, pump, court shoe, etc. Timelessly, the clog has survived the ups and downs of rural life and has now entered city-life finding itself on the podiums with Dirk Bikkemberg, for example.

Others reappear sporadically. This being the case with platform shoes which derive their origins from the *zazous*, or swingers, in the 1930s reappearing with the ska and new wave movements of the 1980s and 1990s. In fact, the first platform shoes appeared during the Vichy regime – a decree was announced which insisted that all the hair, cut off in hair salons, was gathered up and mixed with fibres to make slippers. To defy this, the young kept their long hair by stuffing it into the soles of their shoes – hence the birth of the platform shoe!

13. Woman's shoe, France, 19th century.

14. Bride's shoe, France around 1900.

15. Woman's ankle boot, Paris – around 1875.

16. Evening shoe, France, 1920.

17. Mule with 20 cm heel, decorated with little cabochons, Vienna, Austria – around 1900.

18. Shoe designed by Salvatore Ferragamo in 1923 for Cecil B. de Mille's film *The Ten Commandments.*

19. Ballet pump.

20. Heel-less court shoe, 1950.

21. Duc de Guise, Louis XV heel, Paris – beginning of 20th century.

22. Shoe designed by Massaro for Chanel, 1958.

23. Platform-heeled sandal, 1990.

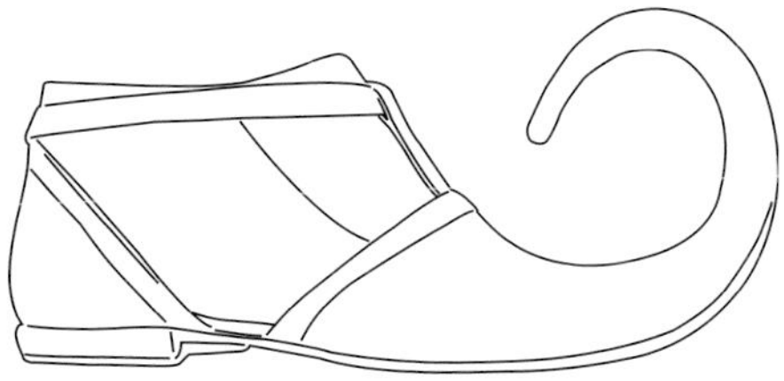

18

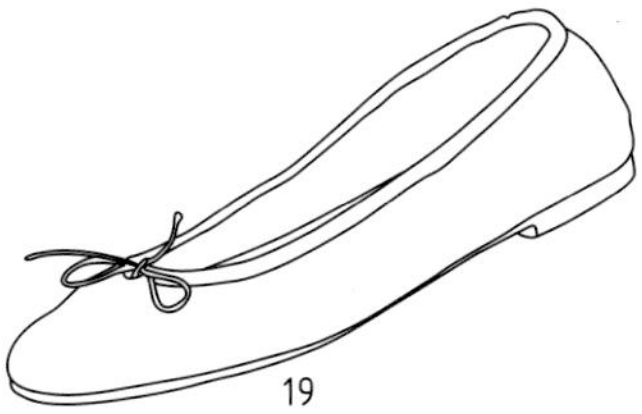

19

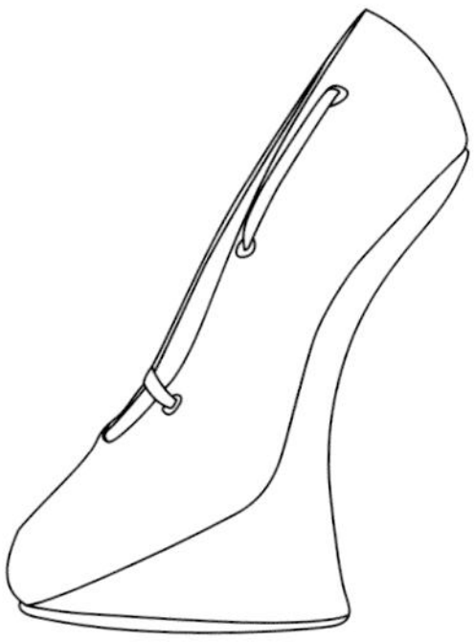

20

21

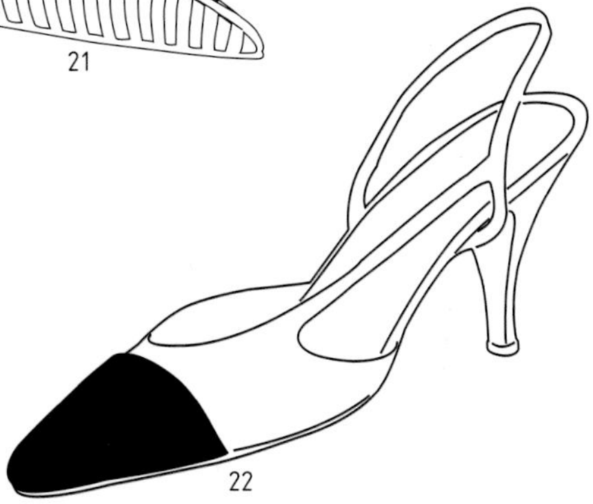

22

23

World shoes

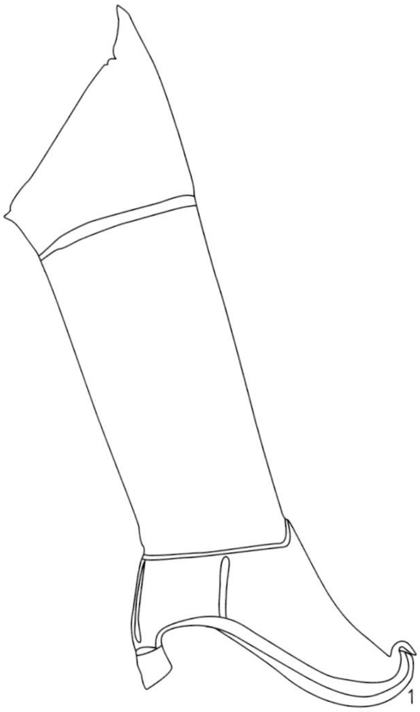

1

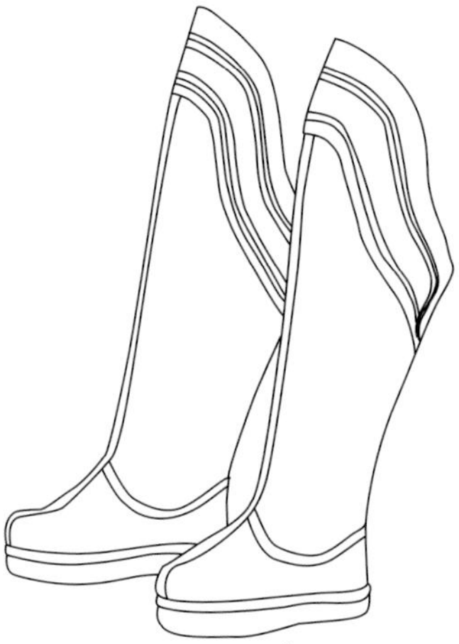

2

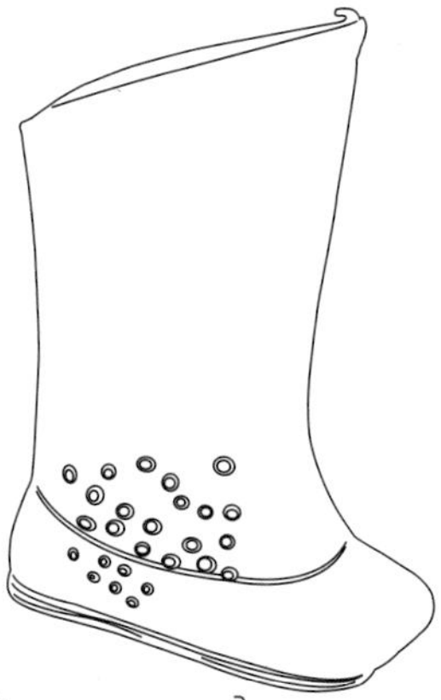

3

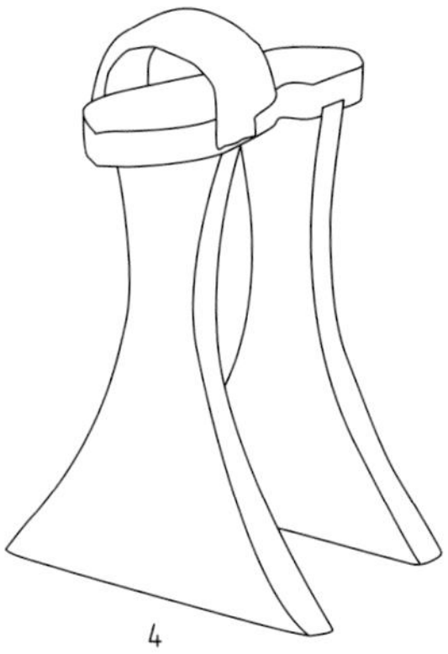

4

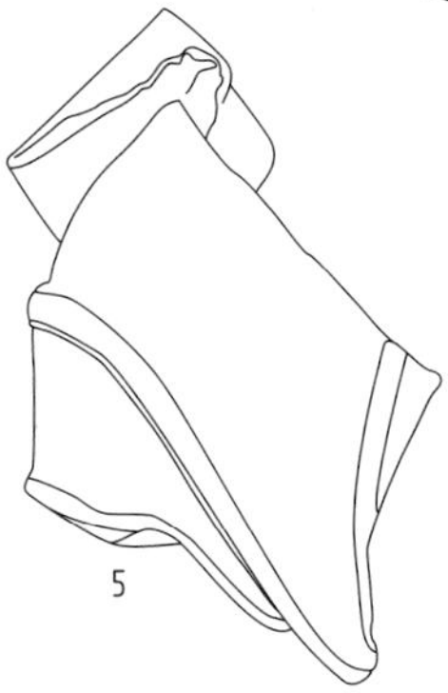

5

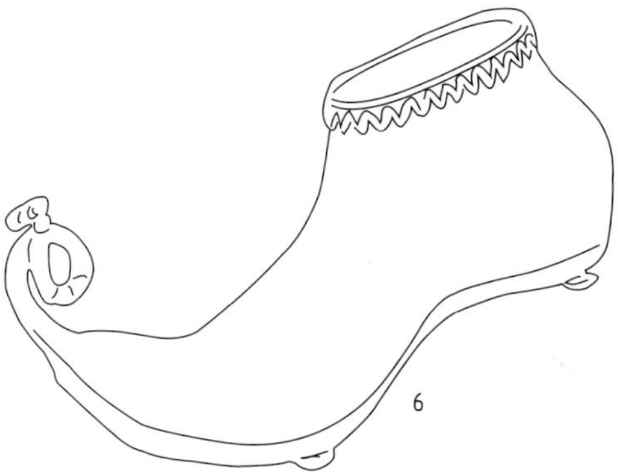

6

Social references

People, and their particular culture, are distinguished by their clothes and accessories. It is essential to emphasise the importance of the social context in which groups of individuals make in their shoe choices, i.e. fabrics, shapes, uses etc.

By making a 'world tour of the shoe' we soon realise that there are many sources of inspiration from the past which have influenced its evolution. The West has adopted several styles from other cultures - the moccasin, which originated from the New World (*figs 8 and 9*), the ballet pump from China (fig. 11*)* and the *babouche* or Turkish slipper, from Morocco (fig.7*)*.

The shoe is not only known for its practicality but also as a symbolic accessory indicative of power and religious persuasion. Several cultures have accessories linked to a rites of passage which mark milestones in one's life such as birth, becoming an adult, marriage and mourning. With the Akan of West Africa, in Ghana and the Ivory Coast for example, sandals inlaid with gold are indicative of royalty.

Particular uses

The foot has frequently played an important part in the history of civilisations with the smallness of women's feet often being highly valued. The, sadly, infamous 'bound feet' of Chinese women and the tale of Cinderella in Western civilisation bear witness to this. In these examples, the shoe can misshape a foot to the point of deformation in spectacular fashion!

The heel is an essential part of the

shoe. Beyond its aesthetic role, the heel plays a particular function as is evident in Figure 4. Here the heel is very high so that the wearer does not get her feet wet once she has stepped out of the bath. This type of shoe was widespread in Turkey and other Eastern countries in the 18th and 19th centuries. In Japan, for example, the geishas also wore high-heels (fig. 10) which protected their feet from the torrential rains.

Nowadays the Birkenstock brand, with their back-to-nature design and anti-fashion statement, has become the archetypal cultural exchange between northern and southern Europeans.

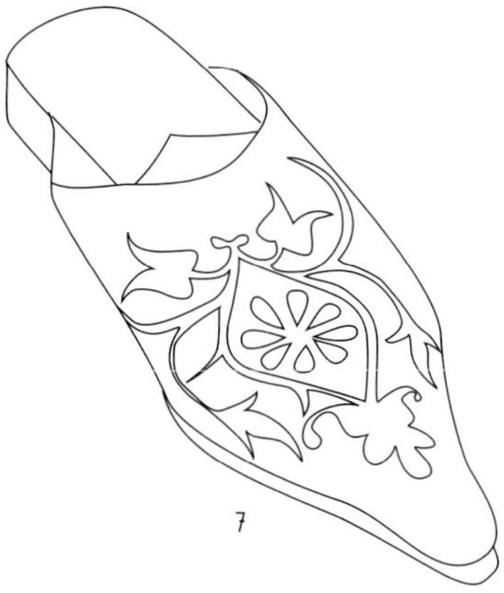

7

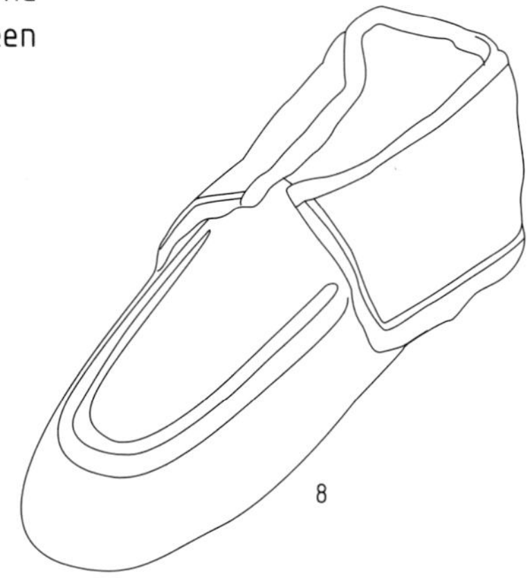

8

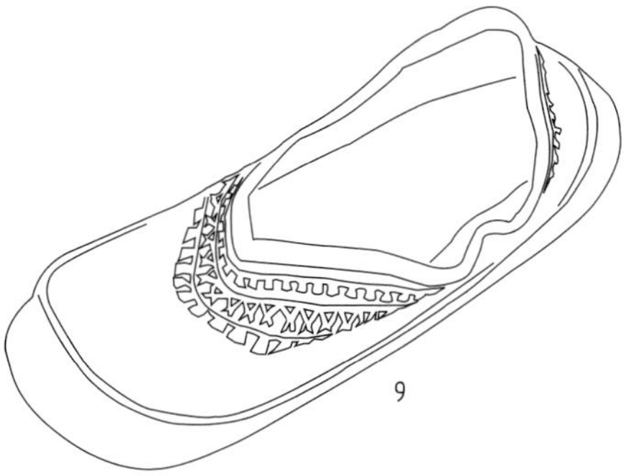

9

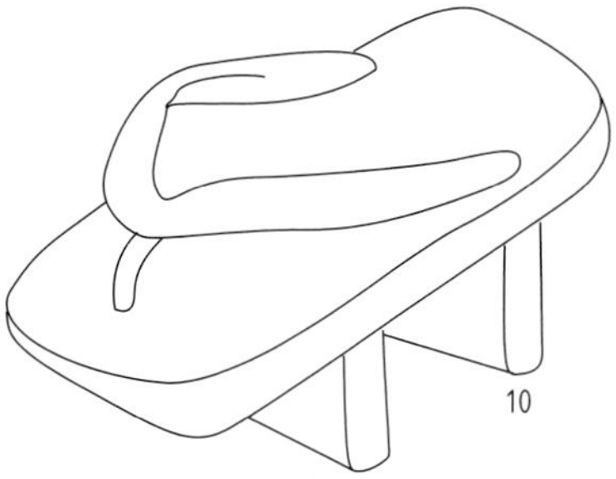

10

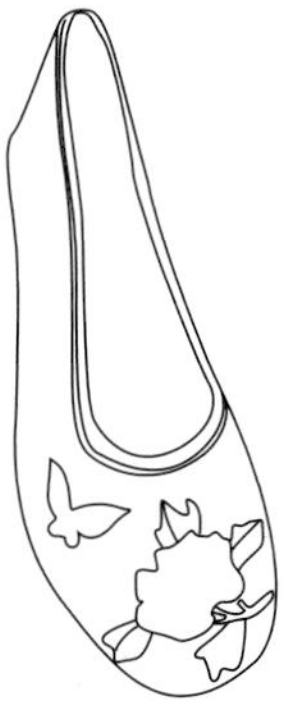

11

1. Riding boots with a deer-hoof shaped heel, Persia, 17th century.

2. Silk Mandarin boots, Kangxi reign, China (1662–1722).

3. Woman's satin boot, embroidered with mirror glass, China, 19th century.

4. Wooden geta shoe, Middle East, 19th century.

5. Wedding shoe, China.

6. Shoe with turned-up point, India.

7. Babouche or Turkish sandal, Morocco.

8. Woman's moccasin, North America 19th century.

9. Man's shoe, walrus and sea-calf, Alaska – beginning of 20th century.

10. Geisha or geta shoe, Japan.

11. Ballet pump, China.

Charles Jourdan's shoe museum

1

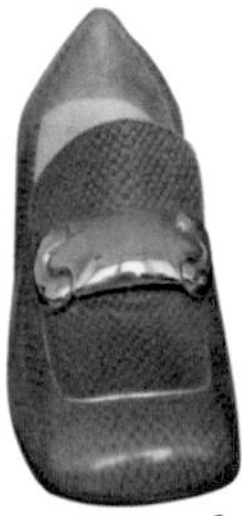

2

3

4

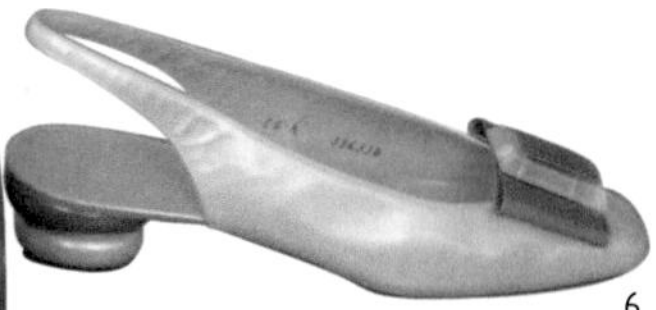

6

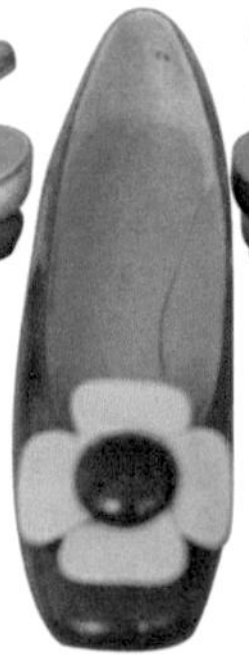

5

7

9

8

Ready-to-wear shoes

The Charles Jourdan brand, which recently disappeared, epitomised French shoe style using more geometric models than those found in Italian shoe designs. In the 1930s Charles Jourdan created a line of ready-to-wear shoes under the name of Séducta whose logo was a pair of stag's antlers. In 1957 Roland Jourdan, the founder's son, launched an idea which brought him international success – that of a court shoe sporting a heel in the style of Louis XV or Charles IX which was available in three widths, twenty colours and every size. In that same year, just one of these styles available in every colour possible, was presented in the boutique which opened in the Rue de la Madeleine, Paris. More than the product, it was the promotion of the brand which was placed in the limelight with Dior quickly signing up the French shoe designer. This paved the way for his entrance into the haute couture world of the 1960s.

A flagship brand

Patrick Cox, who had been the brand's artistic director, believed that Charles Jourdan's architectural design and ground-breaking approach to colour had been the two pivotal elements responsible for the success of the Charles Jourdan company. However, it should be noted that designers such as André Pérugia, Roger Vivier and Hervé Leger contributed equally to this success.

The company has kept a number of styles from this era which are currently on show at the Charles Jourdan museum. This museum works alongside that of Roman's Shoe Museum (Isère) both of which promote the skilled craftsmanship of a region which has specialised in footwear for a long time.

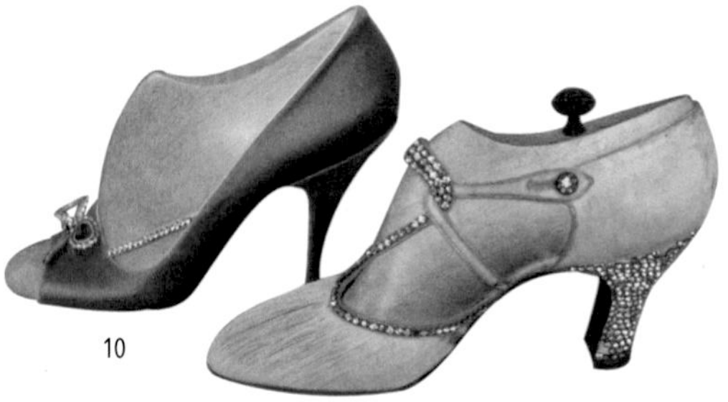

10

11

1. Christian Dior, 1969-1970.

2. Charles Jourdan, 1969-1970, style *Puma 1.*

3. Charles Jourdan, 1969-1970, style *Charlie.*

4. Charles Jourdan, 1967, style *Nankin vert.*

5. Charles Jourdan, 1967, style *Niki.*

6. Charles Jourdan, 1967, style *Oracle.*

7. Charles Jourdan, 1955, style *Agadir.*

8 & 9. Charles Jourdan, 2002-2003, designer Patrick Cox, style *Zoom.*

10. Charles Jourdan, 1950, mock-up « 7595 ».

11. Charles Jourdan, 1924, style *Grure.*

12. Charles Jourdan, 1975, style *Compensee osier.*

13. Charles Jourdan, 1972, style *Sans pan.*

14. Charles Jourdan, 1976, style *Comedia.*

15. Charles Jourdan, 1976, style *Goya.*

16. Charles Jourdan, 1976, style *Elvire.*

17. Charles Jourdan, 1955, *Le Poisson de Braque.*

18. Charles Jourdan, 1980, style *Alicante.*

19. Charles Jourdan, 1980, style *Christel.*

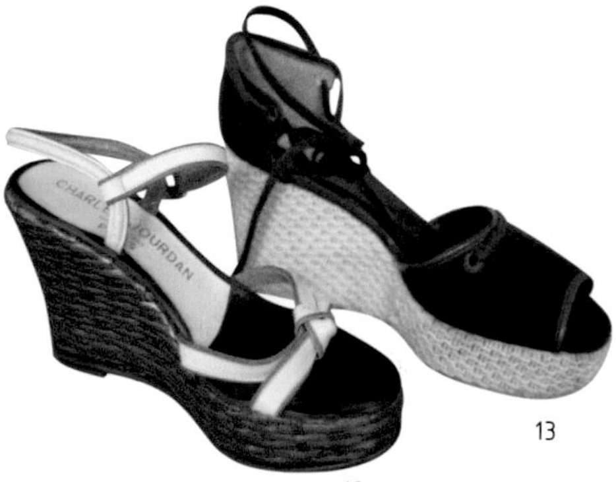

13

12

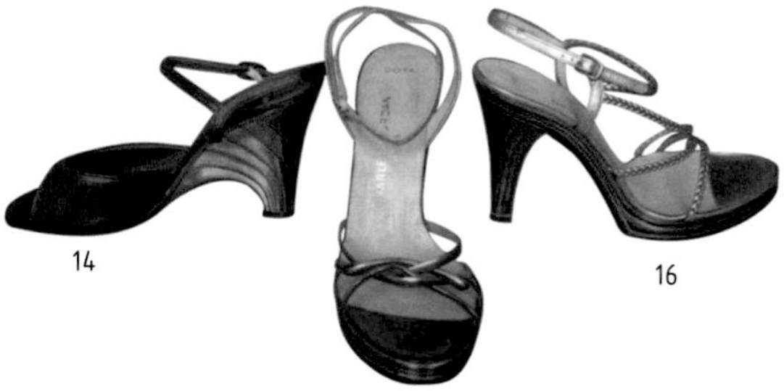

14

16

15

17

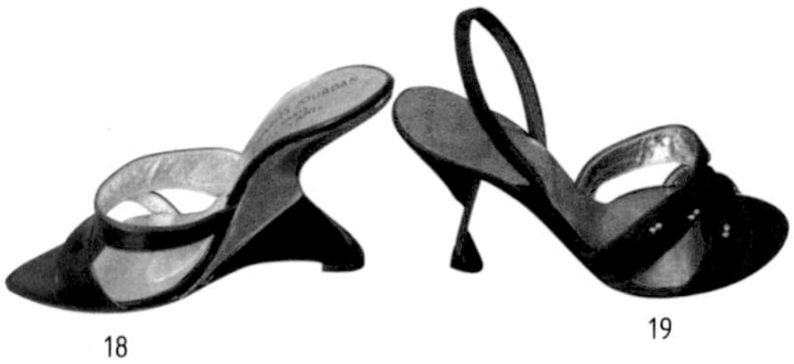

18

19

Didier Ludot and vintage bags

1

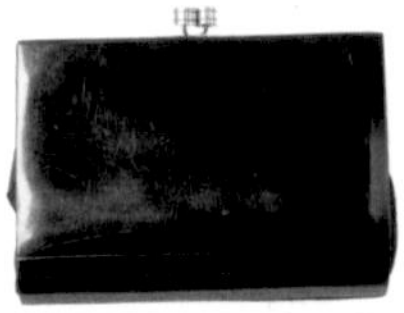
2

3

4

5

6

7

8

9

10

11

12

13

14

The king of vintage

If, in Los Angeles, the vintage trend is led by top models such as Kate Moss and Naomi Campbell then, in Paris, it is Didier Ludot – the famous vintage fashion guru who made his name at the Palais-Royal in Paris. Alongside his numerous themed and retrospective exhibitions of brands and designers – notably those for Dior or Christian Lacroix, he makes sure to keep us up to date with innovative fashion trends by acquiring a trademark piece from a designer. As in the wine trade - from where, in fact, the term *vintage* originates – a piece does not necessarily need to be 'aged' to be valued. Therefore, certain recent creations already make up part of his collection, as is the case with recent pieces by Olivier Theyskens for

15

16

17

18

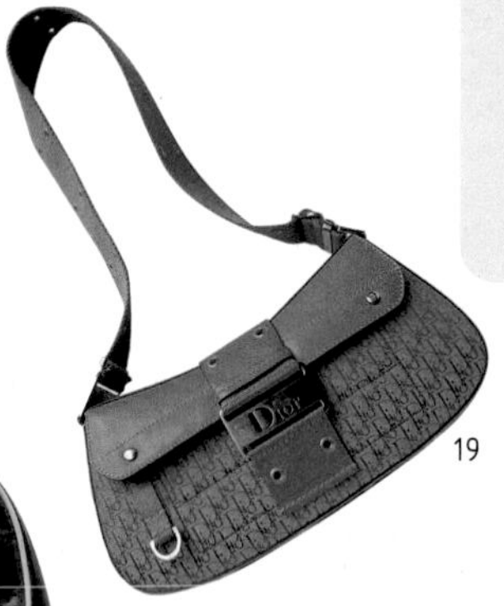

19

20

Rochas or Viktor & Rolf's dresses. Coupled with his keen eye and love of fashion, he is able to discern those items which merit keeping.

A personal take on the accessory

Here, Didier Ludot proposes a selection of vintage bags to illustrate the evolution of this particular product. For him 'there is always a treasured side to a vintage garment: it is not an item which will grow out of fashion as it is no longer fashionable!' For Didier Ludot, the fashion accessory accompanies the garment and its importance is such that a simple change of accessory can totally revive a look.

1. 1920s tapestry clutch-bag taken from a Sonia Delaunay picture.
© Didier Ludot Collection, Paris.

2. 1930s rigid black Bakelite clutch-bag with chrome clasp.
© Didier Ludot Collection.

3. 1930s handbag with thin handle in textured, black leather with chrome and Bakelite clasp.
© Didier Ludot Collection, Paris.

5. 1940s black antelope handbag Reverbere, House of Schiaparelli.
© Didier Ludot, Paris.

6. 1960s Hermes handbag Piano in navy blue, also called Fabiola after the Queen of Belgium who particularly liked this bag.
© Didier Ludot Collection, Paris.

7. 1950s Hermes black crocodile handbag with gilt clasp.
© Didier Ludot Collection, Paris.

7. 1940s Hermes Moto bag made from recyclable materials, brown leather and seal skin with an alterable shoulder strap.
© Didier Ludot Collection, Paris.

8. 1950s black reindeer handbag from Germaine Guerin. Ivory and brown Bakelite flap with twisted braid trimming and monogram.
© Didier Ludot Collection, Paris.

9. 1950s black leather quilted Chanel bag designed by Coco Chanel in 1955
© Didier Ludot Collection, Paris

10. 1966, red square bag by Pierre Cardin.
© Didier Ludot Collection Paris.

11. 1967, Celine , box-shaped handbag with shoulder strap and gilded harness feature.
© Didier Ludot Collection, Paris.

12. 1970s Dior clutch bag in natural-coloured cloth with maroon-coloured motifs.
© Didier Ludot Collection, Paris.

13. 1970s Hermes handbag with shoulder strap in beige leather with canvas insignia of 'Leaning H' , designed by J-C Brosseau.
© Didier Ludot Collection, Paris.

14. 1980s Karl Lagerfield fan-shaped handbag in silver-coloured leather.
© Didier Ludot Collection, Paris.

15. 1980s Renaud Pellegrino evening bag in brightly-coloured duchess satin with gilded ballet dancer's feet feature.
© Didier Ludot Collection, Paris.

16. 1980s Commode, black box-shaped handbag, Rochas by Christian Astuguevieille,
© Didier Ludot Collection, Paris.

17. 1990s Chanel quilted chain handbag with bright blue glass sequins.
© Didier Ludot Collection, Paris.

18. 1990s Prada Bowling bag in bordeaux-coloured leather.
© Didier Ludot Collection, Paris.

19. Year 2000, Dior handbag in beige and white monogrammed cloth with natural-coloured leather trim with wide shoulder strap.
© Didier Ludot Collection, Paris.

20. Year 2000, Gucci handbag in beige and absinthe coloured cotton satin with horse's bit feature in the shape of emerald green sequined snakes.
© Didier Ludot Collection, Paris.

Designers and their accessories

Lanvin: Alber Elbaz

1

2

3

4

5

1.'Orchidee' metal brooch with rhinestones. Spring-Summer 2006.

2. Choker made from jersey-covered pearls with rhinestone insets. Fastened with a satin bow. Autumn-Winter 2005-6.

3. Ring , Spring-Summer 2006.

4. Lambskin court shoe with patent conical heel and ankle strap. Spring-Summer 2006.

5. Ring, Spring-Summer 2006.

6. Necklace of three orchid flowers made from metal, pearls and crystal with a black satin ribbon. Spring-Summer 2006.

7. Handbag with metal finishings in textured and lacquered lambskin. Maroon leather handle with Lanvin medallion and shoulder strap. Spring-Summer 2006.

8. Patent calf-skin pumps. Autumn-Winter 2005-6.

A culture and a style

Alber Elbaz has been the artistic director of Lanvin since 2001. After making a name for himself in the USA, he came to Paris to work with Guy Laroche and Yves Saint Laurent. His belief that fashion is art and imagination, which is his principal driving force, is derived from a plethora of sources – not least from sculpture and literature. A single word 'desirable' illustrates his 2001-2002 autumn-winter collection. It is the white porcelain bodies of the Japanese sculptor from Shanghai, Liu Jianhua which inspired Lanvin's flagship perfume 'Arpège'. Accessories are supremely important to him. Attracted to the colour blue for a necklace or a pair of pumps, for example, because it is reminiscent of the sky in Casablanca where he spent most of his childhood. He has also been influenced by the full moon as it signifies perpetual renewal which has been an important theme in his work.

6

7

Harnessing influences

Couturier, but also designer, Alber Elbaz describes the stages of his creative processes. In the first instance there is the solitary confrontation with the blank page and the drawing. Following that, time is spent researching with great scrutiny shape and form using a tailor's dummy. It was he who was responsible for the design and window dressing of the Lanvin boutique on the Rue St. Honoré in Paris. His understanding of fashion, literature and sculpture has enabled him to produce accessories of great originality – the covered pearl necklace in Figure 2 bears witness to this. Drawing inspiration from around the great capitals of the world he has designed pieces where silk birds nestle into *decolletés* and, after overhearing a woman's conversation where she tells how she conceals her jewellery in her dress, this triggered the idea of covering jewellery. This is all part and parcel of the romance of haute couture. Alber Elbaz loves elegance and perfection but above all, he loves women and to whom he will always leave the last word. For it is she who will determine a style by the particular way she will lace a ribbon or tie a bow.

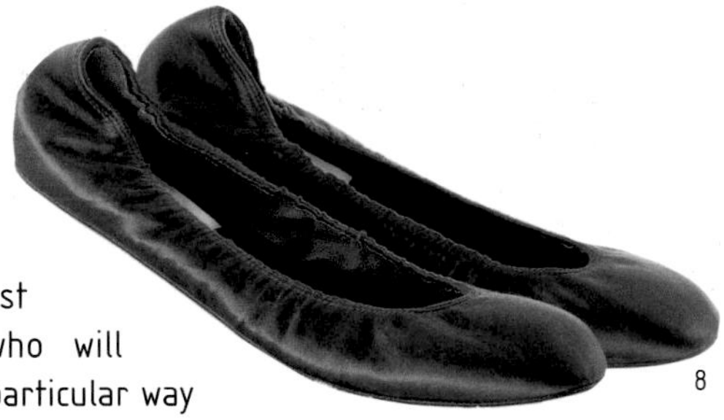

8

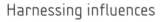

Louis Vuitton and Marc Jacobs

Portrait of Marc Jacobs, creative director of Louis Vuitton, 2003
© Pierre Bailly

In 1898, George Vuitton, son of the founder and creator of the legendary monogram canvas, had already crossed the Atlantic and conquered America. Marc Jacobs, the creative director of Louis Vuitton since 1997, has been inspired by the spirit of travel and innovation held dear to the heart of this renowned *malletier* (leather goods manufacturer) to the point of making it a fashion in itself. His creations are the results of his dynamic, yet relaxed, approach to design coupled with an in-depth knowledge of Louis Vuitton's traditional techniques. This designer, from New York, links history, culture and modernity in his collections by reliving the great transatlantic crossings which gave the brand its success.

Marc Jacobs reinterpreted the grunge-rock culture of Seattle in the 1990s, such as hip-hop and skate-board, by introducing elements of these into the Vuitton style. He transformed a traditional object - the holdall – into a fashionable one. He rendered art accessible to everyone (just as Andy Warhol did with Pop Art) when he asked New York underground artist Stephen Sprouse to design a limited-edition collection of graffiti written over the monogram canvas. Jacobs also invited the Japanese designer Takashi Murakami to reproduce multi-coloured versions of the monogram canvas.

His autumn-winter 2006-07 collections do not only consist of a bit of jewellery but also a profusion of hats, from toques (cylindrical hats) to large baseball caps in the Gavroche style. He uses materials such as lacquered crocodile, mink and – for the first time in the history of Louis Vuitton – alligator skin to create original compositions by combining and super-imposing latex, tweed, fur (notably, leopard), satin and cashmere. Marc Jacobs doesn't hesitate in showing men carrying handbags or shoulder bags and chinchilla earmuffs sporting the initials Louis Vuitton.

1

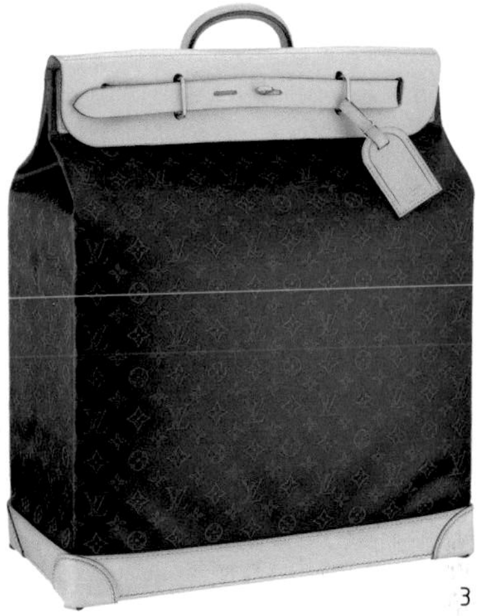

3

2

4

5

6

1. Holdall in silver metallic monogrammed canvas.
© LB Productions.

2. Holdall 50 (50 x 29 x 22 cm) in nomad leather.
© Laurent Bremaud /LB Productions.

3. Steamer bag (45 x 52 x 20 cm) in monogrammed canvas with luggage label, 2004.
© Louis Vuitton.

4. Holdall 50 in monogrammed canvas with silver graffiti and luggage label, 2001.
© Antoine Jarrier.

5. *Noe* in monogrammed canvas with two miniatures attached to the handle: in Mandarin and green leather respectively.
© Patrick Galabert/LB Production.

6. *Alma* in monogrammed canvas with a mini-*Alma* in multi-coloured monogram on white canvas, a mini-steamer bag in green leather and a mini-Alma in black leather.
© Monogram Multicolore is created by Takashi Murakami for Louis Vuitton.
© Patrick Galabert/ LB Productions.

Loulou de la Falaise

1

2

3

A game of materials

For more than 30 years Loulou de la Falaise was Yves Saint Laurent's muse as well as his design collaborator. She created her own label in 2003 where she admitted her passion for natural materials, notably coral. Stones, wood and fur are also amongst her favourites. She uses a combination of glass, pâte de verre and blown glass to make her costume jewellery, known affectionately as *loulouteries* by Saint Laurent. Regarding her design approach, her technique varies according to the piece in hand - 'certain pieces require a drawing whereas others can be made directly', she states. She is not fond of 'things which are too strict, nor principles which are too restricting'. Working from the premise that false pearls are harder than cultured pearls, she embarks on a design in one of her most favoured materials.

An enchanted world

With this designer we see certain colours, such as black (also a favourite with Yves Saint Laurent) as well as bright reds, azure blues and turquoises. The sea has been a constant theme of inspiration since her childhood. She has never forgotten the walks along the shores collecting shells, stones, leaves and flowers. With Loulou de la Falaise, gardens, lichen, bracken, and even the Scottish Highlands, all become potential objects. She likes to 'surprise' with her designs such as the small clutch bag (fig. 6) in python skin with an ebony fastening. She derives inspiration from an eclectic mix of themes - Africa, Asia, sometimes work by Gustav Klimt, other times it is a Chinese lacquered object. 'Childhood has a charming side', underlines the designer who is equally inspired by make-believe. Her logo is inspired by a wolf baying in the moonlight. She particularly likes 'jewellery which evolves' because she aims to 'break the images" by returning all the elements to their original function.

Louise de la Falaise is called Loulou. Her forename could be linked to one of Louis XIV's favourites, with her surname evoking one of Alban Berg's heroines. Possessing a brilliance and multi-coloured facets to her personality, she is nymph-like with a hermaphrodite body. She is impressed by everything and, revelling in the contrasts and extremes which appear, she has an innate ability to make sense of all of this. She is a mixture of exuberant elegance, aristocracy and haughtiness evoking a surprising sensuality which is both intriguing and disturbing. This distant reserve is full of mystery. However, we must not be mistaken for beneath this immodest veil of black lace hides a little girl who is in fact all woman.

Yves Saint Laurent

4

5

6

7

8

1. Loulou de la Falaise. Photo by Rose Deren.

2. Exotic wooden bracelets with parchment cuff.

3. Butterfly-shaped stone brooch.

4. Autographed homage to Loulou de la Falaise by Yves Saint Laurent.

5. Drop earring, metal lacquered interconnecting hoops, 'Fantasie' line, 2006.

6. Python-skinned clutch bag with glossy ebony fastening.

7. Coral brooch, 'Fantasie' line, 2006.

8. Necklace made from glass, coral, red and turquoise jasper.

Yazbukey

1

2

3

4

5

6

7

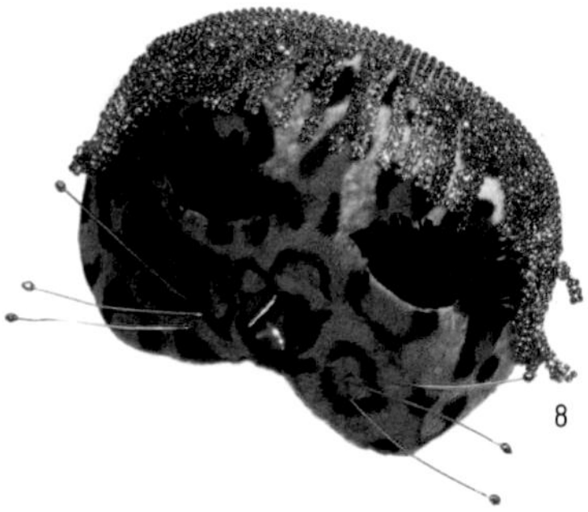
8

Perfumes from the orient

The Yazbukey label was created by the sisters Yaz and Emel in 2000. Yaz was born in Istanbul and Emel in Cairo. Their work is redolent of the fables of the 1001 Nights, inspiring a range of accessories. They organise parties with provocative themes such as 'Let's get physical', 'Let's get animal' and 'Let's get wet'. The singer and performer Bjork propelled Yazbukey into the limelight when she wore their masks during her concerts.

The two sisters worked in different countries before coming to Paris where they currently work. Yaz studied fashion design while Emel worked for three seasons with Christian Lacroix on his prints. They started off with a line of accessories which included jewellery, shoes, gloves, masks, belts and even a clothing range for dogs! Two chihuahuas with painted toe nails have become their mascot and are even presented on the catwalk during their fashion shows.

The two designers work with leather offcuts which they embroider and embellish with pearls and glass beads. They also include recyclable materials as well as crystal and Perspex.

A cosmopolitan inspiration

Their concept is that every object can become an accessory. They draw inspiration from the imaginary world of *Aesop's Fables, The Wizard of Oz* and the Brothers Grimm whilst films by Tim Burton and Alfred Hitchcock are also influential. The illustration of the two sisters (fig. 9) is by the famous American fashion illustrator Cedric Rivrain. The Yaz label is sold in Hong Kong, London and Tokyo. In Paris it is marketed under the PR company Totem. They produce two collections per year, as well as designing jeans and tee-shirts advertising Absolut Vodka in Turkey, and pearl wigs for Gaspard Yurkévitch.

9

1. Perspex and metal necklace from the '*Panthere*' collection.

2. 'Bibi' from the *Panthere* collection.

3. Miniature bag from the *Panthere* collection.

4. Dog cape from the *Panthere* collection.

5. High-heeled fur shoes with pompon from the *Panthere* collection.

6. Metal brooch with perspex charms from the *Panthere* collection.

7. Dog coat from the *Panthere* collection.

8. Mask from the *Panthere* collection.

9. Illustrations of Yaz and Emel by Cedric Rivrain.

Sonia Rykiel: Sonia and Nathalie Rykiel

The woman's wardrobe revolutionised

Sonia Rykiel is perhaps best known for her knitwear – an essential element to any woman's wardrobe and one which she knows how to make very successfully. A committed designer, she has been instrumental in the liberation of attitudes, as well as women. 'I've placed seams on the outside, dispensed with bras, introduced dresses without hemlines, worked on the wrong side of a fabric as much as the right, removed shoulders pads, was the first person to make haute couture clothes available by mail order (3 Suisses catalogue) and made stripes my trademark. It was an era without taboos', she states. Sonia Rykiel has also written a

1

2

3

4

5

6

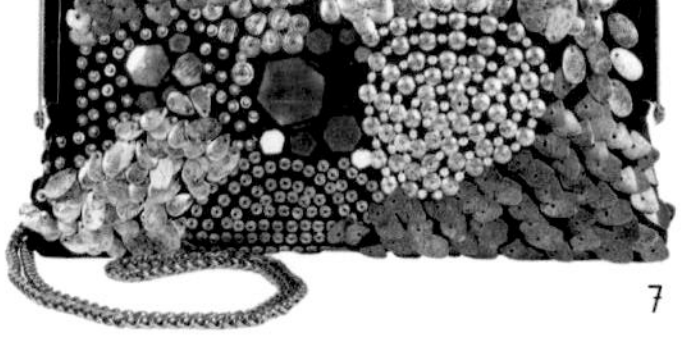

7

8

number of books on fashion and in 1961 when she was pregnant with her daughter Nathalie, she created knitwear maternity dresses. In May 1968 she opened her first boutique in Paris and, in 2001, both Sonia and Nathalie received the Fashion Award from the film director Robert Altman in his film *Prêt-à-Porter* (1994). This was a homage dedicated to a family dynasty in the fashion milieu who were known the world over. It was Sonia who inspired the film's theme in which she played herself.

Mother and daughter

Before becoming artistic director of the label, Nathalie directed the fashion shows. From 1987, she designed various collections and launched Sonia Rykiel Accessories and Sonia Rykiel Shoes in 1992. A shop dedicated to women called 'Rykiel Woman' was opened in Paris in 2002 where fetish-wear found place with cult designs.

In the foreword of *La Dictionnaire des mots et expressions des couleurs* (*The Dictionary of Words and Expressions of Colour*) written by Annie Mollard-Desfours, Sonia writes: 'I am inspired by everything to make colours – I have brought flowers back from all over the world, found sand and coral, collected fragments of wood ....'

For Sonia Rykiel Accessories it is the material which is all important – the knitted striped handbags with glittery rivet details, the 'kiss' and cat motifs made either as brooches or pins. Sequins and glitter guarantee 'eternal femininity' affording the woman a timeless and 'rive-gauche/left bank' style.

This year the company celebrates 40 years of being in business.

9

10

11

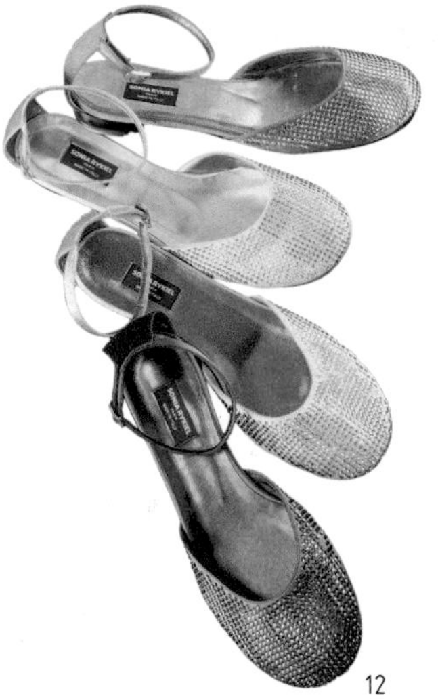

12

13

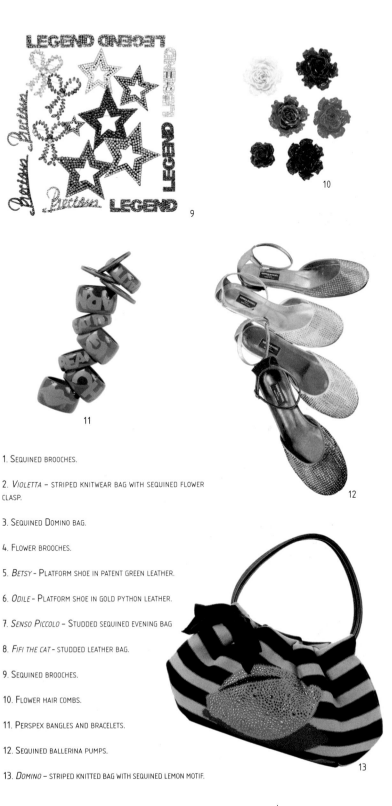

1. Sequined brooches.

2. *Violetta* – striped knitwear bag with sequined flower clasp.

3. Sequined Domino bag.

4. Flower brooches.

5. *Betsy* - Platform shoe in patent green leather.

6. *Odile* - Platform shoe in gold python leather.

7. *Senso Piccolo* – Studded sequined evening bag

8. *Fifi the cat* - studded leather bag.

9. Sequined brooches.

10. Flower hair combs.

11. Perspex bangles and bracelets.

12. Sequined ballerina pumps.

13. *Domino* – striped knitted bag with sequined lemon motif.

Christian Louboutin

2

1

A fascination for the foot

Born in 1963, Christian Louboutin made an early entrance into the Paris fashion scene and its night-life. A notice, forbidding women to enter a museum wearing high-heels for fear of damaging the floor, was to have a big impression on him: he was haunted by this vision and covered his schoolbooks with drawings of high-heeled shoes! Fascinated by Parisian night-life, in particular Le Palace and les Folies Bergère, he dreamt about designing shoes for the dancers. However, he was only met with refusal so decided to follow apprenticeships with Charles Jourdan, Maud Frizon and freelanced with Chanel and Yves Saint Laurent until he met his mentor, Roger Vivier, the legendary haute couture shoe designer.

In 1992, Christian Louboutin opened his first boutique. Here his clients were charmed by the luxury of discussing, over a cup of coffee, their needs and thus a privileged rapport was spawned. The red nail polish of one of his employees was the inspiration for his red lacquered soles – his signature was born!

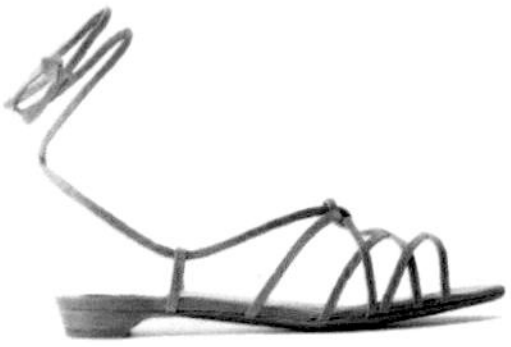

5

4

3

Au Revoir*
Et merci à Olga de .....
s'être mouillée!
christian L

Women's footwear

The shoe is an integral part of body language and defines the silhouette. 'I like it when women see my shoes as beautiful objects, a kind of jewel outside of fashion, standing in its own world. The shoe is not just an accessory – it is an attribute,' he affirms.

For his theme 'Le Love' Christian Louboutin created *Les Inséparables* which is a name given to a variety of doves or love birds. The principle is simple: 'A design in pairs: when the two feet are together the design is complete.' He likes the contrast between raw materials such as cork and flax used for the thick parts of the platforms, and shiny materials used for the upper parts. He also favours exotic leathers and satins. The 'classic woman' has made him appreciate the fundamental basics, he is moved by the 'taste of beauty' as he puts it. 'Today, I am much more interested in the shape of the line than the detail. I design very freely, then I adapt it,' he says.

1. *Vamp* sandal, Spring-Summer 2005.

2. *Pigalle* stiletto-heeled shoes, Autumn-Winter 2004-05

3. *Petit Tour* bags, Spring-Summer 2005.

4. *Cristobag* clutch bag, Spring-Summer 2005.

5. *Neferina* roman sandal, Spring-Summer 2006.

6. *Glamazone* over-the-knee boots, Autumn-Winter 2004-05.

7. *Accroche-moi* ankle boots, Autumn-Winter 2004-05.

8. *Pin-up* stiletto-heeled shoes, Spring-Summer 2006.

8. *Lady Macbeth* clutch bag and *Palace* peep-toe high-heeled 9. shoes, Spring-Summer 2005.

10. *Lady Macbeth* clutch bag, Spring-Summer 2005.

11. *Air France* slippers.

6

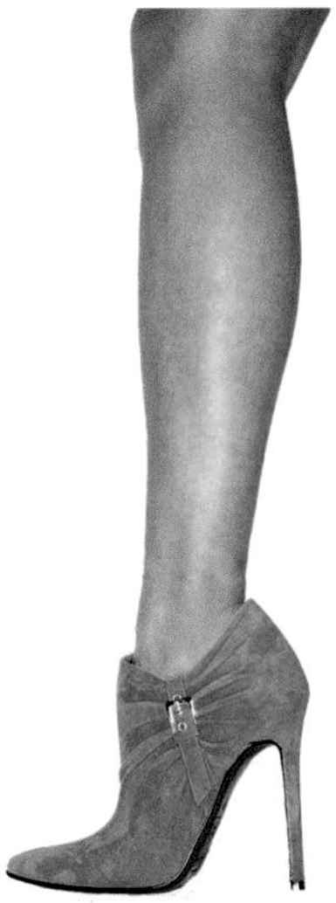

7

8

9

10

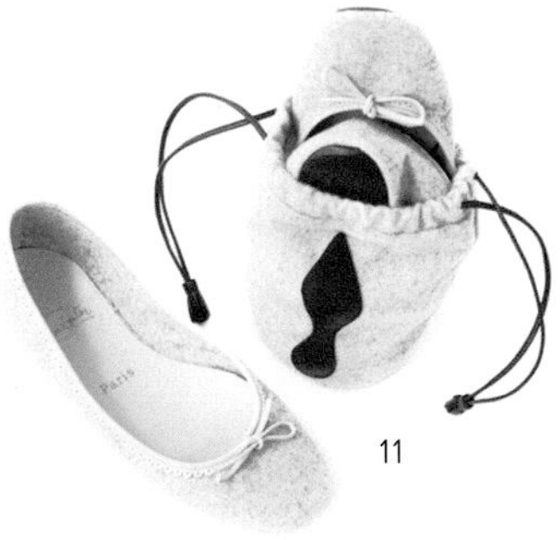

11

Éléna Cantacuzène

1

2

3

4

From Byzantium to Paris

Originating from one of the oldest families from Constantinople, Eléna Cantacuzène derives inspiration for her jewellery from the ancient civilisations: her *Keops* line (fig.5) is evocative of an Egypt from the time of the eponymous Pharoah (IVth dynasty *c.* 2600 BC). 'Everything inspires me from architecture, the shape of a stone, to the colours of the countryside ...,' she says.

After having studied the decorative arts in Paris, she made women's accessories giving away her first attempts to friends as gifts. Eléna feels the relationship between colour, form and material is paramount and considers herself a better colourist than designer. Her passion for minerals and precious stones stems from her childhood when her father, who was a mining engineer, introduced her to the extraordinary variety of rocks that exist.

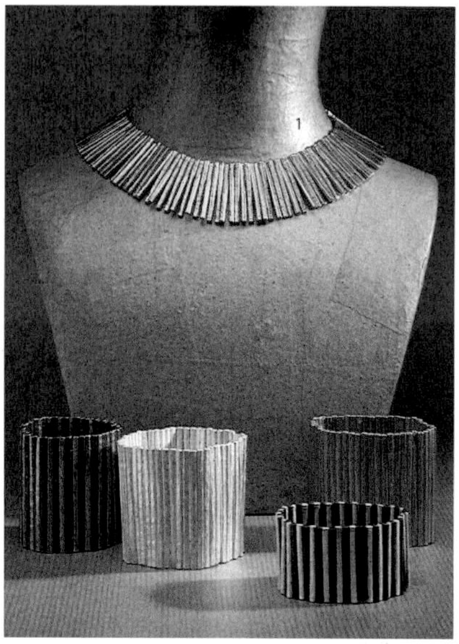

5

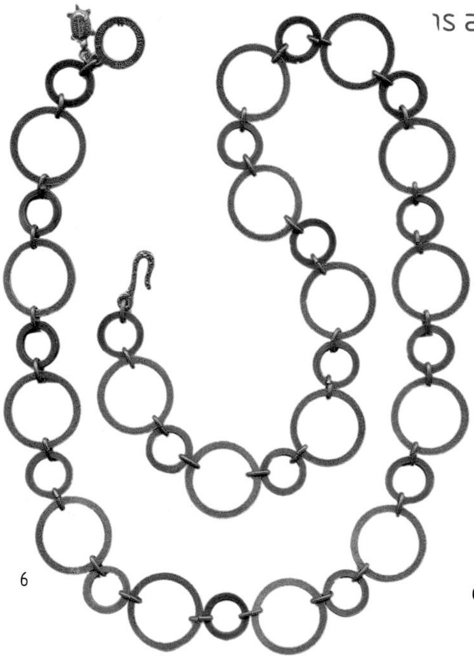

6

ıs and jewellery

In 1993, Eléna Cantacuzène made her mark by opening a studio-boutique in Paris. From that point on each product would be made by hand, *in situ*, with materials coming from a variety of exotic places – turquoise from the Yemen, agate from Afghanistan, horn and macassar from Africa, red coral from the Persian Gulf and glass and crystal from China. She strikes a perfect balance between the brilliance of the materials and the

7

intensity of the colours, which are heightened and diminished accordingly. The ruby turtle which is found on all the clasps has become the trademark of her designs. Eléna produces a woman's collection twice a year, as well as a limited edition of men's accessories. She also works to special commission deriving a great satisfaction from custom-made one-off pieces of jewellery using semi-precious stones. For Eléna Cantacuzène, the gem becomes a veritable work of art in itself.

8

9

10

11

1. Stone and silver-plated drop earrings.

2. Stone and gold-plated drop earrings.

3. Exotic wood and metal bangles mounted on elastic.

4. Exotic wood and turquoise ring.

5. Gold-plated choker with four pewter, silver and gold-plate bangles (three long and one short) from the Keops collection.

6. Bronze and gold-plated hoop necklace.

7. Gold-plate, bronze and stone drop earrings.

8. Bronze and stone necklace.

9. Stone and turquoise two-string necklace and bracelet.

10. Gold-plated choker.

11. Bronze and stone three-string bracelet.

This product is an object where function determines design and which is duplicated after extensive market research and stringent testing for comfort, strength, quality and safety. The majority of accessories retain their initial function. The bag therefore remains a container, the shoe protects the foot, the scarf the neck, the hat the head etc. Spectacles are, in fact, a prosthesis which either corrects sight or offers protection from the sun, or both. On the other hand, jewellery seems to have a purely ornamental function nowadays although originally it served as a social indicator and was associated with religious symbolism.

To simplify the question, we have classified the accessory into two groups: ornamental and functional. It is clear, however, that every object is made for a specific use. In the case of historic jewellery we realise that the symbolic functions preceded the ornamental ones as beliefs and superstitions were at the origins of jewellery design. At that time, men regarded jewellery as either a hunting trophy, or as an object which offered protection against the evil spirits long before it became purely ornamental.

Technical progress, economic and social changes coupled with a particular specialist knowledge, all assist in the transformation and development of an accessory into a product. One can imagine, therefore, the mastering of the stone setting technique afforded to the creation of a pair of spectacles is as valuable as the work involved in the glass and optic manufacture. New innovations are evident with the Oakley brand where MP3 or Bluetooth technology has been integrated into some of its spectacle designs.

We should also note that the development of leisure activities in the 20th century encouraged wide research into sunglasses design with profiled and resistant frames aimed at sportsmen and women. The technological advancements of today have allowed us to create high-protection insulating materials which offer maximum comfort and originality. This evolution is as visible in bag design as it is with shoes, spectacles and scarves, with designers drawing inspiration from the armed forces and top-level sporting personalities who, within their own field, also favour these technical innovations.

Colour, shape and material are all important in accessory designing. As for the choice of material, which is directly linked with function, the insulating properties and suppleness of

Chapter 2 - Products

leather are also used in the creation of gloves, hats and shoes. In the past, leather dyes offered a limited palette whereas nowadays there is a huge range of colours as well as fabric imitations, such as jean material.

Jacques Le Corre, who we present in this chapter, shows some excellent examples of material and shape used to great effect with his reinvention of the hat.

Jewellery, in terms of purely decorative accessories are nowadays incontrovertible products for the big brands and their designers, with certain brands being specialists in this field. There are two types of jewellery: costume jewellery and jewellery proper. Perspex, metal and moulded plastic or acrylic are materials which are used more and more in the costume jewellery world as they offer more scope and freedom when designing. Thanks to these materials it is possible, not only to imitate stones and pearls, but also to be able to offer to a wider audience a more accessible range of jewellery which use unusual colours and materials not found in the natural world. Swarovski is the largest producer and supplier of synthetic stones today.

Products which become the great classics are commonly called *basics*. Their forms are regularly revisited reappearing in different colours and materials, with the combination of several basic designs giving rise to new products. The designer can also offer an innovative concept by diverting the basic from its initial function. Examples of this can be seen in this chapter with Alexis Mabille's bow ties found on belts, brooches and hair slides. His inventive use of materials for accessories, such as straw ribbons on hats, plaited leather trim, as well as contemporary materials, such as over-stitched denim, all of which demonstrate his imaginative approach. Other designs include those decorated with flowers, embroidery, jewellery, crystal or rows of pearls. Alexandra Neel, whose designs are also represented, explains how to maintain a balance between style and merchandising for an accessory collection which is both original and commercial. We are also introduced to Christian Louboutin and Bethony Vernon who use fetishism in their shoes and jewellery. It is essential to be able to identify and list the basic accessory forms in order to grasp the work involved in designing and reinterpreting a form into a new product. It is for this reason that we begin this chapter by listing these basics.

The world of the accessory

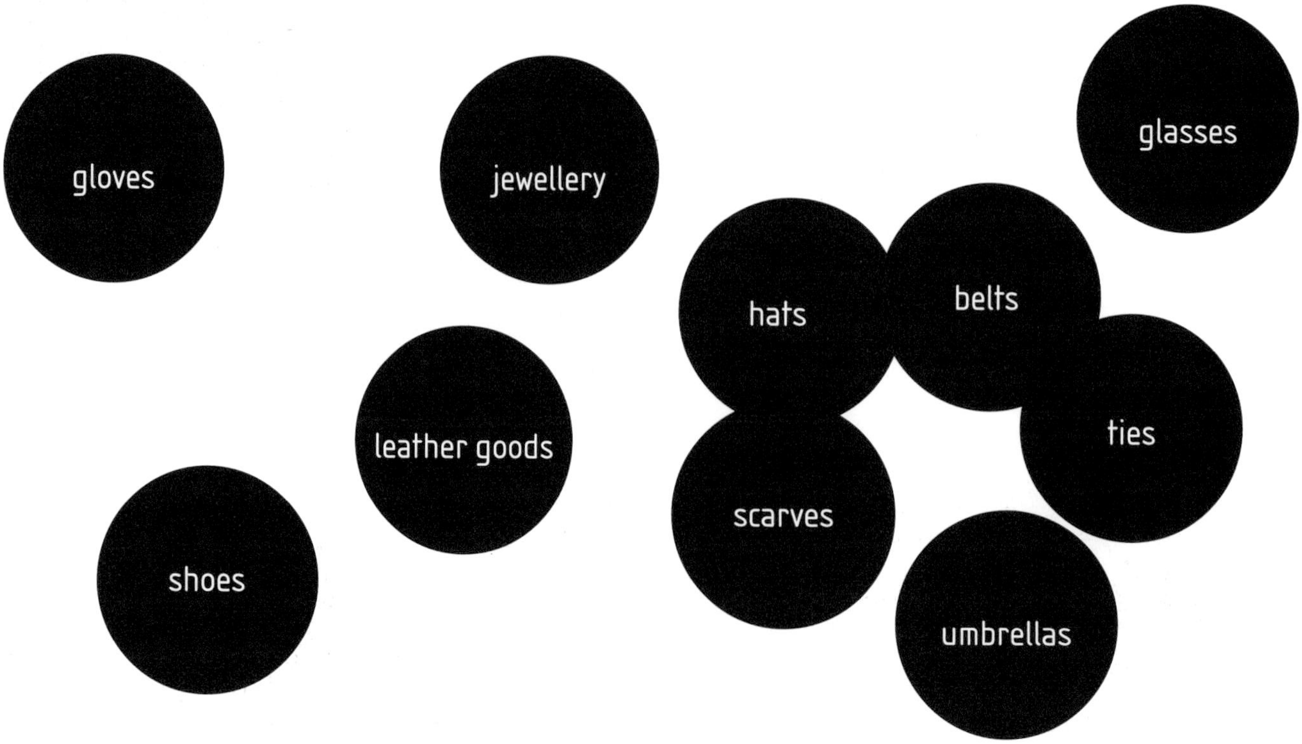

This encompasses a vast range of skills as well as a string of craftsmen and women and technicians. We can cite, in particular, the heel maker who sculpts the heels of shoes, the foundry worker and gilder who casts the metallic parts of jewellery, the milliner who makes the hats, the watchmaker who creates the watch movements, the spectacle-frame manufacturer, the stone-cutter etc. These craftspeople are the creators who perpetuate, each in their own way, these specialised skills.

The work involved in making a scarf, tie or bow tie depends on these very skills – the quality of the silk, its cut, as well as the care afforded to the design, are all proof of the incredible *savoir faire* of the weavers, designers and seamstresses concerned.

Although leather-work today is essentially industrialised, this sector of activity has been able to conserve an authenticity and a certain degree of luxury, as the big names testify. For example, Louis Vuitton and Hermès have both used their skills to successfully combine tradition and innovation in their collections, to the point where their wallets and money belts have become a sign of social distinction.

Sometimes, however, style overrides traditional skills. This has been the case with the house of Prada who started off by making its own fabric for its umbrellas but has ultimately established this material as a genuine concept for its *prêt-a-porter* lines. Although the accessory appears in a variety of guises and serves many functions, it has become at some point an undeniable part of a brand's image, thus completing its range.

The following pages present about 20 accessories, the list being far from exhaustive as we have seen with the Yazbukey brand where a dog can be completely 'accessorised'! They are presented in such a manner as to dispel any difference between those termed 'ornamental' and those referred to as 'functional'.

The layouts propose a snapshot of the different forms and colour ways for each of the products whether it be a handbag, shoe, scarf, bow tie, glasses, hat, hair accessory and finally jewellery. The significant variety of forms and range of colours allow us to appreciate the talent, creativity and infinite generosity of the numerous contributors.

We recognise familiar designers, as well as discovering new ones, such as Philippe Roucou and Kazu Huggler for their handbags, Alexandra Neel and her shoes, Alexis Mabille and Didier Ludot for their scarves and bow ties, Pierre Marly for his spectacles, Jacques le Corre for his hats and finally Bethony Vernon for jewellery.

fans
bags
hair accessories
shawls
tights
socks

The bag

1

2

3

4

5

6

7

8

9

10

The bag is a product which is regarded as a container and is normally falls into two categories: supple and rigid. The messenger or saddle bag, pouch and purse are generally supple; the satchel, briefcase and tote bag being more rigid. There are also back packs, which are a derivation of the army bag, and of course, handbags.

A little history

The oldest bag on record is one that dates back to 3,300 years BC belonging to the famous iceman Ötzi whose body was found in 1991 in the Alps on the Austro-Italian border. It was a type of sack consisting of an armature made from curved larch and hazel twigs tied together with grasses. A calf-skin belt, with a kind of pocket, was also found on his body.

In the West, the forerunner of the handbag would have been exclusively for men's use. It was worn around the waist and called a 'pocket', 'purse' or even 'money-bag'. It was not until the 14th century that the fairer sex adopted them. But from the 15-18th centuries larger dresses were the fashion with hidden interior pockets replacing the waisted purses. Equally, muffs worn by elegant ladies in the 1950s served the same purpose as a handbag, as did the sleeves of the Japanese kimonos.

One had to wait for the Age of Enlightenment, with its change of lifestyle and mentality, before the bag became an essential accessory in the woman's wardrobe. After the French Revolution clothes became lighter and more eccentric sometimes even using semi-transparent fabrics, as worn by the famous Madame Tallien. It was during this era that interior pockets disappeared in favour of the handbag. The bag was only commonly termed a 'handbag' from the beginning of the 20th century.

An accessory revisited

In this chapter we present a selection of basic models which have been reinvented by designers such as Sonia Rykiel who was responsible for reviving the tote bag and the Boston (see photos 5, 8, 13 and 14 on the following pages). Certain travel bags, such as *Grace* by Philippe Roucou (photo 3) were inspired by plumbers, messengers and game bags.

1. Cabin luggage, *Airport* by Philippe Roucou, Autumn-Winter 2006-7.

2. Satin and textured leather handbag with adjustable shoulder strap, *Lampas* by Lanvin, Spring-Summer 2006.

3. Messenger bag, *Grace* by Philippe Roucou, Autumn-Winter 2006-7.

4. Handbag, *Chifonana* by Christian Louboutin, Spring-Summer 2005.

5. Large suede tote bag, *Gavroche* by Sonia Rykiel, Autumn-Winter 2005-6.

6. Tote bag, *Van der Rohe* by Philippe Roucou, Autumn-Winter 2006-7.

7. Boston bag, *Iron Bag* by Christian Louboutin, Spring-Summer 2006.

8. Boston bag, *Popeye,* 'Cruise' collection by Sonia Rykiel, Spring-Summer 2006.

9. Clutch bag with chain, *Casino* by Philippe Roucou, Autumn-Winter 2006-7.

10. Rigid handbag, *Tam-Tam,* by Christian Louboutin, Spring-Summer 2006.

11. Satin and crystal-studded evening clutch bags, *Venus* by Sonia Rykiel, Spring-Summer 2005.

12. Metal minaudiere by Martine Boutron.

13. Mini box bags in patent leather with crystal-studded bows *Fil Rouge* by Sonia Rykiel, Autumn-Winter 2003-4.

14. Studded hand bag, *Lili* by Sonia Rykiel, Spring-Summer 2006.

15. Minaudiere *Manga* by Kazu Huggler, Autumn-Winter 2005-6.

16. Fringed clutch bag, *Louis XIV* by Christian Louboutin, Spring-Summer 2005.

17. Python skin bag, *Ginger* by Sonia Rykiel, Spring-Summer 2006.

18. Knitted basket bags ,*Domino* by Sonia Rykiel, Spring-Summer 2005.

19. Knitted bag, *Domino* by Sonia Rykiel, Autumn-Winter 2005-6.

12

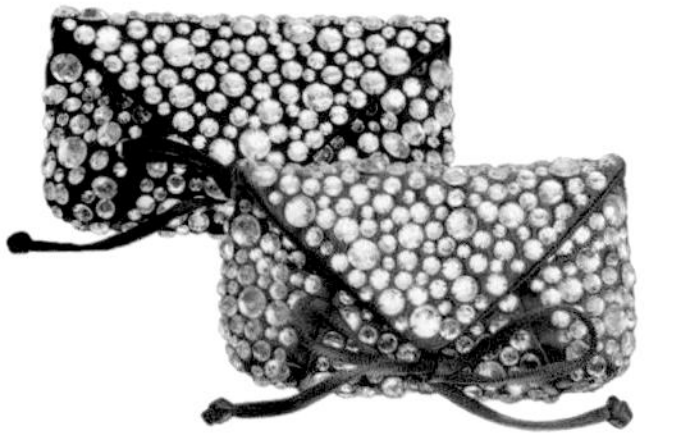
11

13

14

15

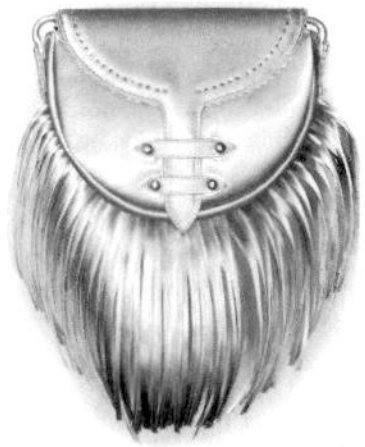
16

17

18

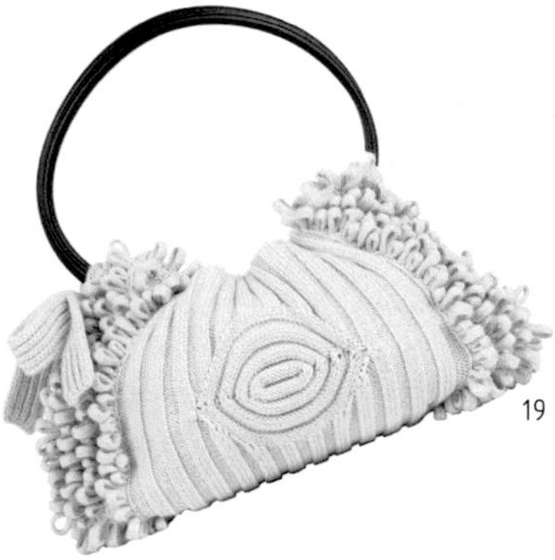
19

Bag designs

From the tool to the accessory

For a long time now the bag has been defined by its function: the doctor's medicine bag, the hunter's game bag, the child's Moses basket, the sailor's bag, the pupil's satchel, the craftsman's holdall, the Boston (holdall) used as an overnight bag, the purse for holding money etc. There are so many designs linked to a specific function. Nowadays, these designs have become the basics of a shop's collection. Here we show the principal ones amongst them.

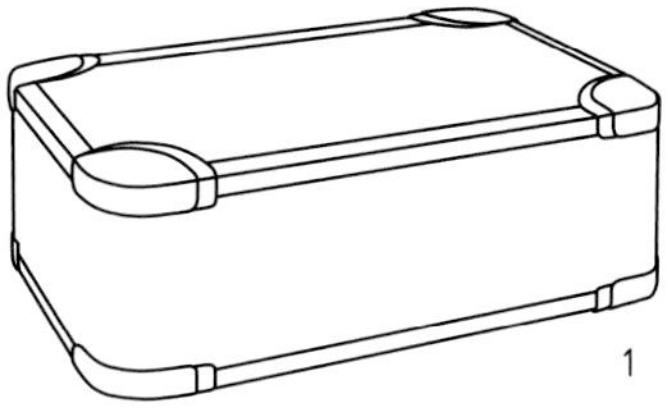

1

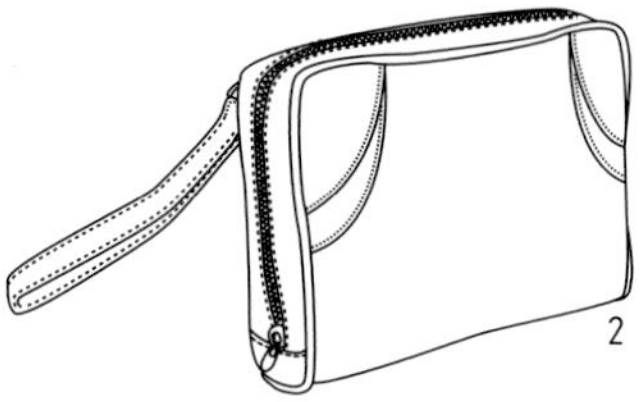

2

3

4

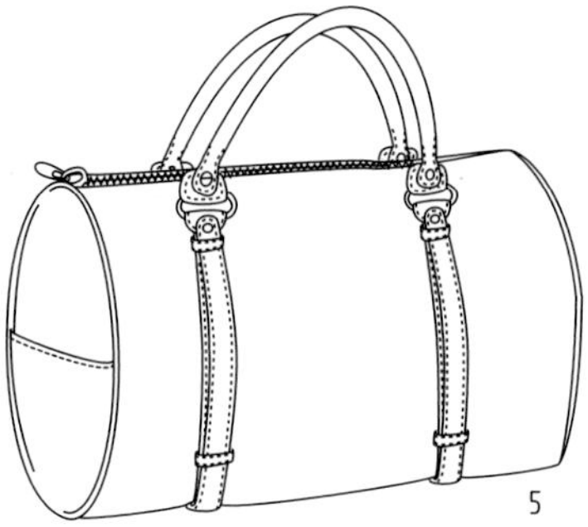

5

7

6

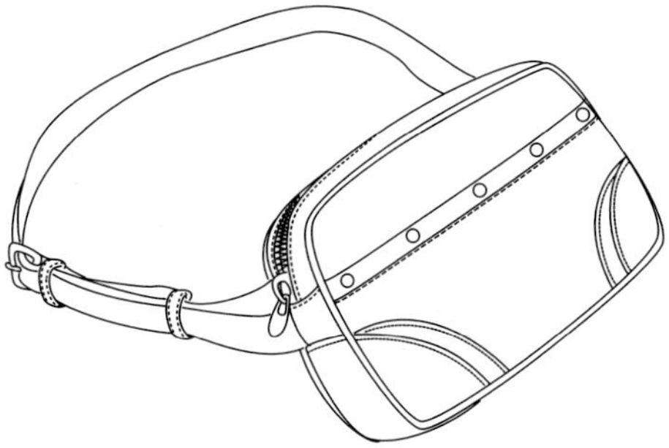

8

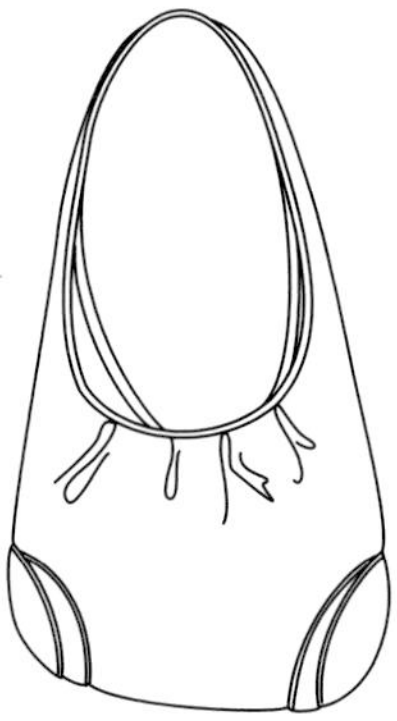

9

10

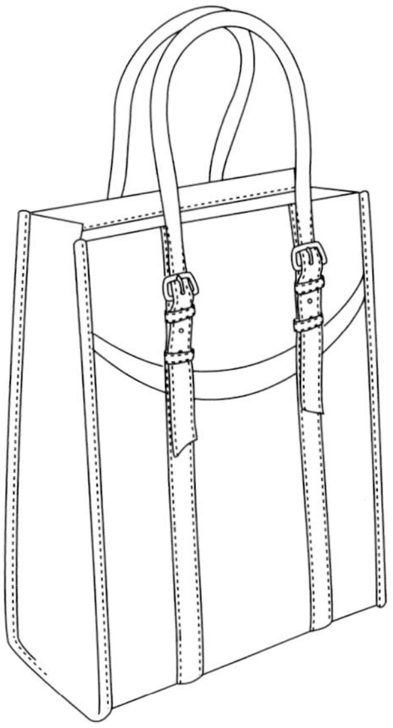

11

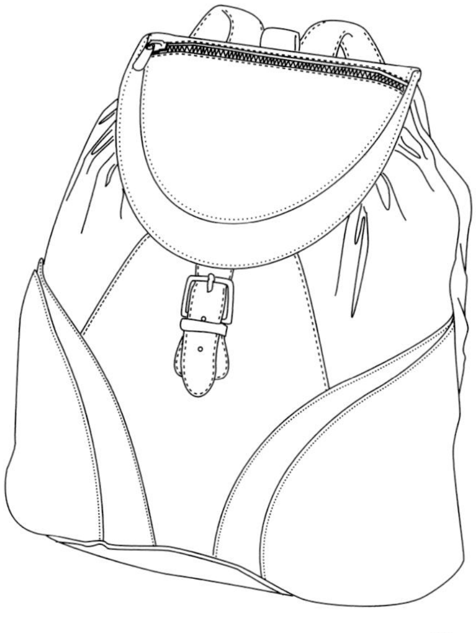

12

13

1. Suitcase
2. Make-up or sponge bag
3. Minaudiere (rigid evening bag)
4. Purse
5. Kit bag
6. Boston or holdall bag
7. Medicine bag
8. Money belt or bumbag
9. Shoulder sling messenger bag
10. Boston (holdall) bag
11. Tote bag
12. Back pack
13. Handbag

The shoe

1

2

3

4

5

6

7

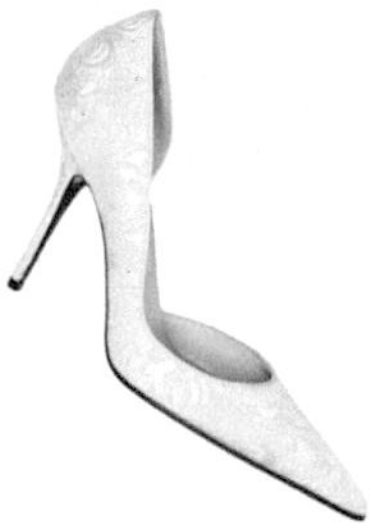

8

First steps

The shoe comes under the guise of many names – slipper, boot, sandal, trainer etc. As early as 13000 BC in the Spanish cave paintings we discover records depicting a man wearing animal skin boots and a woman in fur boots. Similarly, the Persian funeral vases of 3000 years ago bear witness to the existence of shoes. We can follow the history of the shoe through the Egyptian sandals made from plaited and sewn palm leaves, to the Etruscan sandals with their split and articulated wooden soles up to *chopines,* or platform shoes, of the 16th century courtesans.

From the 17th and 18th centuries, the material from which they were made differed according to gender – men generally wore shiny or glossy leather in suede or pig skin whereas brocade, velvet, satin, beaded or moiré fabric was the woman's prerogative.

After the Industrial Revolution, the bourgeoisie, with austere religious principles, could be found wearing sober, black shoes hidden under their long dresses. Whereas the mistresses of rich Parisians and actresses, such as those immortalised by Toulouse-Lautrec, lifted up their skirts to reveal high-heeled boots.

The contemporary shoe

After the First World War and women's emancipation, the skirt became shorter, showing more leg and shoes, more or less open, in such a way as to define the silhouette of the foot. These shoes were also accompanied by gloves and bags. And in 1947, Roger Vivier introduced the haute couture silhouettes with his New Look collection for Christian Dior.

Mary Quant and her muse Twiggy

gave birth to a completely new silhouette in 1965 and Charles Jourdan with his prestigious Séducta collection produced a variety of flat shoes in bright colours with geometric patterns. At the end of 1960s with the beatnik movement and the return to nature, nylon stockings were rejected in favour of open-toed wedge-heeled shoes in cork and other natural materials.

However, in 1971, Yves Saint Laurent presented his vintage collection where he returned to the platform-soled designs of the 1940s.

1. Open-toed platform-soled patent court shoe, *Namur* by Sonia Rykiel, Spring-Summer 2006.

2. Salome shoe with conical heel by Lanvin, Spring-Summer 2006.

3. Satin pumps by Lanvin, Spring-Summer 2006.

4. Ankle-boot by Sonia Rykiel, Autumn-Winter 2005-6.

5. Satin court shoe with conical heel by Lanvin, Spring-Summer 2006.

6. Knee-high boots, *Mailla Botta* by Christian Louboutin, Autumn-Winter 2004-5.

7. Moccasin-style court shoe *Steva* by Christian Louboutin, Autumn-Winter 2005-6.

8. Satin court shoe *Let's Go* by Christian Louboutin, Autumn-Winter 2005-6.

9. Two-tone trotter shoe with laces in patent calf skin with stainless steel heel by Lanvin, Autumn-Winter 2005-6.

10. Satin and crystal-studded court shoe with ankle strap and stainless steel heel by Lanvin, Autumn-Winter 2005-6.

11. High-heeled sandal, *Paramount* by Alexandra Neel, Spring-Summer 2006.

12. Sandal with ankle strap, *Bonny II* by Alexandra Neel, Spring-Summer 2006.

13. Suede mule, *Fame* by Alexandra Neel ,Spring-Summer 2006.

14. Platform-soled and wedge-heeled sandal, *Capri Zeppa* by Christian Louboutin.

9

10

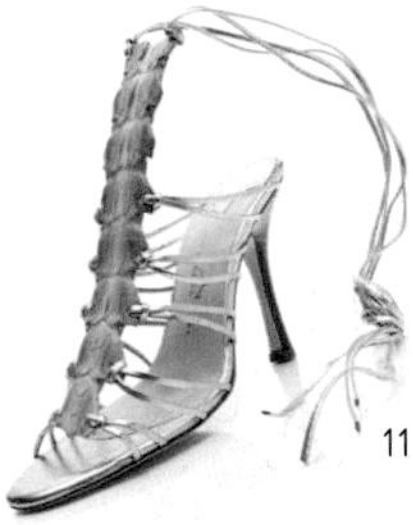

11

12

13

14

15

16

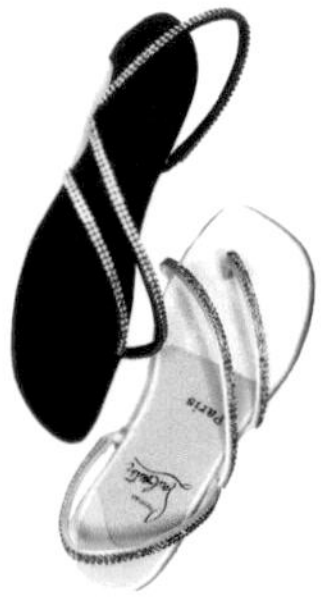

17

18

19

20

21

22

23

24

Shoes today tend to define a character, a style, or a manner more than an era. The fetishists have seized upon the stiletto heels; the moccasin, a classically English style, is often revisited; the Salome and court shoe characterise French elegance; the platforms the avant-garde and the thigh-length boots eroticism with history and world cultures remaining a constant inspiration for new footwear designs.

Here we have chosen a selection of designs by Alexandra Neel, Christian Louboutin, Jeanne Lanvin and Sonia Rykiel to present the basic principles.

15. Stiletto-heeled sandal in leather and velvet ankle strap by Sonia Rykiel, Autumn-Winter 2004-5.

16. Tropezienne sandal, *Caymen* by Alexandra Neel, Spring-Summer 2006.

17. Crystal-studded strap sandals, *Star-Line* by Christian Louboutin, Spring-Summer 2005.

18. Leather and crystal-studded Salome by Sonia Rykiel, Spring-Summer 2005.

19. High-heeled Salome in patent leather with crystal-studded counter *Navarre* by Sonia Rykiel Spring-Summer 2006.

20 .Tango shoe in iridescent leather by Sonia Rykiel, Autumn-Winter 2005-6.

21. Mule, *Light* by Alexandra Neel, Spring-Summer 2006.

22. Open-toed, patent leather platform-soled Salome by Sonia Rykiel, Autumn-Winter 2004-5.

23. Salome *Metallica* by Christian Louboutin, Autumn-Winter 2004-5

24. Leather man's shoe *Fred* by Christian Louboutin, Spring-Summer 2006

Shoe styles

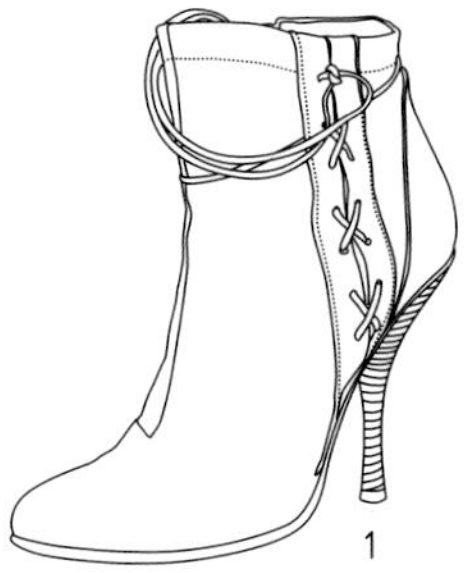

1

2

3

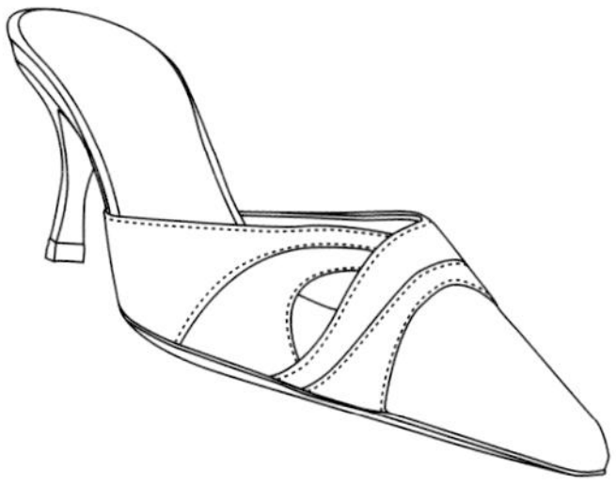

4

5

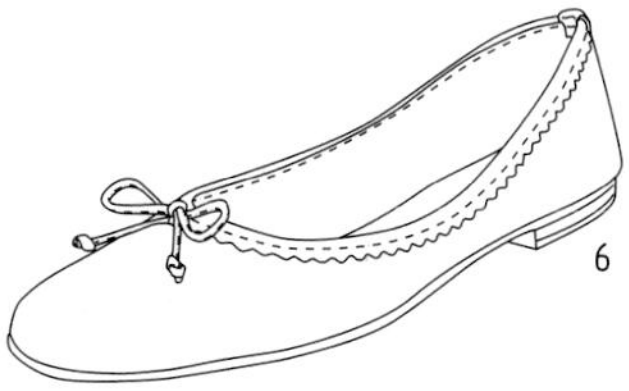

6

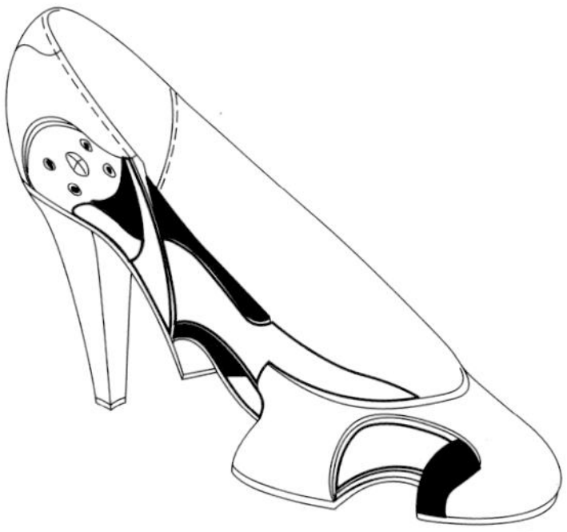

7

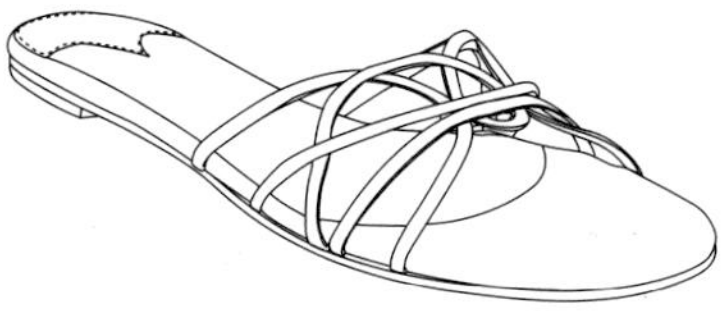

8

10

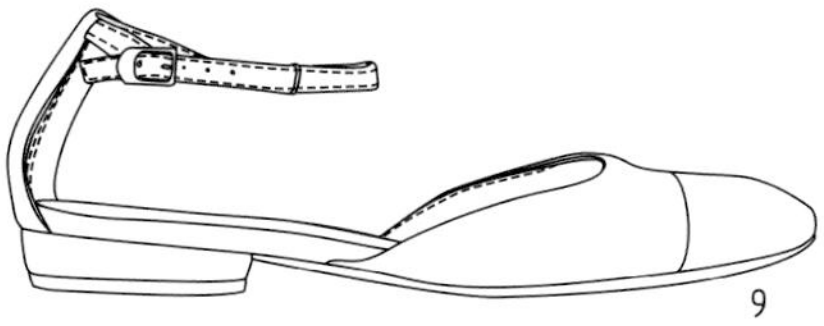

9

11

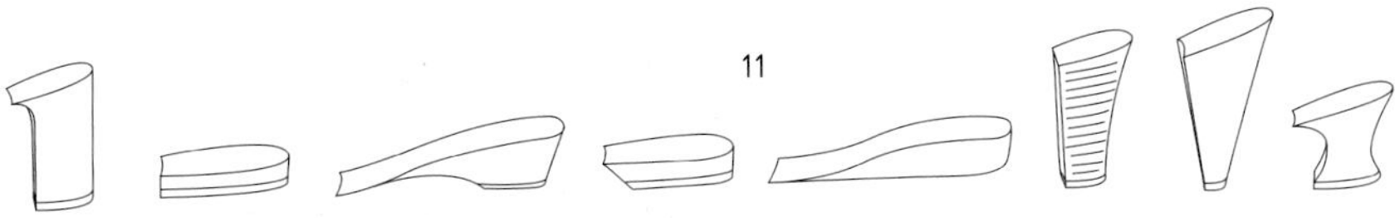

1. Ankle boot
2. High-heeled sandal
3. Sling-back Salome
4. Mule
5. Laced court shoe with open toe
6. Ballet pump
7. Court shoe with cut-outs
8. Mule sandal
9. Ankle-strap Salome
10. Trainer or basket ball shoe
11. Heels:
From L to R: round heel, classic heel, filled-in heel, angled heel, wedge heel, wooden heel, conical heel, bobbin heel.

The scarf and the bow tie

1

2

3

4

Shapes and sources of inspiration

The scarf has the dual function of being ornamental, as well as protective. It always has a simple geometric form: triangular, rectangular or square and can be made with a variety of finishes – rolled edge, straight edge, fringed, embroidered etc. as well as decorated with all sorts of patterns using a rich assortment of fabrics.

At the beginning of the 20th century Paul Poiret mainly used foulard (the fabric) and chiffon in his collections, both of which possessed an oriental aesthetic. In the 1920s Sonia Delauney designed a number of scarves with geometric patterns in collaboration with the couturiers of that era, notably Coco Chanel.

The notion of the Orient and, more significantly the idea of travel, still remains associated with this accessory. The 'Lawrence of Arabia' style with his long white scarves has inspired the couturiers for decades. Illustrations of the first cars showed women dressing up their clothes with long scarves which would either protect their hairstyle or keep their hat in place.

In the 19th century paintings of the Empress Elisabeth of Austro-Hungary show her riding side-saddle, dressed in her shawls, illustrating the stylishness of this accessory. Still continuing with the equestrian connection, the Ascot or the *lavallière*, or floppy neck tie, are also associated with the riding world.

The revival of these accessories

The way in which the scarf is worn, or tied, is in fact the essence of style. It is hard to imagine Madame Grès without her turban. This accessory, which is midway between a hat and scarf, was inspired by a knotted scarf thus defining its style forever. In the 1970s, during the 'hippie' period, Brigitte Bardot and Claudia Cardinale wore scarves under cowboy hats in the film *The Legend of Frenchie King* (*Les Pétroleuses*) 1971.

Didier Ludot's stole (fig. 1) sends us back to the 1950s when it was usual to coordinate it with a muff. Hitchcock's women, such as Tippi Hedren or Grace Kelly, were portrayed at the wheel of a convertible sporting sunglasses and scarves epitomising ultimate glamour. Today, they have taken on a sexy look with the likes of Sharon Stone and her long silk scarves. The scarf is a common theme in Hermès collections as, each season, they revive the twill squares with their anchor patterns for the Spring-Summer collections and the equestrian ones for Autumn-Winter. These types of scarves were normally associated with the classic woman - Jackie Kennedy being a perfect example. However, to give them a contemporary slant they can be tied around a handbag, dressed up with a piece of jewellery, or worn like a bandana. The latter, with its paisley designs, are available in numerous colours. In the 1980s, it was the accessory of choice for the Blood and Crips gangs of Los Angeles, immortalised in the film *Colours* (1988) with Sean Penn and Robert Duval.

The scarf can also be used as another type of accessory such as a strap fastening on a handbag or, as a belt.

Alexis Mabille's bow ties, shown on this page, illustrate another variation of the scarf; today designers have also turned them into belts, cuffs, brooches and even hair accessories.

5

6

7

8

9

10

11

12

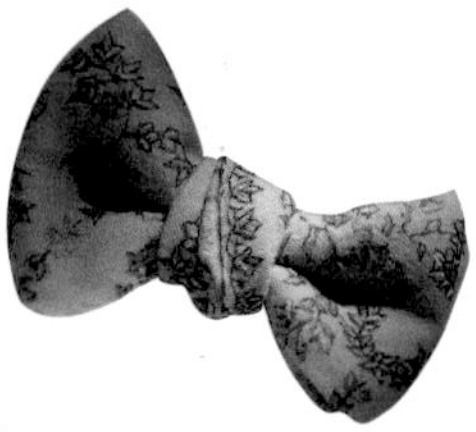

14

13

1. Didier Ludot stole

2. Didier Ludot scarf

3. Yves Saint Laurent scarf

4. Yves Saint Laurent head scarf

5. Hermes square

6. Chanel square

7. Chanel square

8. Hermes square

9. *Mick* - Velvet knotted handkerchief with dotted Swiss pattern by Alexis Mabille

10. *Madona* – organza handkerchief with jewelled buckle by Alexis Mabille

11. *Kate* – rubber bow by Alexis Mabille

12. *Iggy* – flat silk bow with golden embroidery by Alexis Mabille

13. *Paul* - classic tartan bow tie by Alexis Mabille

14. Classic cashmere embroidered bow tie by Alexis Mabille.

Eyewear

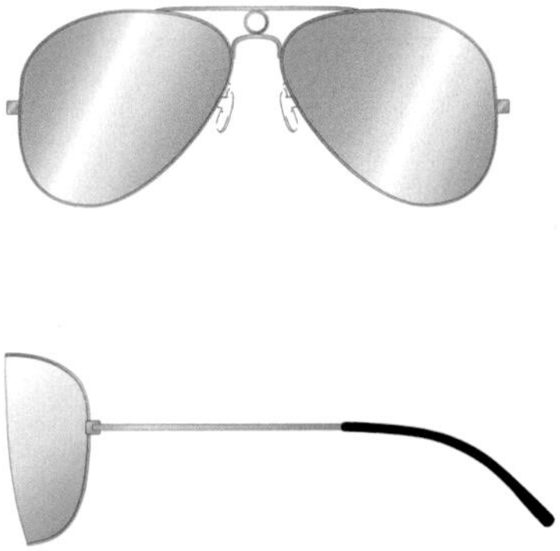

1

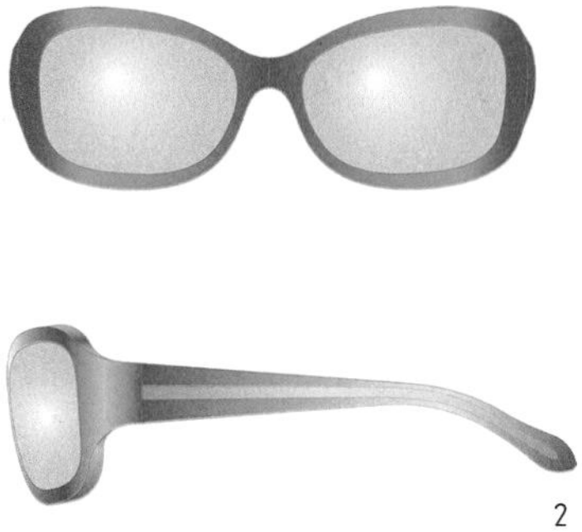

2

3

4

5

6

7

Pierre Marly, Georges Lissac's right-hand man in the 1960s, was the first person to regard spectacles as fashion accessories, rather than just necessary optical prostheses. So, a new accessory was born as he proposed a range of audacious colours, along with creative designs, which took them far away from the familiar, traditional models.

The ones designed for Audrey Hepburn (fig. 8) which she wore in *Charade* (1965), propelled spectacles into the limelight. He also designed a pair for Sophia Loren which were square with white frames, known as 'Sophia Sport' – the inspiration being derived from a television set. The pair designed for Michel Polnareff (fig. 11) became the singer's trademark.

Frame materials

For a long time horn-rim, and in particular, tortoiseshell was the preferred material of spectacle manufacturers. This was due to its extreme lightness and the fact that it could be polished to a high finish. The lighter the colour, the more expensive it was. It demanded a specific skill to produce and there are only three remaining artisans who still work this material, of which two are in Paris. Nowadays, however, it has become outlawed in most countries in the world with tortoiseshell being replaced by buffalo horn.

Frames are normally made from acetate which is a plastic that can be cut and is better quality than injected plastic. It is available in a variety of colours, shapes and thicknesses.

Top-level competitive sporting brands, such as Nike and Oakley, use flexible metal alloys or titanium for their strength, lightness and reliability.

8

9

10

Glass technology

Brands such as Nike and Oakley are amongst the most innovative. They propose glass which is interchangeable, polarised, anti-mist and whose surface allows water to slide off it. Oakley has even planned to integrate MP3 or Bluetooth into their glasses!

There are four intensities of protection: for resting and interiors, a tinted glass for aesthetics, classic intensity (which filters 65-70 % light), and maximum filter intensity of 85 % light. To combat UV rays, polycarbonate glass is used more and more.

Shapes

Inspiration for basic shapes was derived from a number of sources such as military sunglasses, like the Ray Ban (figs 1 and 12) with the US Air Force design or, from the artisan sector such as welders (fig. 13) or even top-level sporting competitors (fig. 9). Highly original shapes are reminiscent of diving masks, alpine hunters' sunglasses or those of the GIs in the desert. The fly, with its facetted eyes, have inspired the disproportional glasses in Figure 2 which have become today's classics.

1. Metal-framed pilot's glasses.

2. Butterfly-shaped square glasses with plastic frames by Pierre Marly.

3. Rimless oval glasses by Pierre Marly.

4. Wooden framed glasses, Pierre Marly collection.

5. Tortoiseshell-rimmed glasses . Pierre Marly collection presented in his boutique in Rue Francois 1er (Paris 8th arrondissement).

6. Binoculars. Pierre Marly collection presented in his boutique in Rue Francois 1er (Paris, 8th arrondissement).

7. Armless glasses. Pierre Marly collection.
Round-shaped *Audrey* design with curved glass, Pierre Marly 1965.

8. Stream-lines competition glasses.

9. Stream-lined competition glasses,

10. Spectacles with oversized frames and large square glass - design *Michel Polnareff* 1970s by Pierre Marly.

11. American Air Force pilot's glasses by Ray Ban.

12. Plastic welder's glasses. Olivier Gerval's collection.

13. Tennis racket glasses by Pierre Marly.

11

12

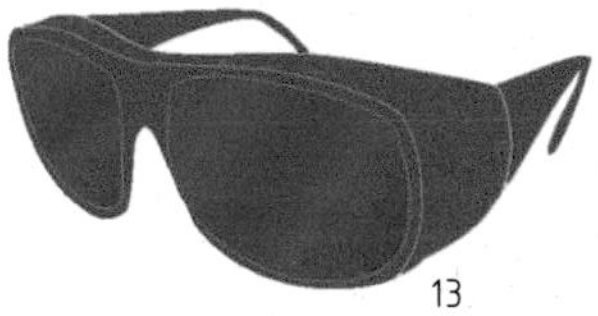
13

14

Hats and hair accessories

1

2

4

3

1. *Couve* by Jacques le Corre.

2. *Bebe Electrique* by Jacques le Corre.

3. *Api* by Jacques le Corre.

4. Stetson redesigned by Jacques le Corre.

Eras and moods

The hat which, for a long time, was only associated with the aristocracy now easily evokes a notion for us of swashbuckling films. It is able to differentiate between the social classes of the XIXth century with the worker's flat-cap and the nobleman's top hat, as well as conjure up a mood. For example, 'so very British' with their bowler hats, or a picnic with people wearing boaters as depicted in the Renoir and Manet paintings on the banks of the River Marne. In the same vein, Marc Jacobs' *Gavroche,* or urchin hat, which he designed for Louis Vuitton in his 2006-7 Autumn-Winter collection, is redolent of this feeling. Coco Chanel evokes the same by giving the boater a particularly feminine aesthetic. New styles are created from the lasting legacy of the hats of colonial days. The beret, for example, whether it be *basque* or military, when coordinated with a tartan kilt and cardigan, spawned the eternal student look.

Couturiers, who established the diktat that a woman could not go out without a hat, gloves and handbag, can themselves be associated with a particular era and be a source of nostalgia. The photographs of Bettina Graziani, the famous model for Jacques Fath and Christian Dior, have immortalised the New Look style where the hat crowned the silhouette. The cloche hats of the 1920s require a particular type of elfin-face, with the nose and the chin slightly turned-up to give the desired effect. Jacques le Corre knew how to reinvent this accessory with his 'tramp's hat' in 1988. Here he used a coloured viscose, which hides the nose, in conjunction with traditional techniques which replaced straw (figs 3 and 6). In his research, Jacques le Corre placed the emphasis on the material, with plaited viscose straw in gold, silver or shiny black. Attracted to the unusual, his choice of materials for accessories are often those destined for garments such as glossy, striped fabrics, denim or even previously unseen animal skins i.e. metallic toad skin. And, he often uses fringes of feathers. He is inspired by men's hats such as the trilby, panama, Stetson or cowboy hat, as well as various caps (gentleman-farmer, military etc.), and adapts them into women's headwear.

Infinite sources of inspiration

Today the hat is an essential part of the religious fraternity's uniform, the army, as well as employees in large stores in the States and Japan. The headwear of nuns, and commissionaires' uniforms, have inspired Jean-Paul Gaultier for a number of his fashion shows.

Moreover, every designer derives inspiration from the different cultures around world whether it be the hats of the Asian rice farmers, the woven Tibetan or Andean bonnets, or the Russian *chapkas* .... Paris Hilton made the Stetson (fig. 4), which originated from the Mexican *sombero*, the latest 'must-have' accessory.

Sport is the other major source of inspiration. The baseball cap is widely used in Jean-Paul Gaultier's collections giving it a type of roguish charm, and by Gucci, who added his monogram, thus rendering it a luxury product. Other headwear such as the sailor's cap or riding hat are often revisited to accessorise a fashion show.

Beyond the hat

Hair accessories such as combs, slides and ribbons, simple as they might seem, can themselves become fashion accessories - the proof being the chignon pins by Odile Guilbert (fig. 5). Another example is Robert Goosen's multicoloured flower hairband, designed by Marc Jacobs, for Louis Vuitton's fashion show in July 2006.

Even a hairstyle can play the role of an accessory as the blond chignon worn by Simone Signoret in Jacques Becker's film *Casque d'or* (1932) testifies.

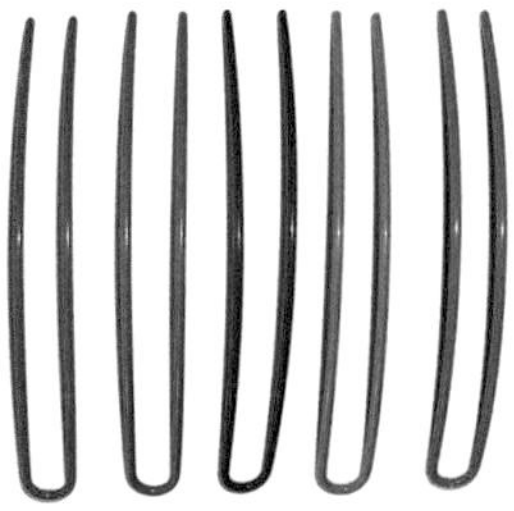

5

6

5. *Compopastel* hair pins by Odile Guilbert.

6. *Api* by Jacques le Corre.

Hat and belt designs

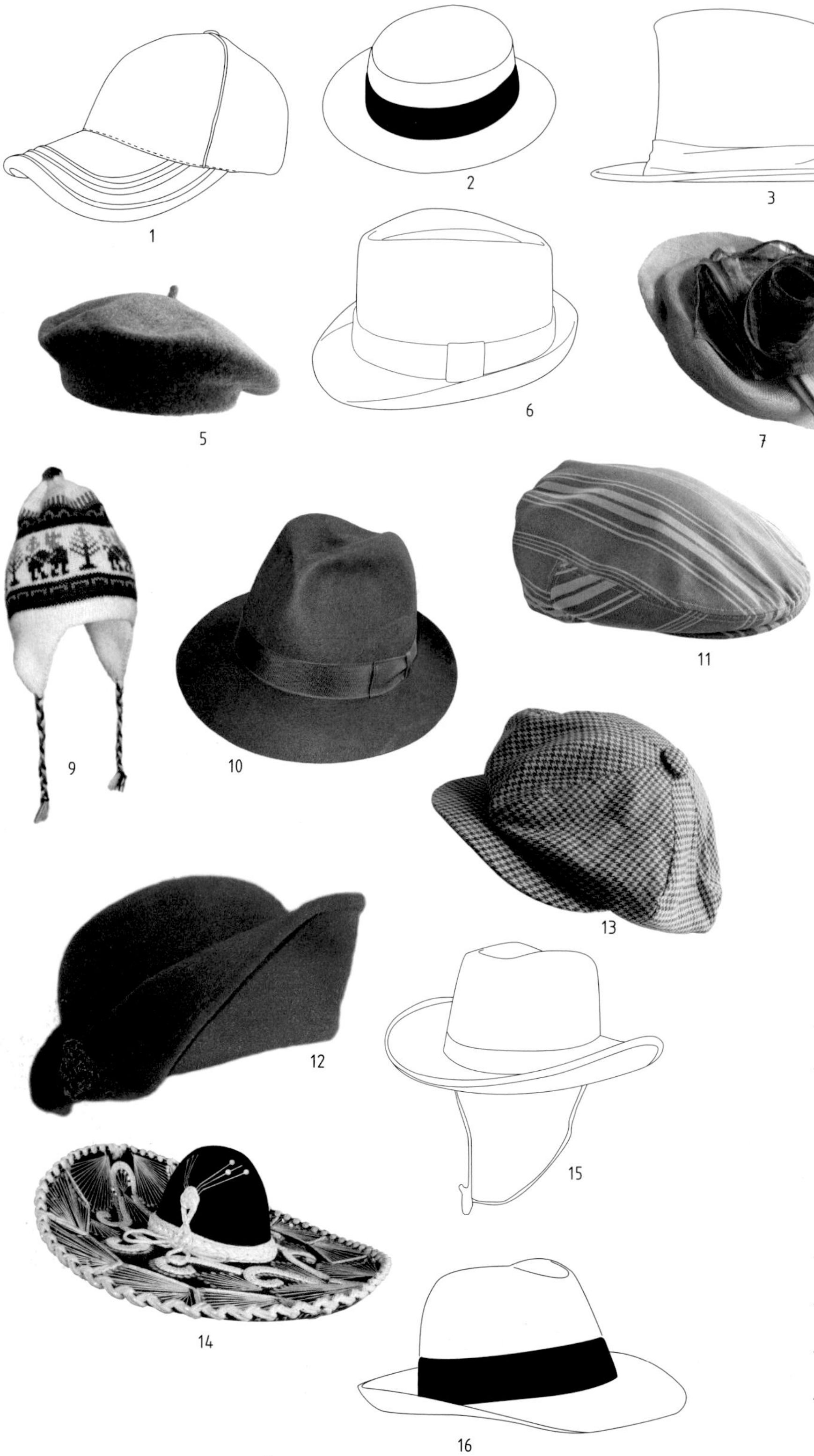

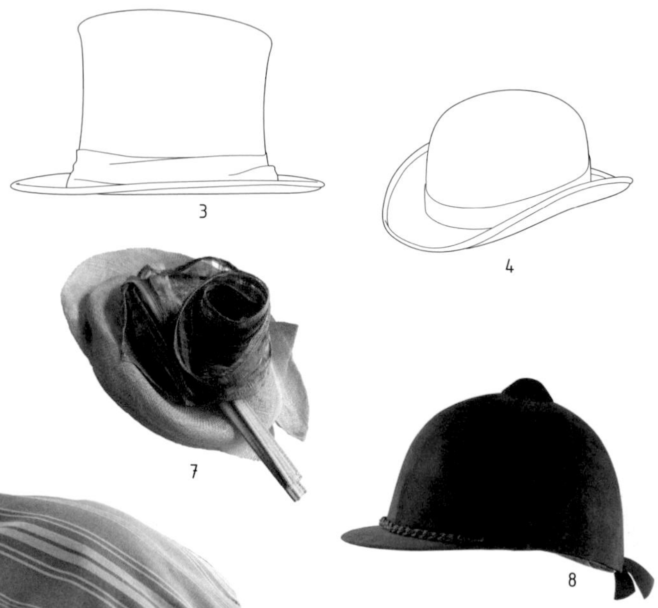

1. Baseball cap
2. Boater
3. Top hat
4. Bowler hat
5. Celine Robert's beret
6. Pork pie hat
7. Celine Robert's Bibi hat
8. Riding hat
9. South American bonnet
10. Borsalino
11. Flat cap
12. Celine Robert's cloche hat
13. Celine Robert's urchin hat
14. Celine Robert's Mexican sombrero
15. Cowboy hat
16. Panama

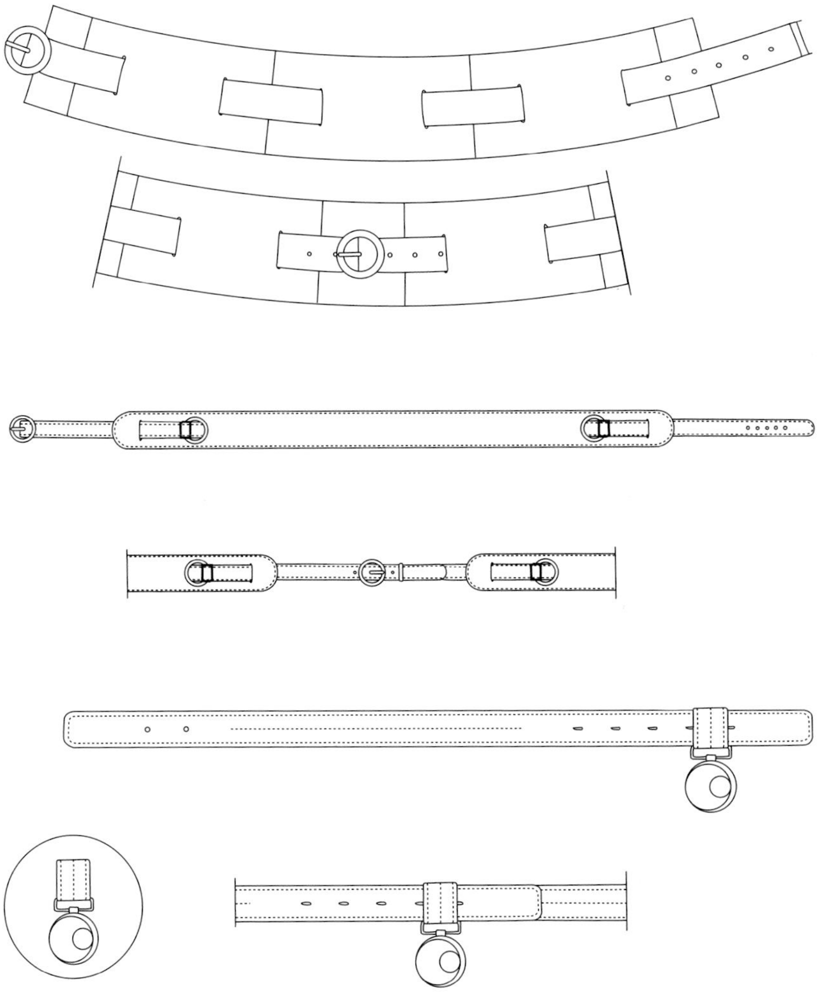

17

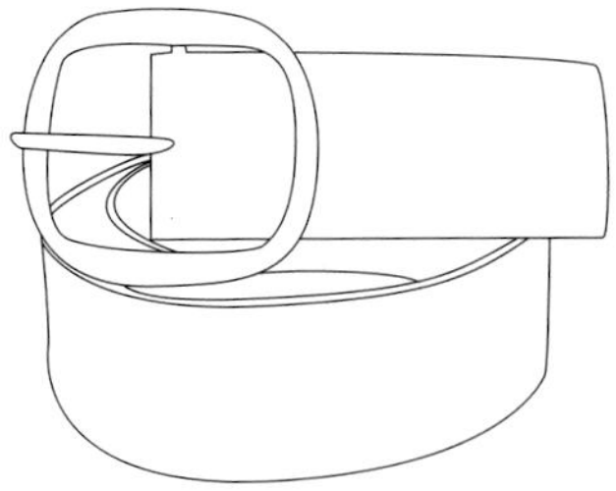

19

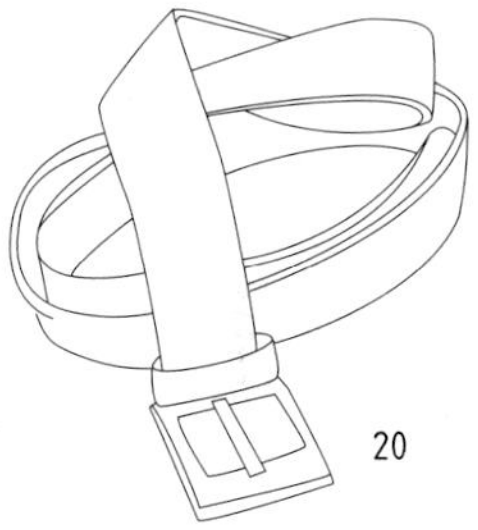

20

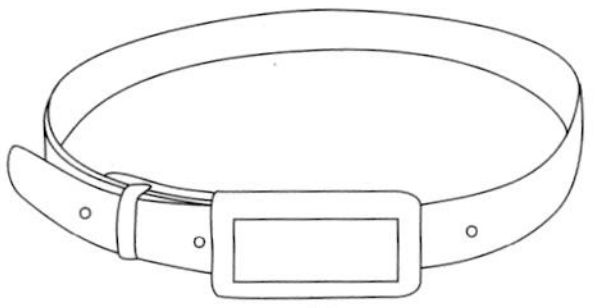

21

17. From top to bottom: wide belt, sliding belt and riveted belt

18. Ornate buckle belt

19. Belt with rounded buckle

20. Belt with fine buckle

21. Classic men's dress belt with rivets

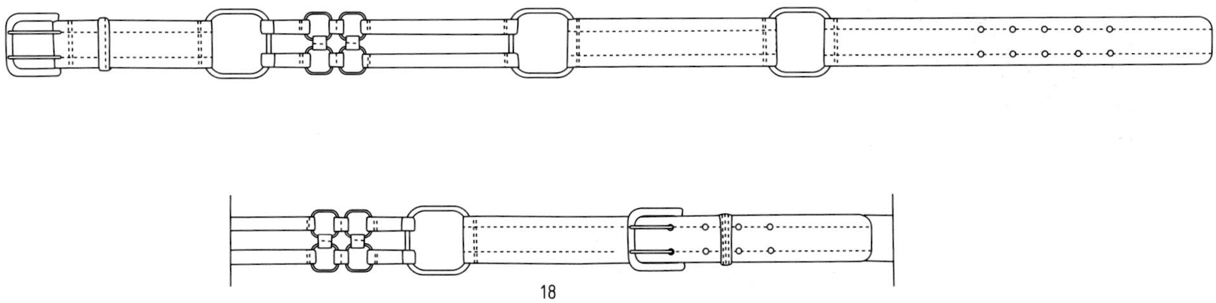

18

Jewellery

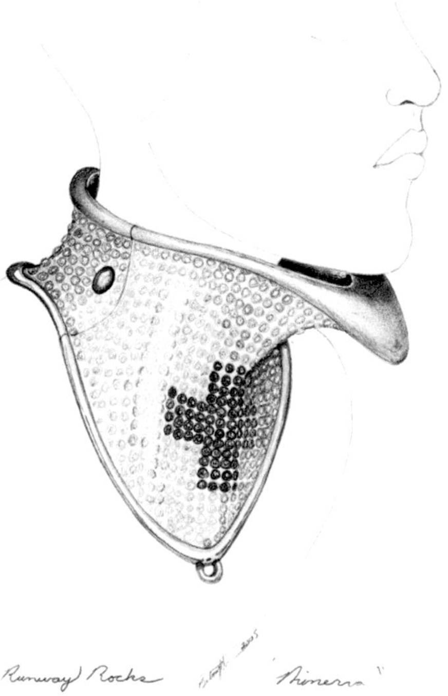

1

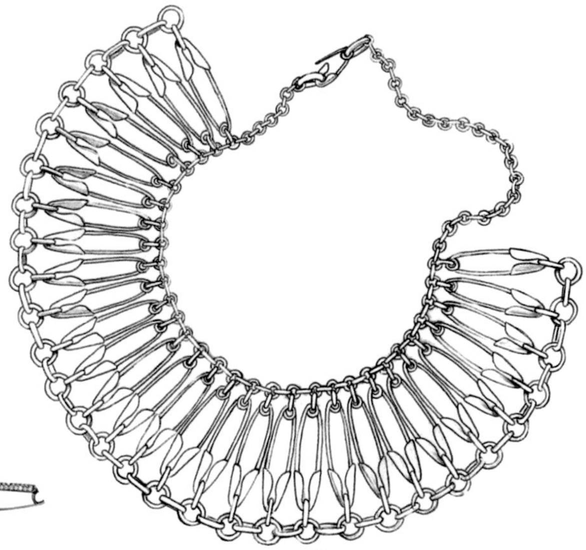

2

3

4

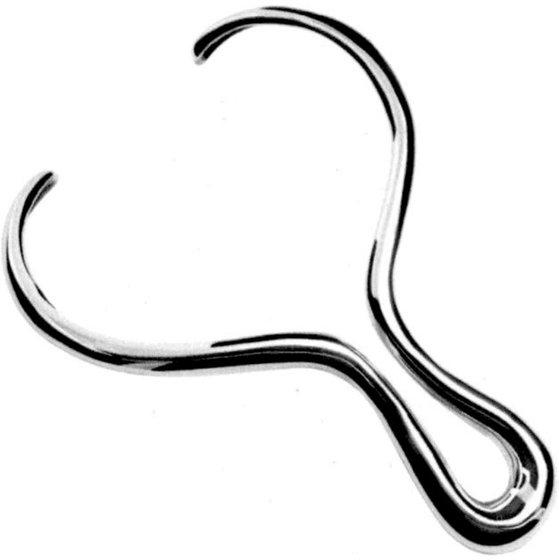

5

6

The origins

The need to adorn oneself with jewellery dates back to prehistoric times: there were pendants, rings made from bone, stone or oval-shaped ivory, as well as jewellery made from feathers, vegetable fibres or fish bones. These types of feather and stone arrangements can be seen in the work of Elena Cantacuzene in Chapter 1 (pp. 38 and 39). Then with the mastery of metal work around 2500 BC, gold and copper bracelets began to be decorated with geometric patterns.

The ancient Egyptians developed the art of stone-setting, wearing bracelets, chokers and necklaces and tiaras with religious symbols. Similarly, Elena Cantacuzene has been inspired by this era – she has used turtles as clasps; the scarab beetle, sacred to the Egyptians, and adapted them into chokers and bangles in silver, gold and bronze. We have to wait until the Greek era, from the end of the 4th century, before a significant evolution takes place and this is when jewellery for the masses ceases and it becomes reserved for nobility and the clergy alike.

Raw materials and techniques

Other than stones and precious metals worked by the jewellers and goldsmiths and cultured pearls which, nowadays, originate from Japan, the principal material used for jewellery in the fashion world today is '*strass*', or crystal. This is a type of lead crystal, coloured with oxides which owes its invention to Georges Frederic Strass (1700 – 1773). Other materials include steel, glass gilded with metal, silver or gold leaf, iron, which has been used in jewellery since the beginning of the 19th century and Swarovski crystal, which is a synthetic form of crystal developed by Daniel Swarovski (1862-1956).

Various types of jewellery

A type of necklace, known as the *Rivière,* was in vogue at the end of the 18th century. It consisted of links of precious stones and was made famous by Alexander Dumas' (1802 – 1870) novel *Le Collier de la Reine* in 1849. This was a historical novel based on Marie Antoinette, the great 19th century bourgeoisie, who revelled in this type of adornment. Bethony Vernon has transformed this necklace into an erotic accessory by replacing the stones with a series of nappy pins linked together (fig. 2). Embellished with crystals in Figure 3 by Sonia Rykiel, they reveal the liberated woman who wears them.

The cameo technique dates back to antiquity. It consists of carving patterns, often the profiles of men and women, onto shells in different coloured layers which are super-imposed. The cameo, which was perhaps best known during the reign of Napoleon III, is nowadays a classic. Queen Victoria particularly favoured this type of jewellery giving it an English feel. Worn as a pendant, ring or brooch, it has been adopted by contemporary designers such as Yazbukey (figs 14 & 16, p. 62). The use of steel by English goldsmiths at the end of the 18th century heralded the advent of large ostentatious jewellery during the Victorian era (1837-1901) in the form of extravagant earrings, watches and other accessories which counterbalanced the somewhat sombre and austere clothing of that period. This kind of jewellery appealed to a certain type of man, notably the dandy, incarnated by Oscar Wilde and it is in this spirit that Marc Jacobs has designed men's accessories which have, up until now, only belonged in a women's wardrobe.

7

8

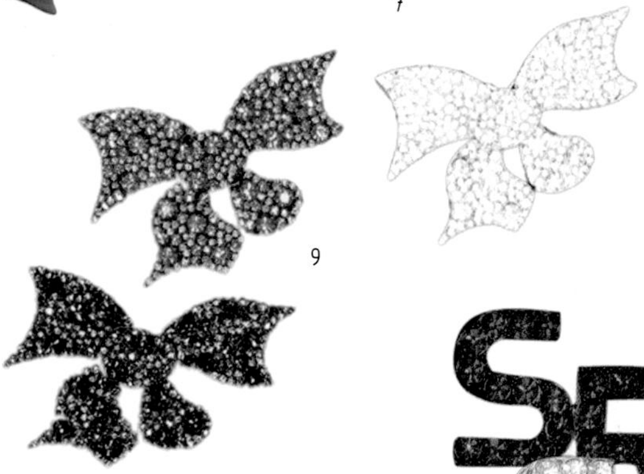

9

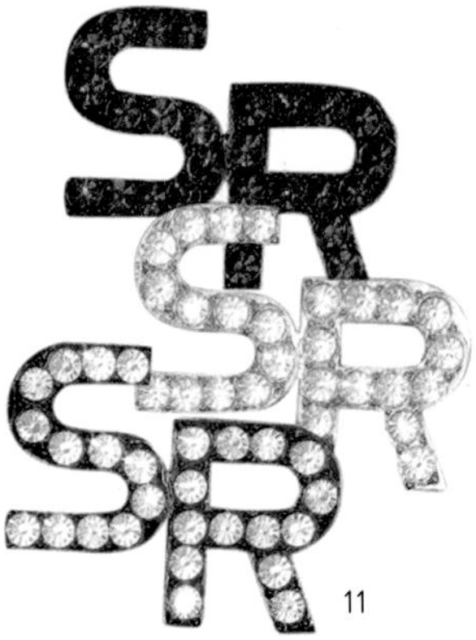

11

10

1. Metal and crystal *Swarovski* collar by Bethony Vernon.

2. *Ferre ,* nappy pin 'riviere' necklace by Bethony Vernon.

3. Crystal brooches by Sonia Rykiel.

4. Crystal brooch by Sonia Rykiel.

5. Silver choker by Bethony Vernon.

6. Crystal brooch by Sonia Rykiel.

7. Painted metal and lustred crystal brooch by Lanvin.

8. Painted metal and lustred crystal hair slide by Lanvin.

9. Metal and crystal brooch by Sonia Rykiel.

10. Painted metal and lustred crystal brooch by Lanvin.

11. Crystal brooches by Sonia Rykiel.

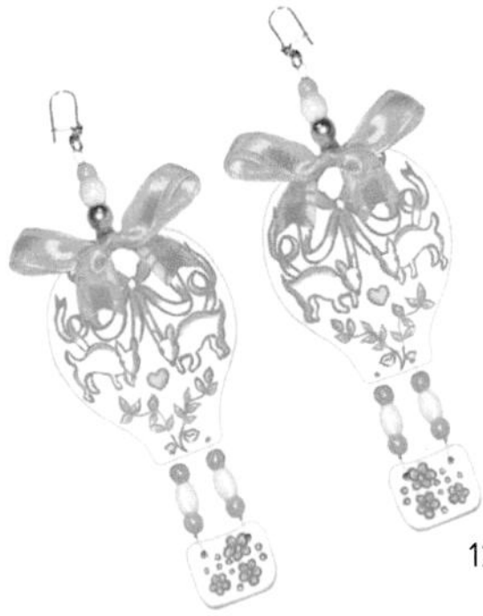

12

13

14

15

16

17

18

19

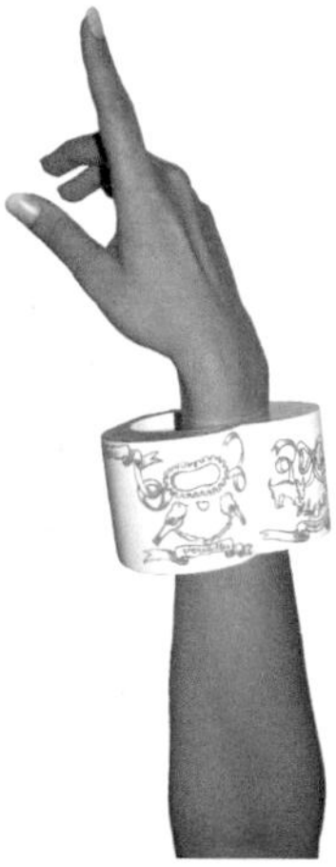

20

21

22

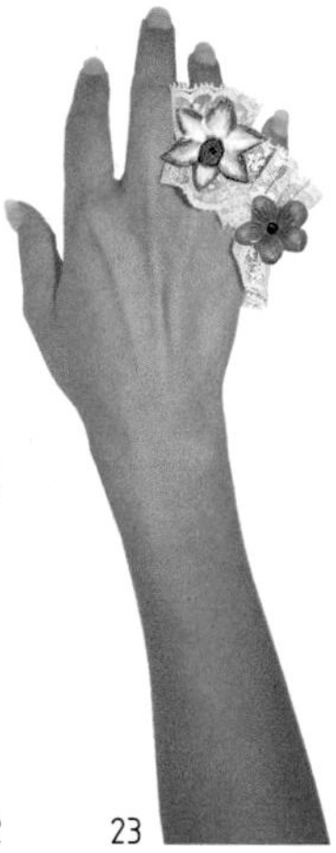

23

Inspirations

The Art Nouveau period, epitomised by Lalique at the end of the 19th century, used glass which had been moulded, reworked and polished as the material of choice for jewellery. This style gave a certain degree of flexibility to rigid materials such as metal or glass. Art Déco jewellery, with its geometric patterns, derived inspiration from Africa, Cubism and Russian ballets.

In the same spirit as the Bauhaus, Karl Fabergé (1846 –1920) heir to the famous jewellery and goldsmith family, tended to distance himself from the *objet d'art* in order to create a piece of jewellery which was a beautifully crafted luxury object in its own right.

The Fabergé egg is, in fact, a symbolic jewel. It was created by Fabergé for Tsar Alexander III at Easter. Each year he would design a new egg with a different function each time e.g. a musical box, watch etc. - more than just a container – the object became a piece of jewellery.

The Rococo period (the term being a fusion between the French word *rocaille* meaning shells, or rocks, and Barocco) appeared during the court of Louis XV. It was here that the distinction was born between day and evening jewellery. The *pâte-de-verre* and shell-like jewellery of Loulou de la Falaise (fig. 24) propels us back to this fantastic era.

By the same token, Yazbukey revisits Marie Antoinette's period with their costume jewellery (figs 12, 18 and 20) by reworking the *toile de Jouy* patterns of the late 18th century and producing them in pastel colours. Still with reference to this period, their multicoloured perspex necklace (fig. 13) has, amongst others, been influenced by a resurgence of ribbons and bows.

Today, virtually every label proposes some form of jewellery to complement their women's collection. Examples include Sonia Rykiel who designs accessories which exude glamour; Alber Elbaz for Lanvin who transforms fabric into metal or plastic creating veritable works of art; Yazbukey who revisits the jewellery of her childhood and Bethony Vernon who creates fetish jewellery.

12. *Balloon* drop earrings by Yazbukey.

13. Garland necklace by Yazbukey.

14. Single strand choker with cameo style pendants by Yazbukey.

15. Choker decorated with narcissus and strawberries by Yazbukey.

16. Baroque brooch with bow by Yazbukey.

17. Single strand necklace by Yazbukey.

18. Heart brooch by Yazbukey.

19. *Cygnes* bangle by Yazbukey.

20. Heart-shaped bangle with ribbon pattern by Yazbukey.

21. *Narcisses* ring by Yazbukey.

22. Bangle decorated with ladybirds and red fruits by Yazbukey.

23. *Narcisses* ring by Yazbukey.

24. *Pate-de-verre* and shell wrap-around necklace by Loulou de la Falaise.

25. *Pate-de-verre* and crystal brooch by Loulou de la Falaise.

26. Tousled necklace in black, red and turquoise coral by Loulou de la Falaise.

27. Drop earring in metal with semi-precious stones of tourmaline, amethyst and citrine.

28. Bamboo coral ring decorated with an amethyst and silver ladybird.

29. Collection of multicoloured lacquered bracelets by Loulou de la Falaise.

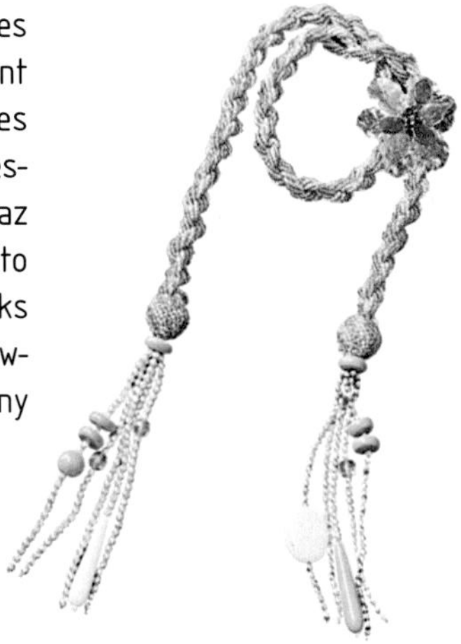
24

25

26

27

28

29

Competition between brands encourages product diversification. For example, a bag can also be a belt, a garment become a bag. New designs enter our consciousness subliminally, triggering a desire to acquire these which we believe have been created especially for us. This 'déjà vu' impression of familiar objects, albeit distant, which are renewed each season, is the result of meticulous work by the designers. With the accessory, the designers' work is directed more towards the product and brand concept. They know how to put together everything we think we desire in the creations with which we identify ourselves. Designers act as visionaries, knowing how to choose, organise information and anticipate our wishes subtly making us believe we want a particular product. Finally, we concede whilst they are already elsewhere working on the next collection.

Working in teams, they determine and illustrate the 'story' for the new collection with the aid of visuals and mood boards. Inspirational photos are presented with potential materials and colours for the products. Colour ranges are organised into colour ways, materials are selected and proposed for the strongest designs. Patterns can also be presented at this stage.

Designers collect, rearrange and assemble information deriving inspiration from a variety of sources which result in new collections. Using iconographic research, they collect photos from magazines which inform shape, material and colour. This is an essential part of the design process as an image has the ability to illustrate a concept very rapidly. The personality of the woman can also emerge from these images, whether she be glamorous or androgynous, for example.

The following pages offer a snapshot of the research carried out by designers whilst they develop a theme which, in turn, defines the collection's direction. Behind the superficial aesthetic of this research is a font of background work: for example, Christian Louboutin's and Élisabeth Guers mood boards and Louis Vuitton's patterns etc. The different designs of materials etc. are also rigorously and thoughtfully researched, demanding just as much work, and requiring a great deal of intuition, savoir-faire and a professional eye.

Style results from a designer's own expression coupled with his, or her, sensitivity, vision and individual approach to shape, colour, volume and fabrics. Each collection can be viewed as a film, or book, into which the whole design team immerses itself. The creative director is the director with each mood corresponding to

Chapter 3 - Concepts and designs

a part of the story-board, which in its entirety, allows us to understand the collection and the message it is trying to convey.

In the first instance, the creative director, and his team, reveal the essence of the story. For example, Marie Antoinette and her luxurious wardrobe. Naturally, artistic licence is applicable for it is not expected to remain steadfastly true to historical facts. What is important in a collection is the detail, which is 'romanticised' by the designer. It is this fantasy of historical abbreviations which give the collection magic, making it more than just a collection of unoriginal theatre costumes. This is also why a theme, completely devoid of any historical roots, such as the 'British Amazone' for example, is almost simpler to develop as it depends mainly on materials and finishes such as buckles and belts etc.

Once the designers have decided upon a particular idea or theme, other ideas will be built around them. The creative director submits these designs to the marketing director who will, in turn, select products which create a balance within the collection plan.

With the accessory, a multitude of collections known as 'lines' are proposed which are identifiable by their materials, finishes and patterns. Contrary to what happens in the *prêt-a-porter* world, accessory shapes are heavily influenced by trends; the originality of these products being in the craftsmanship afforded to their manufacture, as well as the innovative use of materials and colours.

This specificity implies that the accessory designer must have possess a good working knowledge of the technical aspects of manufacture. In this chapter the designer, Élisabeth Guers, shows us the different methods of manufacture involved in the manufacture of her shoe collections. According to her, the work of a designer can be likened to that of the tightrope-walker where one tries to find a balance between the expression of an idea, its production and its marketing. As trends and marketing can be contradictory, sometimes the designer must make allowances for these factors when creating a product. The creative director and the designer must clearly define their target markets before beginning to develop a collection, or product. In order to do this, it is important to travel extensively, not only for inspiration but also for studying different markets such as Paris, Tokyo, London, New York or Milan. This has certainly been the case with Élisabeth Guers who travelled the world as she designed her collections for Jimmy Choo, Maud Frizon, Sergio Rossi, Céline and Thierry Mugler.

Moods, colours and materials

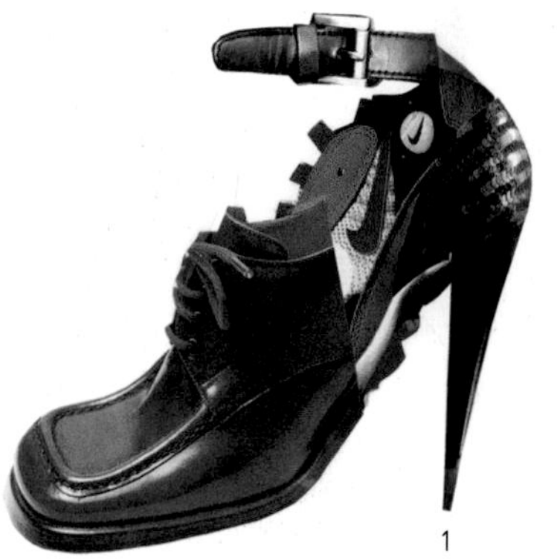

1

2

3

1. Combination of quirky collages, masculine/feminine, sport/sophisticated, heavy/slick. It portrays a snapshot of the fashion world's contrasts and free spirits in one go.

2. Masculine/feminine collage, moccasin/brogue, Chanel toe and bejewelled heel. Here, as well, the associations refer to the contrasts which inspire fashion.

3. This collage represents several thematic combinations: the season's make-up, belted military-style jacket, wide belt worn on the hips, flared skirt worn over drainpipe jeans with open-toed shoes (in winter?!).

4 & 5. The two mood boards illustrate monochrome colour palettes, one in warm tones, the other in neutral tones. Their respective themes being 'fusion' and 'shadows'. The colour swatches are stapled to the boards with the name of the fabrics and colour references.

Inspirations

Freelance designer, Élisabeth Guers, clearly explains how she decides on a trend and why she chooses the visuals, colours and materials she does.

By working on moods and colours simultaneously, she illustrates her initial colour selections by means of visual mood boards. This presentation is achieved by using material samples from leading manufacturers sourced from Italian and French trade fairs.

She uses Bristol board to present her themes and colours where the label, season and material references are also catalogued. The mood boards she produced for Calvin Klein in 2001 (figs. 4 and 5), and her collages of the main products for the pre-Winter season 2002-2003, are also accompanied by written descriptions.

Contrasts

The starting point for Élisabeth Guers' designs originates from what she feels are essential products for the forthcoming season. She will then gather that information together and cut and paste it onto a silhouette. By mixing and matching this patchwork of images, the foundations of the new season's 'must haves' are laid down. The silhouette to the left, combines punk with the somewhat bourgeois spirit of the small hand bag, successfully demonstrating the cultural cross-referencing of these 'compositions'.

The caricature-like feel of these collages accentuates the themes' essence or story-boards – exaggeration being essential. For Élisabeth, there is a fine line between beauty and the grotesque for she feels this is determined by one's

4

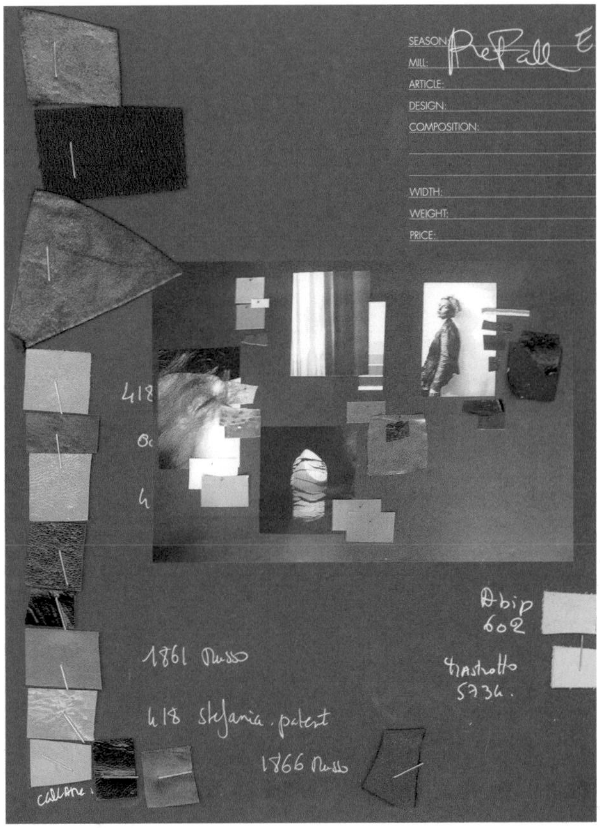

5

culture and sensitivity. Her themes are inspired by personal desires, moods and images as she allows herself to be guided by her instinct and senses. It is in this discrepancy, between materials and volume, that the unexpected shows itself. She is particularly drawn to the association of themes and contradictory images, such as alleged ugliness and alleged beauty, crude, almost vulgar, materials combined with an element of sophistication. Subsequently, she researches different elements of composition thus enabling her to tell her 'stories'.

The theme entitled 'Shadows' (fig. 5) shows the interplay of light and dark constructed around metallic, textured and iridescent materials. In order to give the colours a feminine aspect they have been highlighted as an eye shadow, on the second board – the choice of visuals being determined by this interplay. The women's smooth, shiny skin portrayed in these photos contrast strongly with the hard, raw aspect of the other elements in Figs 4 and 5. Some the colours from each palette will be used for the collection.

The 'Fusion' theme in Figure 4 has been inspired by fire. Here warm, orangey and coppery colours are proposed. This range of spicy tones, chosen for the pre-Winter collection of 2002-2003, are softened by some more sombre tones. The colours bear reference to tanned summer skin tones which evoke a sensation of heat.

Élisabeth Guers tends to choose women's faces to express a certain sensuality in her collections. Due to her love of contrasts, she has selected a face which is wild, yet sophisticated , associating it with a wintry undergrowth scene (fig. 4). This improbable association gives a certain ambiguity to the theme. The style of these very different elements – femininity, on the one hand, with high-heeled shoes and virility, on the other, with a crude leather belt – flags up these contrasts. The three-dimensional effect afforded by these objects breathes life into these boards.

Mood and sketches

1

2

3

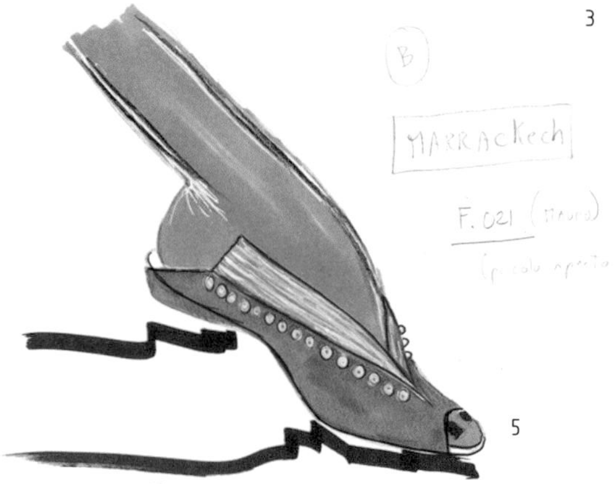

5

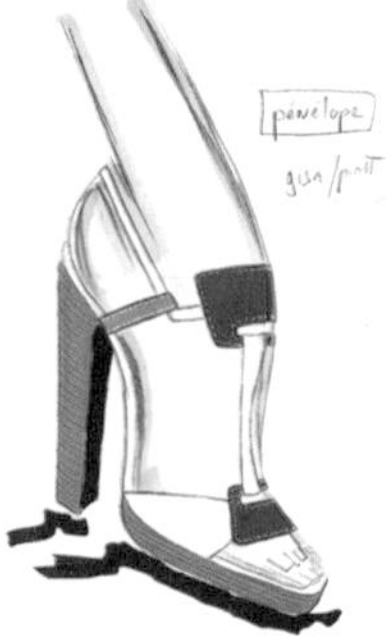

4

6

7

8

9

Mood board

After preliminary research, the designer can introduce, to a greater or lesser extent, an element of his, or her, own personal interests, current affairs, musical and artistic trends. This information-gathering exercise is 'documented' by means of a mood board which gradually determines the direction, mood and general feel of the collection, its lines and details. Its main aesthetic characteristics are presented here in a harmonious fashion. A balance is created on the board between empty and full spaces, images and text and the choice of colours – every element has some significance.

Christian Louboutin's board (fig. 10 – opposite page) illustrates his interest in architectural detail. Whilst observing elements of Islamic-style lattice or fretwork screens, he was inspired to design a shoe buckle in the same vein. Likewise, The Rolling Stones concert ticket shows an interesting colour combination. The presence of diverse comments such as 'PS. Call Dita before 7 o'clock' or 'Go to the Rousseau exhibition before the end of June!!' demonstrates how the designer draws inspiration from everyday life.

Details, such as the tassel-trimmed heel and whimsical buckle, contribute to the theme of the product. A small sketch of the *Robocopina* court shoe in the bottom left-hand corner of the mood board, shows the importance of 'cut-outs' on the shoe. A piece of black satin, embroidered with gold thread and sequins, originating from an 18th century mule, and a photo of leopard skin, define the spirit of the materials.

Christian Louboutin chooses his favourite by encircling it with a red heart, noting alongside the necessary modifications. Historic references are

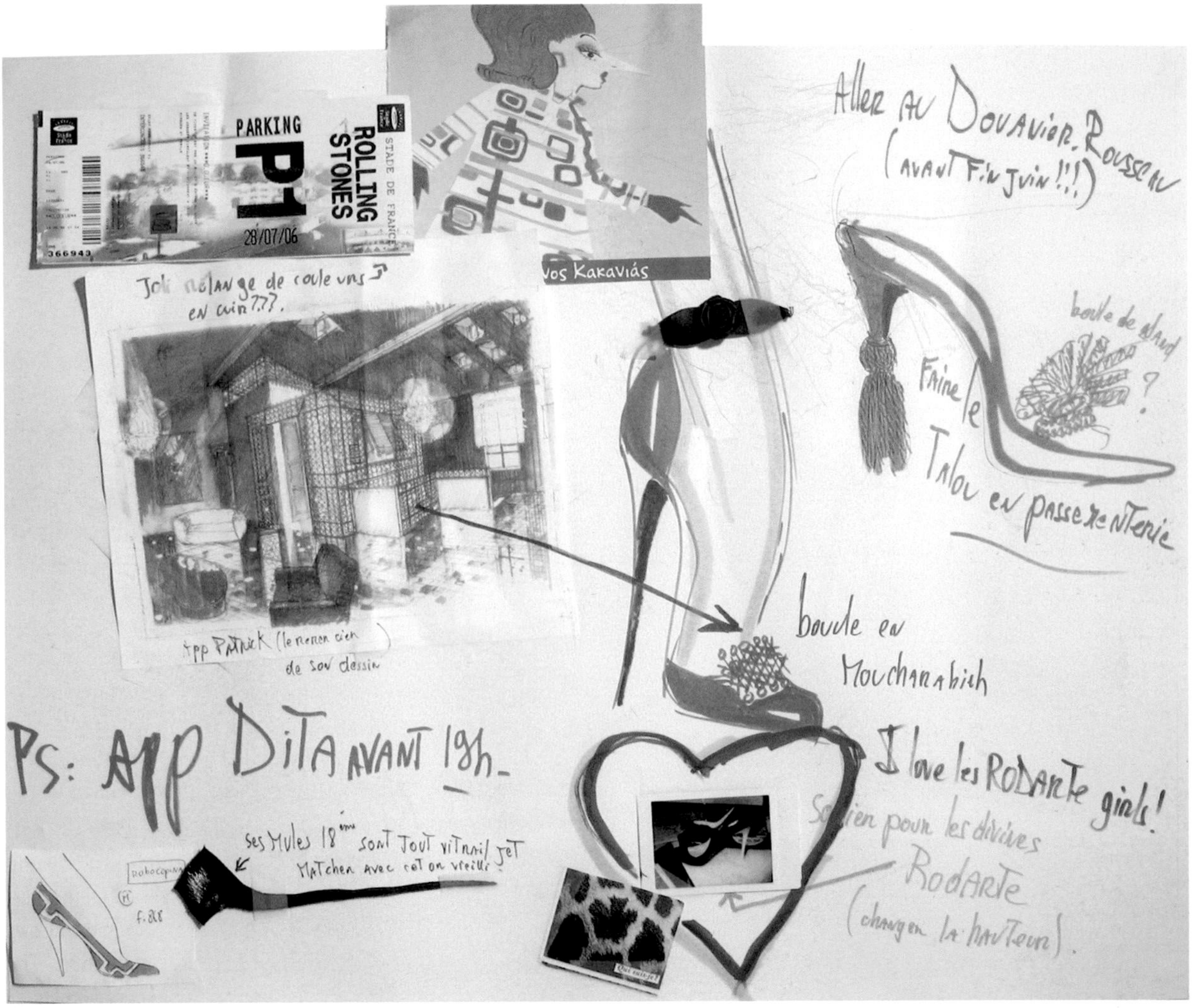

10

revisited, inspirational elements are reinterpreted in a flash and the proportions, volumes, finishes, materials and colours are all suggested.

Style and drawing

In order to personalise a product, the designer needs to find one, or several, original elements which will undeniably distinguish it from the competition. Christian Louboutin has, for example, chosen the colour red for the soles of all his shoes. This detail has now become his trademark or signature.

Figures 1 to 9 show the importance of marker pens in the production of roughs. It is also important to have a good understanding of anatomy so that the correct arch, or instep, is obtained when designing high-heeled shoes.

Three-dimensional roughs, which are a necessity for handbags and other leather goods, require a false perspective in order to convey a sense of depth in the illustration. With jewellery, the drawings require much more technique representing each face of the object i.e. plan, sides and underside view.

In all cases, it is important to master the techniques of rendering light and shadow, both freehand and computer-aided. Some of the colour marker techniques and Photoshop are explained at the end of this chapter.

1 to 9. Shoe illustrations made by Christian Louboutin using a marker pen for his Spring-Summer collection 2006.

10. Mood and inspiration board 50 x 64 cm, made by Christian Louboutin, for Rodarte's Spring-Summer fashion show in 2007.

Themes and designs

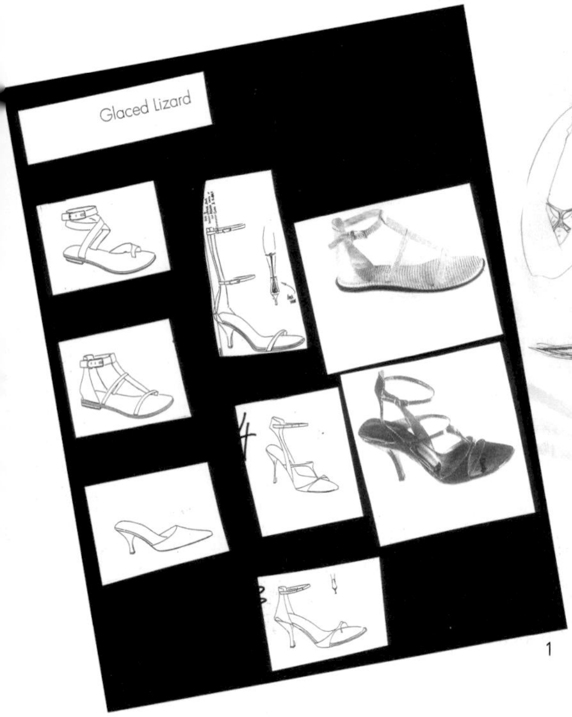

1

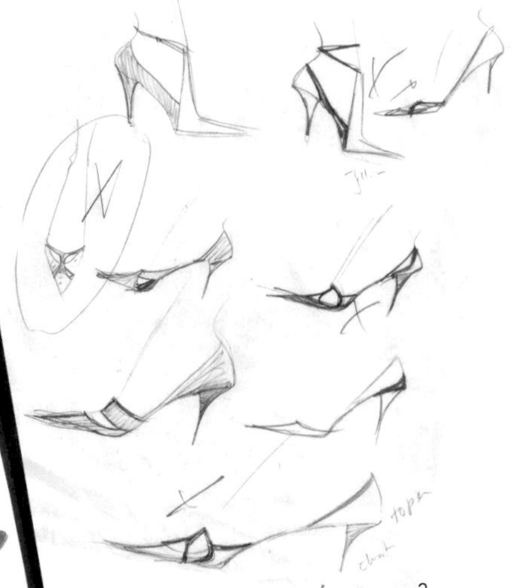

2

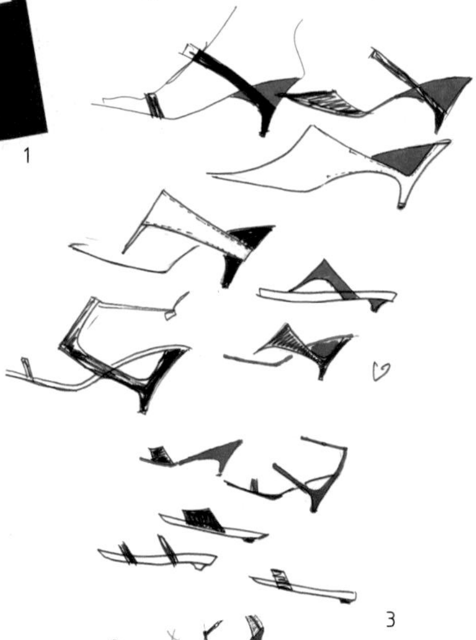

3

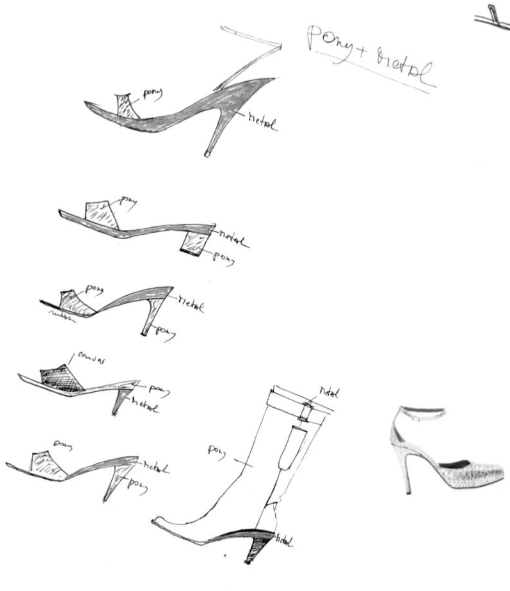

4

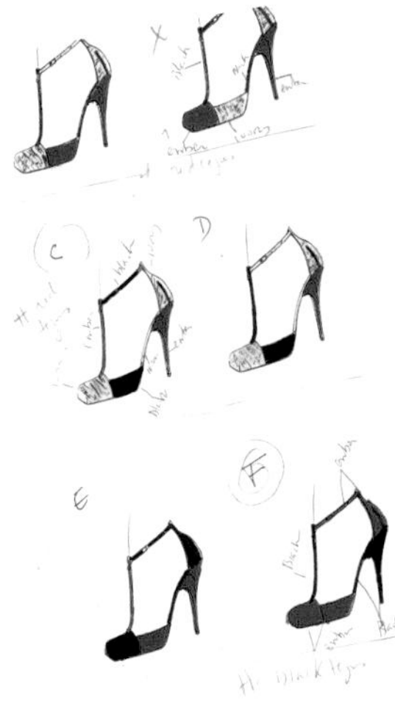

5

Élisabeth Guers uses quick, instinctive sketches as preparation for her design work. From these, a few are selected which will ultimately make up the collection plan. These sketches give a general idea of the themes which have inspired her. This type of rapid design development is essential part of the design process so, by working closely with the heel-maker, the final shape of the shoe comes to life. Élisabeth also includes photographs as a means of research, such as those which she took from an illustration by Antonio Lopez (fig. 8).

The technical drawings in (fig. 1) made subsequently are much tighter and colder having lost some of this creative spontaneity.

The finished drawings do not always allow for the development of as many variants as the sketches. The design of a heel is in fact drawn as exactly as possibly. The sketch is, therefore, an ideal communication tool between the designer and the craftsperson whose close collaboration is essential for the success of the product. As the heel-maker sculpts the heel, bit by bit, so the designer reworks his, or her, drawing; the shape evolves, influencing the designer's subconscious, as it is reinterpreted in these rough drafts.

The first step when making a shoe is the production of a *last*, a hand-carved wooden replica of the human foot, which is then moulded in plastic. A well-fitting shoe and contour of the arch, or instep, depends entirely on the skill of the last-maker. At the same time, the heel-maker makes the heel corresponding to the shape chosen by the designer. The heel can be perceived as a sculpture upon which the whole weight of the body rests. Its centre of gravity and size are the determining factors for a comfortable instep.

Using the last as a guide, the patternmaker cuts out the shoe's upper and lining. A master craftsman then stretches the chosen leather tautly over the last, positioning it tightly using nails, or machines which have been perfected for this purpose. Finally, the sole is chosen and stuck in place.

The secrets of a successful shoe lie in the close relationship between the design and the manufacture.

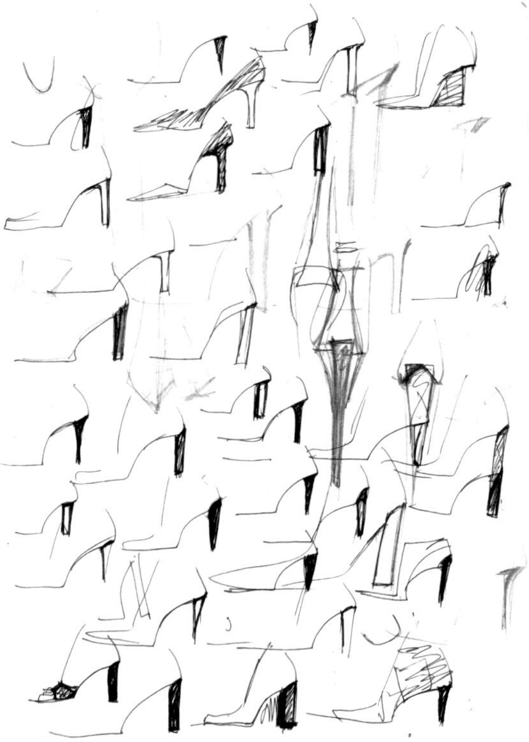

6

Developments

It is essential to have certain ideas in one's head to produce a successful shoe collection. For example, Élisabeth Guers confirms that 'a shoe's success is directly linked to its heel: a lot of women will choose their shoes in relation to this'. The heel, its height and the resulting arch are decisive factors for the physiognomy of the shoe and a badly-arched heeled shoe will not be well-received. Certain women prefer waisted or hourglass heels, Oxford or stilettos whereas some prefer flat or very high heels. The height of the most current heels is in the region of 3, 4, 5 or 7.5 cm with the majority available in three heights. The heel sketches must, therefore, lend themselves to these variations. Colour and material (fig. 5) play an important part in the styling of a shoe so it is important to try several combinations to arrive at the best one. The cut of the upper is also essential for the success of a beautiful court shoe with a low cut will making the foot look more elegant.

To recap, time and effort spent on researching heel sizes and the cut of the uppers are decisive factors for a collection's success.

The same theme could be developed in a very different fashion according to the choice of heel, colour and materials as is the case with the Greco-Roman sandals in Figure 1.

7

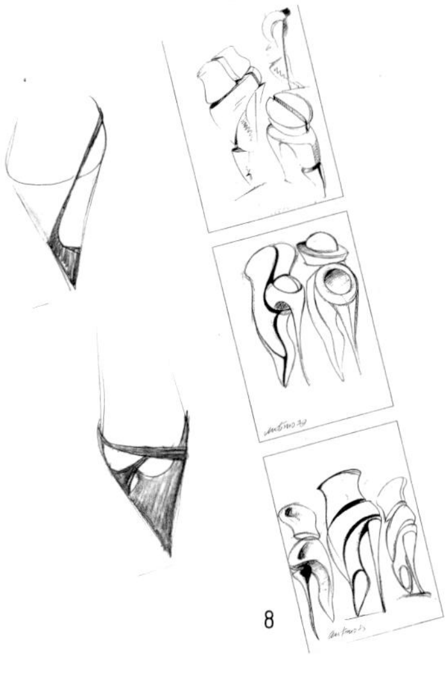

8

1. Design board of technical drawings for variations of a line inspired by a Greco-Roman theme by Élisabeth Guers.

2 & 3. Research sketches of uppers and heels by Élisabeth Guers.

4. First material suggestions for the uppers and heels of varying heights by Élisabeth Guers.

5. Suggested models for Calvin Klein's Winter 2006 fashion 2006, with colour and material variations on the same shoe by Élisabeth Guers.

6. Quick sketch done at an Italian heel maker's in order to decide on the heel size by Élisabeth Guers.

7. Development of the theme '*Jeux de bandes*' on a court shoe, sandal, T- strap and a spuntato (open-toed court shoe) by Éisabeth Guers.

8.Research sketches of a shoe upper inspired by an illustration of Antonio Lopez by Élisabeth Guers.

The collection's structure

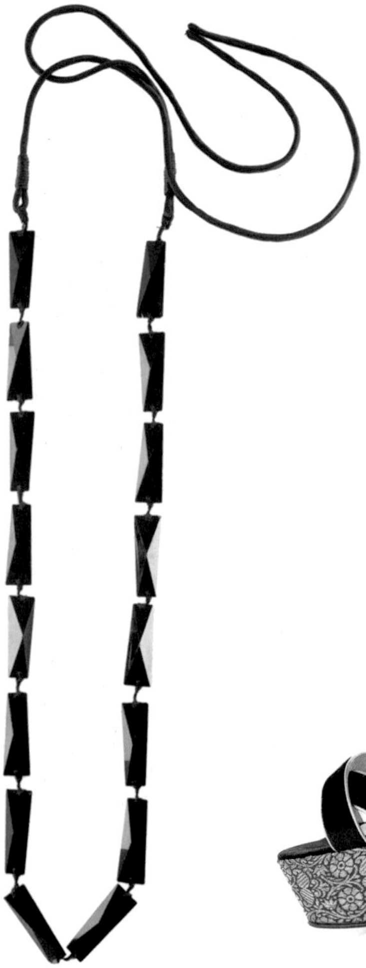

1

2

3

4

5

6

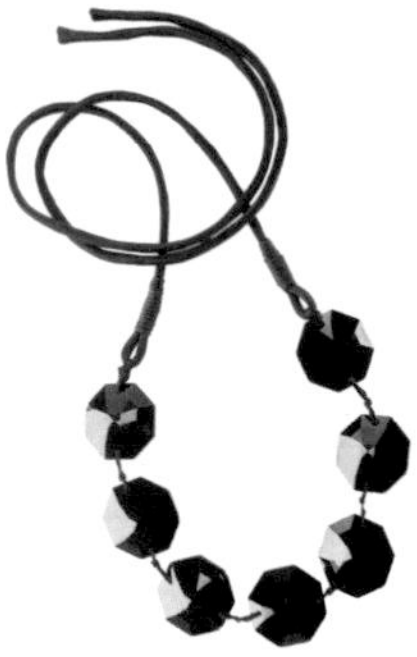

7

8

Brands and lines

Accessory brands propose complete product lines which are enriched by *prêt-à-porter* collections as is the case with Hermès and Louis Vuitton for example. On the other hand, however, prêt-à-porter brands such as Dior, Chanel or Yves Saint Laurent tend to use accessories to complement their clothing collections. Accessory and clothing lines follow the global direction of a brand's collections. Yet they will have their own theme and are developed in collaboration with artistic, marketing and commercial direction. The collections plans are established in order to propose complete, coherent ranges which respond to the brand's identity and market needs.

Designing an accessory line

Each line is designed with special attention being paid to an original visual identity which emphasises the details, materials, colours and patterns, whether branded or not, and which are individual and subsequently developed through all the product lines. See Chapter 2 for an example of the development of a logo which is available on all of the brand's items. These are generally complete lines i.e. cases, handbags, small leather goods, shoes, belts, scarves, umbrellas, glasses, jewellery etc. and they are often available in several colours (figs 3 & 5). Certain series of luxury brands are limited-edition items which make the lines more affordable, thus reaching a larger market.

Big brands such as Louis Vuitton and Chanel tend to develop their classic products in different sizes, i.e. miniature, small, medium and large.

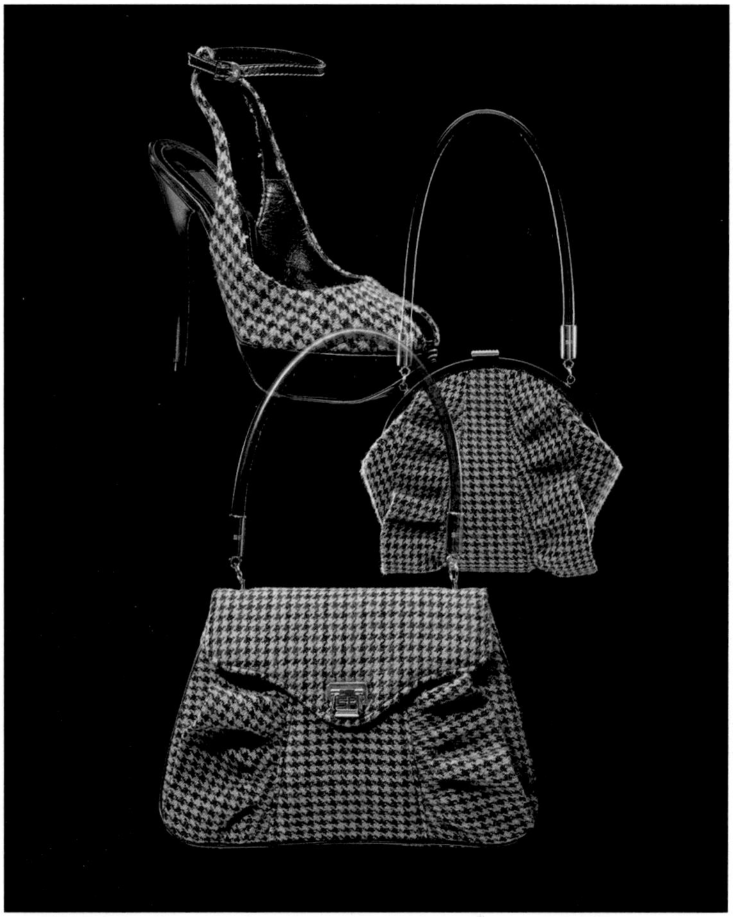

9

Whether it be Lanvin with his shiny crystal jewellery, Louboutin with his ethnic themes or Sonia Rykiel with her chic Parisian style, all the products presented on these two pages are immediately identifiable as to whom they belong.

1. Shiny crystal and satin long necklace by Lanvin Summer 2006.

2. Pearl, metal and shiny crystal necklace by Lanvin, Summer 2006.

3. Flagada ballet pumps and *Totem* handbag by Christian Louboutin, Summer 2005.

4. *Viva Zeppa* platform sandal with embossed golden decoration by Christian Louboutin, Summer 2005.

5. *Totem* handbag by Christian Louboutin, Summer 2005.

6. *Origami* pearl and metal necklace by Lanvin, Summer 2006.

7. Satin and shiny crystal necklace by Lanvin, Summer 2006.

8. Clutch bag and court shoe with embossed golden decoration by Christian Louboutin, Autumn-Winter 2005-6.

9. Clasp handbag, flap handbag and stiletto in hound's-tooth check wool by Sonia Rykiel, Autumn-Winter 2004-5.

Accessory patterns or motifs

1

2

3

4

Patterns, as with materials and details, are essential to the visual identity of an accessory collection. To illustrate this point, we have chosen to present the design process followed by Marc Jacobs with Louis Vuitton.

Vuitton revisited by Marc Jacobs

Marc Jacobs likes a contradiction. Beauty and ugliness complement each other in his surprising creations and he has even been known to describe some of his models as 'Very good but very ugly'! His deconstruction concept, which is more or less unpredictable, provides him with the inspiration he needs before embarking on a design, i.e. a chaos of ideas and experiences. His handbag stems from a combination of several Louis Vuitton bags (of which there are only 28 examples in the world) in a style reminiscent of Cubism. He disintegrates the flowers which he presses, bleaches or soaks in tea, uses butcher's wrapping paper from rue Saint-Denis in Paris, for the flowers made by the feather-maker Lemarié in New York and is inspired by the dots from the Japanese artist Yayoi Kusama in order to produce his own in the form of buttons. The material is transformed by using pattern almost as a form of alchemy.

Reinterpretations

In collaboration with the Japanese artist, Takashi Murakami, this New York-based designer has devised a new motif Multicolour Monogram (fig. 2) for the Louis Vuitton brand. This required more than 33 colour pulls in order to be reproduced by the printing method (which serves as a good deterrent against any forgery). He has also taken the tea towel check laundry bag as inspiration for Louis Vuitton. Equally, Azzedine Alaia has also exploited this with his famous pink checked carrier bags derived from Tati, the large chain store based in Barbès. He has developed an entire range around this famous print including clothes and accessories.

Marc Jacobs often works with artists, such as the aluminium sculptor Sylvie Fleurie who inspired him to design a handbag line. And, in his time, Yves Saint Laurent would make reference to the great artists who influenced him such as Vincent Van Gogh, Picasso, Braque and even Mondrian, who inspired his famous dress, created in 1966. Beyond these complex combinations of materials and patterns, Marc Jacobs has reinterpreted the traditional Louis Vuitton printed cloth into a jean material evoking the notion of eternal youth. In this same contradictory spirit, he takes up Takashi Murakami's motif using it on handbags and white mink muffs. Marc Jacobs maintains it is important to stay in tune with current artistic trends. 'He transforms fashion into images,' says his friend, the New York artist, Elisabeth Peyton.

6

5

7

1. Detail of the Monogrammed canvas, printed motif
(© Louis Vuitton archives).

2. Detail of the Multicolour Monogram, white with printed motif
(© Louis Vuitton archives).

3. Detail of Monogrammed canvas, denim with woven motif
(© Louis Vuitton archives).

4. Detail of Multicolour Monogram on black background with printed motif.
(© Louis Vuitton archives).

5. A miniature *Noe*, *Steamer* and *Alma* placed in front of a *Alma* in Multicolour Monogram white canvas with printed motif.
(© Patrick Galabert/LB Productions).

6. *Neo Speedy* (30 x 32,5 x13 cm) in Monogrammed denim canvas with finishes in VNN and brass with woven motif.
(© Philippe Jumin).

7. White mink *Bum Bag* Multicolour Monogram, detail from the Louis Vuitton's women's fashion show, Autumn-Winter 2006-7, inlaid motifs.
(© Louis Vuitton archives).

CHAPTER 3
Concepts and designs

Materials

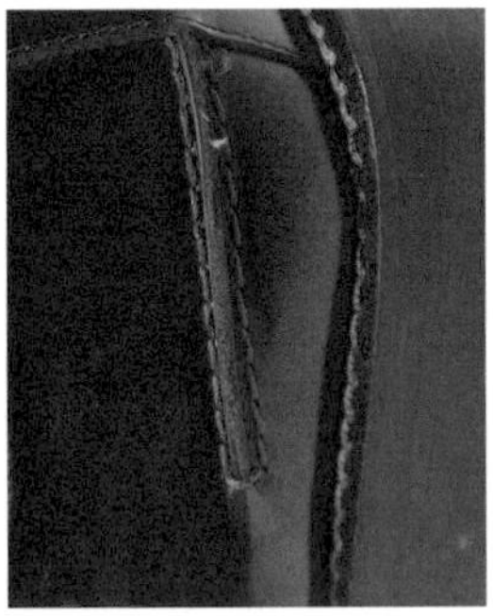
1

2

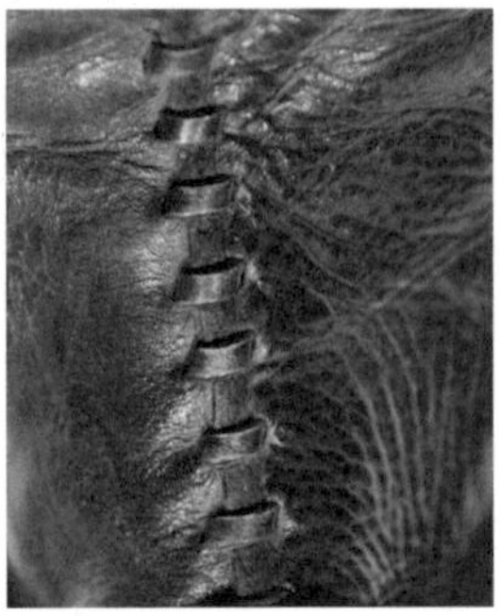
3

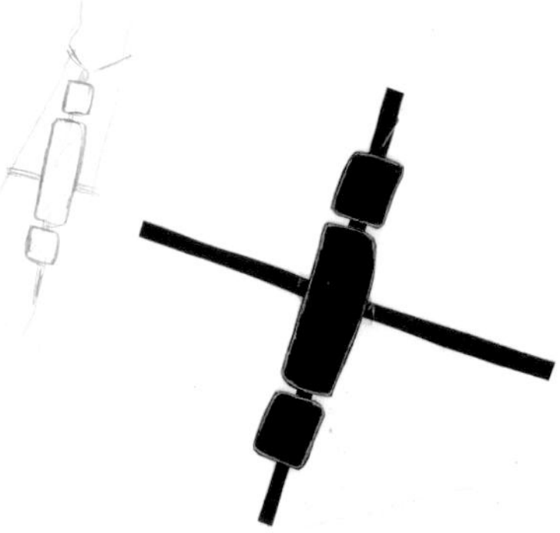
4

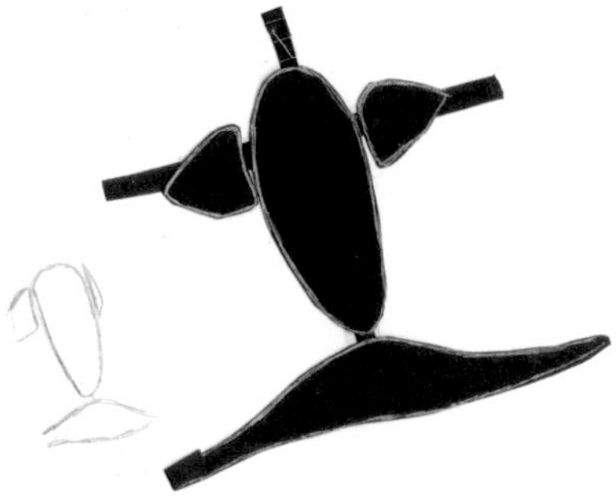
5

6

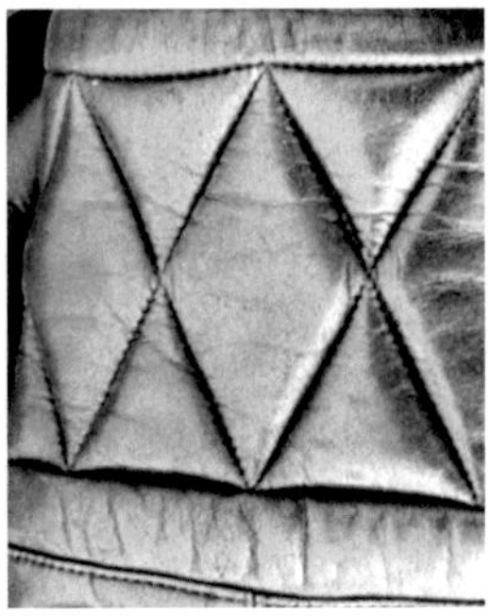
7

8

Materials

The accessory uses materials of which the transformation, itself, can result in new and original lines. Obviously the techniques used to do this are influenced by how the materials have been used in the garments and vice versa. An example of this could be jeans and the famous *stone-wash* used by Marc Jacobs in his collections.

Transformations

There are a variety of technical processes to which materials can be subjected in order to alter their appearance and hence result in new products. For example: coating, assembling, crumpling, folding, engraving, sewing, overlaying, burning, mixing, inlaying and colouring etc.

At the beginning of the 20th century, Fortuny was inspired by Greek *chitons* (type of folded garment) for his famous, finely pleated silk dresses. More recently, the Japanese designer, Issey Miyake developed a line of handbags called *Pleats Please* linked to a permanent pleating technique for synthetic materials using a heated pressing technique; the bags are perfectly flat when empty, however, open like an accordion when full.

In the 1980s Martin Margiela, along with Marithé and François Girbaud, were amongst the first to consistently deconstruct their collection prototypes in order to transform them from new garments into customised ones. Today this practice has become current in many accessory collections.

It is possible to obtain a variety of contrasting results. Due to designers' demands, fabric suppliers have a greater tendency nowadays to pay more attention to the visual and technical finishes of a fabric. The designer destroys, modifies or deconstructs the original material turning the fabric into an innovative concept in itself. These are the slogans of a new generation of which Marc Jacobs is living proof.

Influences

The assimilation and reinterpretation of images and/or ideas into new arrangements are also at the root of new concepts. Any image, whether it be of an apartment block in Shanghai at night (fig. 13), of moss on a wall, tree bark, a potpourri of petals etc. ... all can play a part in this process. Major events such as armed conflicts and wars can also inspire designers. Famously, Rei Kawakubo made use of this theme with her 1995-96 Autumn-Winter fashion show causing a great scandal. It has to be noted, however, that her use of bandages was an innovative use of materials which prompted a range of totally new weaves. This is an example of an innovative concept being transferred into an industrially-

Shapes, materials and patterns

The designer's talent and modern techniques has encouraged the development of new materials such as heat-regulating fabrics used in skiwear with patent research and development being as essential in the accessory world as it would be in any other field.

A pattern is closely linked to the material. For example, leather could inspire an abstracted tyre mark, or a stitched headlight pattern, relating to the world of the motor cyclist (figs 6 & 8); a lace threaded through the leather is reminiscent of a native American's moccasin (fig. 3) with a contemporary twist.

Certain shapes involve the use of one material above another. It is very important not to lose sight of the object in question, particularly in the case of shoes upon which one has to walk, for example! It is not unusual to see catwalk models being unable to walk properly due to a shoe being too heavy or too arched. This is reminiscent of the shoes Marc Jacobs designed for Louis Vuitton where the heels where so heavy that the models lost them. Faced with this type of problem, it is essential to conduct feasibility studies on suitably adapting the product.

9

10

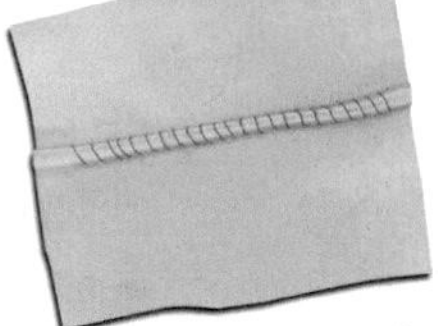
11

12

13

14

1. Saddle-stitched leather.

2. Contrast of materials obtained by inlaying a net pattern on the shoe upper.

3. Moccasin effect achieved by laced leather seam.

4/5 Sandal upper templates. Élisabeth Guers cuts out different shoe elements using a flexible cardboard in order to visualise the effect on the foot. If the proportions are suitable, the design will be given to the pattern cutter with the corresponding template.

6. Quilted leather with tyre mark-inspired pattern.

7. Quilted leather with geometrically-inspired pattern.

8. Quilted leather with motorbike headlight-inspired pattern.

9. Photo and material sample board researching crumpled texture and over-stitching.

10. Crumpled leather. This effect is achieved by heating the leather making it more supple.

11. Moccasin-type seam.

12. The shiny appearance of the leather is contrasted by a line of saddle-stitch.

13. Light and shade contrast: this optical effect is portrayed by strips of leather linked together by chrome plaques. This composition has been inspired by a photo of an illuminated apartment in Shanghai.

14. Crumpled and sewn piece of fabric with its inspiration photo.

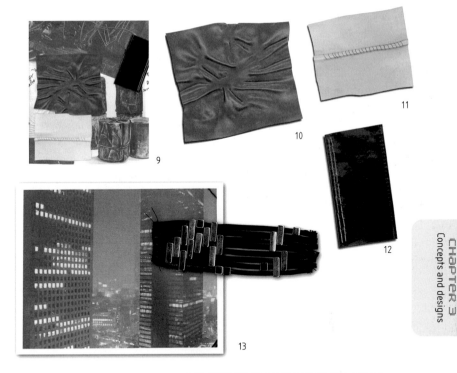

Themes and products

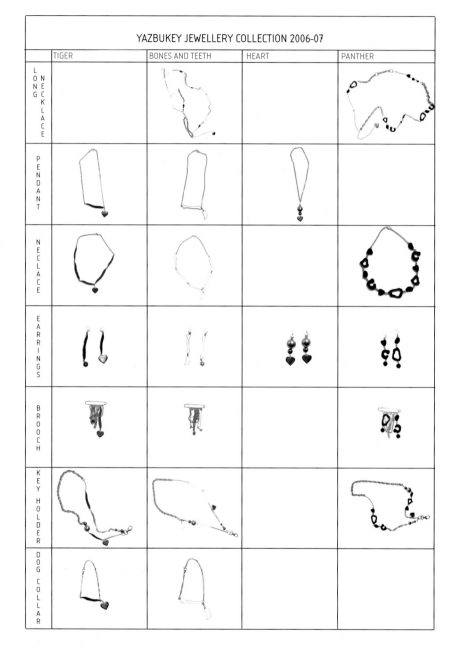

YAZBUKEY JEWELLERY COLLECTION 2006-07				
	TIGER	BONES AND TEETH	HEART	PANTHER
LONG NECKLACE				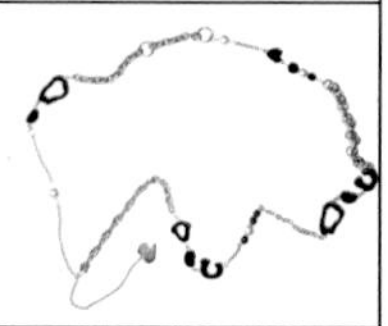
PENDANT				
NECKLACE				
EARRINGS		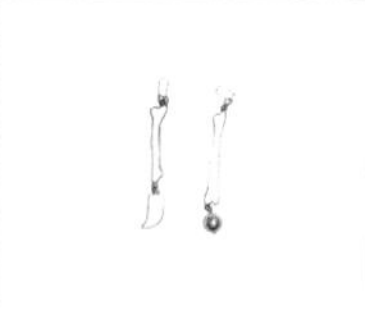		
BROOCH				
KEY HOLDER				
DOG COLLAR				

In the following section, the creative director, Jean-Philippe Bouyer explains his collection plan concept. His impressive curriculum vitae involves, most notably perhaps, designing for Dior from 1989–1995 and then for Paco Rabanne from 2000–2005. At the beginning of the 1980s he worked for Charles Jourdan until the company closed and he has also been creative director in Japan and Russia.

Analysis and definition of a collection plan

Accessory collections always respond to trends and, of course, illustrate the seasonal themes which have already been defined by the brand. The way in which a collection is structured is determined by the collection plan. It is also the starting point for designers (contrary to *prêt-a-porter*). This plan is, in fact, a document which defines the composition and quantity of accessory elements.

An accessory is defined by a product, which is a response to commercial demand. The collection plan is generally established from prospective market research studies which have been carried out by the head of product development, who could also be the marketing director. These studies are based on analyses of buying and selling made at a particular brand's retail outlets. This information defines, as closely as possible, the client's profile.

The plan helps to structure, as well as provide an overview of the collection with its number of themes, lines and models and relevant manufacturing processes. It is based upon different criteria relating to quantities i.e. number of themes, materials and items in each theme or sub-theme.

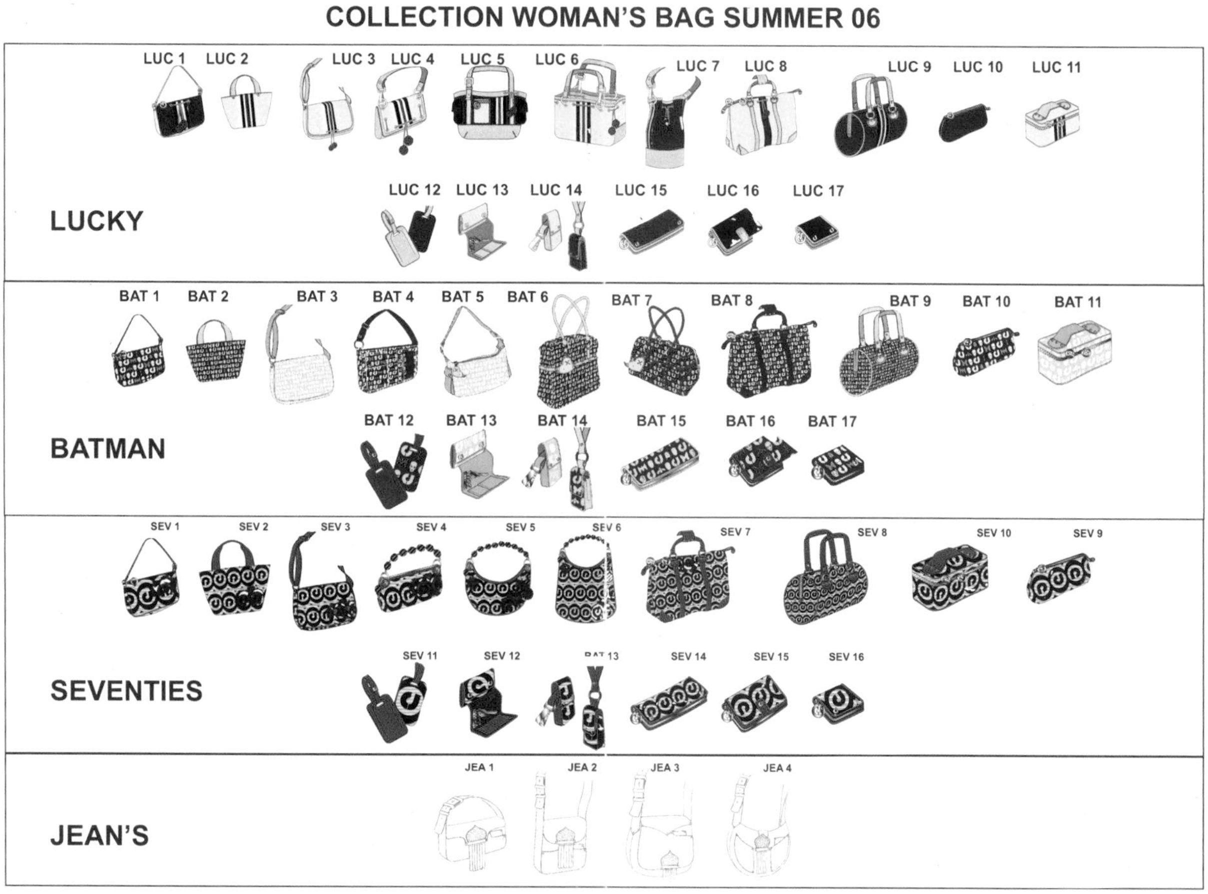

CHARLES JOURDAN
Spring/ Summer 2006

Collection plan development

Accessory collection plans are very rigorous and continually developing. They are designed in several stages at various points along the collection's development.

First stage: A brief idea of the plan. This is done before the designer really starts work. The marketing section prepares a chart for him/her showing the product lines i.e. shoes, bags, scarves etc. (See illustration opposite for Yazbukey's jewellery, p.78.) Another chart states, for each line, the number of materials and models proposed. And, depending on the product, the number of colours to be used in the collection will also be indicated on this. This is particularly the case with scarves as the precise number of colour variations is often required.

Second stage: The development of the collection plan. It is honed down to include the material and colour choices. Once chosen, these elements will assist the designer in his or her job. The collection plan is displayed in the design studio for all the team to see. It also helps to punctuate other necessary aspects of the collection, i.e. marketing, manufacturing and sales.

Third stage: After the collection. This plan serves as a basis for the conception of a sales book/catalogue. It can also used as a presentation document for sales teams or press agencies. By offering an overview of the products, the plan can help with determining the 'look' of a fashion show.*

The collection plan defines all the essential and indispensable products giving the designer all the necessary information in order to optimise results.

* See *Fashion: Concept to Catwalk*, chapter 1, page 59 in the same series.

Colour rendering using a marker pen

Equipment

The marker pen is one of the designer's basic tools as it allows for rapid colouring of a sketch or rough. It can be used for project presentations on the condition that it is used in conjunction with other techniques such as coloured crayons, paintbrushes, pens etc. The marker pen is simple to use resulting in a good quality work.

A large choice of colours are available and by mixing different colours together a variety of shades can be obtained. Marker manufacturers propose neutral tones - cool and warm - for monochrome drawings which can be used for accentuating shadows etc. and they are available with different shaped interchangeable nibs, i.e. wide, fine, round, square, angled, rigid or flexible which allow for a variety and precision of line. The nibs are available in either felt or fibre. The felt ones are stronger and are used for quick colouring and flats. To obtain more detailed colouring a fibre nib is more suitable.

Specific papers known as *layout paper* is the most suitable for use with marker pens as the ink does not come through the other side, nor does it bleed over the outline of the drawing.

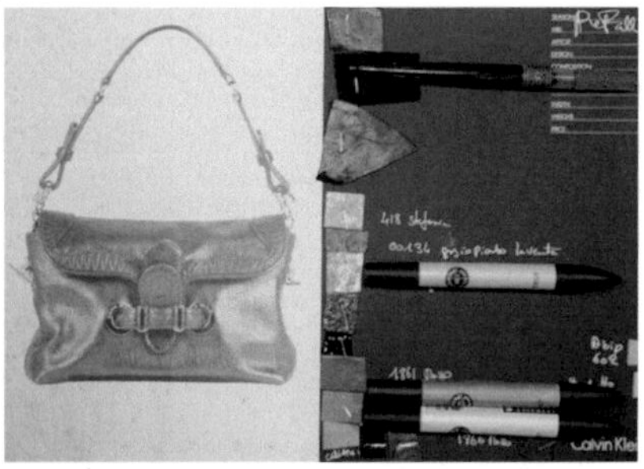

1. Select a marker pen in relation to your chosen colour range. Preferably, use one with a lighter shade so that more contrasts can be given to the bag. Brush and ink will eventually be used to accentuate the shadows.

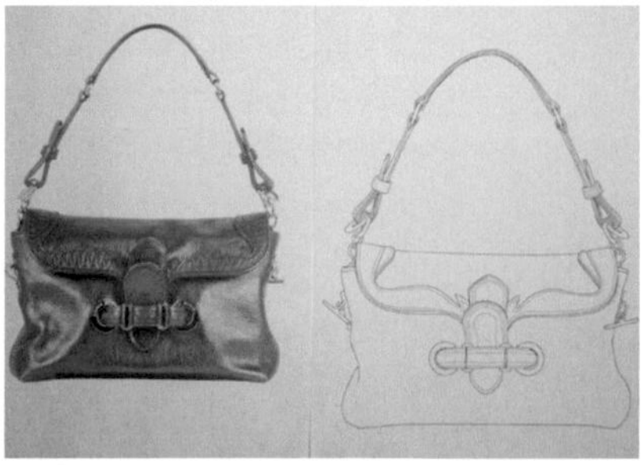

2. Using a 0.4 felt pen the outline of a handbag is traced which is identical to that of a Sonia Rykiel bag. In the photo, the contrasts between the light and shade are clearly defined which helps with the understanding of the volume of the bag. Use a 0.1 or 0.05 felt pen for a more precise areas of the drawing, i.e. details, stitches, buckles etc. For shadows, a felt pen with a thicker nib i.e. 0.8 will give the drawing a more contrasting effect. For this we have chosen to use ink and a paintbrush.

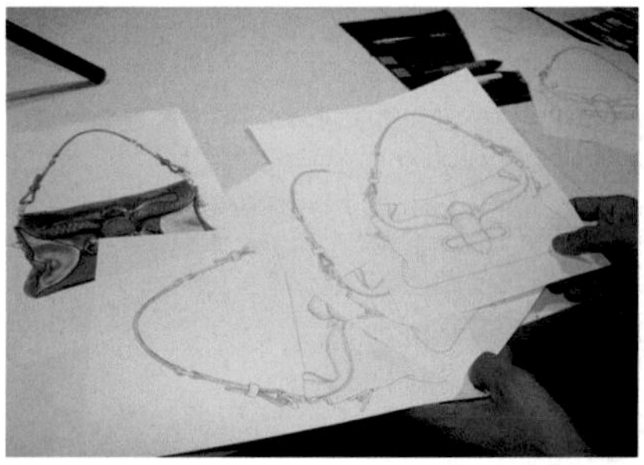

3. Make several photocopies of the drawing as this will allow you to make several colour ways and material tests. If a mistake is made then the rendering can be restarted without having to re-trace the outline of the bag. Incorporating the material effects is essential when designing an accessory.

4. On the original photo, the highlighted areas can be selected. However, in the absence of one, try to imagine one, or more, lateral light sources coming from either the right, or left, of the bag depending on the amount of contrast required. By doing this light and shade can be added to the drawing.

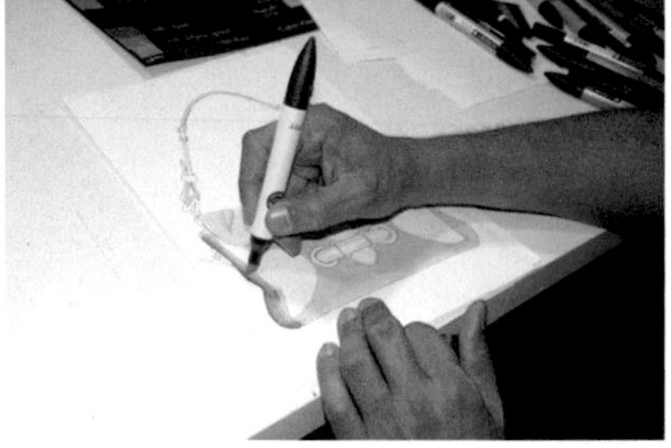

5. Using a marker with a medium-sized nib, mark the highlighted areas before beginning the solid areas of colour.

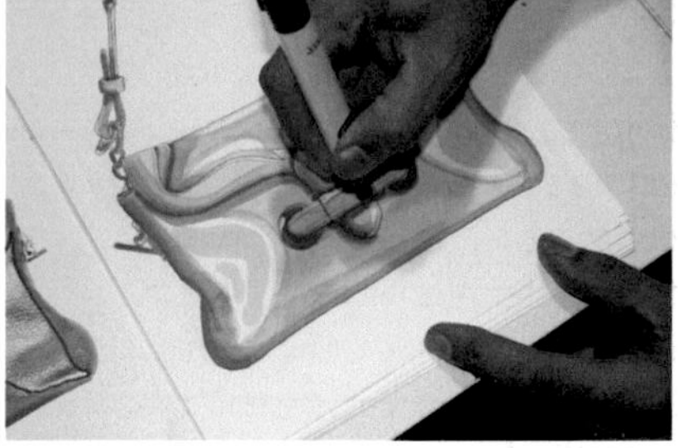

6. Colour in the bag using an angled marker. Carefully fill in the colour allowing a margin on the inside of the outline so that the colour does not go over the line. It is important to apply the colour quickly so that a solid block of colour is applied, because once the ink has dried, any overlaid colours will leave marks.

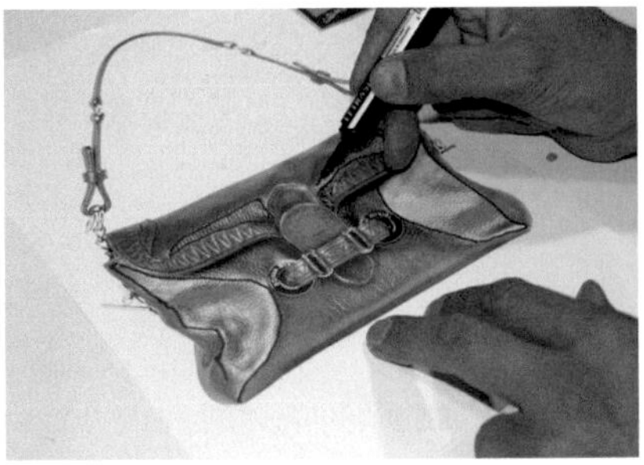

7. The first colour is applied uniformly in order to obtain a good solid colour. The highlighted areas will then stand out. To recreate a textured aspect to the material, place the drawing over a textured support, then apply another layer of ink over that. The texture will then become apparent.

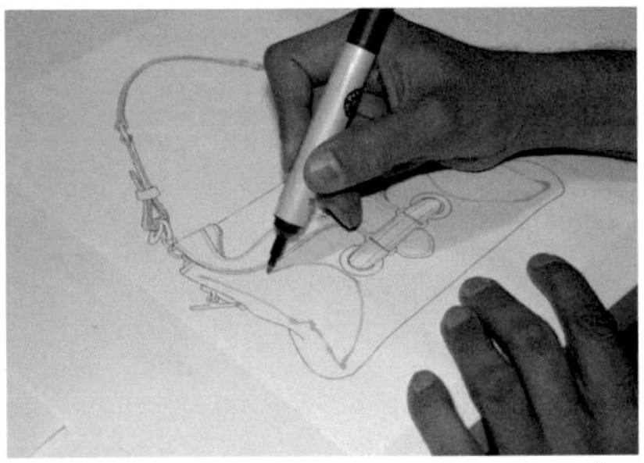

8. Colour in the shaded areas. For a matt finish, accentuate the shadows with opaque colours. However, if the material has a shiny finish emphasise the highlighted areas in order to restore a shiny aspect. To accentuate the shadows, apply several layers of ink with the marker. Allow a bit of time for the ink to dry in between layers. Using complementary colours also accentuate shadows, for example, to achieve a very contrasted effect a pink can be added to a green. It is very important to be able to contrast your drawing so that the volumes can be emphasised.

9. Use a slightly darker shade for shaded areas and material effects as this will give a quilted effect.

10. It is advisable to use a watercolour crayon to enhance the colours and accentuate the look of the material. Use a white one for highlights, a metallic one for details such as buckles etc. and use darker colours to emphasise the folds.

11. Use a paintbrush with white acrylic paint to achieve reflections from the metal finishes.

Sonia Rykiel handbag

Preparation

Before adding the colour, place the drawing on a pad of rough paper which will not only protect the table, but also allow for a better absorption of the ink avoiding any bleeding over the drawing's outline. The designer's position is also important as he, or she, should sit front-on to the table to avoid any back problems. Finally, it is possible to make a colour photocopy of the drawing on photographic paper in order to achieve a more contrasting and realistic look.

Coloured drawing

Example of colour rendering a shoe

To colour render a shoe, use the same techniques and equipment as for the handbag. The colour of the heel and shape of the shoe is of utmost importance. Place the drawing over a layout pad, or a pad of rough paper, so that the marker pen can be absorbed. A colour photocopy of the drawing on photographic paper will give a more contrasting look to the finished piece.

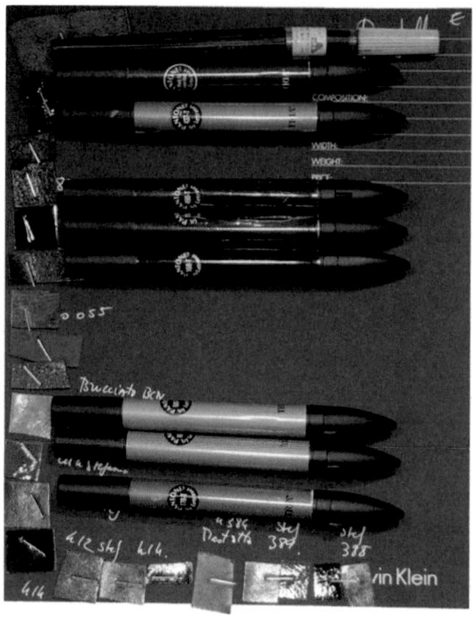

1. Select a range of marker pens in relation to the chosen colour ways. Preferably use lighter coloured ones as these will give more contrast to the shoe. To accentuate the shadows we have used a brush and black ink.

2. We have used a 0.4 felt pen to trace the outline of a shoe identical to a Sonia Rykiel model. In the photo, the areas of light and dark are clearly defined. For more precision, use 0.1 or 0.5 felt pens on the details. For the shadows, use a felt pen with a thicker nib 0.8 or 10 as this will give a more contrasting effect. We suggest using ink and a paintbrush rather than a black marker pen. Photocopy the drawing several times so that various colour ways and material effects can be tried out. If a mistake is made, then the colour rendering can be done again without having to retrace the entire shoe.

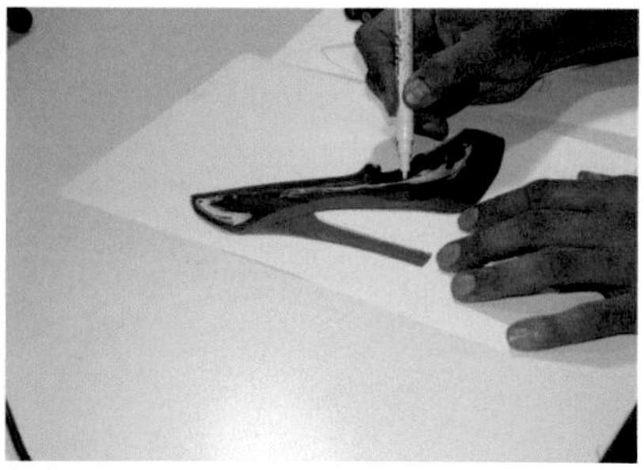

3. On the original photo, select the highlighted areas, however, in the absence of one, try to imagine a lateral light source.

4. Using a marker with a medium-sized nib, mark the highlighted areas before beginning the solid areas of colour. The patent leather of the shoe requires particular attention. It is a question of enhancing the shininess of the material by studying the contrasts of light as this will distinguish the volume of the shoe.

5. To colour the shoe use an angled marker. Carefully fill in the colour allowing a margin on the inside of the outline so that the colour does not go over the line. Use a marker with a medium nib for the strap. It is important to apply the colour quickly and graduate it, paying particular attention to the black and shiny areas.

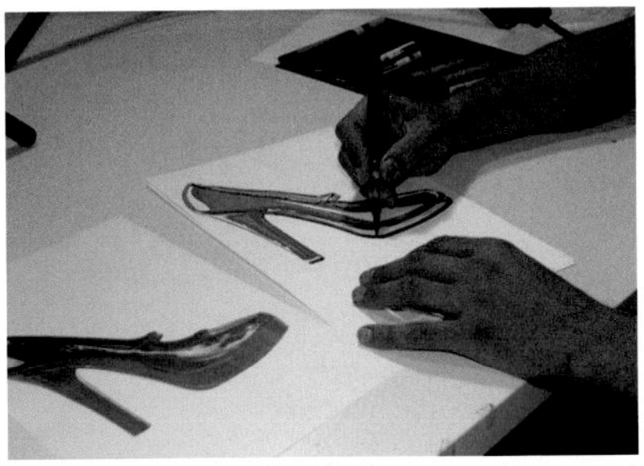

6. To accentuate the shadows, apply several layers of ink with the marker. Allow a bit of time for the ink to dry in between layers. Using complementary colours can also accentuate shadows, giving a very contrasting effect which will emphasise the volume as well.

7. Watercolour crayons will enhance the colours and accentuate the look of the material. Use a white one to highlight the metal details such as buckles/fastenings etc. and use darker colours to emphasise the folds.

8. To make the patent leather look shiny, use a paintbrush with white acrylic paint to achieve reflections.

9. For the black, use ink and a paintbrush, not forgetting to leave the white areas which will show the shininess of the material.

Sonia Rykiel shoe

Coloured drawing

Colour rendering using Photoshop®

Trace the outline of the handbag, making sure that there are no breaks in the line as this will make the work easier. Designing a bag using a computer follows the same set of rules as colour rendering using a marker pen. Use a variety of different nib sizes, i.e. 0.5 to 0.7 for the outlines, and 0.1 to 0.3 for the details and cut. In addition to this, the material, from which the bag is made, can be selected in Photoshop® and applied to the image giving a very realistic result.

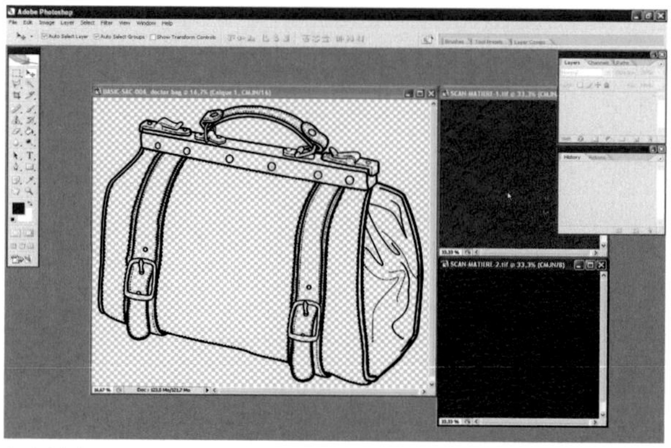

1. A high resolution scan will show all the details of the bag. Scan the drawing in at 600 dpi and the materials at 300 dpi. Once the bag and the materials have been scanned open these files in Photoshop.

2. Use the magic wand in the toolbox to overlay materials onto selected areas of the handbag. Select all the areas of the bag which correspond to one of the materials that you want to apply by clicking inside this area. It will become highlighted. This magic wand also allows you to select areas of colour and tones.

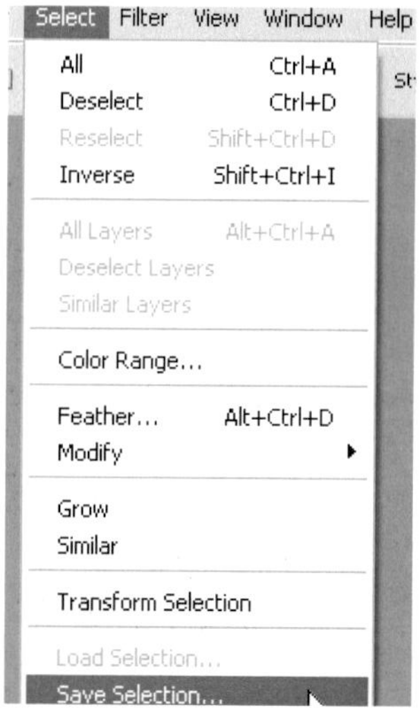

3. To add another area to the selection, use the Shift key on the keyboard. A little + sign will appear next to the cursor. To reverse the operation in the case of a mistake, press the Alt key and the – sign will then appear. If you click in the selected area inadvertently, then just Deselect it. It is advisable to use the Zoom tool from the toolbox to show all the small areas enabling you to work them in more detail. It is possible, therefore, to zoom in and out at will, then re-use the magic wand and finish the selection. So that it can be continued to be used, it must be saved. This can be done by going to the Select menu and clicking on Save Selection.

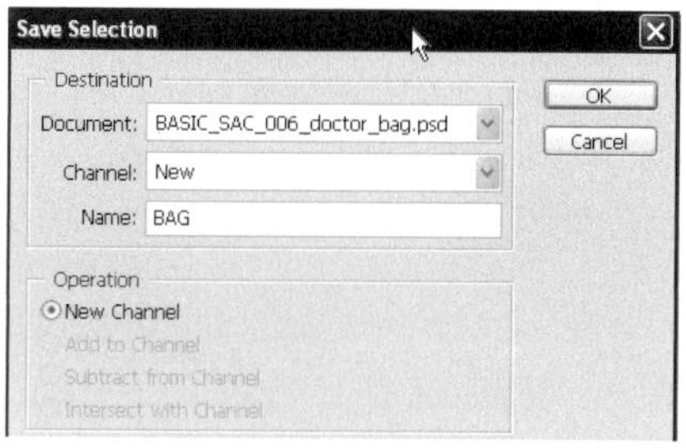

4. A dialogue window will appear. In the Name field, type the name of this selection then confirm by clicking OK (fig. 4). Repeat this process of Select and Save for the other areas of the bag.

Importing

Once the preparation has been done, the chosen material can be imported into the document. Just select the document containing the chosen material and open it at the same time as the bag document.

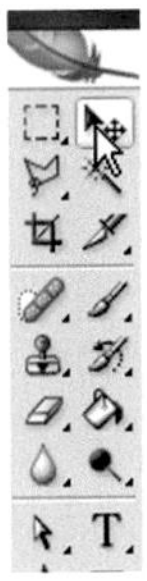

5. A simple click on this image will activate this document. Select the Move icon in the toolbox, click on it and drag the material image over the handbag document.

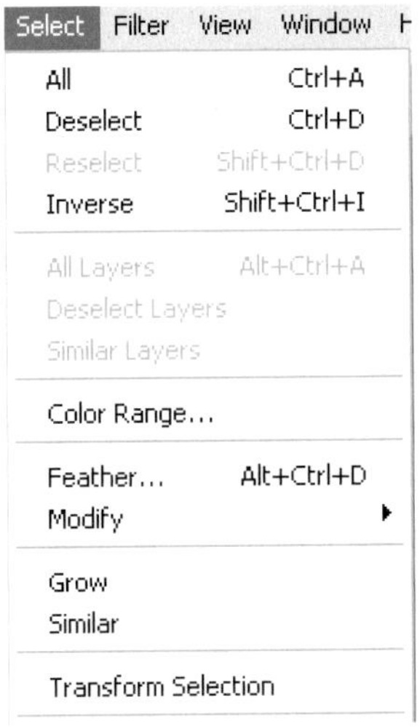

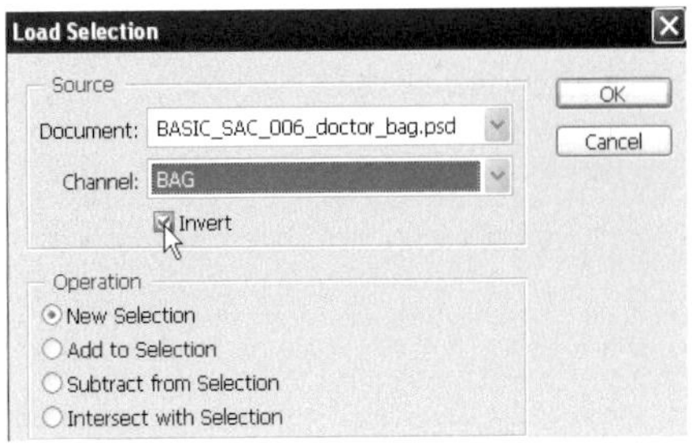

6 & 7. As in No.3 (NB: See highlighted/grey areas in illus. for Load Selection instructions.)

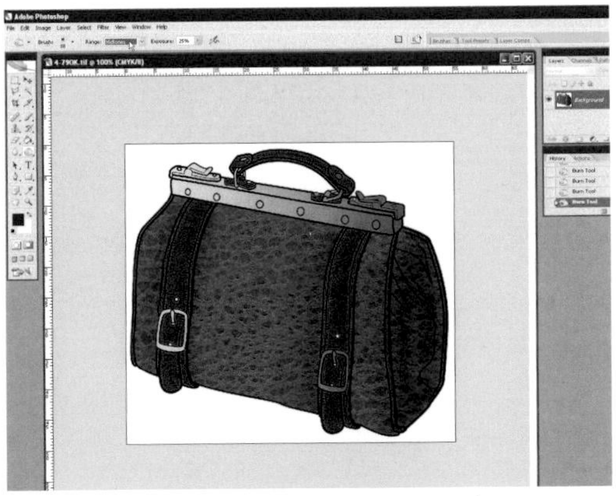

8. Then, on the keyboard, press the Remove (or Delete, or Backspace) key to remove all the material on the outside of the bag outline. The material is now overlaid on the bag giving a more precise and realistic idea of the bag and the material it is made from.

9 & 10. Finally, to push the idea a little further, use the Density tool to give shadows and volume to the bag.

The production of an accessory involves some very specific manufacturing techniques which combine innovative technology with traditional skills. When a skilled craftsman uses new materials and components, he stamps his trademark onto the objects which result in highly original products. The craftsman is, therefore, a very important component/cog in the industry. Although labour and manufacturing costs are very high in France, large luxury brands continue to use these exceptional skills and knowledge in the production of their models which, in turn, affords a certain exclusivity to the product in the eyes of the client. This policy helps to safeguard the incredible technical heritage which has been passed from generation to generation in the heart of the design studios.

Chapter 4 - Craftsmanship and manufacture

Whether it be with leather goods, shoes, scarves, jewellery, France has, in fact, kept a certain number of these ateliers alive; as precious as they are rare, they are also world-renowned archival temples. The large fashion houses to whom we owe this continuing survival are namely, Louis Vuitton with his atelier and travel museum at Asnières in the Haut-de-Seine region; Charles Jourdan with his shoe museum at Romans, in the Drôme, and Marc Rozier whose manufacturing studio houses at least a 150 years' worth of archival material.

Equally, the up-and-coming generation of designers endeavour to integrate skilled craftsmanship into their products. This is evident with the young Japanese shoe and handbag designer Ryusaku Hiruma, whose work, and label Sak, is presented in this chapter. In the *prêt-à-porter* market, the Kitsuné label also uses these manufacturing skills and materials to exceptional effect.

Luxury brands are constantly researching new concepts which combine tradition with the contemporary and one of the principal challenges of creative directors such as Marc Jacobs for Louis Vuitton, Alber Elbaz for Lanvin or Jean-Paul Gaultier for Hermès, is to continue to surprise and delight their public.

We have invited Louis Vuitton, Marc Rozier, Sak, Éléna Cantacuzène and Charles Jourdan (one of the foremost shoe designers of the Isère whose brand disappeared in 2007) to open their studio doors and allow us an insight into their world which we present on the following pages.

Tradition and modernity at Louis Vuitton

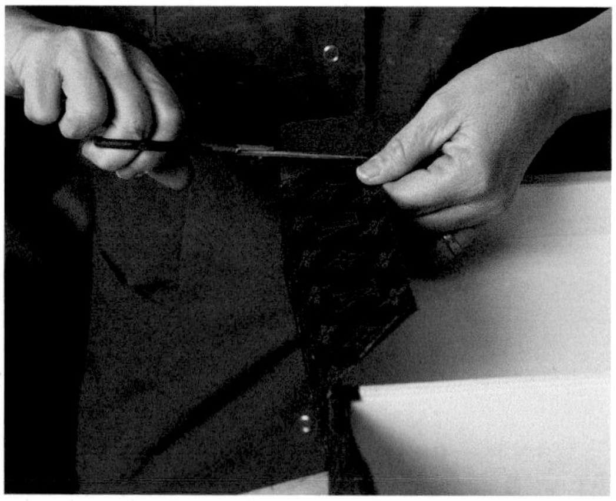

1

2

In the family home at Asnières, Louis Vuitton established a studio where limited edition and specially commissioned pieces are made. This building also houses the Travel museum where the brand's one-off, signature pieces are exhibited. He organises temporary exhibitions here presenting his concepts which range from architecture to design and development.

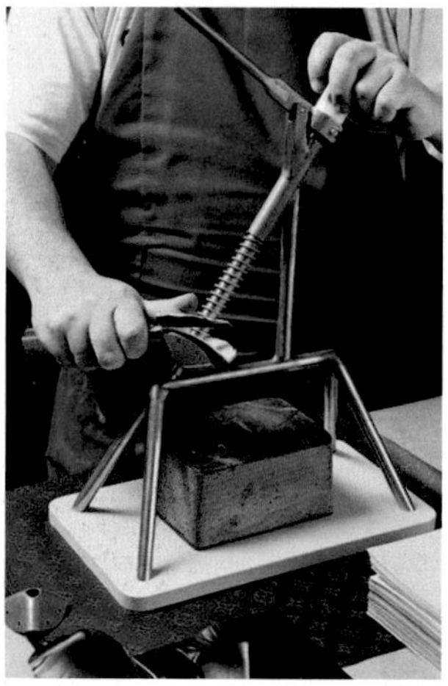

3

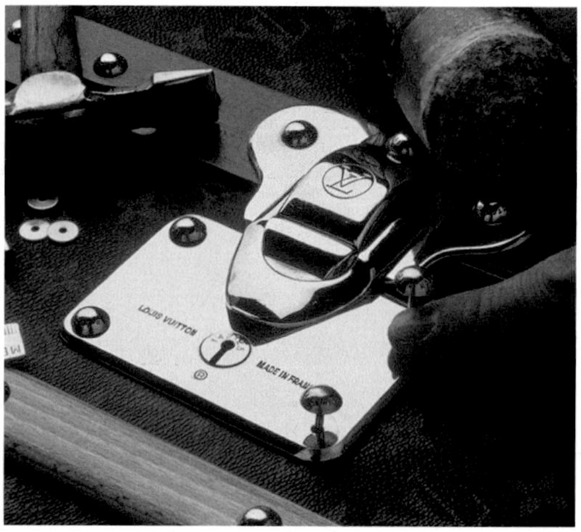

4

5

LOUIS VUITTON'S MANUFACTURING STUDIO AT ASNIÈRES

1. Monogrammed canvas stretched over a wooden frame. This operation requires extreme precision with the motif being perfectly aligned at each seam or join.
© Emmanuel Layani

2. The angles and edges of the rigid luggage items are reinforced by using lozine. This is a particularly strong vulcanised fibre exclusive to Louis Vuitton. Here the *lozine* is carefully nailed in place using a hammer. Several thousands of nails can be used in the manufacture of a trunk.
© Emmanuel Layani

3. Making a case corner in natural calf skin.
© Antoine Rozes

4. Fixing a brass lock onto a rigid bag. Invented by Georges Vuitton in 1890, these multiple tumbler locks are still in use today. The customer has a unique number for the lock and can, if so desired, request a single key which will open all his bags.
© Jean Larivière

5. Placing a hinge onto a rigid bag. The hinges of a Louis Vuitton bag have always been made from two pieces of cotton sewn together then stuck on the inside and outside of the frame.
© Emmanuel Layani

Opposite: Saddle stitch is done using a two needles and thread coated with beeswax. This is just one of the traditional techniques still carried out in the Asnieres studio. It is used to reinforce the stitches on the calf-skin trunk handle.
© Antoine Rozes.

Manufacturing a *Lockit* bag

1

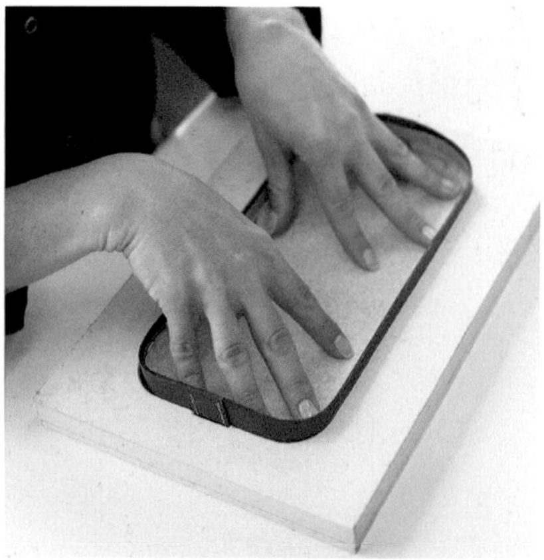
2

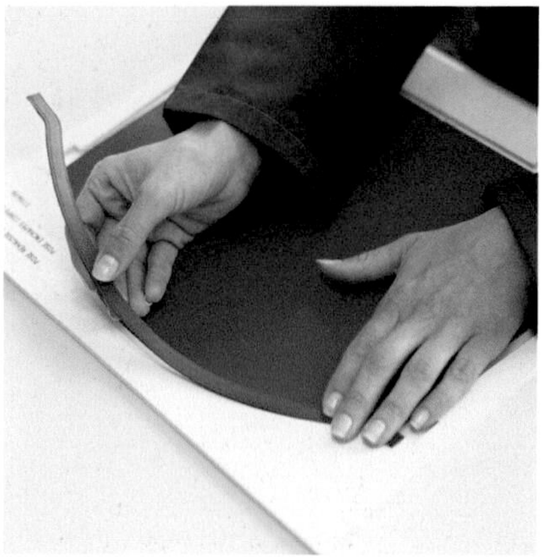
3

4

5

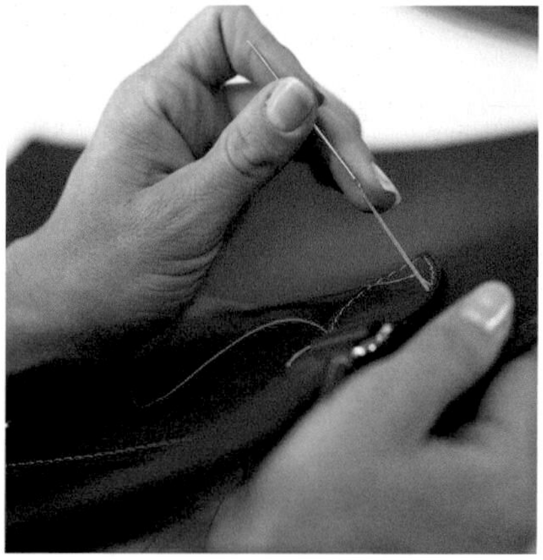
6

Continuing the tradition of handmade products, Louis Vuitton takes advantage of the brand's traditional skills which offers a certain exclusivity to the objects. Here we present some photographs which show the principal stages of making a *Lockit* handbag.

PRINCIPAL STAGES OF MANUFACTURE OF A *LOCKIT* BAG IN THE PRODUCTION STUDIO AT ASNIERES.

1. Cutting the leather by hand.
© Eric Leguay

2. Assembling the base.
© Eric Leguay

3. Assembling.
© Eric Leguay

4. Colouring the edges.
© Eric Leguay

5.& 6. Sewing the reinforcing piece by hand.
© Eric Leguay

7. Burning the threads.
© Eric Leguay

8.& 9. Final check.
© Eric Leguay

10. Extract from *Women's Autumn-Winter Accessories* book showing three-quarter view of *Lockit* handbag (29 x 28 x 12 cm) in caramel Nomade leather.
© Laurent Bremaud/LB Productions.

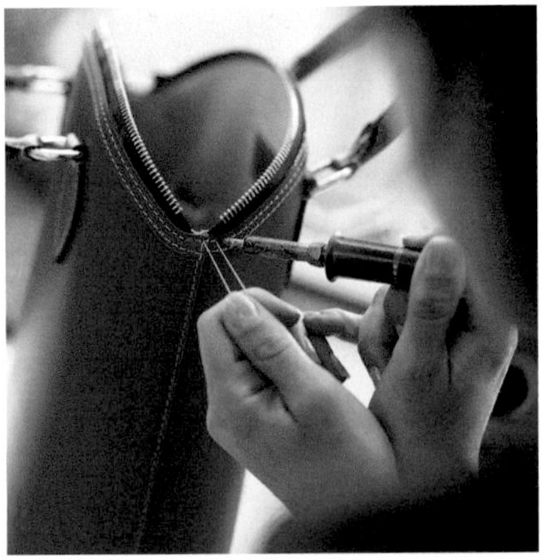

7

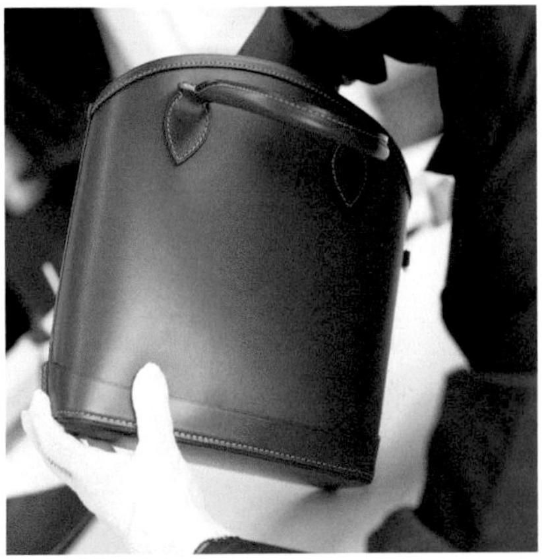

8

9

10

Details and finishing features for bags

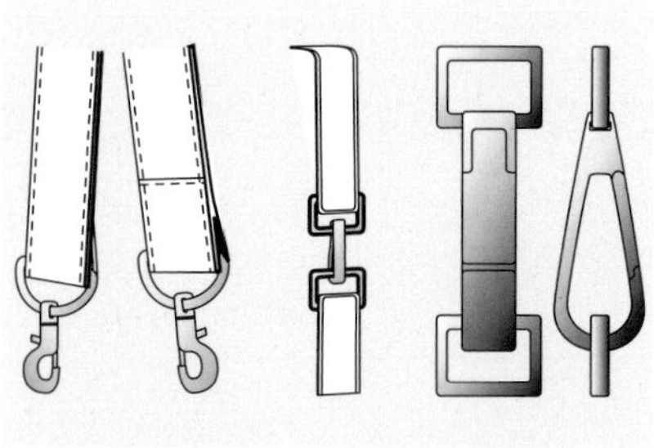

1

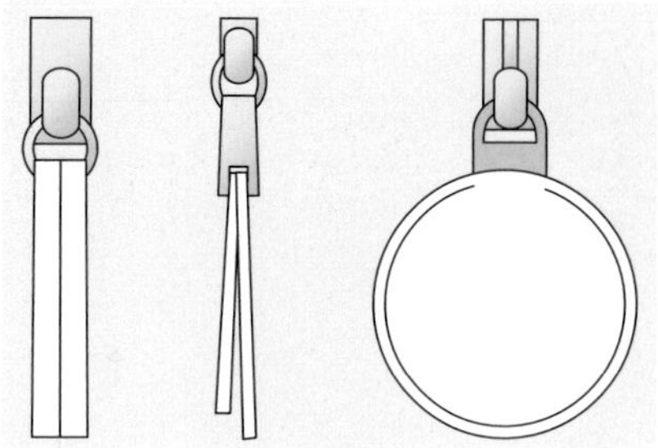

2

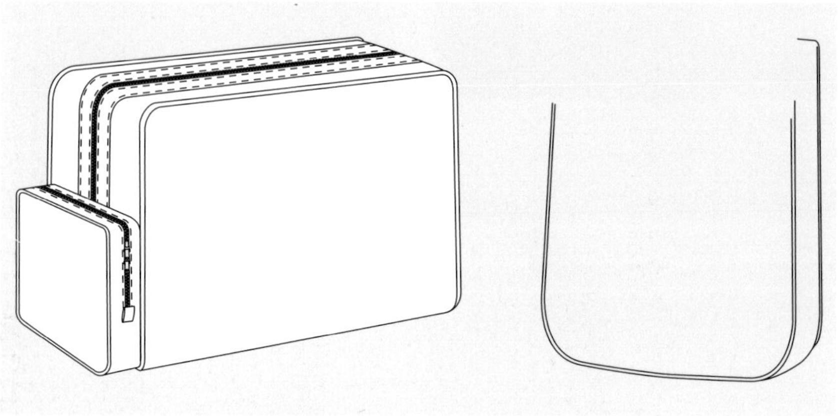

3

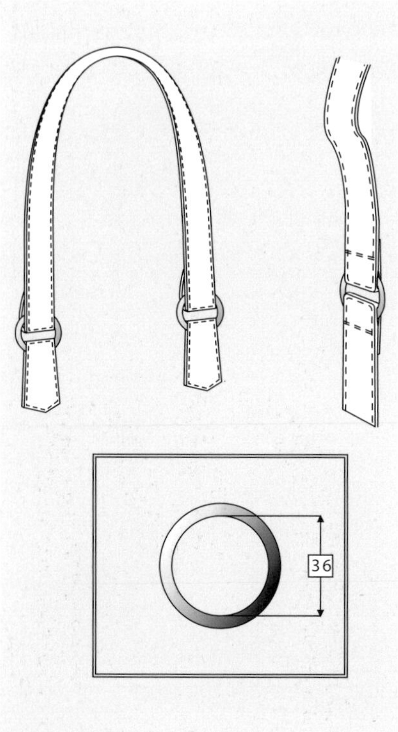

4

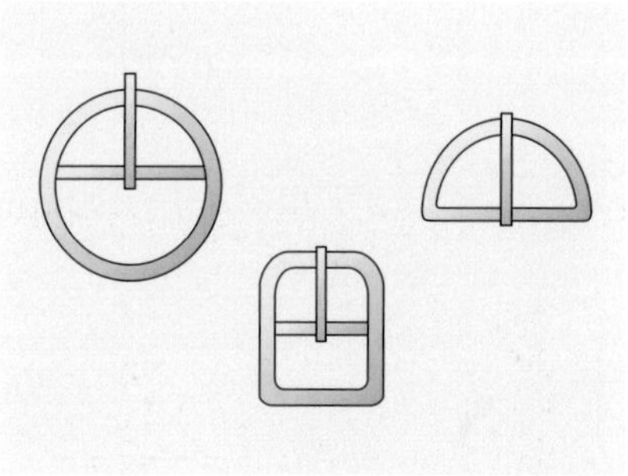

5

6

The various choices of finishing features, such as buckles, clasps, rivets etc. are essential prerequisites which need to be determined prior to any accessory manufacture. This is because these elements will define the width of straps, length of openings and the necessary pattern shapes.

There are specialist trade fairs, like Mod'amont in Paris, which designers visit each season in order to keep up to date with the latest trends and products in this field. Large companies themselves are regularly visited by manufacturing representatives who propose samples, although in an attempt to remain exclusive, certain brands will make their own easily-identifiable features. However, these are in the minority, as young designers tend to use standard elements for ease of restocking and in order to keep costs down.

1. Snap clasp or hook
2. Zip pullers
3. Piping
4. Ram rings
5. Belt buckles
6. Nails and rivets
7. Detail of a shoe ring
8. Clasps
9. Non-adjustable shoulder strap
10. Top stitches
11. Handles and straps
12. Zip fasteners
13. Adjustable shoulder straps

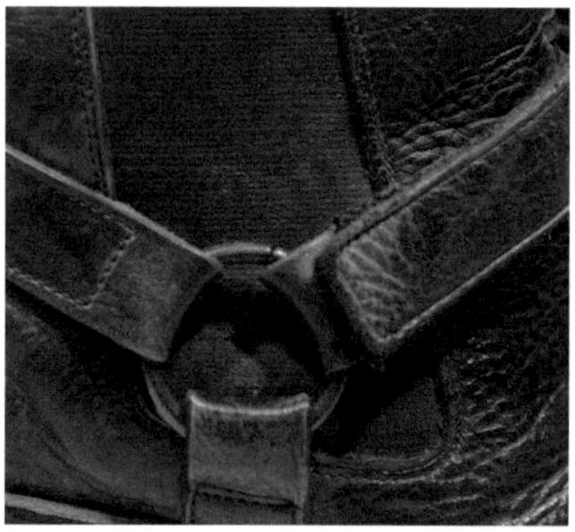

7

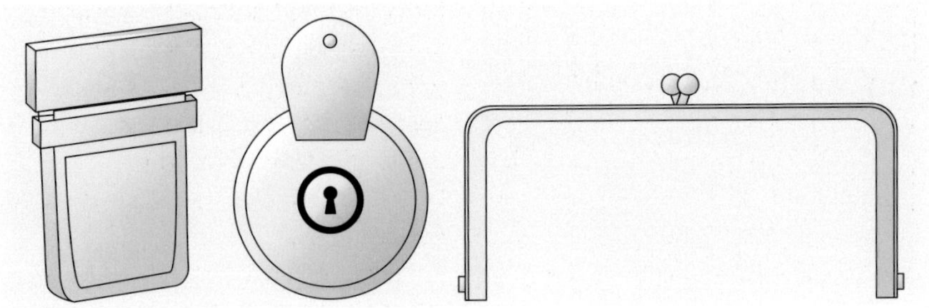

8

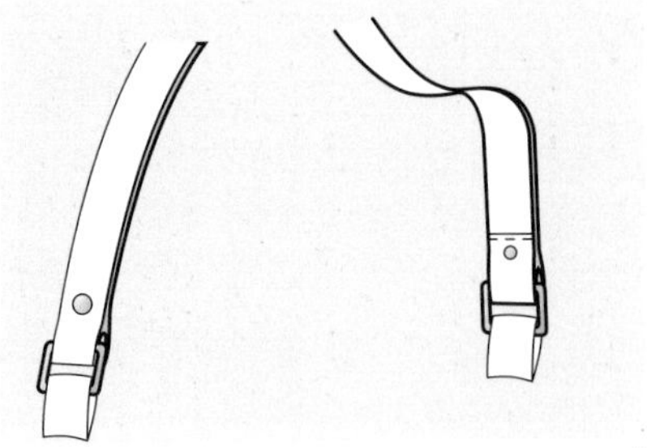

9

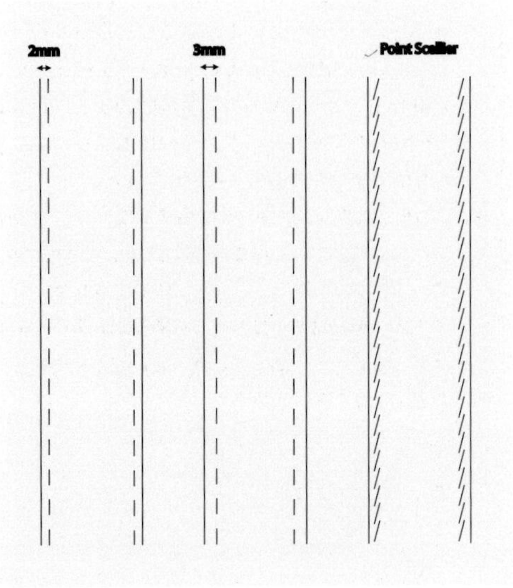

10

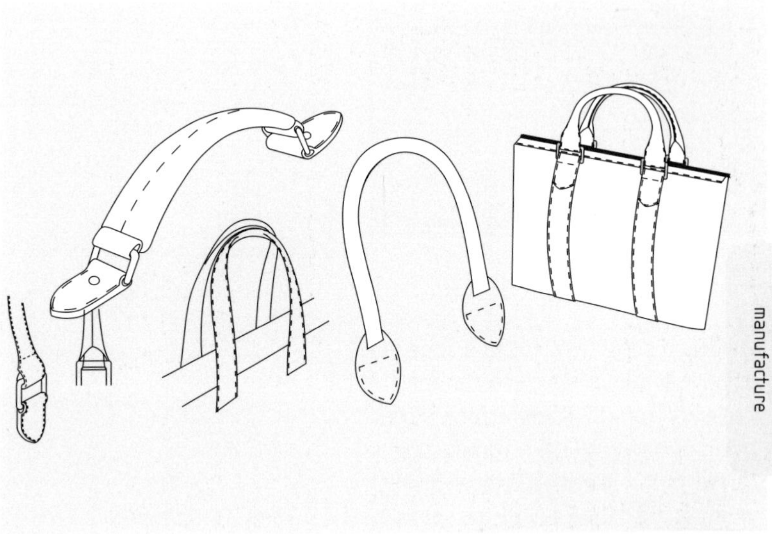

11

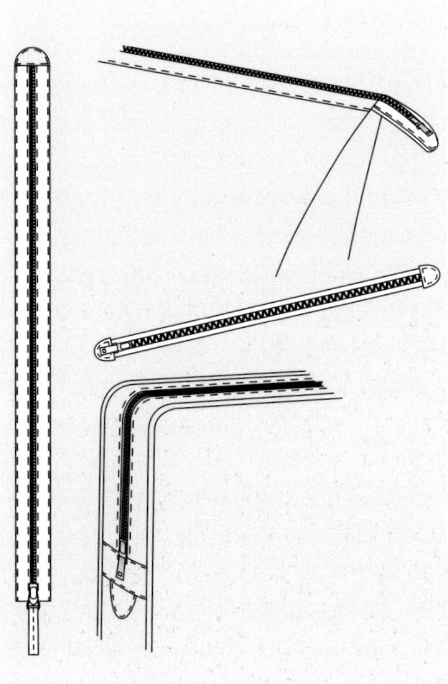

12

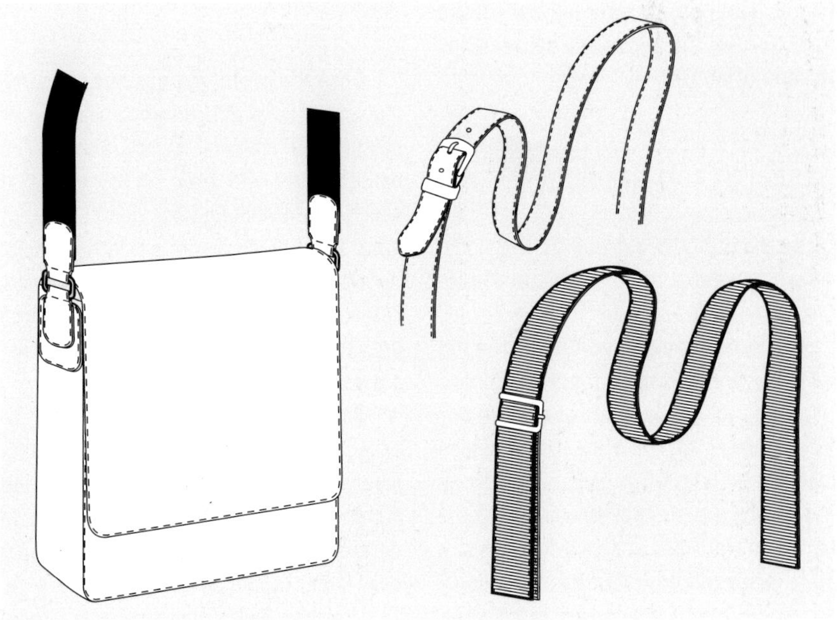

13

Industrial shoe manufacture

1

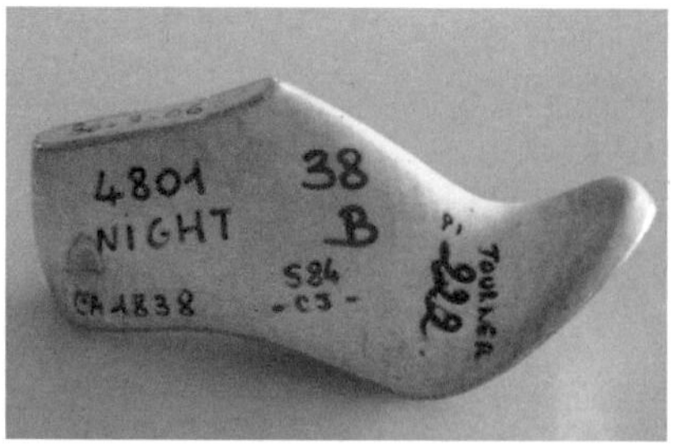

2

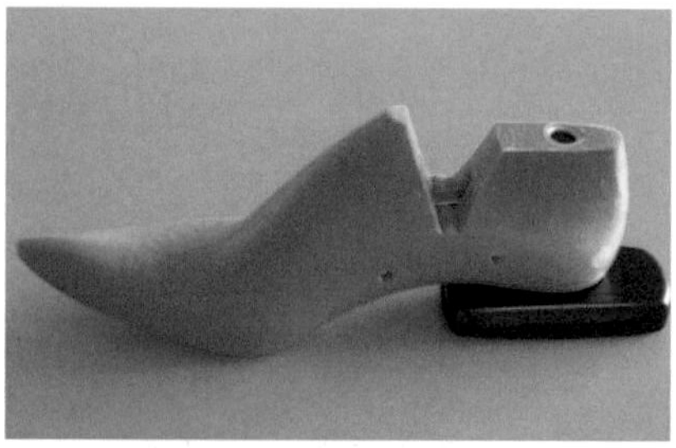

3

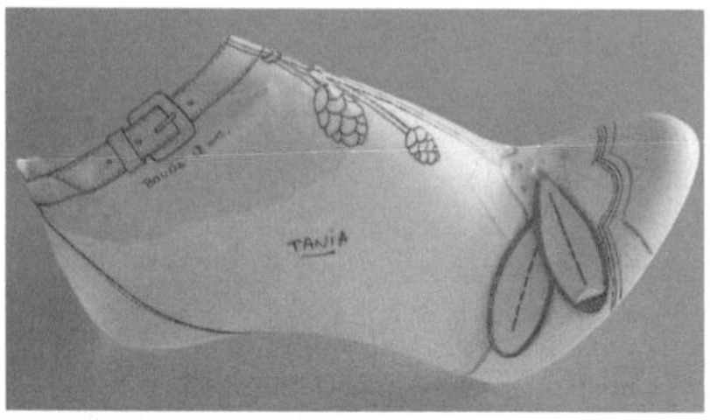

4

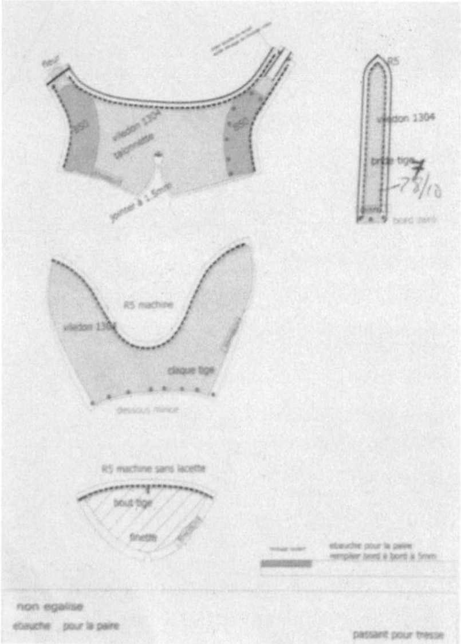

5

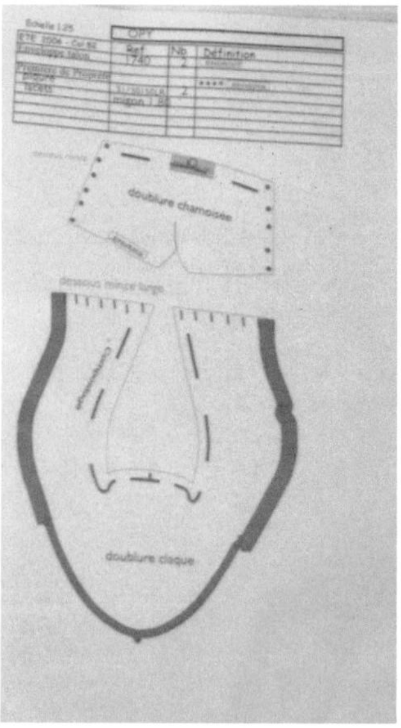

6

It takes an entire year to put a shoe collection together, of which six months are necessary for its manufacture. For a Spring-Summer collection, production is started in the previous October so that the shoes are delivered into the shops by the end of February. And for an Autumn-Winter one, production begins in the April so that the shoes are delivered by the end of August.

Research and development

Using the designer's drawings, the model maker recreates the models in three-dimensions on a wooden former or *last* (fig. 2). The volume of the shoe and the flat patterns are adjusted; these cardboard templates will be used to cut out the different pieces of the shoe. Once assembled, a pre-series of six pairs is made from this prototype so that the shoe can be tested on a number of people who are size 38/5. After this research has been done, any modifications needed are carried out.

Once the prototype has been passed, the shoe is produced in a variety of colour and material combinations. The model maker will then 'industrialise' it which means making a range of different sizes for it. Each model has a nomenclature (figs 5 & 6) which includes its name, reference, number of materials, design and technical drawing of model, accessories used, linings and finishes.

The model maker must take into account the manufacturing costs involved including labour (cutting) and materials (leather). It is also his job to determine the factory, or cost price, of each shoe, as well as manage production. This involves being in charge of the number of hours worked in the studio, any design modifications, ordering and buying of materials and finally, quality control. All these operations are expected to be done within very tight deadlines.

The patterns and materials are either laser-cut or made by using a water-jet. A shoe is subjected to 70 interventions including positioning the *counter* (a stiffener for the shoe's back), sticking in the lining materials, placing the metal reinforcing bar for the sole. A finisher takes care of the sole, heel and decoration or details of the shoe. A felt pen, in the same colour as the shoe's material, is used to touch up the edges or outline of the shoe. The final phase of

7

8

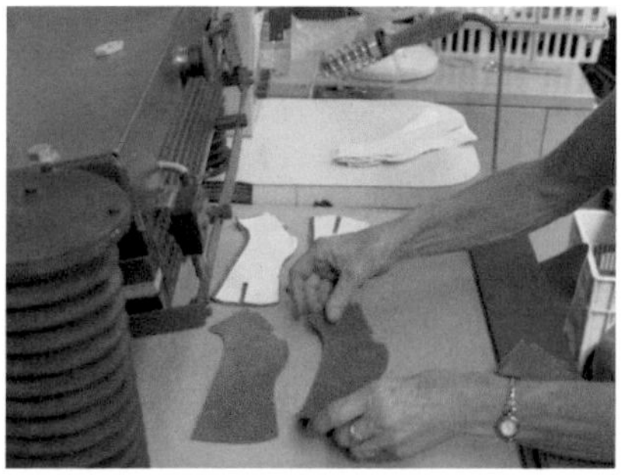

9

10

11

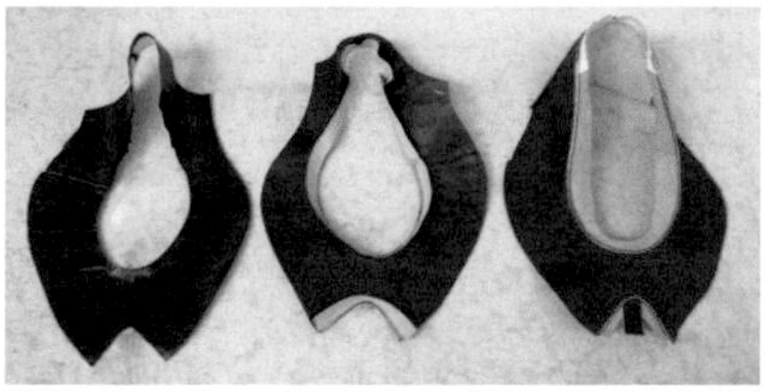

12

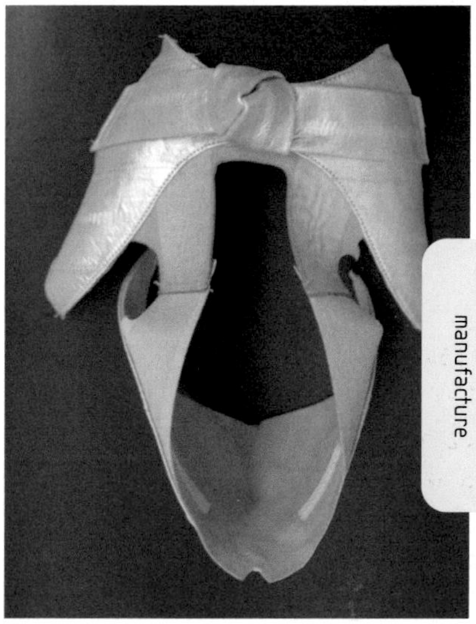

13

production involves adjusting the shoe leather upper snugly over the last. Nowadays, the majority of this is done industrially, using automated machinery which replaces the craftsman. However, the designer Sak still uses these skills which we can see on the following pages. The knowledge and supervision of these skilled technicians is essential for good shoe manufacture. This savoir-faire, which is unfortunately disappearing, is increasingly sought after within luxury brand manufacture. Finally, the last stage consists of cleaning and checking the shoe before it is carefully wrapped and put in its box.

Heel and last making

The shoe maker Charles Jourdan generally designs a line of seven different shoes from just one shape and one heel.

1. Rolls of leather from which shoe patterns will be cut.

2. Wooden last or former. This prototype will be used to make the shoe.

3. Plastic moulded former. It has a hole so that the heel can be nailed in place. This one will not be used for a high-heeled shoe, however.

4. Plastic moulded former for a high-heeled shoe with designs drawn on it.

5 & 6. Technical drawing

7 & 8. Positioning the different pattern pieces on the leather.

9. Stiffening the different pieces of the pattern which make up the shoe.

10. Shoe with its corresponding pattern.

11, 12 & 13. Sewn uppers ready to be assembled onto the sole and heel.

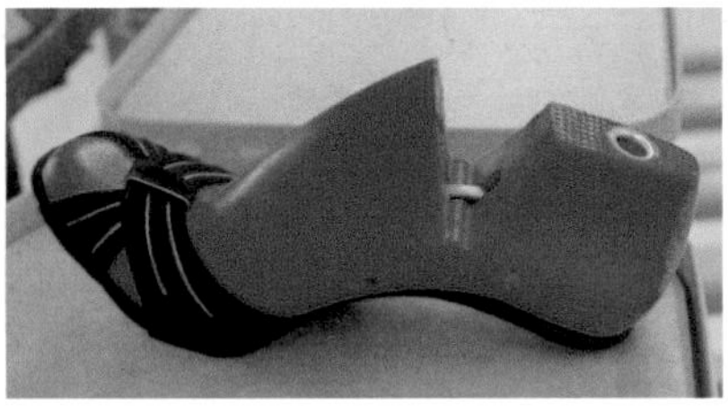

14

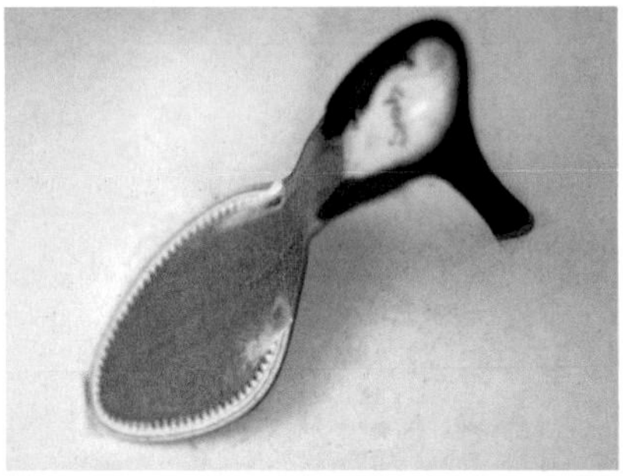

15

16

17

18

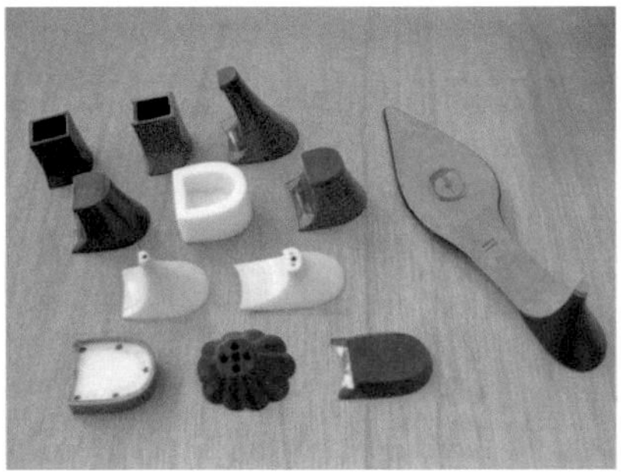

19

20

Last making is the largest and most important investment in shoe production because it is essential to recreate a last for each style and subsequently each size. At the top end of the market, half-sizes are also made which, in turn, increases the investment cost.

The last is initially made from hand-carved wood then reproduced in a very strong plastic material for mass-production. Each last consists of an individual in-step and shoe-fit. In the 1950s, the lasts were made up to size 36 whereas nowadays they go up to size 38/5. It is very important to anticipate the manufacturing constraints whilst developing the prototype taking into account the different thicknesses. For example, four thicknesses of leather are necessary for the production of a classic shoe. They can, therefore, modify the shape of the shoe in such a way that the result can be very different from the original concept. However, with tighter and tighter deadlines, there is no room for error: only one alteration is allowed per prototype. Elisabeth Guers annotates/sketches her designs in crayon on the wooden last in order to visualise the shoe. At Charles Jourdan, each last was hand-carved in the studio, listed and then placed in the archives for a period of five years. The lasts are then recycled at the end of this period.

In the meantime, the designer develops the heel prototypes with the heel maker. The ideal situation is to design them with the prototype of the wooden last as this allows for a better visualisation of the general shape of the shoe and helps the heel maker adjust the heel accordingly. The heights of the most currently used heels at Charles Jourdan were 2, 5, 6, 7, 8 and 9 cm.

The plastic last has a vertical hole

21

22

23

24

25

(fig. 14) in the heel so that a nail can be inserted in order to fix the sole to the heel. A badly-fixed heel will break very easily. This hole, which is placed in the shoe's centre of gravity, strengthens the heel. Underneath the sole, metal plates/rods reinforce the shank or arch support. A decision is then made as to whether the last can be carried through into production.

The heel can be made from either wood or resin. The wooden one is made using a metal-brushed grinding wheel. Moulds are then made of the heels which are then cast in different alloys. Finally a variety of finishes are proposed for the heel. This work demands great skill and a perfect understanding of the technique. Elisabeth Guers considers heel- and last-makers to be great virtuosos as one of the difficulties lies in the ability to combine beauty with comfort without compromise. The comfort of a heeled shoe, even if it is very thin, depends on the heel's centre of gravity, the arch support, enough room at the widest part of the foot and the upper. Charles Jourdan designed a particularly comfortable sole known by the Italians as a '*fondo* Jourdan'. This thin, curved sole allowed for the manufacture of thin, yet roomy, shoes.

The three distinctive elements of shoe production - the last, heel and sole are generally made in separate studios. However, at Charles Jourdan, all the stages of manufacture had been integrated into the factory – the heels, shoe lasts and accessories were made in-house.

14. Plastic last with upper in place.

15. Sole and heel before the rod is assembled.

16. Heels with covering material.

17. Leather-covered heel.

18. Different heel finishes.

19. Choice of different heels.

20. Shoe manufacturing stage.

21. Plastic production lasts.

22. Storage of card patterns.

23. Production shanks before finishing.

24. Resin being poured into heel moulds.

25. Sole die-cutter.

Handmade shoe manufacture

1

2

3

4

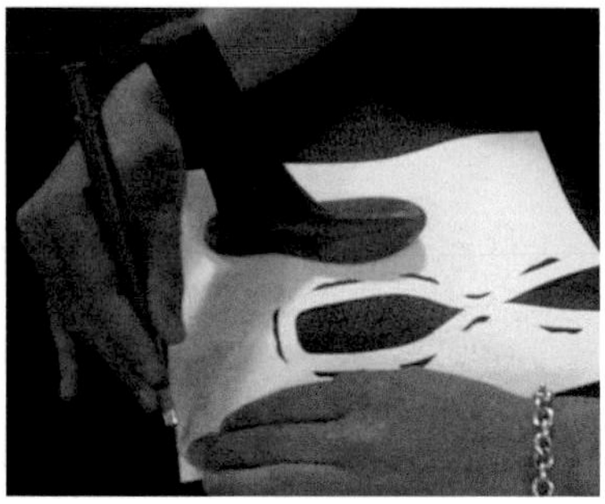

5

6

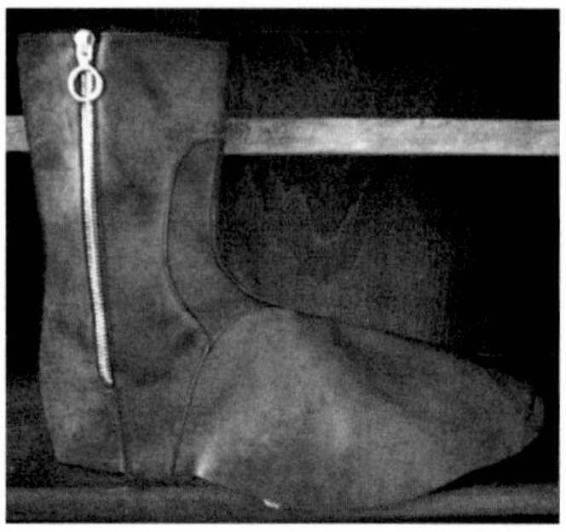

7

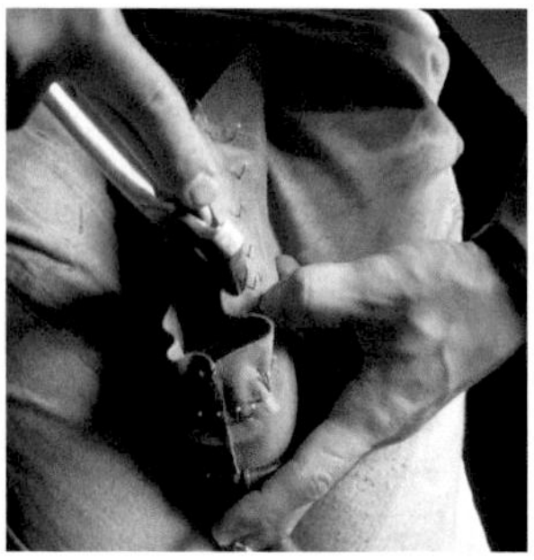

8

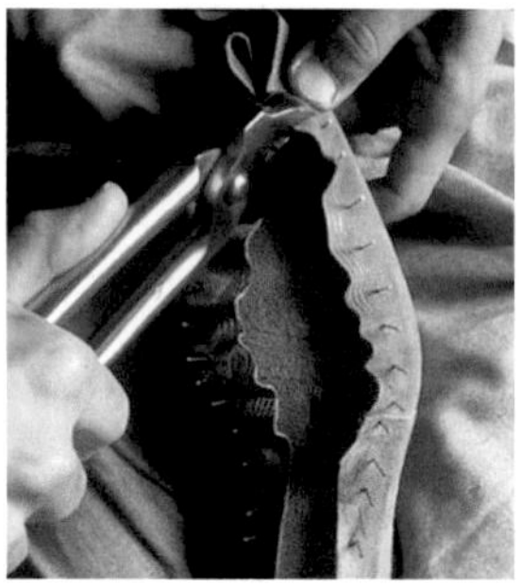

9

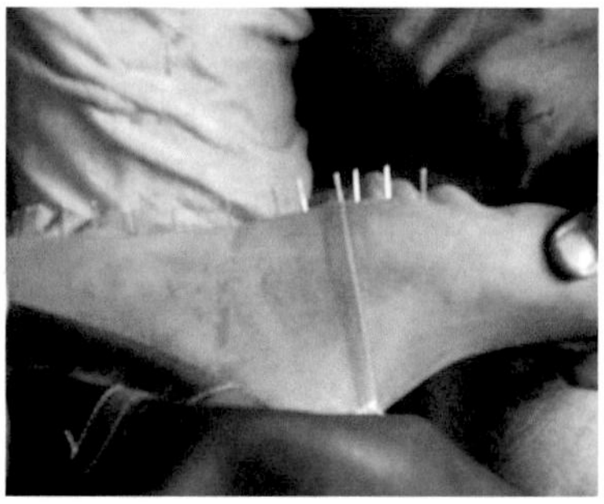

10

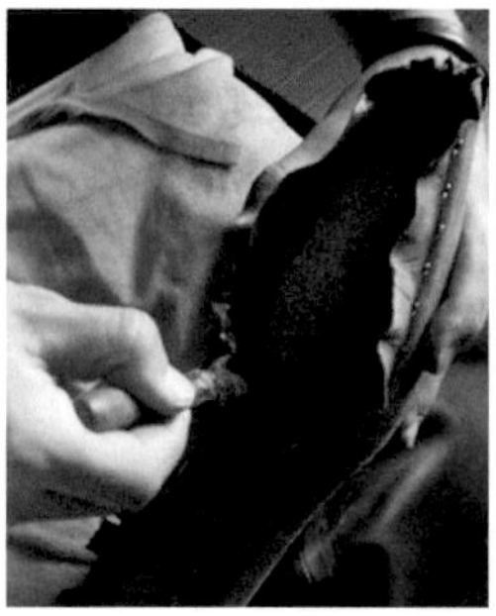

11

Sak – a young designer label

Handmade production demands a less structured organisation than industrial manufacture and depends on versatile, skilled craftspeople who are able to turn their hand to any aspect of the manufacturing process as was the case with the shoemakers at the beginning of the 20th century.

Ryusaku Hiruma is an accessory designer specialising in shoe and handbag design. In 2004, he created his first shoe collection under the Sak label and presented it in Paris. This young Japanese designer, now living in Florence, owns a collection of vintage bags and old shoes from which he recycles the leather to reproduce new shoe styles.

He makes individual, artistic shoes which do not belong to either the ready-to-wear or industrial sector, seeing his shoes as 'works of art'. In 1998, when he was working in London, his first creations were inspired by London streets and contemporary art. From 2002, Hiruma moved to Italy where he discovered the studios and knowledge of

12

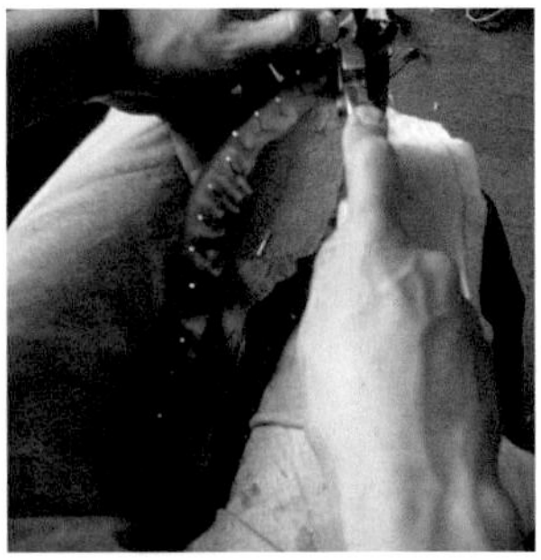

13

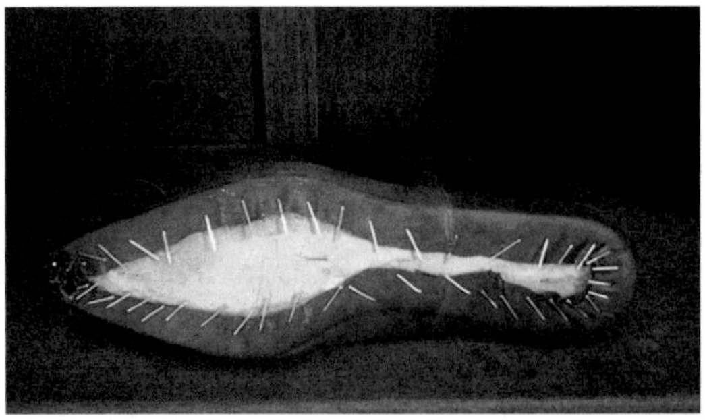

14

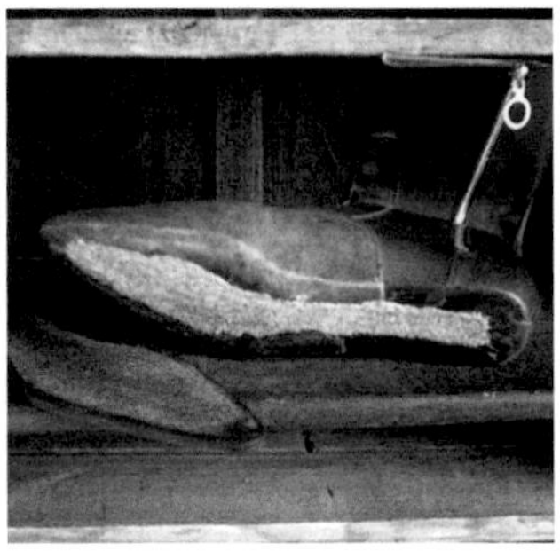

15

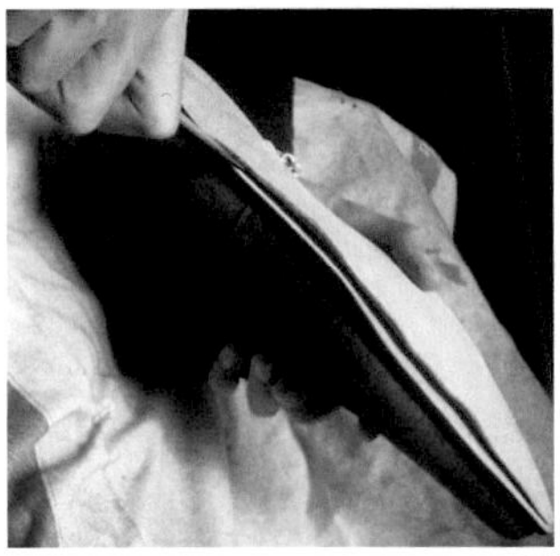

16

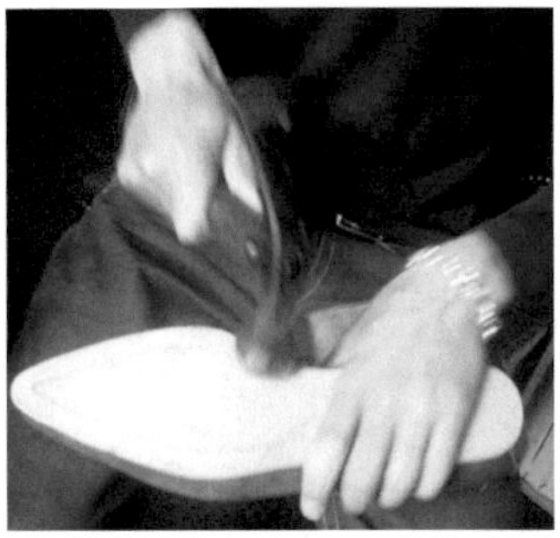

17

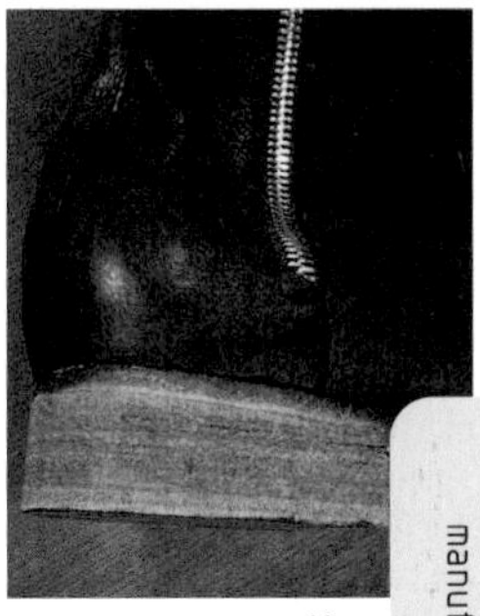

18

Italian craftsmen, going back to the Renaissance, and from which he derives enormous inspiration.

Ryusaku Hiruma presents his collections in Europe, the United States and Japan. His first line of handbags date back to the 2005 Spring-Summer collection. Also in 2005, he made some shoes for the American artist Vincent Gallo which became the starting point for his 2005-6 Autumn-Winter collection.

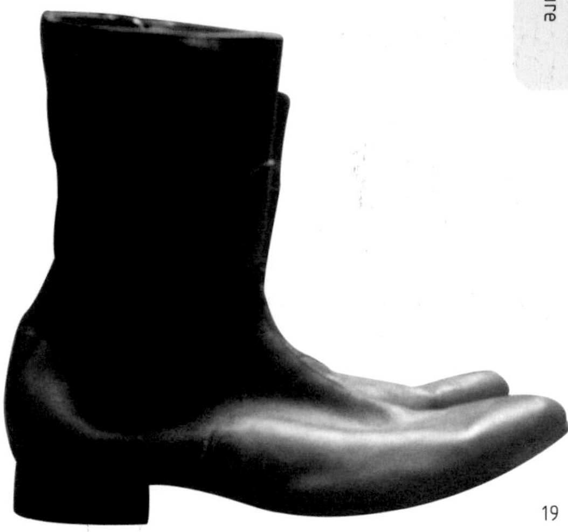

19

1 AND 2. SHOES DESIGNED BY SAK.

3. TOOLS USED IN SHOE MANUFACTURE: PINCERS, PLIERS, CALLIPERS AND HAMMER.

4. CORNER OF WORKBENCH USED FOR SHOE-MAKING.

5. CUTTING OUT A LEATHER SHOE PATTERN.

6. SEWING THE ZIP IN PLACE. THIS CORRESPONDS TO THE AREA WHERE THE LEATHER UPPER MEETS THE LINING UPPER.

7. SEWN ZIP. (

8. NAILING THE SHANK TO THE WOODEN LAST BY HAND.

9. USING PLIERS, THE LEATHER IS STRETCHED ALLOWING FOR ADJUSTMENT OF THE FINAL ASSEMBLY ON THE WOODEN LAST.

10. ON THE WOODEN LAST, NAILS ARE FIXED AROUND THE SHANK BEFORE ASSEMBLING.

11. NAILED SHANK, THEN STUCK BEFORE BEING FINALLY FIXED IN PLACE.

12. BOOT'S UPPER BEFORE ASSEMBLING.

13. NAILING THE LEATHER UPPER ONTO THE WOODEN LAST.

14. SHANK NAILED AND SEWN IN PLACE, BEFORE SECURING THE SOLE AND HEEL.

15. WEATHER-PROOFING AND STICKING THE CORK INSOLE TO THE SHANK.

16. CUTTING AND STICKING THE OUTER SOLE TO THE SHANK.

17. HAMMERING THE SOLE IN PLACE.

18. ADDING THE HEEL.

19. FINISHING TOUCHES: COLOURING THE SOLE AND THE HEEL, POLISHING THE BOOT. THE LAST IS REMOVED AND THE BOOTS ARE FINISHED.

Industrial scarf manufacture

1

2

House of Marc Rozier

The scarf, along with lingerie, is one of the most important and oldest items of one's wardrobe. Originally, it was reserved for the rural population. It was very popular with the women who worked in the fields as it protected their hair and kept the sweat off their faces, becoming a key item of clothing. According to Éric Provent, the great-grandson of Marc Rozier, who founded the famous factory, it is the beauty of the scarf which is the at the origin of the Provençal patterned *Gavroche* hat in cotton.

Founded in 1890, the Marc Rozier company began by designing little Provençal patterns for cotton prints. Four generations have perpetuated this family tradition and savoir-faire and today, Éric and Didier Provent have taken up the reins of the company which now consists of three factories : a weaving factory, printing manufacture and a sewing and finishing studio. The company houses more than a century of information in its archives. Marc Rozier works with a number of couture and *prêt-a-porter* brands, as well as lingerie and leather goods labels such as Dior, Chanel, Vuitton, Cartier, Jean-Louis Scherrer, Sonia Rykiel, Agnès b. etc. The fashion house produces fabrics by the metre to make their collections of scarves, shawls and stoles. Marc Rozier is a specialist in all sorts of chiffon: woven, printed, flocked, devoré as well as sophisticated Jacquard-weave mixes of wool, silk, linen and cotton.

1. Weaving tools from the Marc Rozier archives.
© Ninjin Puntjag.

2. Twill scarf from the Marc Rozier archives.
© Ninjin Puntjag.

3. Finishing the selvedge of the fabric on an overlocker machine.
© Ninjin Puntjag.

Vega
FICHE ARTICLE
date :
ROZIER
Réf. : 521
Collection : ETE 2007

1

2

3

4

5

6

Weaving at Marc Rozier's

Design studio

The design studio (fig. 3) creates original patterns from scratch (fig. 5) or develops designs from already purchased material samples for printing scarves or fabric by the metre. The motif, which is drawn in black and white or in colour, is printed or woven. A number of choices need to be made from the original design i.e. colours need to be separated, threads chosen whether matte or shiny, whether the motif is the same, or different, colour, which tones or hues are to be used, as is the case with striped shiny satin and chiffon etc. The motif must then be arranged so that it can be repeated all over the fabric to form a pattern.

Developing a woven fabric

Marc Rozier buys his thread from China and Brazil on cones (figs 6 & 7) and makes different weavings which are white initially, then printed in colour. Weaving is a method of producing a fabric using a particular arrangement of warp and weft threads, known as a 'weave'. There are three main types: plain, twill or satin weaves; however, these constructions can be mixed to produce more sophisticated fabrics.

Weaving with different thread tensions can result in a variety of very different fabrics. For example, canvas and seersucker are both plain weaves but one has a regular appearance, whereas the other has a puckered effect. The double ladder stitch is very fine, open-work weave. Gradated weaving is achieved by using different threads which get increasingly closer together thus giving the fabric a gradation of colour.

The combination of coloured threads gives rise to distinct fabrics such as gingham check, for example. This is a plain weave which is a result of alternat-

7

8

9

10

11

12

ing white and coloured threads giving squares of various sizes. As for motifs which are in relief, these would require a different technique such as devoré or flock printing.

The textile engineer will produce several samples using a variety of weaves and threads. This is done by trying different thread and colour combinations using a computer. By using CAM (Computer-Aided Manufacture), the technician is able to programme the type of weave required. The warp threads (fig. 11) come down from the top with the weft threads coming from the sides. The threads are distributed by a spool which regulates their tension whilst the weaver feeds the warp from the weft threads.

1. Textile design archives.

2. Printed samples in Marc Rozier's design studio.

3. Marc Rozier's design studio.

4. A technician working on a Jacquard card.

5. Maquettes and archives.

6&7. Cones of thread.

8. Automated weaving loom

9. Reels of thread bobbins.

10. Arrival of threads on the loom.

11. Loom with warp threads.

12. At work on the loom – a technician adjusts the combs which sort the threads.

1

2

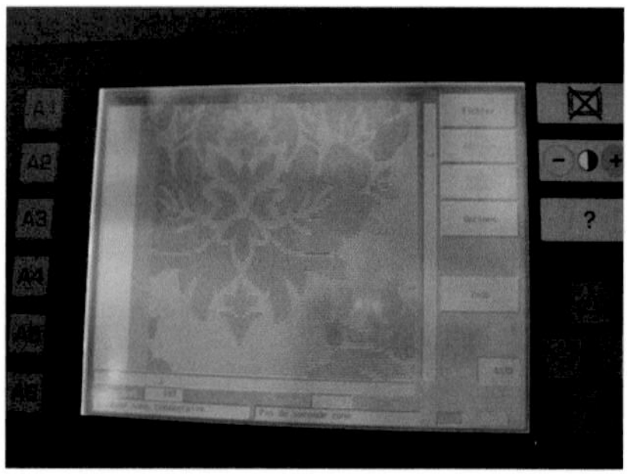

3

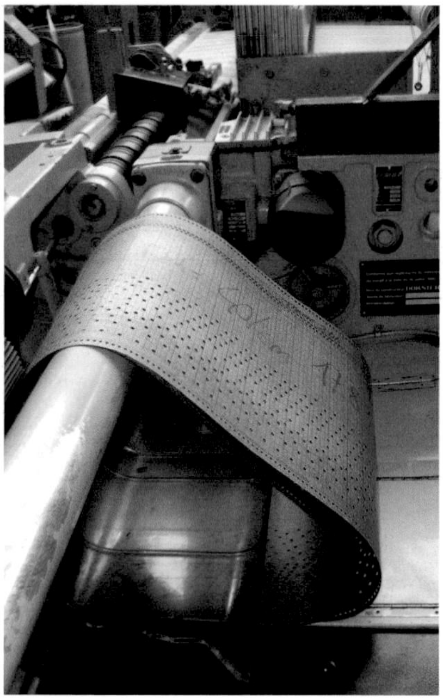

4

5

6

Jacquard weave

The jacquard pattern is achieved by mechanical weaving using a computer-generated perforated card upon which the pattern has been punched (fig. 4). Each row corresponds to one row of the design, which guides the warp thread so that the weft thread will lie above or below it. The fabric weave is symbolised by a grid on the computer screen (fig. 4, p. 102). The black and white points represent the jacquard pattern. Sample pieces are produced on the loom (fig. 6) so that the pattern can be tested on the fabric. A control panel or screen (fig. 3) on the machine shows the pattern which is in the process of being made. If the result is successful, the fabric will be produced in a given size and quantity. Normally, samples are made in measurements of 40 x 140 cm for small items and in 60 x 160 cm for larger items and stoles.

Preparing the dyes

The colourist researches which dyes are to be used in relation to the season's trends. Depending on the desired quality, different types of dyes are used with acid colours for silks and reactive, or dispersed, colours for polyamides or synthetics.

The dyes used are in paste form. Their preparation, which requires a certain knowledge of chemistry, follows a precise recipe. The dyes are prepared and mixed in a laboratory using ladles to measure the necessary quantities (fig. 12). After each use, all the utensils are carefully

7

8

9

10

11

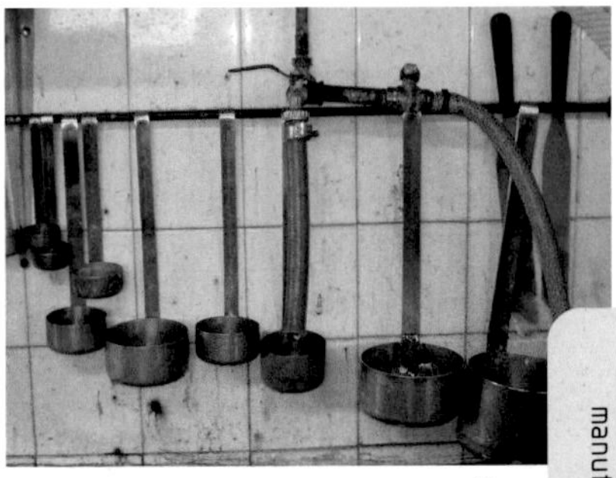
12

washed to avoid any chemical cross-contamination with the other colours. Nearly 400 pigments, as well as chemical products, of which the majority are in powder form, are kept in the 'back kitchens'.

Other than colour, the dye consists of gum, different acids and thickeners which are mixed together in a container with soft water to the right consistency and uniformity adapted to the material. The resulting colours are then catalogued with reference codes which relate to the different ingredients and quantities used. This helps the colourist reproduce them when necessary. Colour tests are carried out on samples of the material in order to establish how the dye interacts with the fabric and also to see how it reacts to washing and drying.

1. Weft threads on a jacquard machine.

2. Arrangement of warp threads so that a striped fabric can be made.

3. Detail of jacquard pattern on the control panel screen.

4. Jacquard punch card.

5. Detail of the combs.

6. Producing a jacquard pattern.

7&8. Preparing the dyes.

9. Dye bath.

10. Mixing the dyes using a mixer.

11. Dye tests.

12. Measuring ladles for each dye tint. By mixing them together, the desired colour is obtained.

1

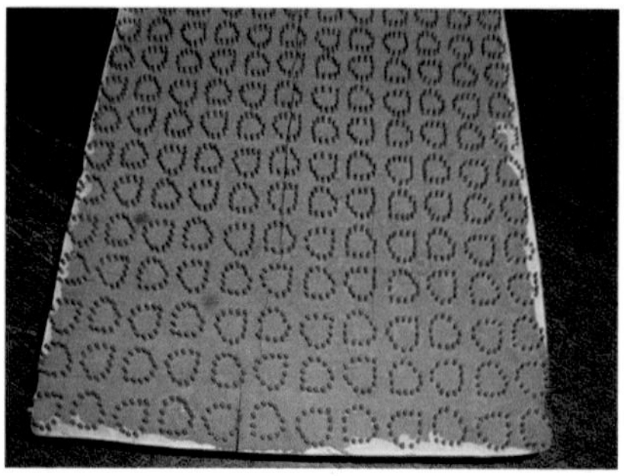

2

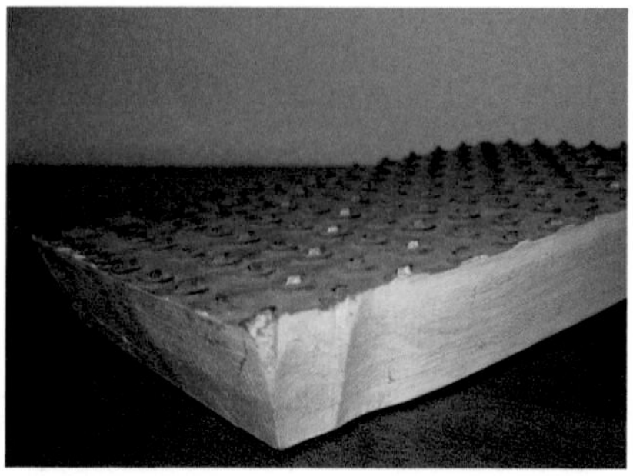

3

4

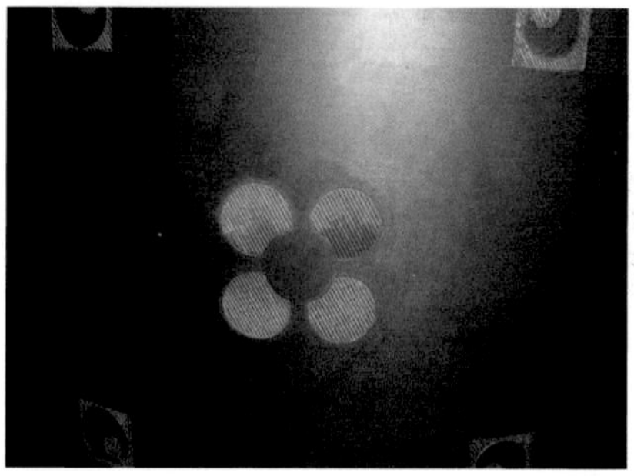

5

Printing techniques for scarves

There are a variety of printing techniques: roller, rotary or flatbed printing presses, automatic or semi, transfer or ink-jet. In Marc Rozier's factory only automatic and semi-automatic flatbed printing presses are used.

Flocking is a technique which consists of printing a glue onto the fabric then projecting small fibres/velvet onto these printed areas. The motifs are normally one colour. Devoré, which gets its name from the French word *devoré* or 'eaten', on the other hand, means that some of the surface of the fabric has a resist applied to it then either, acid-etched or, burnt away to create the pattern. Some dyes or tints can be manually applied as is the case with ombré chiffon which is soaked in dye baths to give a more exclusive feel to the product.

Roller printing

Although used less and less nowadays, this process does allow for very neat, distinct prints of which the most suitable are small patterns or motifs. The repetition of the pattern depends on the circumference of the printing roller or cylinder. The pattern is engraved onto either a brass, copper or nickel cylinder (figs 4 & 5) to which the dye is applied. The excess dye is scraped off the roller's surface, leaving it in the engraved sections only.

A second cylinder is wrapped with a large blanket of soft, absorbent material which forces the fabric to be printed into the engraved areas. This soft material also absorbs any excess dye. The fabric is printed by passing between the cylinders.

Rotary screen printing

This process allows for continuous printing. In basic terms, the printing dyes are inside rotary drums or cylinders. The cylinders are perforated and the dyes are forced out through these holes onto the fabric. This is not a very sophisticated technique and tends only to be used for mass-production fabric printing.

1.2 & 3. Old manual printing plates.

4. & 5 Copper cylinders used for printing squares of cotton fabric. There are about 50 cylinders similar to these in Marc Rozier's archives.

6

7

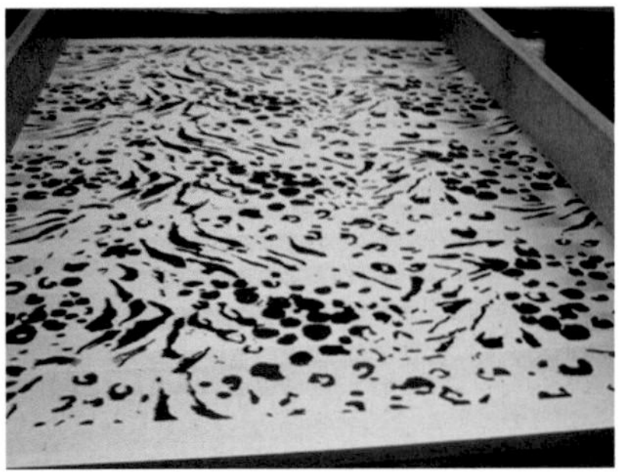

8

9

10

11

Automatic flatbed printing

With flatbed printing, also known as printing *a la lyonnaise* (fig. 9), larger patterns can be achieved with this technique than with roller printing. The size of the pattern varies in relation to the screen size. The screen has a gauze or stainless steel mesh stretched over it onto which a stencil of the pattern is applied either manually or photo-chemically. The pattern areas to be printed are left open so that the dyes can be forced through onto the fabric.

The pattern will have had its colours separated as each colour requires a separate screen. The more screens there are, the denser the final pattern will become. There are some very complex prints which require more than 20 printing screens - an example being Louis Vuitton's Multicolour fabric (see p. 74). With automatic flatbed printing, the fabric passes intermittently along the printing conveyor belt (although it is stationary when a colour is applied). The screen is raised then lowered and the colour is applied to the mesh using a squeegee. Very fine and delicate fabrics such as chiffon must be placed on calico beforehand which acts as blotting paper for the excess dye which seeps through. After printing, this calico material is washed and recycled.

6. Unrolling the fabric prior to printing.

7. Virgin fabric secured on the conveyor belt prior to printing.

8. First colour printed.

9. Second colour screen placed on fabric.

10. Automatic printing.

11. The printed material unrolls onto the printing table.

12

13

14

15

Semi-automatic flatbed printing

This technique is more for small-scale production than the others requiring a certain amount of manual intervention. The pattern needs to be very precise in order to achieve a successful engraving. This process involves printing the fabric using wet printing dyes, rather than the paste-like ones used in the other techniques. This is why this type of printing is done as 'wet on dry'. However, this process can make the image less sharp. Contrary to the automatic flatbed machine principle, with this method the fabric does not move along the printing table automatically. A technician is needed to manually move the length of fabric along the table which measures 37 metres long. Two technicians are involved in this printing process – an engraver and a printer. A number of the stages are not automated. For example, the controls are manually operated with a technician positioning the registration marks for the pattern repeats (fig. 15), pulling the squeegee and checking that the colours are right.

Final stages

After printing, the fabric is stretched and dried. Once the colours are dry, the printed fabric is plunged into a fixing tank for a certain period of time. This is dependent on the quality of the material. After this operation, the fabric is machine-washed in order to fix the colours, then spun and finally dried. It is at this point that a technician carries out a colour control. If the pieces of fabric conform, then a finishing treatment is applied in order to stabilise the dyes.

16

17

18

19

20

21

12. The fabric is washed after printing and then placed in different tanks to fix the colour.

13. Washing the fabric.

14. Detail of a printing screen.

15. The technician positions the registration marks to where he is going to place the screen.

16. Colour control on a sample fabric.

17&18. Manual printing screens.

19. The printed fabric after the initial printing.

20. Final stage: Drying the fabric before rolling it.

21. Storage area for the printing screens.

Jewellery making with Eléna Cantacuzène

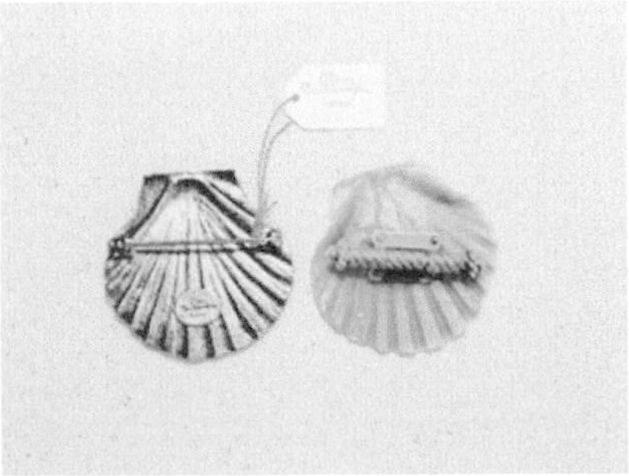

1

2

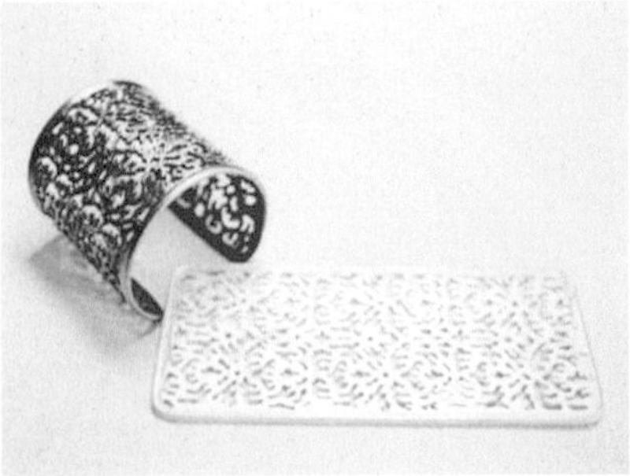

3

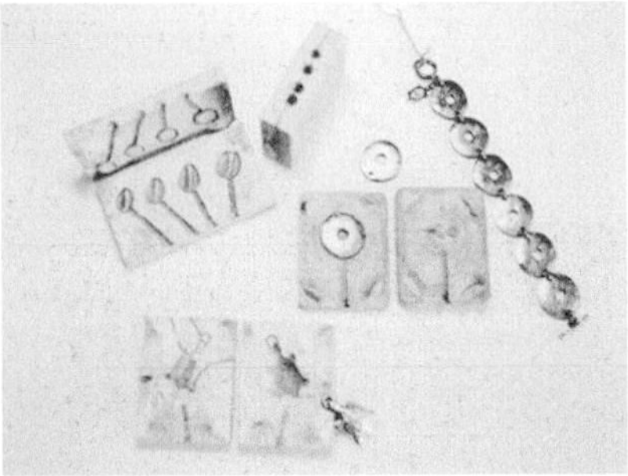

4

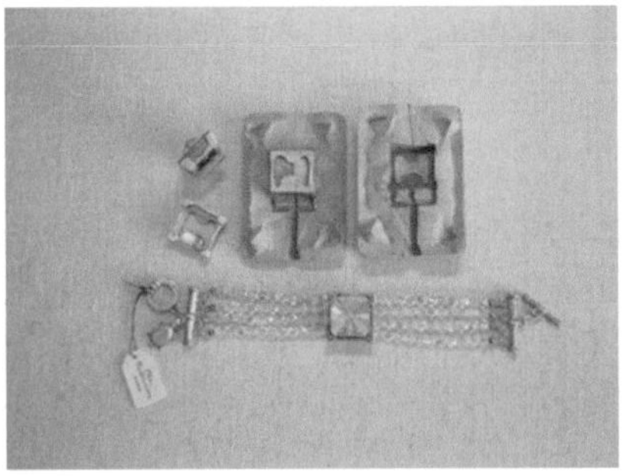

5

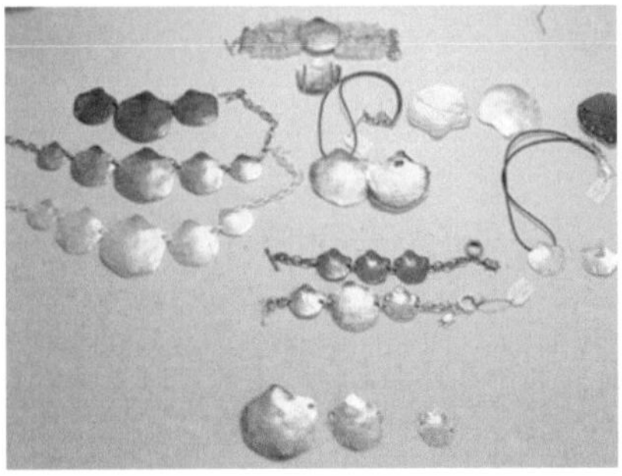

6

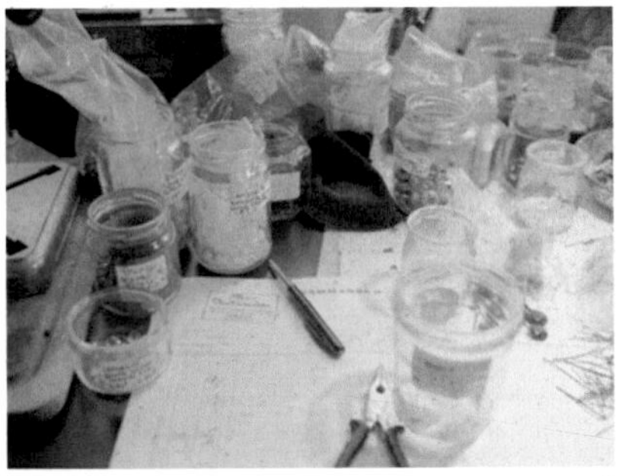

7

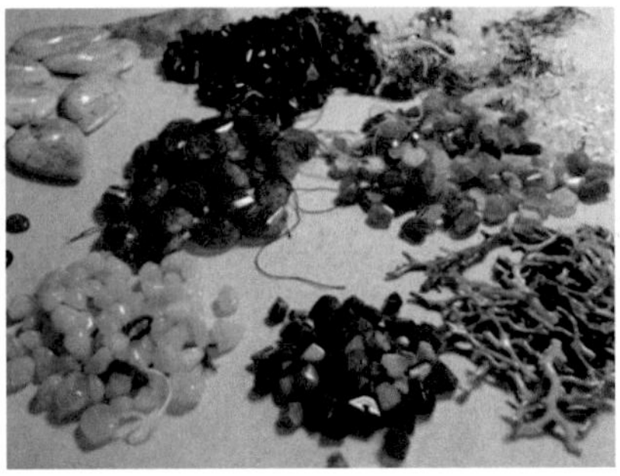

8

9

In collaboration with her assistants, Éléna Cantacuzène designs the main pieces for her collection, which will be ultimately made into ranges. A model maker produces prototypes from her original designs which she checks afterwards. Once agreed, they are sent to a gilding foundry where a mould is made for the pilot production. Ten examples are produced in three colours (gold, bronze and platinum). Cantacuzène makes three versions of the same model in different sizes: small, medium and large. These models will then be made into a brooch, pendant and bracelet. The sets are produced following orders placed at specialist trade fairs such as Bijorca in Paris etc.

Germany supplies the carved stones on demand. The shells, mother-of-pearl and wood come form the Philippines; the glass and crystal from China and the blown glass from Murano in the lagoon in Venice. The beads she uses the most of are made from natural and freshwater pearls, shells, glass and plastic. For the natural and freshwater pearls Éléna uses vegetable dyes with colours ranging from white, pink and golden. The pearls need to be soaked in the dyes for six months and naturally this needs to be taken into account when orders are placed.

She lists the most frequently used precious and semi-precious stones used in her jewellery as follows: amethyst,

10

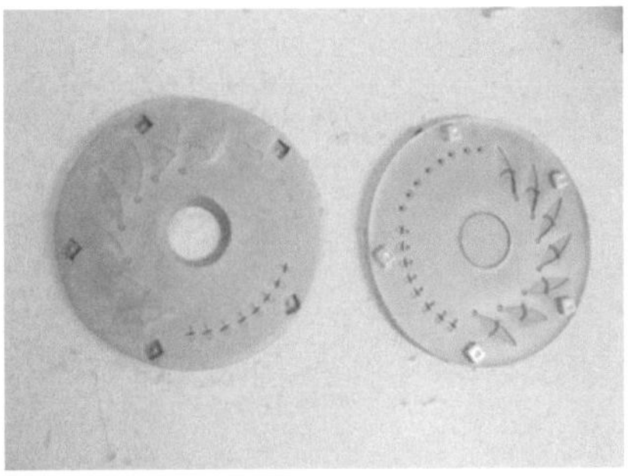
11

12

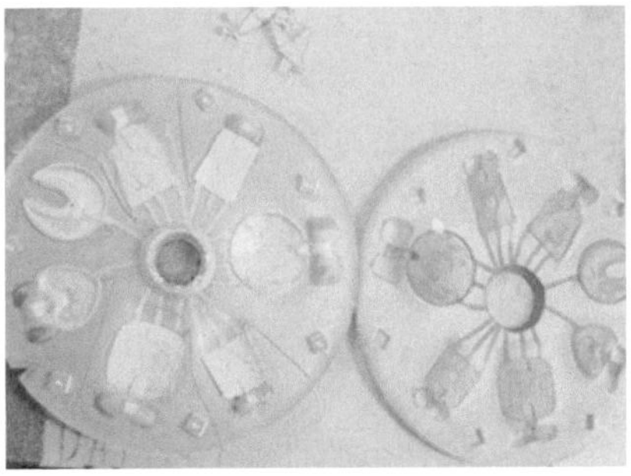
13

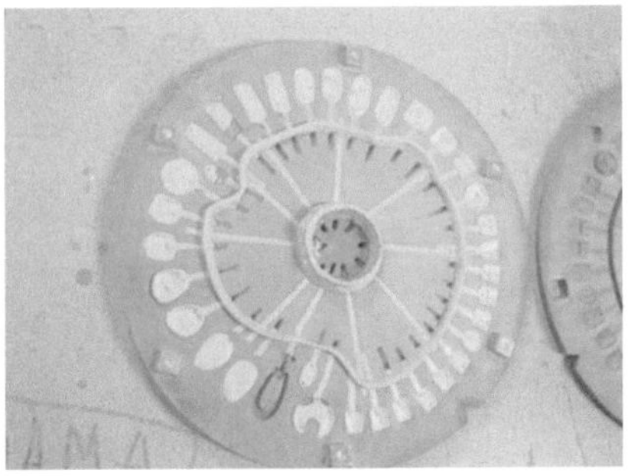
14

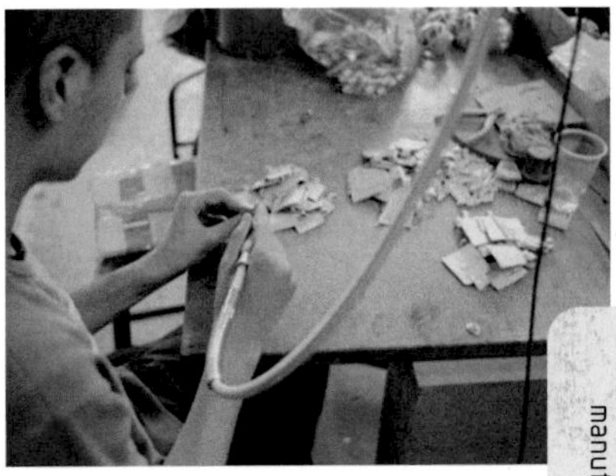
15

16

17

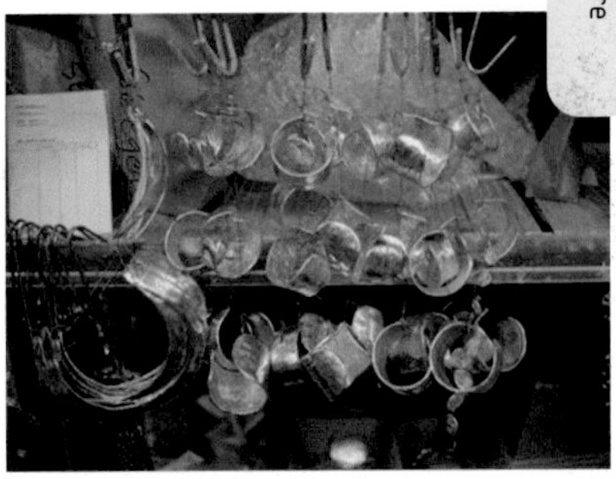
18

rose or smoked quartz, turquoise, rock crystal, cornelian, green rutile, serpentine, agate, red or green garnet, chrysoprase, fossilised jasper, amber, calcite, obsidian, moonstone, chalcedony, lava, coral, opal, and aquamarine. The accessories, stems, clasps, wires, etc. are supplied by different manufacturers.

1. Shell brooch and resin prototype (on the right).

2. Bangles and rings.

3. Gilded metal cuff bracelet and tin plate prototype before being shaped.

4. Flat ring moulds (on the left).

5. Moulds (at the top) for synthetic crystal and bracelet.

6. Shell forms with bronze, gold and platinum effect.

7. Containers for glass beads.

8. Glass beads.

9. Threading the beads.

10. The gilder preparing the resin moulds.

11. Models and moulds.

12. The mould is filled with pewter.

13&14. Pewter casts in the mould.

15. Once the moulded pieces are removed, the gilder grinds off any bumps etc.

16. The polished pieces are galvanised with a protective layer of zinc.

17. The polished pieces are soaked in an acid bath.

18. The finished pieces are rinsed and hung up to dry.

M*aroquinerie* or leather goods usually refers to a group of products which are made from leather such as wallets, purses, handbags etc. and which are covered one way or another in order to protect the material. The shapes will vary depending on what they are required to contain, i.e. make-up bags, sponge bags, overnight bags etc.

Keeping abreast of the times, designers have introduced new materials such as vinyl or neoprene either to compliment or, at times, replace leather. The techniques and basic shapes are continually revisited. However, the techniques remain unchanged and a good working knowledge of these methods greatly helps in the manufacture of certain bags.

There is a distinction between rigid and supple bags. Rigid

Chapter 5 - Step by step

ones are made in materials which require very specific sewing techniques; supple ones, on the other hand, are made from leathers which can be sewn and then turned inside out. In this chapter, the rigid and supple bags are made from stiff cardboard and felt respectively; the cardboard more or less imitates rigid materials whereas the felt, being a non-woven material, is likened to supple leathers. The techniques and methods used in the manufacture of soft bags are close to those used in garment-making.

With leather goods, the finishing stages require special tools. A style can have a smooth edge which is finished with piping i.e. cylindrical trim – or require a particular finishing technique. Each brand has its own methods and trademark – for example, Hermes and its saddle-stitch, or even Louis Vuitton's coated canvas items which are reminiscent of travel trunks.

In this chapter we present the basics – a tote bag and a shoulder bag with a flap. The bags with handles, or shoulder straps, and the one with gussets, made by Fatron Hosoi in felt, make up the basis for the supple bags. The techniques described for the rigid bag offer great scope for a number of variations on a theme. These are explained step by step and result in a finished prototype.

In order to understand the work involved when working with leather, we have chosen to list in detail the process. However, we have simplified certain stages for a better understanding of the working methods.

Tools

1

2

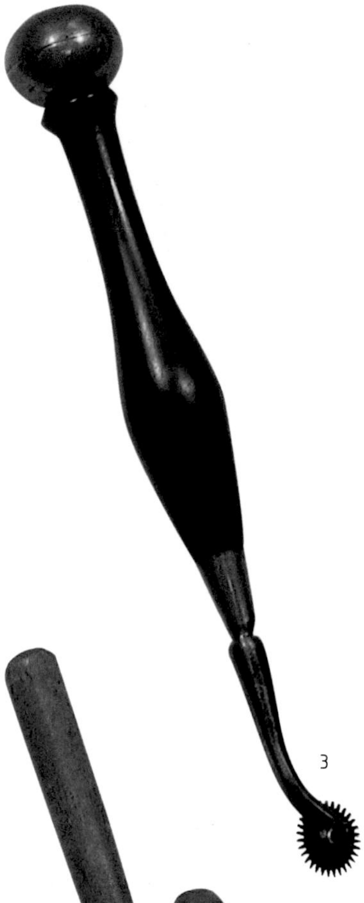

3

4

5

6

7

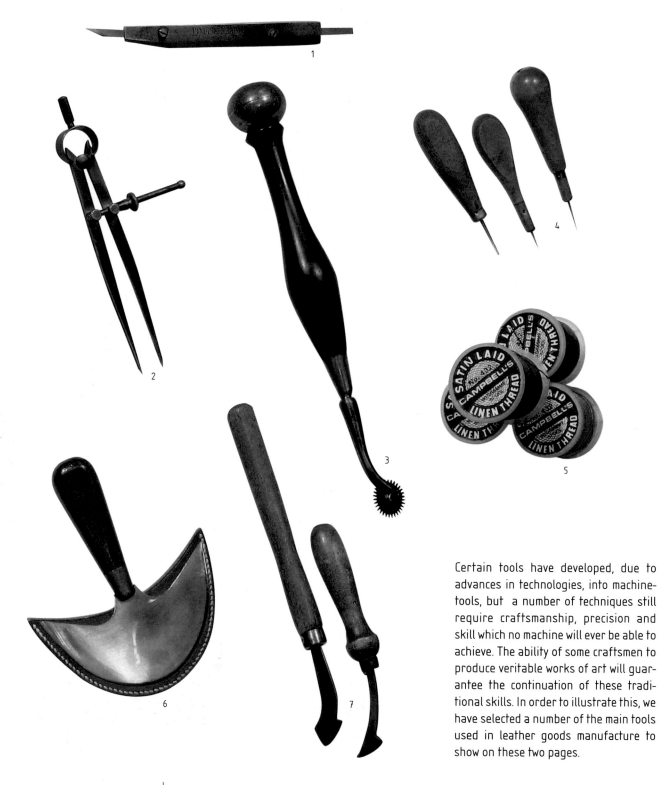

Certain tools have developed, due to advances in technologies, into machine-tools, but a number of techniques still require craftsmanship, precision and skill which no machine will ever be able to achieve. The ability of some craftsmen to produce veritable works of art will guarantee the continuation of these traditional skills. In order to illustrate this, we have selected a number of the main tools used in leather goods manufacture to show on these two pages.

1. Leather knife.

2. Adjustable compass: tracing tool used mainly to transfer measurements.

3. Roulette: Tracing tool used to mark stitch holes at regular intervals. Griffe/claw tools can also be used. They have fairly long and evenly spaced teeth. Either one or other is used depending on the type of stitching to be done.

4. Awl: Piercing tool used for making holes in the leather.

5. Linen thread: Used for hand stitching.

6. Head knife: Cutting tool.

7. Threading irons: Cutting tools which, when hot, allow the leather edges to be threaded by marking them.

8. Paring knife: Cutting knife used to reduce the thickness of the leather. It is used by scratching the underside of the leather.

9. Hole puncher: This cutting tool is used to remove a pre-determined shape in conjunction with a hammer. It makes the necessary holes for rivets, press studs etc. It can also be used for making holes in belts and straps.

10. Bone folder: tracing tool used for finishing details and flattening stitches. Pliers have the same function.

11. Metal ruler: Used for measuring and tracing lines.

12. Silver-ink biro: Used on the reverse of the leather for tracing lines so that no marks show.

13. Glue pot: Special glue made from a gum base, normally used by shoemakers. It is used to secure the leather pieces before stitching.

14. Crepe: Rubber used to remove all traces of glue.

15. Weights: Necessary for holding the pieces down.

Making card prototypes

1 - Tote bag

A prototype is the first object which is made to scale, so that the proportions of the model can be fully understood. If it is approved, it will then serve as the pattern for the bag's final manufacture.

The bag's pattern which is illustrated here is constructed symmetrically, i.e. we will work on half of the bag. Generally, in the case of a symmetrical bag style, the right side will be the same as the left. On the other hand, an asymmetrical one is treated in the same way but its modifications are taken into account.

In order to make it easier for the reader in the following step by step photos, we have labelled the top and the bottom of the bag with letters 'h' and 'b'.

This bag is trapezoidal in shape with stitching along the edges. It is made up of five main pieces : a front and identical back, two identical sides (or gussets) and a base. The enchapes – reinforcing pieces where the handle buckles are attached – are drawn on the front of the bag ; these show the position of the handles. The first stage of these step by step photos show how to make the templates which are used to make the patterns. Secondly, we demonstrate how the prototype is assembled.

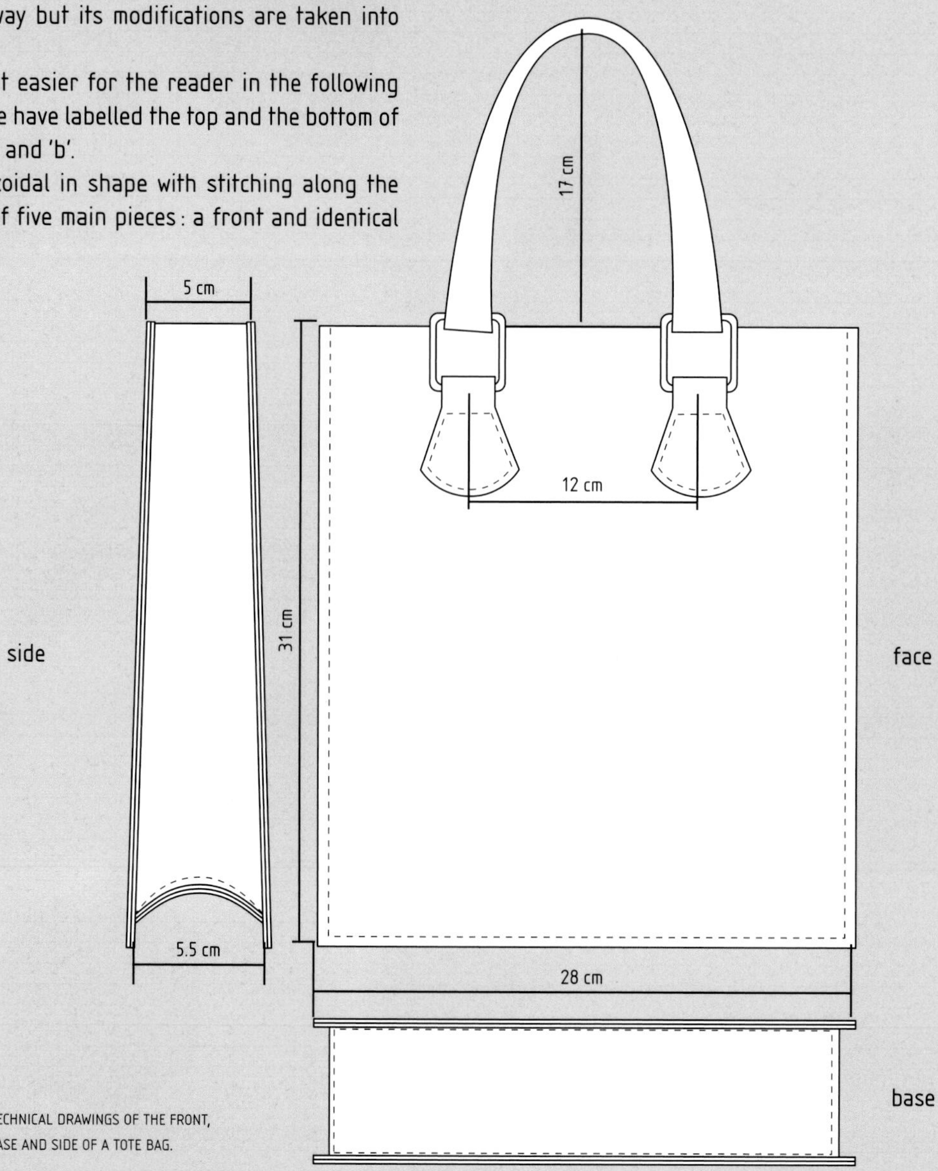

TECHNICAL DRAWINGS OF THE FRONT, BASE AND SIDE OF A TOTE BAG.

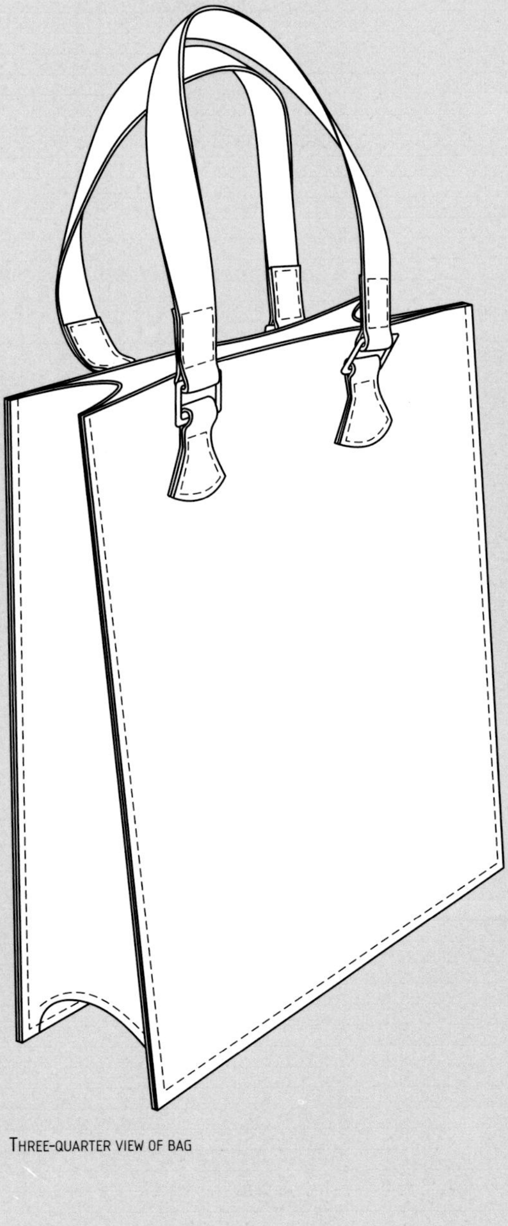
Three-quarter view of bag

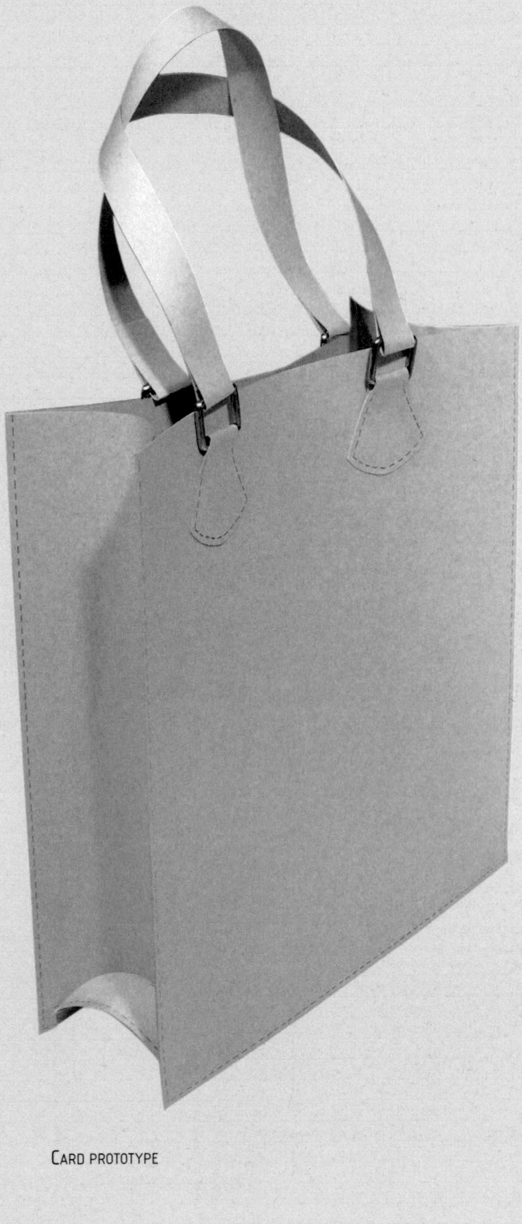
Card prototype

1 - Tote bag

Front template

This template, which we have called the 'front', is used to make the front and back pieces of the pattern - the pieces being identical.

1. Cut a piece of card slightly larger than the dimensions of the front of the bag.

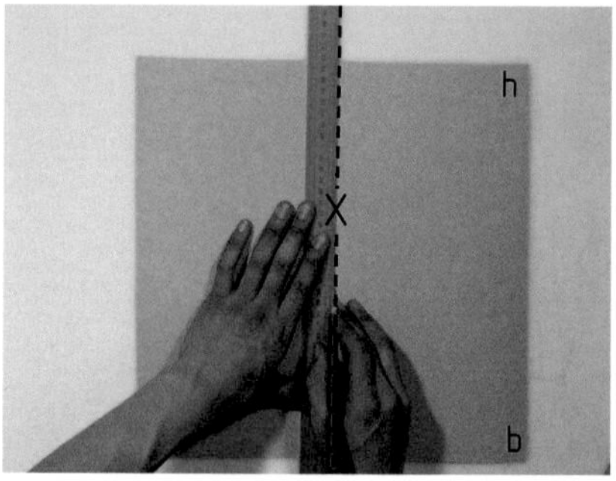

2. Using a cutter and ruler, score the vertical axis X, apply a slight pressure to help with the folding. This axis will be the centre-front of the template. The letter 'b' corresponds to the bottom of the bag with the letter 'h' being the top.

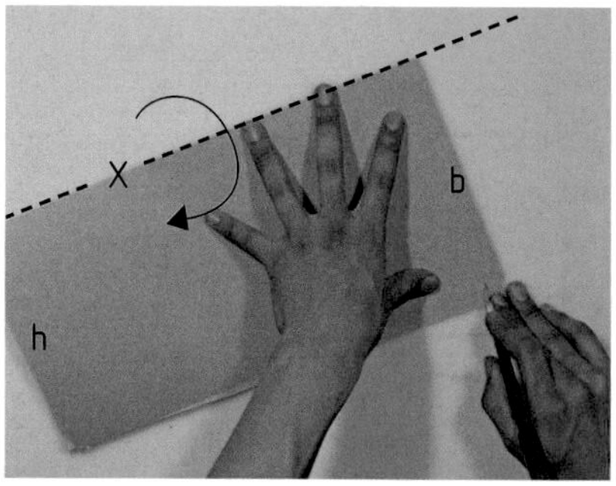

3. Fold the piece in two along the X axis, then in the bottom of this piece use the cutter to make a small incision through the two thicknesses – this is called a 'notch'. These incisions will serve as location points for the bottom line of the template.

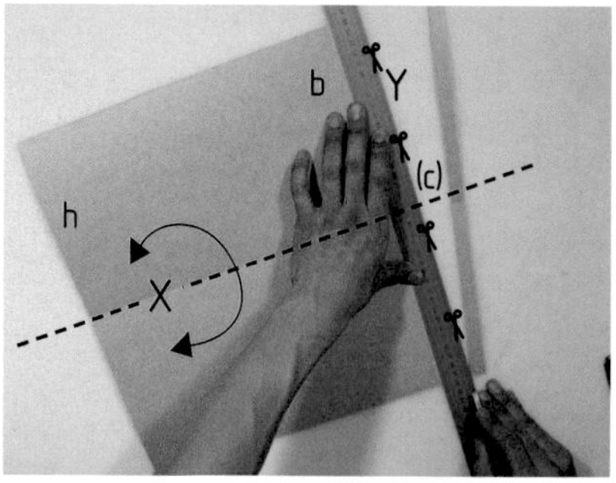

Unfold the piece of card and draw a line connecting the two incisions to make the bottom line of the template . Call this line Y. Cut along the traced line. This is a way of achieving perpendicular lines without using a set-square. Line Y is perpendicular to the axis X in the centre back. Place the biro point (c) at the intersection of the lines X and Y.

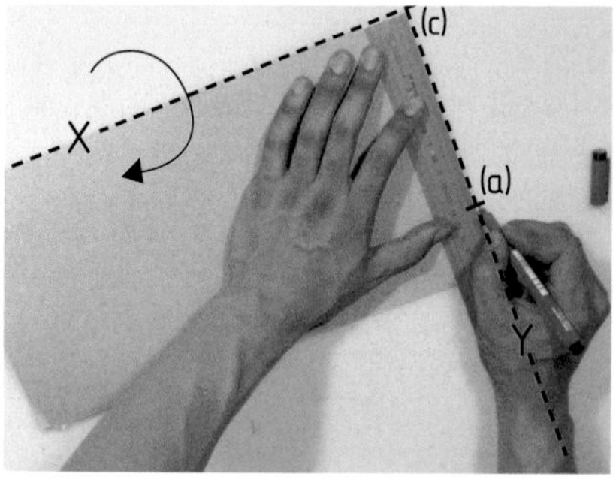

5. Once the card has been cut following line Y, trace half the width of the bottom of the template. Fold it again along the vertical axis X. Measure half the length of the bottom of the bag along line Y from point (c.) being 14 cm (for a bag whose width is 28 cm) and mark this point (a) with the biro.

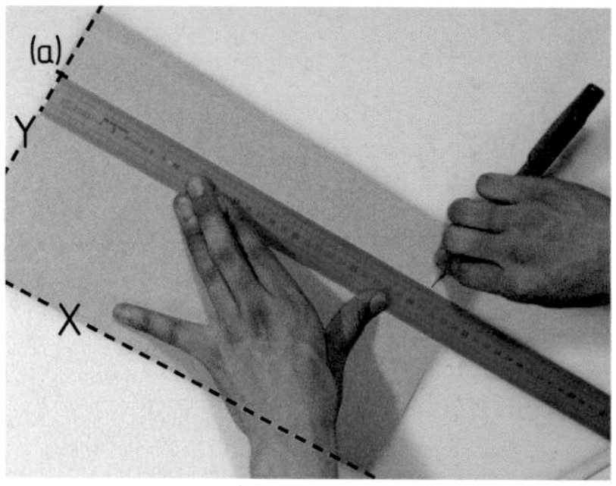

6. From point (a) measure a parallel line from axis X to the top of the bag, in this case 31 cm, and make an incision through the two thicknesses of card with a cutter.

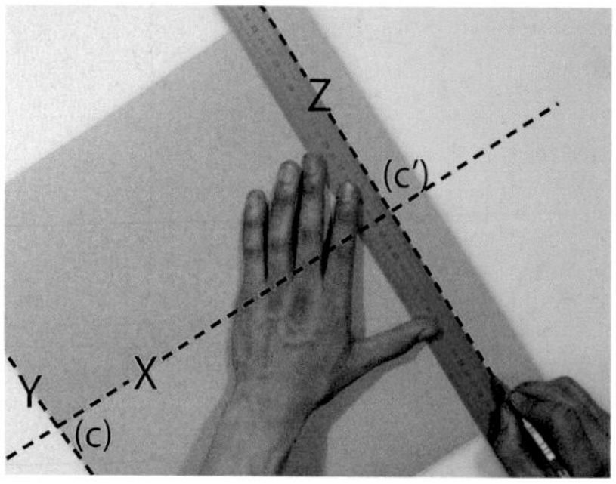

7. Unfold the card and, using a biro, connect the notches in order to draw the top of the template. Call this line 'Z'. Place the biro point (c.) at the intersection of lines Z and Y.

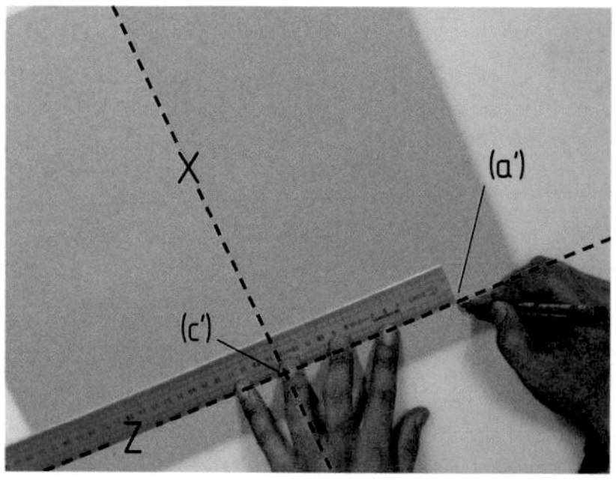

8. To determine half the measurement of the top width of the front template, place a biro point (a) on line Z, being 13.5 cm from point (c.) (for a bag with a top width of 27 cm.).

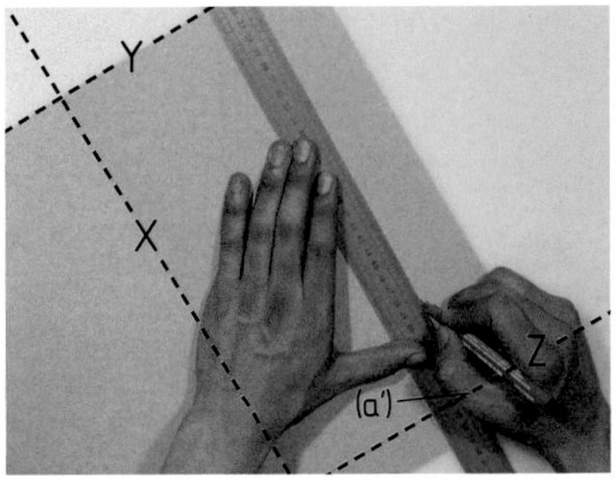

9. Connect biro points (a) and (a') to trace the side line of the template : this will make the front template of half the bag.

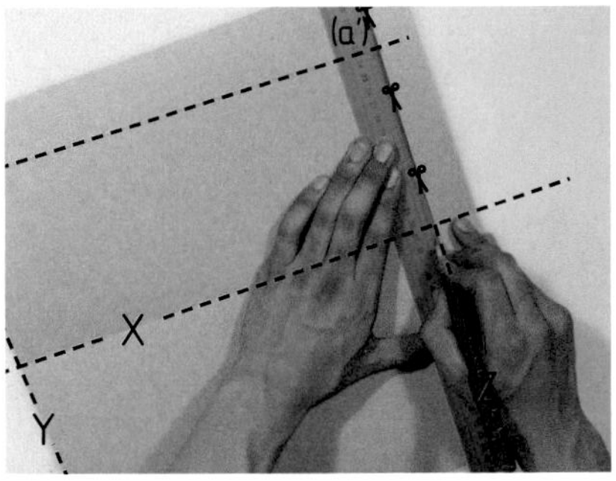

10. To cut half the template, place the ruler on line Z. Using the cutter, cut the card between points (a') and (c') remove the surplus card by cutting line X, starting from point (c') up to the top of the card.

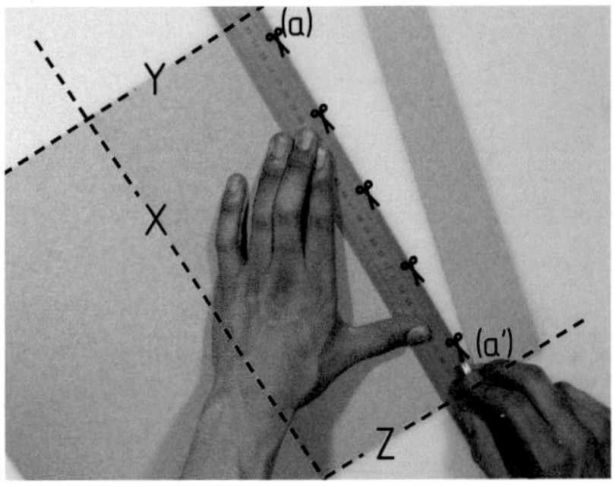

11. Using the ruler, draw a line along the side line (a' a) and cut the card following this line.

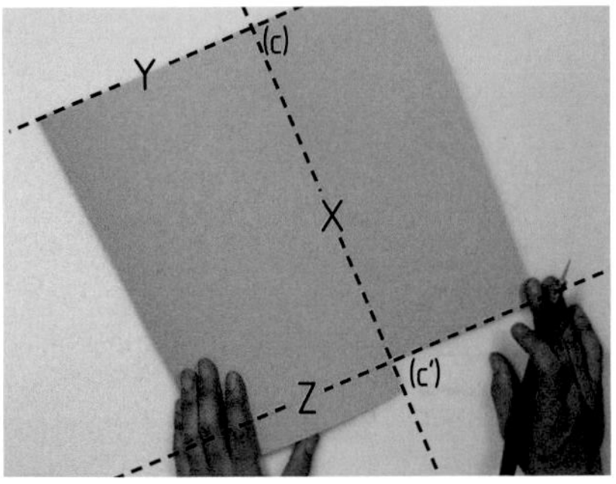

12. Half of the front template is now achieved.

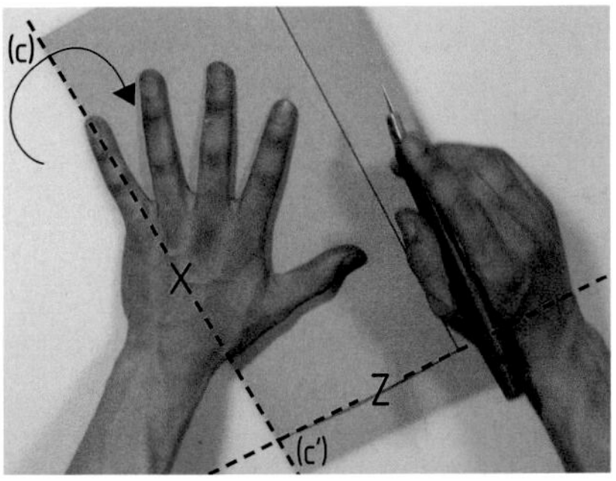

13. Fold along line X then fold the cut half (c a a' c') over onto the other side cutting it off symmetrically.

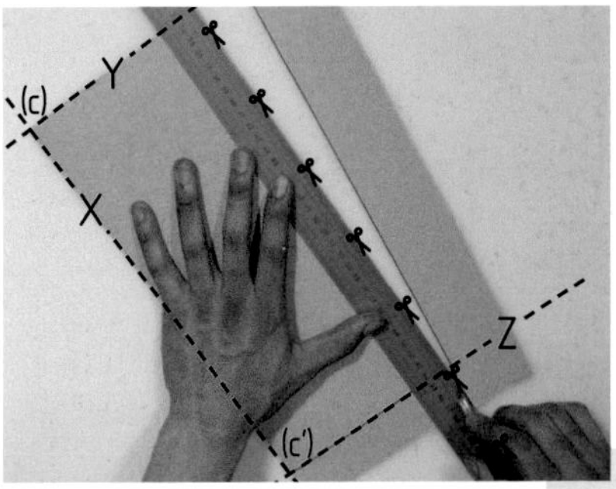

14. Place the ruler onto line (a a') and cut the side off.

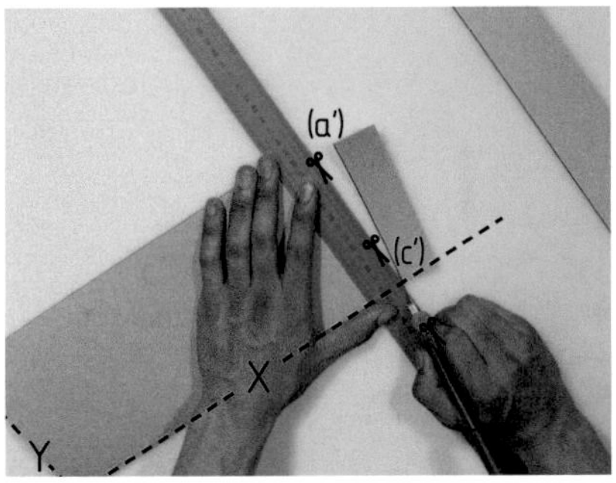

15. Place the ruler onto line (a' c') and cut along this line.

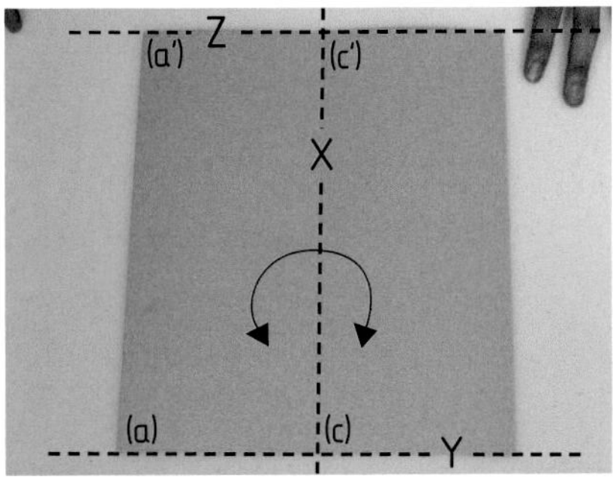

16. Open the template up: we now have the template of the front of the bag.

CHAPTER 5
Step by step

Enchapes pattern

The enchapes are the pieces of leather which hold the handle rings or buckles on the front and the back of the bag. Draw the enchapes onto the front of the template (fig. 1) placing them symmetrically in relation to the centre front. In this case the enchapes are trapezoidal but they can be any shape : triangular, rectangular etc. depending on the design. The top part of the enchape is determined by the width of the chosen buckles.

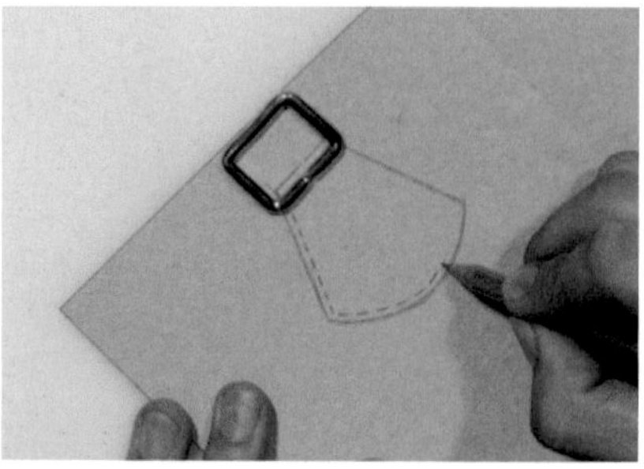

1. Draw the enchape shape onto the front template, on one side only – in this case on the left side. This shape serves as the pattern for the enchapes. It is folded in two to enclose the buckle . For a height of 5 cm, the pattern should be twice that, i.e. 10 cm.

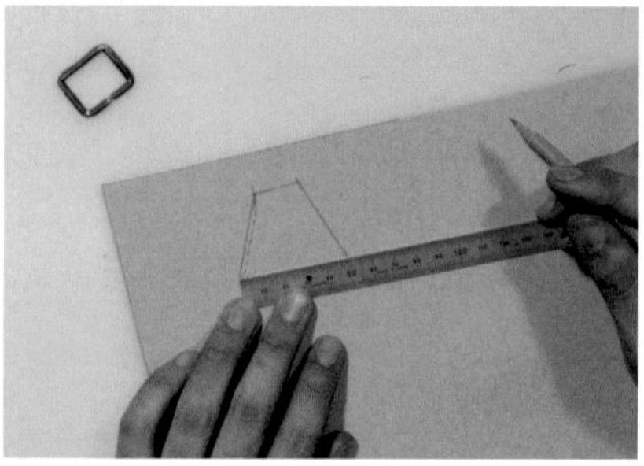

2. Mark off the measurements of the enchape (5 x 5 cm). These correspond to the size of the finished enchape once it is on the bag. This measurement is multiplied by 2 for the height, i.e.10 cm h for a width of 5 cm wide.

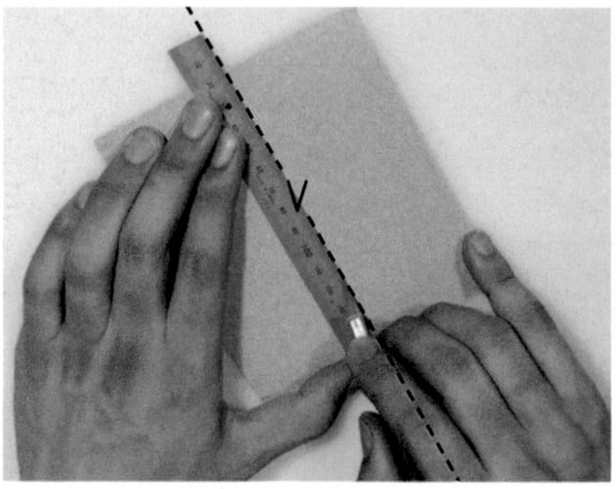

3. Cut out a piece of card bigger than the finished enchape, i.e. 15 x 10 cm for one being 10 x 5 cm. Place the card in the direction of its height then, pressing slightly, use a cutter to score the vertical line V in the middle of the piece of card.

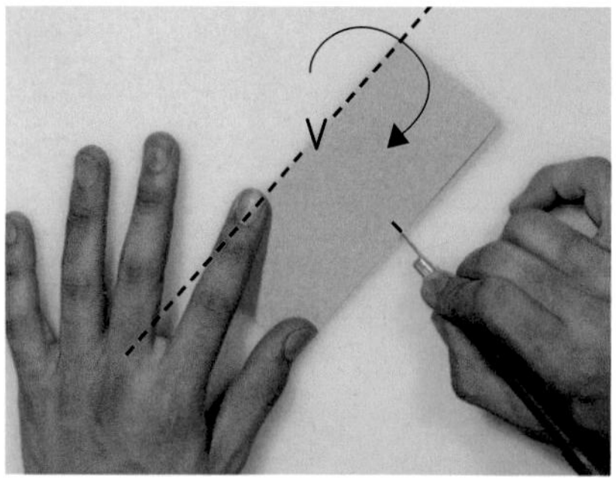

4. The horizontal line H must intersect the V line at the halfway point and these two axes should be perpendicular to each other. To mark the H line, fold the card over symmetrically on the V line. Mark the sides with the cutter making sure to go through the two thicknesses.

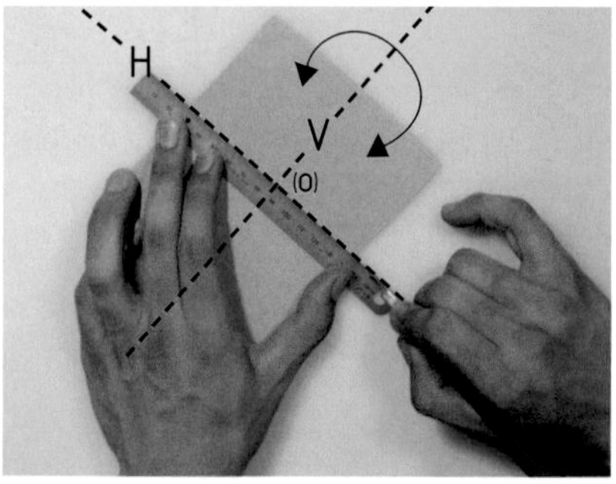

5. Treat the same way as the template for the front of the bag, i.e. once unfolded, draw a line joining the two points. This will produce the horizontal line H. The point where the two lines intersect will be the centre of the card. Pressing lightly, use the cutter to mark line H. Mark (o) at the intersection of lines V and H.

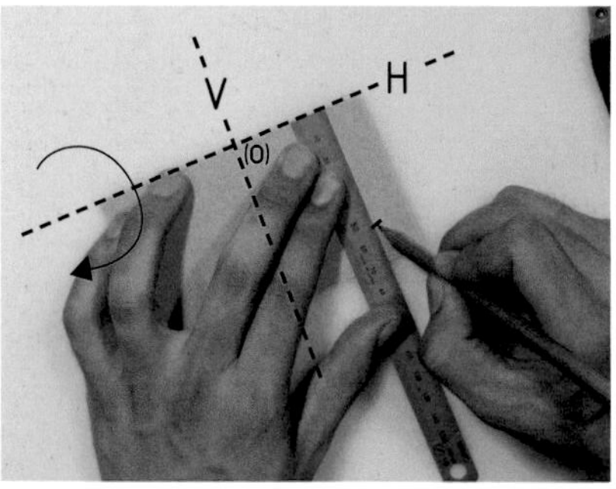

6. To trace half the height of the enchape, fold the card along line H and make a pencil mark 5 cm underneath this line (for a height of 10 cm). Make sure it is symmetrical in relation to line V.

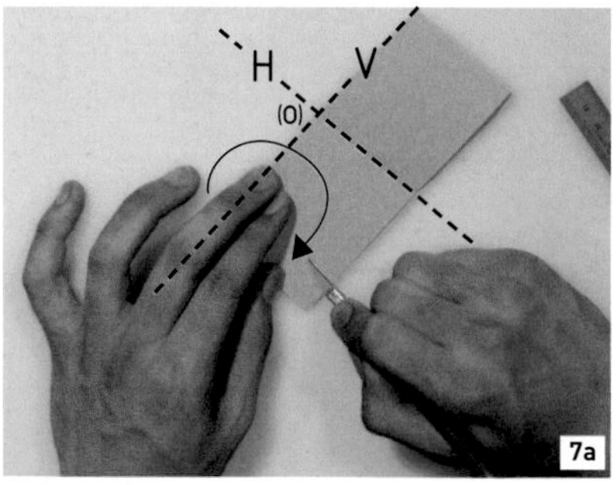

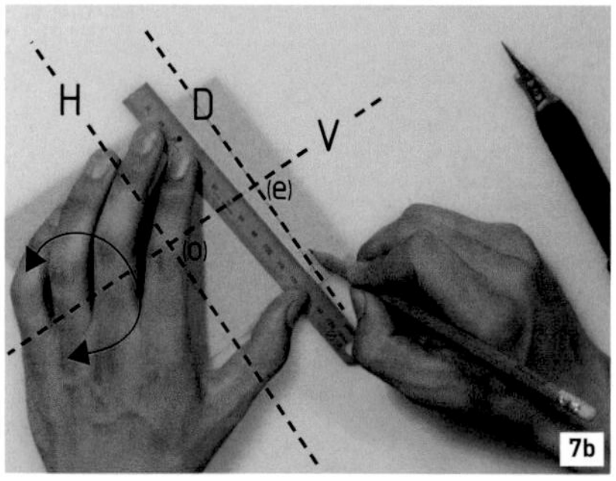

7. Unfold the card and fold it along line V. Mark this point with a cutter (fig.7a). Unfold, then using a pencil, join up these marks. This will produce line D which corresponds to half the height of the enchape (fig. 7b). Mark point (e) at the intersection of line D and the V axis.

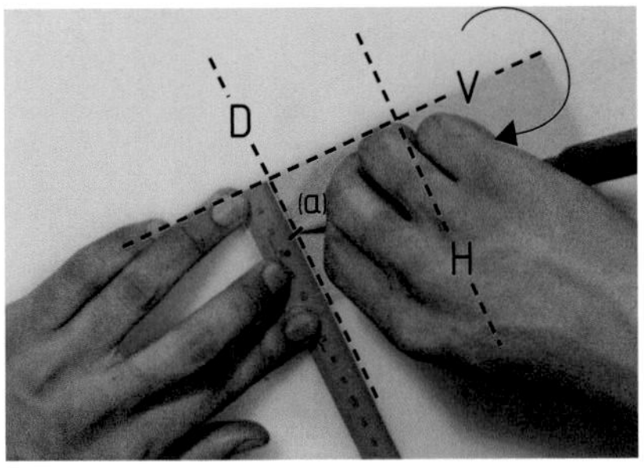

8. To trace half the width of the enchape, fold the piece of card along the V axis and make a pencil mark (a) 2.5 cm underneath this on line D (for a enchape with a 5 cm width). Make sure this point is symmetrical to the H axis.

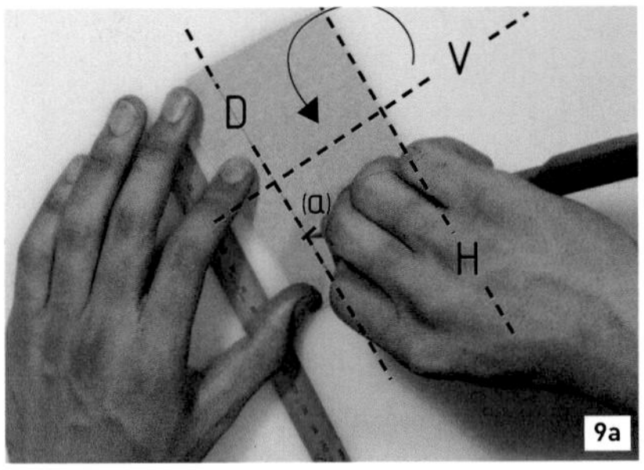

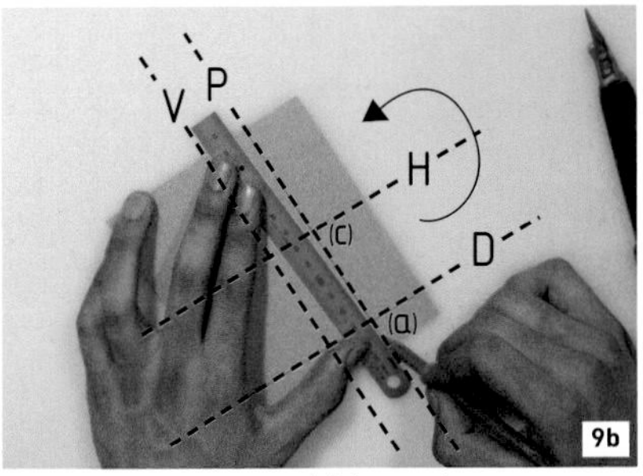

9. Unfold the card and refold along the H axis. Use a cutter to mark point(a) (fig. 9a). Unfold, then use a pencil to join up the marks: this will give you line P which corresponds to half the width of the enchape (fig. 9b). Mark point (c) at the intersection of line P and the H axis.

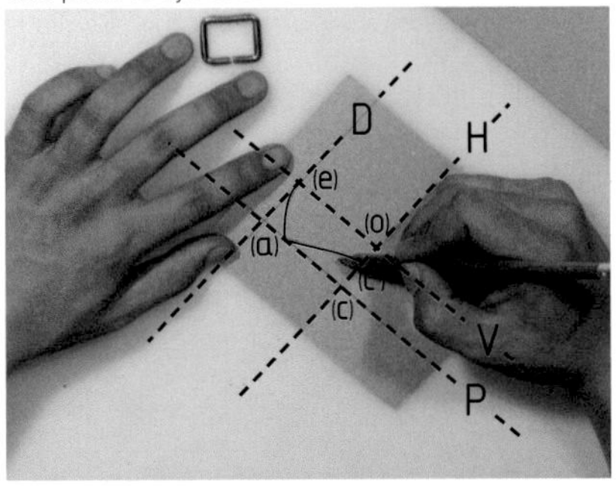

10. Axis H corresponds to the fold of the enchape which will contain the buckle (see the result in fig. 13). Position point (c') so that line (oc') is equal to half the width of the buckle, i.e. 1 cm for a buckle which is 2 cm wide. In the rectangle (ocae), starting at point (e) and going to point (c'), draw a quarter of the enchape's shape. This is then symmetrically reproduced to obtain the whole shape of the enchape.

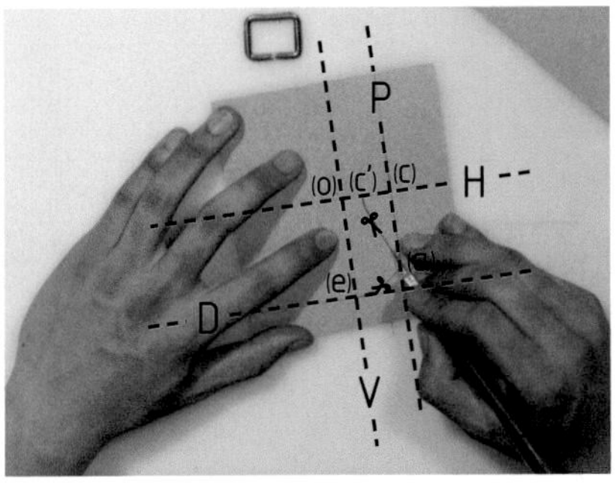

11. Cut out a quarter of the enchape.

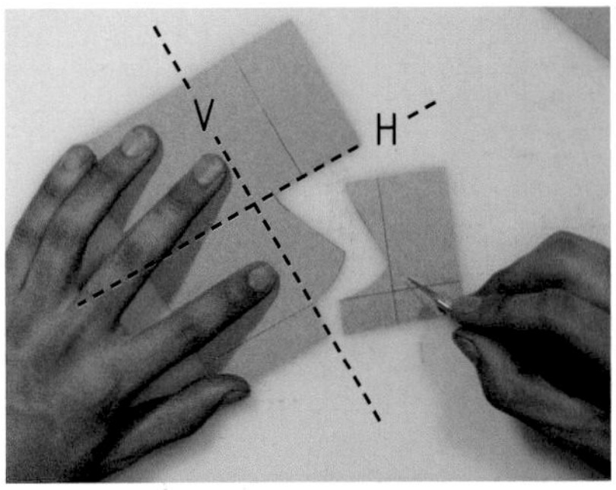

12. Remove the excess card using the cutter and duplicate this quarter by folding along the H and V axes.

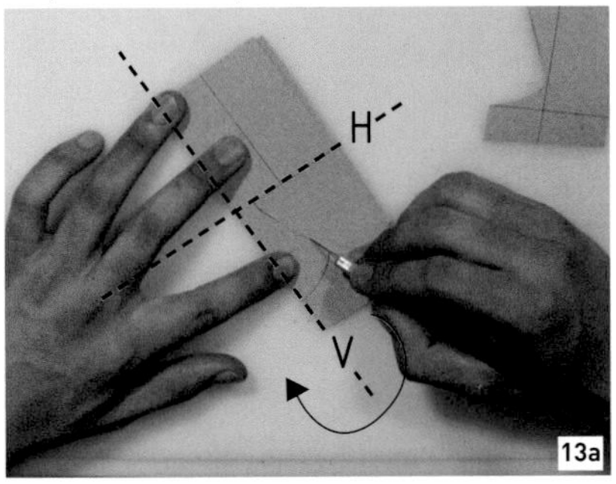

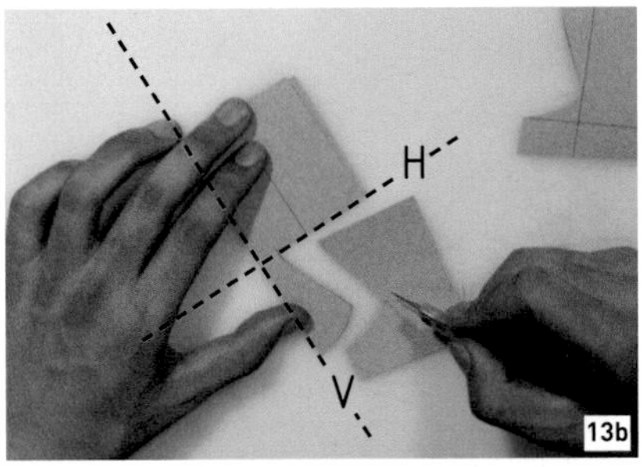

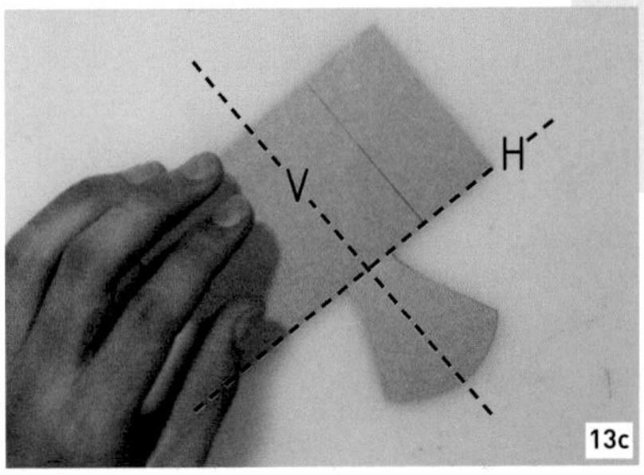

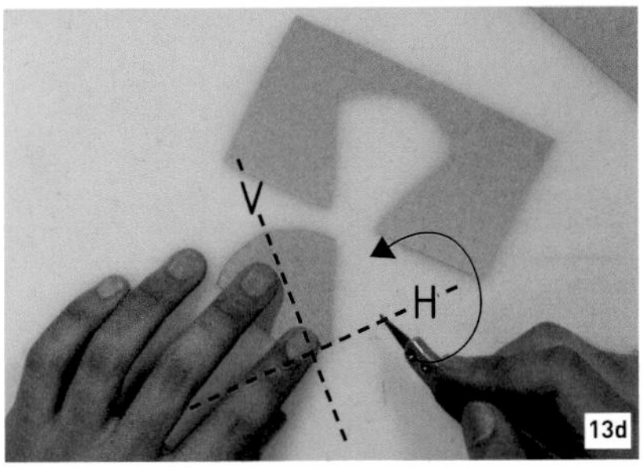

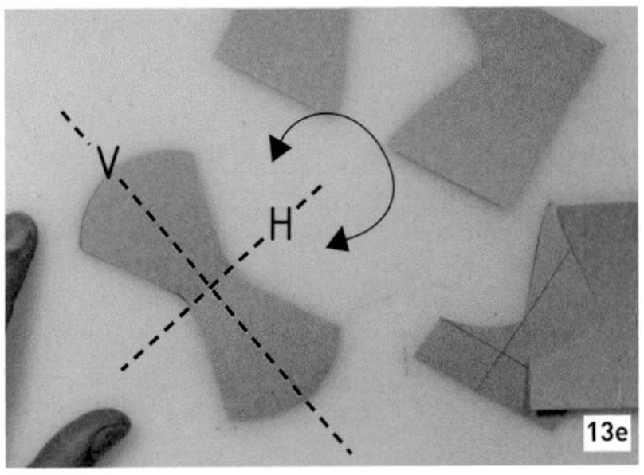

13. Fold along the V axis (fig.13a) then cut the second quarter symmetrically (fig. 13b). This will give you half the enchape (fig.13c). Fold along axis H and cut again (fig.13d). Unfold (fig.13e) the card to reveal the finished pattern for the enchape.

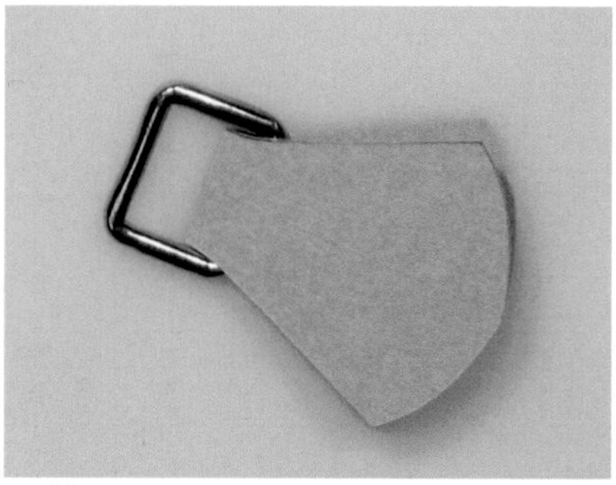

14. Check that the handle buckle fits comfortably into the enchape.

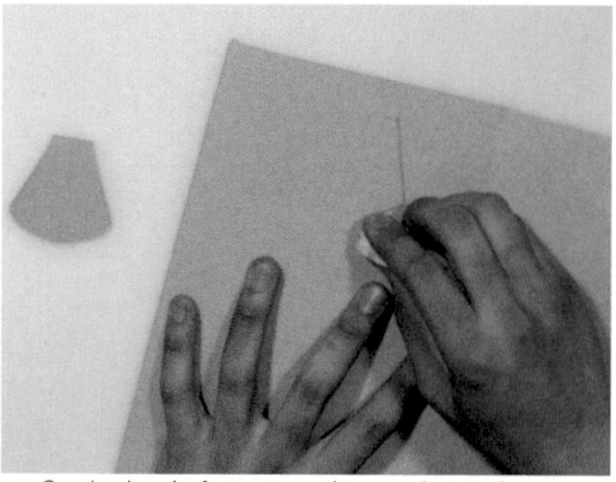

15. On the bag's front template, rub out the previously drawn enchape. Now the correct enchape can be traced onto the front template. To do this, place the enchape pattern onto the folded side of the template. The outline needs to be placed symmetrically so that the other half can be perfectly traced onto the other side. The slightest discrepancy is likely to set the whole bag off-balance both practically, as well as aesthetically.

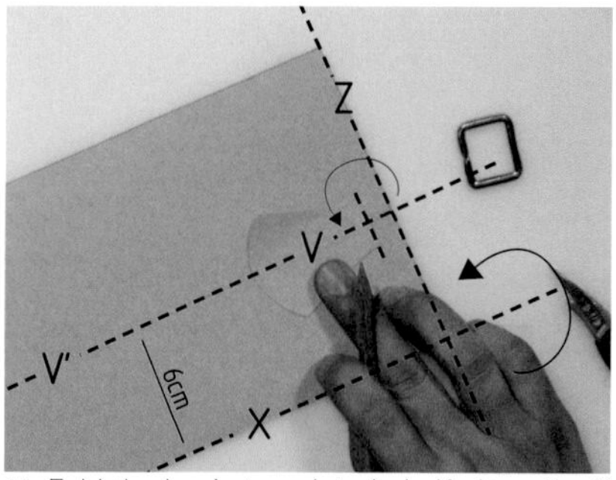

16. Fold the bag's template in half along the X axis. Then, onto the folded template trace a straight line V', parallel to the X axis (centre-front of the template) at a distance of 6 cm from it. Refold the enchape pattern along the H axis. Place the enchape pattern on the front template carefully lining up the V axis on the pattern and the straight line V' on the front template.

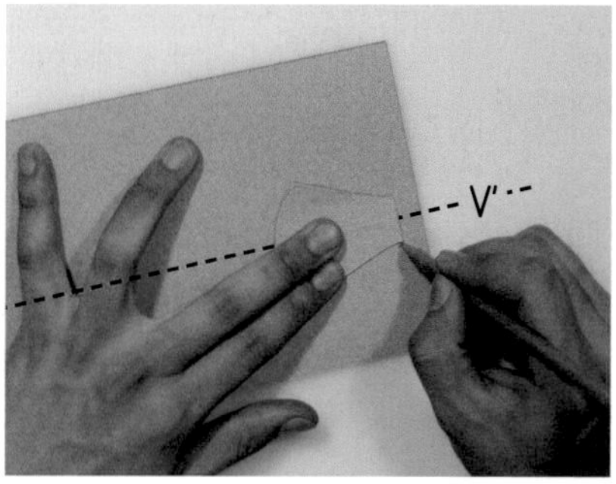

17. Use a pencil to draw the outline of the enchape onto the front template.

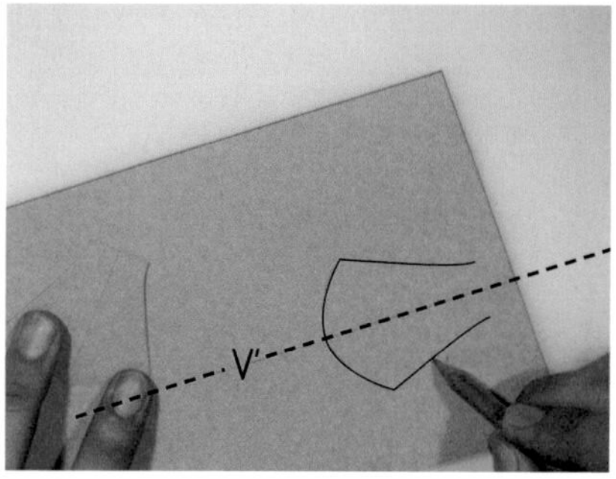

18. Redraw the pencil lines a bit harder, if necessary.

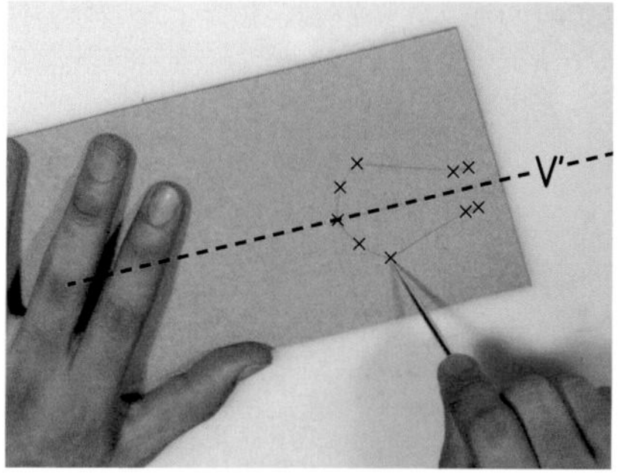

19. Using an awl, prick out the outline of half of the template, making sure to press quite hard to ensure going through two thicknesses of card. The crosses in the photo illustrate important points to mark with the awl.

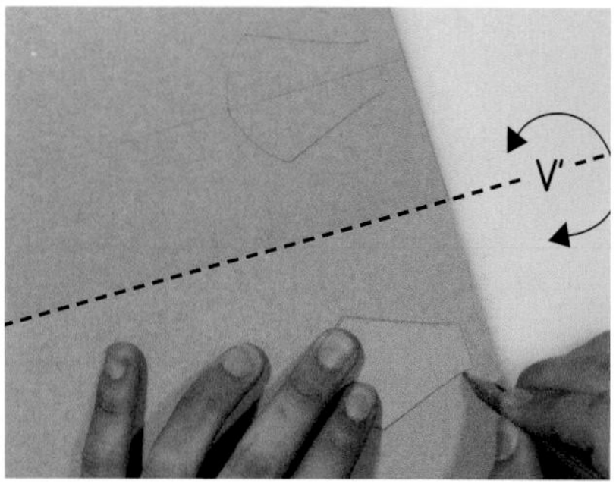

20. Unfold the front template. On the second half of the template, place the enchape template on the awl marks and trace the outline using a pencil.

21. Redraw the pencil lines a bit harder if necessary.

Template for the sides (or gussets)

The front template is also used to construct the gussets.

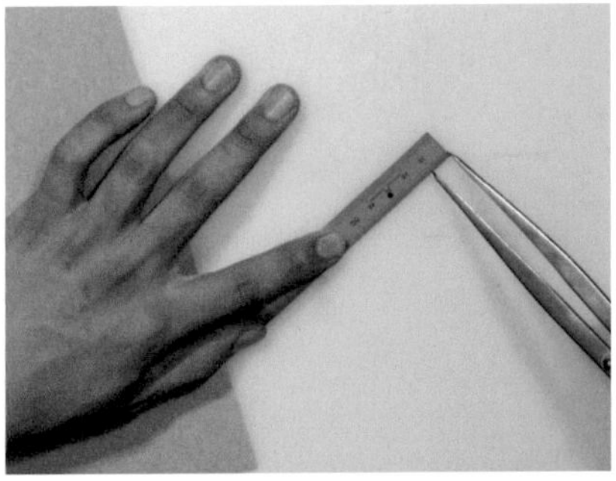

1. Set the adjustable compasses, or dividers, to measure 1cm.

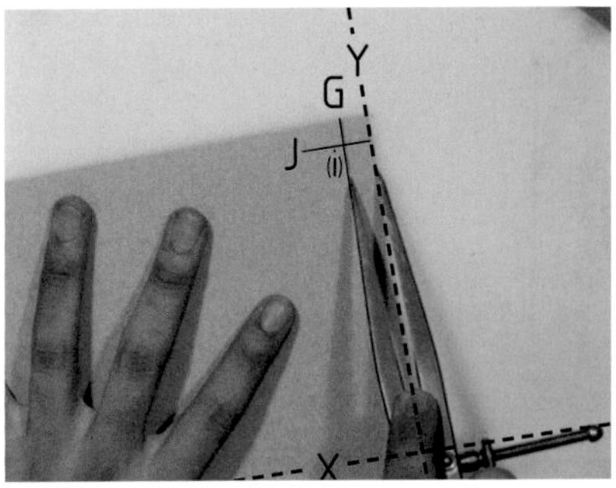

2. Using the compasses, and being guided by the edge of the template, trace a line G parallel to line Y (bottom of the template), and line J, parallel to the edge of the front template. Mark a point (i) where lines G and J intersect; this point allows you to make the base of the gusset.

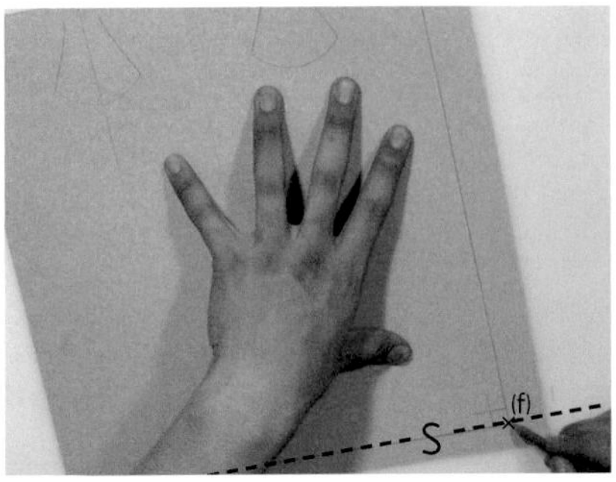

3. The gusset width is 12 cm and the bag height is 31 cm. With the front of the bag being trapezoidal, the length of the side is slightly bigger than the height of the front. It is important to get the exact height of the side (which will obviously be bigger than 31 cm). Cut a piece of card bigger than the gusset i.e.15 x 35 cm. Position the front template on this piece of card allowing about 1.5 cm on the side. From line Y on the front template, trace a pencil line S, onto this piece of card. Where the side line and line Y intersect, mark with a pencil point (f).

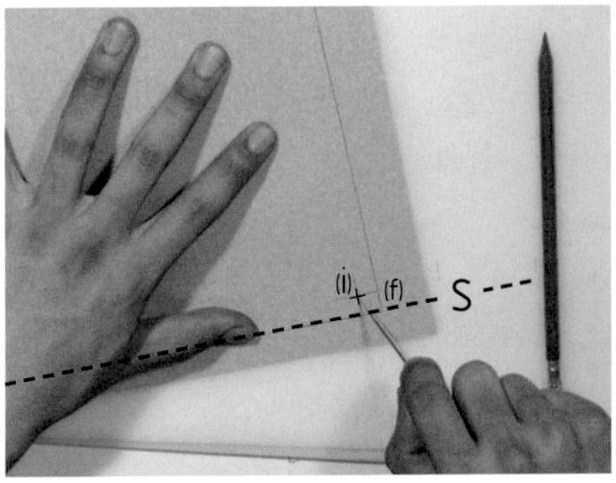

4. Use an awl to prick point (i) pushing quite hard in order to go through two thicknesses.

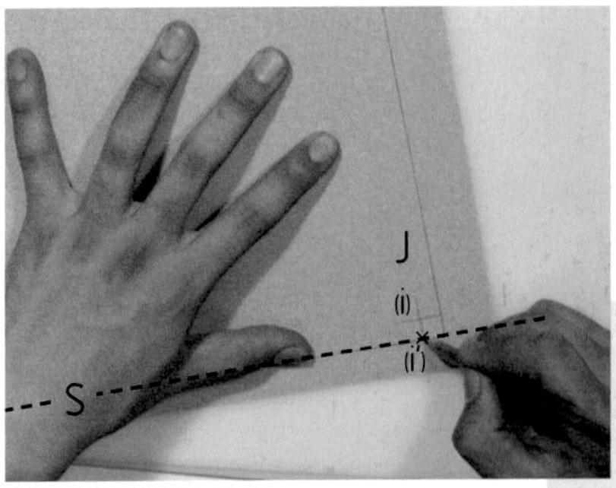

5. Mark point (I') at the intersection of line J, on the front template, and line S on the gusset.

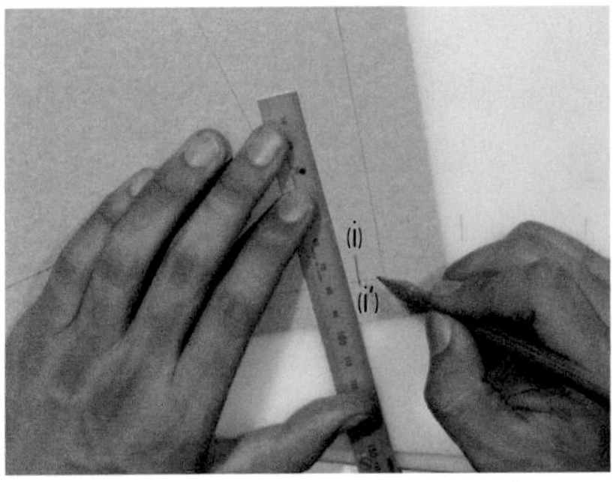

6. Remove the front template then, on the gusset, join up points (i) and (I') with a pencil line.

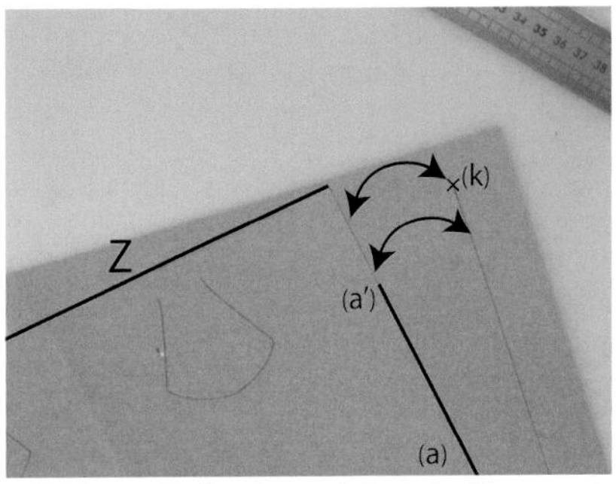

7. Replace the front template onto the gusset. At the intersection of the side line (a' a) and line Z (top line of the front template), mark point (k) on the gusset. Join up points (k) and (f) to trace the height of the gusset.

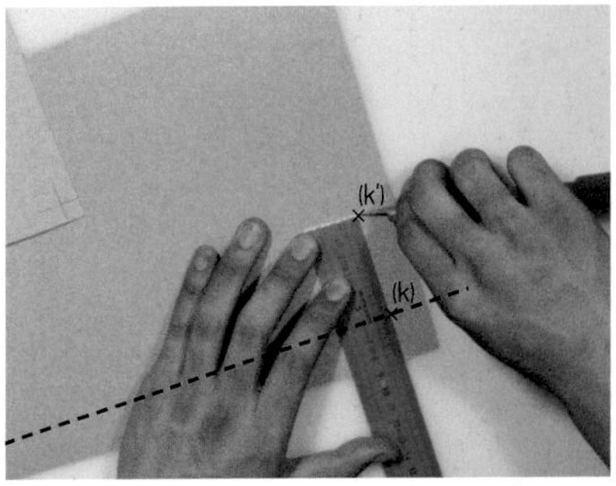

8. The gusset measures 12 cm wide. To construct this width, the vertical axis V of the gusset must be traced on. This V axis is parallel to the straight line (fk). With a cutter, mark point (k') 6 cm from point (k) which is perpendicular to the straight line (fk).

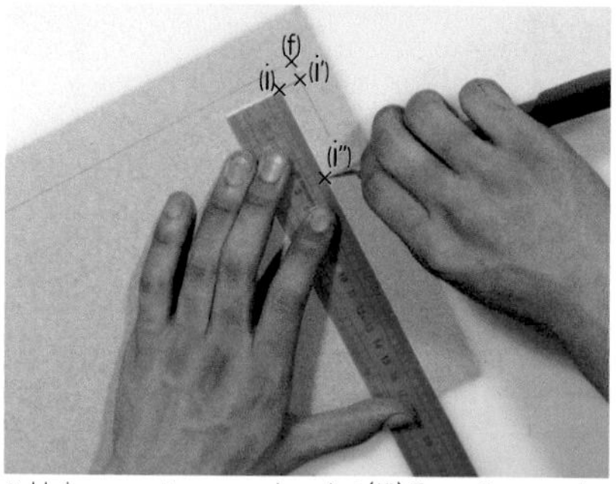

9. Using a cutter, mark point (I'') 5 cm from point (i) which is perpendicular to the straight line (fk). In simple terms, 1 cm has been deducted from the compass line.

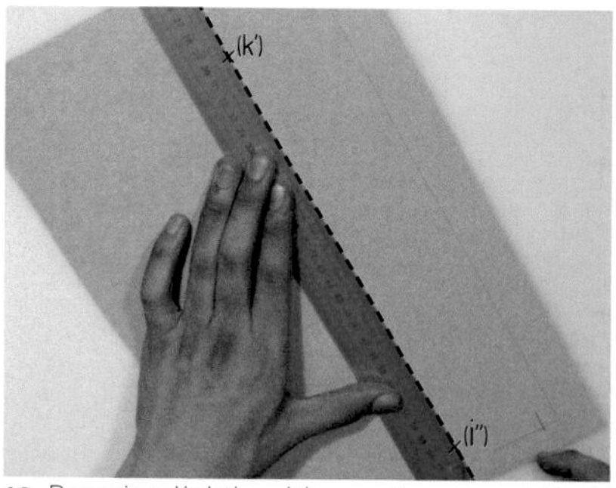

10. Pressing lightly with a cutter, score the V axis of the gusset by joining up points (I'') and (k').

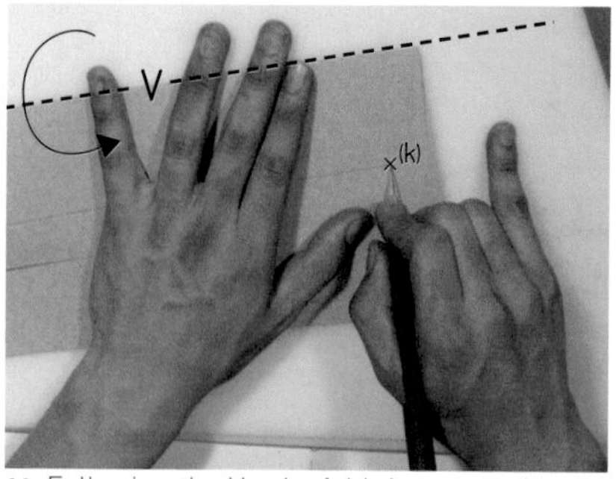

11. Following the V axis, fold the gusset in two. With the cutter, transfer symmetrically point (k) of the gusset onto the other half of the card.

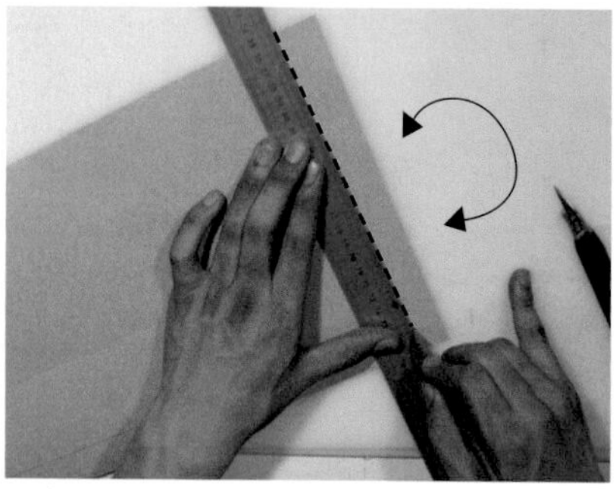

12. Unfold, then join up the two points using a pencil line. This line will create the top of the gusset.

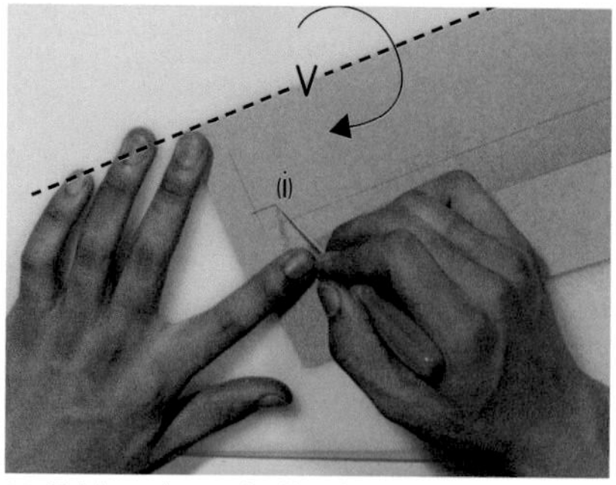

13. Fold again on the V axis then using an awl prick through point (i) to the other half of the card.

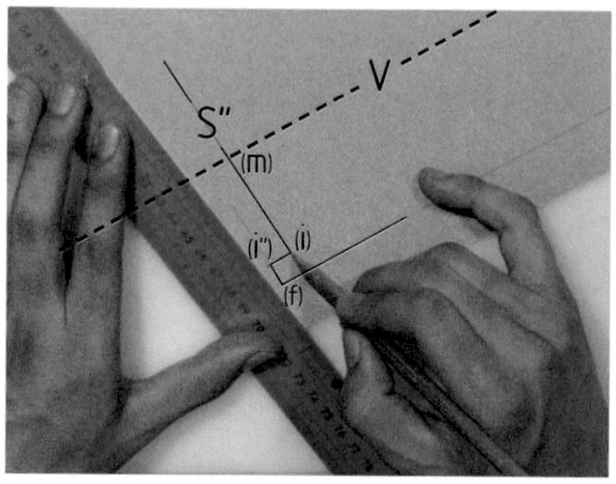

14. Unfold and join up point (i) and the other point created by the awl on the other side. Call this line S. At the intersection of the V axis and line S, mark a point (m). The line which passes through points (m), (i), (I'') and (f) shows the shape of the bottom half of the gusset. At the side and the bottom of the gusset there will be an area of 1 cm by 1 cm: this will be necessary for the final assembling.

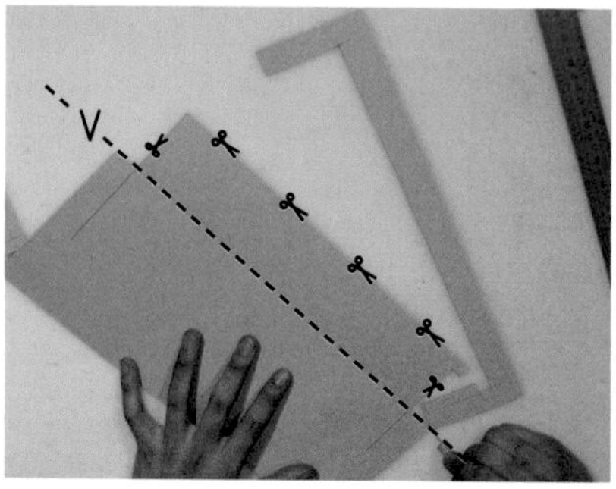

15. Cut away the half drawn area stopping at the V axis.

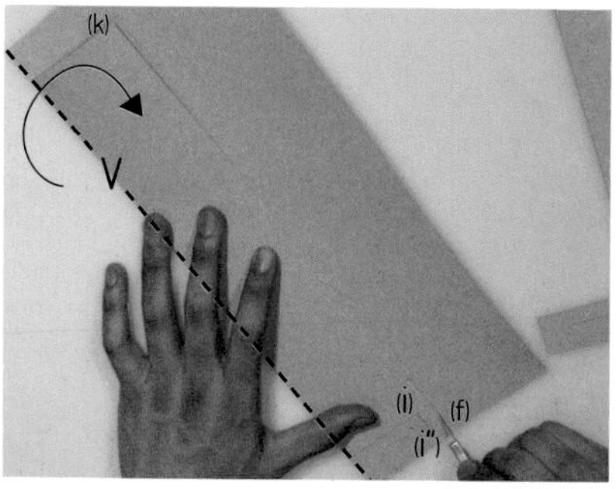

16. Fold in two along the V axis.

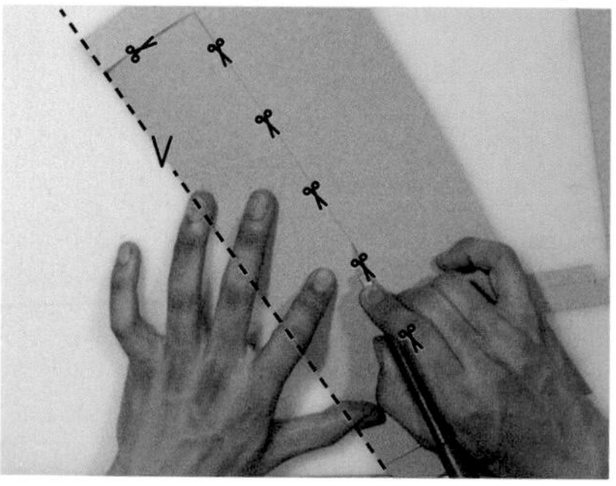

17. Cut the side of the gusset symmetrically.

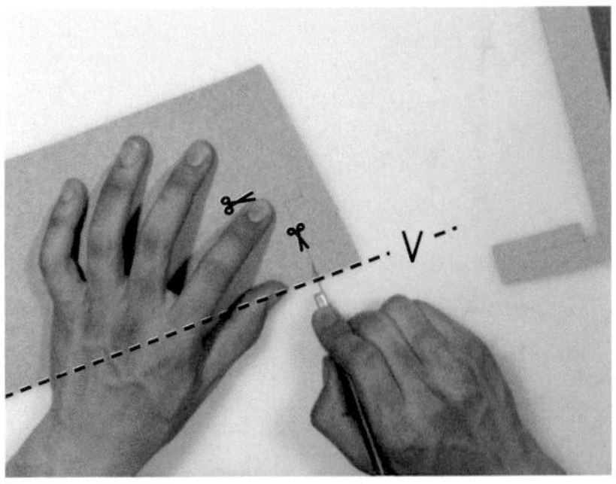

18. Cut the top symmetrically.

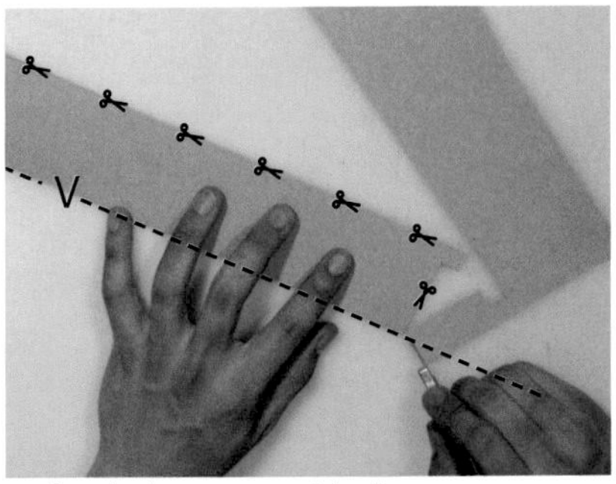

19. Cut the base symmetrically.

20. Unfold to achieve the gusset.

Base pattern

To make the base pattern, cut a piece of card larger than the dimensions of the base, i.e. 35 x 20 cm if the base is 28 x 12 cm. Place the card vertically, then using a steel ruler and cutter, lightly score the horizontal axis H in the middle of the card.

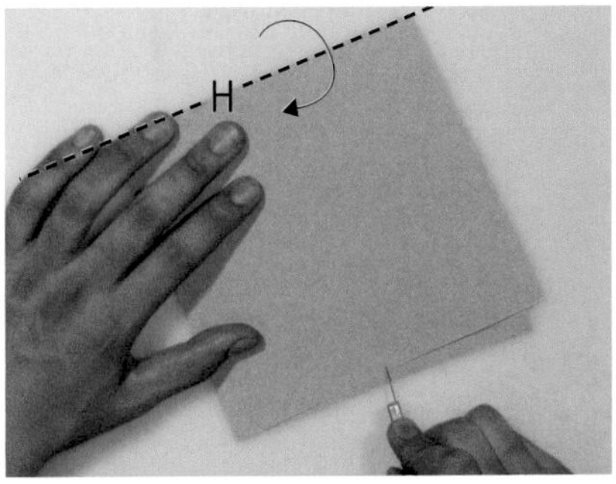

1. Fold in two along the H axis and using the cutter, mark off the edge of the card as is shown in the photo. Apply enough pressure to mark the two thicknesses of card.

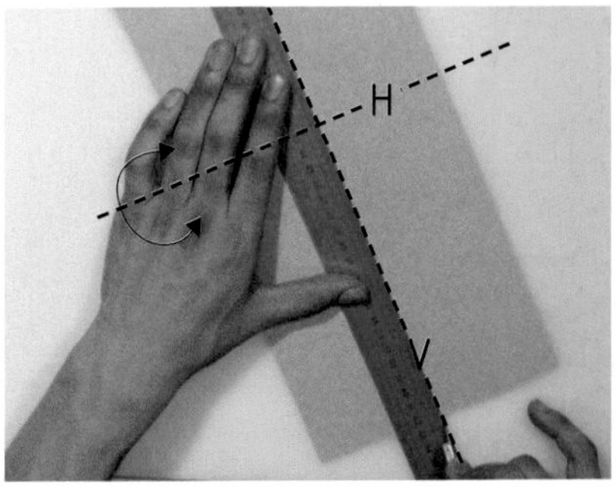

2. Unfold and join up the two cutter marks . Press lightly to score a vertical Axis V. The H and V axes are perpendicular and intersect each other in the middle.

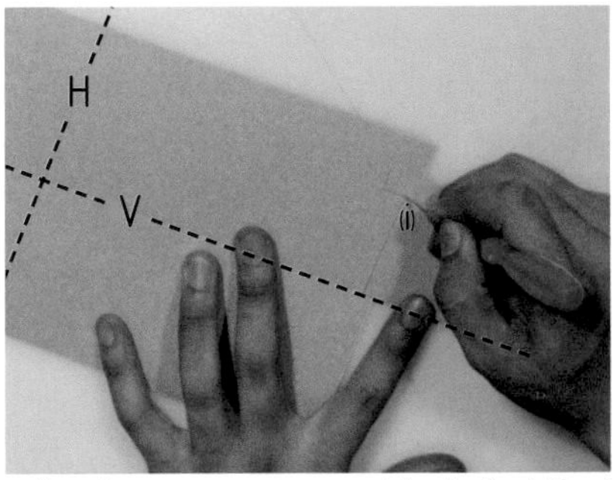

3. Use the gusset to trace out the half-width of the base. This corresponds to the distance between points (m) and (i) on the gusset, added to the distance between points (i) and (i"). Place the gusset onto the base, along the edge of the card, lining up the V axis on the gusset with the V axis of the base. From the V axis on the base, use an awl to transfer point (i) on the gusset onto the base.

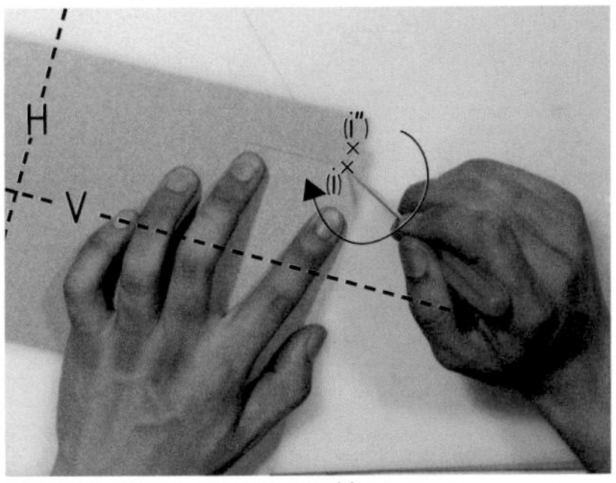

4. Leave the awl on point (i). Use this as a rotation point then pivot the gusset 90 degrees clockwise around this axis.

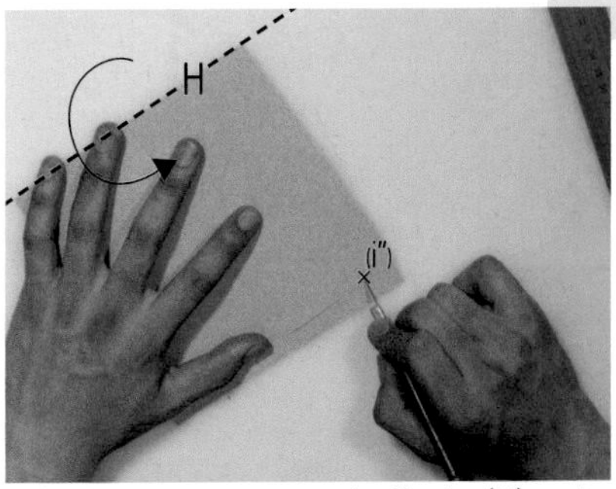

5. On the base pattern, mark off point (I") on the gusset. Fold the base pattern in two along the H axis and mark off point (I") with a cutter so that it goes through the two card thicknesses.

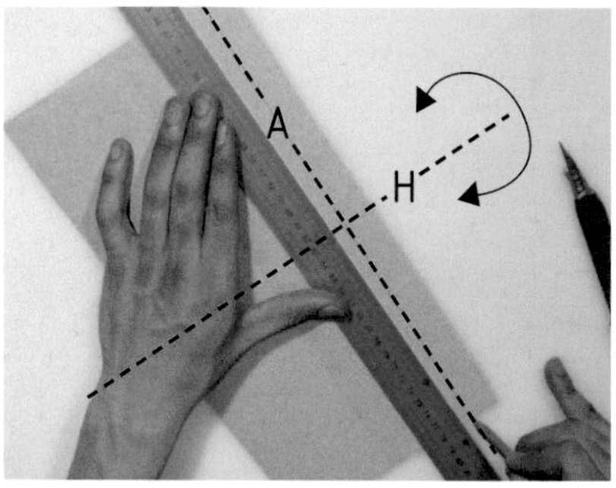

6. Unfold then join these two points with a pencil. You will now have line A which corresponds to half the width of the base.

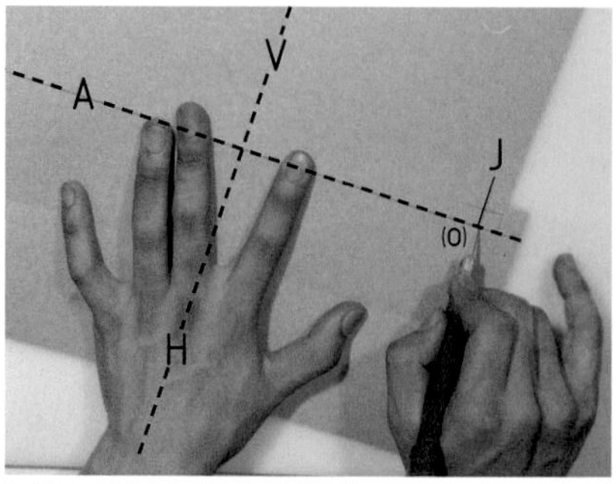

7. Place the bottom of the front template along line A, lining up the V axis of the front and the H axis of the base. Mark off with a cutter point (o), which corresponds to the intersection of line J, on the front, and line A, on the base.

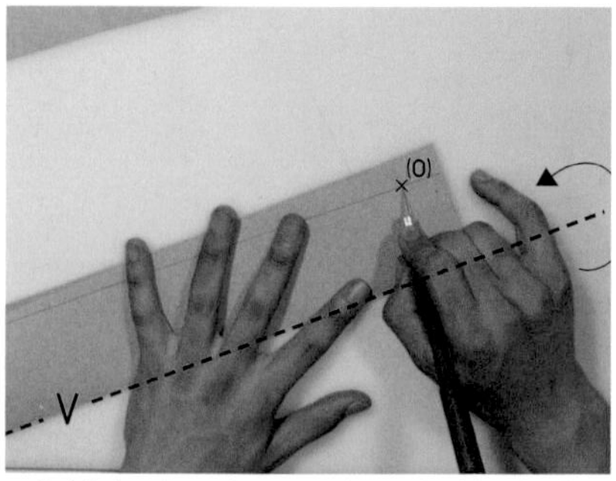

8. Fold the base in two along the V axis then mark off with a cutter point (o) through both the thicknesses of card.

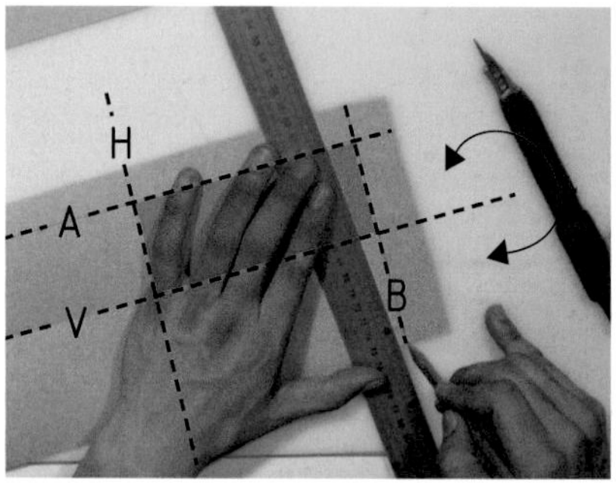

9. Unfold and join up these two marks. This will give you line B which corresponds to half the length of the base. The area between lines A and B and the axes H and V (marked in orange on the photo) corresponds to a quarter of the base of the bag.

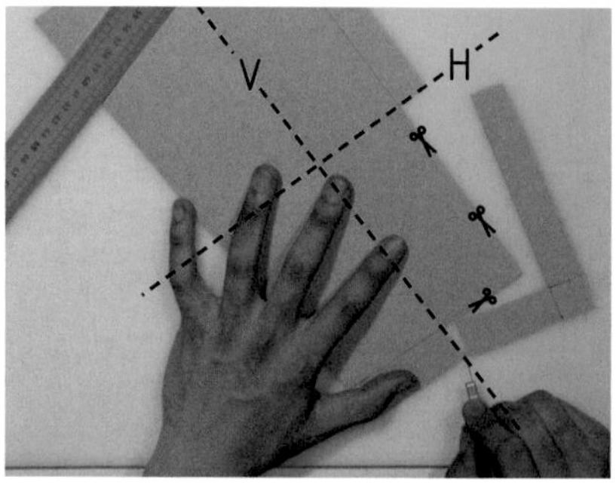

10. Cut out this quarter of the pattern with a cutter making sure to stop at the H and V axes.

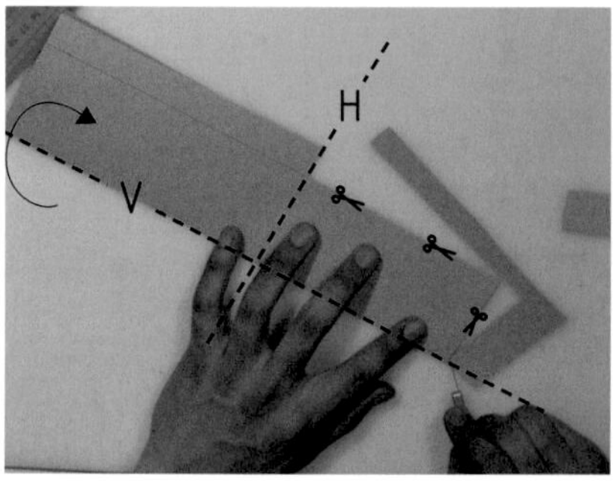

11. Fold the base along the V axis, cutting it symmetrically then unfold it to obtain half of the base.

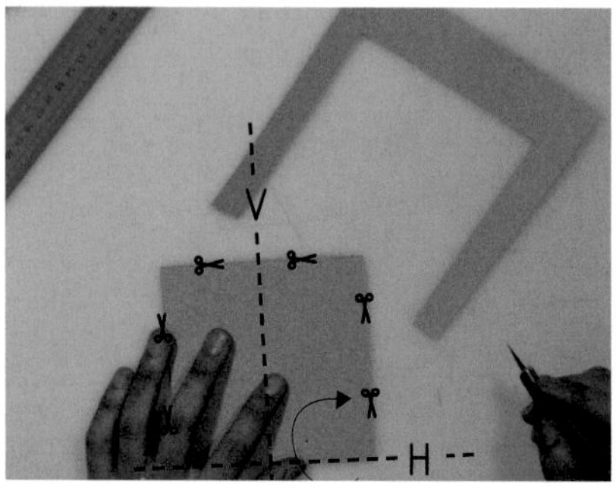

12. Fold along the H axis and cut the other half symmetrically.

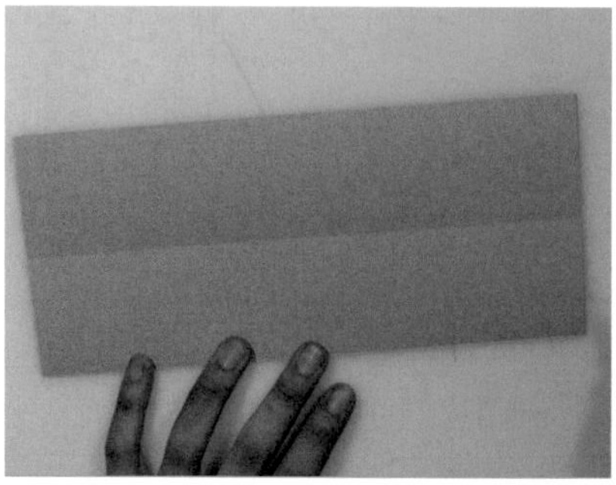

13. Unfold this to achieve the base pattern.

Assembling

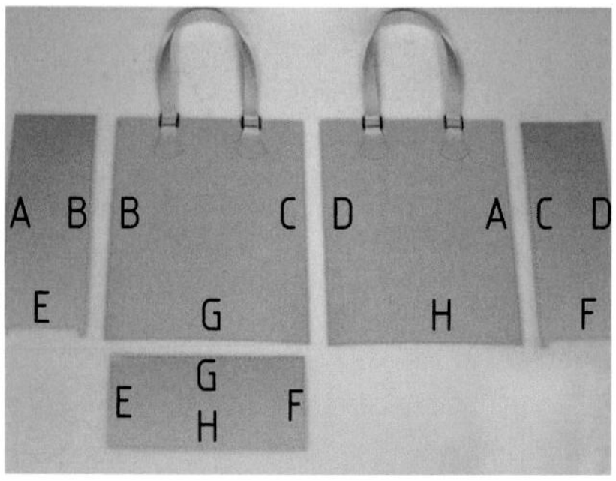

1. Using the resulting patterns, cut out a front, a back, two gussets, four enchapes, a base as well as two handles. Draw the top stitches 0.3 cm from each edge, then use a cutter to mark a fold inside these stitches. This photo shows the different sections of the bag and its method of assembling, i.e. part A joins with part A, B with B, etc.

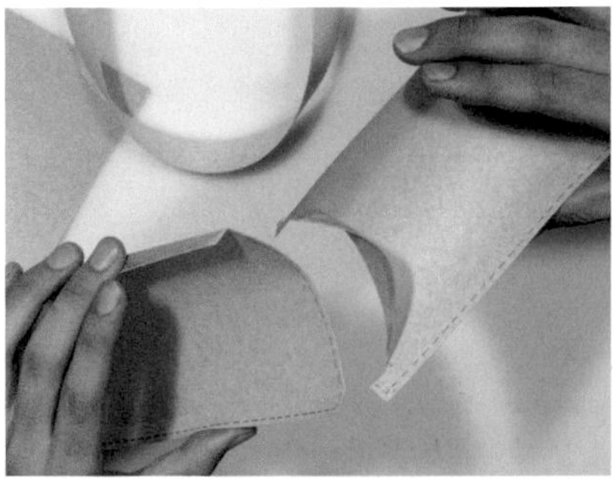

2. Stick the first gusset to the base, taking care not to fix the seam allowance of the gusset as this will be joined to the front and back pieces.

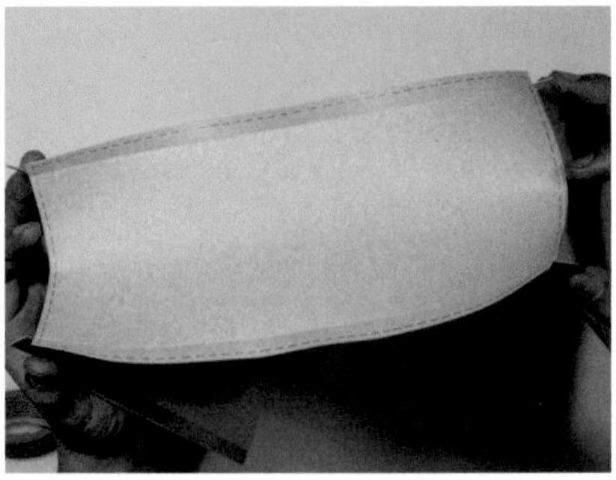

3. Stick the second gusset to the base in the same way as the first.

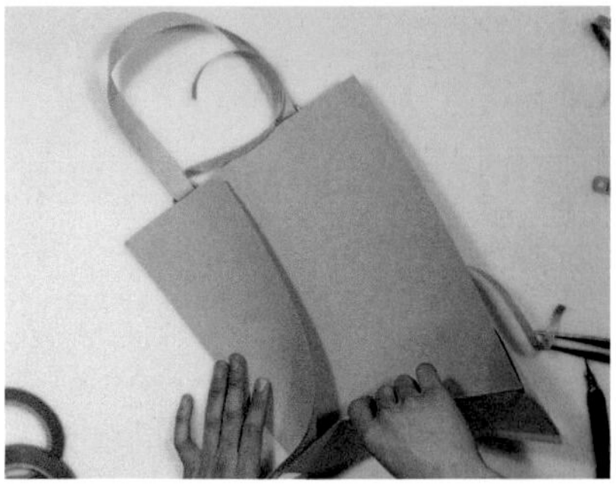

4. Stick the first gusset to the front.

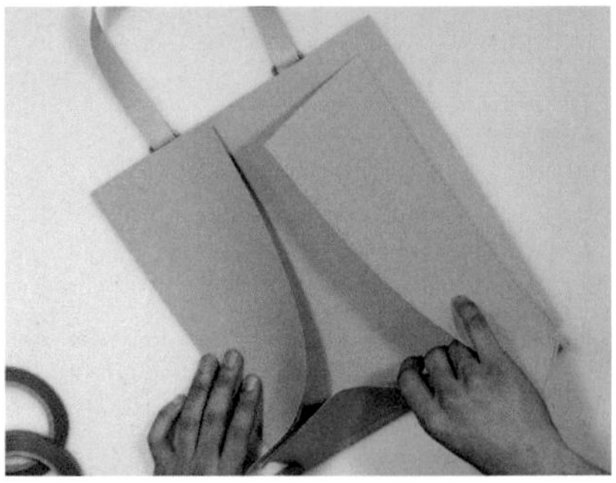

5. Stick the base to the front.

6. This photo shows the gusset's seam allowance stuck against the front with the bottom of the gusset stuck against the base.

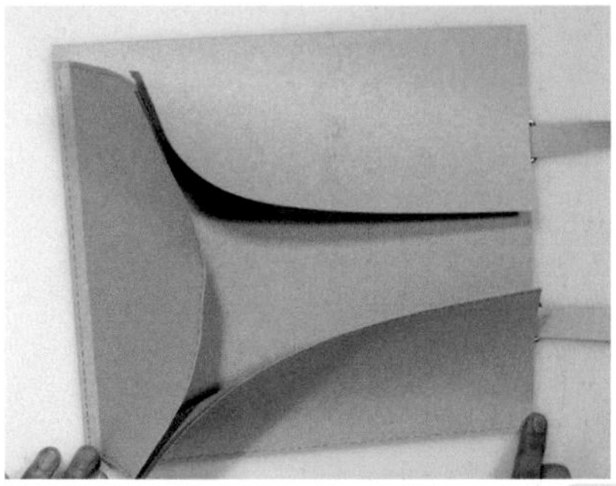

7. Stick the second gusset onto the front. Once the gussets and the base have been stuck to the front, stick them all onto the back.

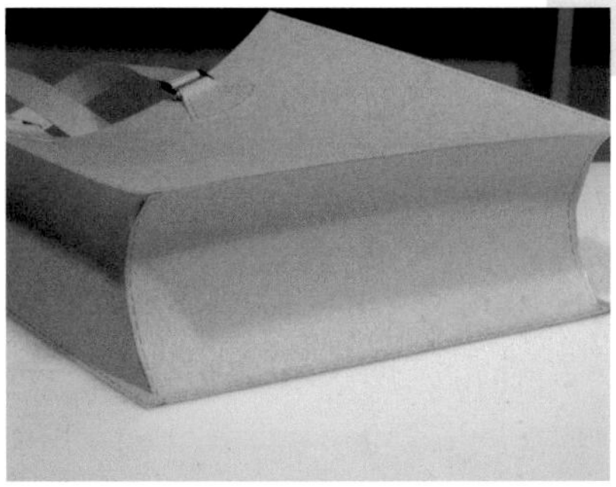

8. Some detailed photos showing how the pieces are joined to each other. The prototype is now finished.

Making card prototypes

2 - Messenger/shoulder bag

This bag, with a shoulder strap and flap, is normally designed for men. Working from the same template, we will make the patterns for the front and the back, and that of the flap. The front and the back are assembled underneath the bag and joined together by an inside seam. The flap is pinned and sewn onto a piece of the back. This type of bag does not have a separate piece for the base. All the pieces are assembled edge to edge, as with the previous tote bag, with the exception of the front and the back, which are joined together by an inside seam.

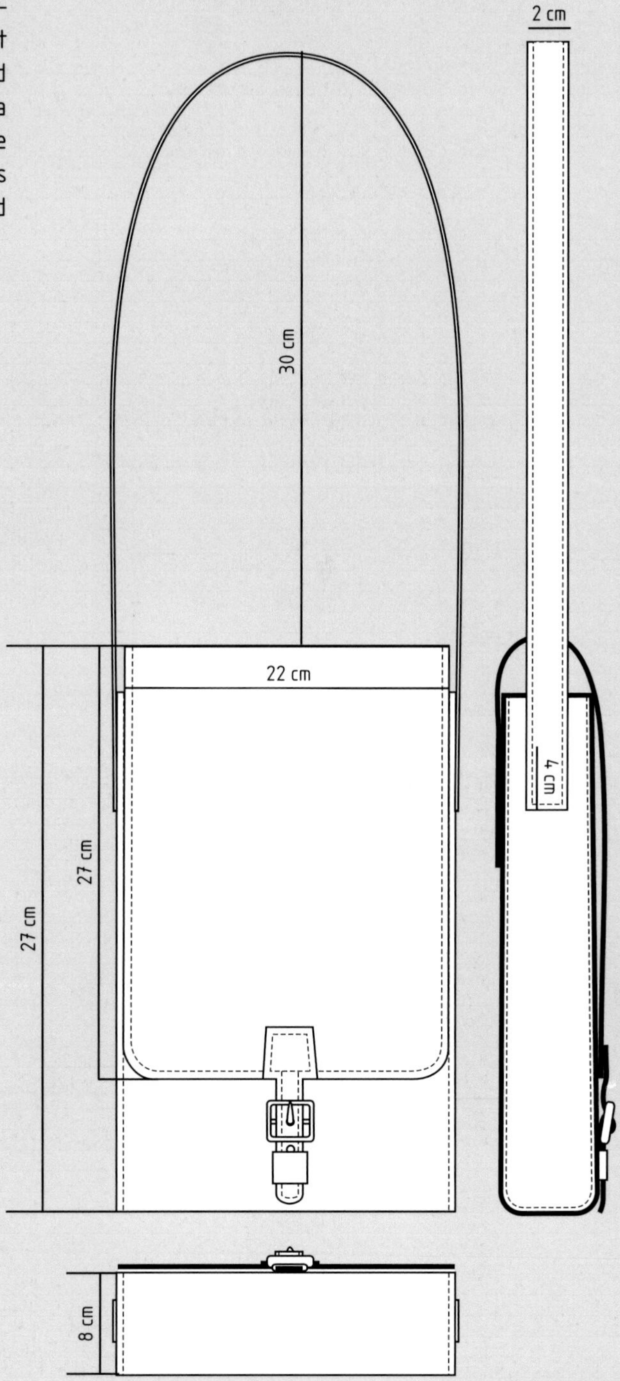

Technical drawings of the bag

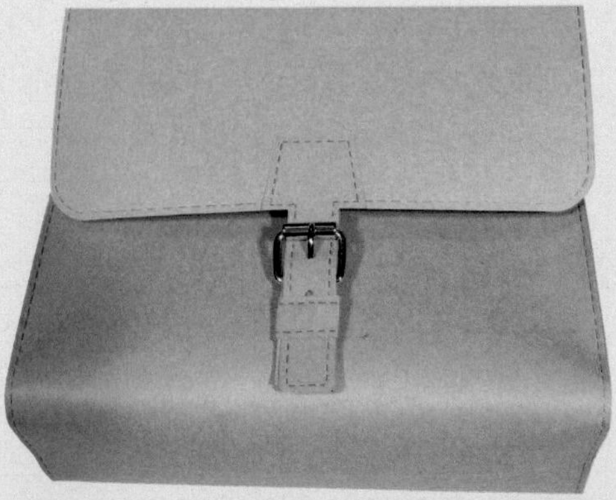

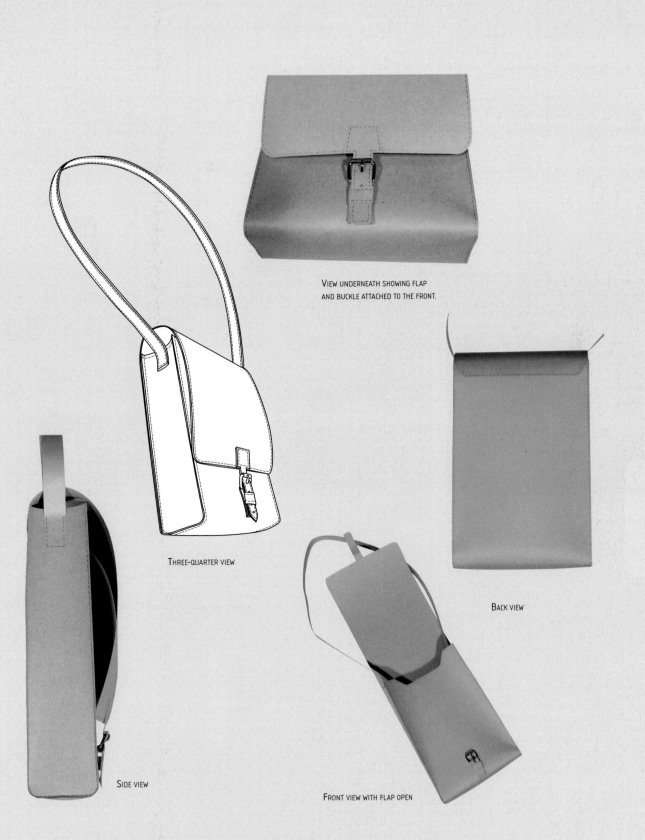

View underneath showing flap and buckle attached to the front.

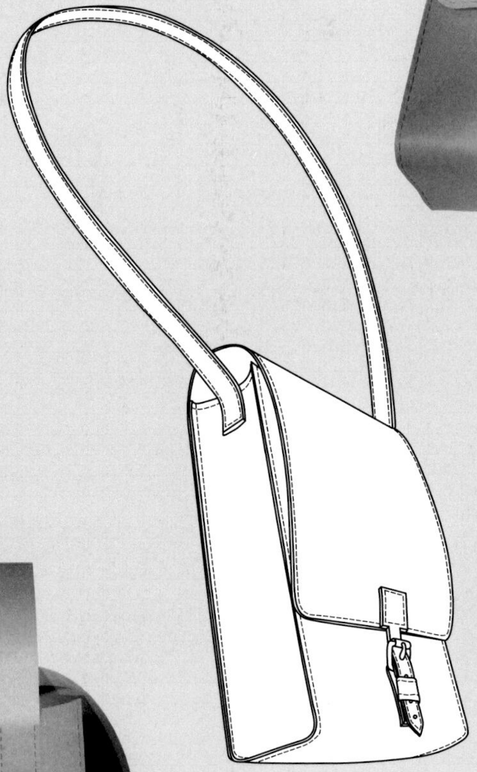

Three-quarter view

Back view

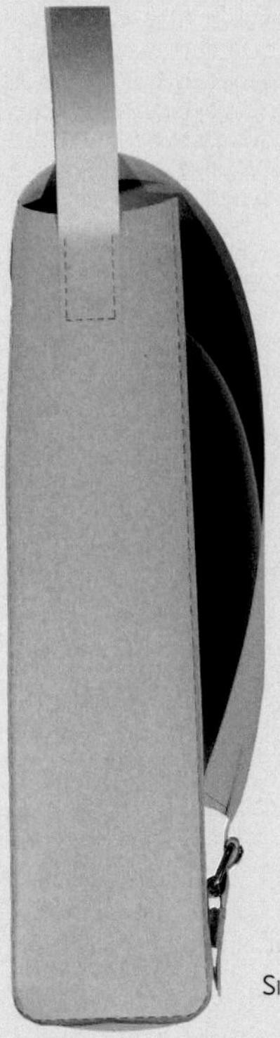

Side view

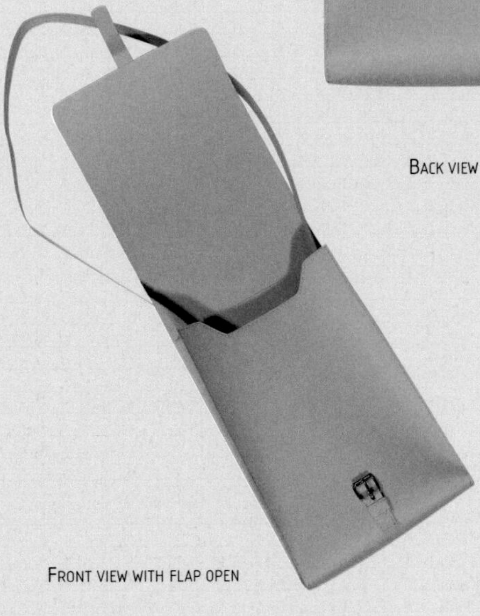

Front view with flap open

Side or gusset pattern

To make this bag, we have to start with the side, or gusset, which will serve as the basis for construction.

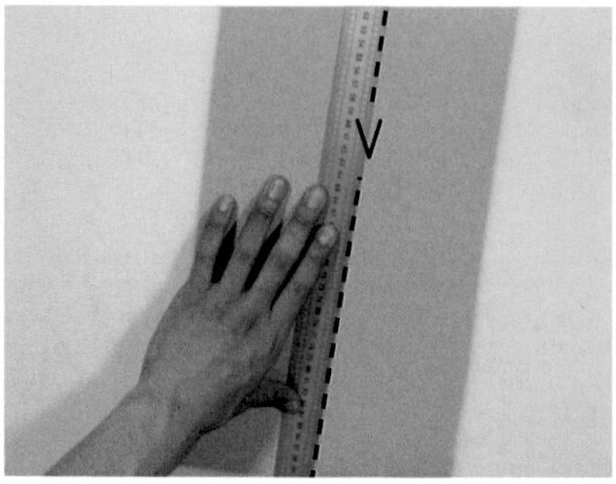

1. Cut out a piece of card slightly larger than the gusset, i.e. 40 x 15 cm for a gusset measuring 31 x 8 cm. Lightly score the vertical axis V with a steel ruler and cutter so that the card can be easily and cleanly folded in two.

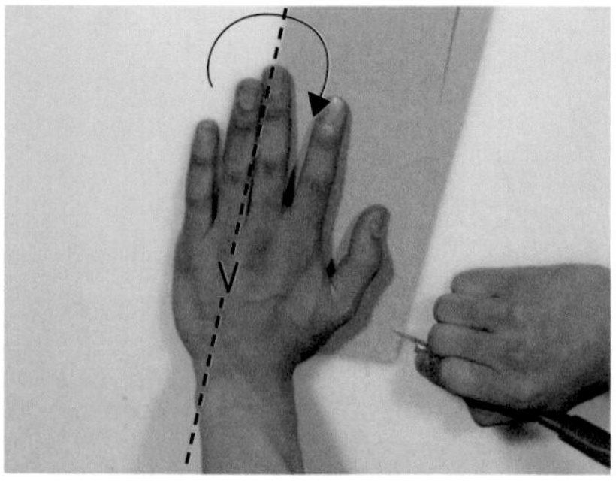

2. Fold the piece in two along the V axis and trace the line of the bottom of the gusset (called Y). Mark off the side of the piece 3 cm from the bottom, pressing quite hard so that the two thicknesses of card are marked.

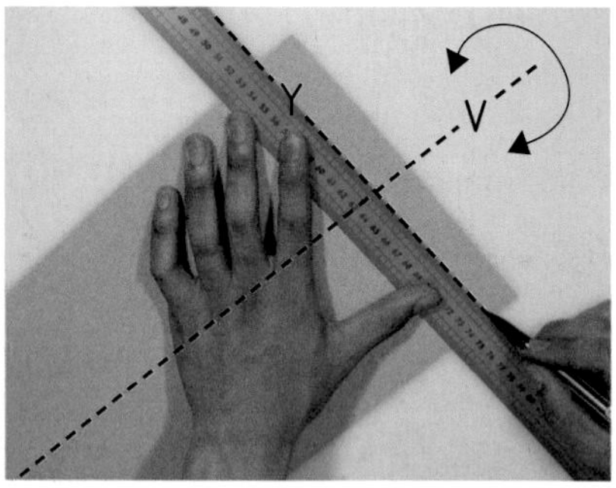

3. Unfold. Here we have two symmetrical points. Join up these two points using a pencil and trace line Y.

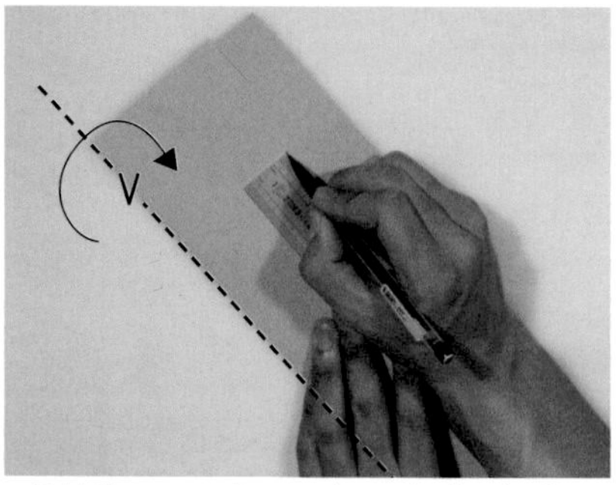

4. Fold the gusset in two along the V axis. From line Y, measure off the height, i.e. 31 cm.

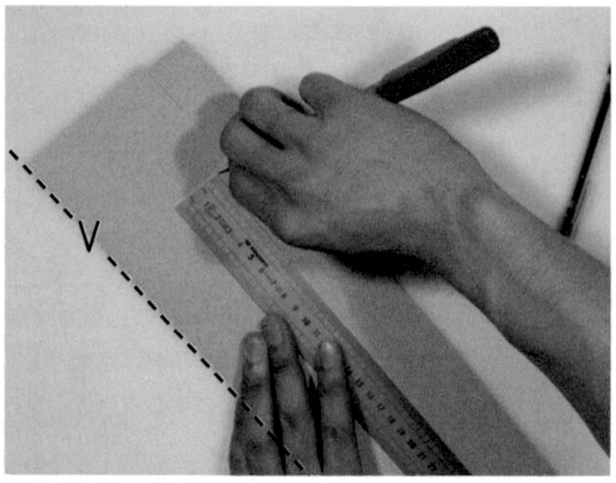

5. Mark off this point using a cutter, pressing hard enough to go through two thicknesses.

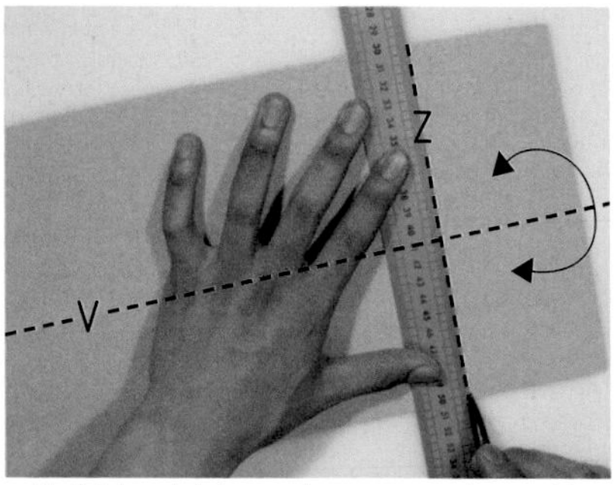

6. Unfold and join up these two points with a pencil. This will make the top line of the gusset called Z.

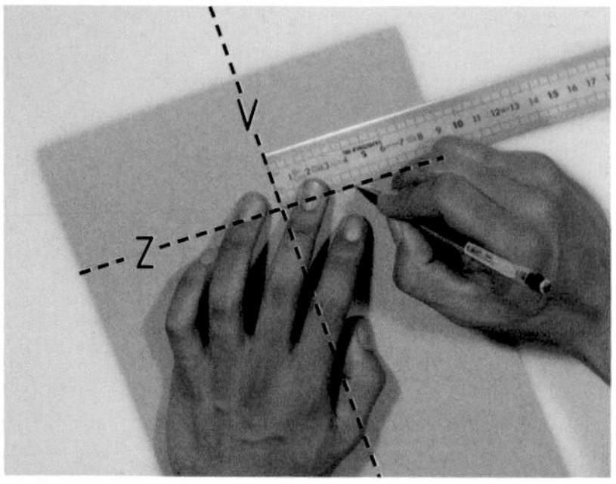

7. On the right of the V axis, mark with a pencil the half-width of the gusset (4 cm) along lines Y and Z.

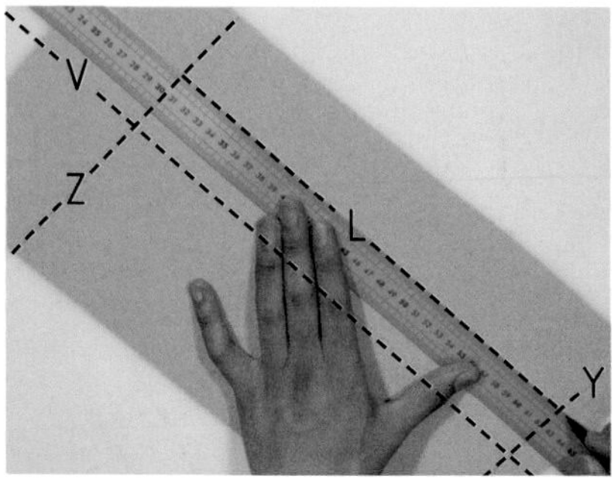

8. Join up these two points with a pencil line which we call L. This creates the half-width of the gusset.

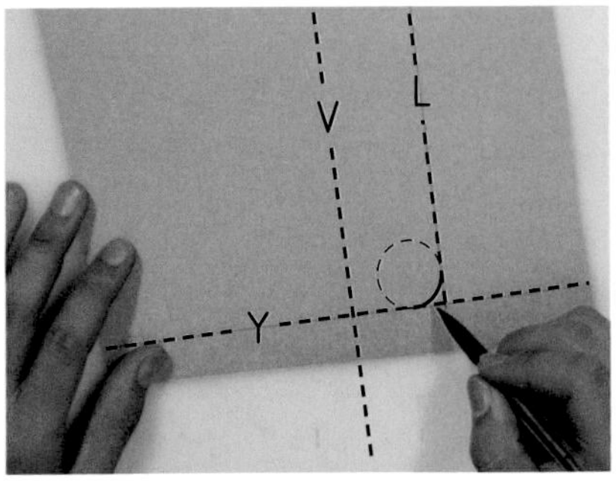

9. Draw the curve of the base of the gusset on the right-hand side of the V axis. This curve corresponds to a quarter circle with a diameter of 4 cm at tangents to lines Y and L. We have just drawn half of the gusset.

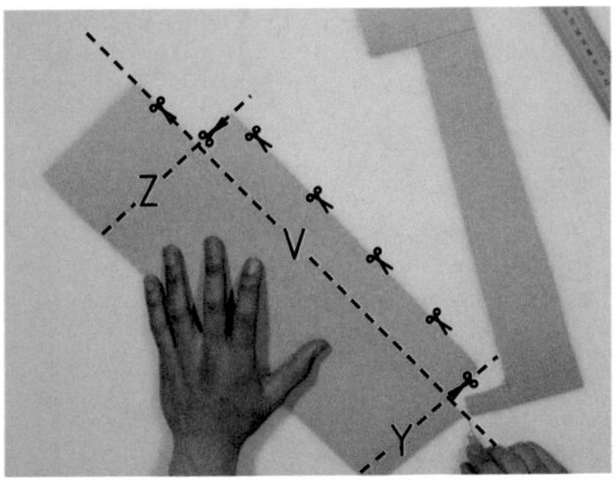

10. Cut the half which has just been drawn stopping short of the V axis.

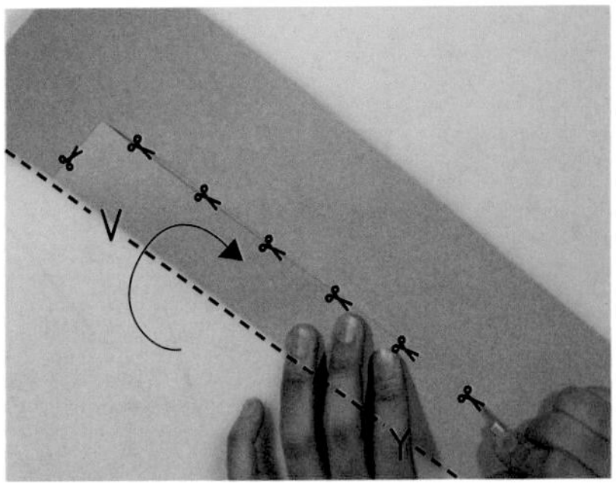

11. Fold the gusset in two along the V axis and cut symmetrically the second half of the piece using the outline of the first half as a guide. The gusset pattern is finished.

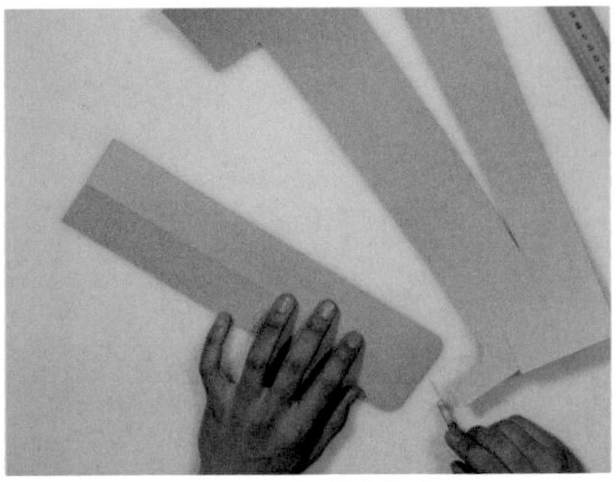

12. The gusset pattern is finished.

Construction template

This template will help us create the patterns of three different pieces: the front, the back and the flap.

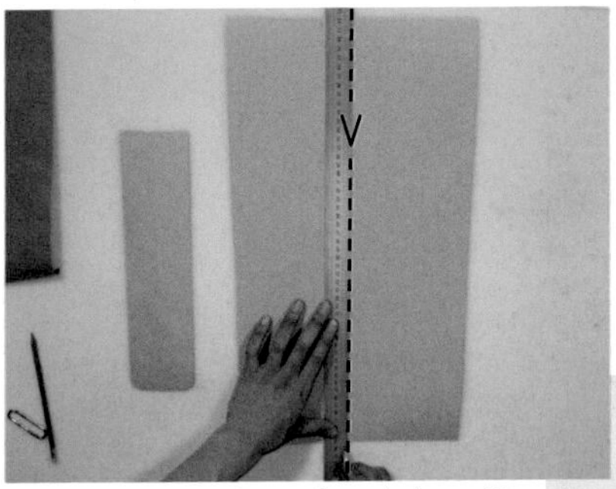

1. We have cut a piece of card about 40 x 30 cm for a bag which measures 34 x 22 cm. In the middle of the vertically positioned piece of card, lightly score the axis V using a cutter.

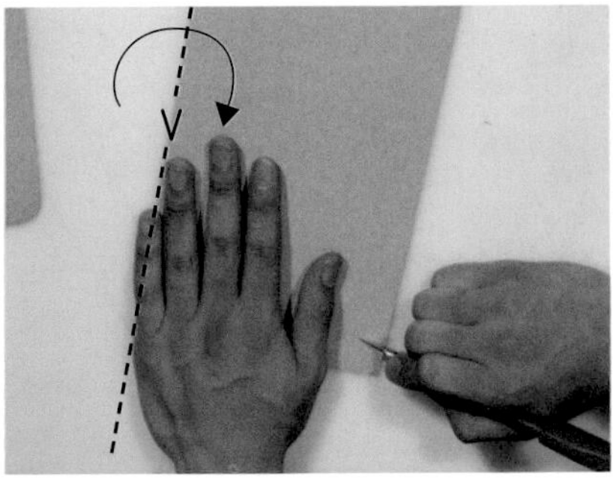

2. Fold it in two along the V axis and use a cutter to mark off about 3 cm from the bottom on the right-hand side of the card. Press quite hard to mark through two thicknesses.

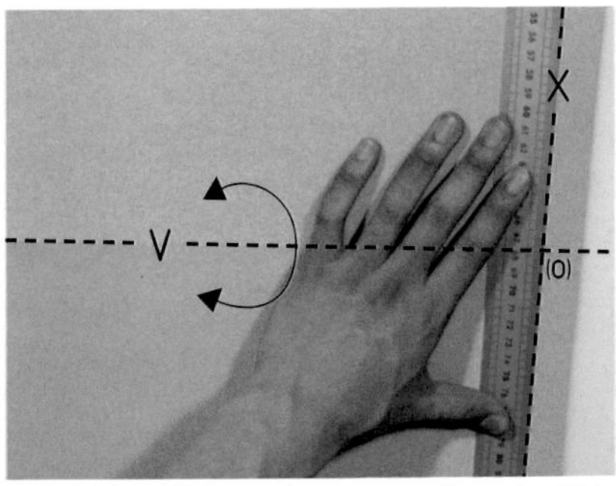

3. Unfold and join up the two pencil marks. This line is called X and makes the bottom of the template. Where the axis V and line X intersect, mark a point (o).

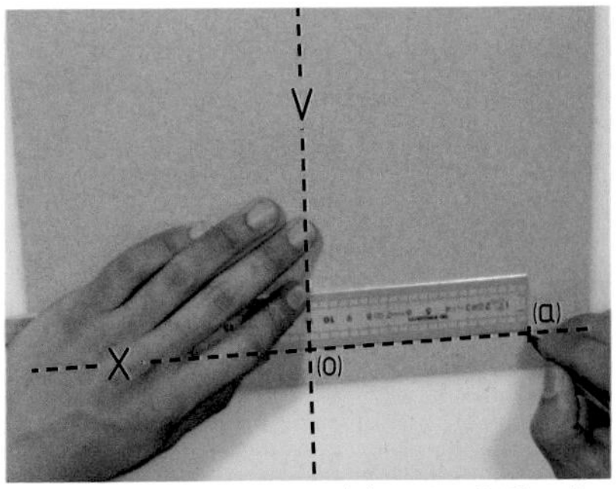

4. Mark with a pencil point (a) on line X. The distance between points (o) and (a) is equal to half the width of the bag, i.e. 11 cm.

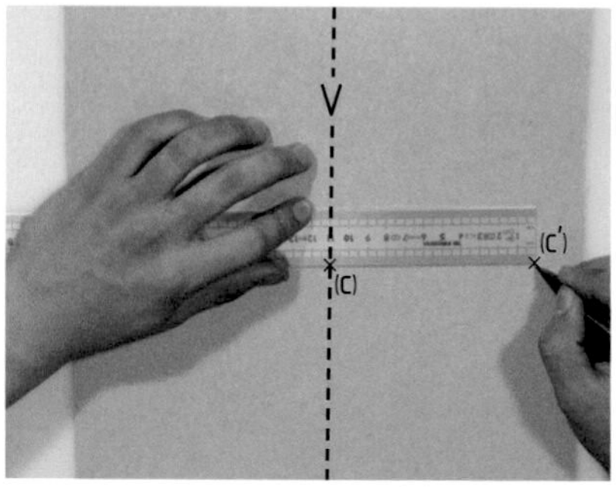

5. Along the V axis, mark point (c). The distance between points (o) and (c) is bigger at the top of the bag i.e. 40 cm. Point (c') is placed perpendicular to the V axis at 11 cm from point (c).

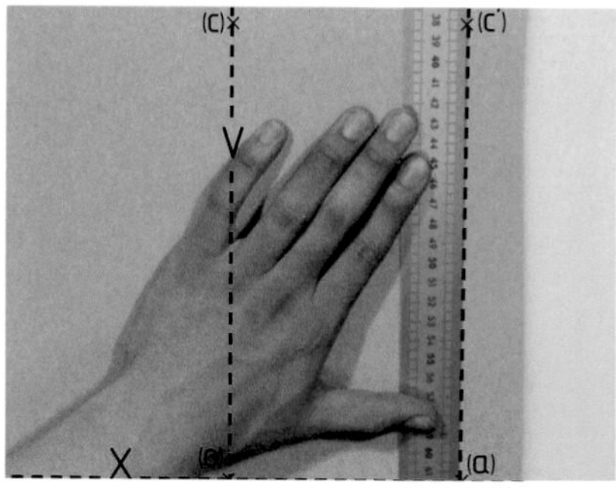

6. Join points (a) and (c'). We now have the line of the side of the template.

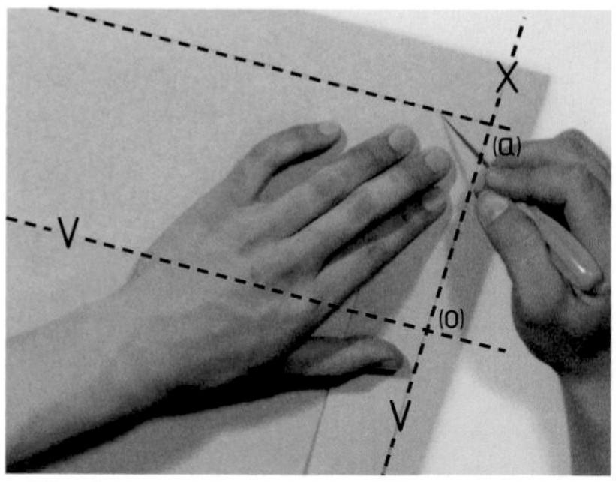

7. The front piece, and that of the back, are the same height, i.e. 31 cm. These two pieces are assembled underneath the bag and make up the base. The width of the base must be divided by half between the front and back pieces and added to the 31 cm of the height of the bag. As the sides of the bag are curved, we will use the gusset to transfer, by pivoting, the measurement of this curve onto the straight line (ac') in order to determine the height of the template. Fold the pattern of the gusset along its V axis. Place the folded gusset pattern on top of the front template. The V axis of this pattern must coincide with X axis of the front template. Position the bottom of the folded gusset pattern against the straight line (ac'). The curve is placed towards the top of the front template. Use an awl to mark off the beginning of this curve on the folded gusset making sure to go through the two thicknesses of card.

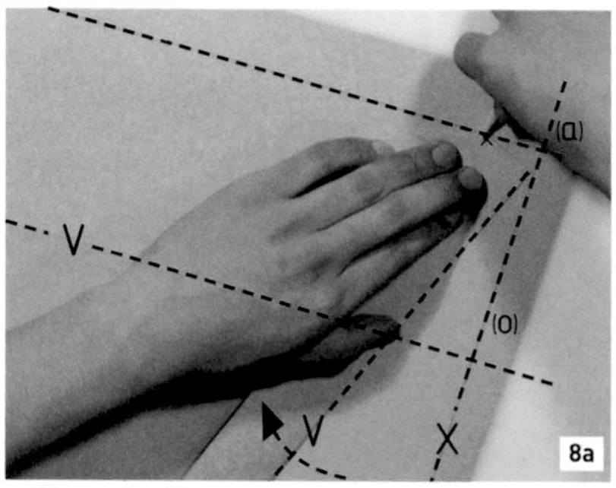

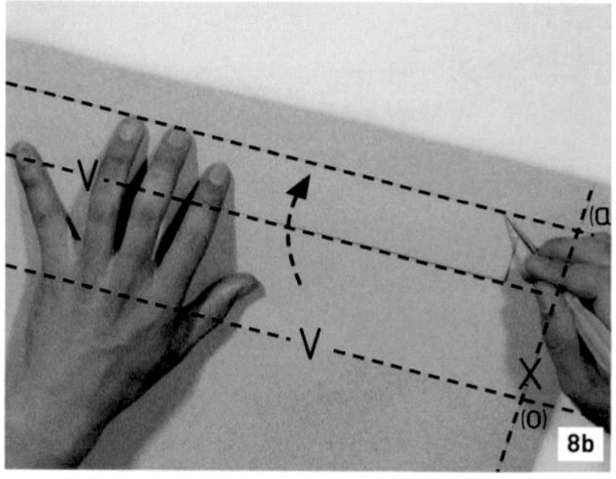

8. The awl will act as a pivot around which we will carefully rotate the curve of the folded gusset, making the curve 'roll' along the straight line (ac' C'). This operation allows us to transfer, precisely, the measurement of half the base of the bag and its height. Move the awl all along the curve of the folded gusset (fig. 8a) and repeat this operation until the height of the folded gusset is aligned with the straight line (ac') (fig. 8b).

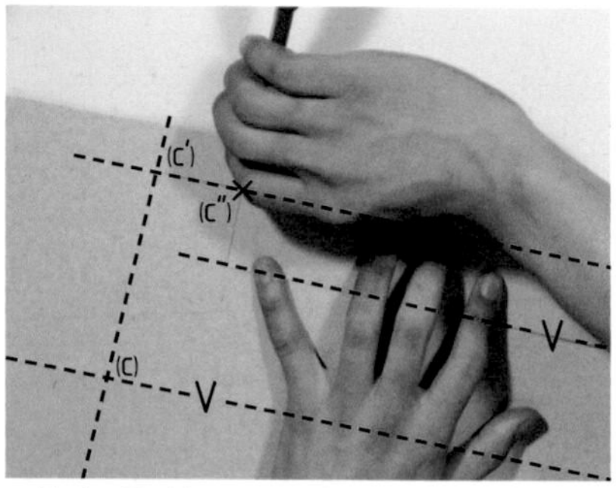

9. Mark off with a cutter the height of the folded gusset onto the template and mark point (c").

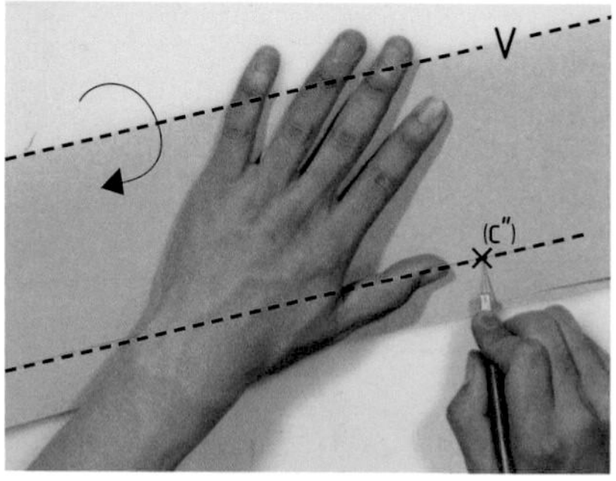

10. Fold the front template in two along its V axis. Transfer symmetrically point (c") onto the other half of the front template, marking off with the cutter into the two thicknesses of card.

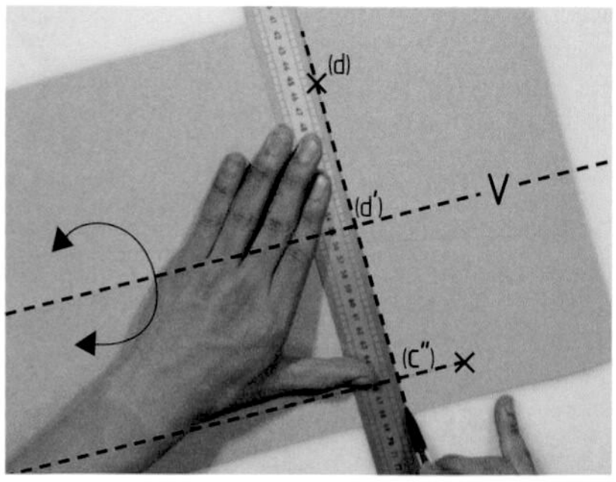

11. Unfold and carry point (d) to the marked spot. Join points (c") and (d). We now have the top line of the template. Put point (d') at the intersection of the Axis V and the straight line (c" d).

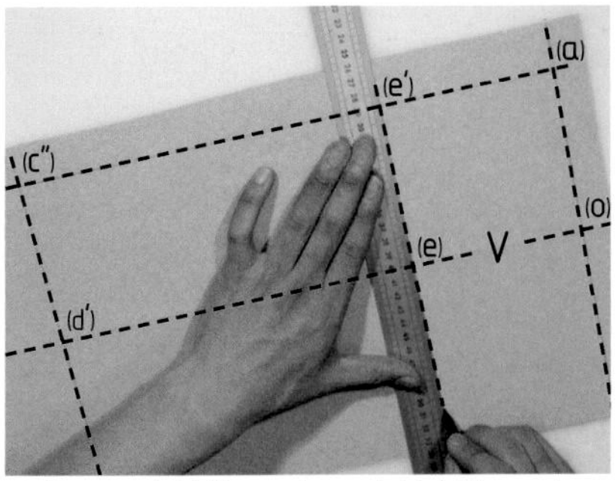

12. From point (d'), mark a point (e) 27 cm along the V axis. From point (c"), mark point (e') 27 cm along the straight line (c" a). Join points (e) and (e') and extend this line up to the edge of the front template : we now have the height of the flap. This operation is very important for the subsequent ones.

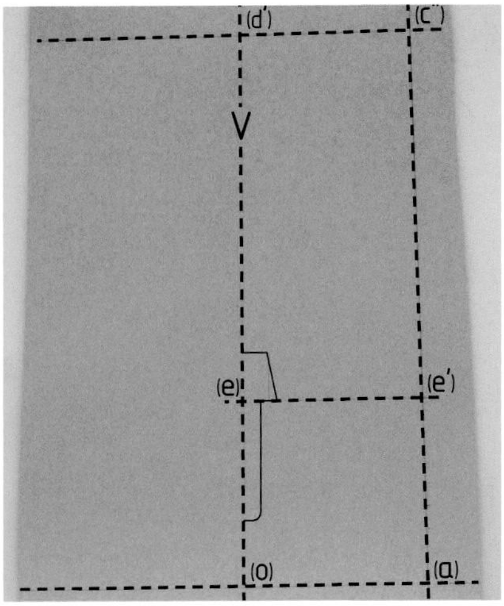

13. On the right-hand side of the V axis, draw half of the tab which will close the flap.

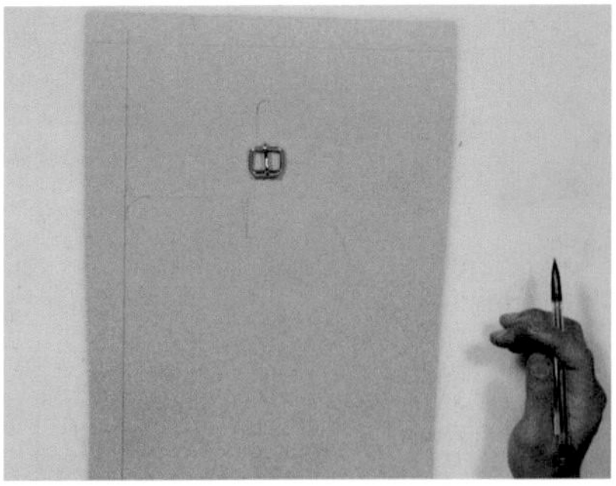

14. The tab will close the bag when it is passed through the buckle once it is fixed onto the front. Place the buckle on the drawing of the tab so that its position can be determined. Now half of the front template is drawn.

15. Cut the drawn half stopping short of the V axis.

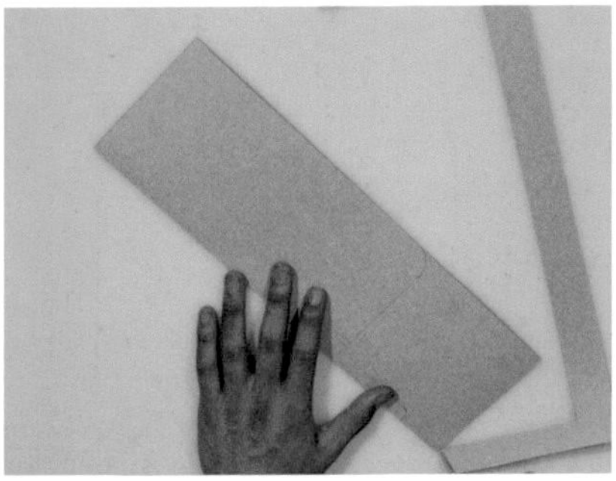

16. Fold along the V axis and cut the second half symmetrically. The templates of the front, back and flap have now been achieved. This will be used to construct the pattern pieces of the front, back and flap sections.

Front pattern

We will use the templates for the front, back and flap to trace off the patterns for these three pieces. We will add seams to the front, and back pieces in order to assemble them. The other parts are assembled edge-to-edge and so do not require any extra seam allowances.

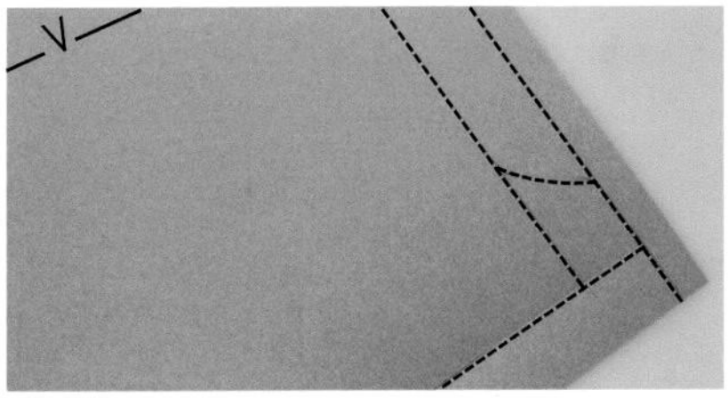

1. Cut out a piece of card measuring about 40 x 30 cm. Using a cutter, lightly score the V axis in the centre of it. Pin the template onto this piece aligning precisely the V axis of the template with the V axis of the pattern. Using a pencil, transfer the template's outline onto the pattern. 4 cm under the top line of the pattern, trace a parallel line and then a diagonal one between these two lines. This creates half of the opening of the bag giving enough room for putting a hand inside.

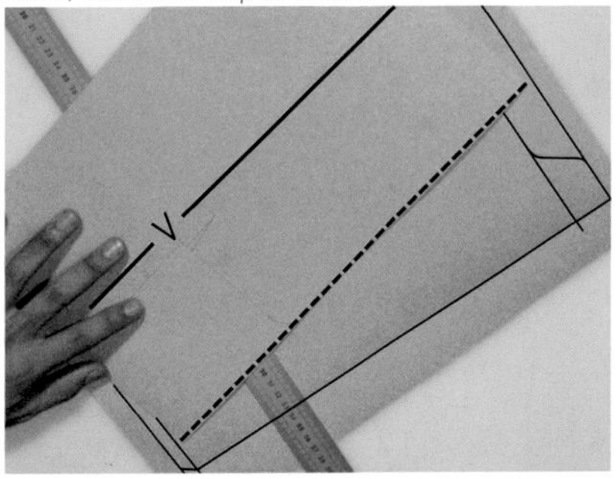

2. At the bottom of the front pattern, add a seam allowance of 1 cm so that the back and the front pieces can be assembled using an inside seam.

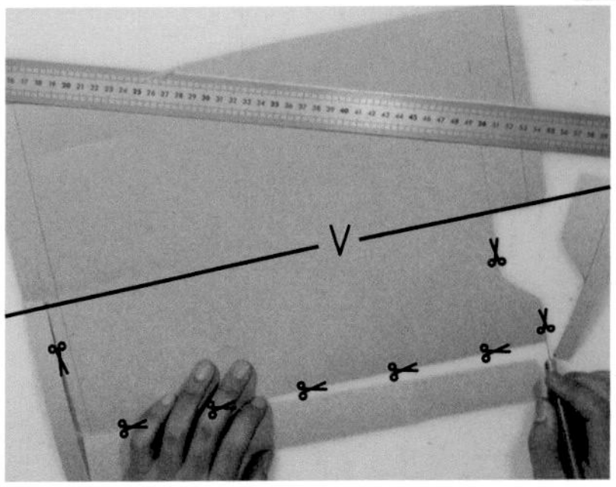

3. Cut out half of the piece stopping short of the V axis.

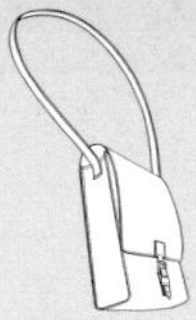

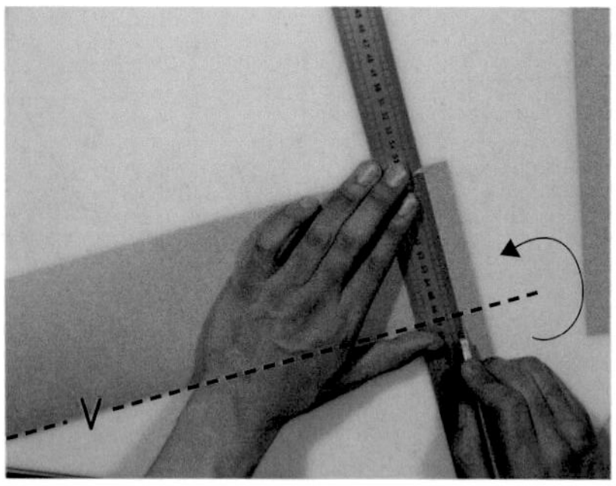

4. Fold the piece in two and cut the second half symmetrically.

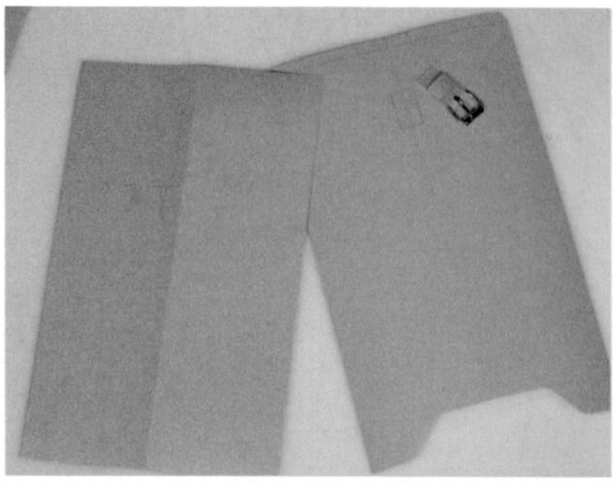

5. Think about drawing the enchape pattern and that of the tab for closing the flap. The size of the enchape depends on the buckle which is to be used. Do not forget to make a hole in the middle of the enchape for the tongue of the buckle. The position of this enchape will have been decided when the template was made.

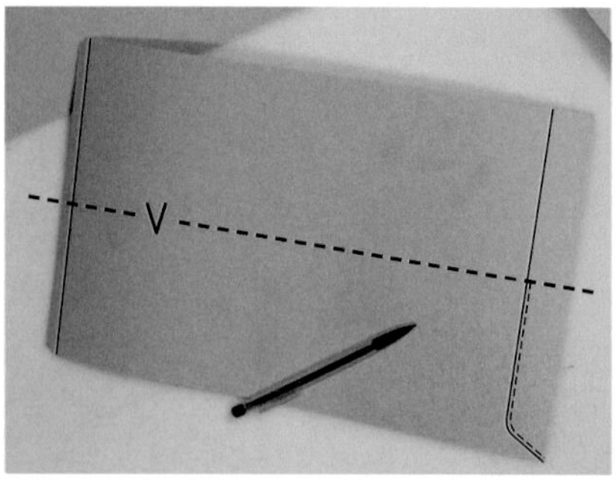

6. For the back pattern, proceed in the same way as for the front pattern because these two pieces are the same size. Trace a parallel line 4 cm under the top line: this will determine the position of the flap on the back. Stop this seam line 4 cm from the side and join the upper angle of the bag diagonally. Slightly curve the traced angle. At the bottom of the back pattern, add a 1 cm seam allowance so that the front and the back pieces can be joined by an inside seam.

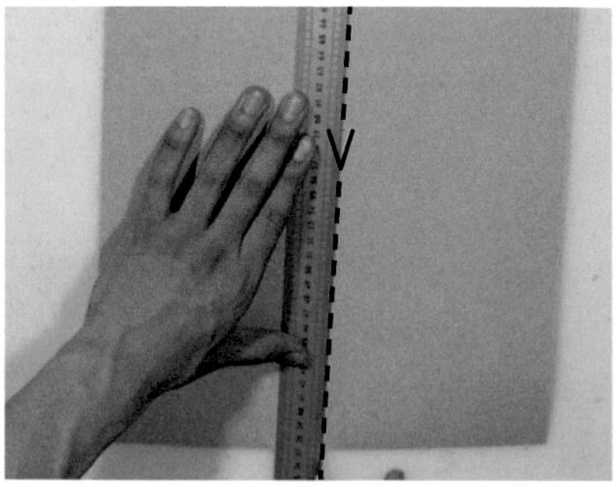

7. We are going to use the back pattern to make the flap pattern. Cut out a piece of card about 40 x 30 cm. Using a steel ruler and cutter, lightly score the vertical axis V in the middle of it.

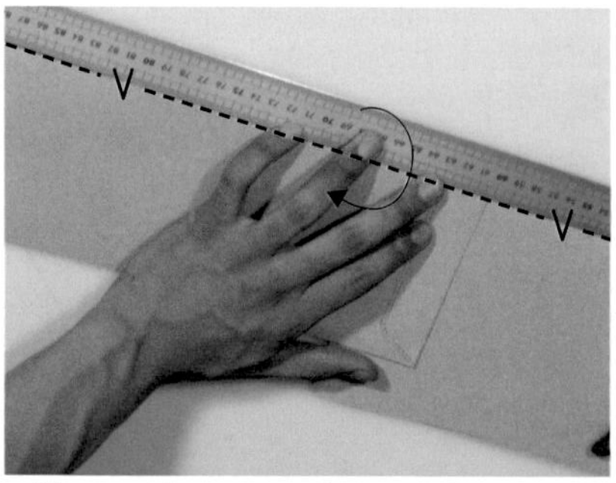

8. We are going to transfer, onto the card, the outlines of the flap position which has been drawn on the back pattern. To do this, fold the card along its V axis. At the same time fold the back pattern. Then place the back pattern onto this card aligning the V axis of the card with the V axis of the back pattern. These two pieces must overlap each other by 6 cm (approx.). The ruler can help align the two pieces.

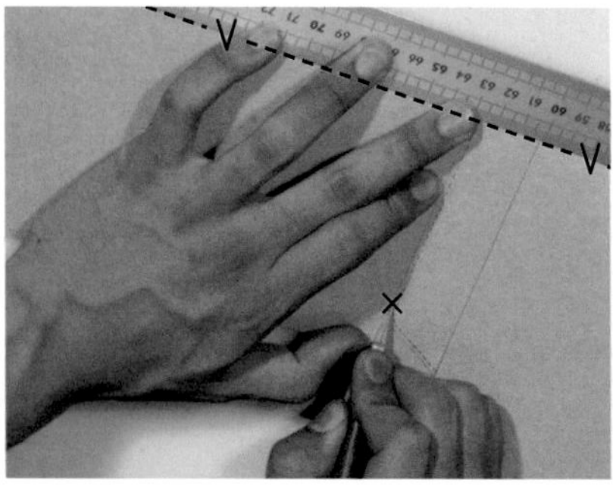

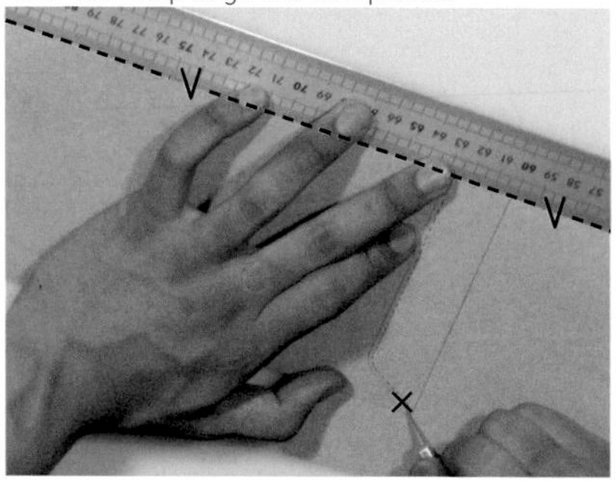

9. To trace the top of the flap, we use the cutter to transfer the drawn shape of the top of the back pattern onto the piece of card. The straight lines and curve are pricked through. The exact shape is transferred onto the card by pricking through at different points along the form. In order to produce an identical round shape add more points, closer together, along the curve.

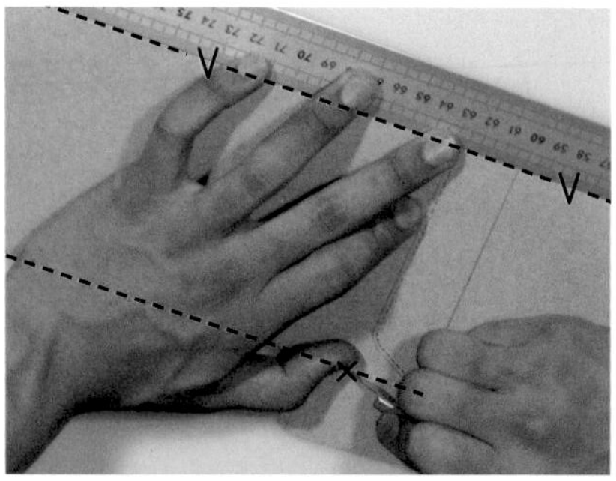

10. In order to determine half the width of the flap, transfer half the width of the back pattern by marking with the cutter.

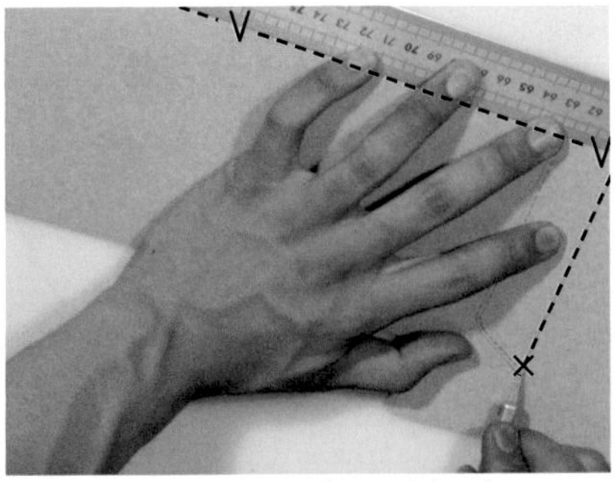

11. To determine the position of the flap seam, transfer the top of the back pattern onto the piece of card by marking with the cutter.

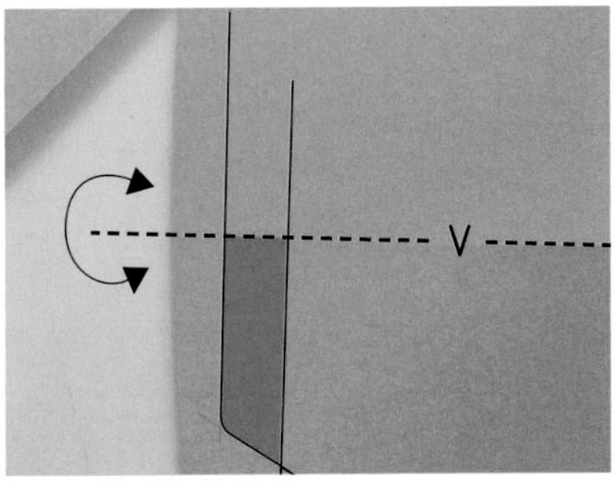

12. Unfold and join up these points using a pencil; we have now produced the top of the flap. The band which has been obtained, known as the 'attachment band' will be stuck, then oversewn. This will fix the flap to the back.

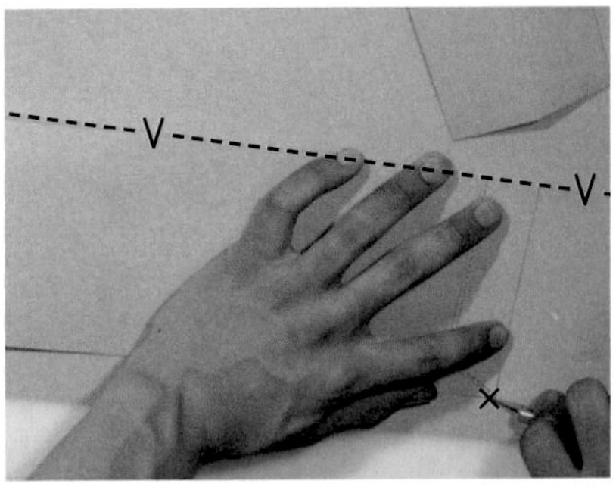

13. The width of the flap is equal to that of the back. We use the back pattern to transfer the its width onto the card by marking it at its two extremities.

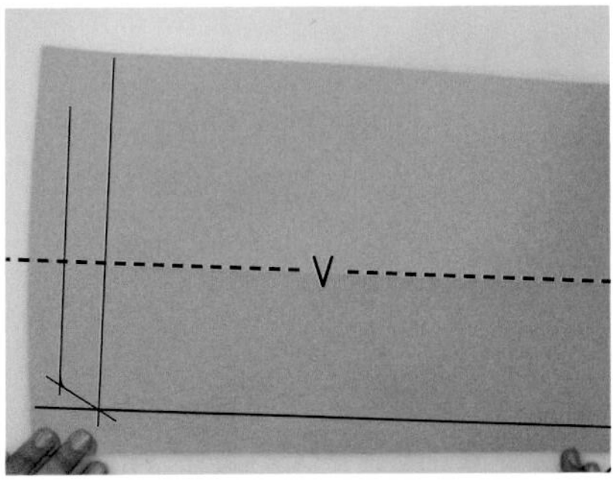

14. Join up these two points to trace off the half-width of the flap.

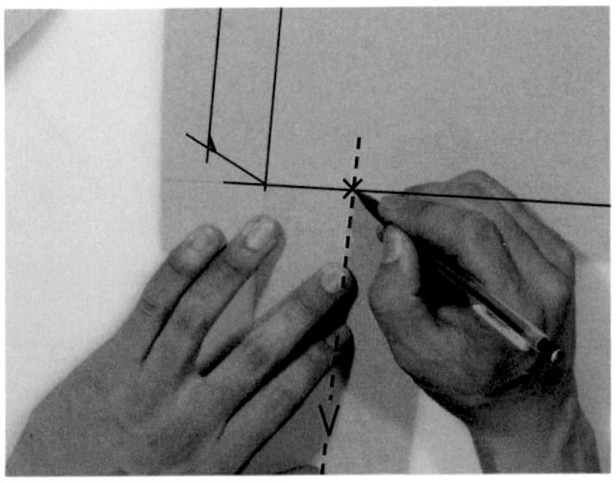

15. Here we determine the height of the flap. On the edge of the flap, transfer the necessary measurements : the attaching band of the back, the size of the gusset and the section folded over the front. We already have the measurement of the attaching band ; we add on the half-width of the gusset by placing the top of the gusset pattern onto the side line of the flap.

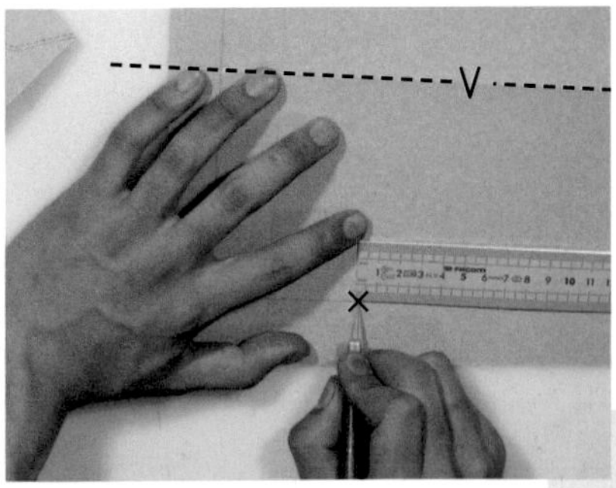

16. Move this point 0.2 cm towards the bottom to take into account the thickness of the leather. Mark off using the cutter.

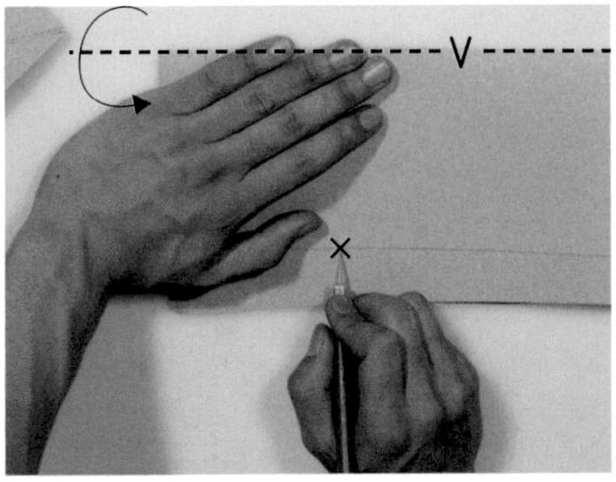

17. Fold the piece of card along its V axis and mark off again symmetrically.

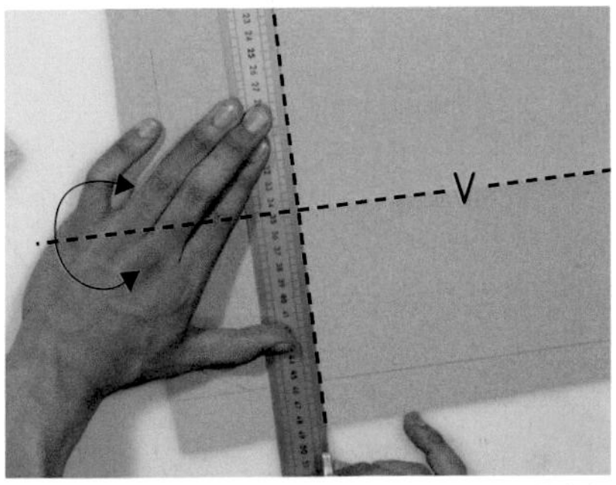

18. Unfold and join these two marks by lightly scoring the card so that it can be easily folded.

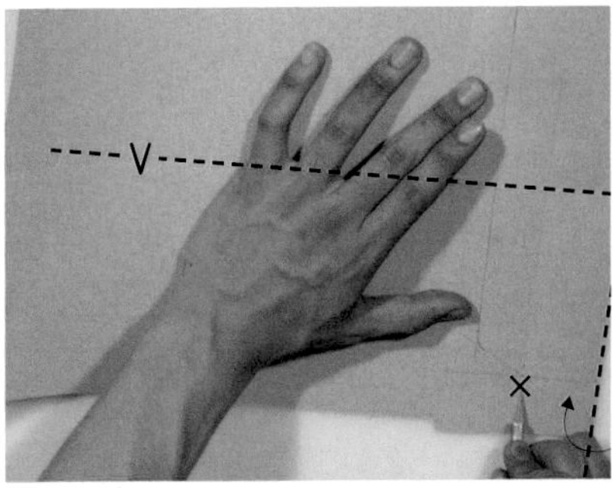

19. Fold the card along the line which has just been traced, then transfer half the measurement of the gusset by marking off with the cutting through the two thicknesses of card.

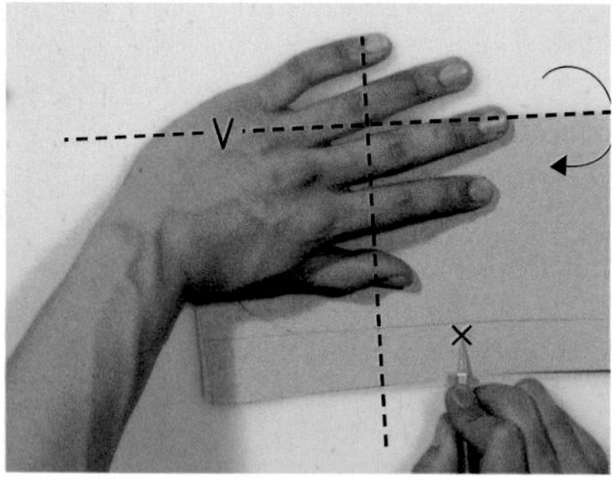

20. Unfold, then refold along the V axis transferring symmetrically with the cutter the point which has just been marked.

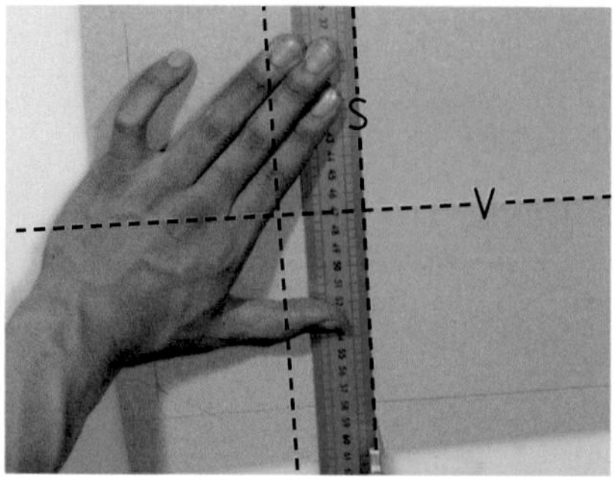

21. Unfold and join these two marks with the cutter by score lightly. This line, known as S, determines the size of the gusset.

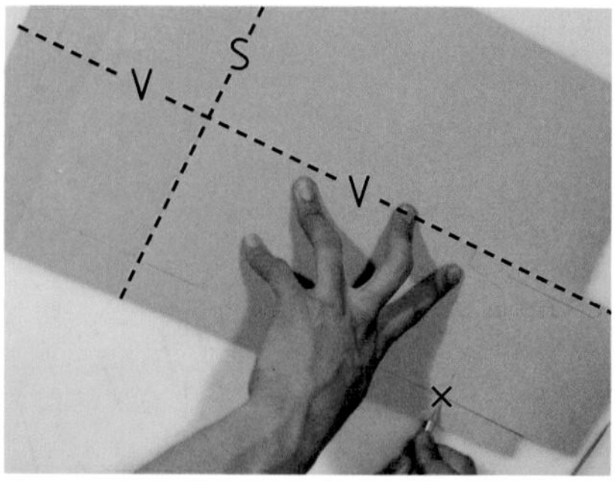

22. We are going to trace the last section of the flap by using the front, back and flap templates. Place the top of the template under line S and, using a cutter, transfer the flap measurement onto the piece of card.

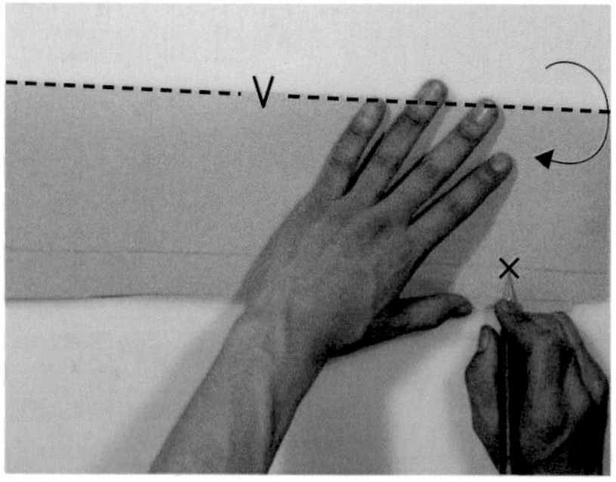

23. Fold the flap pattern in two along the V axis and transfer symmetrically the height of the flap onto the other side.

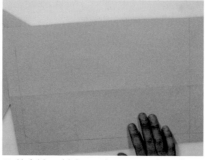

24. Unfold and join up the two marks using a pencil line to trace the bottom of the flap.

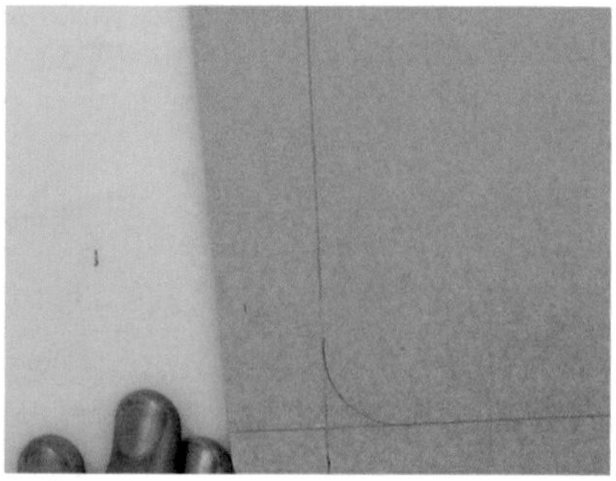

25. Draw the curve of the bottom of the flap on one side.

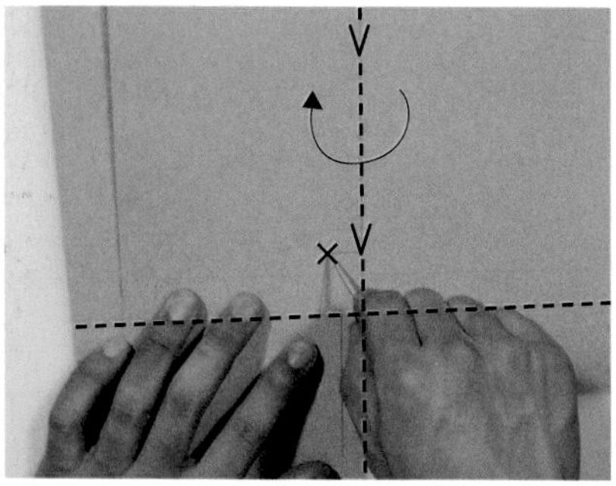

26. Fold the template along its V axis then place it on the flap pattern. Line up the V axes of the pattern and the template and make the line of the flap template coincide with that of the pattern. With the awl, transfer the outlines of the fastening tabs onto the pattern pressing hard enough to pierce through two layers of card.

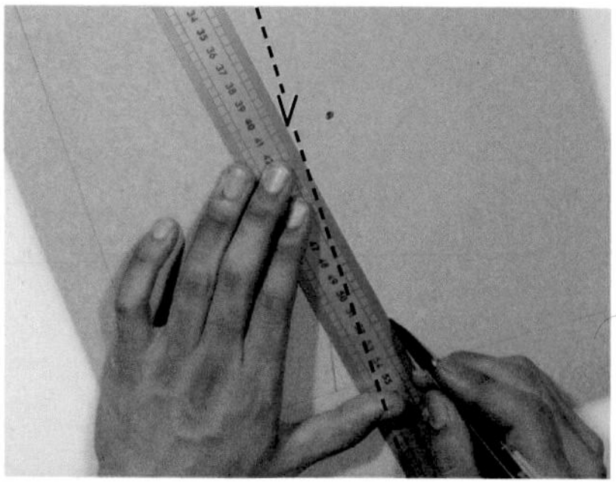

27. Draw the section where the tab is fixed onto the flap pattern and join up these marks with a pencil line.

28. The construction of the flap pattern is finished.

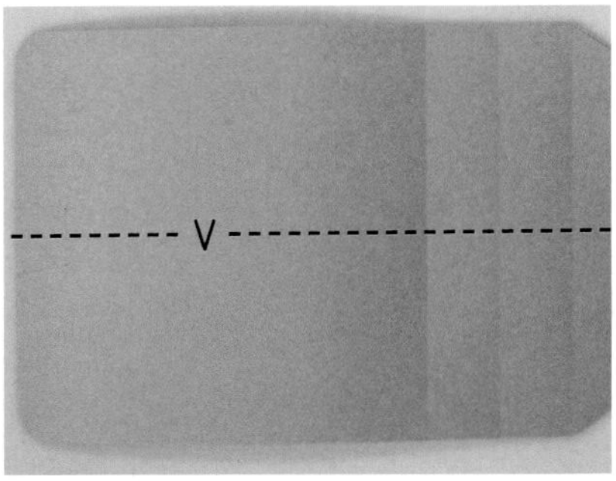

29. Cut out half of the pattern stopping short of the V axis, fold in two and cut symmetrically to achieve the finished flap pattern.

Cutting and assembling

We now have the pattern for the bag which consists of a back, a front, a flap, a side, a shoulder strap, a fastening tab, an enchape and a strap which goes through the buckle. We have made the pattern of a shoulder strap of 70 cm long and 2 cm wide. All that is left to do is cut out the pieces and assemble them.

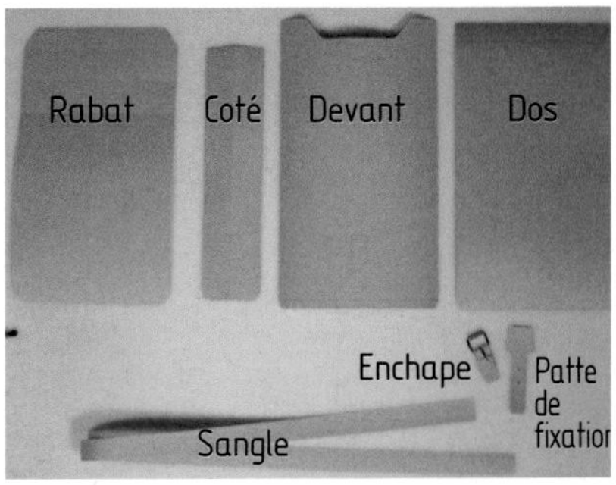

1. At each end of the strap, we add a seam band of 4 cm in length so that the gussets can be assembled. To make the pattern for the fastening tab, the traced drawing must be transferred onto the front template. Also, trace the pattern of the enchape and transfer this onto the front template. (NB: the drawn section only represents half of the enchape, its length is twice as big as the drawing when it is folded in two to enclose the buckle.) The strap, which measures 3 cm long and 0.5 cm wide, will be fixed into the seams of the enchape.

2. With the help of the patterns, we are going to cut out the parts of the bag : two sides, a front, a back, a flap, a fastening tab, an enchape, a buckle strap and a shoulder strap. Place a weight onto the pattern whilst cutting to hold everything in position.

3. Use an awl to prick out important assembly points. For example, mark where the position of the enchape is on the front, or the position of the fastening tab on the flap.

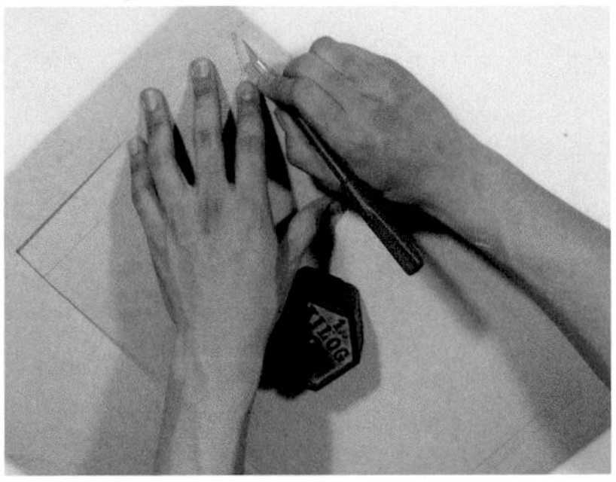

4. Cut out following the outlines of the patterns. Make a light cutter mark in the first instance then go over this pressing a bit harder.

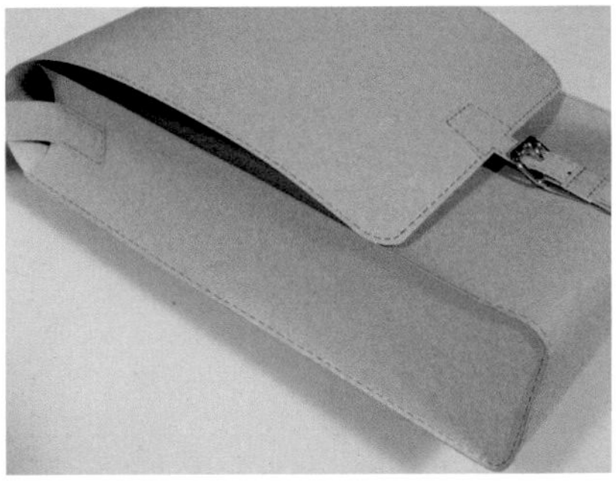

5. Use glue to stick all the pieces together. To fix the fastening strap to the flap, place the buckle into the enchape, fold the two halves over and stick them together, enclosing the two ends of the fastening strap. Stick the enchape to the front, then each end of the shoulder strap to a gusset. Assemble the front and the back, then the flap and the back. The assembling of the gussets to the front and the back are done edge to edge with the seams inside out.

6. The final piece.

Making felt prototypes

1 - Cylindrical bag

Flexible or supple bags are made in a leather which can be sewn inside out then reversed. Felt possess the same characteristics and is the material chosen to make this bag which consists of four main parts: two round sides, and an identical front and back. The pattern of this bag also has some small pieces: handles, straps and tabs. This bag is, in fact, a false cylinder as its base is flat. Finishing details must also be considered : 16 x 0.5 cm rivets, 1 x 25 cm zip and 4 detachable rivets.

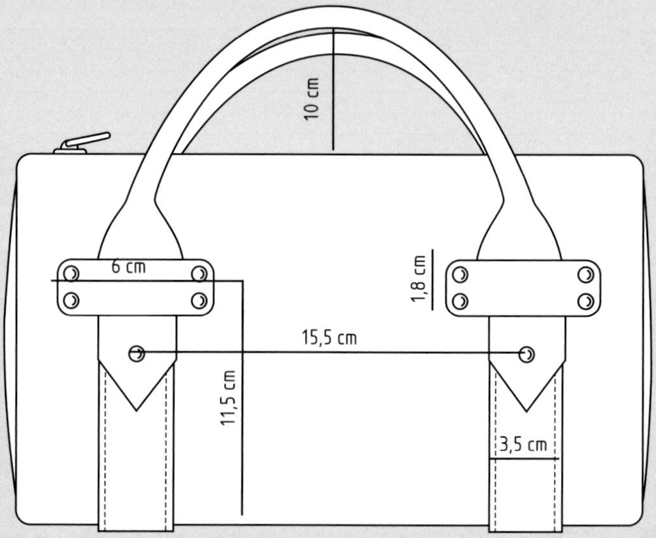

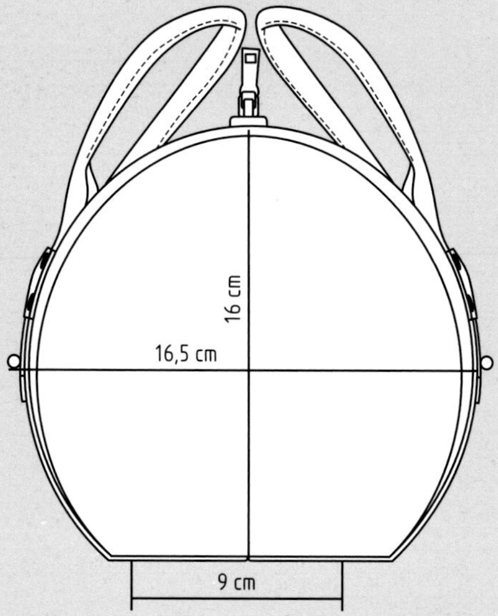

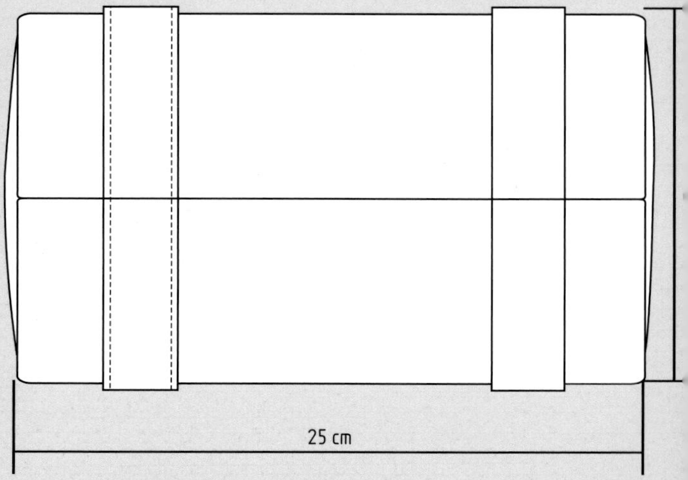

Technical drawings of the side, front and underside of the bag

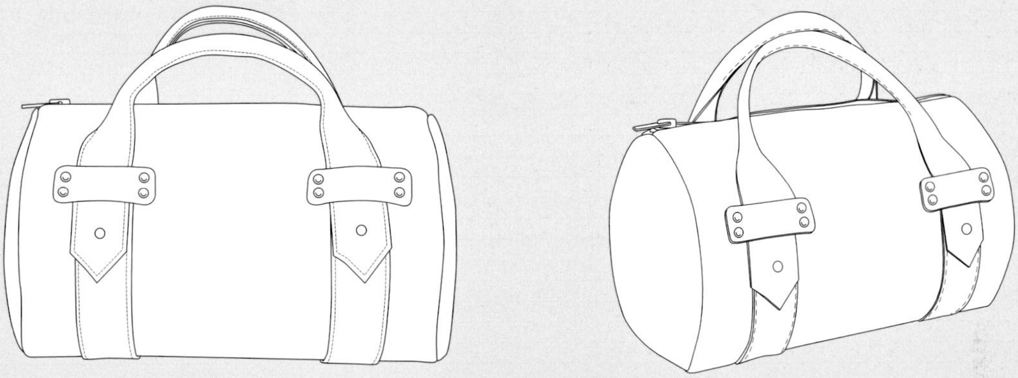

Drawings of the front and three-quarter view of the bag.

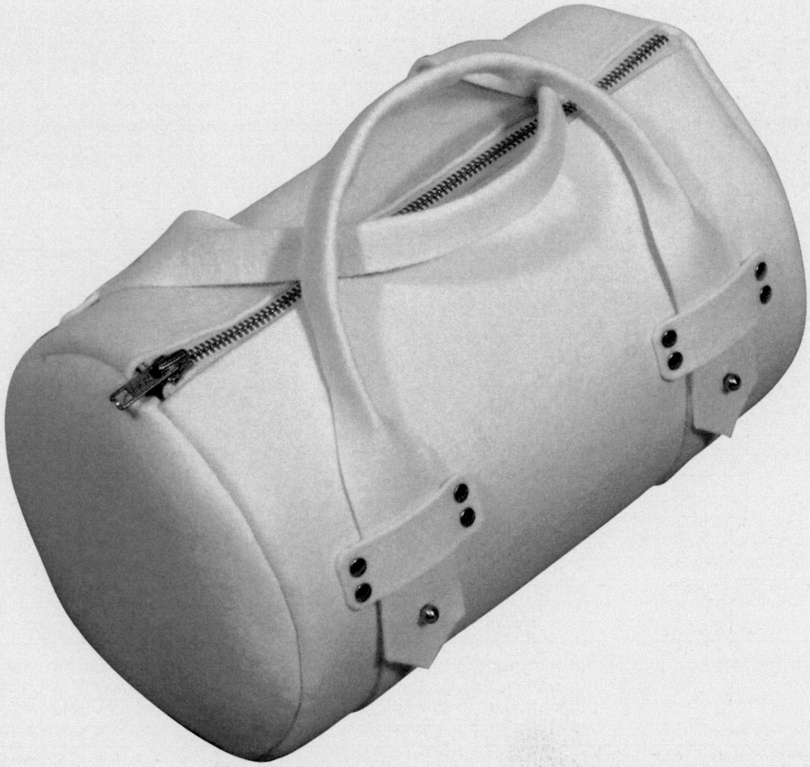

Three-quarter view of the top of the finished prototype.

1 - Cylindrical bag

Preparation

First of all, it is most important to determine the bag's proportions by drawing the flattened shape onto the card .

Draw the flat shape of the bag onto the card. To choose a comfortable length for the handles, place your hand onto the drawing and make a fist to trace around.

Side Template

The side template allows you to make the side pattern. Start by tracing the cylindrical shape of the side; add onto this the seam allowance.

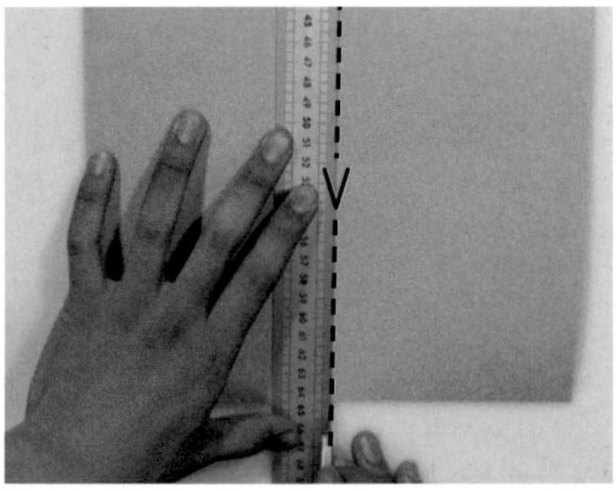

1. Cut out a piece of card slightly larger than the side, i.e. 20 x 20 cm for a bag with a 16.5 cm diameter. In the middle of the card, use a ruler and a cutter to lightly score and make a vertical axis V for the template which can be folded in two.

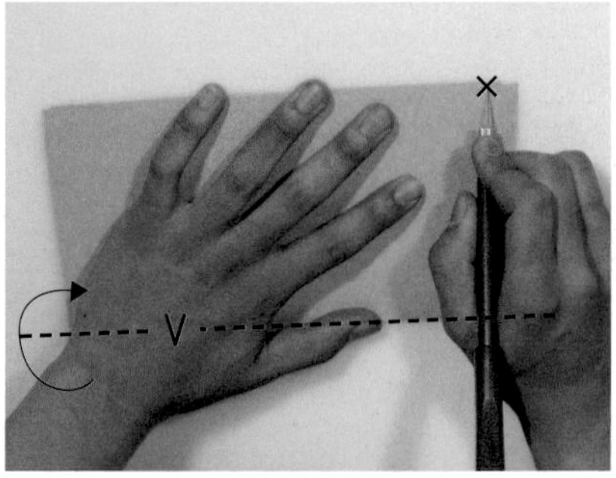

2. Fold the card on its V axis. Use the cutter to make a mark on the side of the card at the bottom right-hand side of the V axis. Press hard enough to go through the two thicknesses of card.

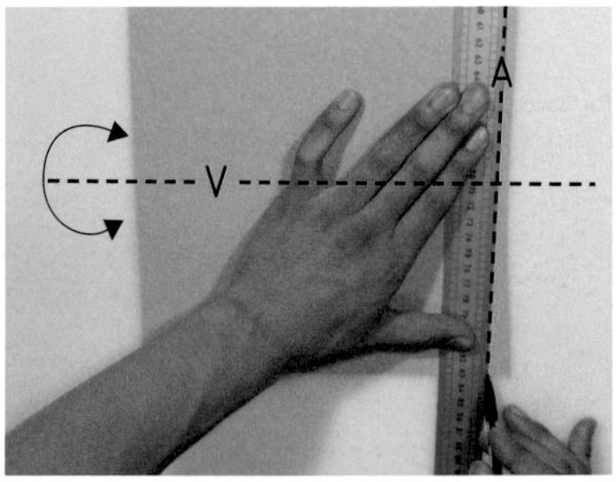

3. Unfold. We now have two perfectly symmetrical marks. Join them up using a pencil line to trace the bottom line of the side template. We call this line 'A'.

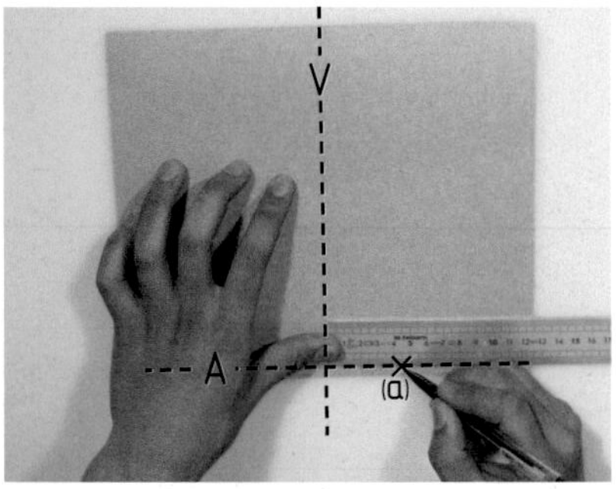

4. The base of this bag is flat; it is from this point that the tracing starts. On line A and right of the V axis, indicate with a pencil mark half the width of the bottom of the side (4.5 cm for a base which is 9 cm). We will call this point 'a' .

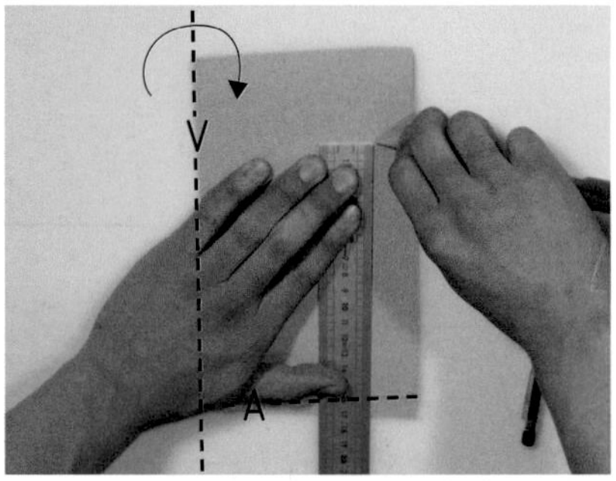

5. Fold the card in two along the V axis. On the side of the card, place a ruler perpendicular to line A and, with a cutter, mark off the height of the side, i.e. 16 cm. Press fairly hard so as to pierce through the two thicknesses of card.

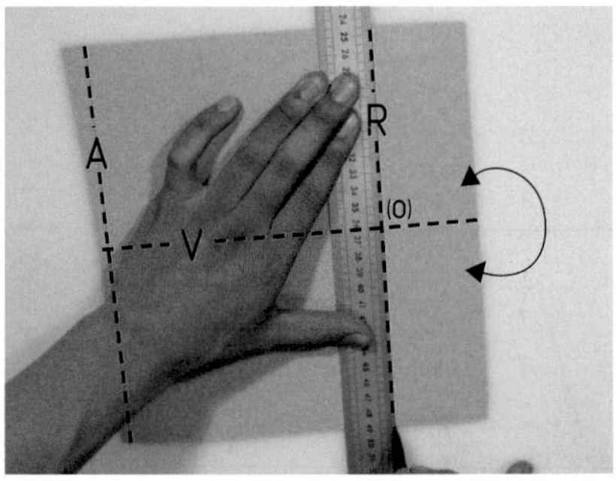

6. Unfold the card and join up these two marks. This will give the top line of the side template. We will call this line 'R'. Place a point (o) at the intersection of line R and the V axis.

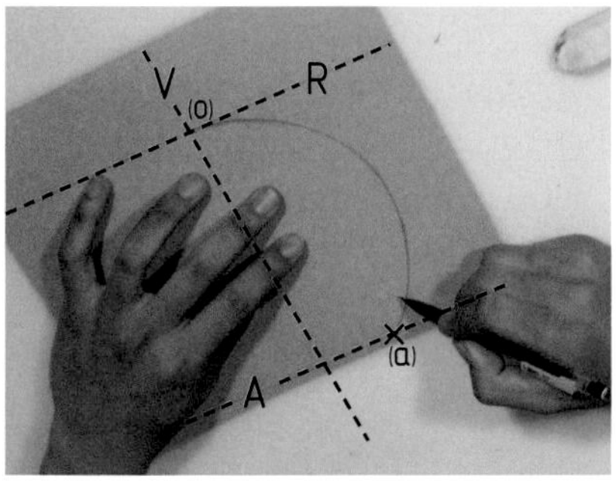

7. Join points (o) and (a) by tracing an arc freehand. Its centre is in the middle of the V axis giving a diameter of 16.5 cm (approx.). To trace this arc, start at a tangent with line R going up to point (a). A French curve will give you a very good line !

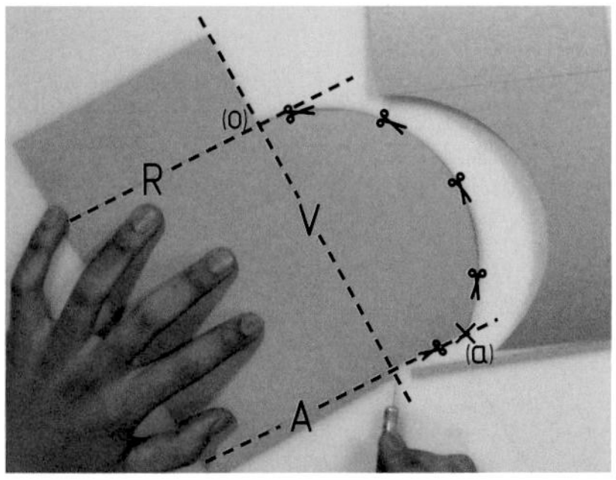

8. Using a cutter, cut out this curve from point (o) to (a) stopping short of the V axis. Use a French curve to cut out the curve properly afterwards.

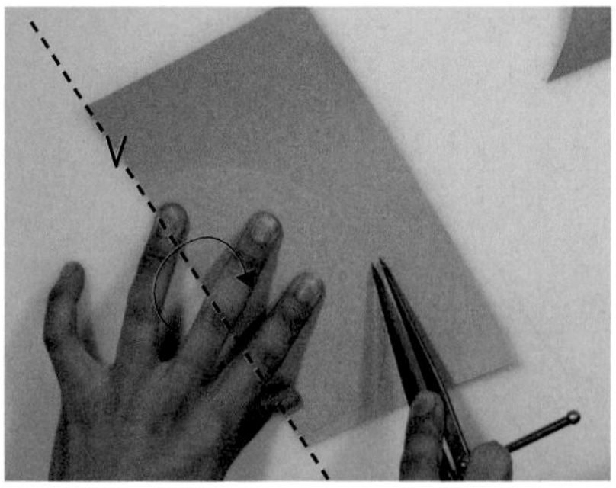

9. Fold the card in two along the V axis. With the dividers measure 0.5 cm and trace a seam allowance of 0.5 cm following the outline of the folded half.

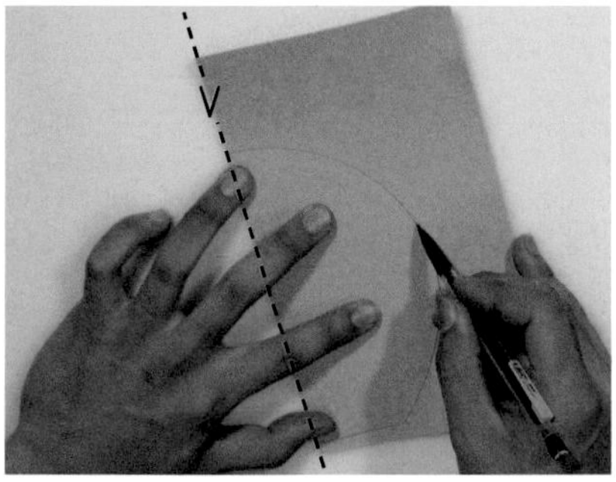

10. Use a pencil to transfer the outline of the folded half onto the other half of the card. We will call this line C. With a pencil, trace the seam allowance into the mark left by the dividers. This outside line is called D.

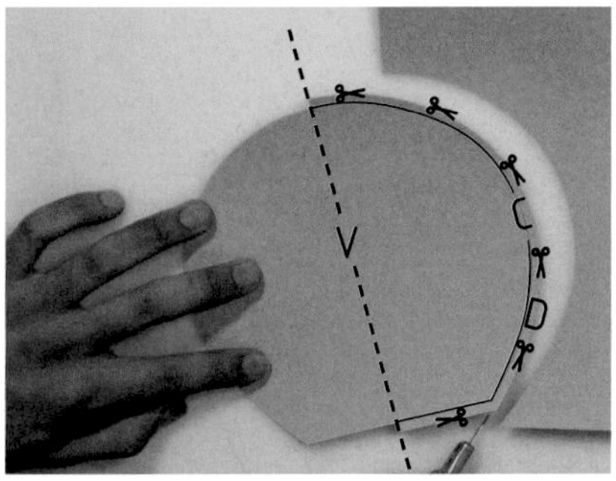

11. Unfold the card and use a cutter to cut along line D. The side template is finished.

Front and back pattern

As the front and the bag are identical, there is only need for one pattern. We will call this pattern 'front pattern'. Details, such as the straps and tabs, are also included on this pattern.

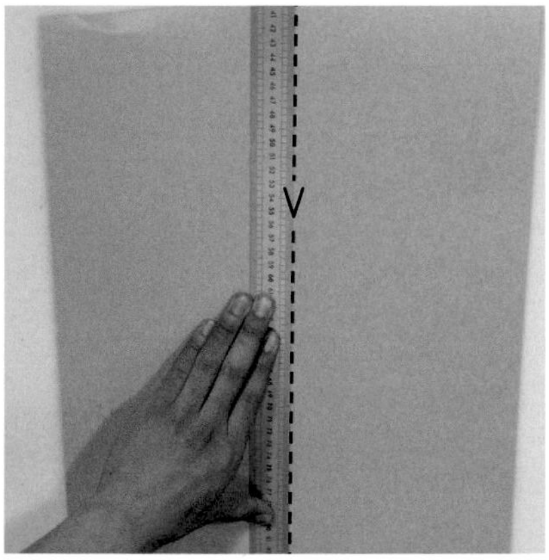

1. Cut out a piece of card about 40 x 30 cm for a bag measuring 16 x 25 cm. Place the card in the direction of its height. Lightly score its vertical axis V using a cutter and ruler so that it can be easily folded.

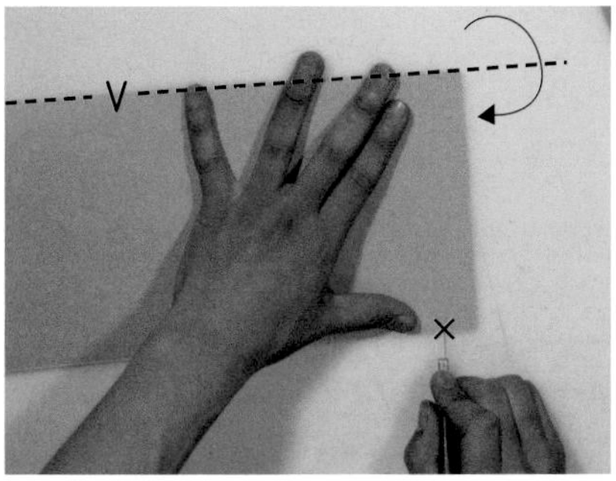

2. To construct the bottom line of the pattern, fold it in two along the V axis. Mark off with a cutter on the side of the card, at the bottom, on the left of the V axis.

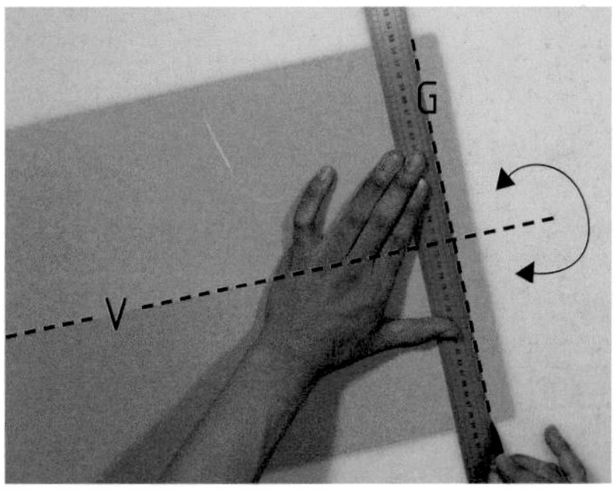

3. Unfold and join the two points with a pencil line. This will make the bottom line of the front pattern. We will call this line G.

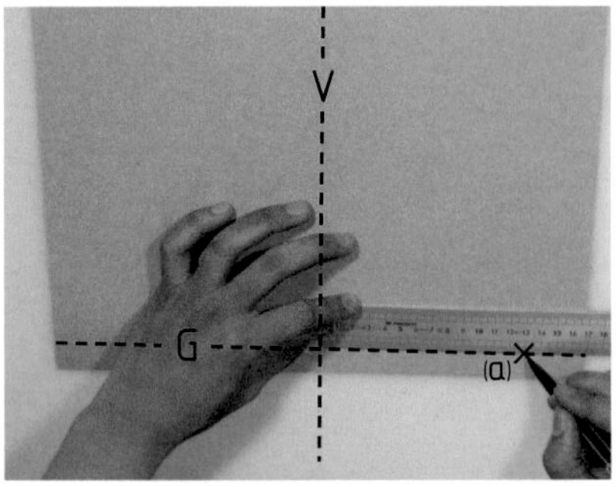

4. Now trace the side line of the front pattern. On line G and on the right-hand side of the V axis, mark off half of the length of the front (12.5 cm) with a pencil. We will call this point "a".

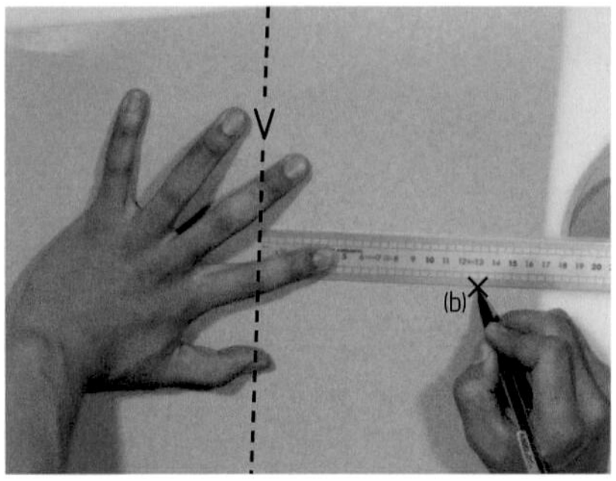

5. Use a pencil to transfer this measurement higher up the card (12.5 cm) perpendicular to the V axis. We will call this point b.

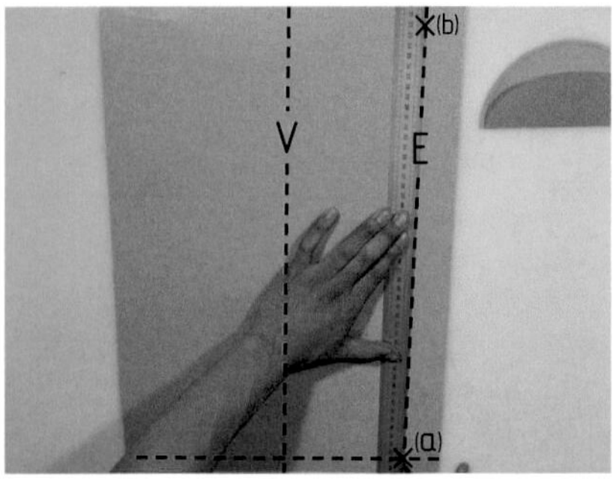

6. Join up these two points to make the side line of the front pattern which we will call E.

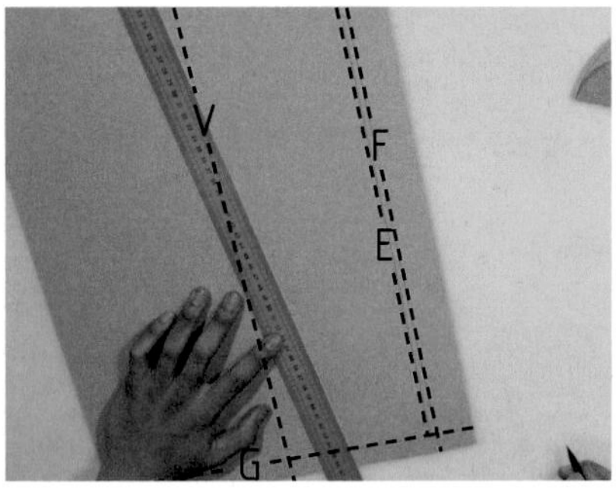

7. At 0.5 cm right of line E, trace a parallel line from E for a seam allowance. This new line is called F.

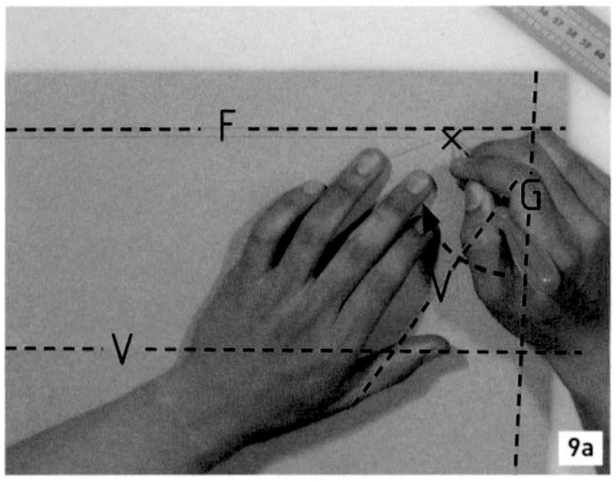

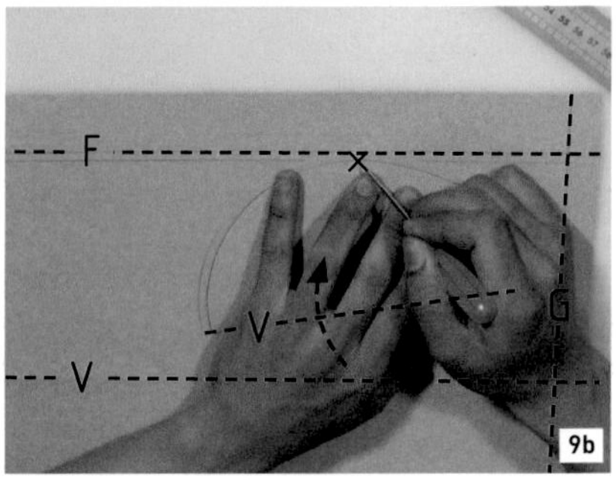

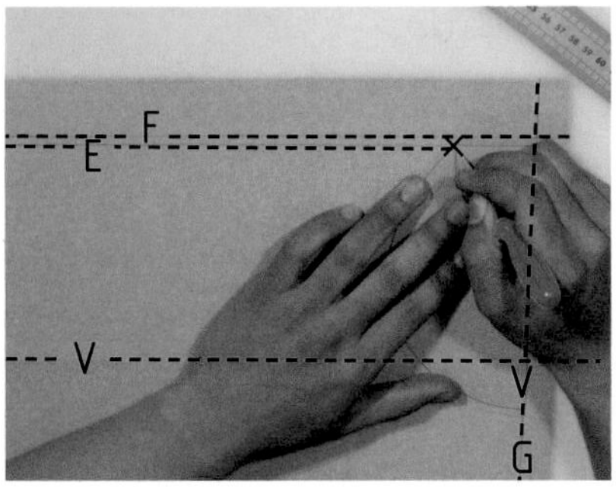

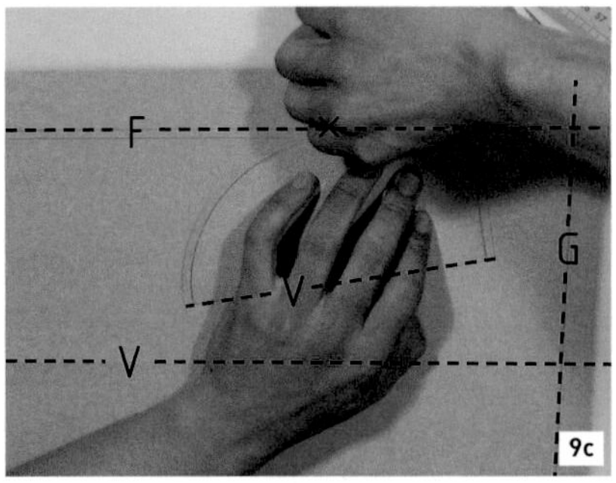

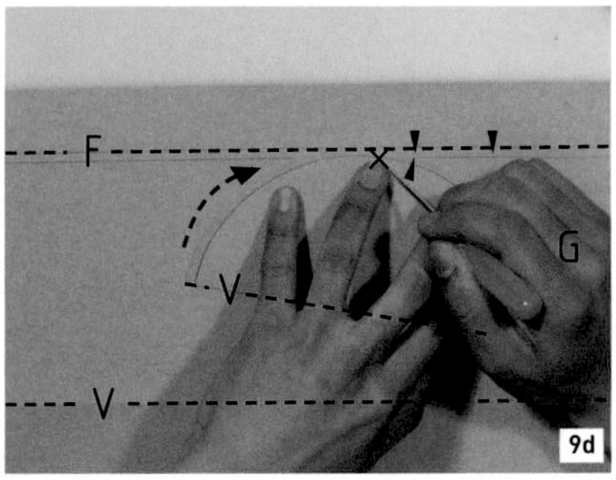

8. To determine the height of the front piece and so that it assembles perfectly, we are going proceed in the same way as for bag 2. Fold the side template in two. Place this template on the front piece aligning exactly the angles of the base of the bag onto lines F and G. At the start of the curve, use an awl to pierce through at intervals what is now three thicknesses of card.

9. We can use the awl as a pivot to carefully rotate the folded template. This is done by 'rolling' line D (corresponding to the side line of the bag with seam included) along line F. This operation allows the measurement of half the bottom of the bag, and the height, to be transferred exactly. Move the awl along line F and repeat this operation up to the V axis of the template which is perpendicular to line F of the front. Nick the template and front with the cutter at regular intervals. Press fairly hard to mark all the card thicknesses.

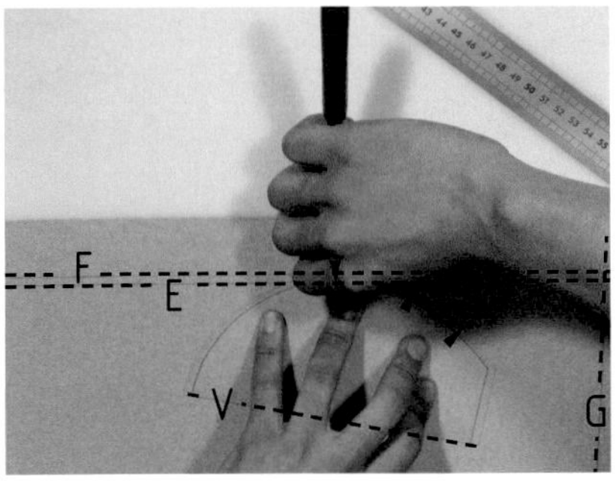

10. At regular intervals, clip the seam allowance of the side template on the front/back pattern. This clipping will prevent any deforming of the seams when the bag is assembled. Press hard to mark through the two thicknesses of card.

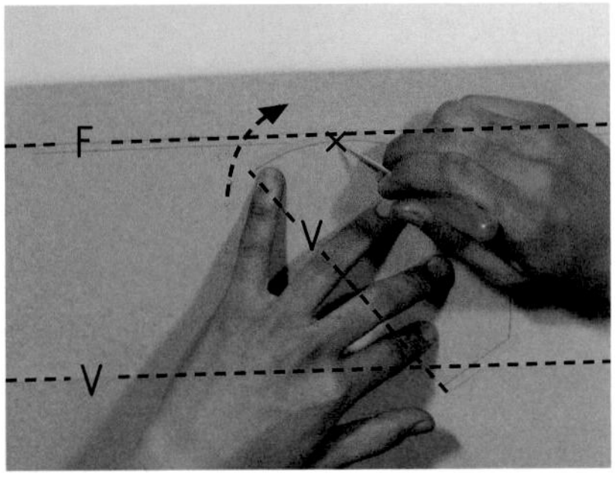

11. Repeat these operations clipping at regular intervals, at the rate of a clip every two rotations around the awl. It is necessary to mark then pivot the template, mark again then clip with the cutter, move the template and repeat.

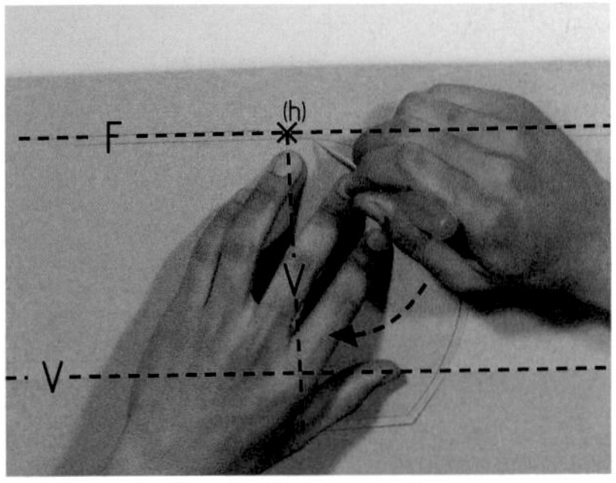

12. When the V axis of the template is perpendicular to line F of the front, mark for the last time with the awl. This last mark indicates the real height of the front pattern. We will call this point "h".

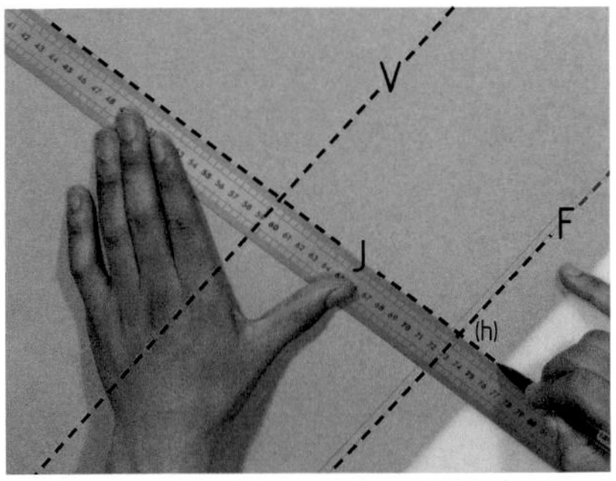

13. Remove the side template, fold the front pattern in two along its V axis and reproduce point (h) symmetrically onto the two halves of the card.

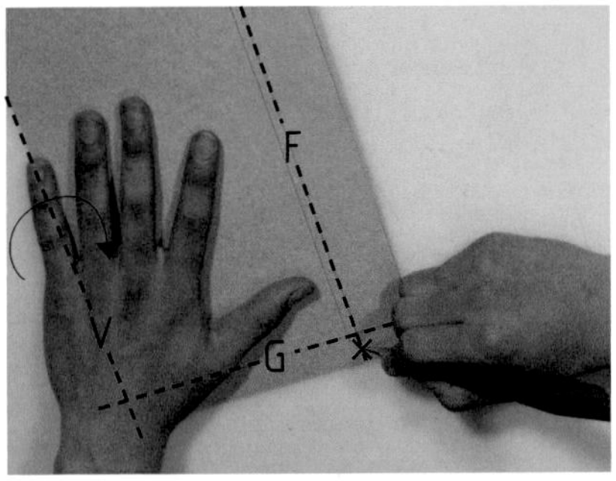

14. Fold the front pattern along its V axis. Mark off with the cutter 1 cm under line G pressing fairly hard to mark through the two thicknesses of card.

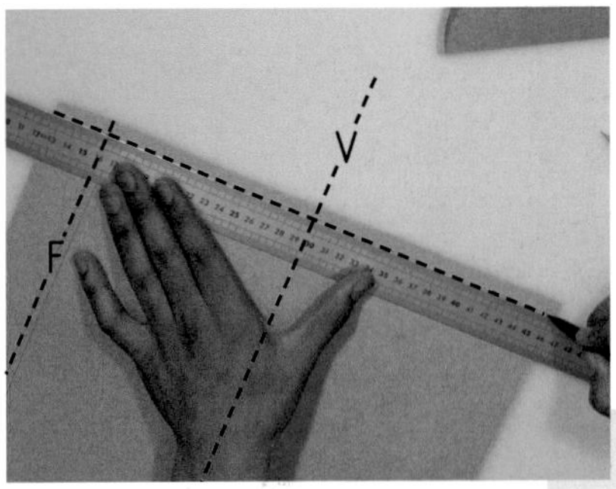

15. Unfold it and join the marks up with a pencil line. We have just traced the seam measurement for the bottom of the front pattern.

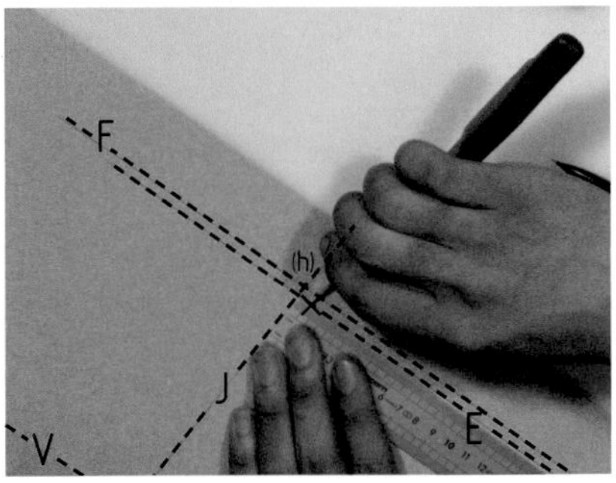

16. This bag is closed by a zip linking the back and the front. We are now going to take off half the width of the zip width i.e. 0.7 cm. Using the cutter, mark off 0.7 cm underneath line J.

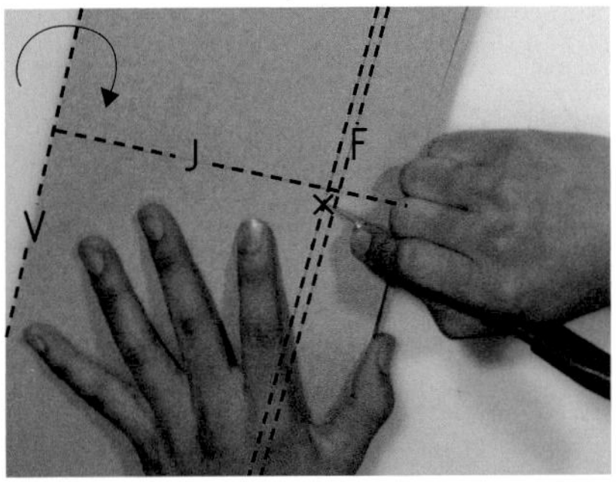

17. Fold the front in two along the V axis and transfer this mark symmetrically onto the other half of the front.

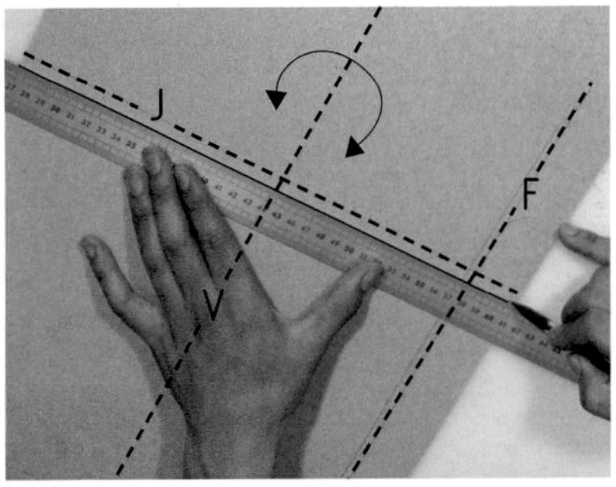

18. Unfold and join up the pencil marks. We have just traced the line of the zip. The front and back sections have now been achieved.

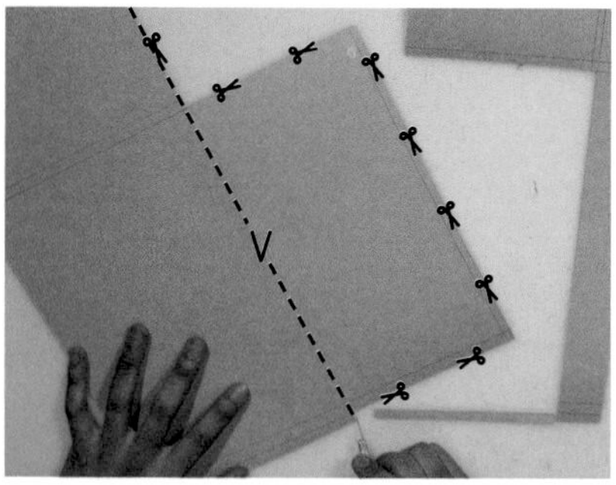

19. Cut out half of the piece stopping short of the V axis.

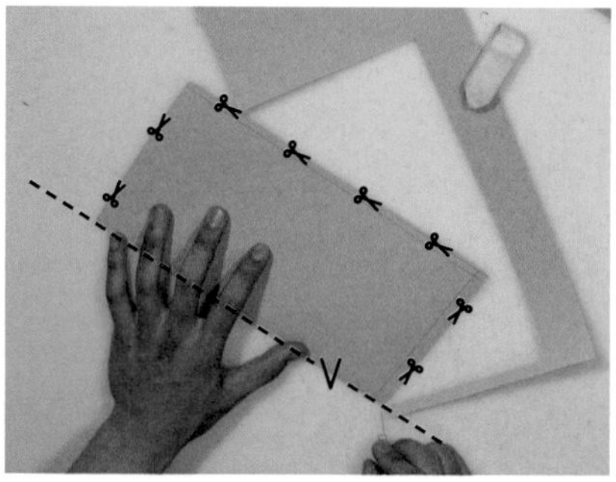

20. Fold and cut out the other half symmetrically.

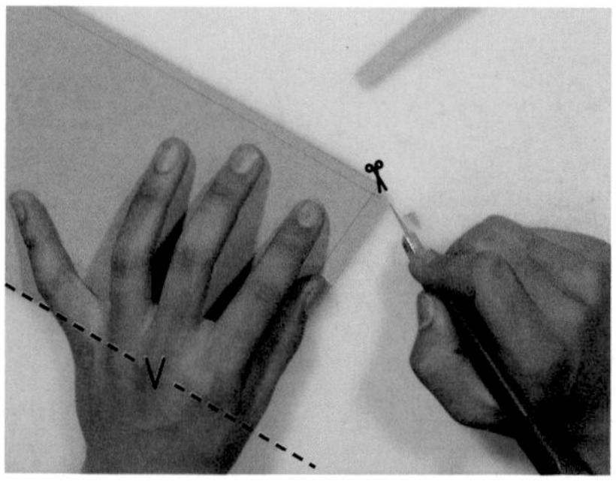

21. Cut the seam at the bottom diagonally as this will help in the assembling and transfer the clipped notches symmetrically onto the side.

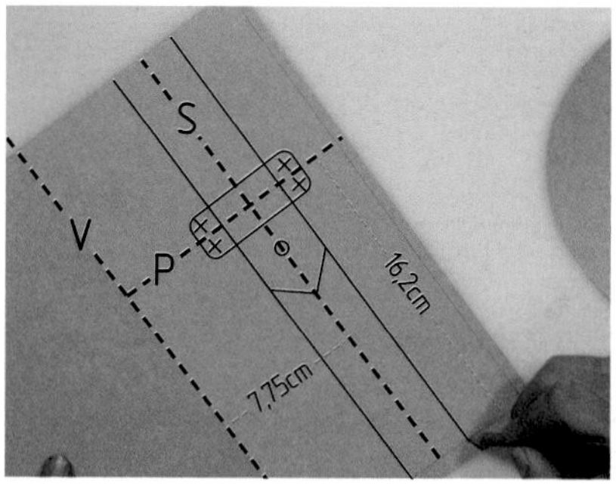

22. Trace the position of the shoulder strap onto the right half of the front pattern. Trace a parallel line the middle of this strap, i.e. 7.5 cm from the middle of the front. We will call this line S. Equally divide the width of the strap and that of the S axis (1.75 cm i.e. 3.5 cm/2). To mark off the height of the strap, trace a line perpendicular to axis S at 16.2 cm from line G of the bottom front. Trace this line P from Axis S up to the side of the front. On the S axis, place a point 13 cm from line G of the front. This reference mark corresponds to the position of the handle fixings.

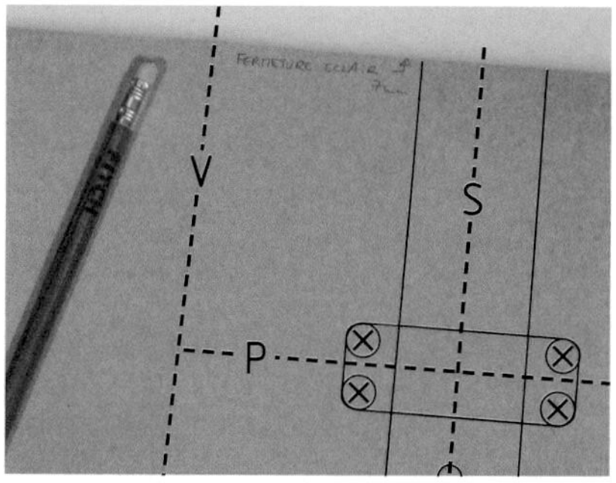

23. On each side of line P, we divide symmetrically the measurement of the height of the fastening tab : i.e. 1 cm above and below for a tab which is 2 cm high. We also divide symmetrically the measurement of the width of the tab on both sides of the S axis, i.e. 3 cm each side for a tab which is 6 cm wide. To curve the angles of the fastening tab, trace a circle 1 cm diameter at tangents to each angle of the tab. The centre of each circle corresponds to the position of the rivets. On the front pattern, make an awl mark for the position of the four tab rivets, the fixing points for the handle on the front, as well as the angles which define where the shoulder strap is placed. Fold in two along the V axis and transfer these points symmetrically onto the other half. When assembling, we will transfer these points onto the felt sections in order to define the exact position of these items on the front and back pieces.

Side pattern

We are now going to make the pattern for the side which will be used for both sides.

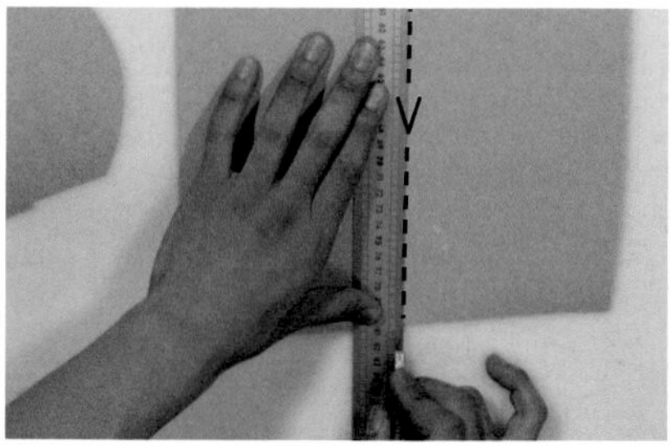

1. Cut a piece of card about 20 x 20 cm for a side measuring 16.5 cm diameter.. Score the vertical axis V in the middle of the pattern using a ruler and a cutter.

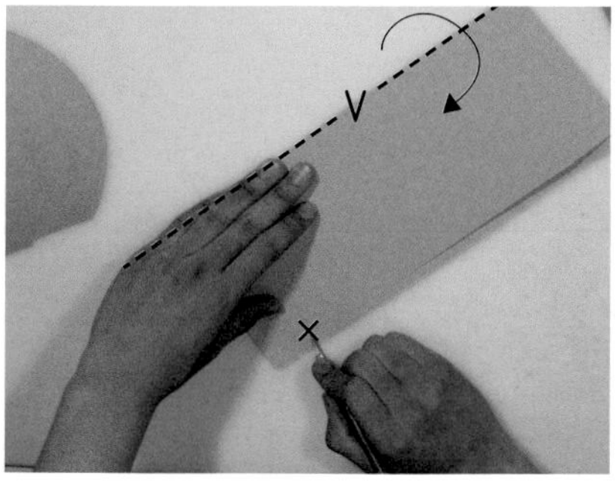

2. Fold the card along the V axis and mark off with a cutter 2 cm situated at the bottom right of the V axis on the side of the card.

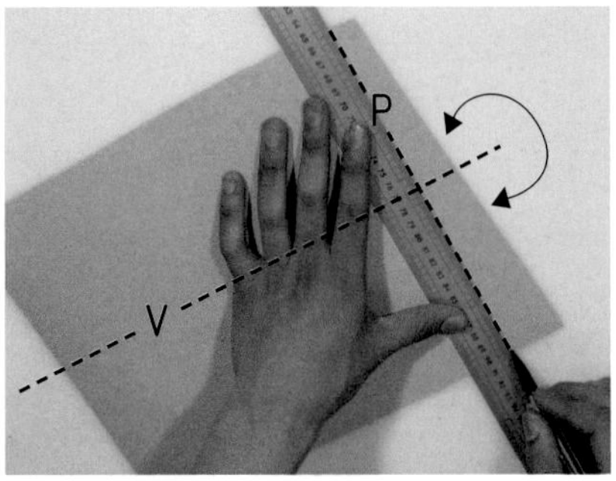

3. Unfold and join the two marks with a pencil line. This will make the bottom line of the pattern. We will call this line P.

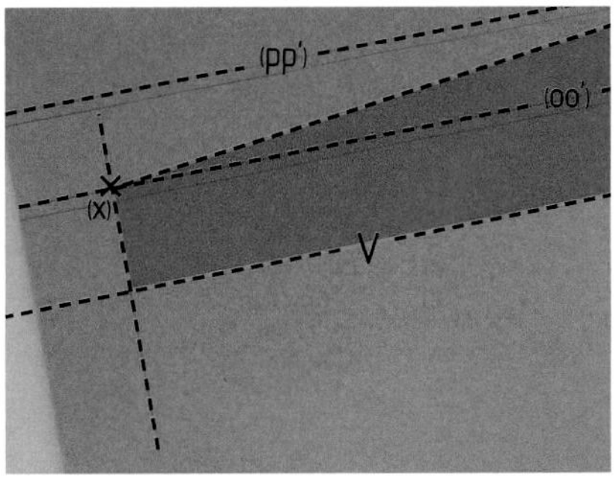

4. Fold the card again along the V axis. Fold the template in two along the V axis. Place the template onto the card lining up precisely the V axes of the template and the card as well as line D, on the bottom of the template, and line P on the card. Cut the card with a cutter following the outline of the template.

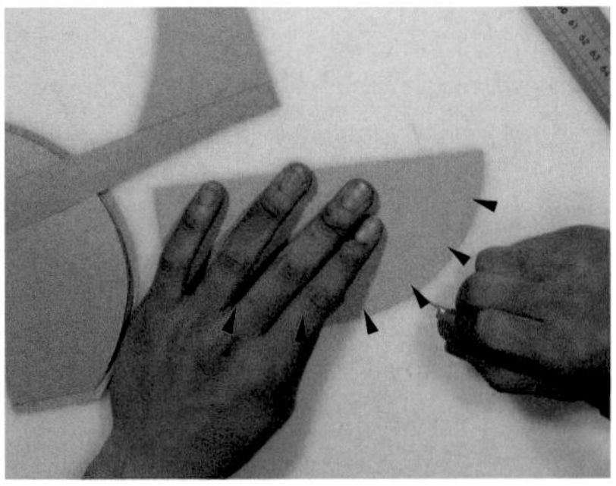

5. Transfer the notches of the template onto the pattern using a cutter. Press fairly hard so as to pierce through the two thicknesses of card.

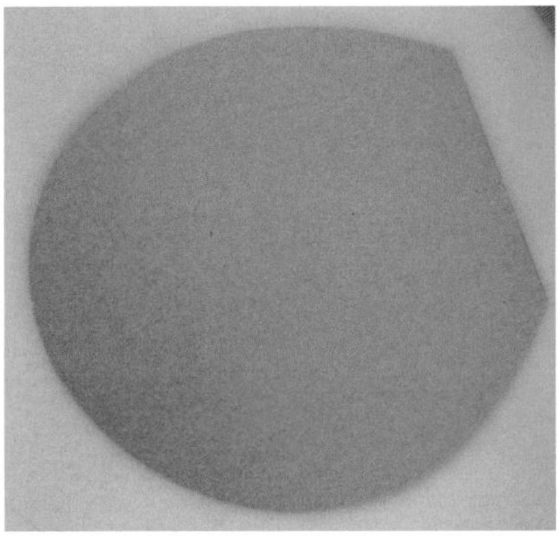

6. The pattern of the sides is now finished.

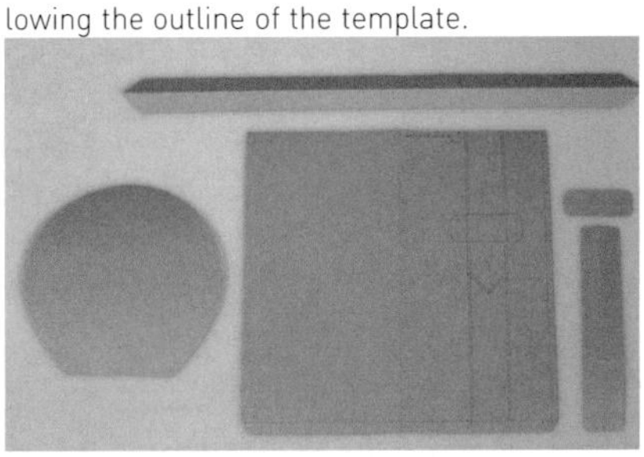

7. Using the front pattern, construct the patterns for the fastening tabs, straps and handles of the bags. The pattern consists of a piece for the front and back, and a piece for the two sides. To make the pattern for the straps and fastening tabs, use an awl to transfer the marks of the front pattern onto the pieces of card and cut. For the handle pattern, cut a strip of card 47 x 3.5 cm. On this strip, transfer the drawing of the ends as it is appears on the front pattern, remembering to mark the fixing point.

Cutting

The prototype of this bag is going to be made in felt. The choice of felt is important: a sewing machine needle is likely to break if a thick felt is used, however, one that is too supple will not give enough rigidity to the bag. We have opted to use a felt of 0.3 cm thickness.

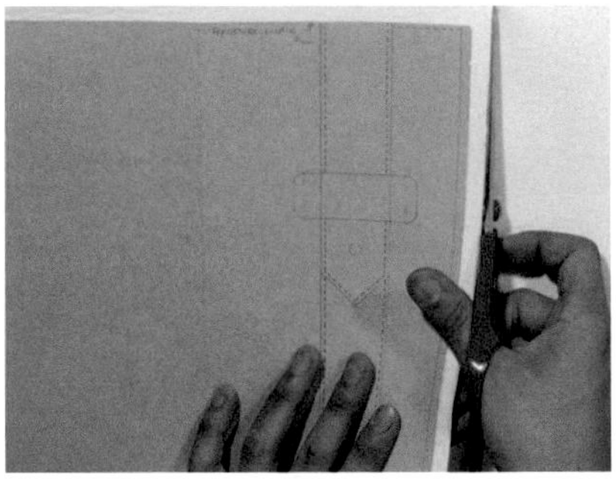

1. Place the pattern onto the felt. Using scissors, cut a piece slightly bigger than the measurements of the front pattern.

2. Place a weight on top of the pattern in order to hold the felt in place.

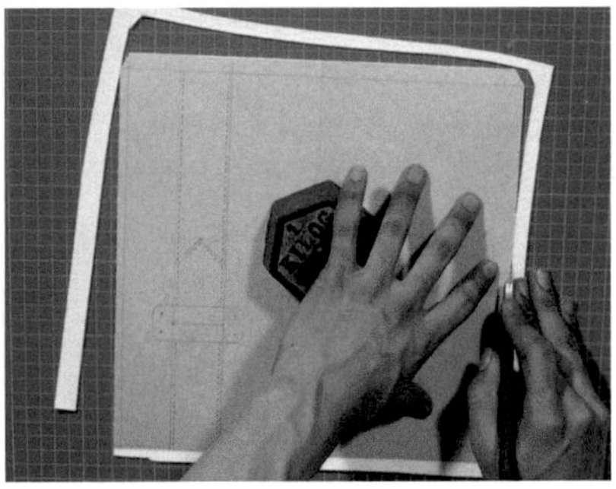

3. Cut the felt with a cutter carefully following the pattern outline.

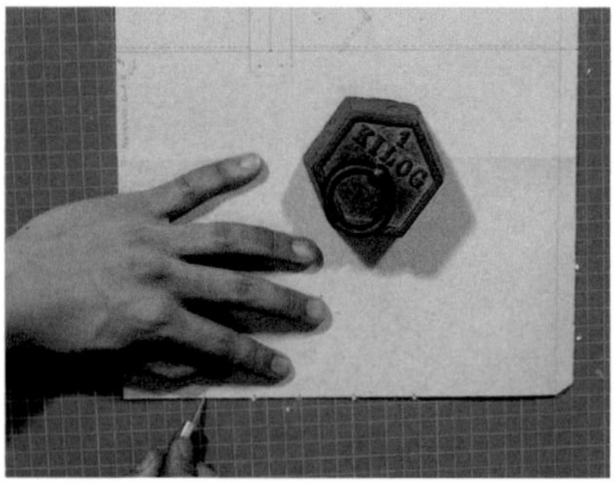

4. Transfer the pattern notches onto the piece of felt.

5. Use a fabric pencil to mark the position of the rivets and strap outlines.

6. Use a fabric pencil to mark the position of the handles.

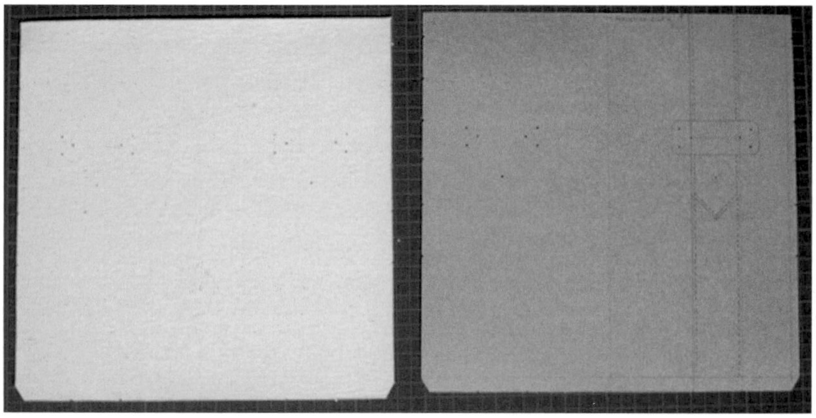

7. On the piece of felt we can see the notches and marks that we have just transferred.

8. Repeat the process for cutting the back, as this piece is identical to the front.

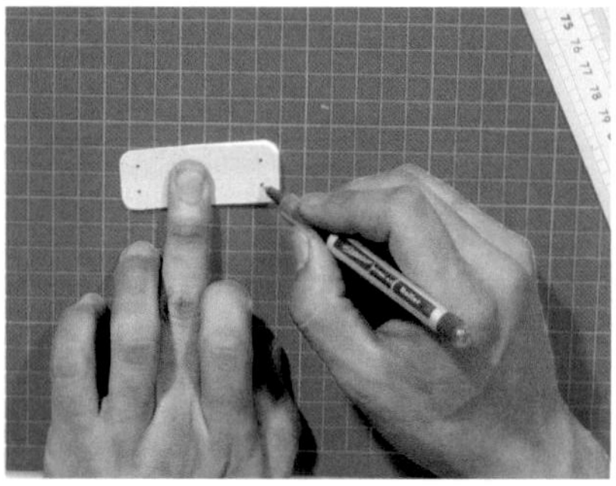

9. Cut out the small pieces for the tabs, like here, taking care to transfer each time the position of the rivets with a fabric pencil onto the felt.

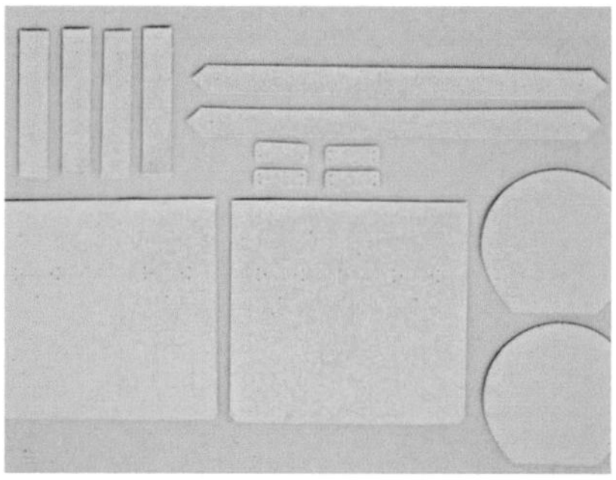

10. We have just cut out a front, back, two sides, four straps, four tabs and two handles.

Assembling

This bag is sewn first, then reversed. We will assemble the different pieces inside-out, then reverse the bag so that the stitches are on the inside, therefore invisible.

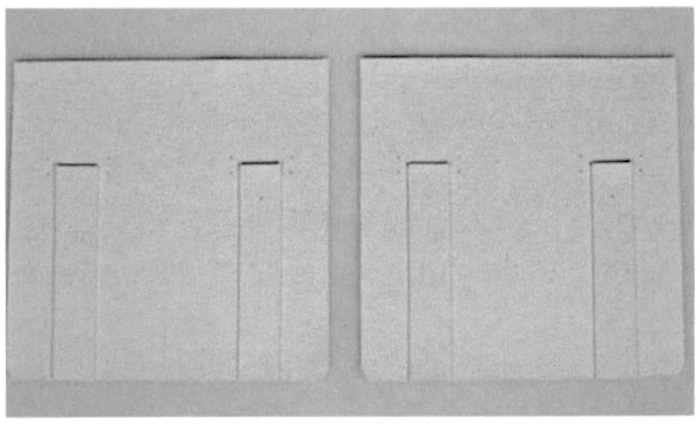

1. Stick the straps onto the front and the back so that they do not move once the sewing starts. The rubber-based glue, is used by shoe makers; it can normally be found in DIY shops.

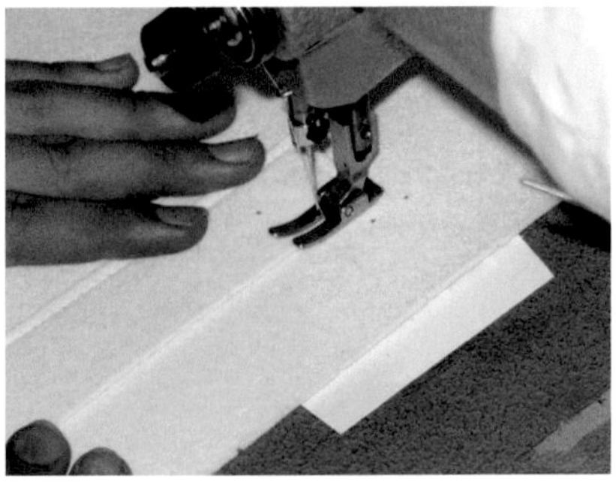

2. Machine sew the straps to the front and the back, using a 0.3 cm length stitch. Work slowly so that a rectangular over-stitch can be made.

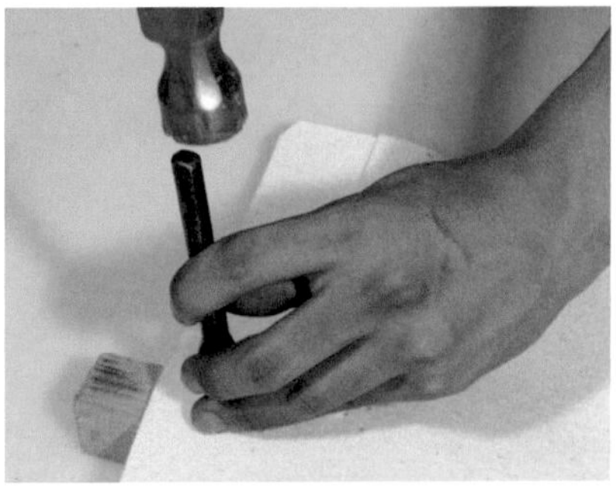

3. Make a hole using a hole pincher for the position of the rivets on the front and back pieces.

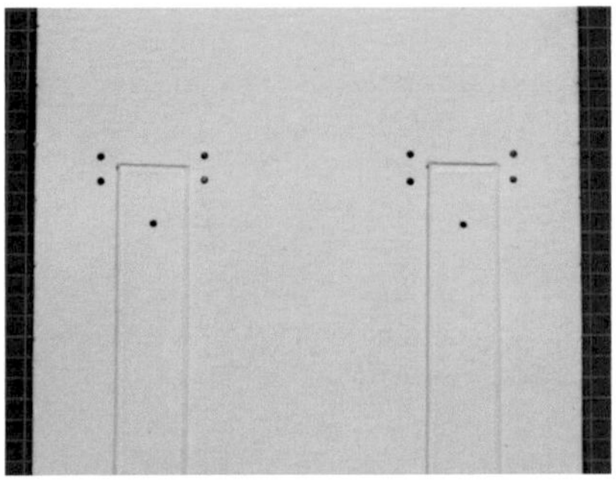

4. Here we have eight rivet holes and two fastening studs for the handles.

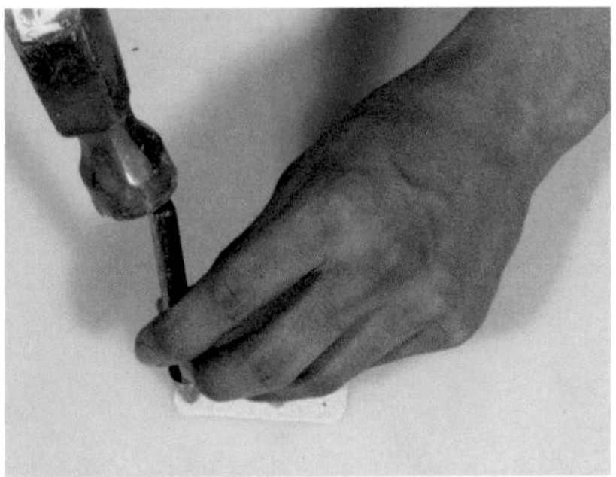

5. Make a hole using the hole puncher for the position of the rivets for the four attachment tabs.

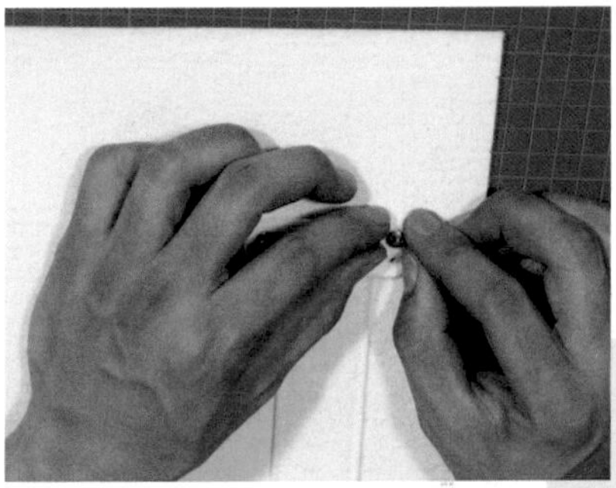

6. Fix the attachment tabs to the front and the back with the rivets.

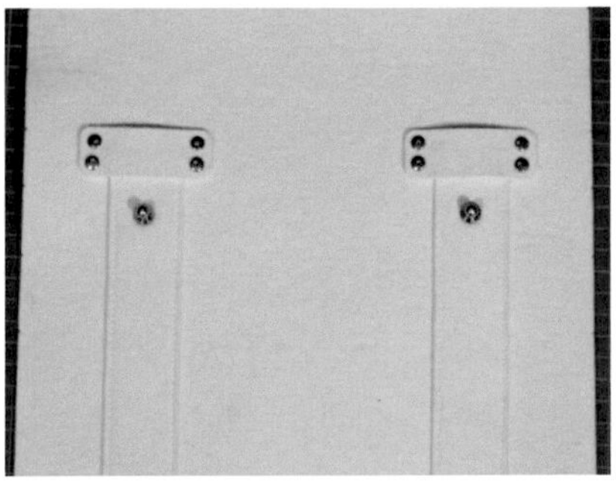

7. Screw the handle fastening studs to the front and back.

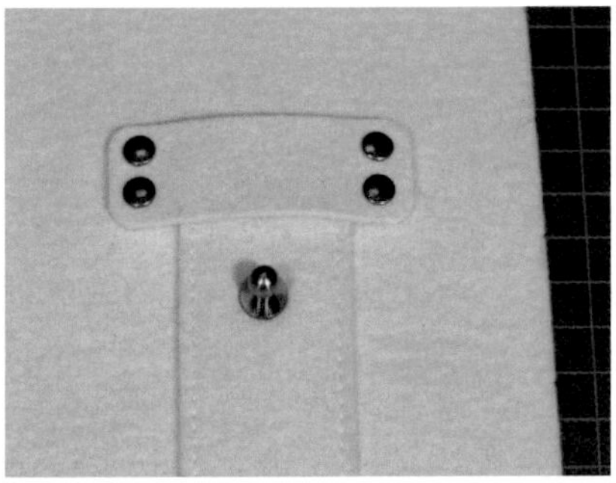

8. Here we have the rivets and studs secured to the front and the back.

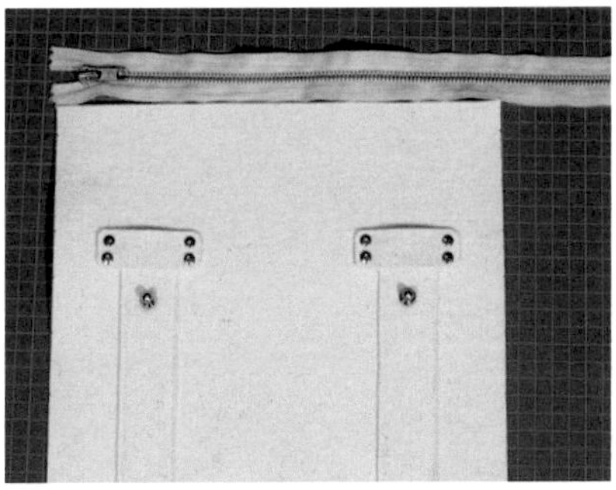

9. The front and the back are now ready to be assembled.

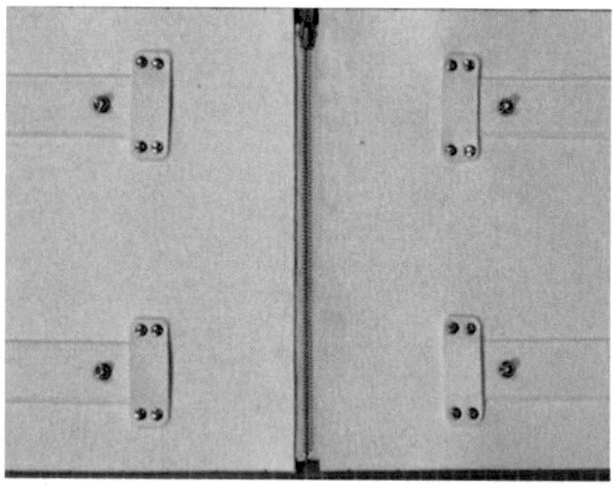

10. Stick the zip to the front and the back

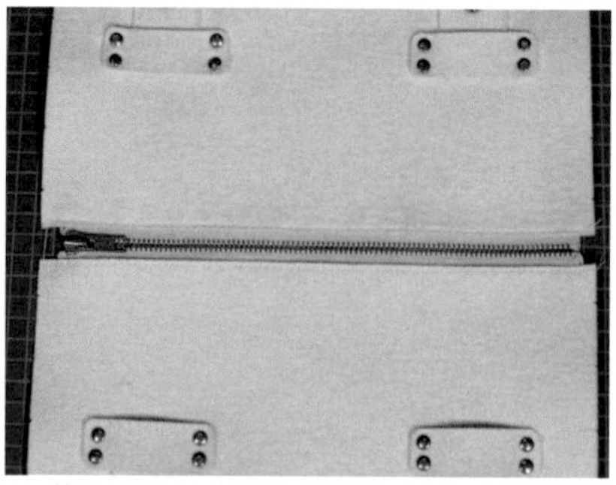

11. Secure the zip by machine sewing.

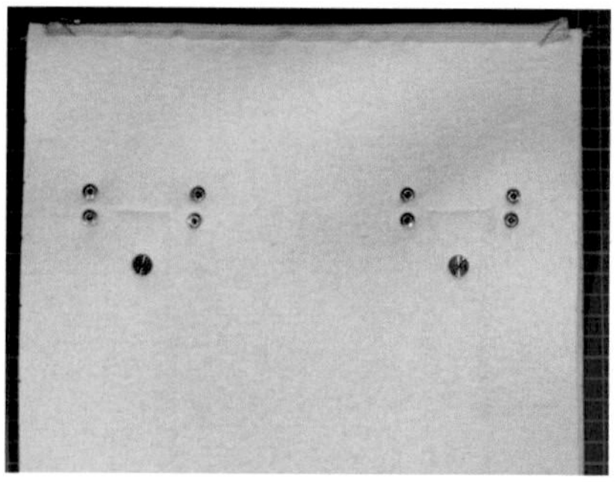

12. Fold the front and the back, right side to right side, to assemble the two pieces back to front.

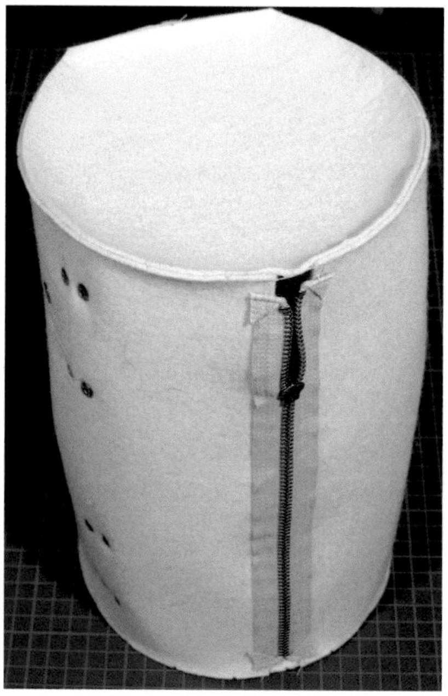

13. From this point on we work on the reverse side of the bag. Stick a side piece to the front and back, right side to right side. Use the notches to assemble the pieces together.

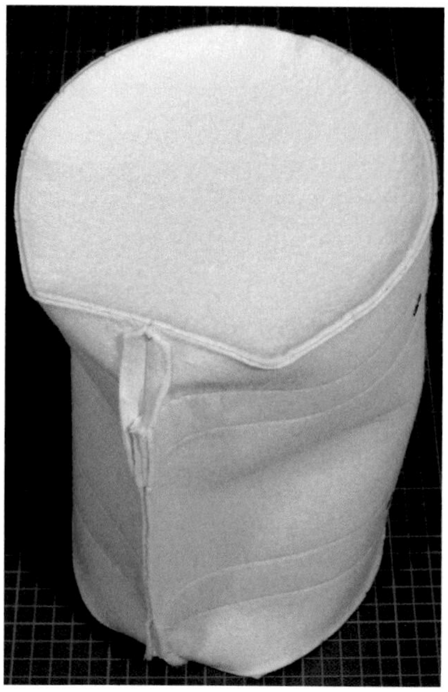

14. Before sticking the second side, open the zip slightly, otherwise it will be difficult to open it once the bag is reversed. Stick on the second side piece remembering to use the notches to position it.

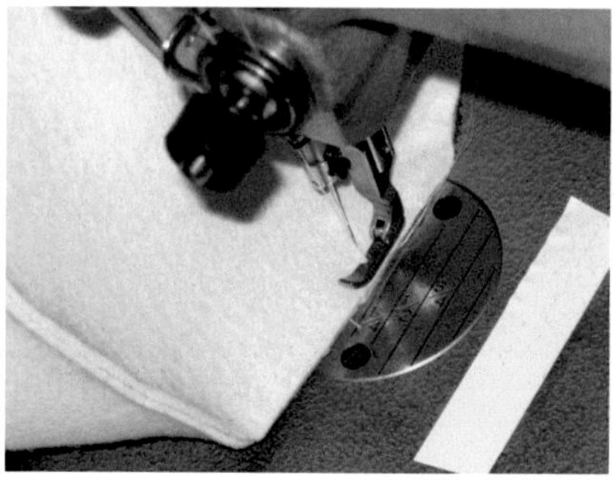

15. Sew the sides to the front and the back; choose a claw foot for the zip fastening. Place the claw foot onto the outside edge of the seam.

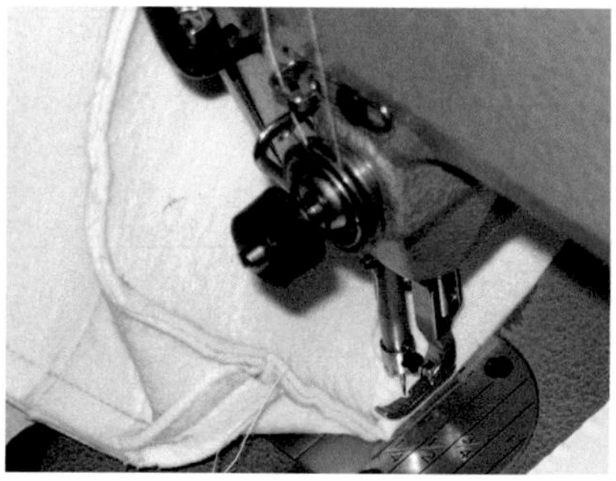

16. The angle formed by the bottom of the bag and the curve is the most delicate part to sew. When the needle gets to this angle, it must be sewn into the seam. Lift up the claw foot and pivot the piece, then lower the claw foot and continue sewing. For the difficult parts, control the speed of the machine by manually moving the wheel.

17. The machine sewing is completed.

18. The seam and the zip have been left slightly opened.

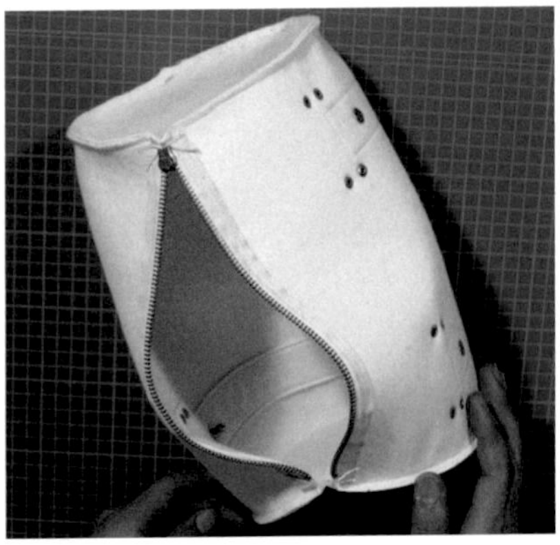

19. All that remains to be done is to open the zip and reverse the bag again. Flatten the seams with pliers and a folder.

20. Fold the handles in two, right side to right side. Then stick and sew them together to form a rib, stopping 8 cm from each end. Slide the handles through the attachment tabs and fix them to the front and the back. The bag is now finished.

21. Side view of the bag.

22. Front view.

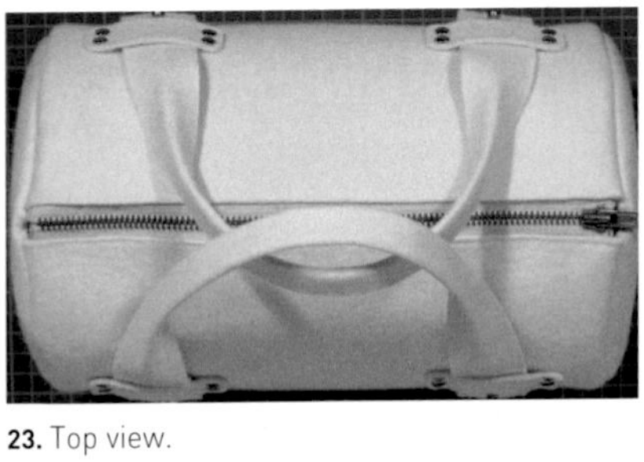

23. Top view.

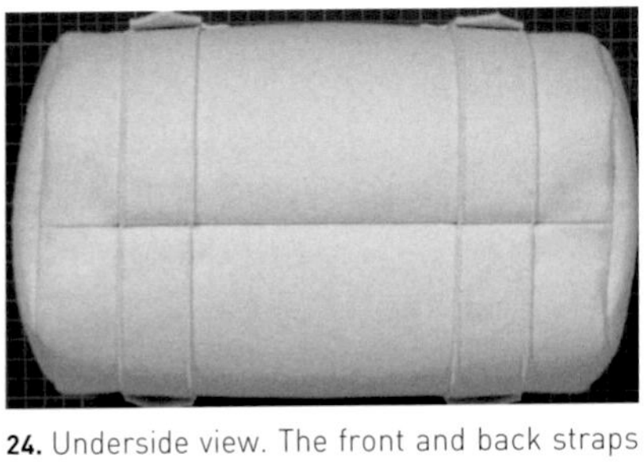

24. Underside view. The front and back straps have been incorporated into the seam between the front and the back.

Making felt prototypes

2 - Tote bag

Here is another example of a tote bag. With this bag we are going to make each side and half of the base from one piece, without a seam. The two sides and the two halves of the base, are assembled by a seam underneath the bag. There are five principal pieces: a front and an identical back, two sides incorporating the half base and a handle fixed to the sides, which allows the bag to be carried from the shoulder. Finally, the trimming strips, which are top-stitched onto the front and the back, are incorporated in the seam of the sides and the bottom. The technical difficulty of this bag is in the construction of the sides, which are larger at the base of the bag then at the top.

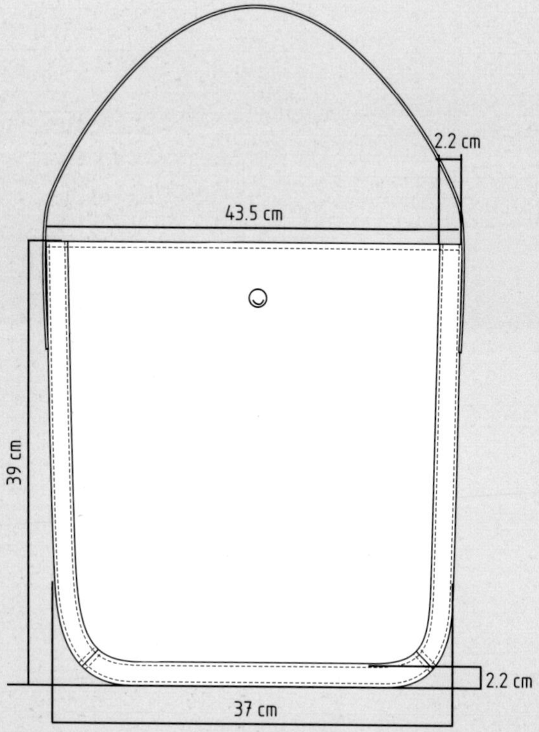

Technical drawing of the front and the back.

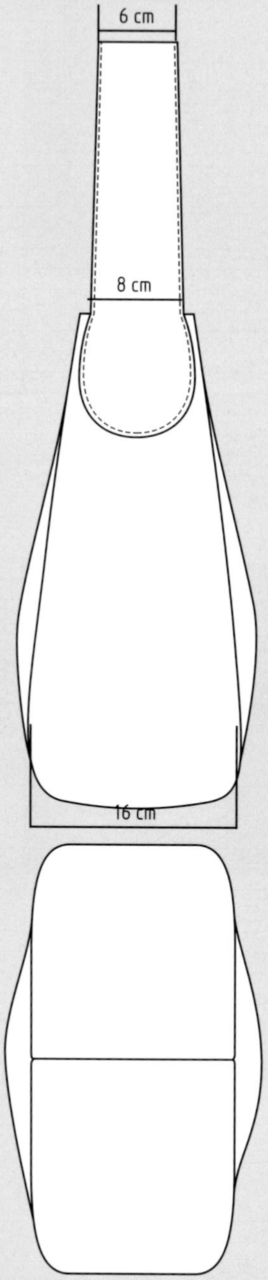

Technical drawing of the side and bottom of the bag

BOTTOM VIEW

TOP VIEW

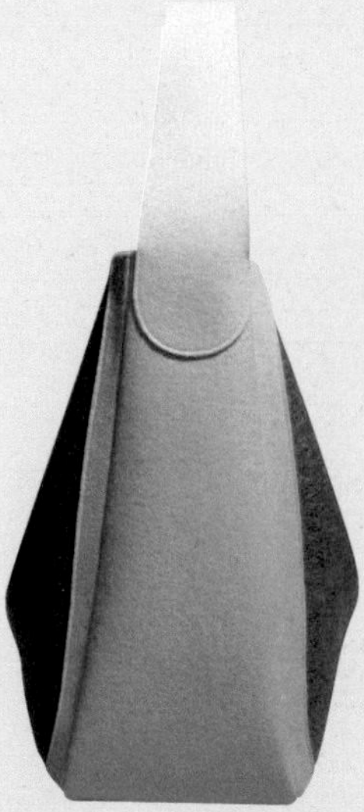

SIDE VIEW

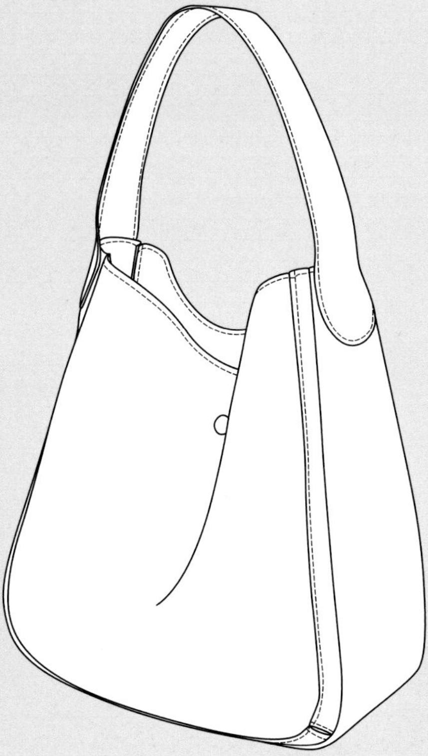

THREE-QUARTER VIEW DRAWING

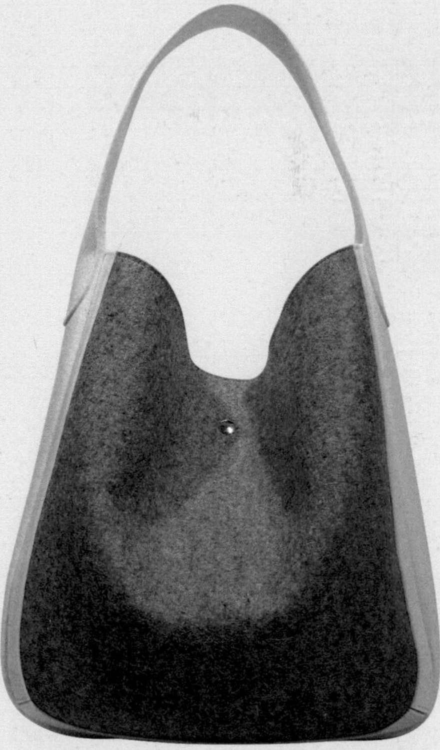

FRONT VIEW.

Front and back template

This template which we will call 'front' will be used for the back as well as the two pieces are identical.

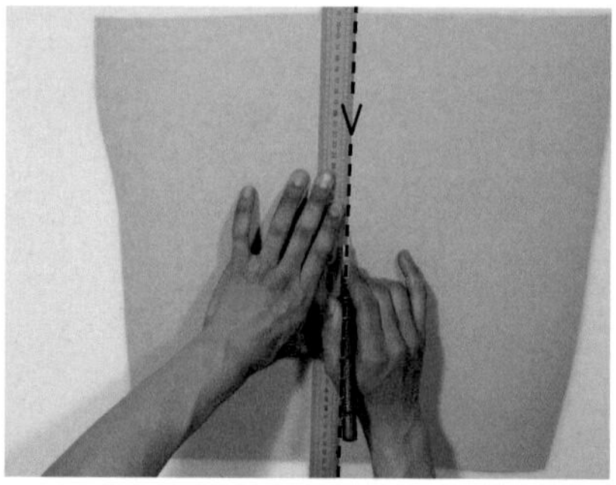

1. Cut a piece of card slightly bigger than the front and back measurements, i.e. about 50 x 50 cm for a front which measures 43.5 x 39 cm. Pressing lightly, score the vertical V axis of the template using a ruler and cutter, so that the piece can be easily folded in two.

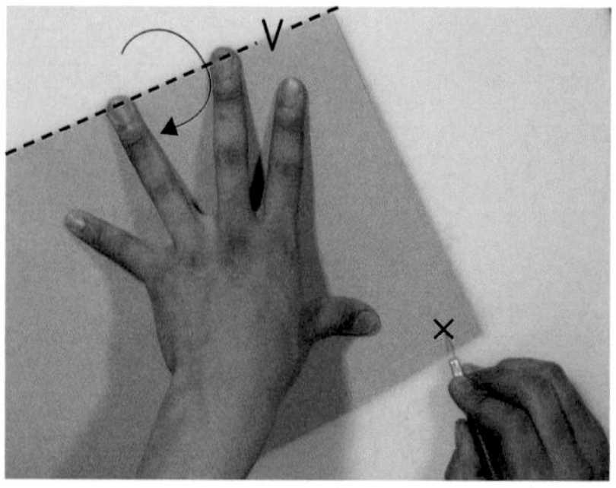

2. To trace the bottom line of the template, fold the card in two along its V axis, and using the cutter, make a mark at the bottom left hand side of the V axis. Press quite hard so that the two thicknesses are marked.

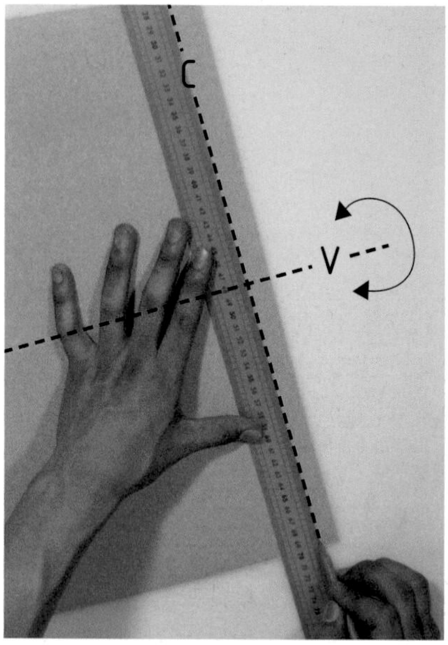

3. Unfold the card: we now have two perfectly symmetrical points. Join these two points with a pencil. We have now traced the bottom of the template which will call C.

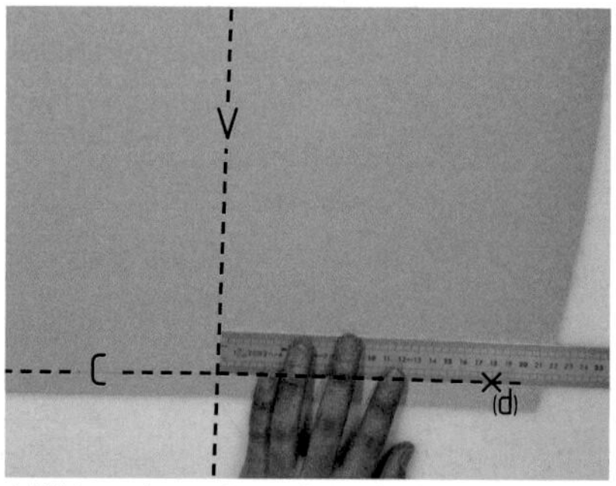

4. With a ruler and pencil, mark off on line C, half the width of the bottom of the front, i.e. 18.5 cm (37/2) the right of the V axis. Call this point 'd'.

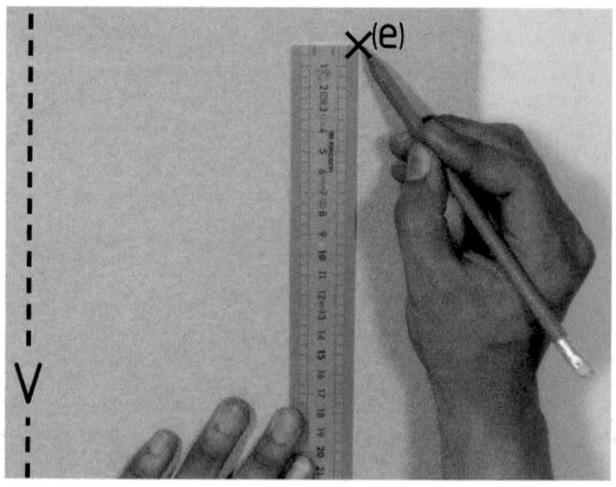

5. To trace the top line of the template, place the ruler perpendicular to point (d). Use pencil to mark the height of the front, i.e. 39 cm from line C. Call this point 'e'.

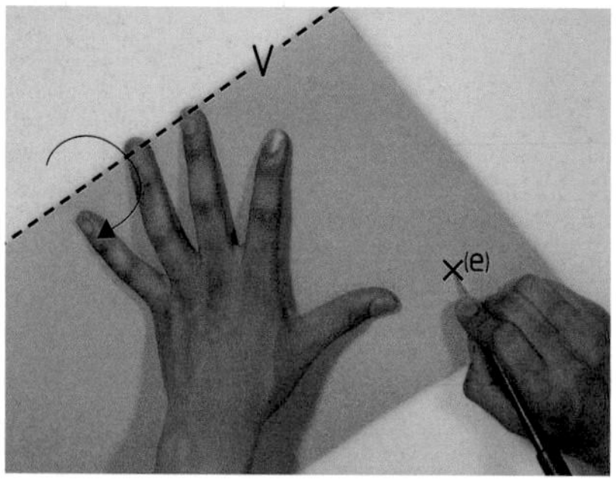

6. Fold the template along the V axis and transfer with the cutter point (e) onto the other half of the template.

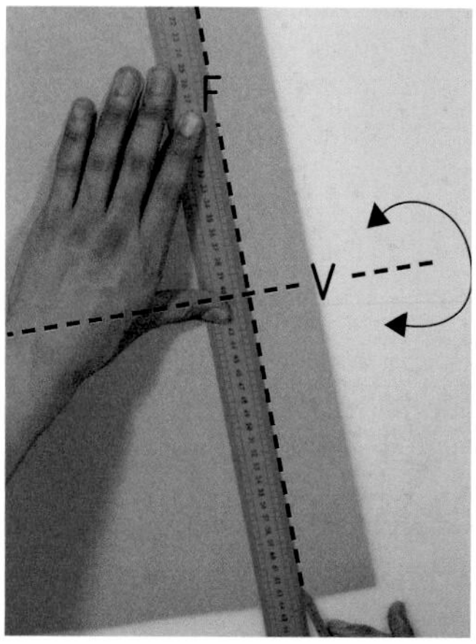

7. Unfold and use a pencil to join up the two cutter marks making the top line of the template. We will call this line 'F'.

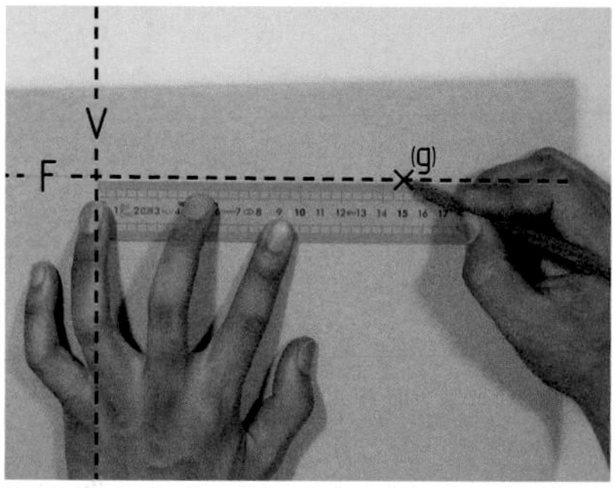

8. Unfold. On line 'F' on the right-hand side of the V axis, measure half the width of the height i.e. 21.75 cm (43.5 cm /2) and put a pencil mark; this is point 'g'.

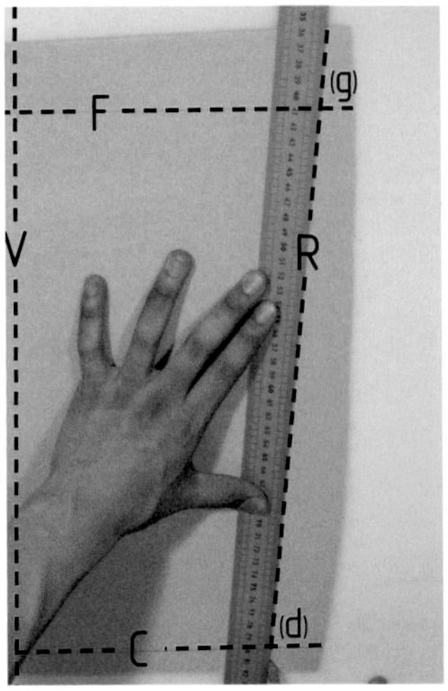

9. Use a pencil to trace the side line of the template joining up points (g) and (d). Call this line 'R'.

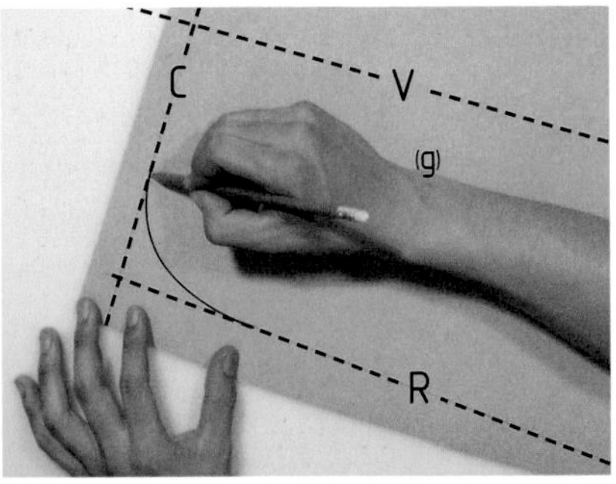

10. Draw a rounded pencil line on the base of the template. Use a French curve to trace a softer curve. We have now traced half the front shape.

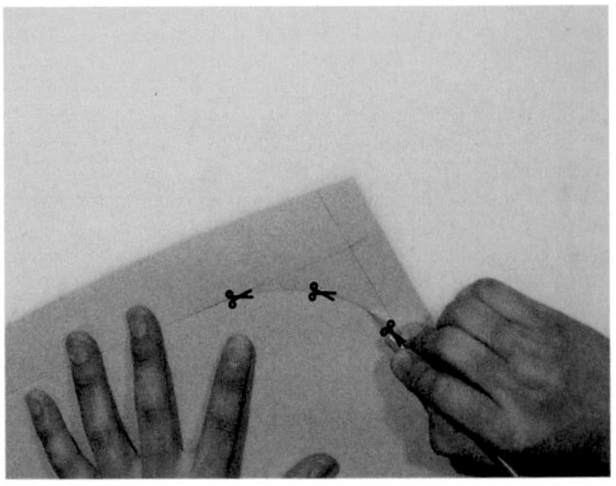

11. We are now going to cut out half of the template using a cutter, or French curve, as a guide.

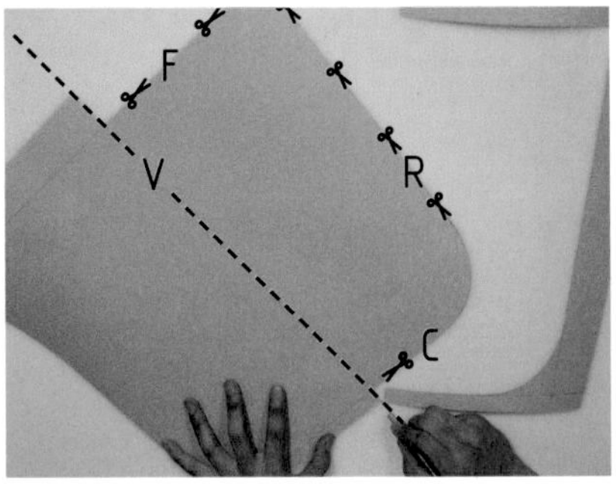

12. Cut around line F starting at the V axis following around line R to line C up to the V axis on the other side. Remove the excess card

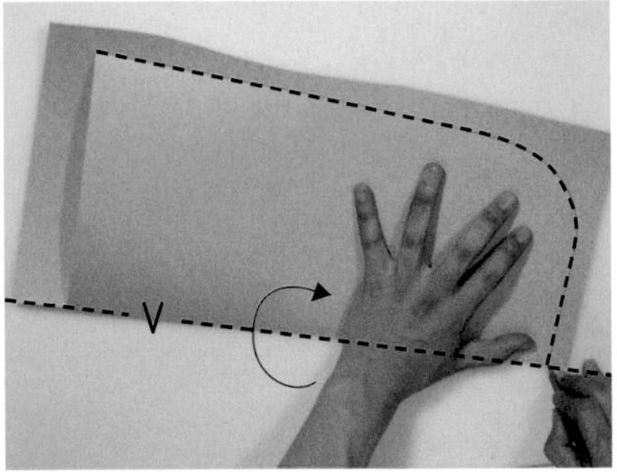

13. Fold the template in two along the V axis and transfer the outline of the cut half using a pencil.

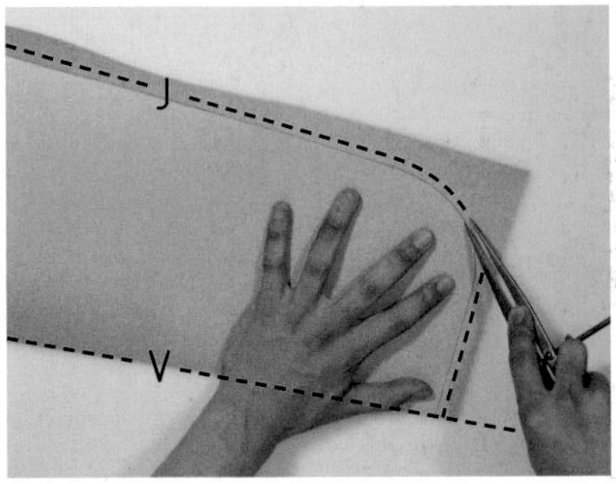

14. With the dividers/compass measure 0.5 cm from this line for the seam allowance onto the second half of the template using the cut side as a guide. This seam line is called 'J'.

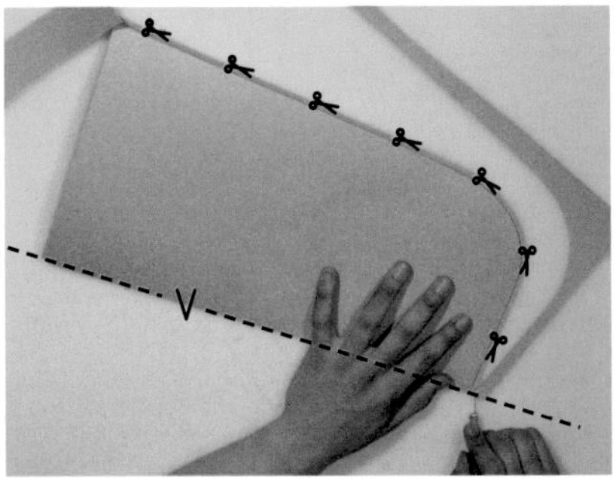

15. Cut along line J using a ruler and cutter for the straight parts. Mark off the curve with a cutter and go over it several times to cut it out.

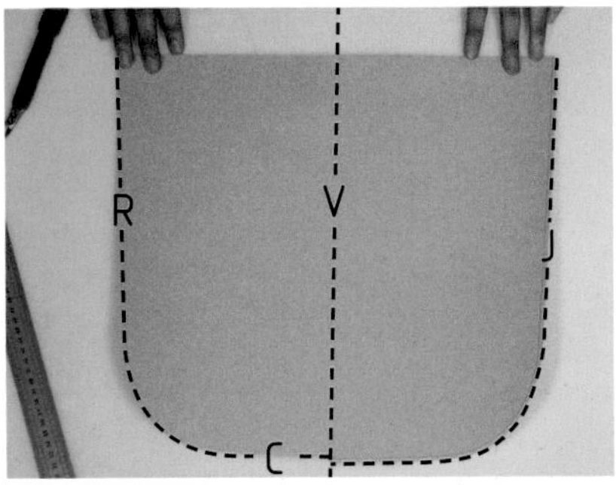

16. Unfold the template and turn it over so that line J is on the left hand side of the template. The front template has now be achieved.

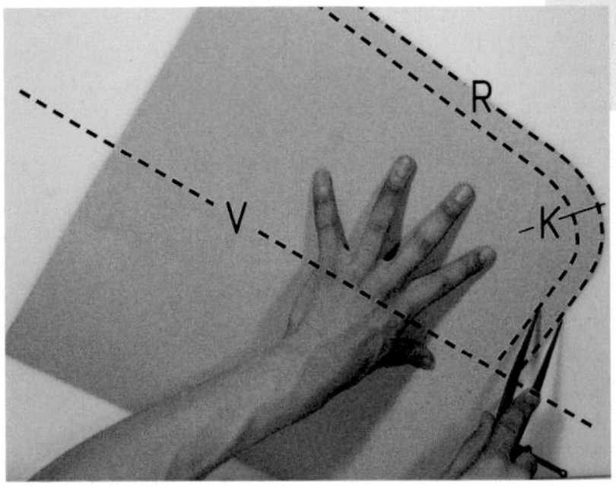

17. Draw the bands of stitching detail onto the right half of the template where there is no seam allowance. With a compass/dividers measure 2.2 cm and trace the width of this band using the outline of the template as a guide. To make it easier and more economical whilst cutting out this band, we are going to fold it in two. Trace out this cutting line 'K' onto half of the curved base.

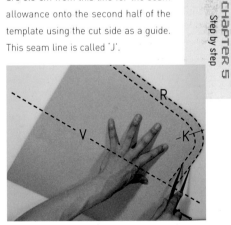

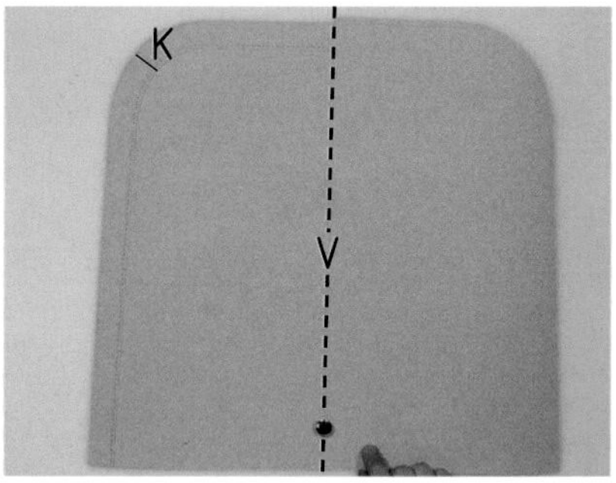

18. Draw the top stitches 0.3 cm from the band. Place the press stud onto the V axis so that the front can be attached to the back, thus marking its position on the template. We now have the front and back sections of the pattern.

Side template

The two sides of this bag are identical. The difficulty in their construction lies in the fact that they start from the centre of the underside of the bag and that they are larger at the bottom than at the top. Before making the pattern for the sides, we must make a template in one piece only which includes the two sides and the base of the bag. We will call this template the 'side template'.

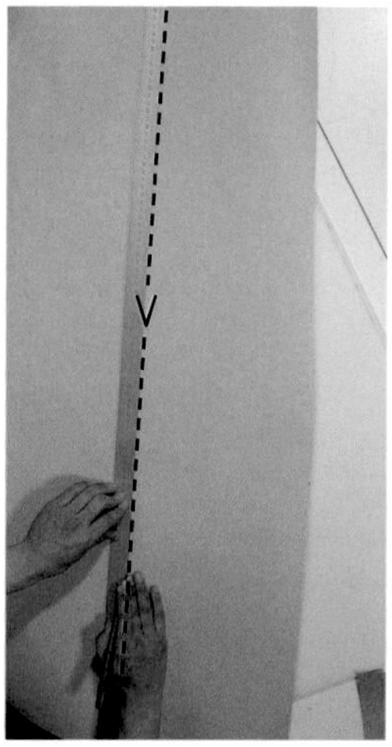

1. Cut a strip of card about 130 x 25 cm for a bag which measures 39 x 37 cm. Use a ruler and cutter to mark off the template's vertical axis V along its length.

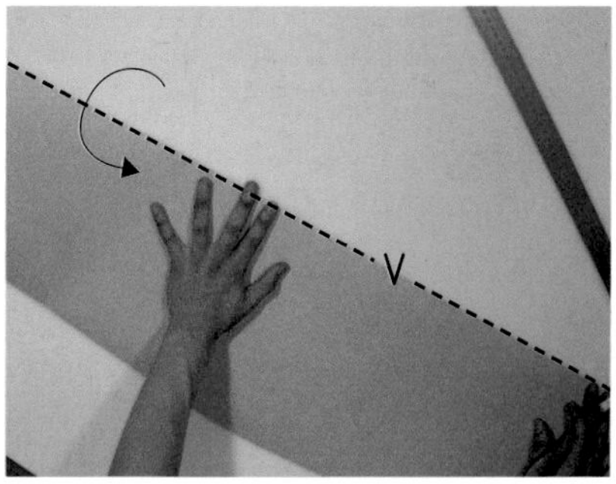

2. Fold in two along the V axis.

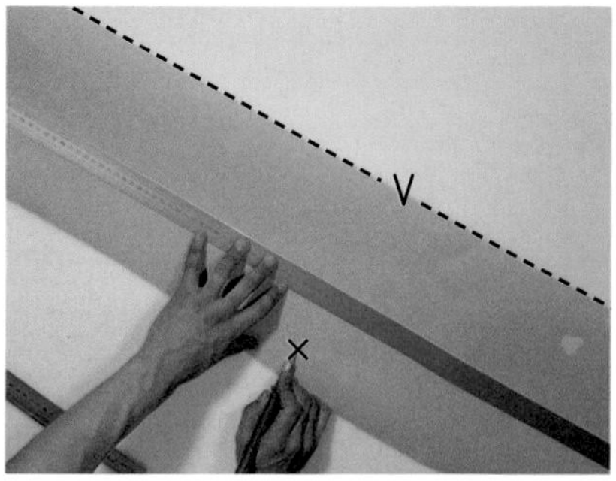

3. Mark the side of the card with the cutter halfway along the strip, i.e. 65 cm for a length measuring 130 cm. Press quite hard to pierce through the two thicknesses of card.

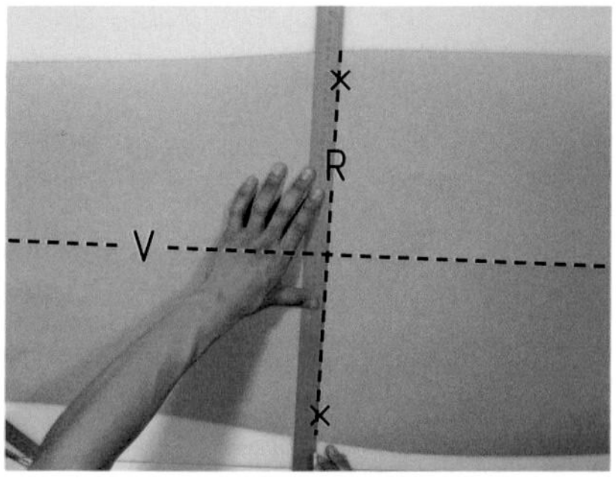

4. Unfold and use a ruler and cutter to join up these two marks which make the template's horizontal axis R .

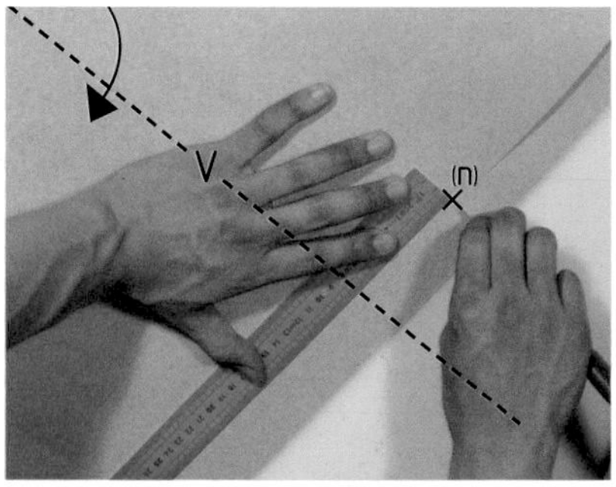

5. Fold the card along the R axis. We are now going to trace four lines parallel to the V axis. On the card's edge, mark point (n) with the cutter, 8 cm above the V axis. Press fairly hard to mark through two thicknesses of card.

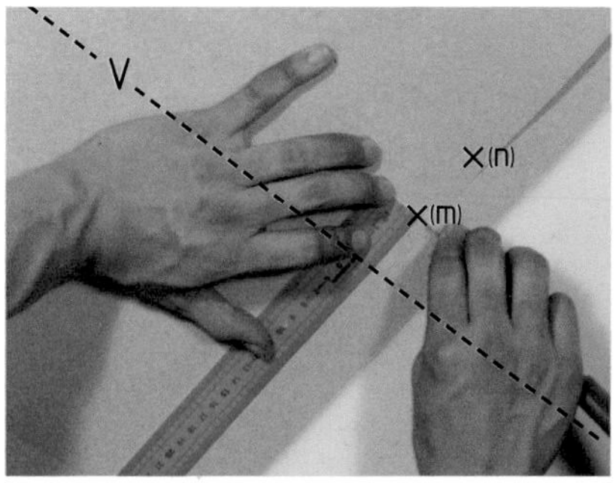

6. Mark a second point (m) with the cutter, 4 cm above the V axis. Press fairly hard to mark through two thicknesses of card.

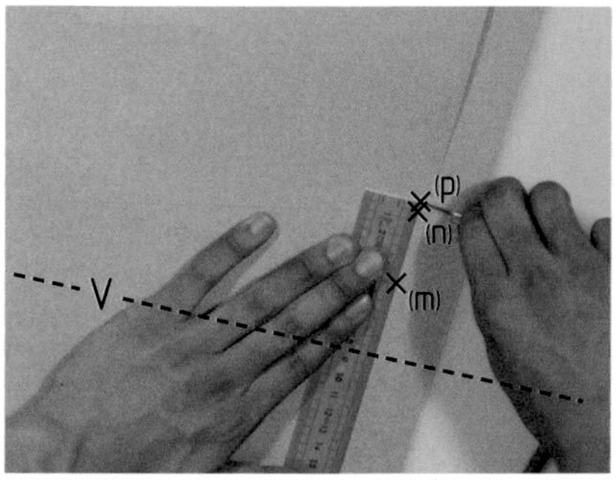

7. Mark a third point (p) with the cutter, 8.5 cm above the V axis. Press fairly hard to mark through the two thicknesses of card.

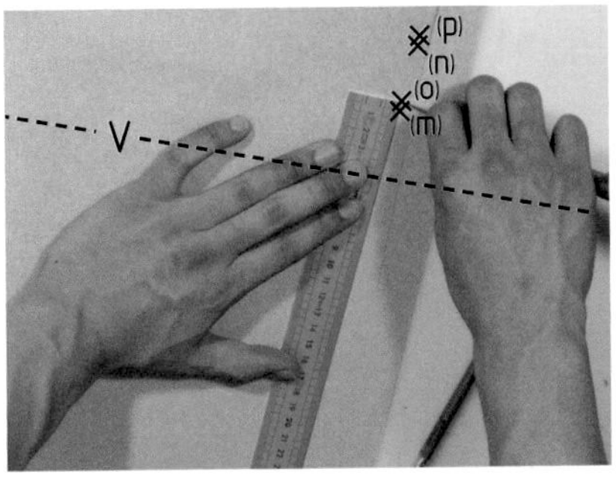

8. Mark a fourth point (o) with the cutter, 4.5 cm above the V axis. Press fairly hard to mark through the two thicknesses of card.

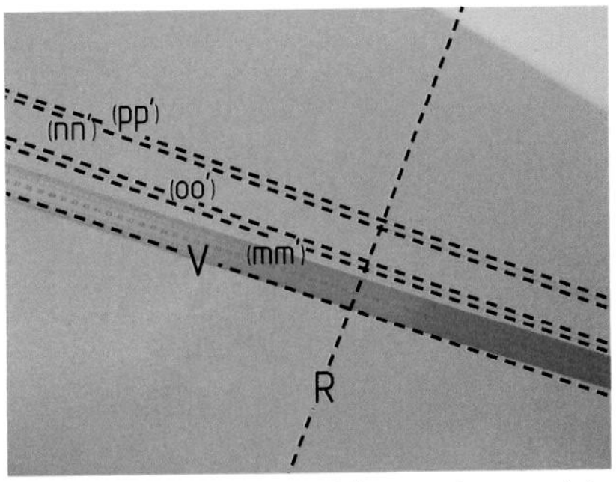

9. Unfold the template. We now have points (m'), (n'), (o'), and (p') symmetrical to points (m), (n), (o), and (p) in relation to the R axis. Join up (m) and (m'), (n) and (n'), (o) and (o'), (p) and (p'). Line (mm') corresponds to half the width of the height of the side. Line (oo') corresponds to its seam allowance. Line (nn') corresponds to half the width of the bottom of the side. Line (pp') corresponds to its seam allowance.

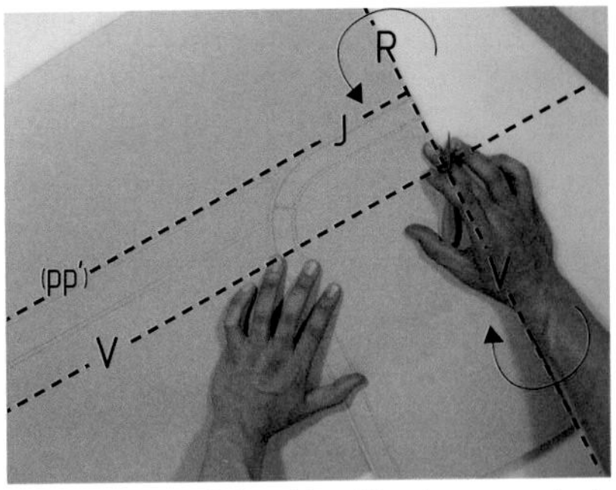

10. The width of the side will get progressively smaller from the bottom towards the top of the bag. The base of the bag has the same width as the bottom of the side. We are now going to construct this shape. To do this, fold the side template in two along its R axis. Fold the front template along its V axis. Place the front template onto the side template carefully aligning the V and R axes of the two pieces. Equally, align line J of the front template with line (pp') of the side template.

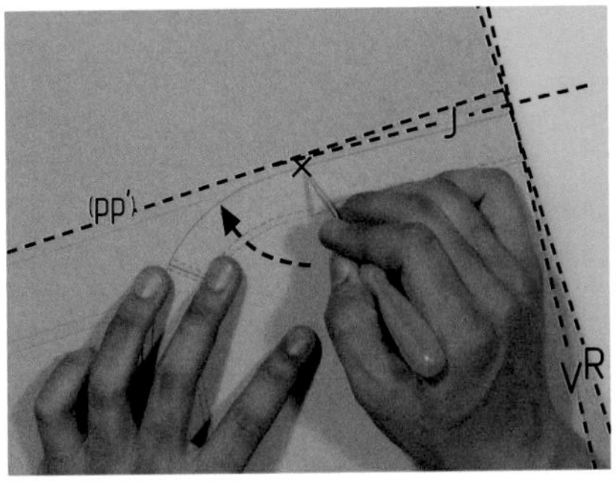

11. Place the awl on line R of the front template, right at the beginning of the curve. Notch this point with a cutter. The awl acts as a pivot point around which we can carefully rotate the folded template, 'rolling' along line J of the front onto line (pp') of the side. This operation helps achieve the exact curve of the bag, as well as the height of the side.

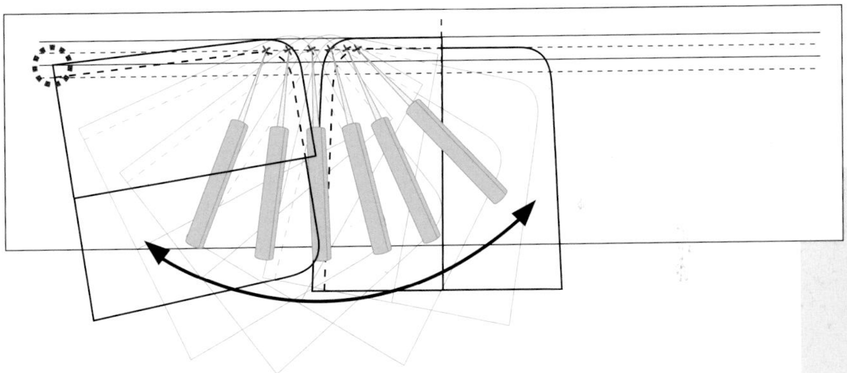

12. On this diagram, we have shown the transfer of the outline of the front template onto the side template.

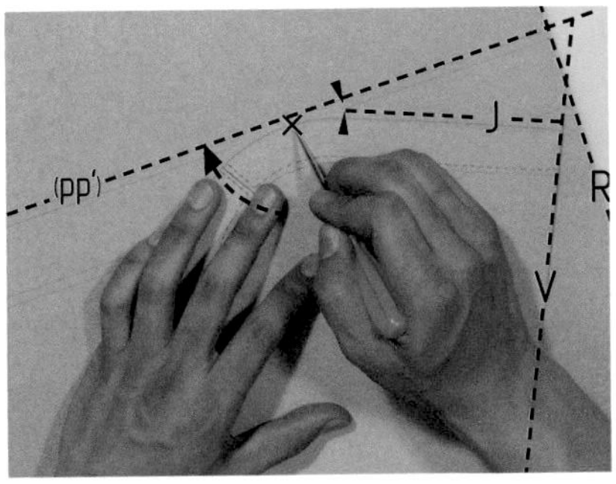

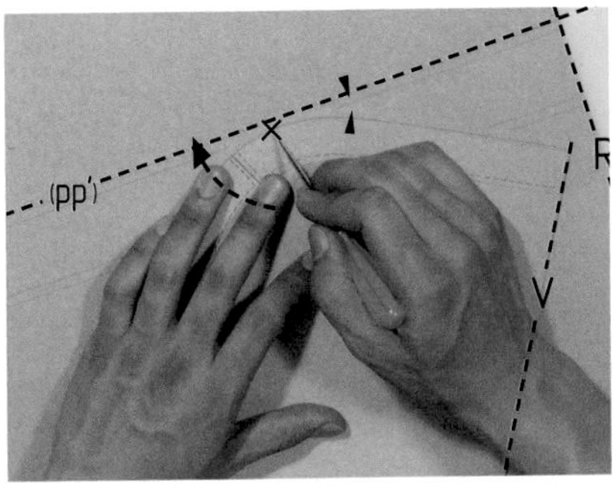

13. Move the awl along line R of the front template so that it 'rolls' on top of line (pp') of the side.

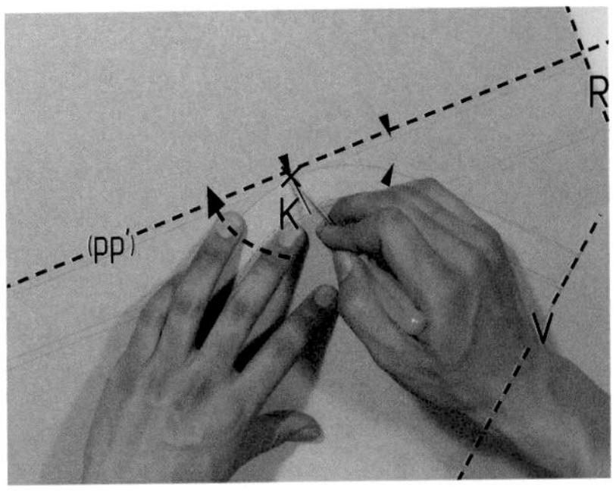

14. Place a notch in the middle of the curve at the top of line K. Press fairly hard in order to mark the front and side pieces.

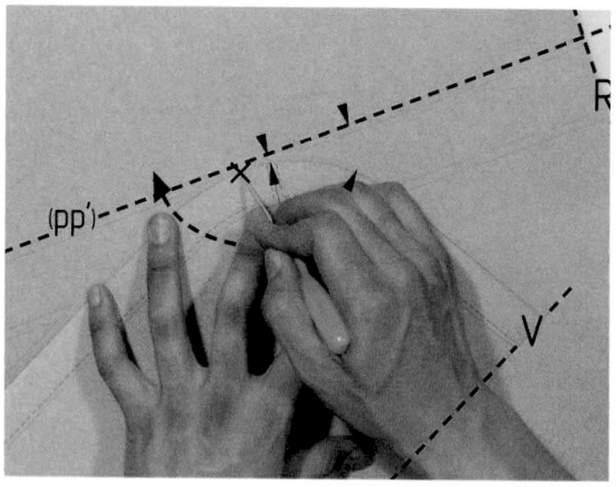

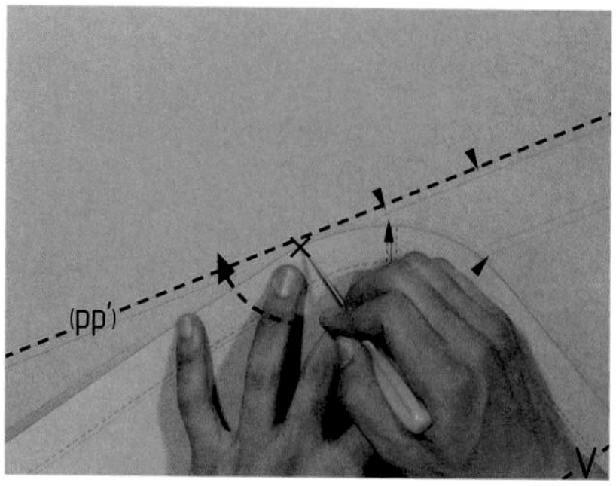

15. Move the awl along line R of the front template so that it 'rolls' on top of line (pp') of the side.

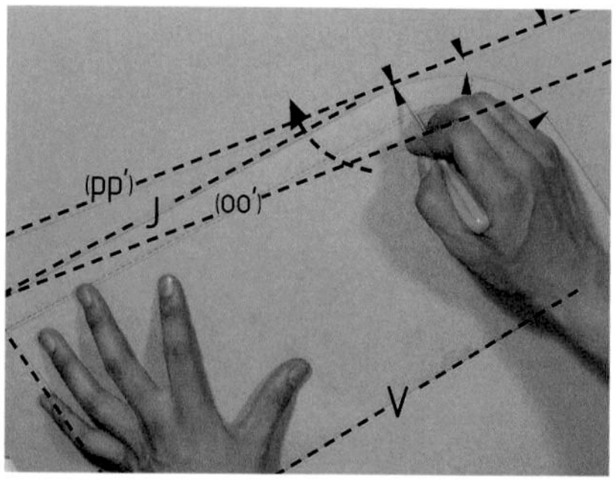

16. Pivot the front template until line J crosses line (oo') of the side template. Notch the end of the front curve. Press quite hard to pierce the thicknesses of card of the front then mark the front and side pieces. This point is important when assembling later.

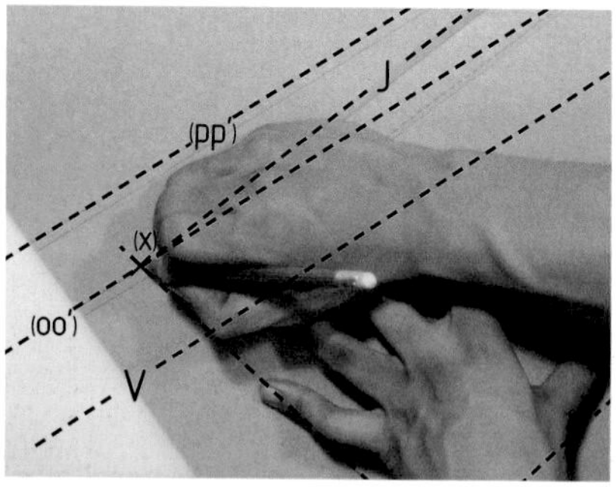

17. Mark with a pencil the intersection of lines J and (oo'). This point (x) determines the exact height of the side template.

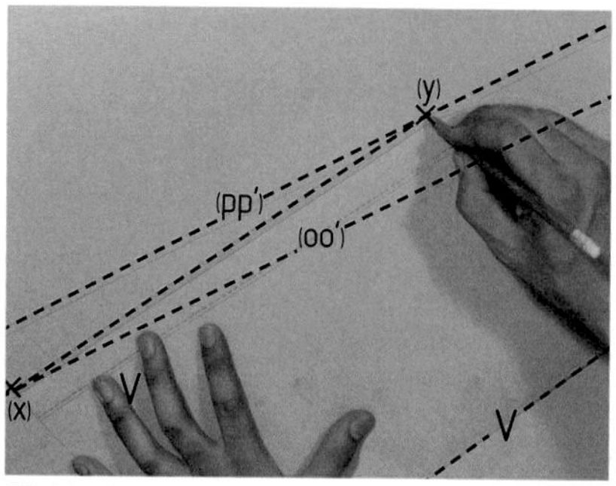

18. Mark with a pencil the end of the front template's curve on line (pp') of the side. Call this point (y). Use a pencil to join points (x) and (y) using the front template as a guide.

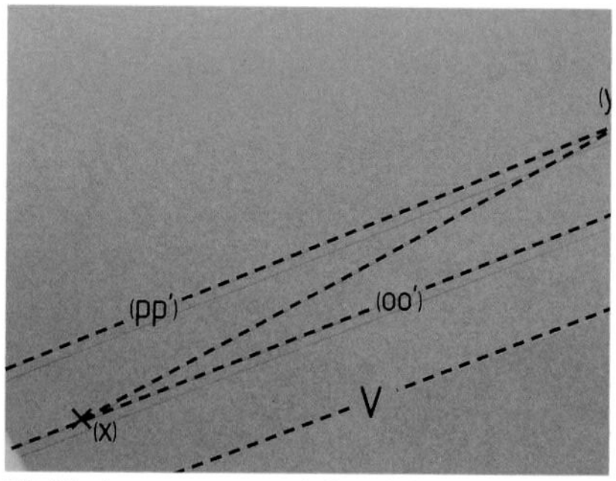

19. We have now traced the shape of the side.

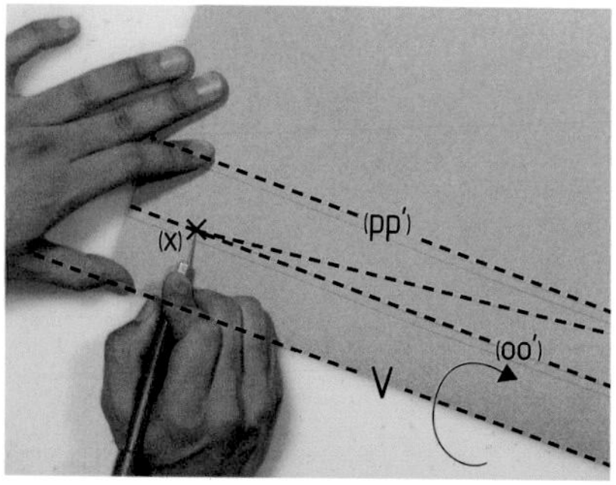

20. Unfold the side template and fold it along its V axis. With a cutter, transfer point (x) symmetrically onto the other half of the template.

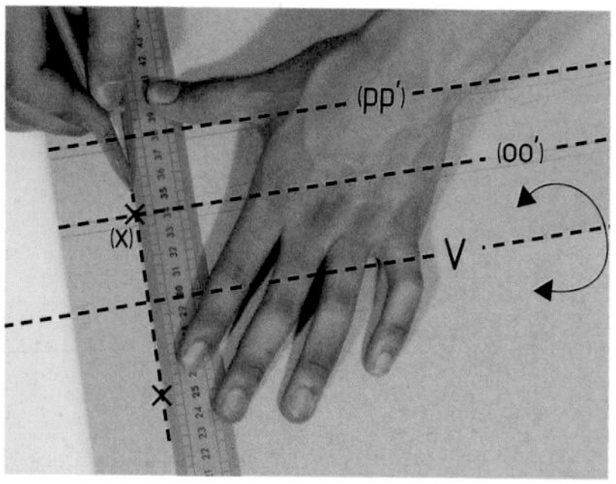

21. Unfold and join the two marks with a pencil. We now have the top line of the side.

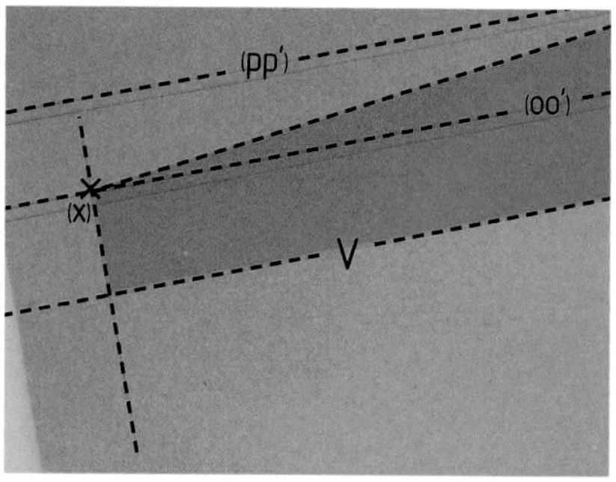

22. We have drawn a quarter of the side template shape.

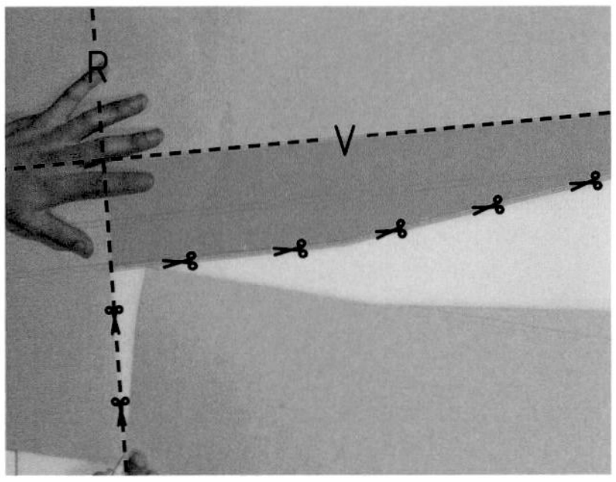

23. Cut out this quarter of the template.

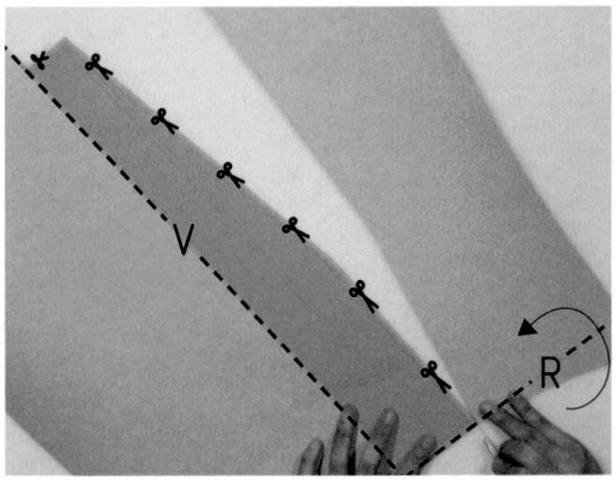

24. Fold the template in two along the R axis and cut it symmetrically, copying the outline of the first quarter.

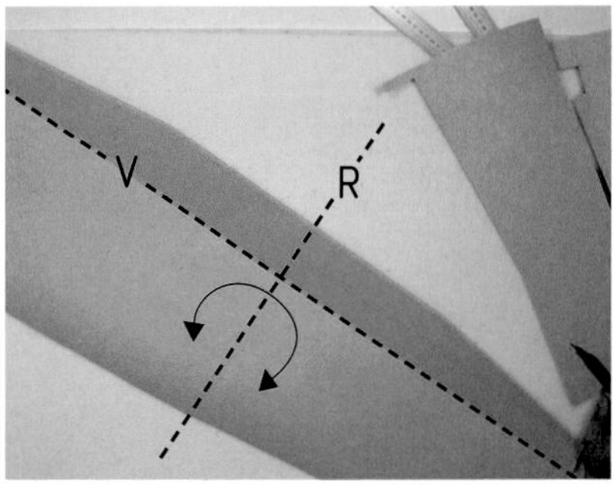

25. Unfold the template.

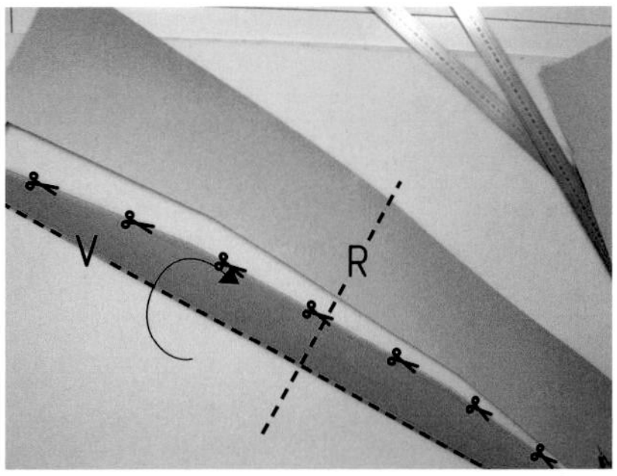

26. Fold the template along its V axis and cut it symmetrically again, copying the outlines of the first half.

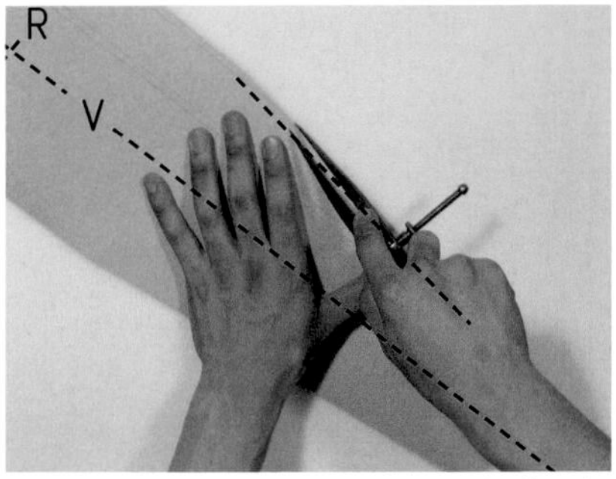

27. Fold the template in two along its R axis. With a compass, measure 0.5 cm to trace a seam allowance using the outline as a guide.

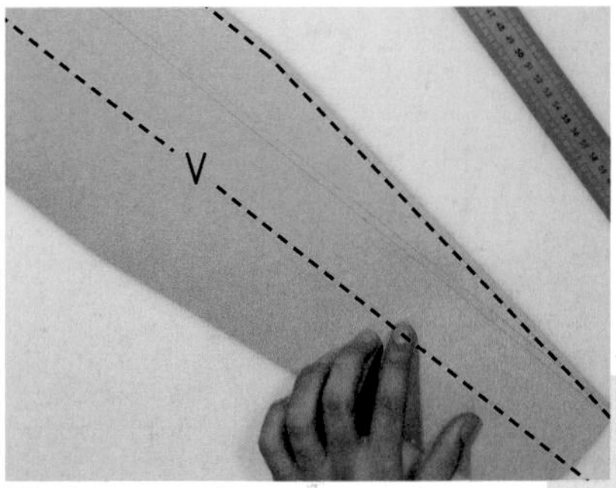

28. Use a pencil to go over the compass mark.

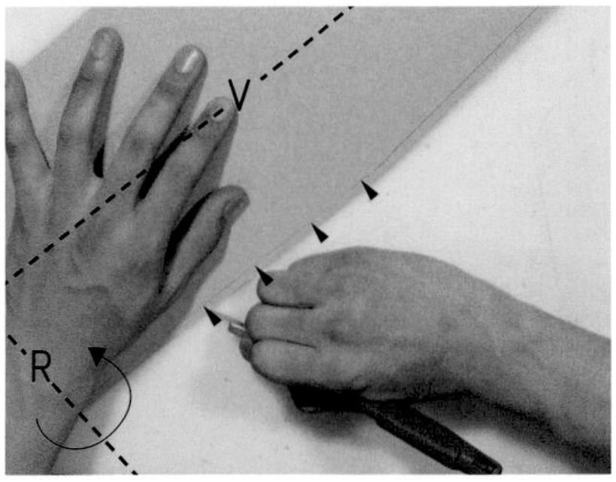

29. Fold the template along its R axis. Transfer symmetrically the notches of the curve.

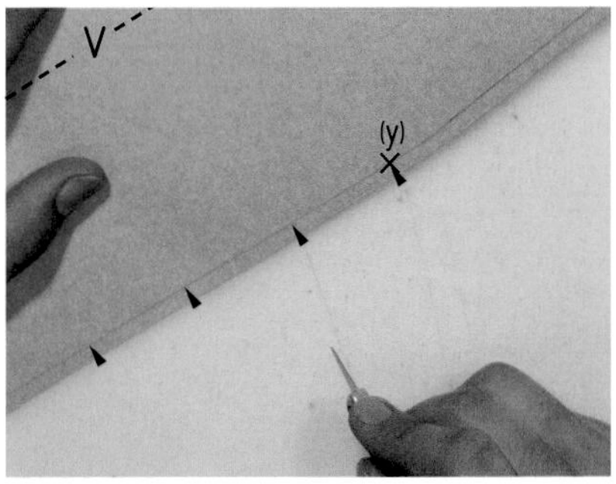

30. The four notches are visible.

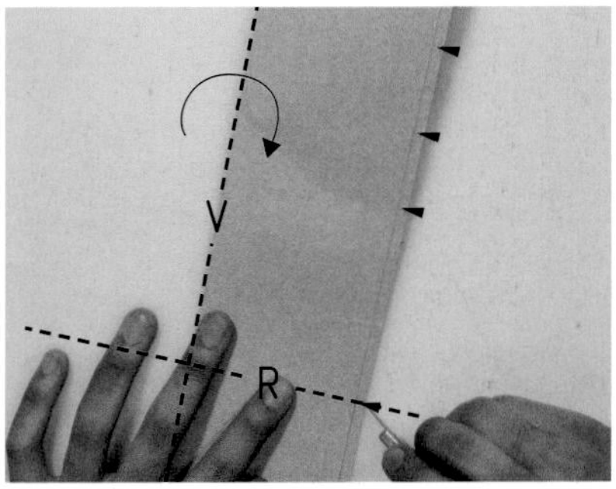

31. Fold the template along its V axis and transfer the notches symmetrically. The gusset, or side template, has now been achieved.

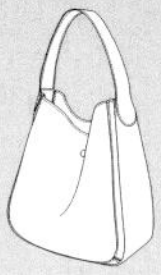

Making front pattern

We are now going to make the pattern for the front and back pieces from the template.

1. Cut out a piece of card slightly bigger than the front measurements, i.e. 50 x 50 cm.

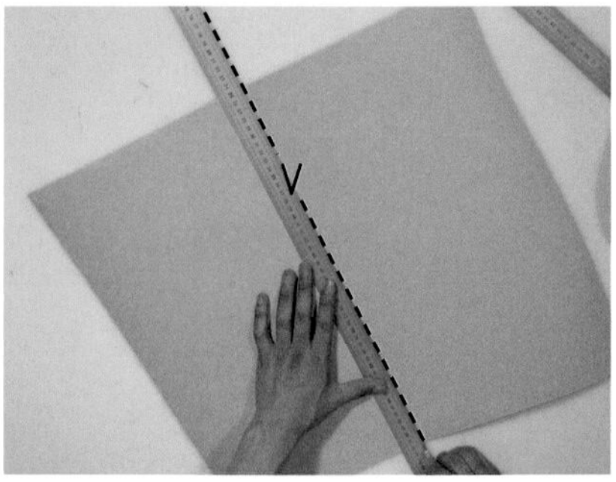

2. Using a cutter and ruler, mark off the V axis of the pattern scoring lightly to mark the fold.

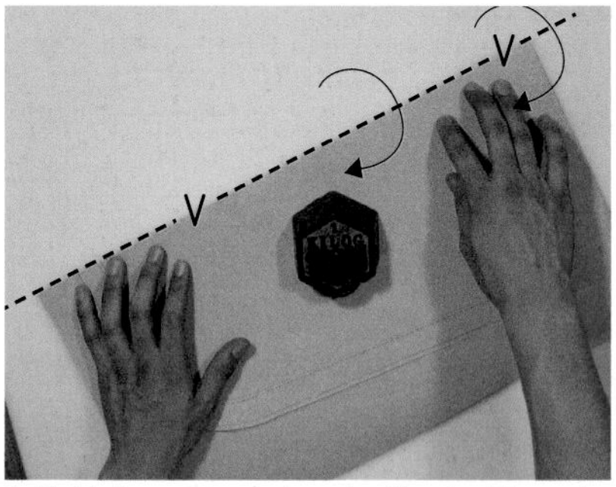

3. Fold the pattern along its V axis. Place the front template, which is also folded on its V axis, onto the piece of card, carefully lining up the V axes. Position a weight on top of these two pieces.

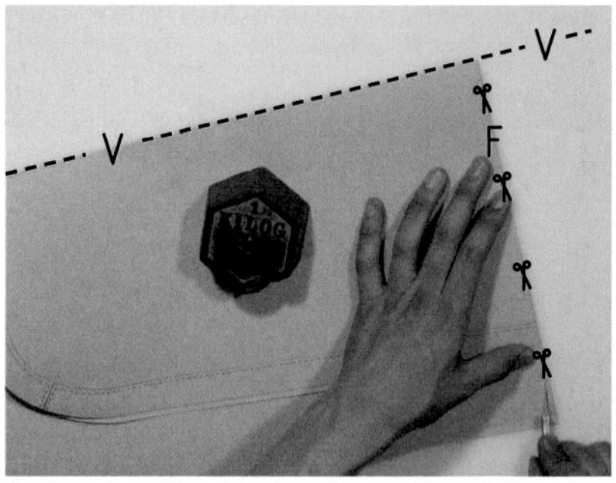

4. Cut along line F using the outline of the template as a guide.

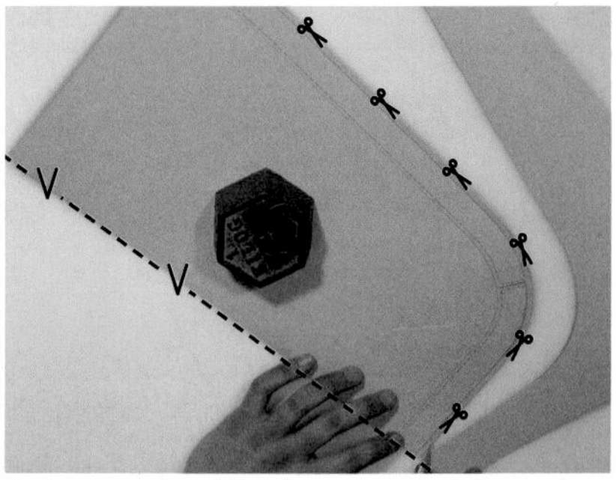

5. Cut out the side, the curve and the underneath in the same way.

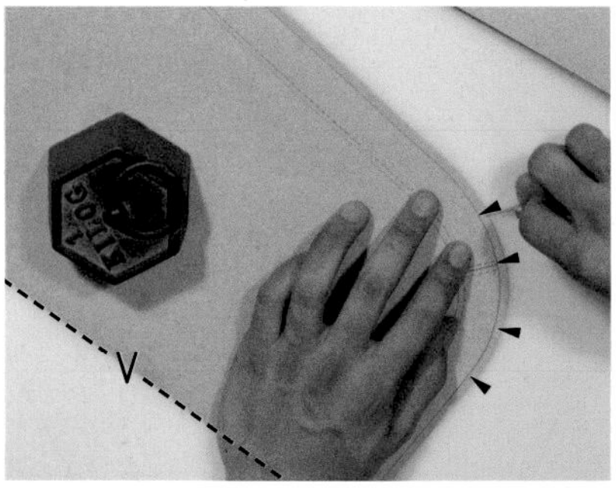

6. Transfer the notches of the template onto the card.

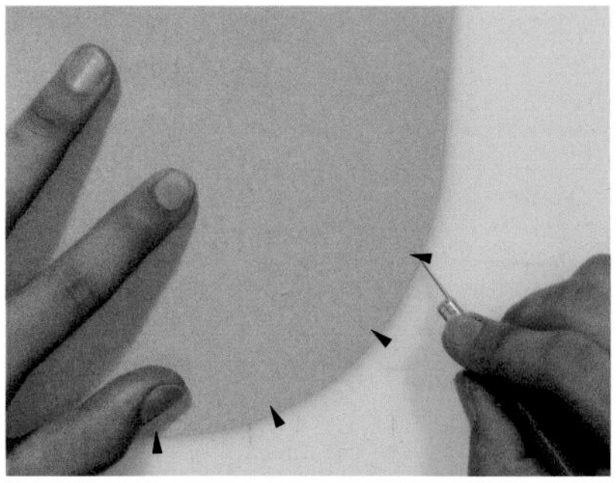

7. Remove the template and correct the badly-cut notches as it is not easy to cut through two thicknesses of card in one go.

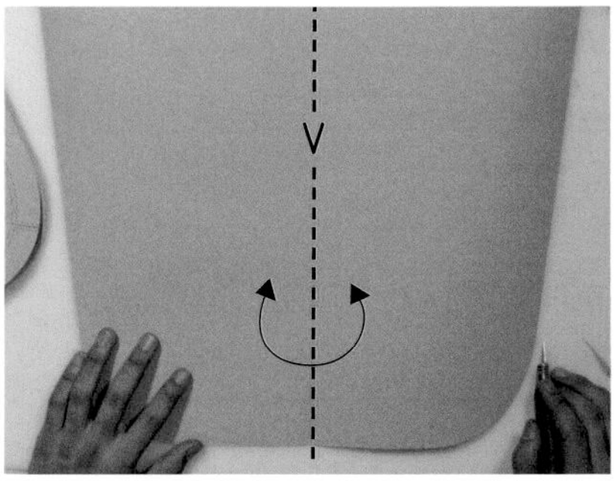

8. Unfold the card.

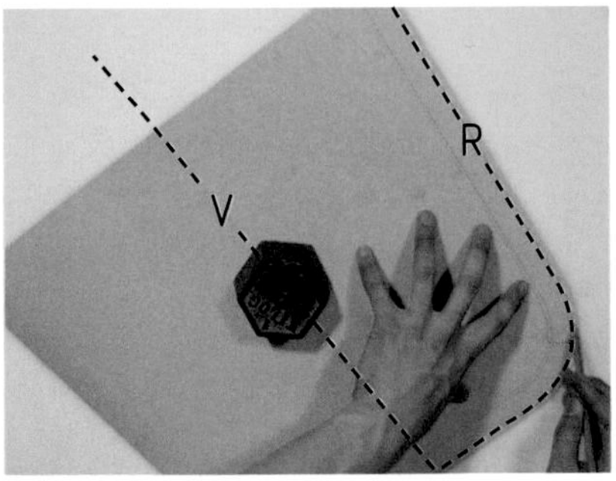

9. Place the front template onto the card lining up the two V axes precisely. With a crayon, transfer line R of the template for a the seam allowance. Use an awl to mark the position of the press stud.

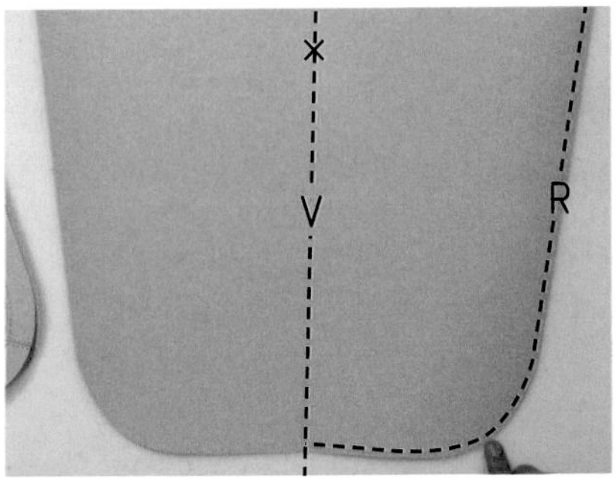

10. The front pattern is now finished.

Making the side pattern

It is possible to cut out only one piece for the two sides and the underside of the bag, however, the size of the material will restrict this, as is the case with crocodile skin and *shagreen* (a type of sharkskin) which are smallish in size. We, therefore, are going to cut out two pieces which will be assembled by a seam underneath the bag.

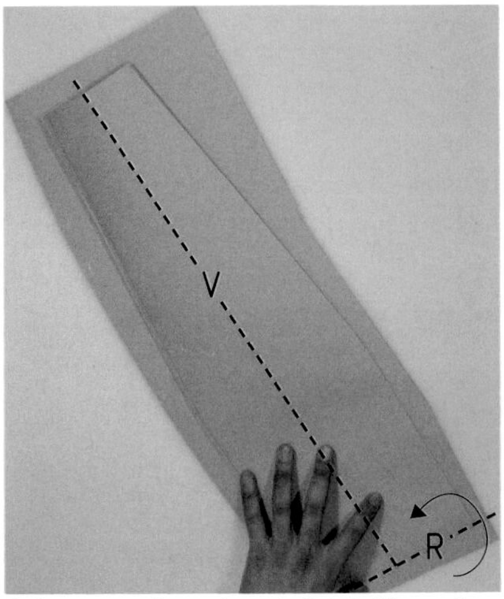

1. Cut out a piece of card slightly bigger than the side template folded on its R axis, i.e. 65 x 20 cm.

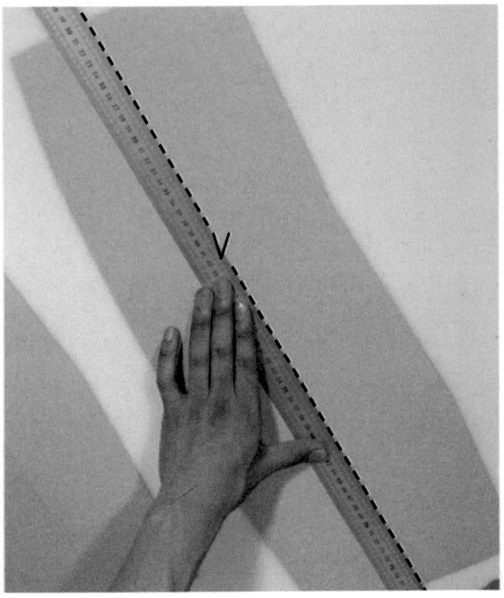

2. Use a ruler and cutter to mark lengthwise the pattern's vertical axis V.

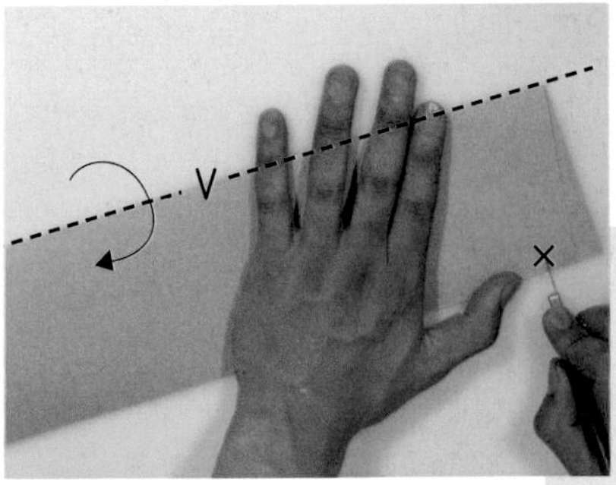

3. To trace the bottom line of the side, fold the pattern along its V axis and use a cutter to mark the edge of the card on the bottom left hand side of the V axis, 2 cm from the end of the card.

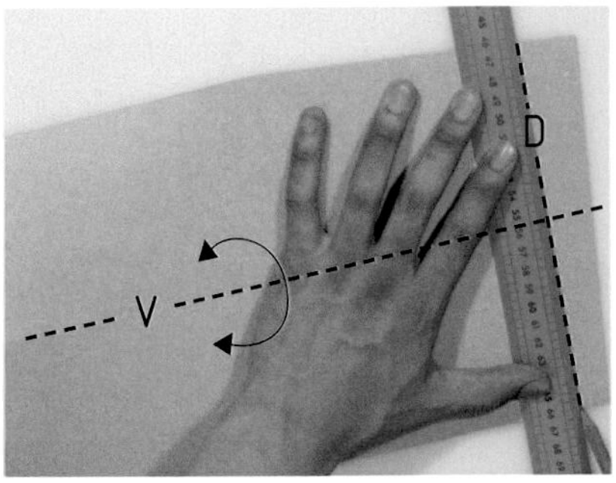

4. Unfold and join up the two marks with a pencil. This will make the centre line of the underside of the bag. Call this line D.

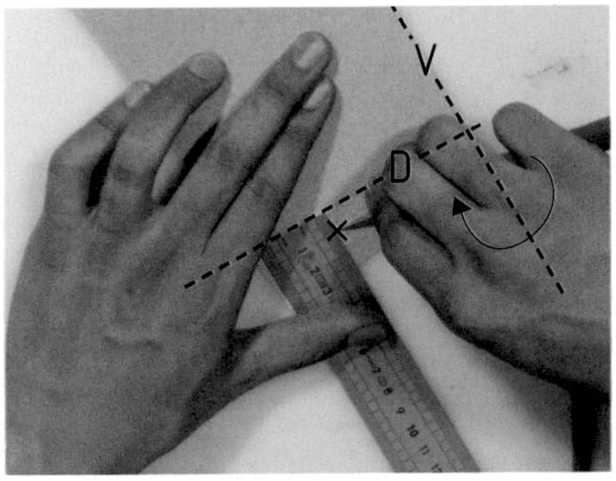

5. To include the seam allowance, fold the pattern again along its V axis. Then mark off 1 cm underneath line D using a cutter making sure to go through two layers of card.

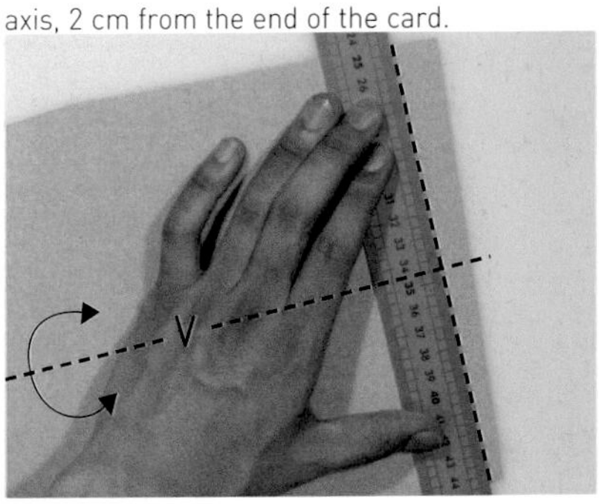

6. Unfold and join up these two marks with a pencil line.

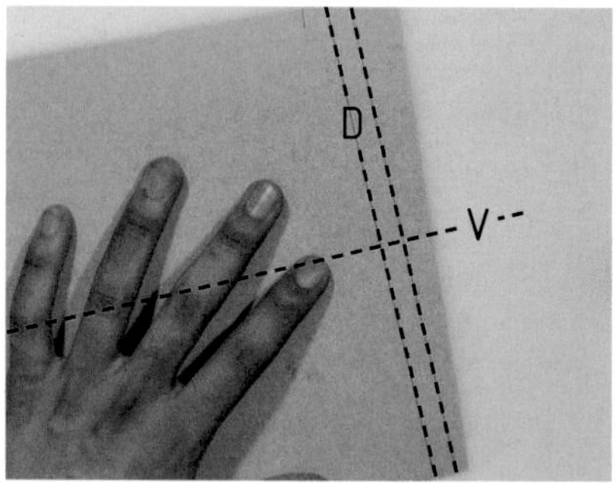

7. We have just traced the seam allowance allowing us to assemble the two halves of the side.

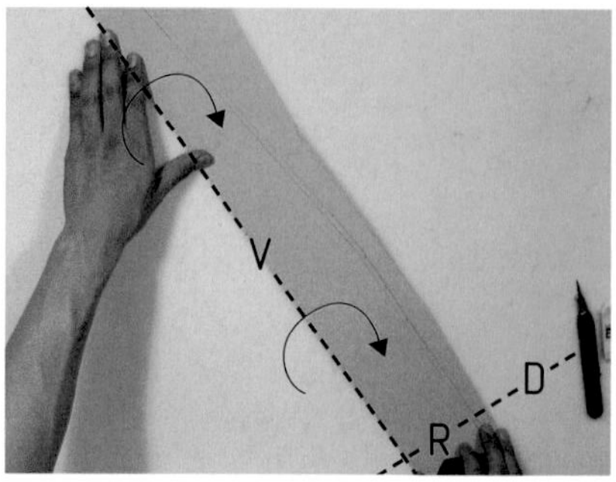

8. Fold the pattern in two along its V axis. Fold the side template of the bag along its V axis. Place the template onto the pattern, lining up precisely their V axes as well as the D axis of the template and line R of the pattern.

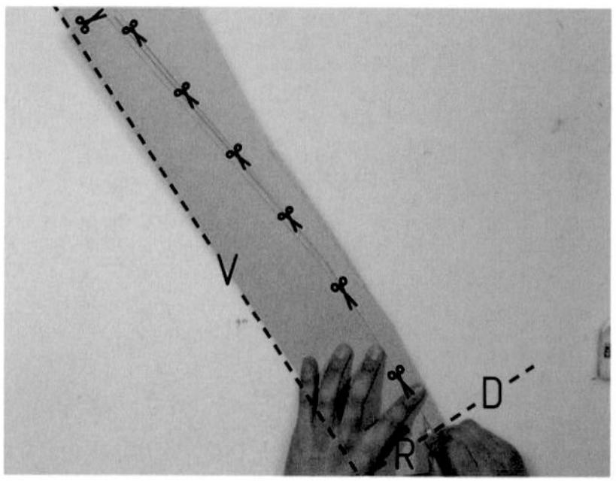

9. Cut the pattern out using the template as the guide.

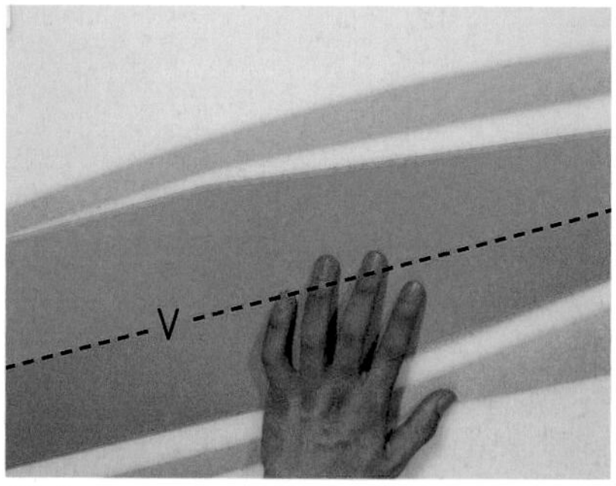

10. Remove the template and unfold the pattern.

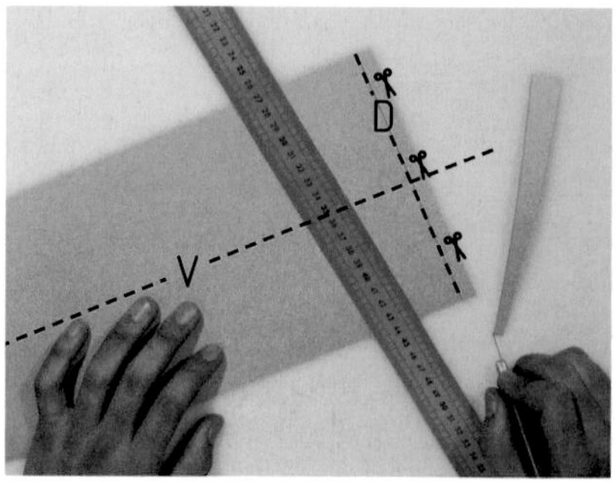

11. Cut the pattern's seam allowance line.

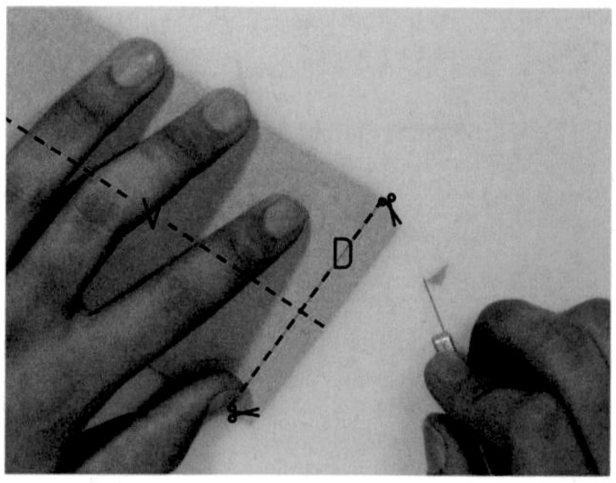

12. Cut diagonal angles on the seam as this will prevent any problems of thickness when assembling the bag.

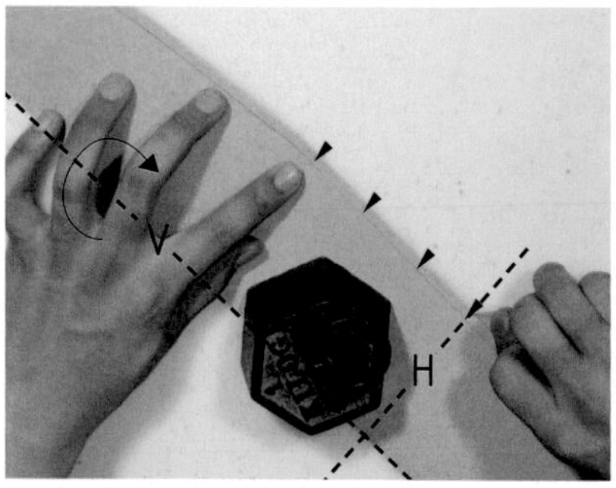

13. Fold the pattern in two along its V axis. Fold the template in two along its V axis. Reposition the template on the pattern making sure to align their V axes, as well as the R line of the template and the D line of the pattern. Transfer the notches of the template onto the gusset or side.

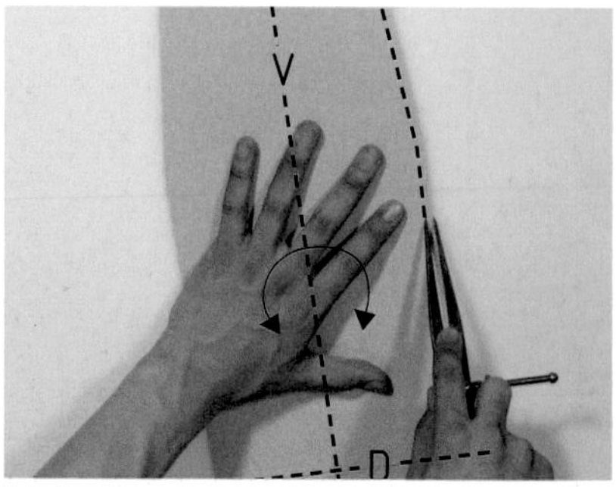

14. Remove the template and unfold the pattern. Using a compass or dividers measure 0.5 cm to trace the seam allowance.

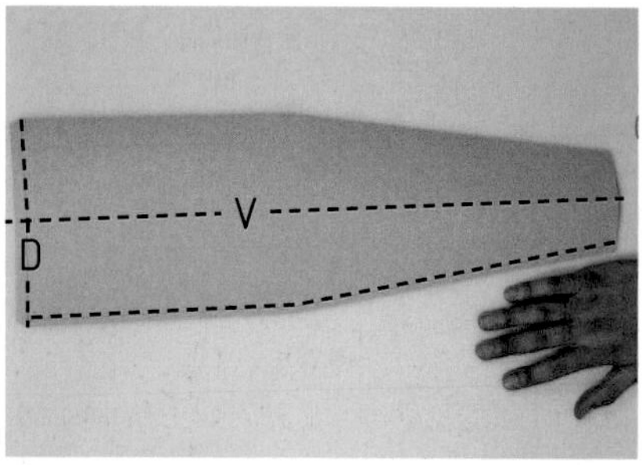

15. Use a pencil to remark the compass line: the pattern which will be used to cut out the two side pieces is now finished.

Making the handle pattern

The handle of this bag which is sewn to the two sides allows it to be worn on the shoulder. We will use the side template to construct its pattern.

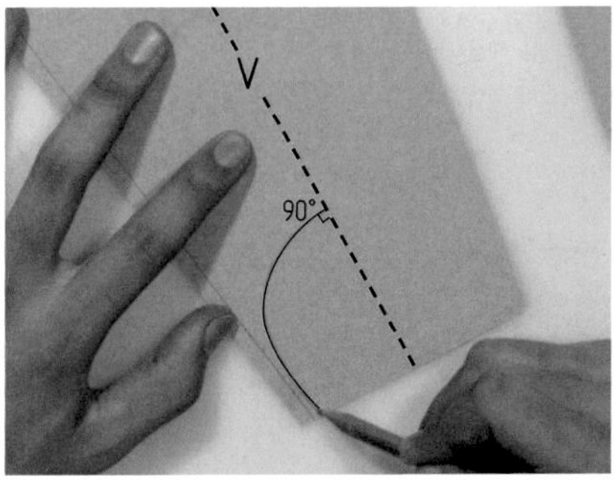

1. Draw the position of half of the handle where it sits on the side template. Use a French curve to achieve a perfect arc of a circle.

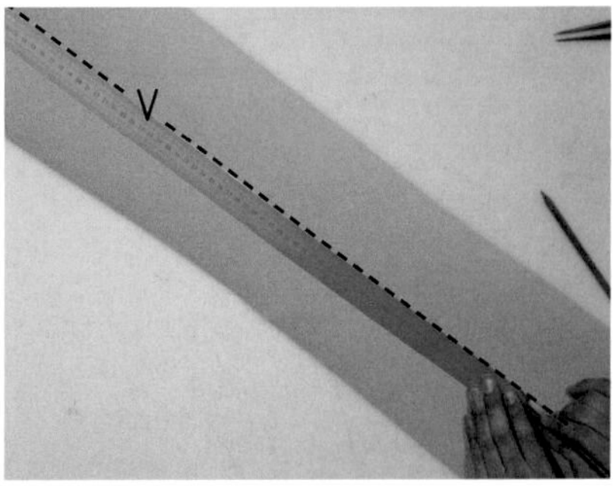

2. Cut a strip of card about 90 x 15 cm. Use a ruler and cutter to mark the pattern's vertical V axis lengthwise.

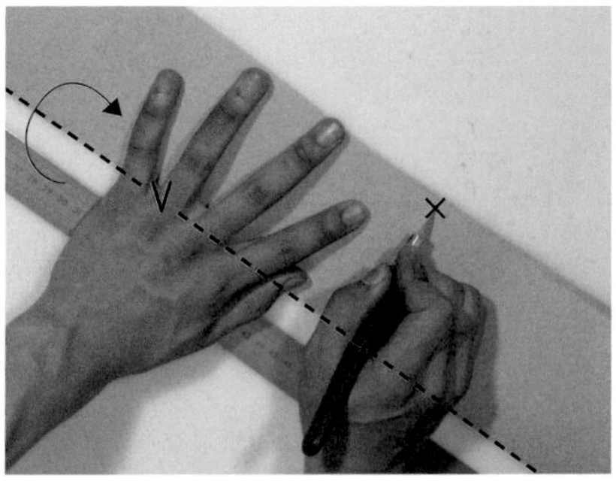

3. Fold the pattern in two along the V axis and, on its edge, place a halfway mark along the length of the card with a cutter.

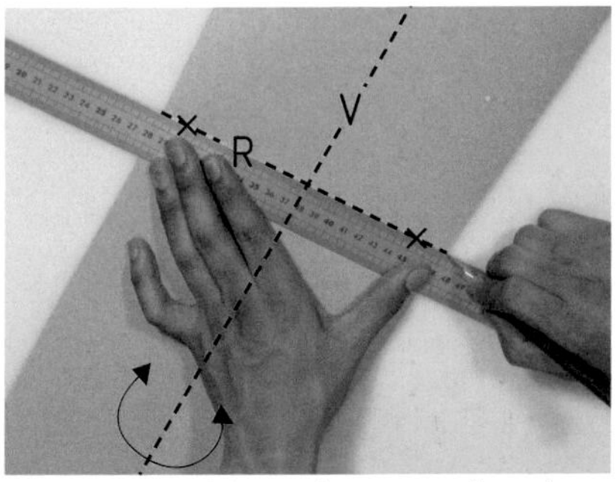

4. Unfold and join up the two marks using a ruler and a cutter in order to find the horizontal R axis.

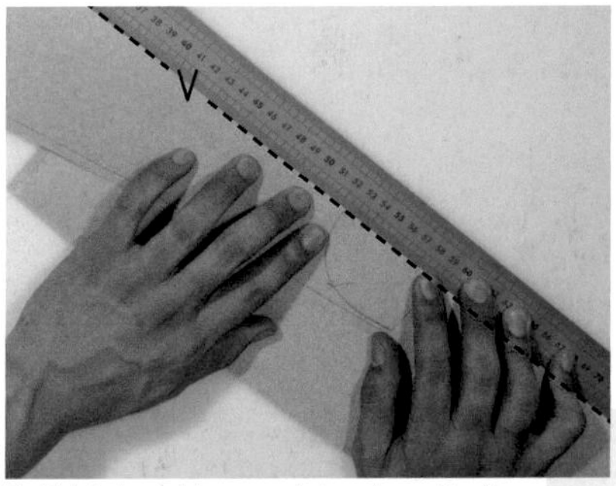

5. Fold the side template along its V axis. Fold the handle pattern along its V axis. Place the side template on top of the pattern lining up their V axes precisely. (The ruler helps to line up these two pieces.) The far edge of the side template must be placed 32 cm from the R axis of the pattern.

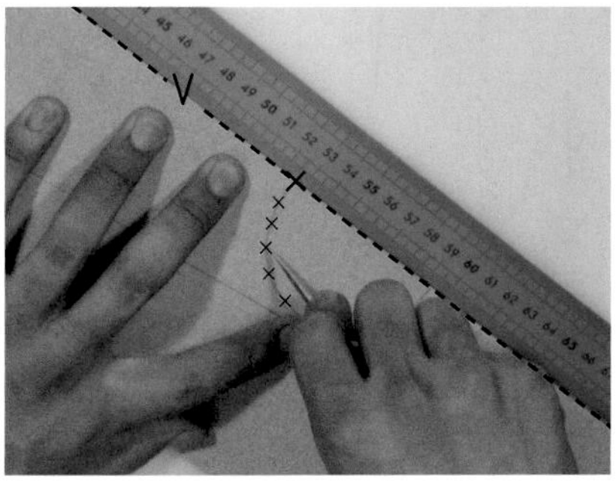

6. Use an awl to mark off at regular intervals (approx. every centimetre) the position of half of the handle. Press fairly hard to ensure going through four layers of card.

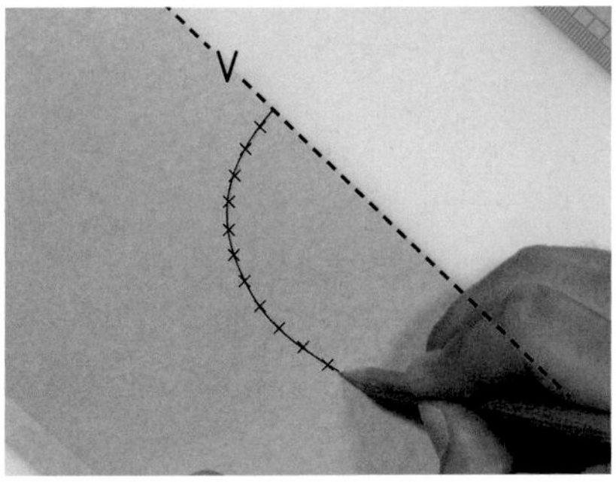

7. Remove the side template but do not unfold the pattern. Onto this pattern join up the awl marks with a pencil.

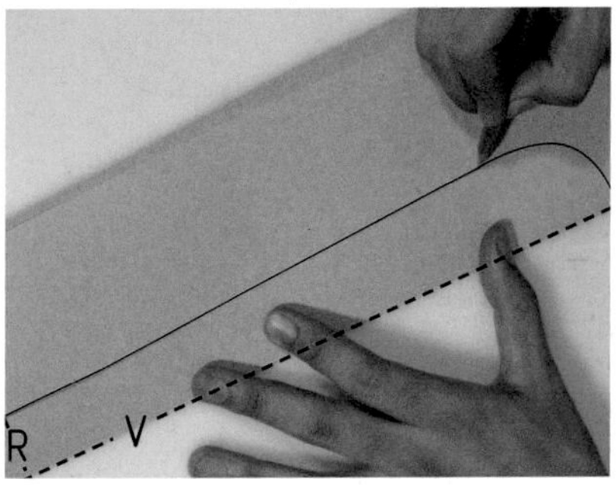

8. On the R axis of the pattern, use a pencil to mark half the width of the handle 3 cm from the V axis. Connect this point with the edge of the curve. We have now drawn a quarter of the bag's handle.

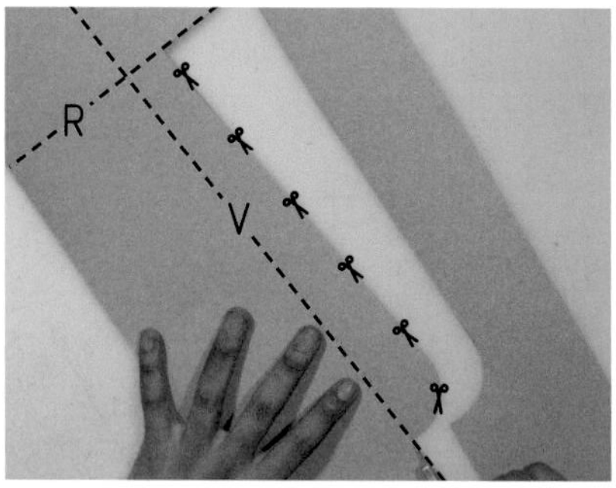

9. Cut out this first quarter.

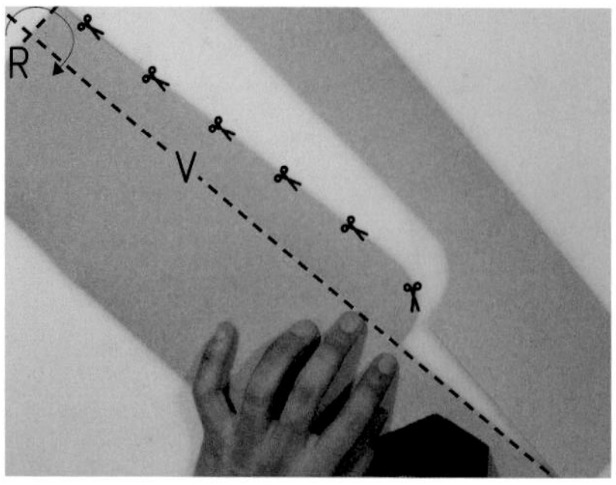

10. Fold the pattern onto its R axis and cut it out symmetrically to obtain half of the handle.

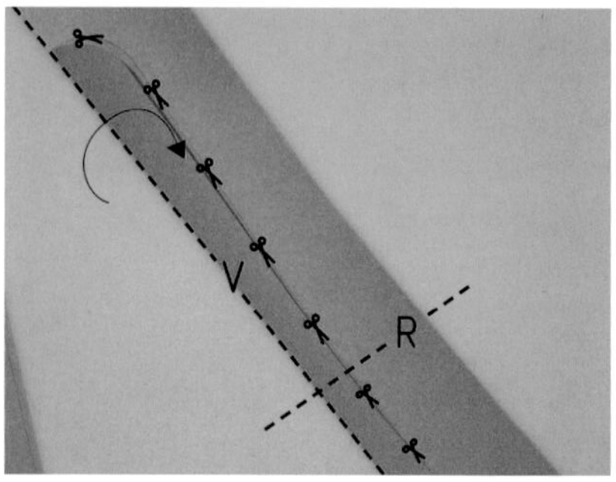

11. Unfold and fold the pattern along its V axis. Cut it out symmetrically.

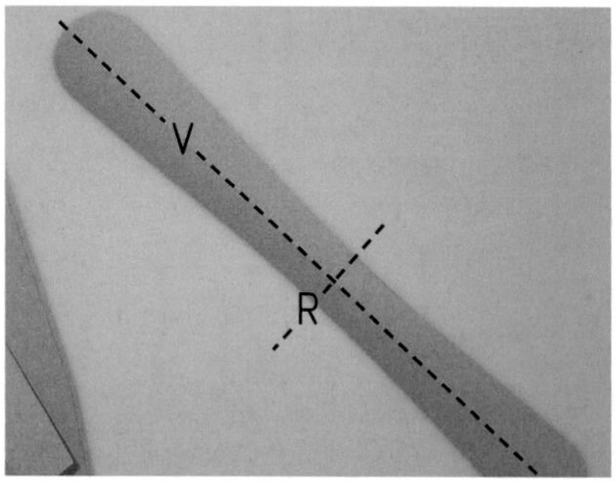

12. The handle pattern is now finished.

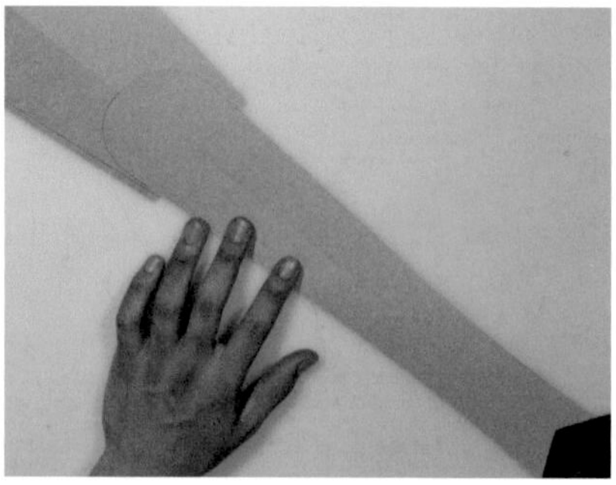

13. The pattern can be placed onto the side template to check that its position is correct.

Making the side trimming strip pattern

The bag's side trimmings will be stuck and then top-stitched onto the front and the back of the bag. The side seams therefore will have three thicknesses: the front or the back, the trimming strip and the side. We will begin with the pattern of the strip of the front and back sides.

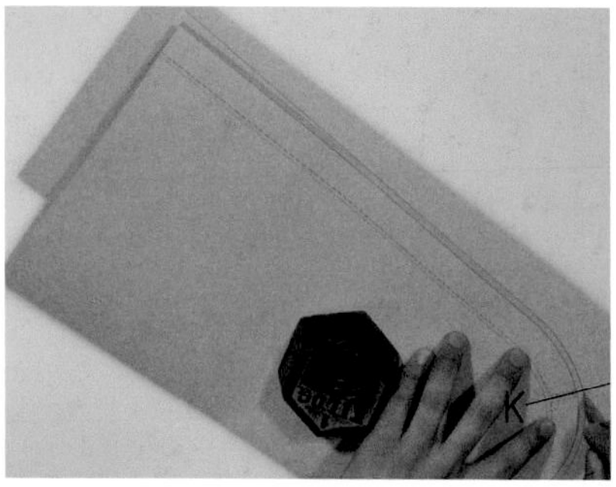

1. Place the front template onto a piece of card so that the exterior outline of the strip can be traced.

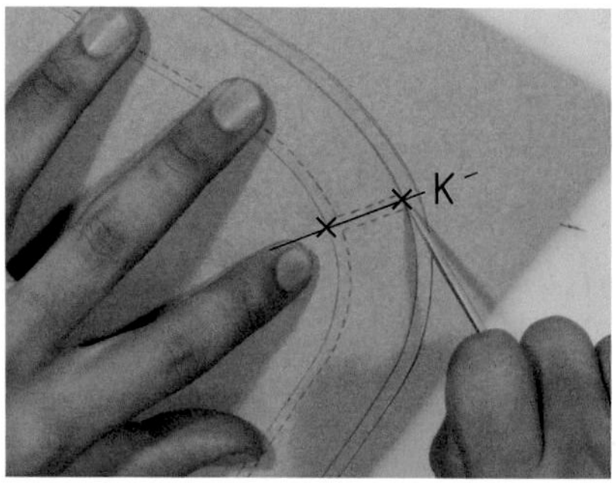

2. Use an awl to mark the width of the strip on line K of the front. Press fairly hard in order to go through the layers of card.

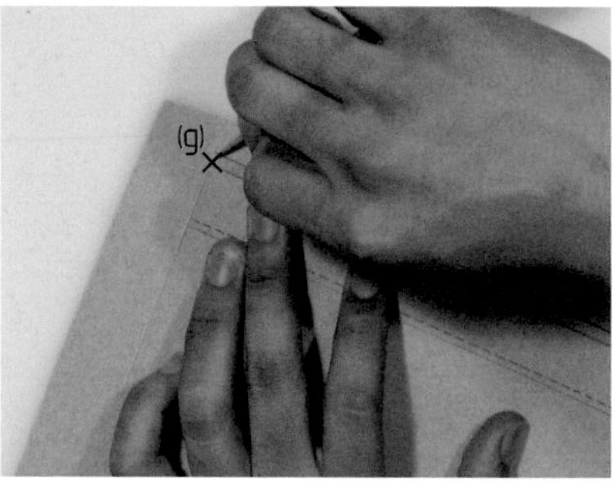

3. With the awl, mark point (g) of the front template.

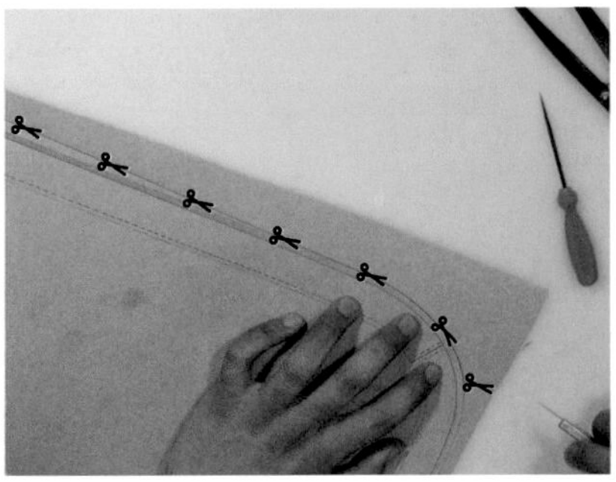

4. Cut the strip pattern using the front template as a guide.

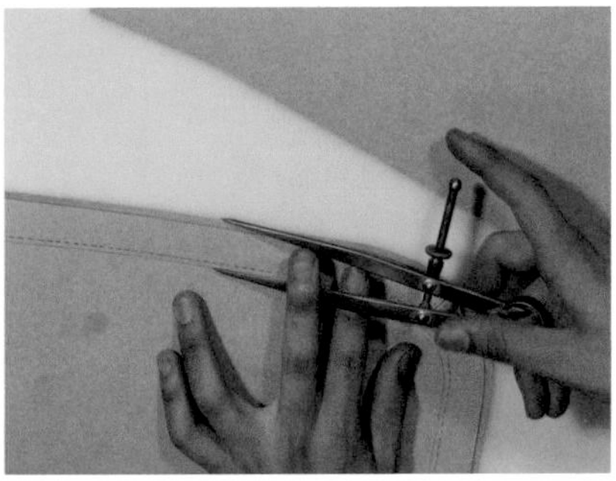

5. Using the compass, plot the width of the strip, including its seam, i.e. 2.7 cm (allowing 2.2 cm for the width of the strip and 0.5 for the seam).

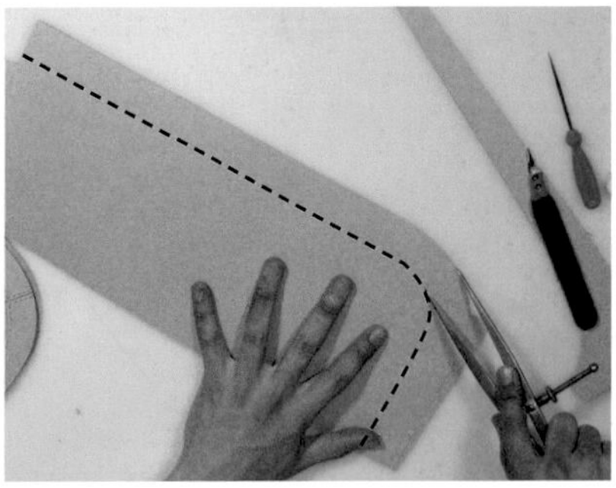

6. Transfer this measurement onto the side strip pattern.

7. Re-do the compass mark with a pencil.

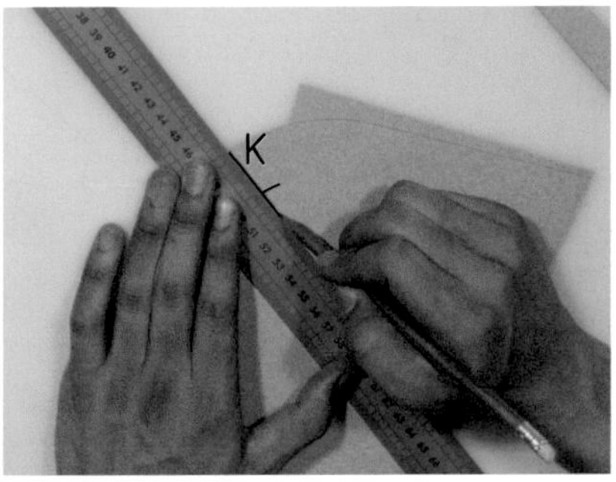

8. Join up the awl marks using a pencil which will give line K on the pattern.

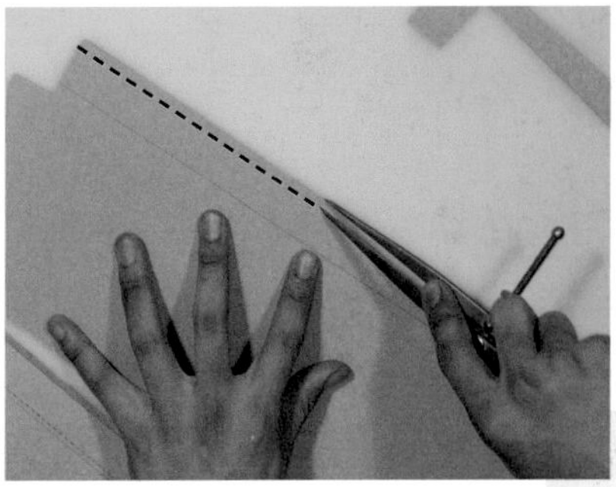

9. Set the compass to 0.5 cm and trace the size of the seam onto the outside edge of the pattern.

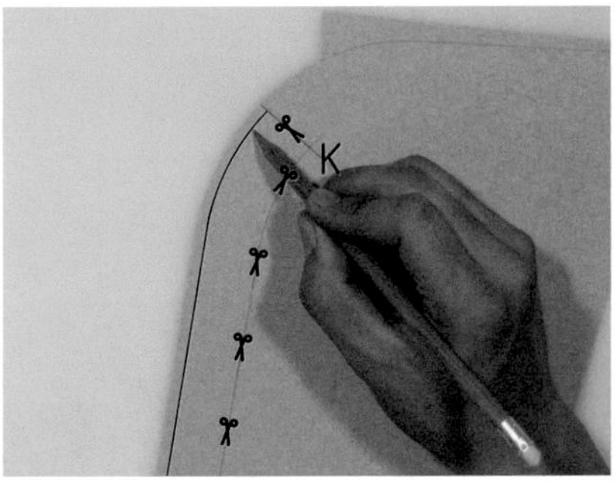

10. Re-do the compass mark with a pencil. Cut along line K and the inside of the strip.

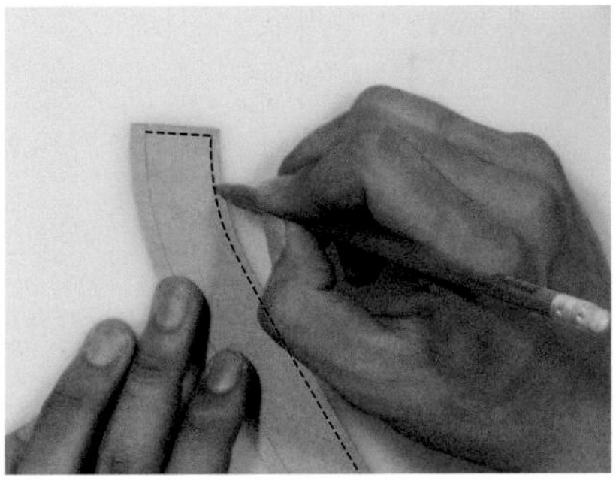

11. Draw the top stitches at 0.3 cm intervals on the inside of the strip.

Making the pattern for the bottom of the trimming strip

The bottom of the front and back strip is divided in two by the symmetrical V axis on the front of the bag. We can therefore construct half its pattern and then transfer it symmetrically, which was impossible with the side strip.

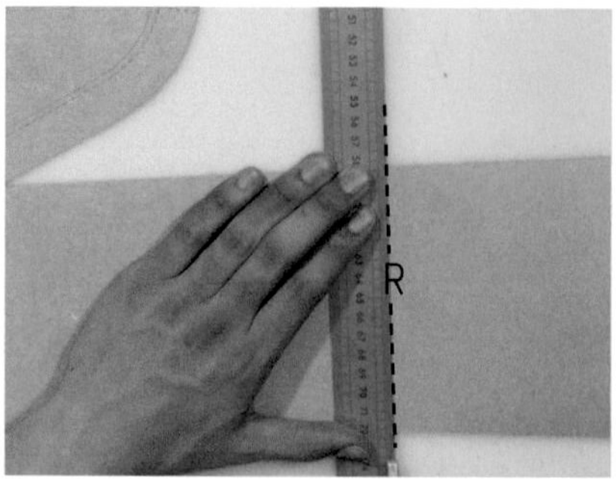

1. Cut out another strip of card about 40 x 10 cm. Use a cutter to mark the horizontal R axis of the bottom-front strip pattern.

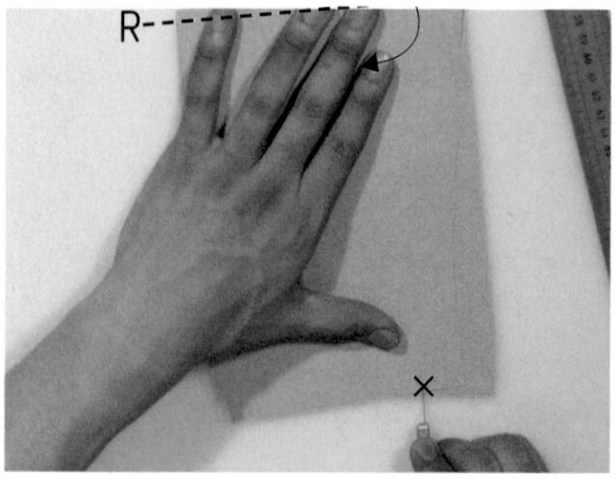

2. Fold in two along the R axis. Use a cutter to mark the edge of the card which is opposite to the R axis. Unfold and join up these marks with a pencil; we have now traced line B on the bottom of the pattern.

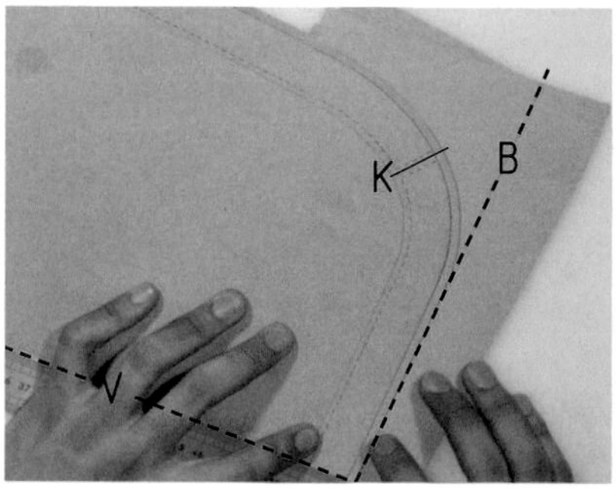

3. Fold the front template in two along its V axis. Fold the bottom strip pattern along its R axis. Place the front template onto the strip pattern lining up very carefully the template's V axis and the pattern's R axis, as well as the bottom line of the template and line B of the pattern.

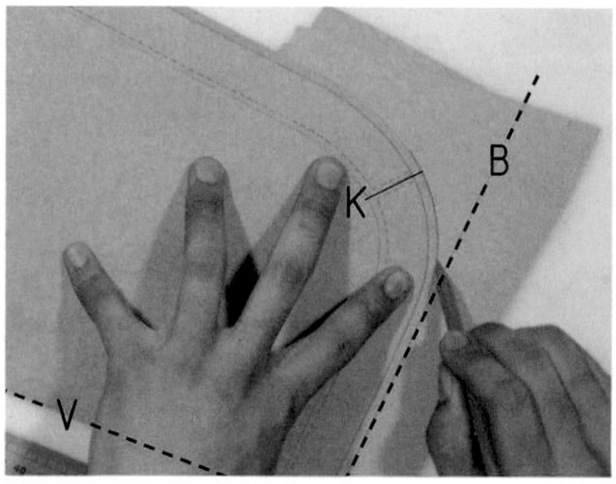

4. Use a pencil to transfer the curve of the template of line K up to line B, stopping at the notches of the curve.

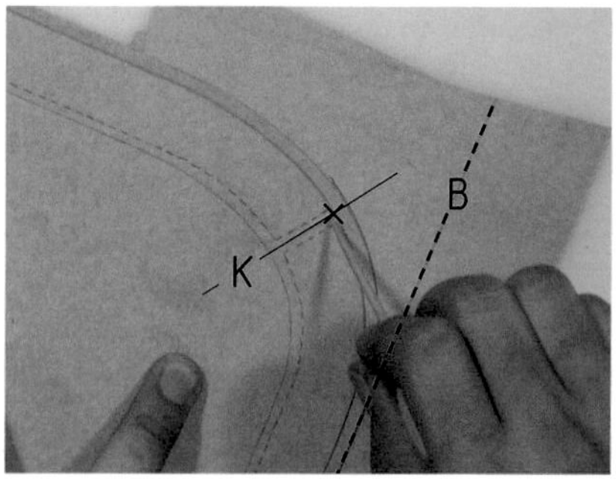

5. Use an awl to plot the width of the trimming strip from line K on the template onto the pattern, starting on the outside line.

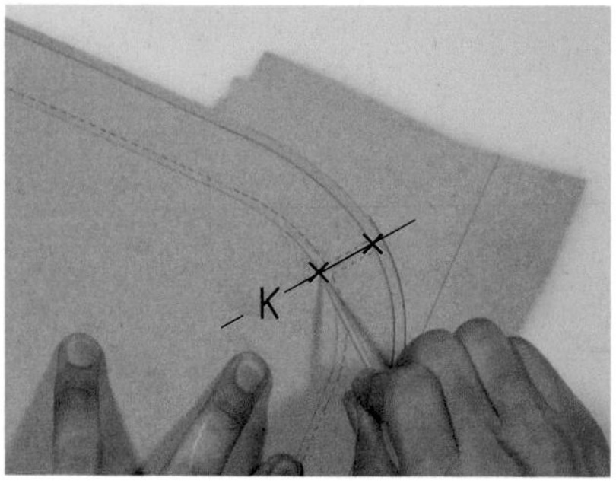

5b. Do the same on the inside line.

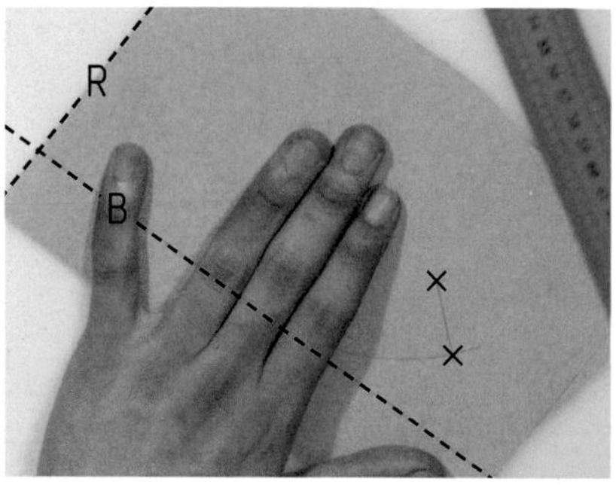

6. Remove the template and join up the marks with a pencil.

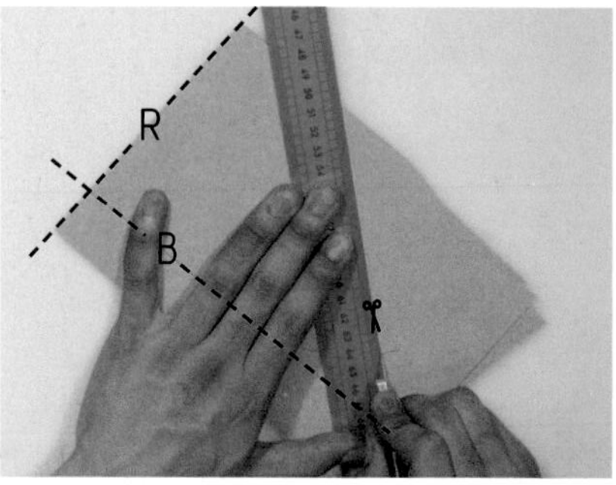

7. Use a cutter to cut out this line [pressing quite hard to ensure going through two layers of card.

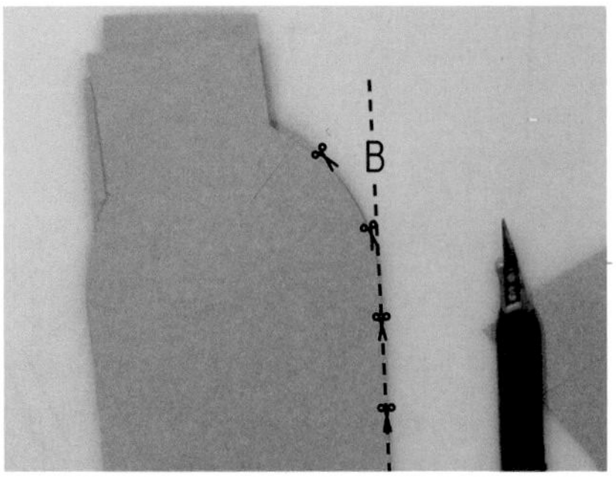

8. Cut the curve as well as line B up to the R axis.

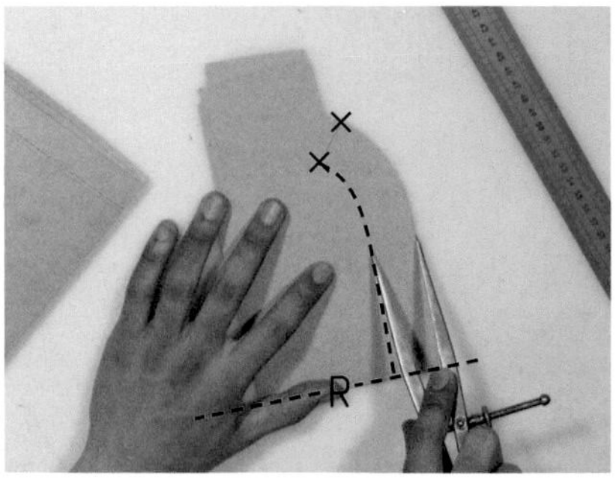

9. Use the compass to plot the width of the strip, including the seam. Transfer this measurement (2.7 cm) using the cut outline as a guide.

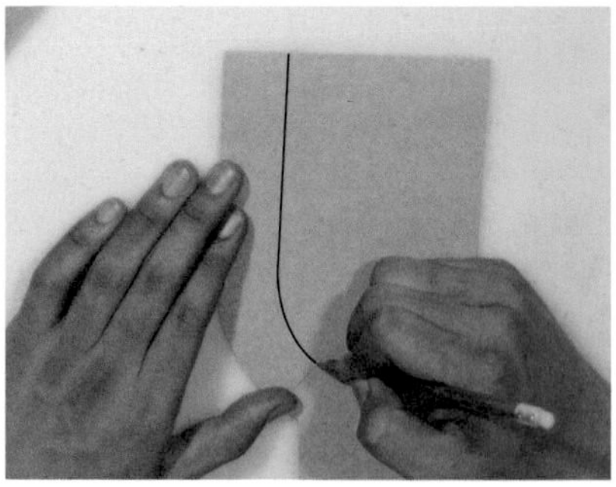

10. Re-do this compass mark with a pencil.

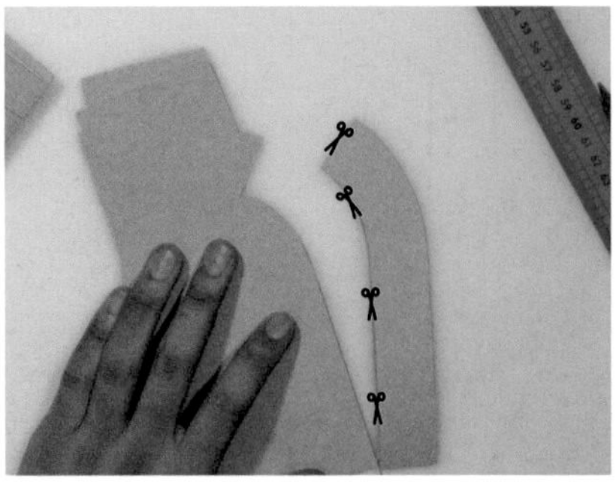

11. Cut it out.

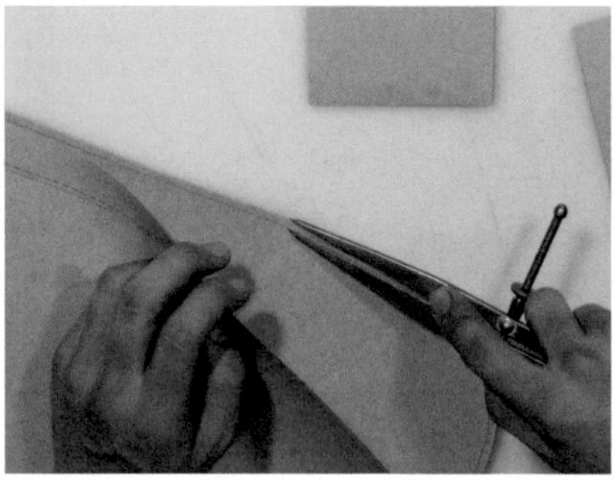

12. On the front template, measure the seam allowance, i.e. 0.5 cm.

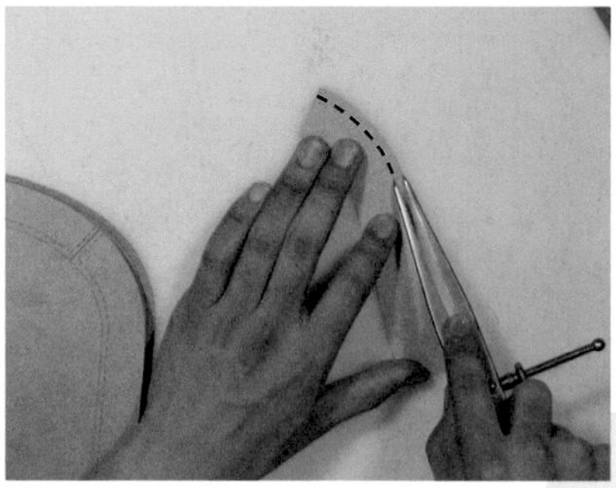

13. Transfer this measurement onto the bottom of the pattern.

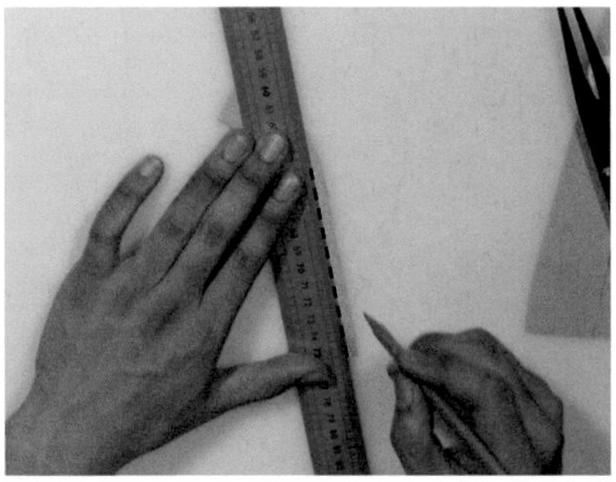

14. Go over this mark in pencil.

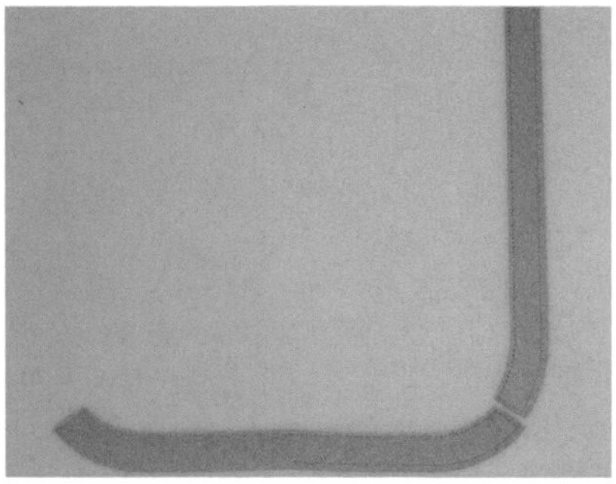

15. Unfold. The trimming strips are now finished. This photo shows the top stitches and the added seam allowance for assembling it to the sides.

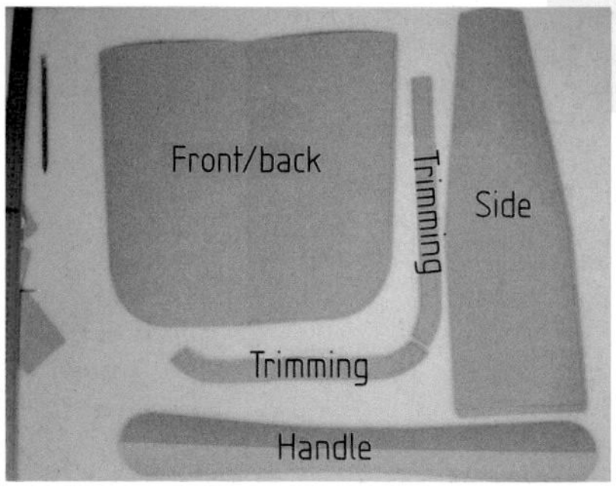

16. The bag's pattern is now finished. We have made patterns for the front and back pieces, the two sides, the handle, the two trimming strips for the bottom of the front and back, as well as four trimming strips for the sides of the front and back. Even for a bag which appears fairly simple, the pattern making can be quite involved and relatively long to make.

Cutting and assembling

This bag is sewn first then reversed. We will assemble the different pieces inside-out then reverse the bag so that the seams are on the inside and therefore invisible. Different coloured felts can be used.

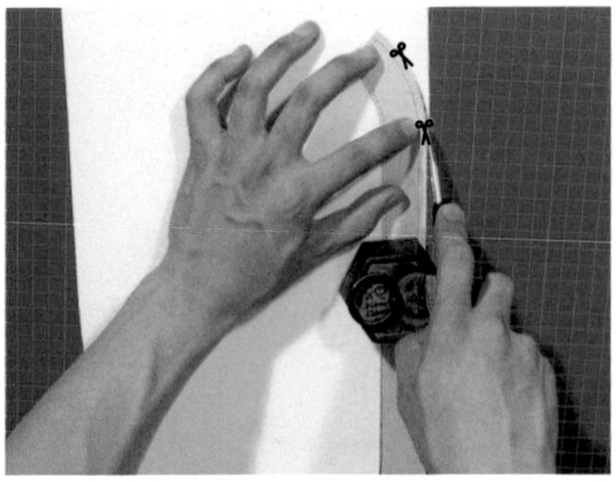

1. Place the bottom trimming strip pattern onto a piece of felt using a weight to secure it. Cut around the pattern's outline. Cut a second piece from this pattern and repeat for the four side trimming strips.

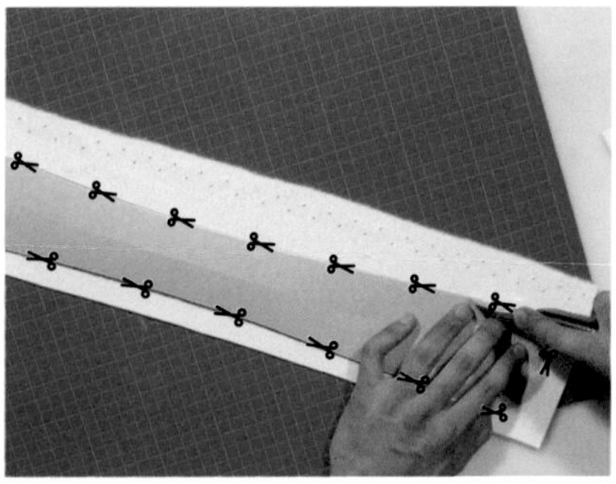

2. Place the handle pattern onto a piece of felt and cut it out. (Be careful not to place the pattern on the selvedge.)

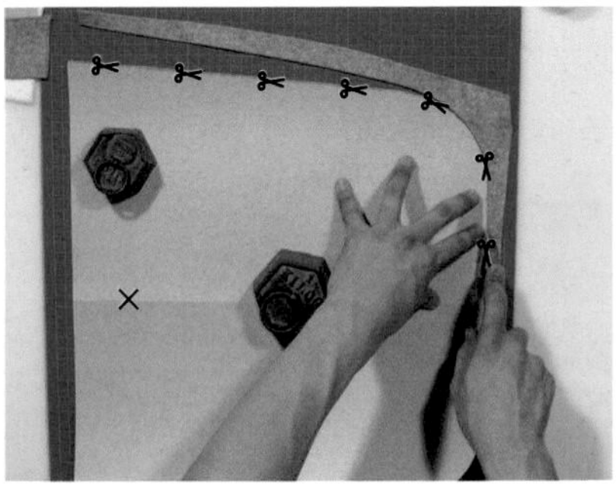

3. Cut out the front and the back. Use a fabric crayon to mark the position of the press stud onto the felt.

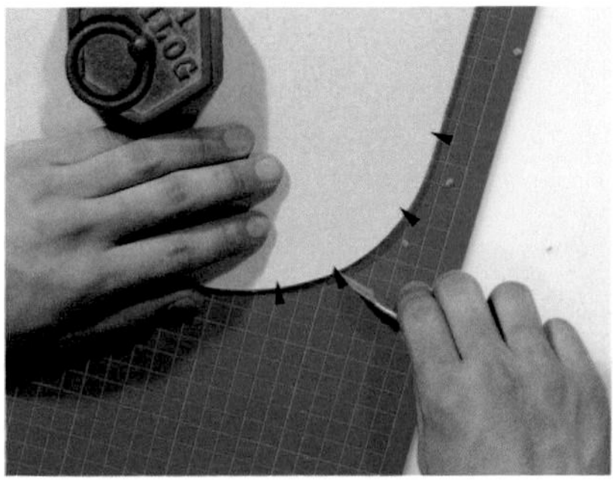

4. Transfer the pattern notches onto the pieces of felt.

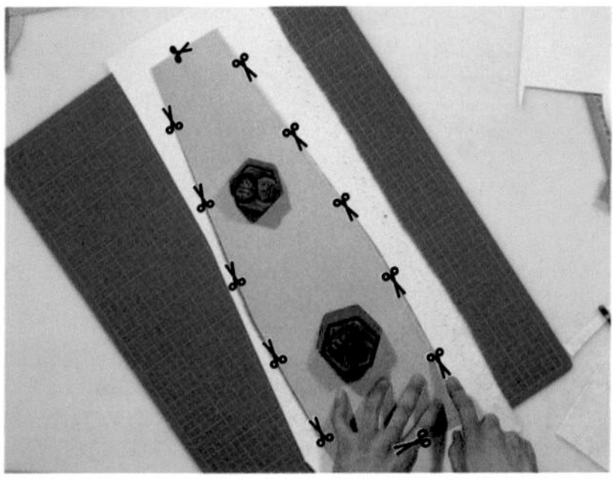

5. Cut out the two sides.

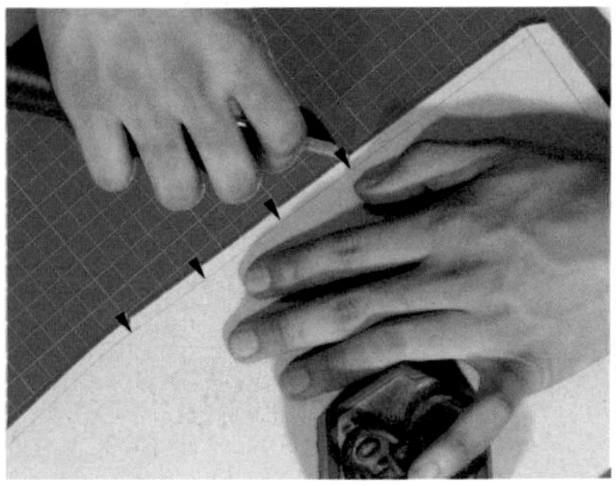

6. Transfer the pattern notches onto the pieces of felt.

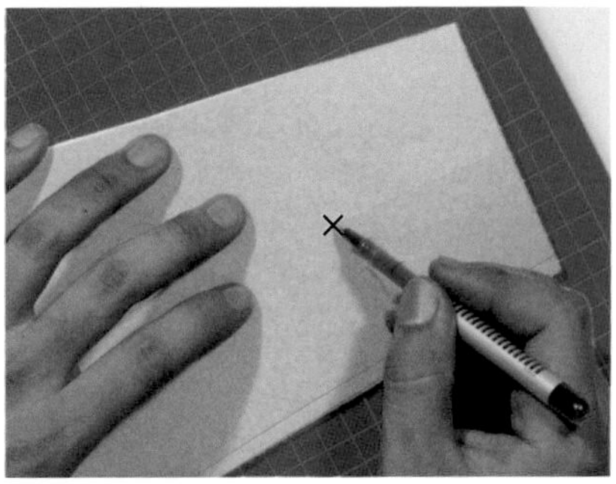

7. Use a fabric crayon to mark the position of the handles on the felt so that it can be correctly positioned when assembling.

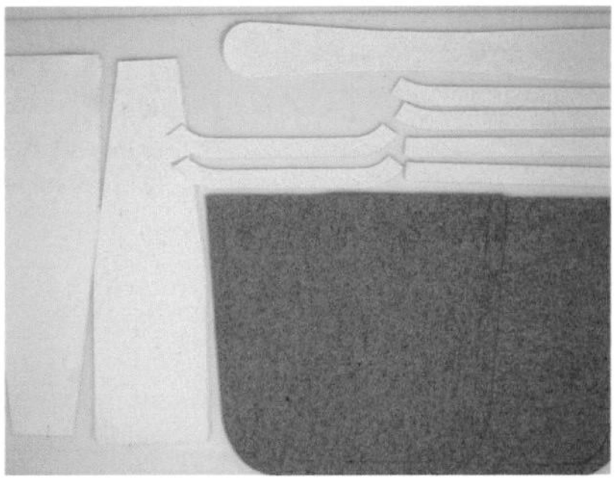

8. In all we have cut out eleven pieces: a front, a back, two sides or gussets, two bottom trimming strips, four side trimming strips and a handle.

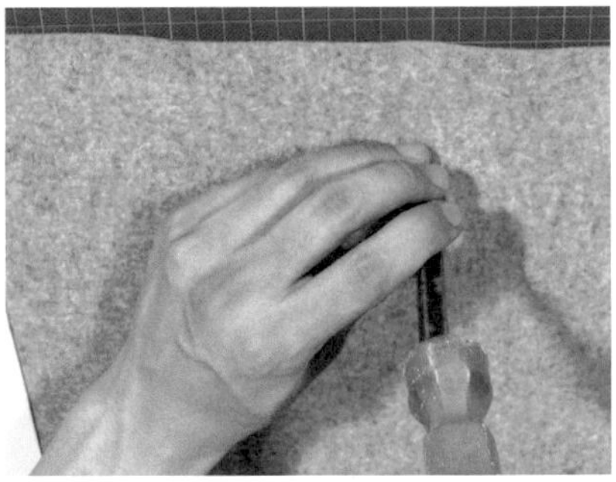

9. With a hole puncher and a hammer, make a hole for the press stud position on the front and back. It is strongly recommended to place something underneath the felt so as not to mark the table.

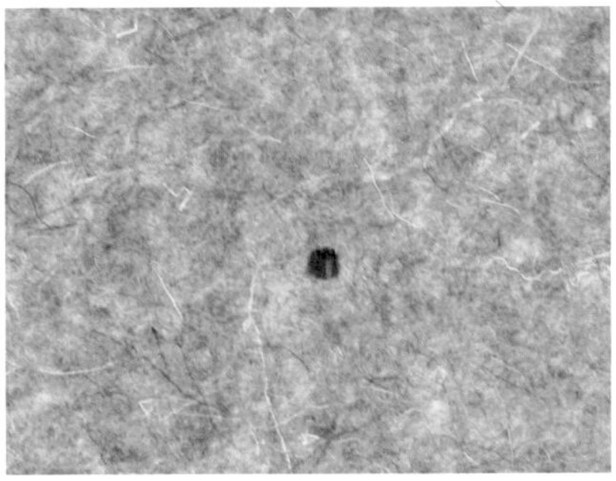

10. The hole puncher and the hammer will make a neat hole for the press stud and prevents the fabric being distorted when assembling it.

11. Fix the female part of the press stud on the underside of the back piece. This press stud is fixed by a rivet, however, there are other types which can be clipped into position. Fix the male part of the press stud onto the front, on the reverse side.

12. Stick the trimming strips onto the front and back pieces. This rubber-based glue can be easily found in DIY shops. Machine-stitch the strips onto the front and the back using a 0.3 cm length stitch.

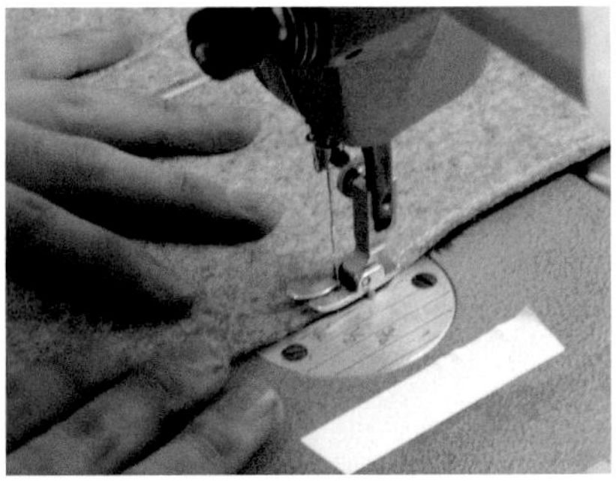

13. Stitch the top of the front and the back.

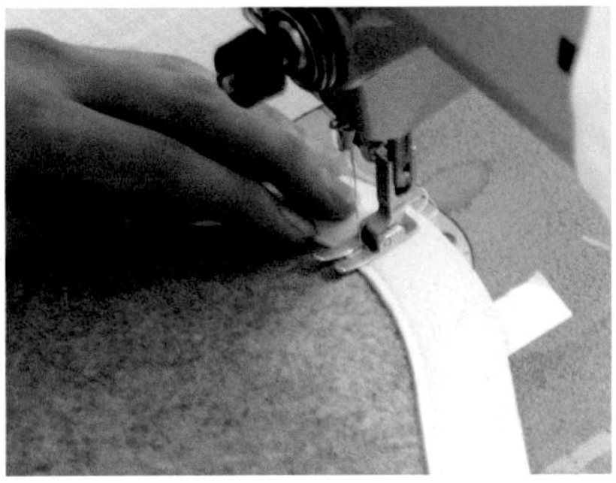

14. Stitch each side of the cut out sections.

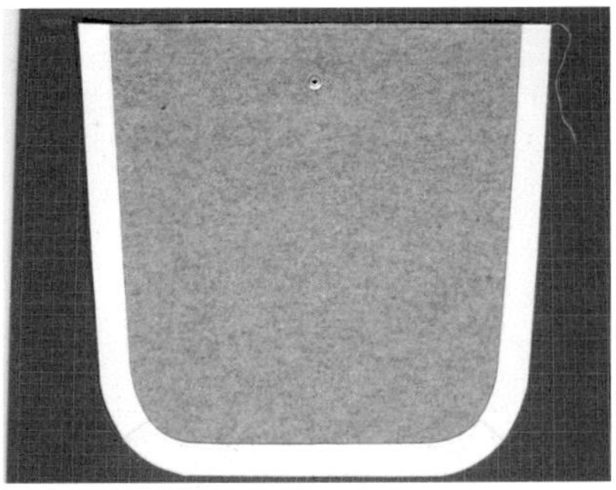

15. The trimming strips have now been successfully joined to the front and back.

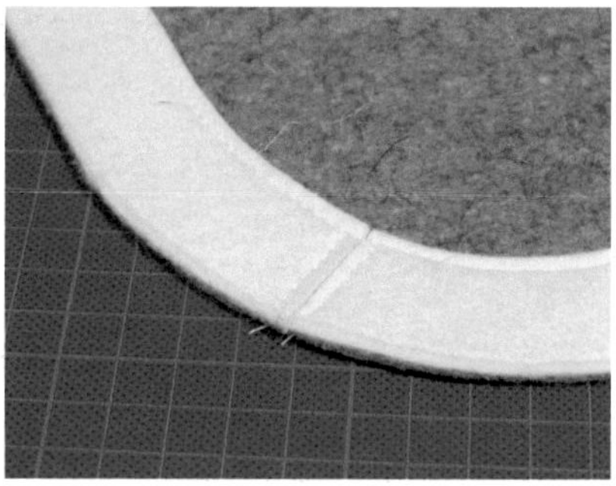

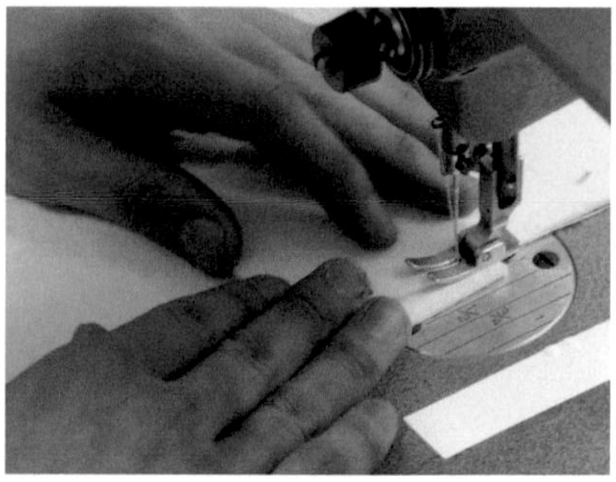

16. Detail of the trimmings and stitches.

17. Detail of the top stitches at the top of the front and back.

18. Stick the handle onto the sides and assemble it all using the machine with a 0.3 cm stitch along the edge.

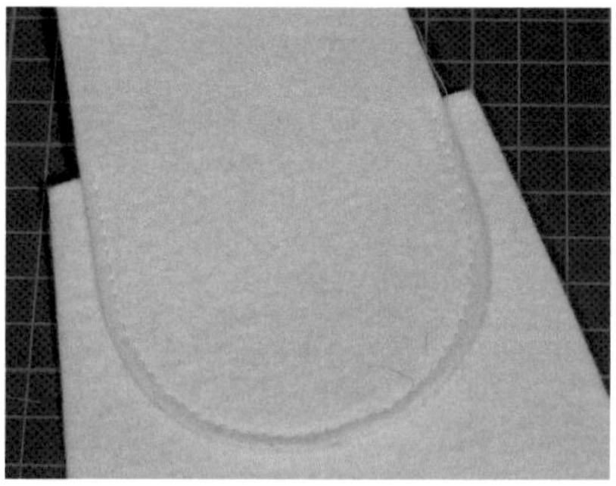

19. Detail of assembling the handle to the side.

20. Stick the seams inside-out underneath the sides and machine sew them. The handle and the two sides will form a single piece.

21. To assemble the front, back, sides and base, stick the pieces right-side to right-side, taking into account the assembling notches.

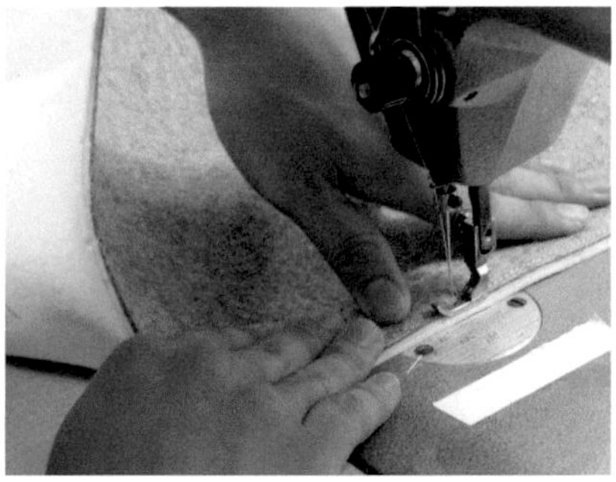

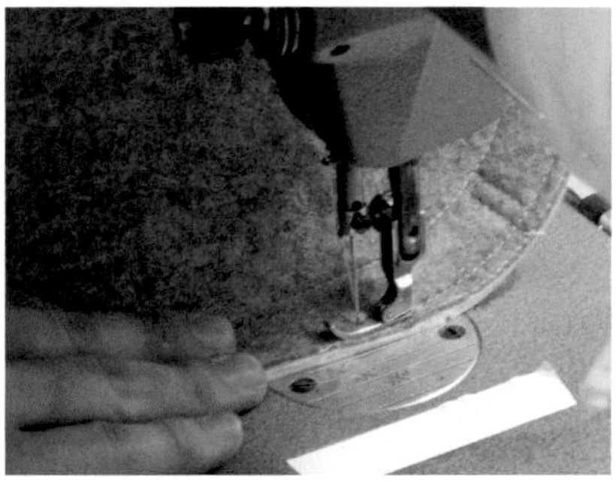

22. Sew together the sides and the base with the front and the back. Choose a claw foot for the zip fastening. Place the outside edge of the claw foot on the outside edge of the seam. The curved part of the bag is the most difficult to sew, therefore use the machine wheel manually to control the stitch speed.

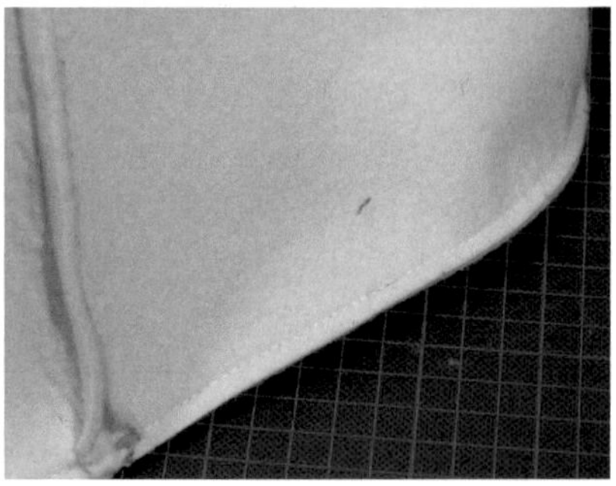

23. Detail of the base seam.

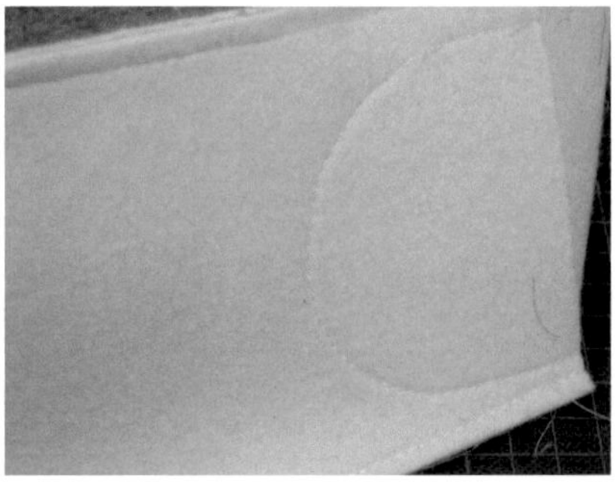

24. Detail of the reverse of the handle seam. The sewing has been completed. All that remains to be done is to reverse the bag so that the seams are on the inside. Flatten the seams with a bone folder.

Making felt prototypes

3 - Toilet/sponge bag

This bag, which is a rounded rectangular form, is one which is fastened by a zip. It is made up of front piece, with a pocket, a back piece, a side/underneath piece, a top piece with a zip and a shoulder strap. To make its pattern, we will use the same method as those used for the previous cylindrical bag and tote bag.

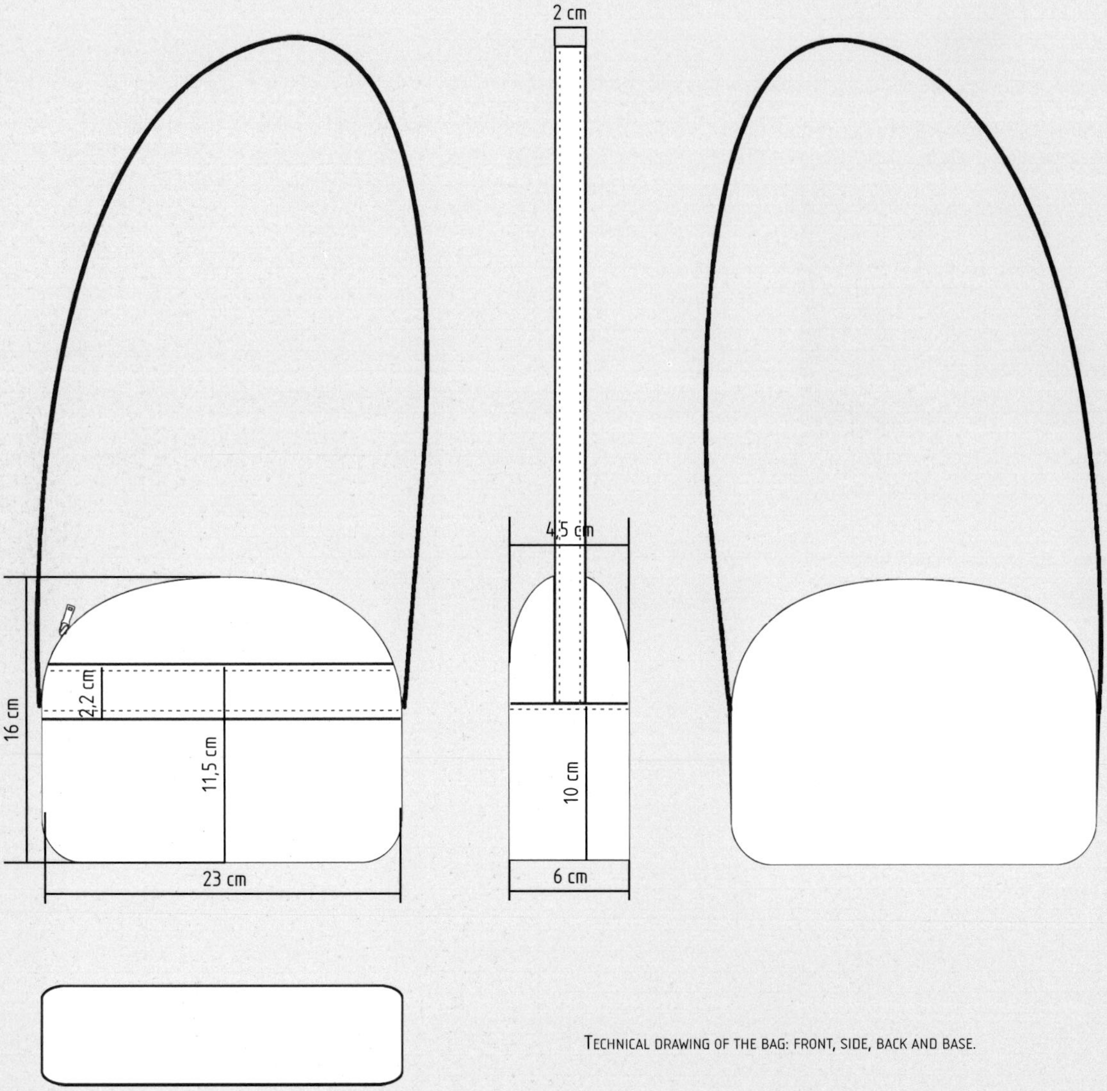

TECHNICAL DRAWING OF THE BAG: FRONT, SIDE, BACK AND BASE.

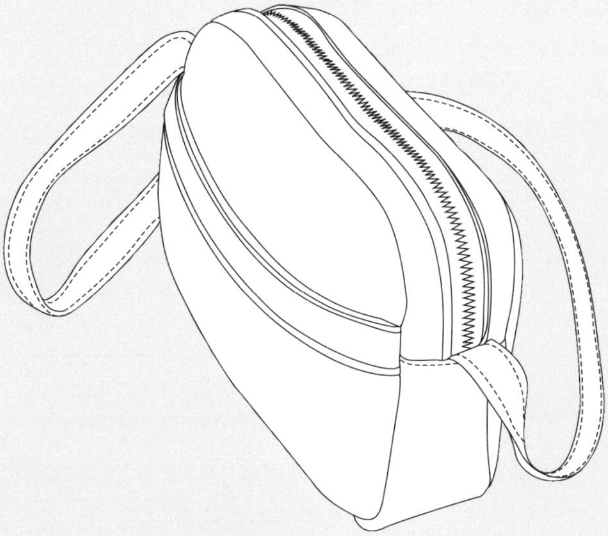

Three-quarter drawing

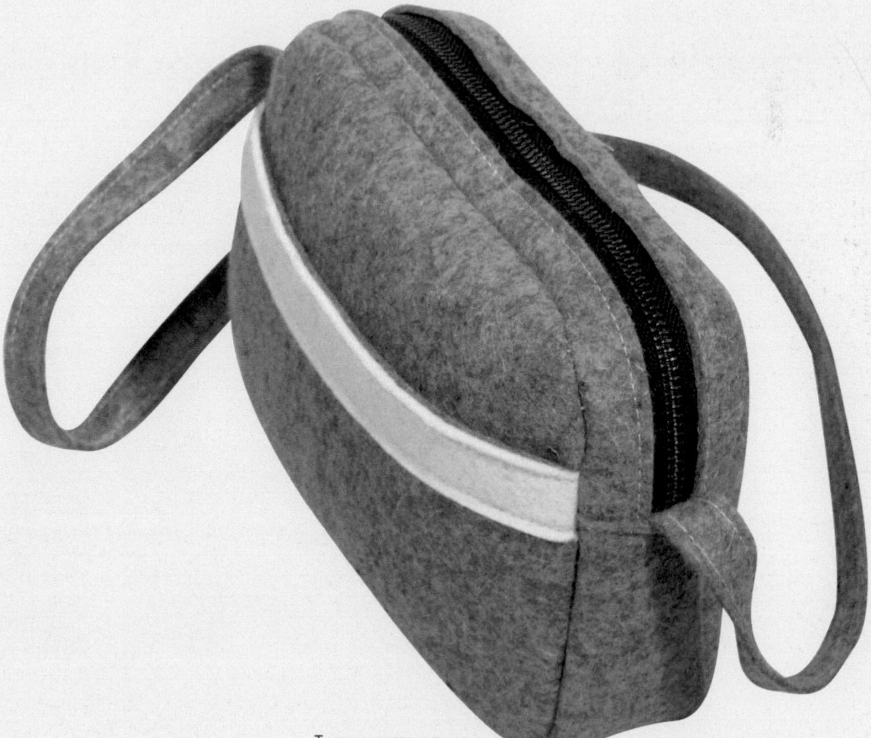

Three-quarter view of finished bag.

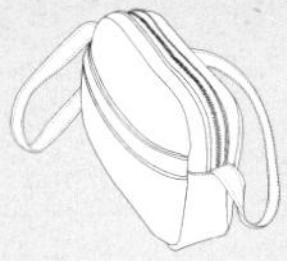

Front template

This template, which we will call the 'front', is used to construct the back and the front (which are identical) as well as the front pocket. It is necessary to begin by drawing the front shape, then add the seam allowance.

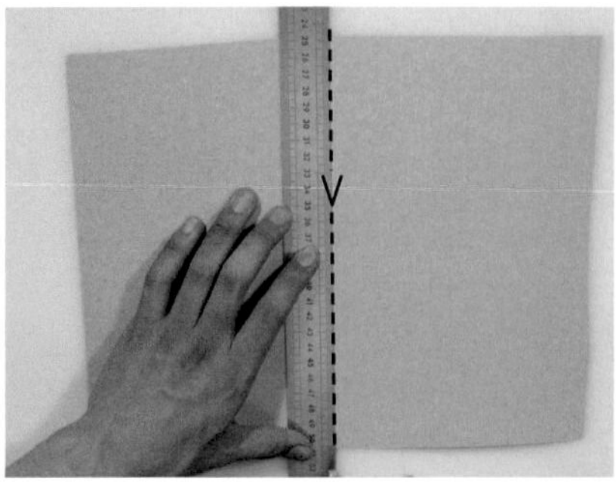

1. Cut a piece of card slightly bigger than the front of the bag, i.e. about 30 x 20 cm for a front measuring 23 x 16 cm. In the centre of the card, use a ruler and cutter to mark the vertical V axis of the template placing it widthways.

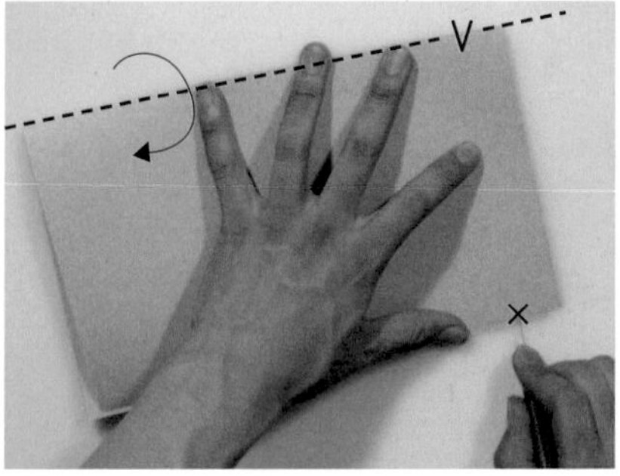

2. To trace the bottom line of the template, fold the card in two along its V axis, use the cutter to mark a point on the edge of the card on the opposite side to the V axis. Press fairly hard to mark through the two thicknesses of card.

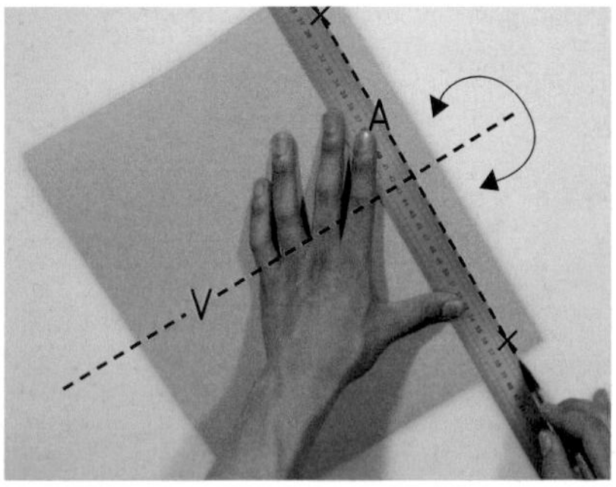

3. Unfold the template: we now have two marks which are perfectly symmetrical to the V axis. Join up these two marks with a pencil to trace line A, the bottom of the template.

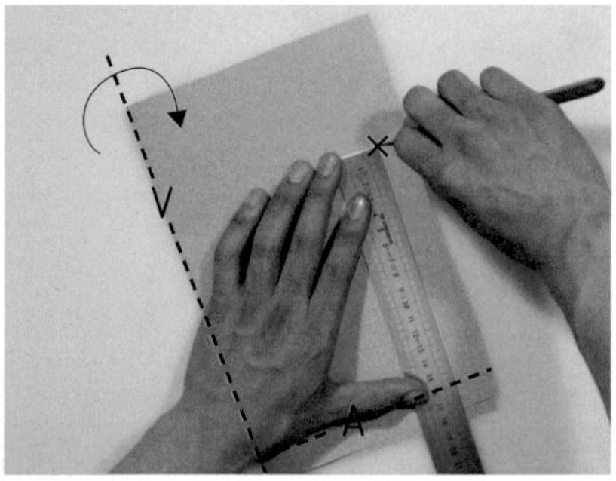

4. To trace the template's top line, fold again along the V axis. Place the ruler perpendicular to line A on the edge of the card, on the right-hand side of the V axis. Use a cutter to mark a point 16 cm from line A. Press fairly hard to pierce through the two layers of card.

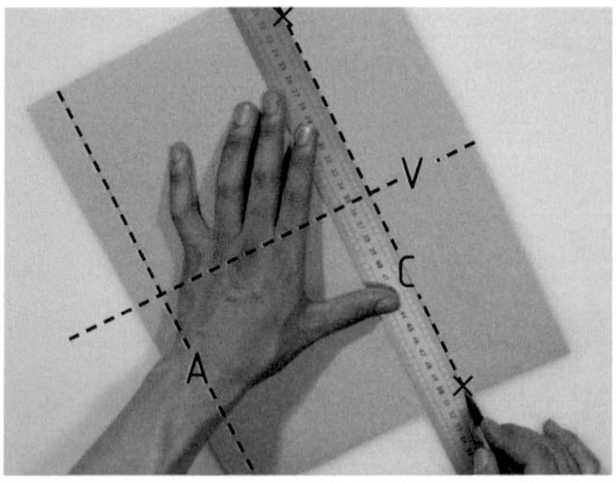

5. Unfold the template and join up the two points with a pencil. We now have traced line C, the top of the front template.

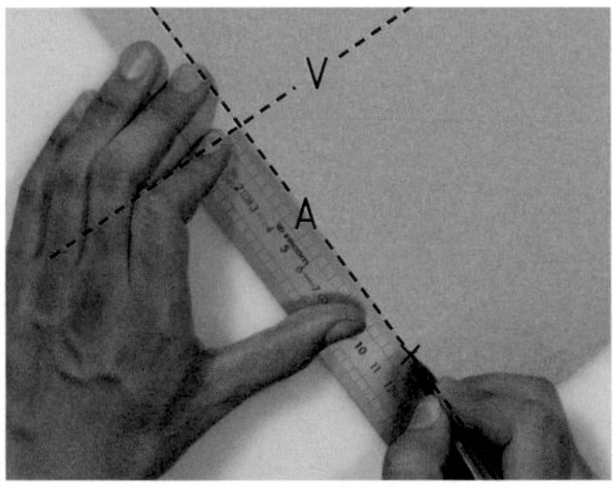

6. Now trace half the width of the template. On line A, and right of the V axis, use a pencil to mark half the width of the front, i.e. 11.5 cm for a front of 23 cm. Repeat this process on line C.

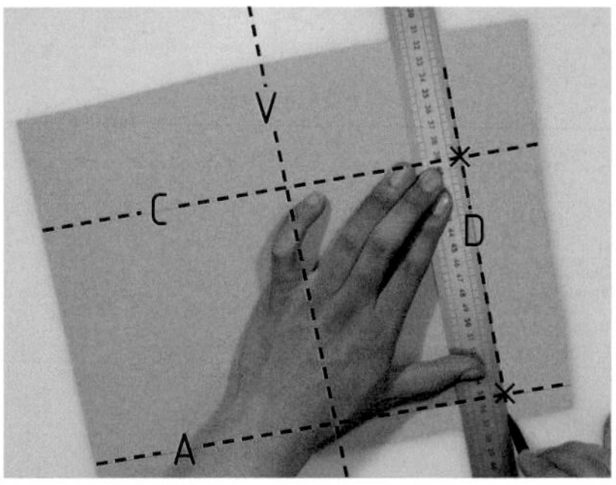

7. Join up these two points to achieve line D which is the side of the front template.

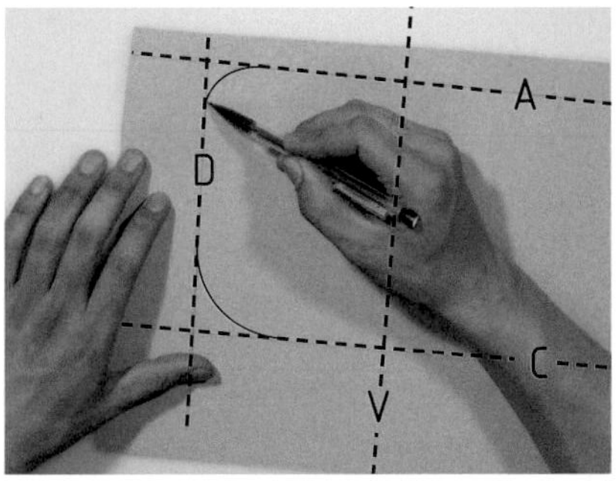

8. Draw the curves of the side. A French curve helps to trace a softer curve.

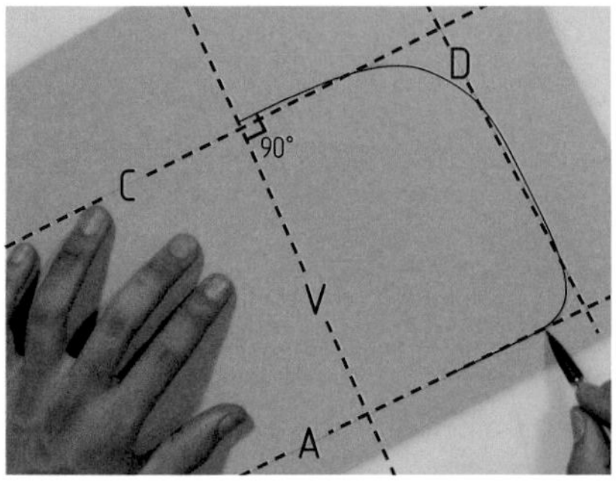

9. To give the bag a softer aspect, we are going to draw the shape by rounding the top and the side. The tracing will slightly go over lines C and D by 0.5 cm maximum.

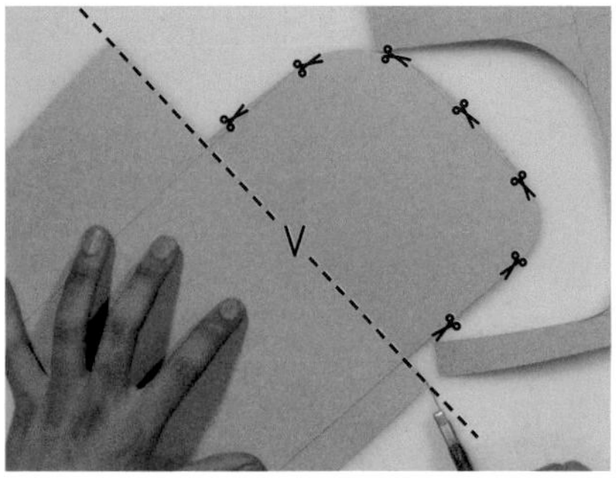

10. Cut half of the card stopping short of the V axis.

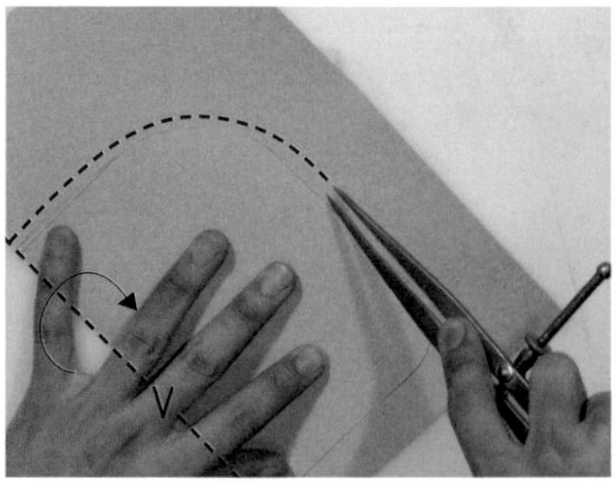

11. We are now going to add the seam allowance. Fold the template in two along the V axis. Set the compass to 0.5 cm, and trace the seam allowance, onto the other half, using the

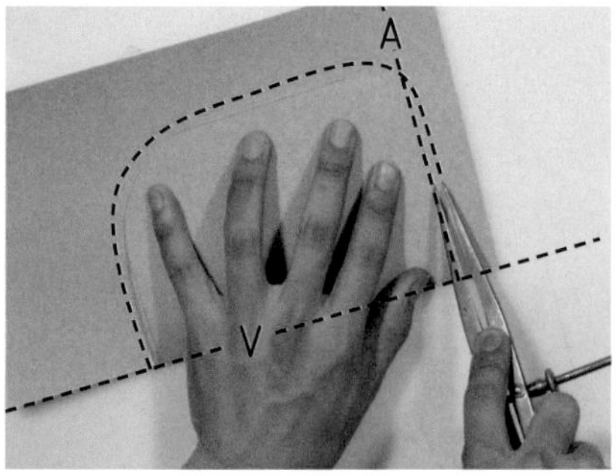

12. Start at the top and work towards the bottom along the V axis.

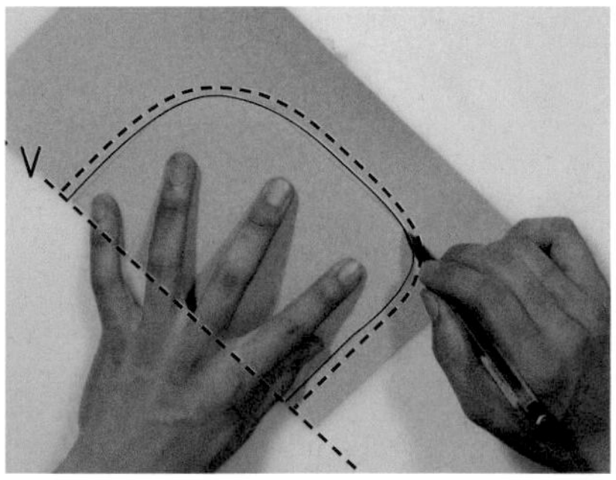

13. Use a pencil to trace the outline onto the other half.

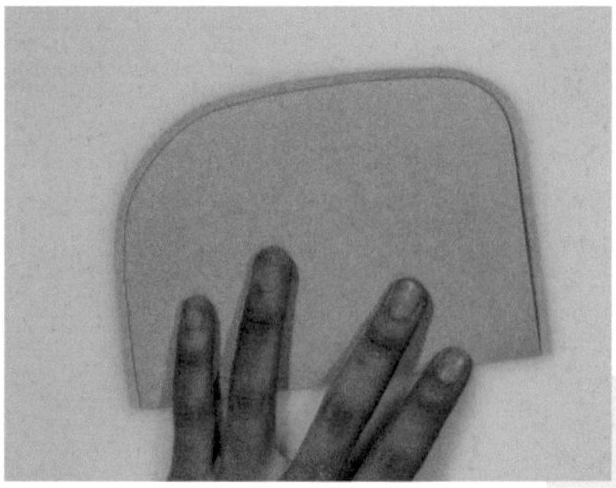

14. We have cut the second half with a cutter following the seam allowance mark.

15. We will now draw the pocket and trim strip (which is stuck onto this pocket) onto this template. Fold the template along the V axis. On the edge of this card, mark off with a cutter point (e) 11.5 cm above line A and perpendicular to this line. Unfold the template and, placing the ruler onto these two marks, trace the top of the pocket i.e. line P, onto half of the template, stopping short of the V axis. Fold the template again and mark off 2.2 cm under point (e) a point (f). Unfold the template and, placing the ruler on these two marks, trace the width of the trim i.e. line G, onto half of the template stopping just short of the V axis. Draw the top stitches measuring 0.2 cm on the inside of lines G and P. The template of the front, back and pocket is now finished.

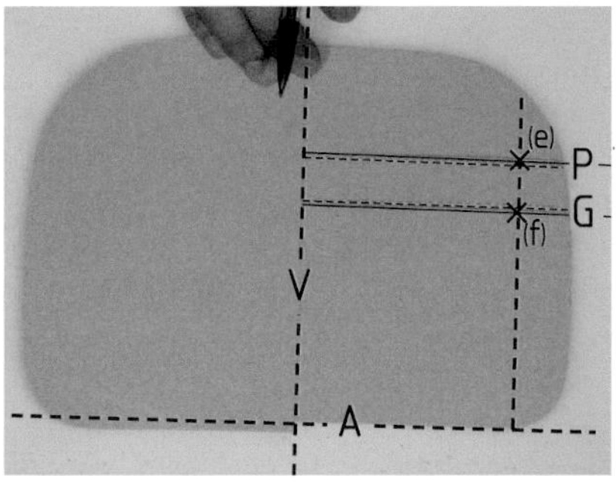

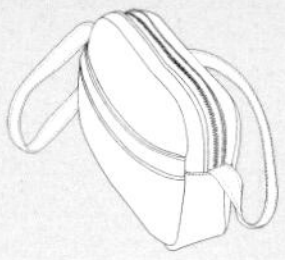

Pocket pattern

To make the pocket pattern we need to use the front template, where the pocket position has been drawn, and add the outline to this.

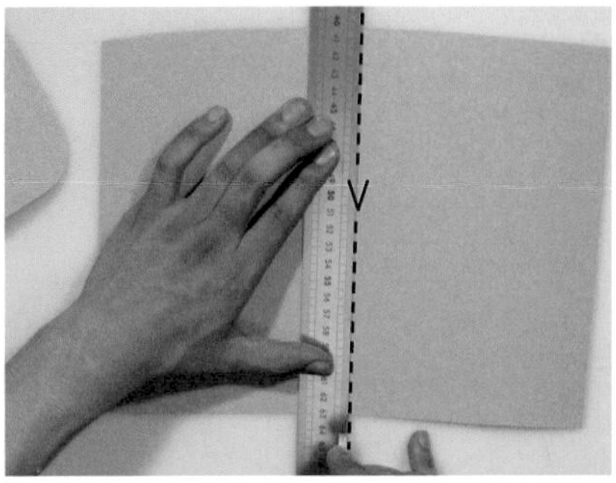

1. Cut a piece of card about 30 x 15 cm for a pocket measuring 23 x 11.5 cm. In the middle of the card, use a ruler and cutter to score the vertical V axis of the pattern in a widthways direction.

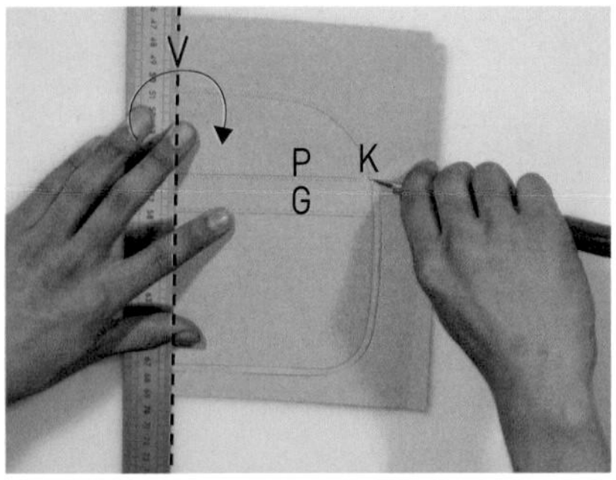

2. Fold the pattern in two along the V axis. Fold the front template in two along the V axis. Place the front template on top of the pattern carefully aligning the two V axes.. Transfer a mark on the far right of line P, pressing fairly hard to go through four layers of card. Call this point 'k'.

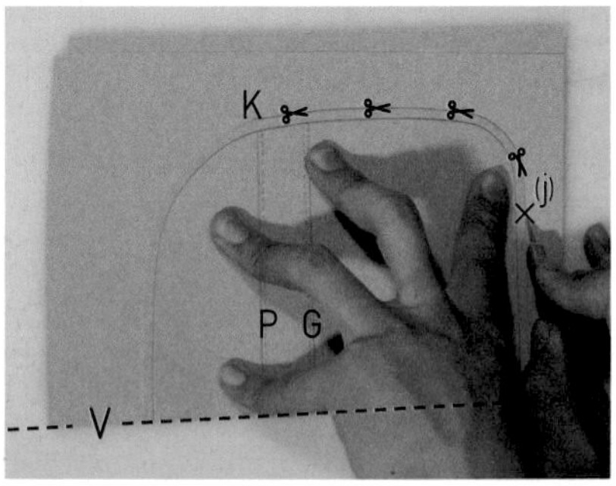

3. Use a cutter to cut through two thicknesses of card following the line of the template's seam allowance. Start from line P and stop at the end of the bottom curve. Call this point 'j'. Mark a notch in the card, without removing the excess.

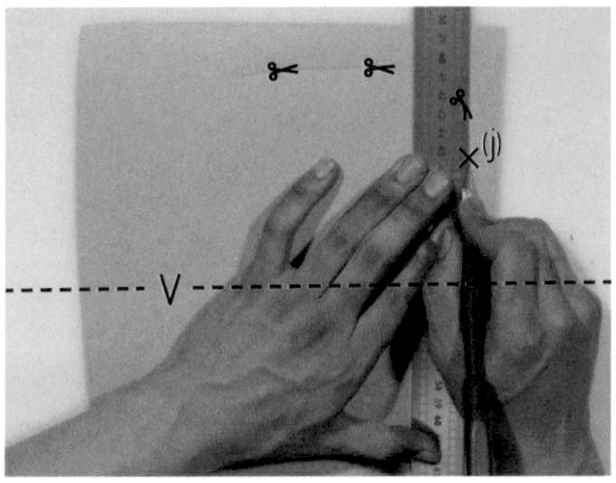

4. Remove the front template. Unfold the pattern. With the aid of a ruler and cutter, cut out the bottom of the pocket joining point (j) with its point which is symmetrical to the V axis. Cut the top, joining point (k) with its point which is symmetrical to the V axis.

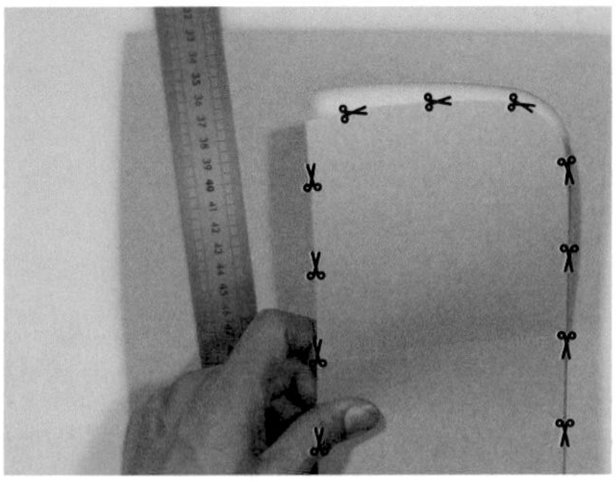

5. We have now cut out the front pocket pattern.

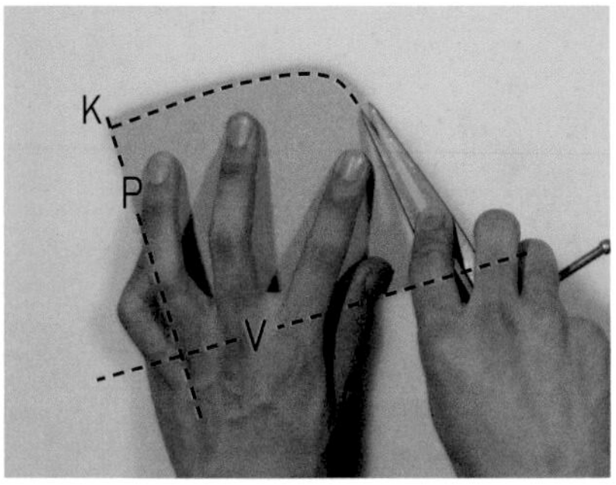

6. Fold the pattern in two along its V axis. Use a compass set at 0.5 cm to trace off the seam allowance starting at point K, using the edge of the card as a guide. With a cutter, transfer a line onto the pattern 2.2 cm under line P on the far right of line G.

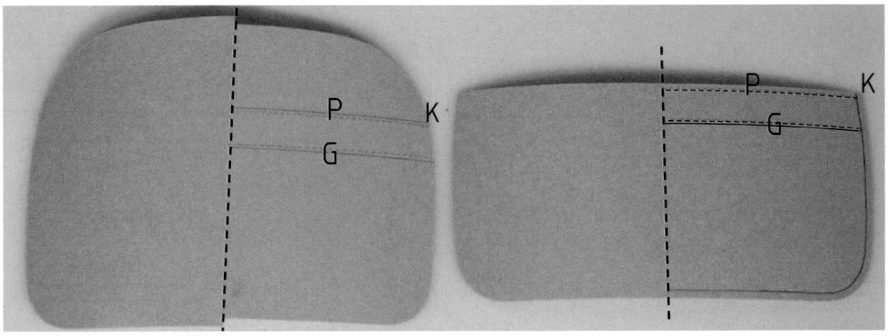

7. Unfold the pattern and join up the two marks with a pencil stopping at the V axis – like on the template – this will trace line G onto the pattern. Re-do the seam allowance mark with a pencil.

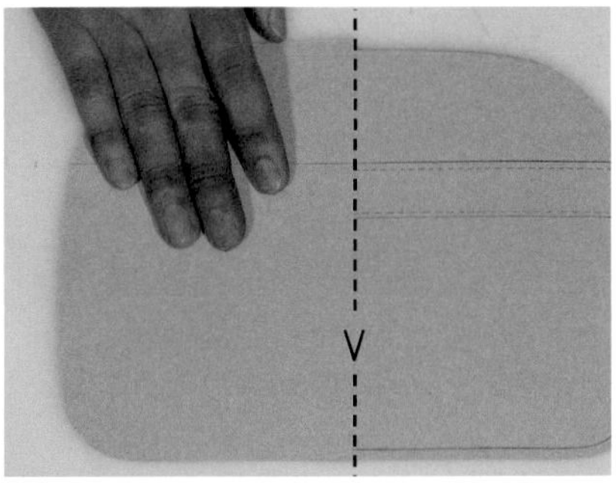

8. The pocket pattern is finished. It can now be placed on the front template to check that it is the correct size.

Front pattern

We use the front template then add the seams to trace the front pattern.

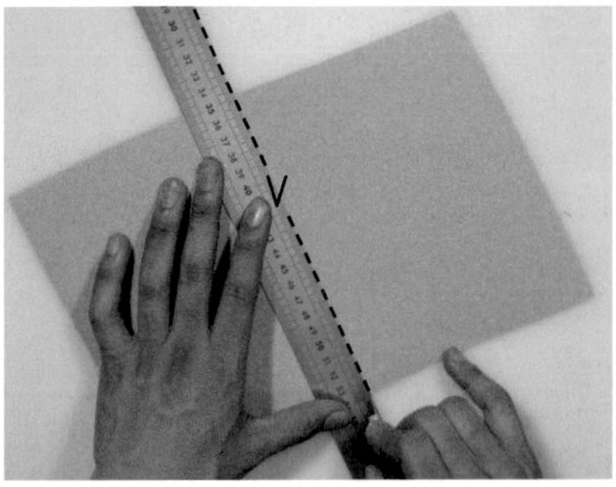

1. Cut a piece of card about 30 x 20 cm for a front of 23 x 16 cm. Use a cutter to score the V axis in the centre of the card.

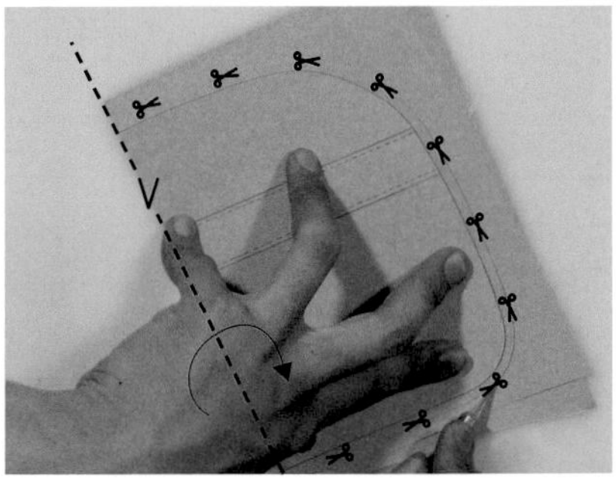

2. Fold the pattern in two along its V axis. Fold the front template in two along its V axis. Place the template onto the pattern lining up carefully the two V axes of both the pattern and the template. Cut it out with the cutter using the template's outline as a guide.

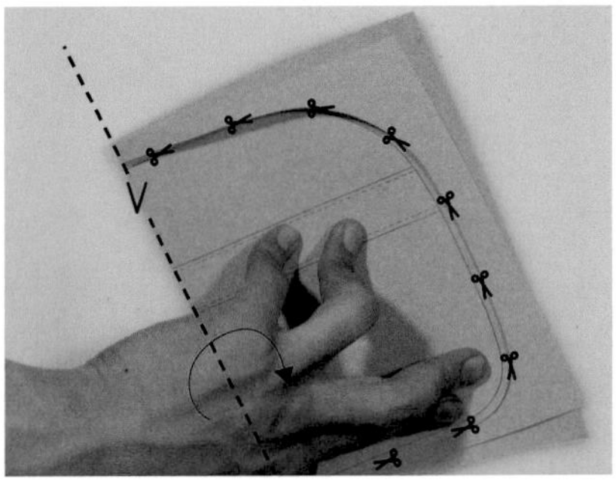

3. It will take several attempts to cut through the two thicknesses in one go.

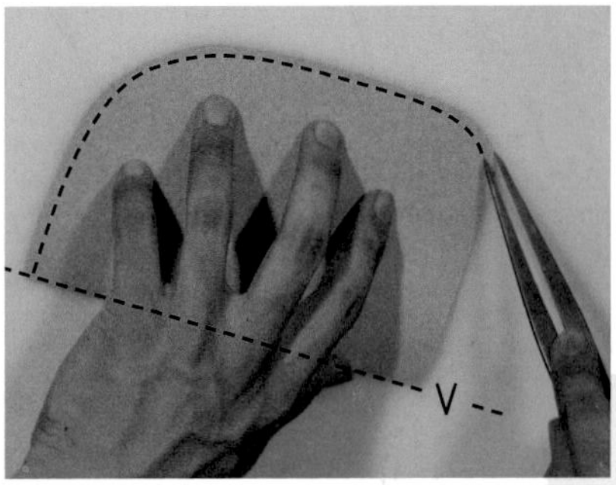

4. Remove the template. Set the compass to 0.5 cm and trace the seam allowance using the edge of the card as a guide.

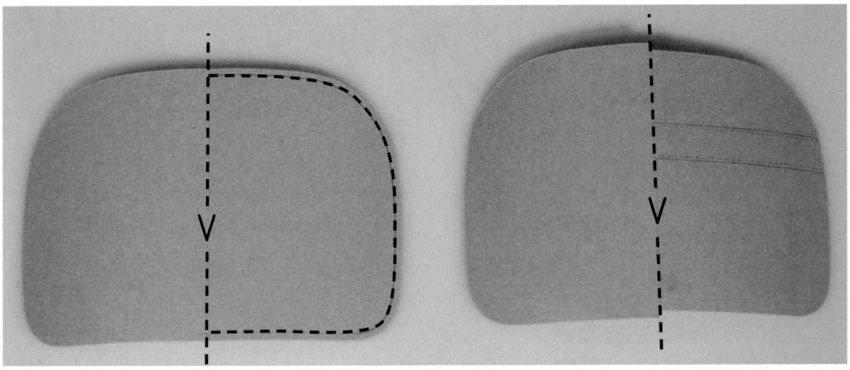

5. Re-do this marking with a pencil. The pattern of the front and back pieces is now complete. We now have the exact measurements of the template and the pattern.

Side template

The side of the bag is the most complicated piece to make. Like the previous tote bag, the bottom of this bag is slightly bigger than the top. The two sides and the base are made from one piece, which begin at the top of the pocket band. The top is made from two pieces which will be held together by the zip. Therefore, we will make a one piece template which will include the top, sides and underside pieces.

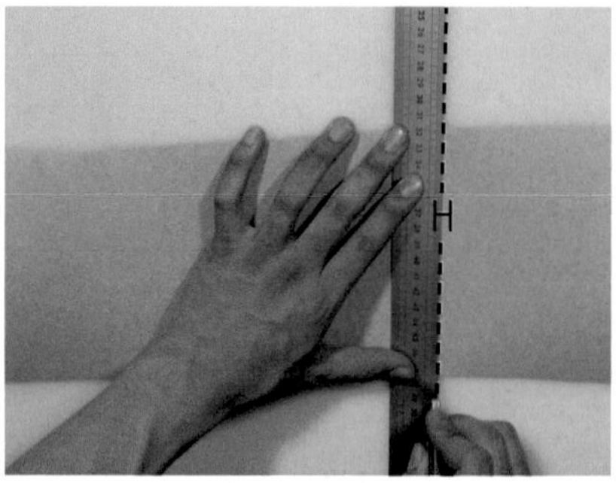

1. Cut a strip of card whose length is bigger than the total measurements of the top, the sides and the base i.e. 90 x 15 cm for a bag of 23 x 16 x 6 cm. Score the centre of the card widthways using a ruler and a cutter. This becomes the vertical axis H of the template.

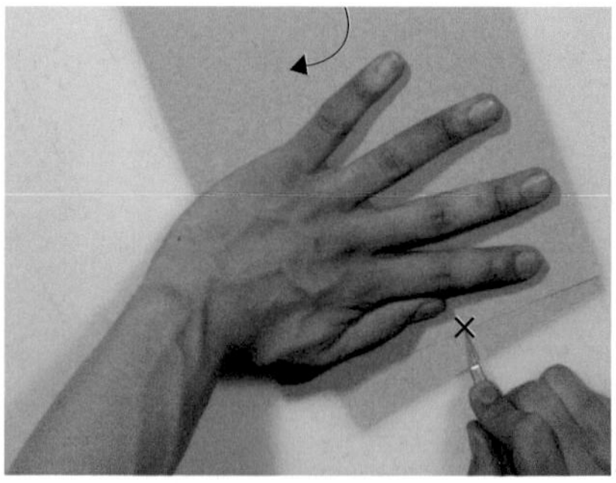

2. Fold in two along the H axis. Use a cutter to mark off the centre of the width on the edge of the card opposite the H axis.

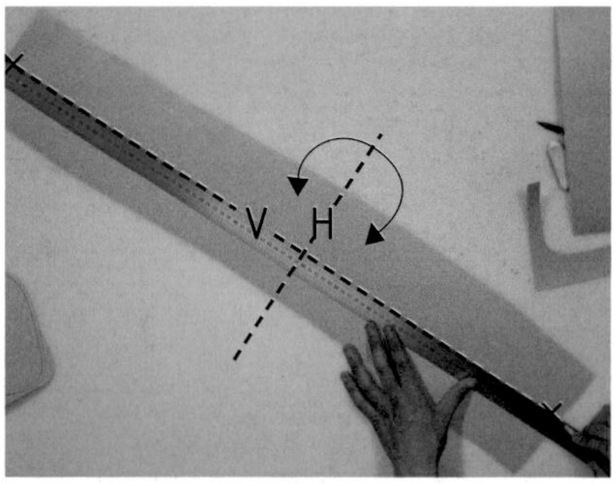

3. Unfold and score a line between these marks with a cutter. This will trace the vertical V axis.

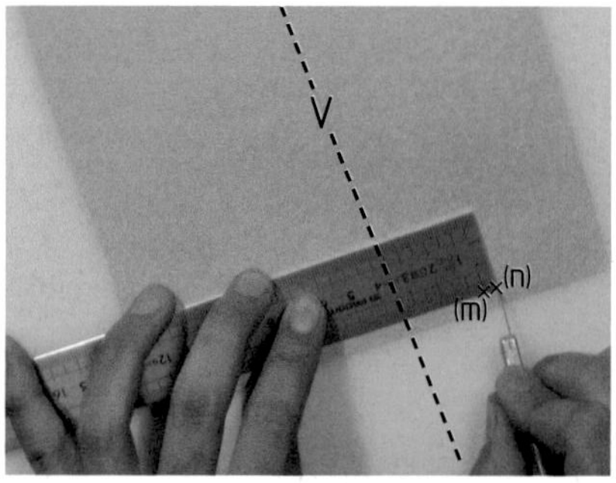

4. Fold the card along the H axis. We are going to trace four lines parallel to the V axis. On the edge of the card, mark a point (m) with cutter 3 cm above the V axis. Press fairly hard to mark the two layers of card. Mark off another point (n) 3.5 cm above the V axis. Again, press fairly hard in order to go through the two layers of card.

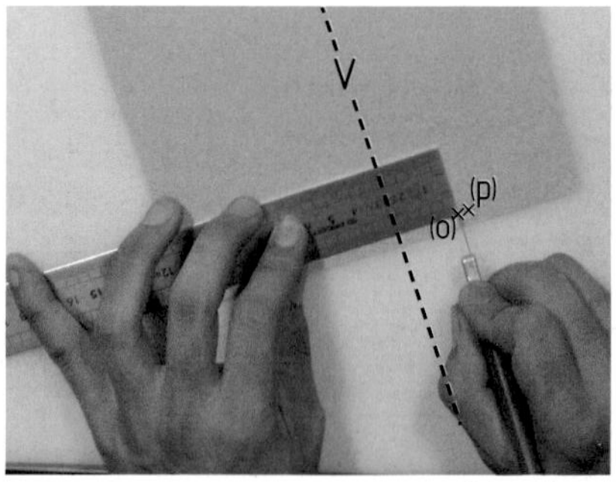

5. Place the cutter at a third point (o) 2.25 cm above the V axis. Press hard again to make sure the two layers of card are marked. Then mark off a fourth point (p) 2.75 cm above the V axis. Press hard again.

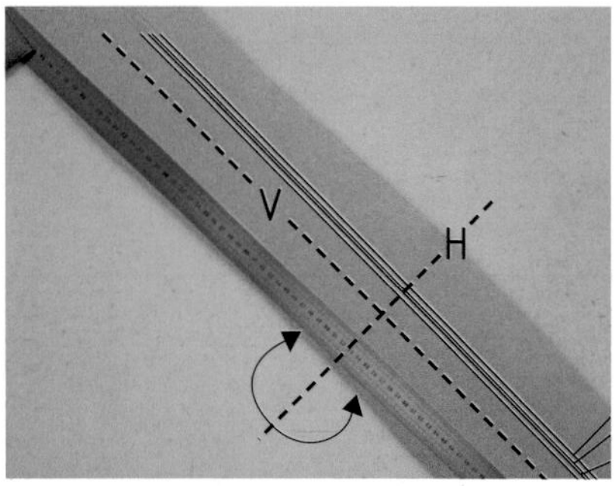

6. Unfold the template. We now have points (m'), (n'), (o') and (p') which are symmetrical to points (m), (n), (o) and (p) in relation to the H axis. Join (m) to (m'), (n) to (n'), (o) to (o') and (p) to (p'). Line (mm') corresponds to half the width of the bottom of the side. Line (nn') corresponds to its seam allowance. Line (oo') corresponds to half the width of the top of the side. And line (pp') corresponds to its seam allowance respectively.

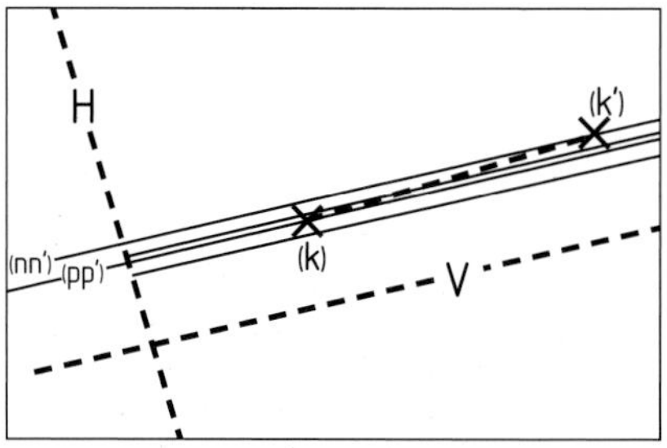

7. Fold the side template along its H axis. This axis corresponds to the middle of the underneath of the bag. On the right-hand side of this axis, put a pencil point on line (pp'); call this point (k). 15 cm to the right of the H axis, put a pencil point on line (nn'); call this point (k'). Join up points (k) and (k'); this line (kk') corresponds to the place where the bag widens.

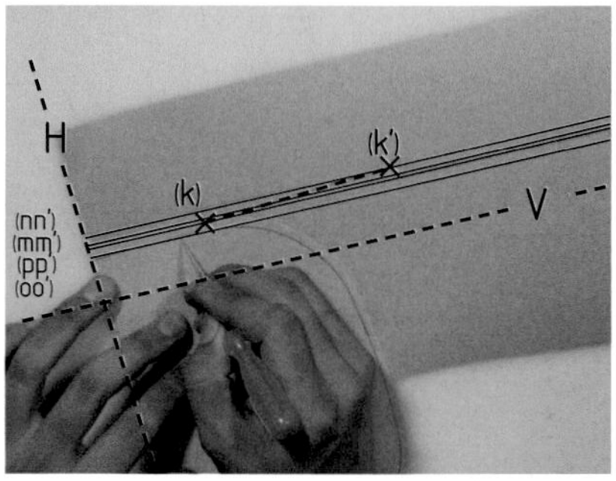

8. Fold the front template along its V axis. Place this template onto the side template, lining up the V axis of the front template precisely with the H axis of the side template, as well as the seam allowance line of the front template and line (pp') of the side template. Place the awl on the front template's outline. Use the awl as a pivot around which the front template can be 'rolled' along the side template, along lines (pp'), (kk') and (nn').

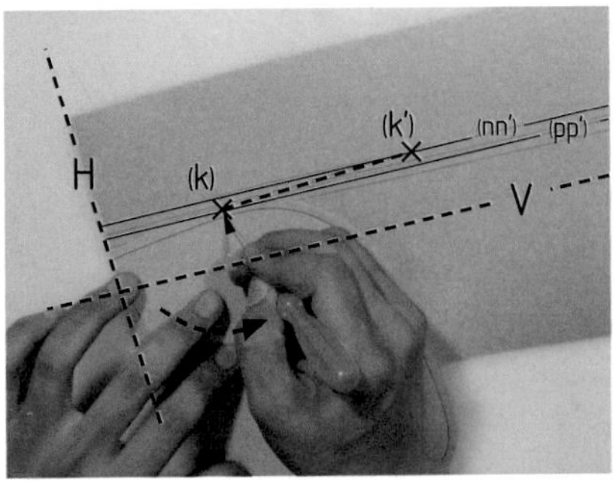

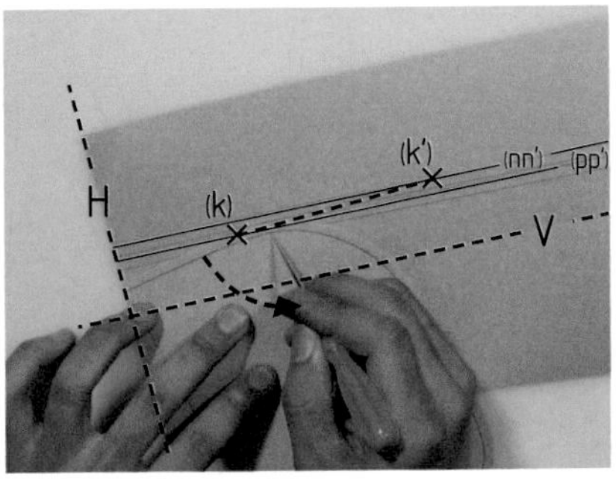

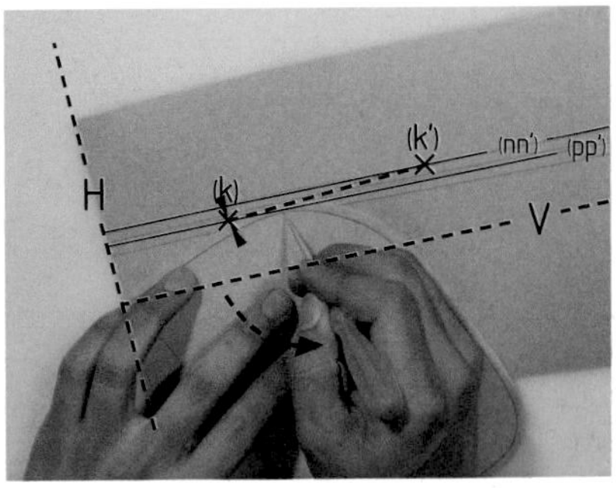

9. Move the awl along the front template's outline so that it 'rolls' along line (pp') of the side. At the top of point (k), notch the two pieces with a cutter. Press hard to mark through the four layers of card. This notch will act as a reference point whilst assembling the front and the back pieces to the sides.

10. From this point, pivot the front template along line (kk').

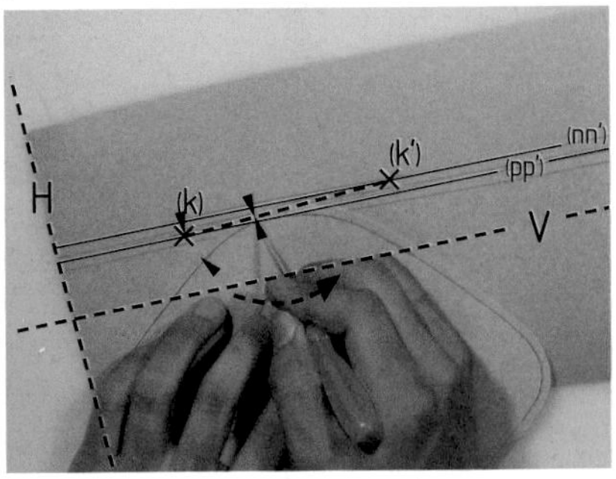

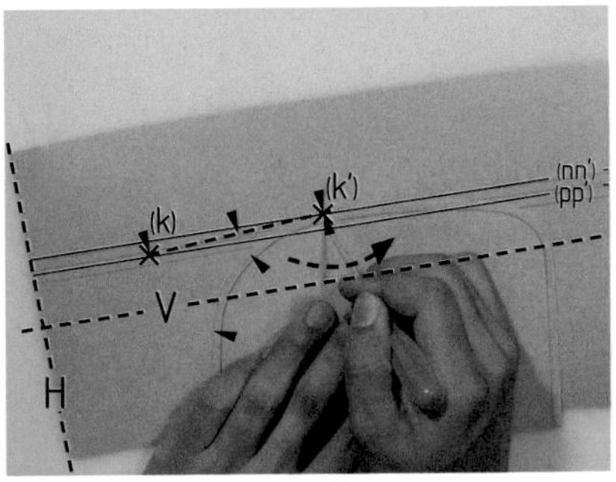

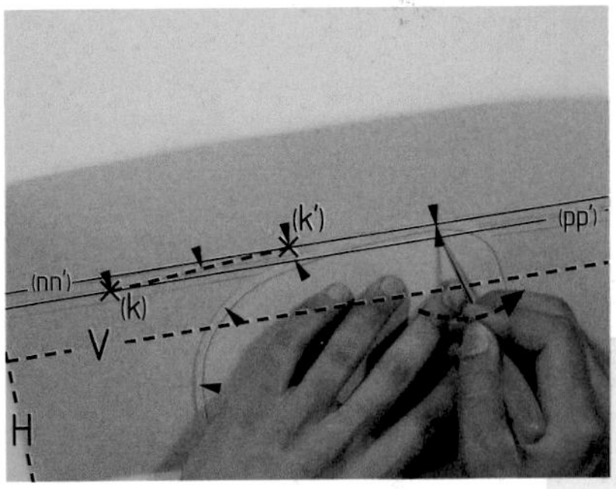

11. In the middle of the curve, notch the two pieces with the cutter, pressing hard enough to go through the layers.

12. At the top of point (k') on the side template, notch the two pieces with the cutter. Press hard to go through the four layers.

13. From this point, 'roll' the front template along line (nn').

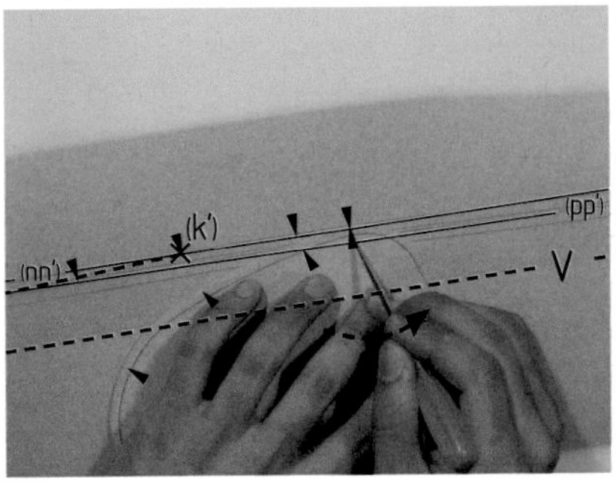

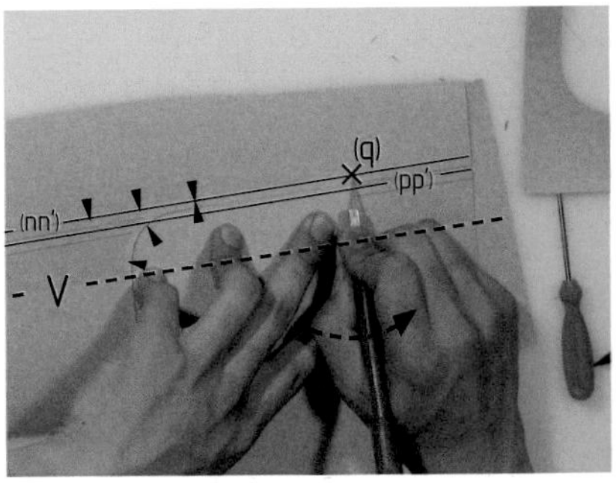

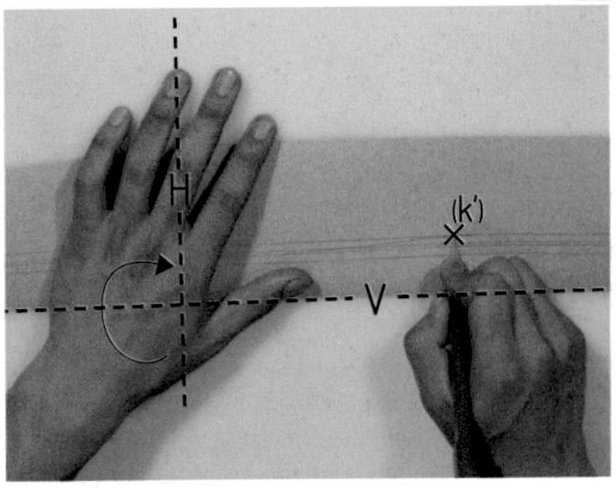

14. Mark a notch at the beginning, in the middle and at the end of the bottom curve.

15. Mark a notch at the position where the V axis of the front template is perpendicular to line (nn') of the side template. This point, which we call 'q' corresponds to the middle of the bottom of the bag. This includes the measurements from the H axis and point (q) which corresponds to the half-width around the bag.

16. Remove the front template. Unfold the side template and fold it along the V axis. Transfer point (k') with a cutter and point (q) symmetrically onto the other half of the card.

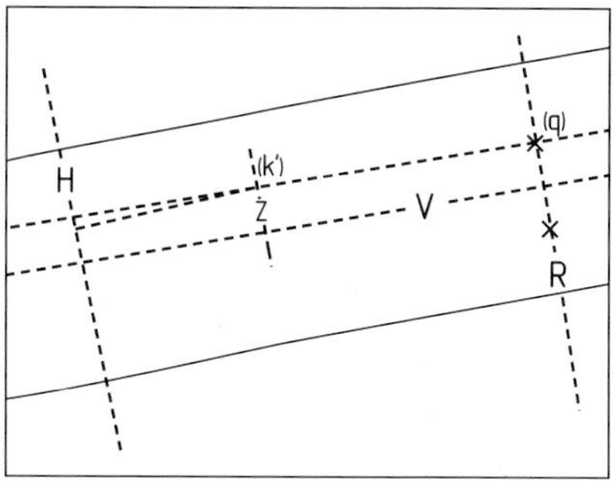

17. Unfold and join point (q) and its point symmetrical to the other side of the V axis. Trace a line which is the middle of the base and call it R.

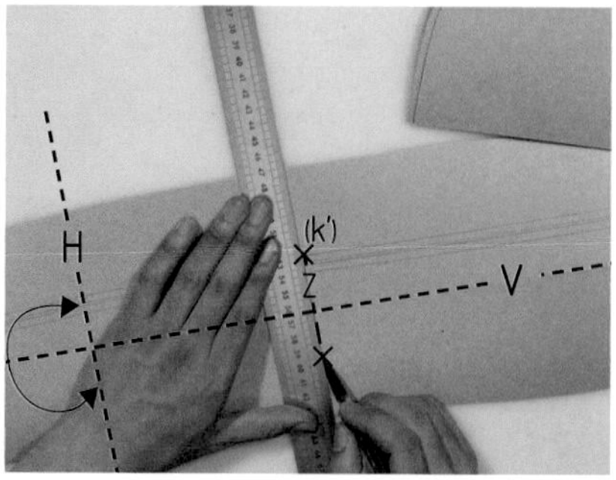

18. Join point (k') and its point symmetrical to the other side of the V axis. This point corresponds to the outside of the zip. Call this place Z.

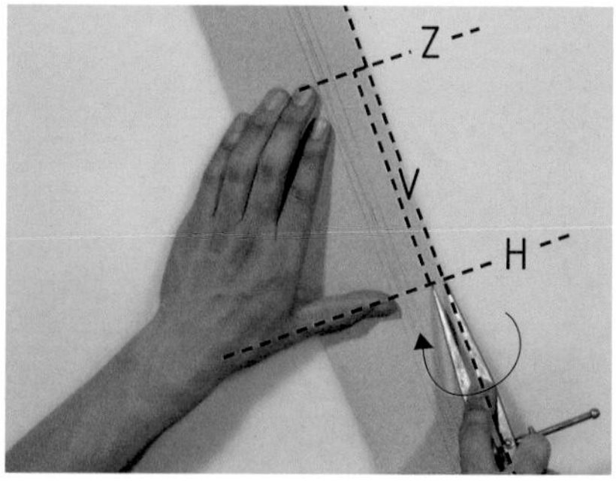

19. To trace the width of the zip, set the compass to its width. Fold the template in two along the V axis. Use the compass to trace the half-width of the zip between the H axis and line Z. Turn the template over and repeat the process on the other side, then unfold.

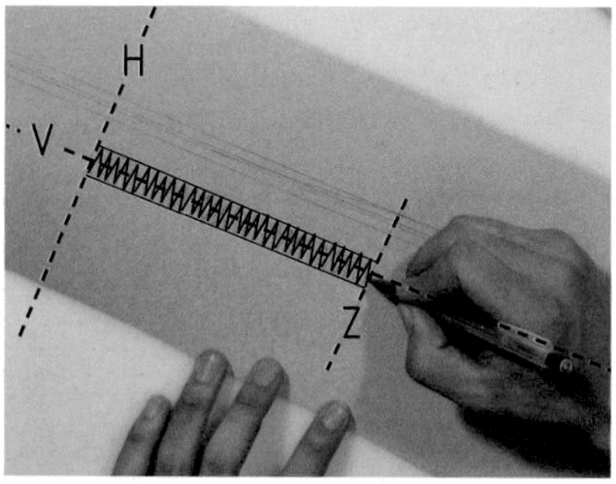

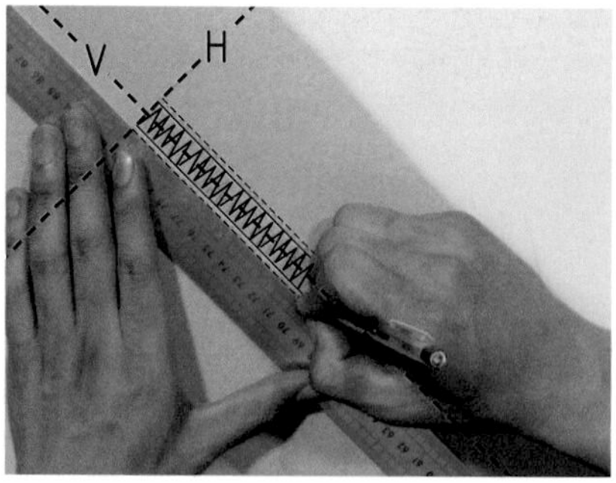

20. Draw the zip and its top stitches in pencil on to the template.

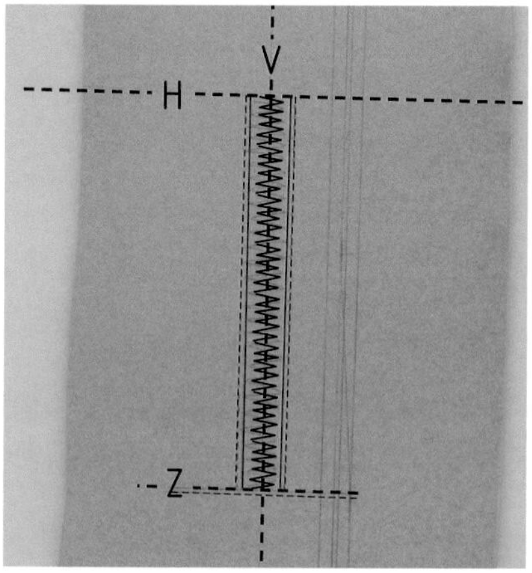

21. The construction of the side template has now been achieved.

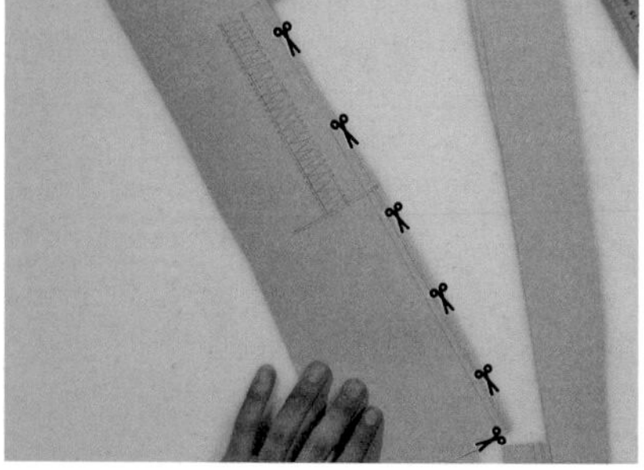

22. Fold the card in two along the H axis and cut out half the template, following the exterior outlines stopping just short of the H and V axes. Unfold and fold along the V axis, then cut out symmetrically the second half of the template.

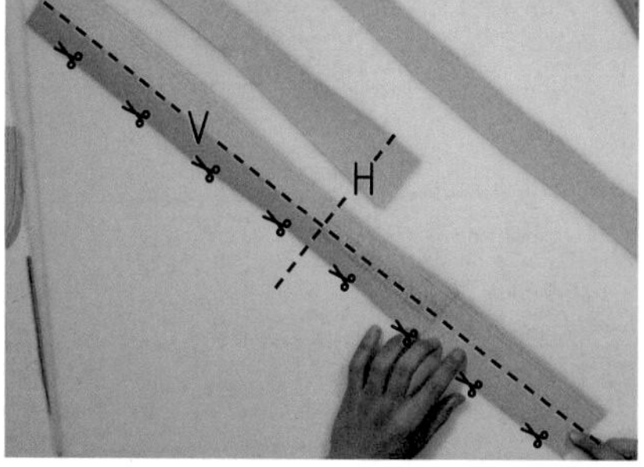

23. Unfold. We have now cut the outlines of the template.

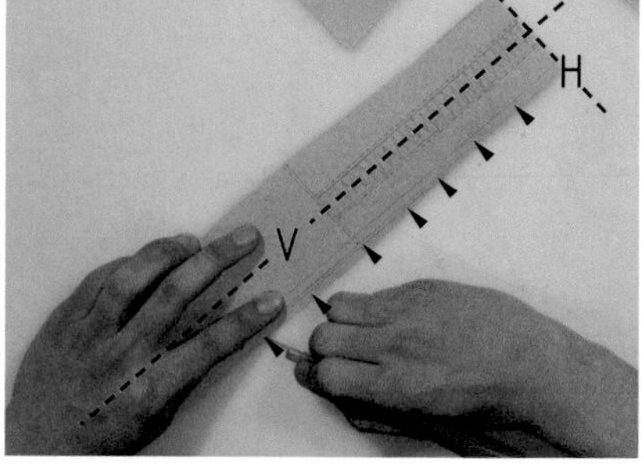

24. Fold the template along the H axis and transfer the notches symmetrically.

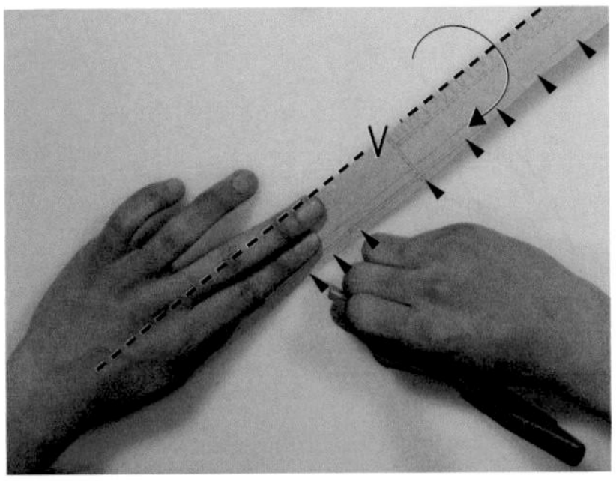

25. Unfold and fold along the V axis to transfer the notches so that they are perfectly symmetrical. The template is now finished.

Side: top pattern

This piece consists of the top and the sides up to the join.

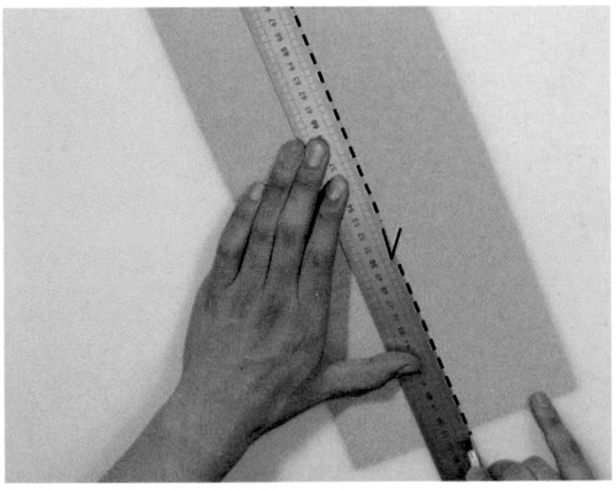

1. Cut a piece of card about 35 x 10 cm. Mark lengthways, with a cutter, the V axis of the pattern in the centre of the card.

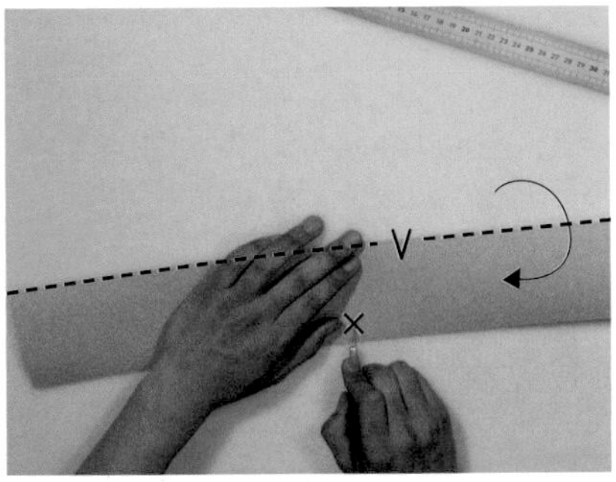

2. Fold in two along the V axis and mark off the middle of the piece on the edge of the card.

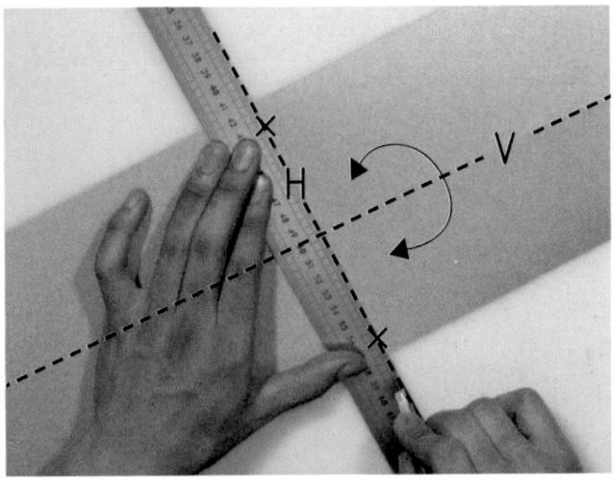

3. Unfold and join up the two marks with a cutter so that the H axis of the top pattern is scored.

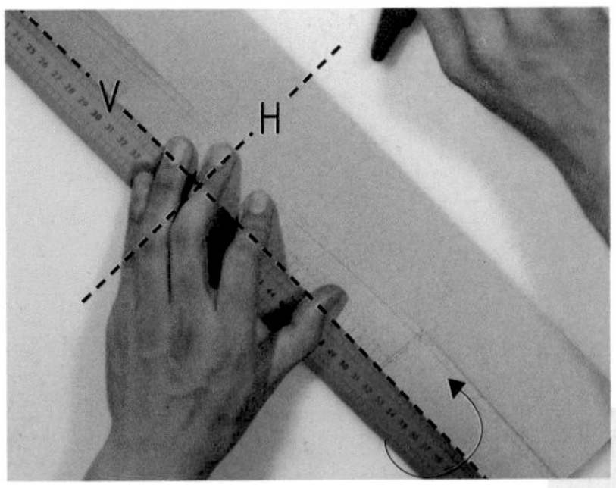

4. Fold along the V axis. Place it on the side template pattern, folded on its V axis, lining up carefully the H and V axes of the two pieces.

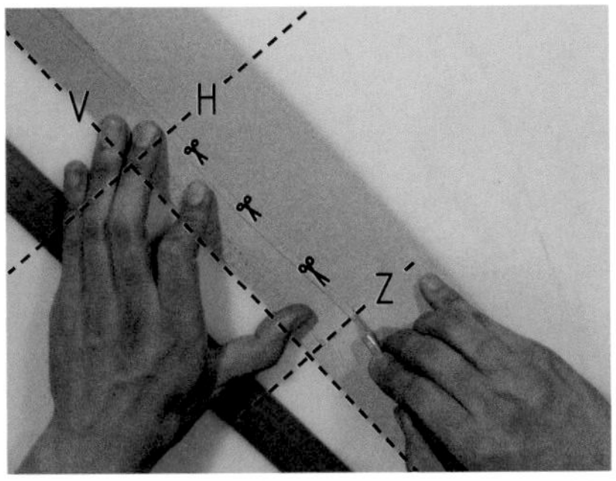

5. Use a cutter to transfer the outline of the side template. Start at the H axis and stop at line Z.

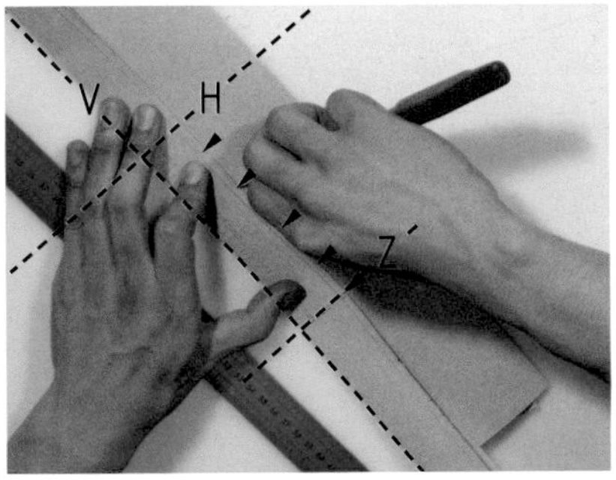

6. Transfer the notches of the template onto the top pattern.

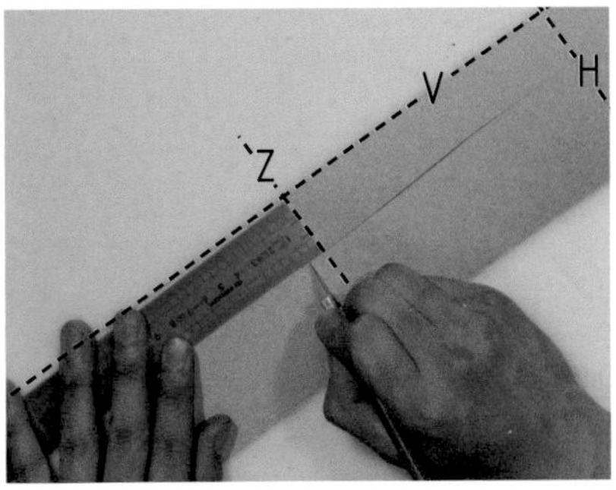

7. Add a I cm seam allowance to line Z which allows the top and side pieces to be assembled.

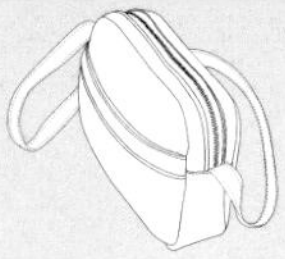

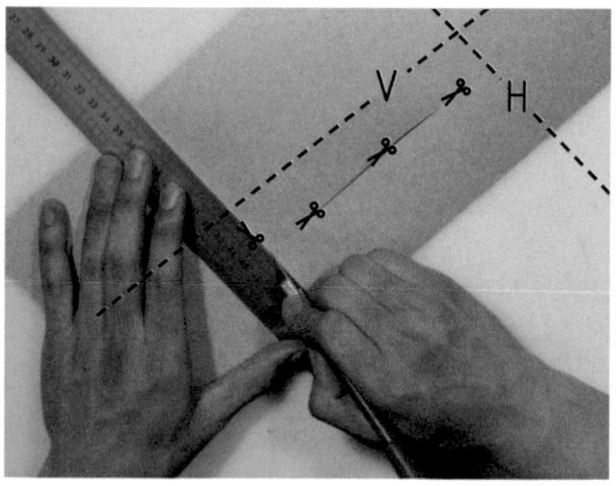

8. Unfold and use a cutter to cut out the seam line starting at the V axis.

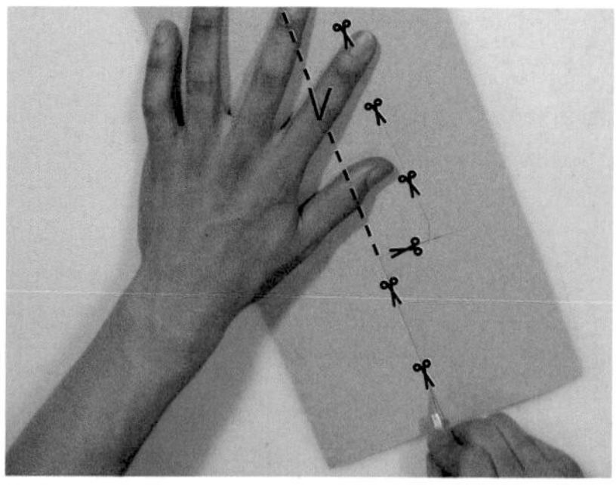

9. Cut the first quarter out stopping at the V and H axes.

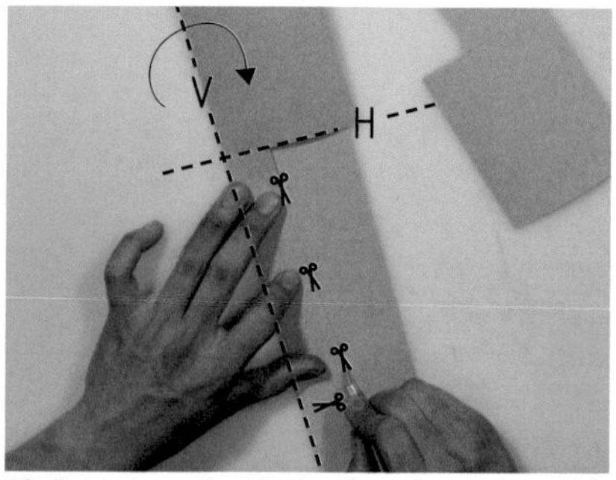

10. Fold along the V axis. Transfer and cut this quarter symmetrically onto the other half of the card. Unfold and fold along the H axis. Transfer and cut symmetrically the second half of the pattern.

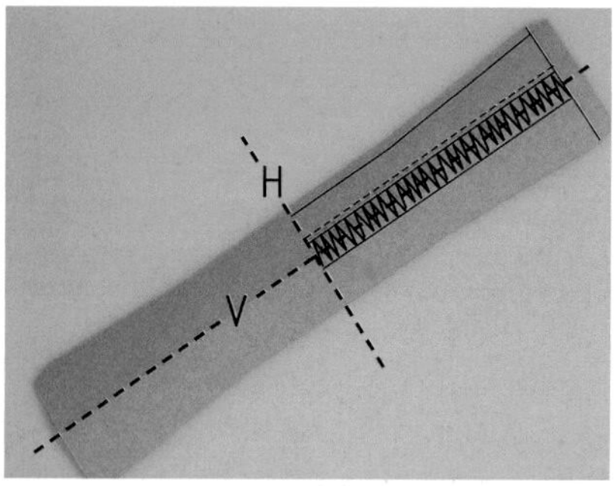

11. We now have the top piece of the bag. With the compass set at 0.5 cm, add the seam allowance using the edge of the card as a guide, then go over this with a pencil. Set the compass to 0.7 cm, trace the lines of the edge of the zip on each side of the V axis. Go over this again with a pencil to symbolise the zip, the top stitches and line Z.

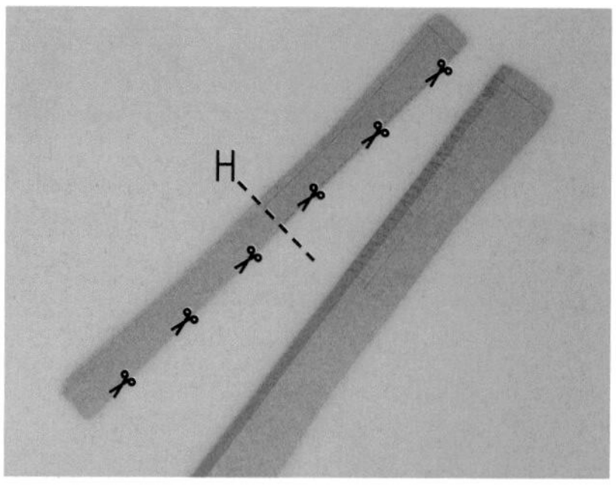

12. Fold along the H axis and cut the line on the edge of the zip. We have cut out the half-width of the zip on the top pattern. Unfold. The top pattern is now finished.

Side: side/underside pattern

We use the top and side template, onto which we add the seams, in order to trace the side and underside patterns.

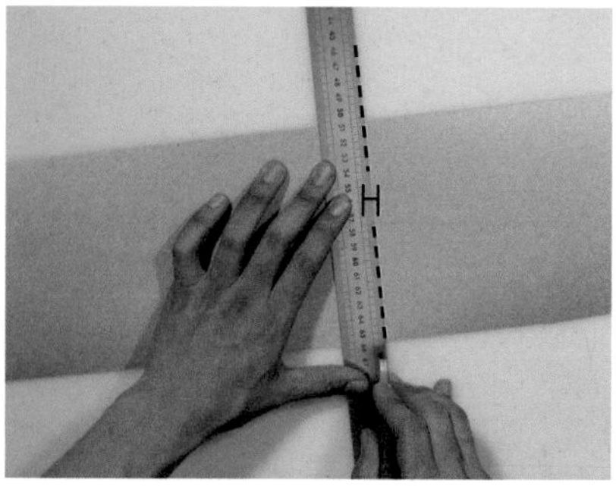

1. Cut out a piece of card about 60 x 15 cm to trace the bottom and sides of the bag. In the middle of the card use a cutter and ruler to score, widthways, the H axis of the pattern.

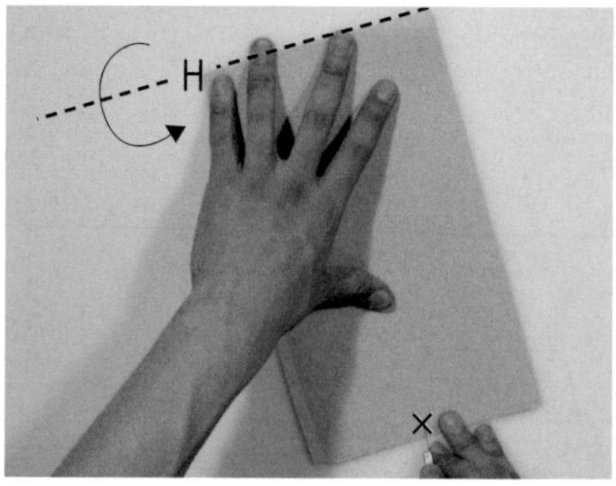

2. Fold the pattern in two along the H axis. Use a cutter to mark off the centre edge of the card.

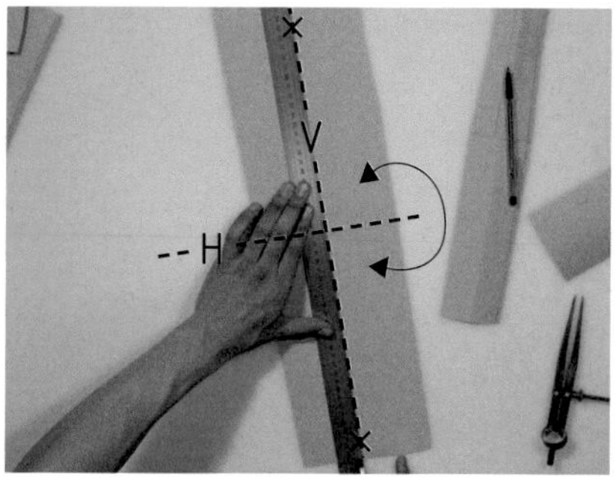

3. Unfold and join up the two marks with a cutter to score the V axis of the pattern.

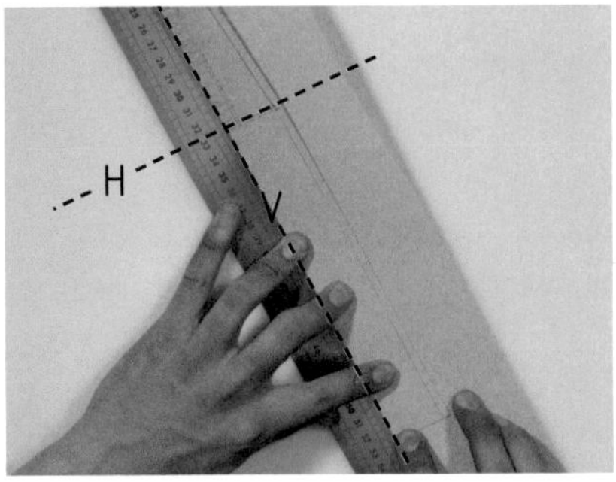

4. Fold the side template in two along its V axis. Fold the pattern along its V axis. Place the side template on the pattern lining up carefully the two axes. Align line R on the template with the H axis of the pattern.

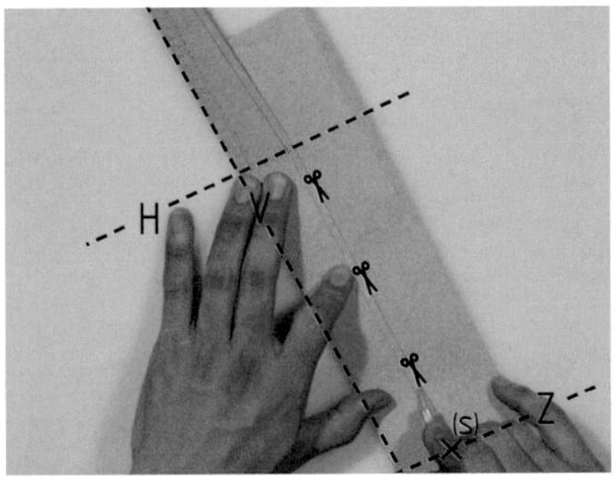

5. Cut the pattern out using the template outline as a guide. Start by cutting at line Z on the template and stop at line R on the template. Use a cutter to mark off the outside of line Z on the template pressing hard enough to go through two layers of card. Call this point (s).

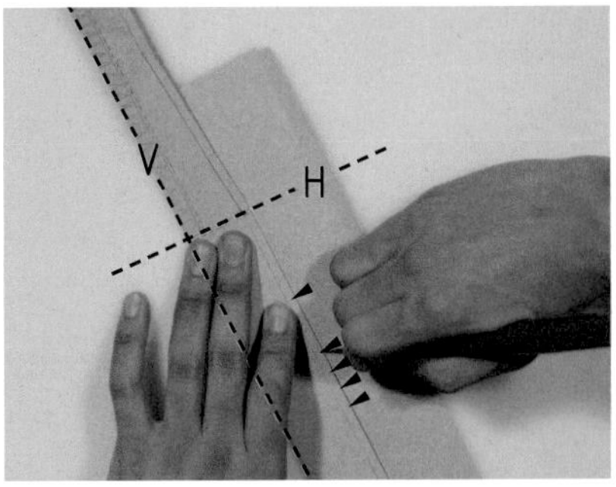

6. Use a cutter to transfer the notches of the template onto the pattern.

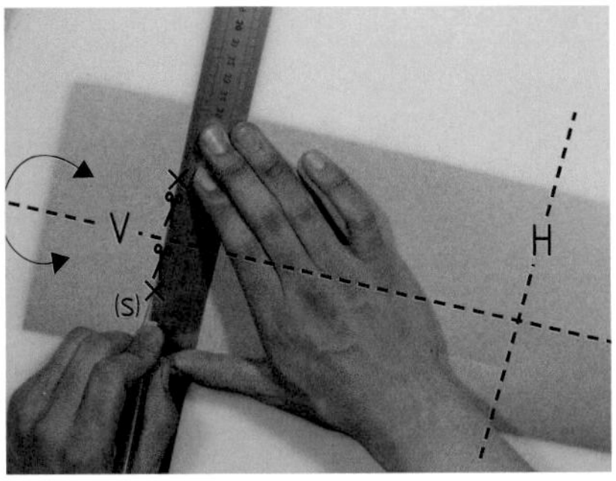

7. Remove the template. Unfold and cut the line between point (s) and its symmetrical point on the opposite side of the V axis, stopping short of the V axis.

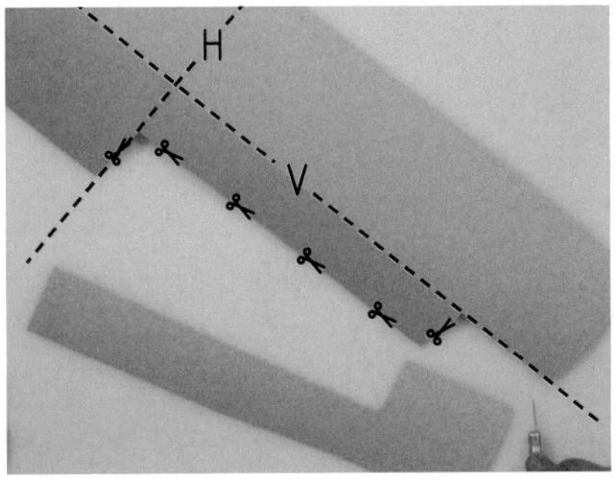

8. Cut out a quarter of the pattern stopping at the V and H axes.

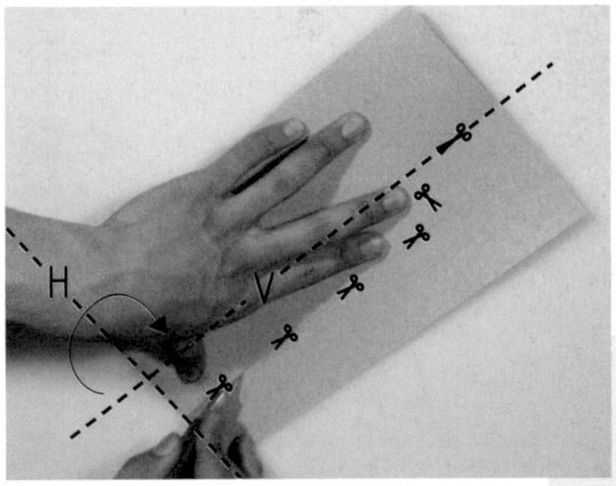

9. Fold along the H axis. Transfer and cut this quarter symmetrically on the other side of the card.

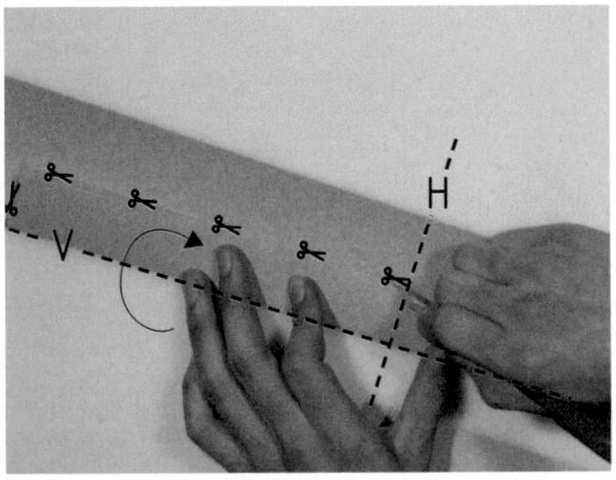

10. Unfold and fold along the V axis. Transfer and cut out symmetrically the second half of the pattern.

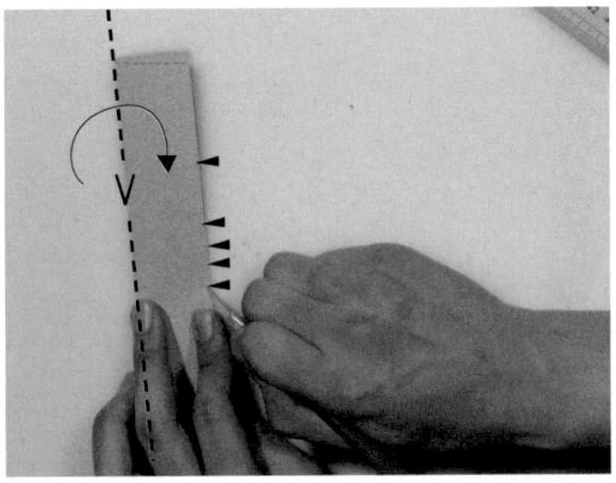

11. Fold along the V axis transferring the notches symmetrically. Unfold. Fold along the H axis and transfer the notches symmetrically again.

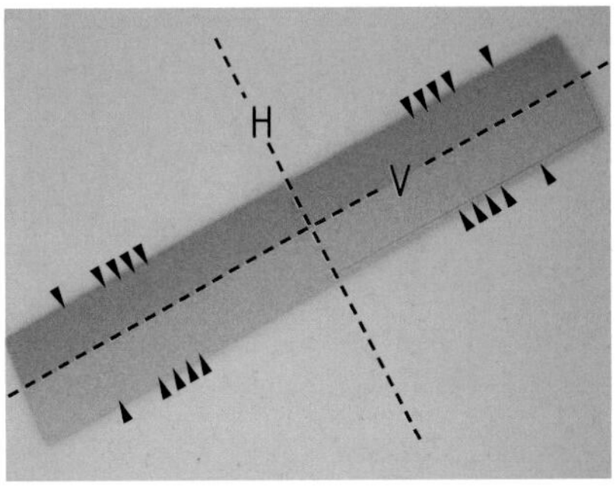

12. Set the compass to 0.5 cm to trace the seam allowance, and draw the top stitches on. The pattern has now been achieved, as well as the pattern pieces which form the sides.

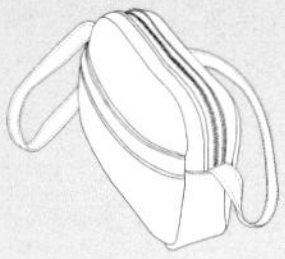

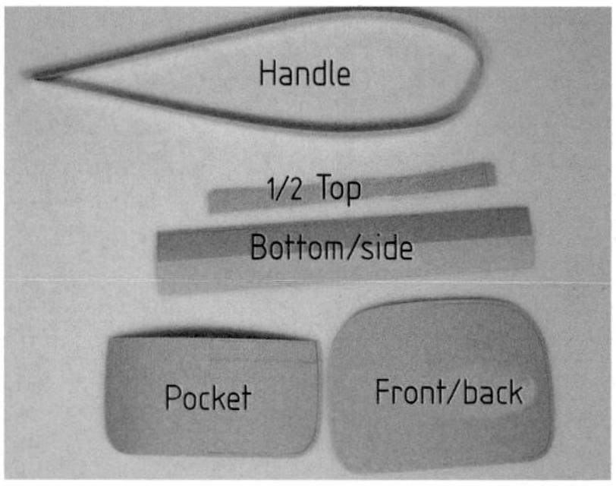

13. We now have a pattern for all the pieces; the front and back, the pocket, half of the top, and one for the underside and sides. All that is left to do is to make a pattern for the strap and another for the top band of the pocket. The strap is a strip of 82 x 2 cm. Make the pocket band pattern by transferring the measurement of this band onto the front template.

Cutting and assembling

We cut out the pieces of the bag from felt, then assemble them with their right-sides together. At the end, they are reversed so that the seams are on the inside. Use the assembling notches to line up exactly.

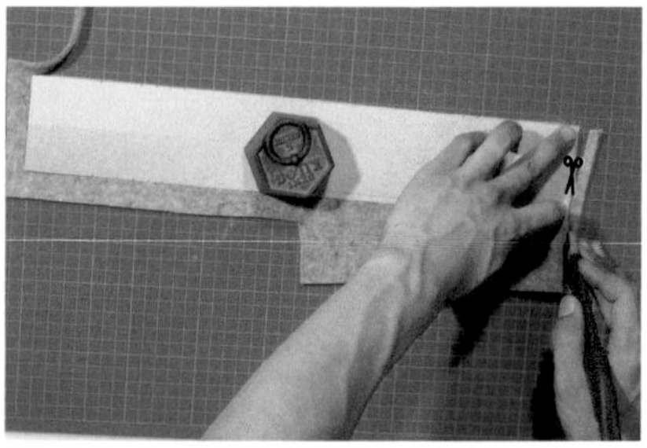

1. Begin by cutting out the base/side pieces.

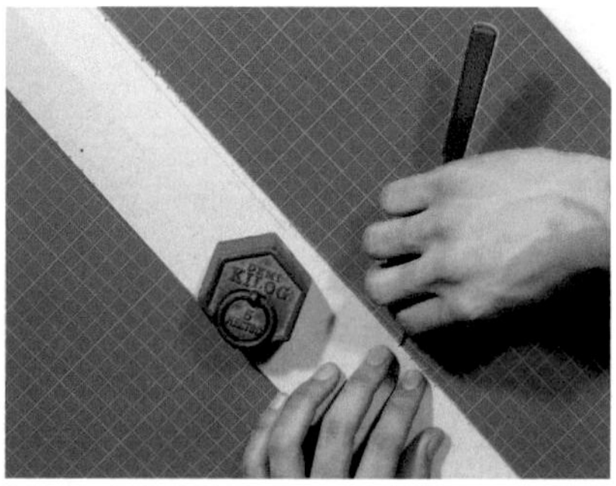

2. Once the outlines have been cut, transfer the pattern notches onto the piece of felt.

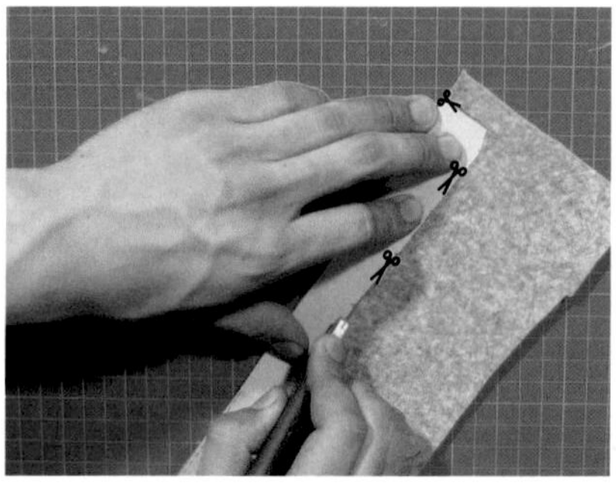

3. Cut out the top piece. Reverse the pattern and cut a second piece.

4. Once the outlines have been cut, transfer the pattern notches onto the piece of felt.

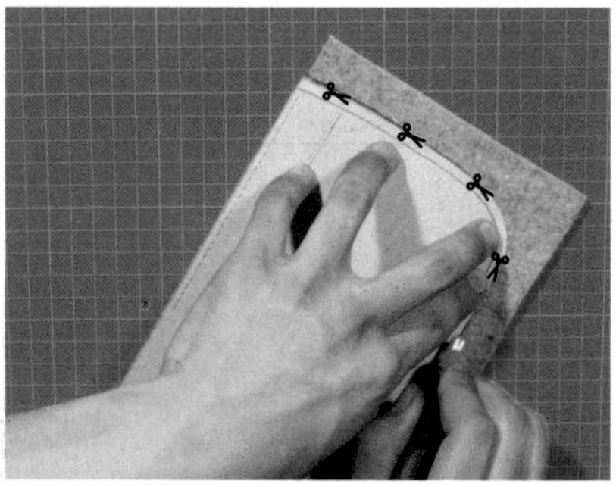

5. Then cut out the pocket piece, transferring the pattern notches onto the felt.

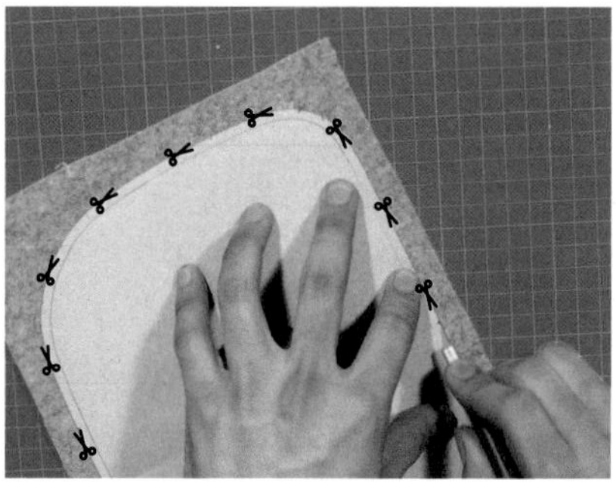

6. Cut the front and the back then mark the notches.

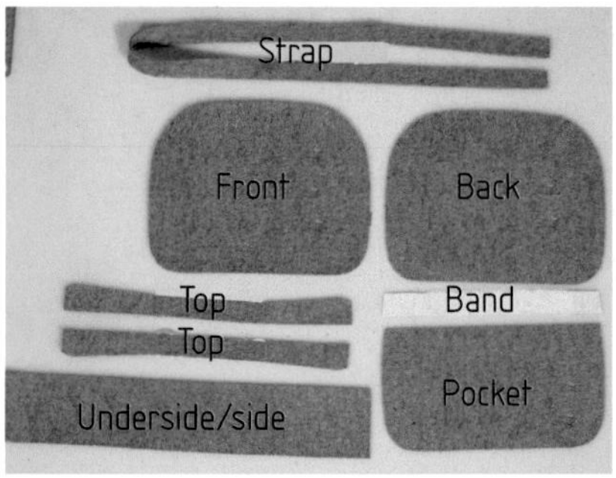

7. We have cut out eight pieces: a front, a back, an underside/sides, a pocket, a band, two tops and a strap.

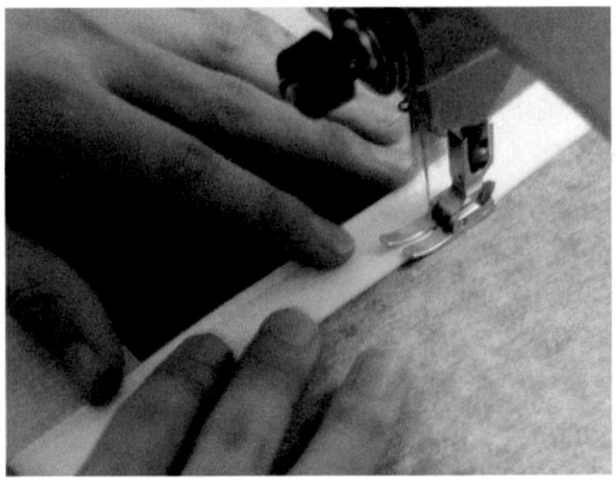

8. Stick the band onto the pocket, then stitch the two pieces 0.3 cm from the edge. Stitch the top first, then the bottom. (It is not necessary to stitch the sides of the band as they will be included in the side seam.)

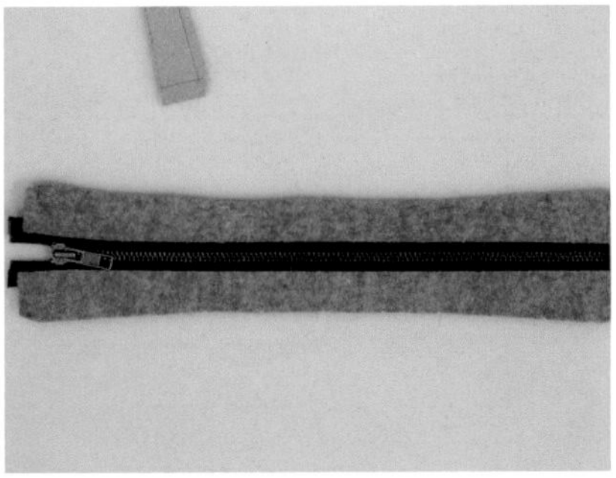

9. Stick the zip to the two top pieces.

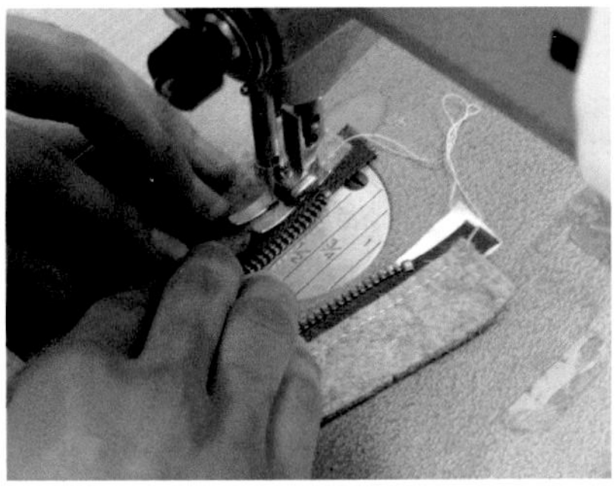

10. Stitch the top to the zip 0.3 cm from the edge.

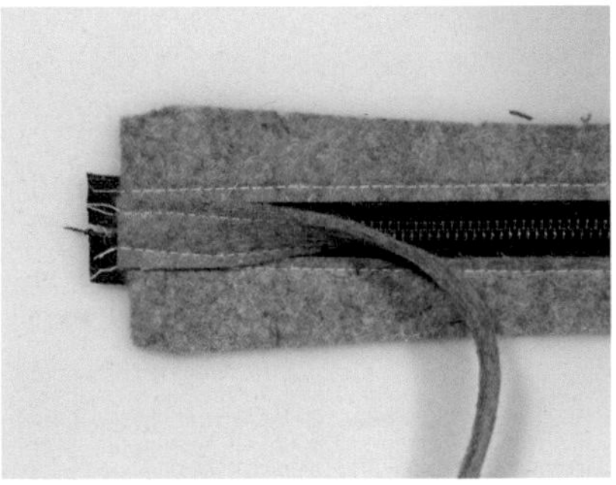

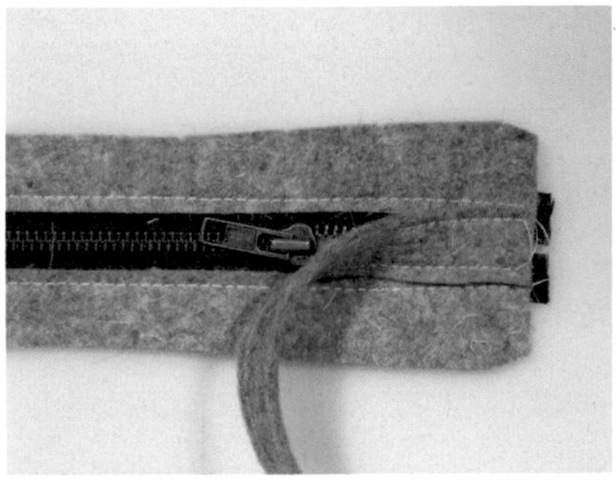

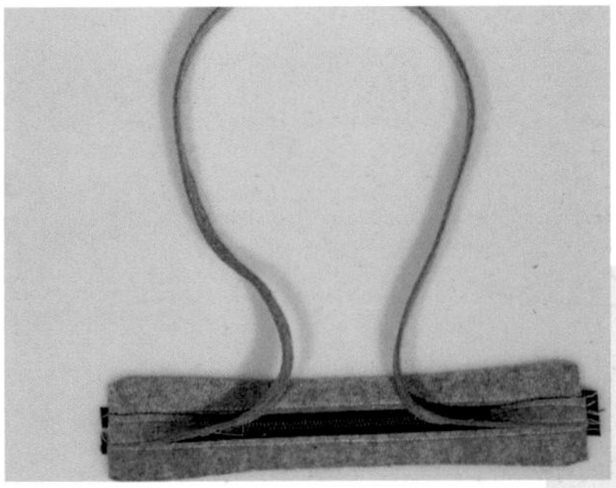

11. After having stitched the strap 0.3 cm from the edge, stick it onto the top piece, wrong side onto the right side of the top.

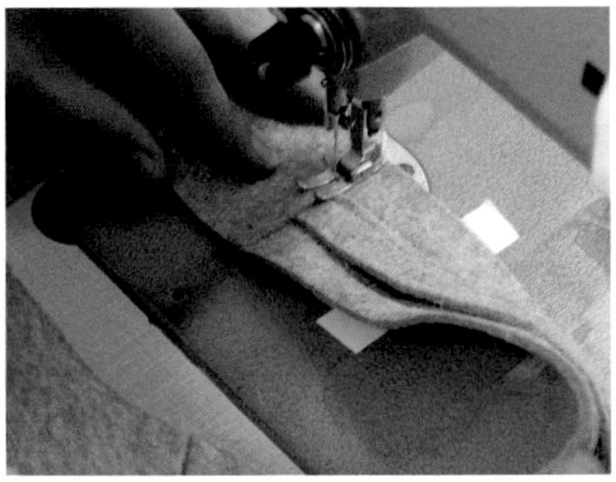

12. Stick the bottom of the side onto the top so that the ends of the strap can be hidden. Stitch them in place 0.3 cm from the edge.

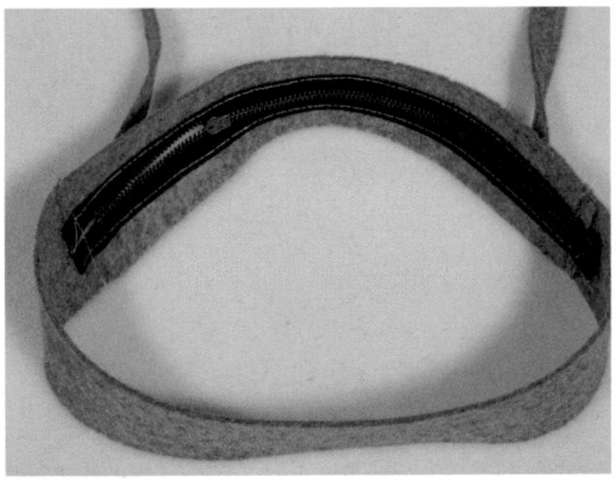

13. The assembling of the band which encircles the bag is finished.

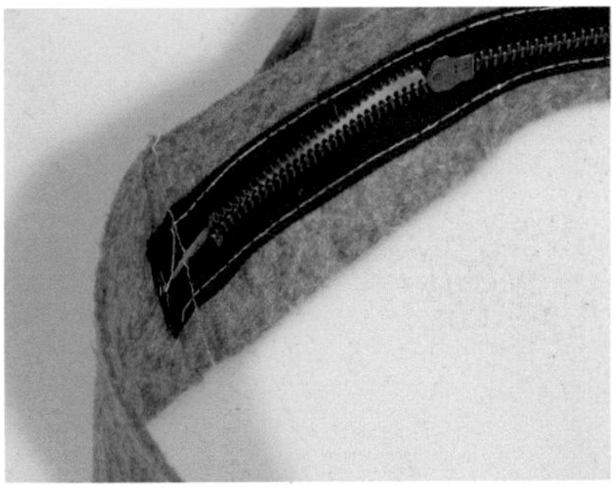

14. Detail of the inside top-stitching.

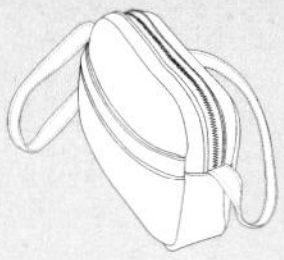

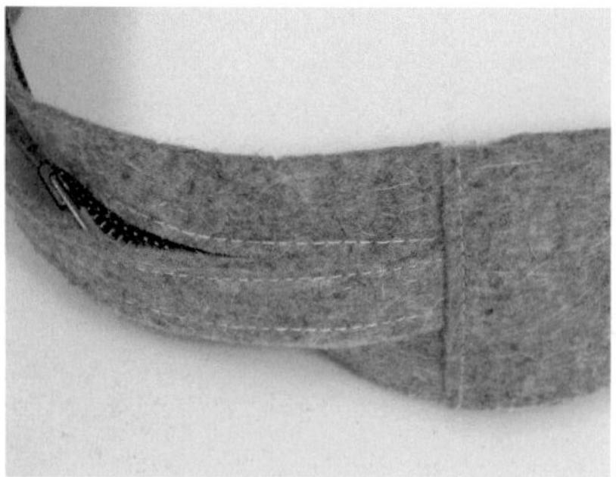

15. Detail of the outside top-stitching.

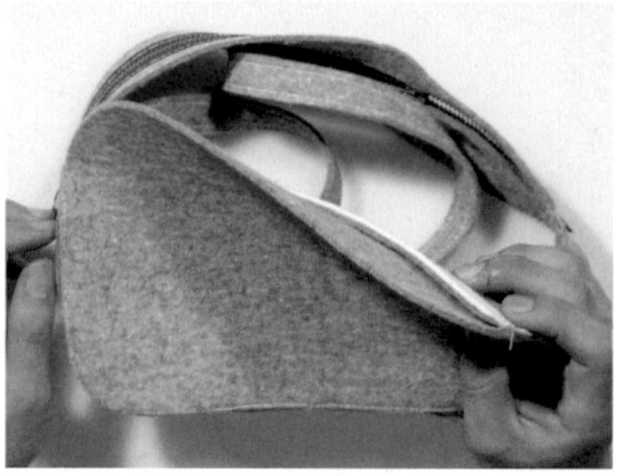

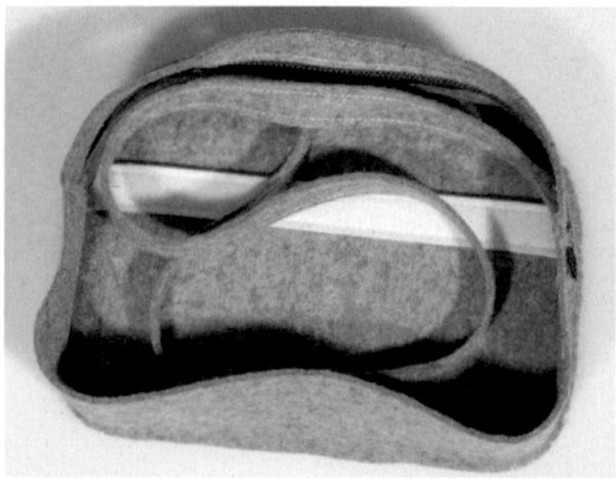

16. We are now going to assemble, on the wrong-side, this encircling band to the front and the back. Glue the seam allowances onto the front and back. Assemble the two pieces, right-sides together, using the assembling notches as guides. (Before sticking the back, slightly open the zip, otherwise it will be difficult to open once the bag has been reversed.)

17. Glue the seam allowances onto the back piece. Assemble the back onto the band, right-sides together, using the assembling notches as guides.

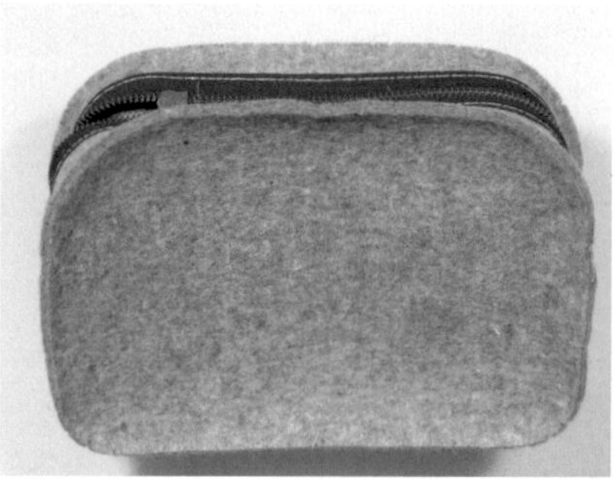

18. The bag is assembled inside-out and the zip is slightly open.

19. Choose a claw foot to assemble the band, the front and the back and the zip fastening. Place the outside of claw foot on the outside edge of the seam. The curve of the bag is the most difficult part to sew so use the sewing machine wheel manually to control the speed.

20. The bag is now assembled.

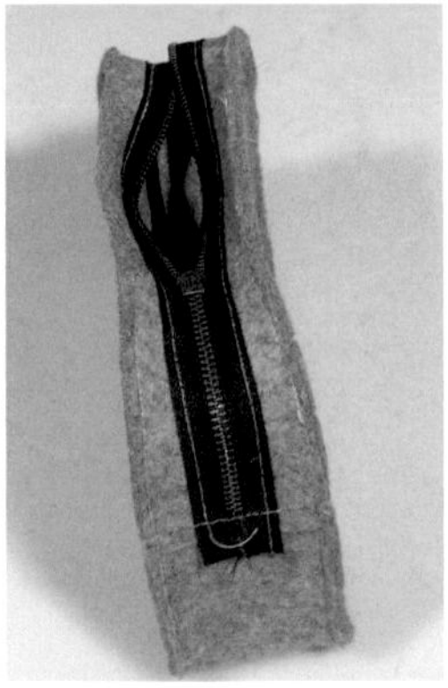

21. Completely open the zip and reverse the bag.. Use a bone folder and pliers to flatten the seams and soften the curve of the bag.

22. Front view of the bag.

23. Side view.

24. Back view.

25. Top view.

Making leather prototypes

Small tote bag

This leather bag is particular in the sense that it is made up of two identical pieces each consisting of a front or a back, as well as a side and half of the base. These two pieces are assembled from the base on a diagonal.

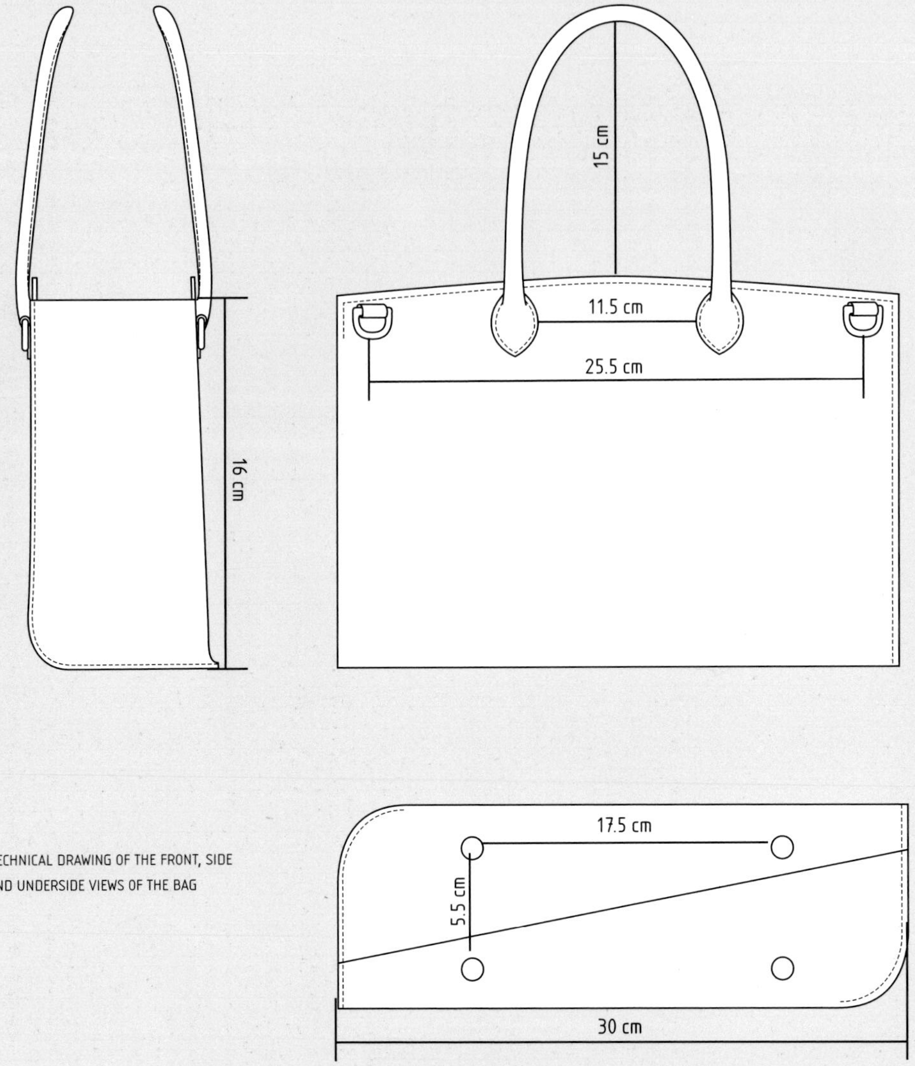

TECHNICAL DRAWING OF THE FRONT, SIDE AND UNDERSIDE VIEWS OF THE BAG

Side view of bag

Three-quarter drawing of the bag.

Underside view. The assembly seam and feet are visible.

Three-quarter view of closed bag

Three-quarter view of open bag

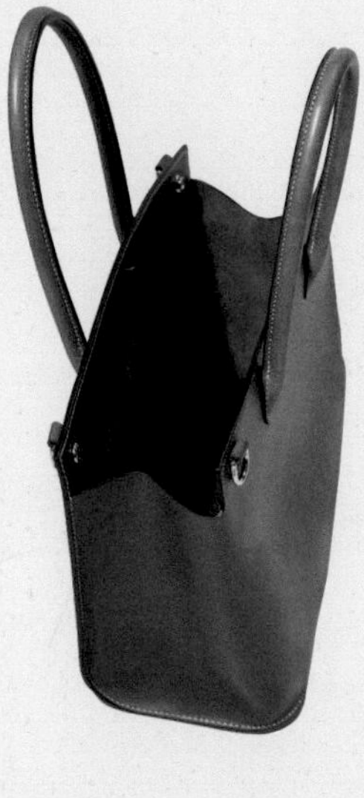

Three-quarter view of top of open bag and interior

Principal stage of manufacturing

Do some sketches, choose one, then make a small-scaled model of it. If it works then it will be possible to scale up and manufacture.

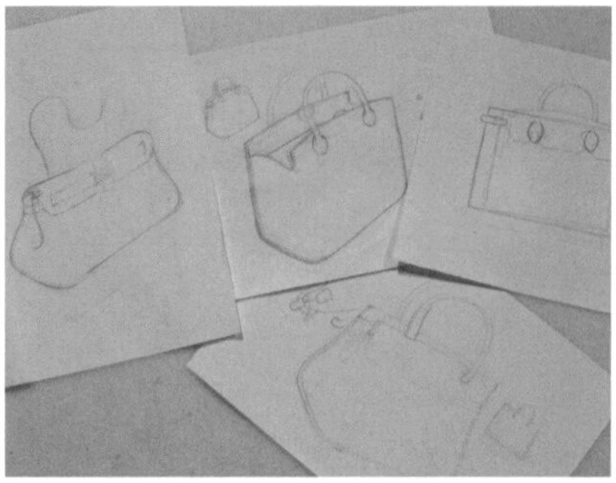

1. Work begins by researching the shape through a series of drawings on paper. We are going to use the one in the centre of the photo for our bag.

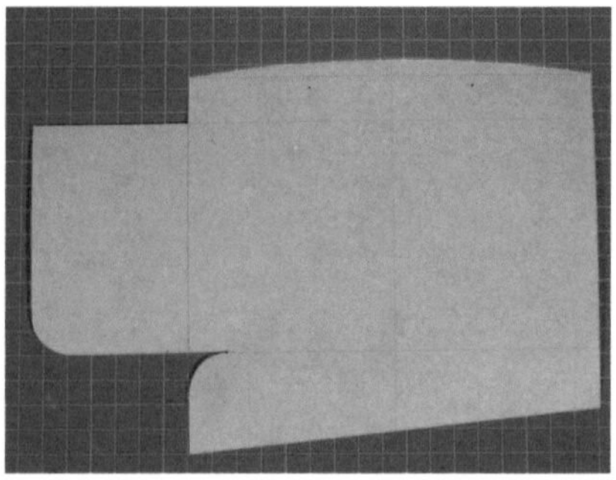

2. We then make a mini-pattern about 1:10 of the normal scale.

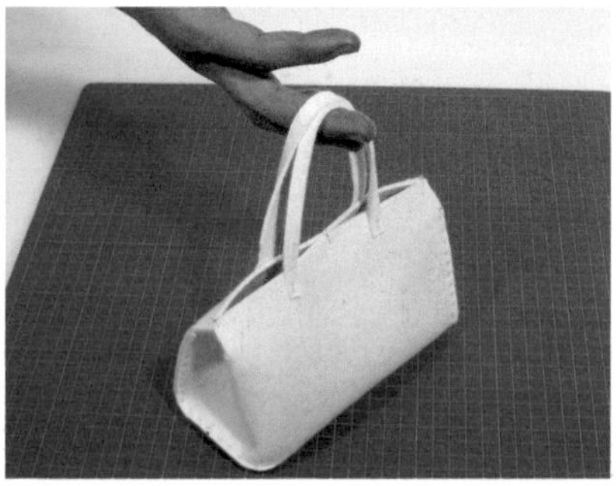

3. From this mini-pattern we make a mini-prototype in felt. This helps us gauge the possible difficulties we might encounter when making the full-size one. It also enables us to see the bag's proportions and rectify them if necessary.

Making a curved template

To help with the bag's construction, we will make a curved template which assists with tracing the bag's curves.

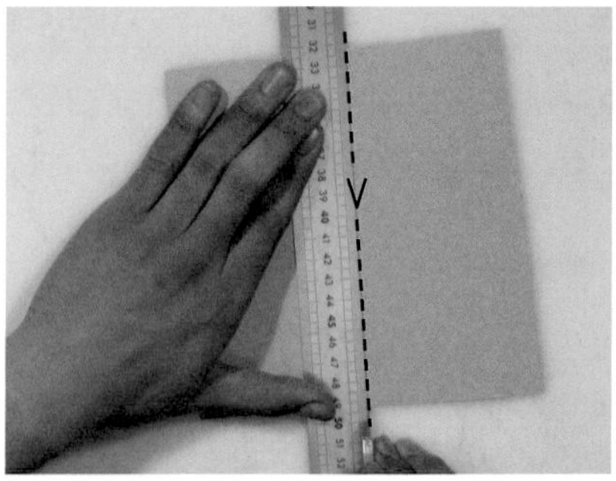

1. Cut out a piece of card about 20 x 20 cm. Use a ruler and cutter to score the V axis in the middle of the card.

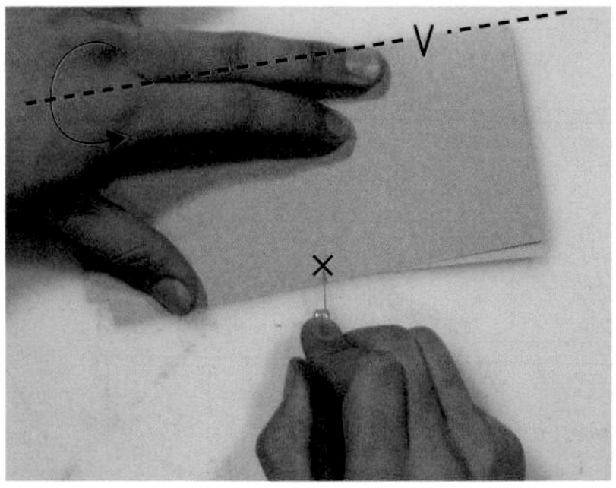

2. Fold the curved template in two along its V axis. Mark off in the middle of the edge opposite the V axis. Press hard enough to go through the two card thicknesses.

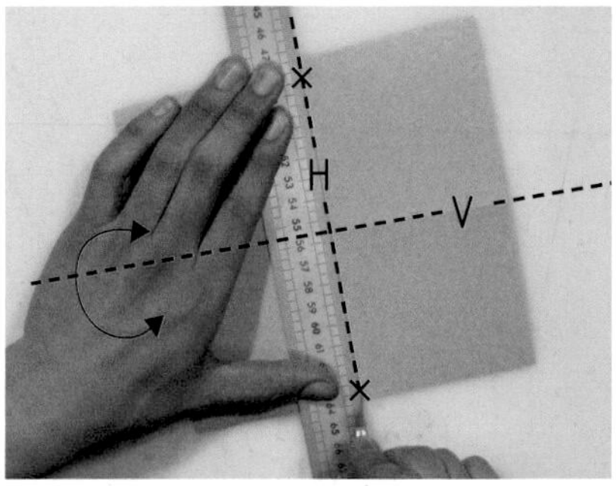

3. Unfold and join up the two marks to trace the template's H axis.

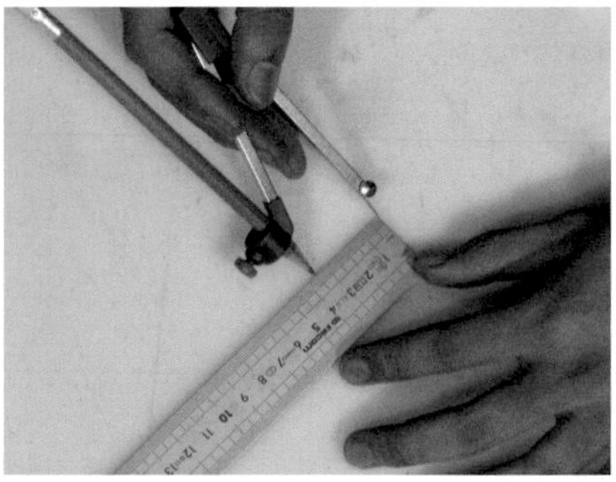

4. Set the compass to 3.5 cm (this measurement corresponds to the R radius of the template).

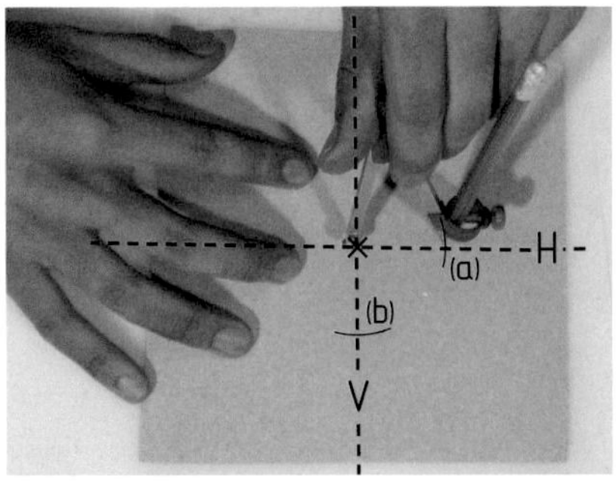

5. Place the compass point at the intersection of the H and V axes. On the H axis, right of the V axis, transfer the radius' measurement. Call this point (a). Transfer the same measurement onto the V axis below the H axis; call this point (b).

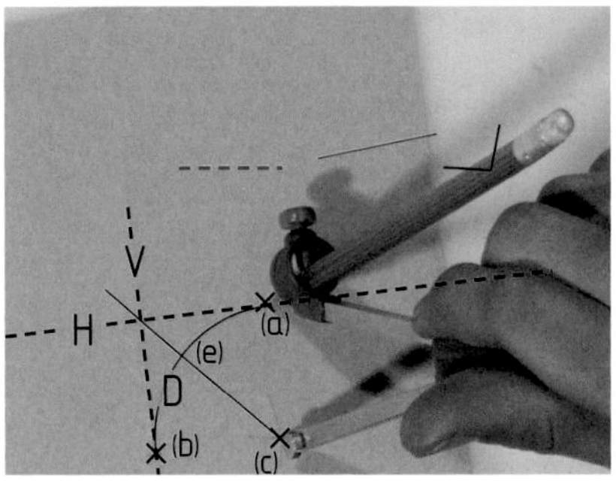

6. Place the compass (still set at 3.5 cm) onto point (b) and trace an arc right of the V axis. Place the compass onto point (a) and trace an arc below the H axis. These two points intersect at a point which we will call (c). This point is the centre of the template's curve. Place the compass on point (c) and trace an arc D connecting points (b) and (a). Trace a straight line with a pencil passing through point (c) and where the V and H axes intersect. This line cuts arc D in its centre; call this intersection point (e).

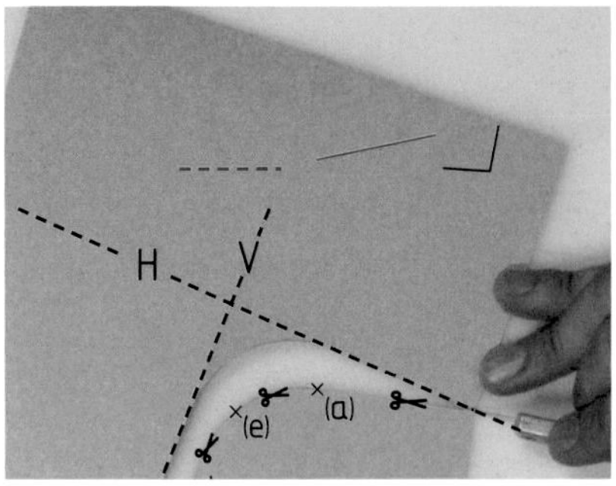

7. Cut out a quarter of the circle along the V and H axes. Use a pencil to mark points (a), (b) and (e).

Making the template for the length

We will now make the template for the flattened-out length which will be used to construct, precisely, the straight and the curved sections, so that they can be perfectly assembled. This template corresponds to the length of arc D when it is flattened out.

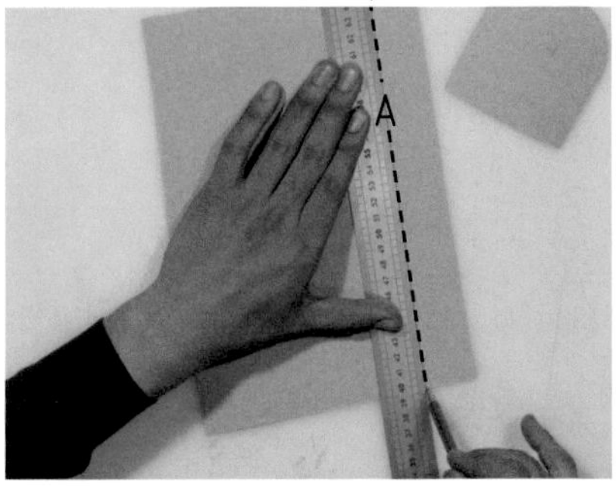

1. Cut out a piece of card about 20 x 20 cm. Trace a straight line A, 3 cm from the edge. It is on this straight line that we are going to transfer the length of arc D.

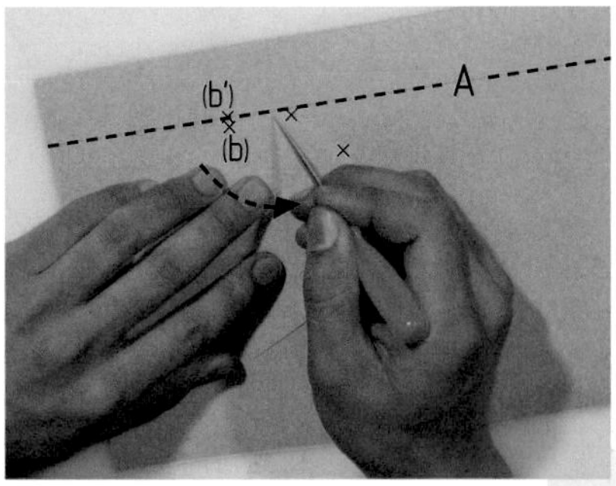

2. To do this, mark on line A, a point (b') 3 cm from the edge. Place the curved template on line A lining up precisely point (b) of the curved template onto point (b') of the straight line A. Place the awl on point (b). Use the awl as a pivot around which the curved template can be 'rolled' along line A. Move the awl along gradually.

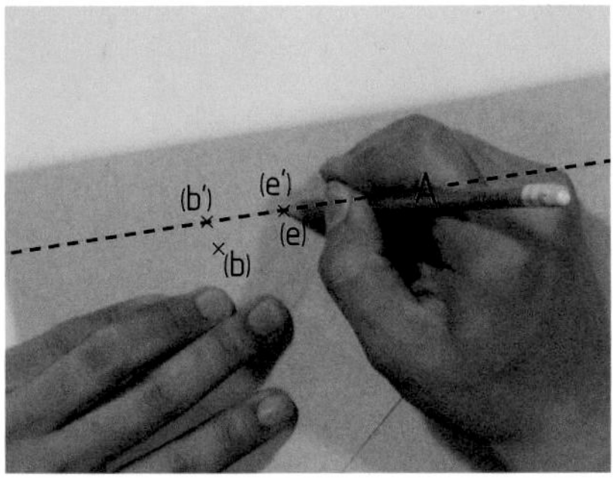

3. Repeat this process until point (e) of the template is at a tangent with line A. Transfer point (e) onto line A. Call this point (e').

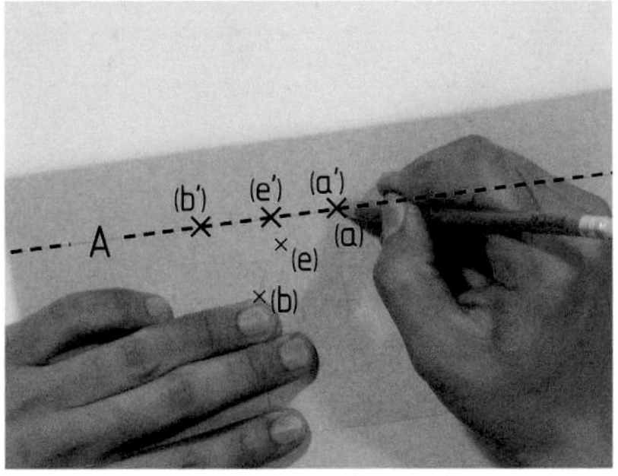

4. Continue to 'roll' the curved template on line A up to point (a) on the template. Transfer point (a) onto line A using a pencil. Call this point (a').

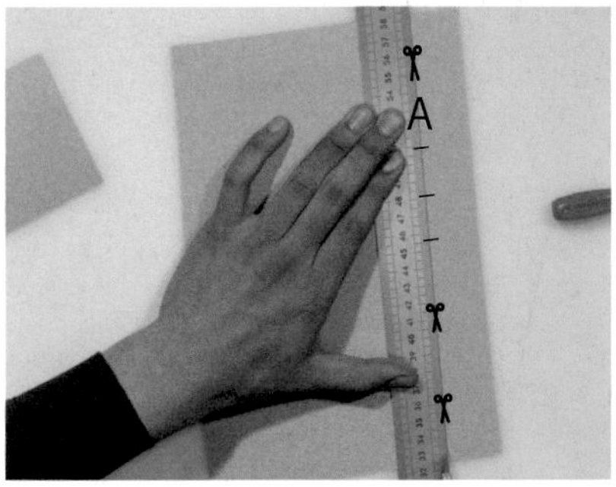

5. Cut the whole length of line A using a cutter.

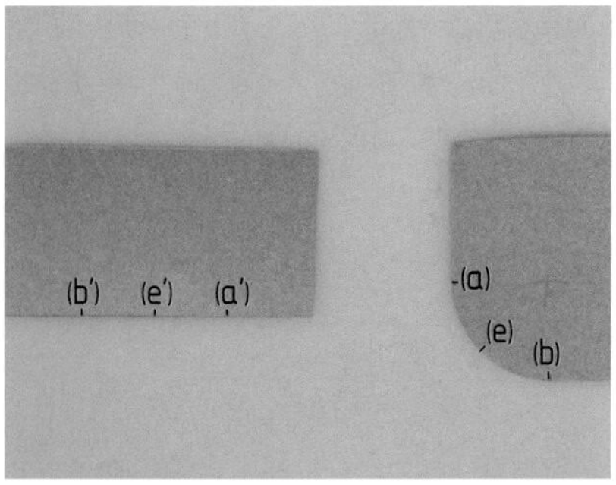

6. We have just made two templates, one with a curved part and the other with a straight part and both have three reference points: the beginning, the middle and the end. The measurement between points (b) and (a) of the curved template is equal to the measurement between points (b') and (a') of the other template.

Pattern making

From the template, the pattern is made including the seam allowances.

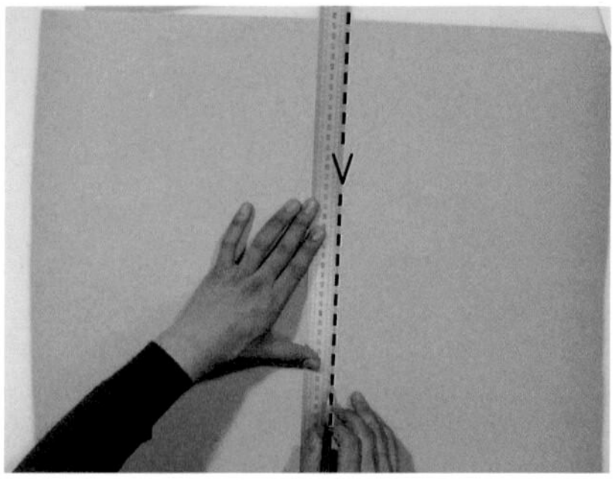

1. Cut out a piece of card about 70 x 50 cm. In the middle of the card score its vertical V axis widthways using a ruler and a cutter.

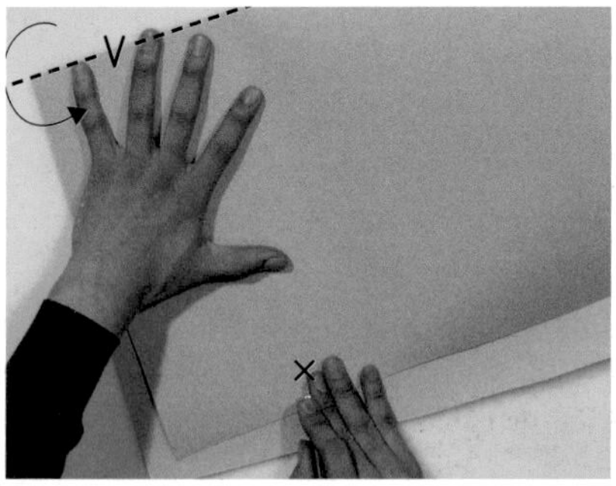

2. Fold along the V axis. Mark with a cutter, on the opposite edge to the V axis, roughly a quarter of the height of the piece of card, i.e. about 12.5 cm from the bottom.

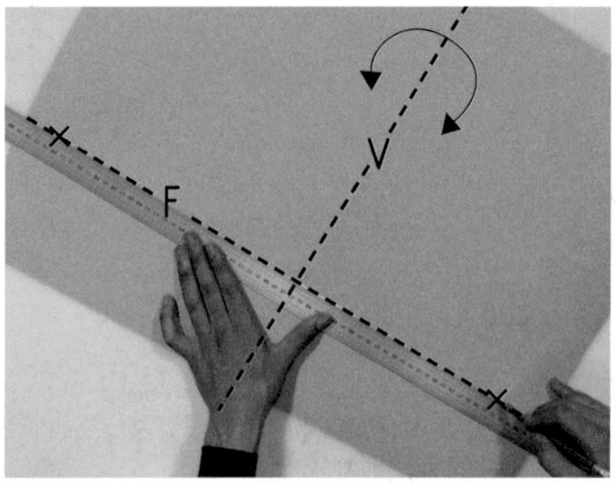

3. Unfold and join the two marks with a pencil to trace line F, this corresponds to the bottom line of the bag.

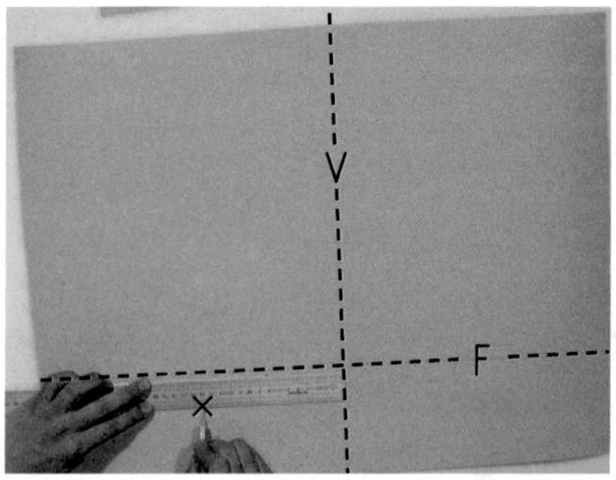

4. We are going to make the side line of the front which we will call G. At the bottom left of the V axis, mark with a cutter half the measurement of the width of the front, i.e. 15 cm perpendicular to the V axis.

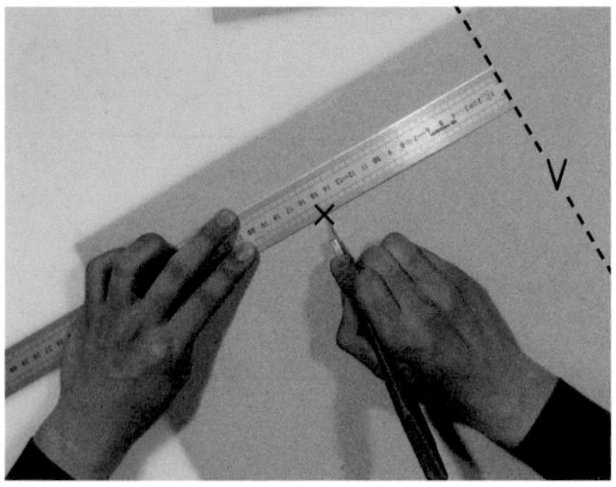

5. Mark this 15 cm measurement with the cutter onto the top left of the V axis.

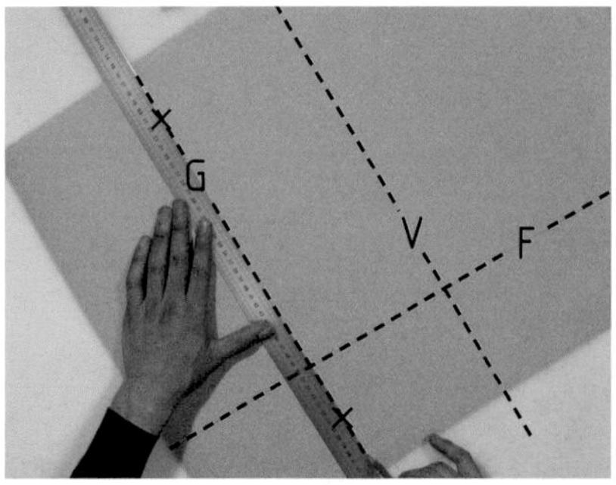

6. Join these two marks with a pencil to trace line G.

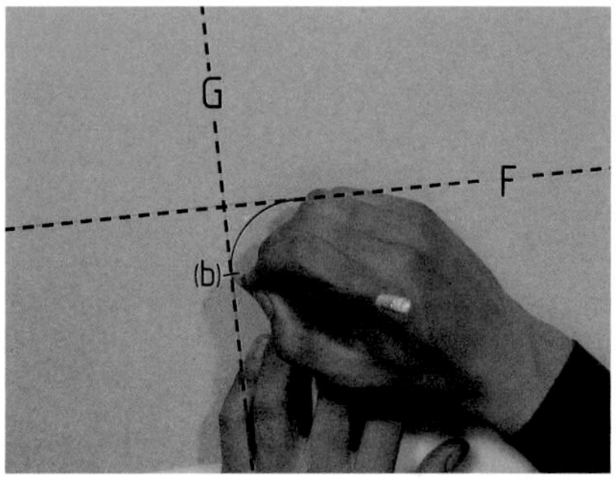

7. Place the curved template on the right of line G under line F.

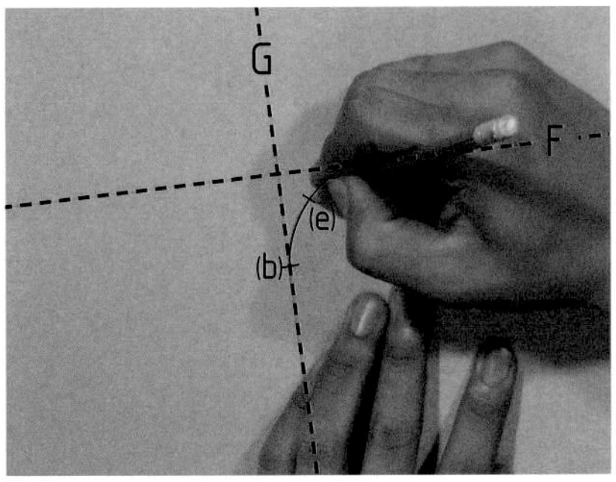

8. Use a pencil to transfer the outline of arc D of the template onto the pattern: draw a pencil line between points (b), (e) and(a) of the template onto the pattern.

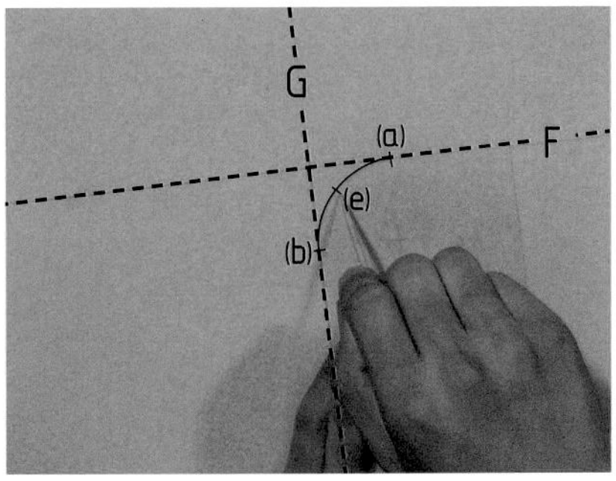

9. Use the awl to mark point (e) on the pattern.

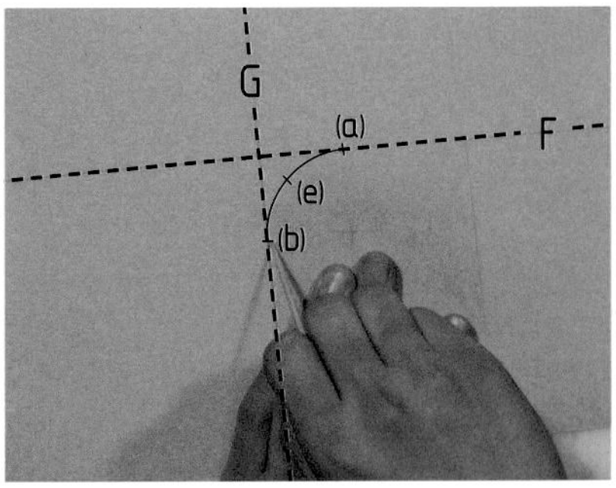

10. Mark point (b) on line G. We call this point (h).

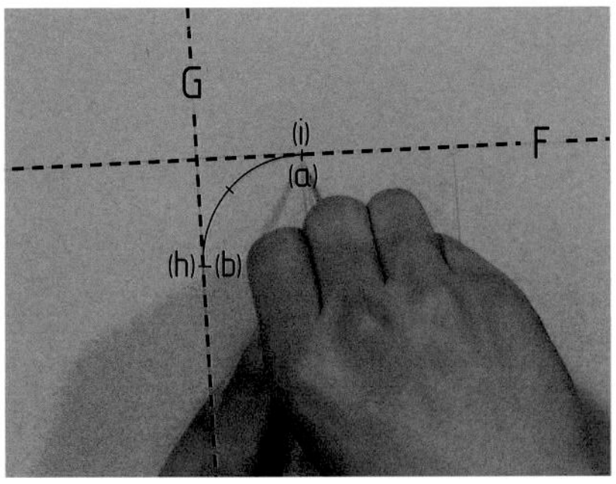

11. Mark point (a) on line F. We call this point (i).

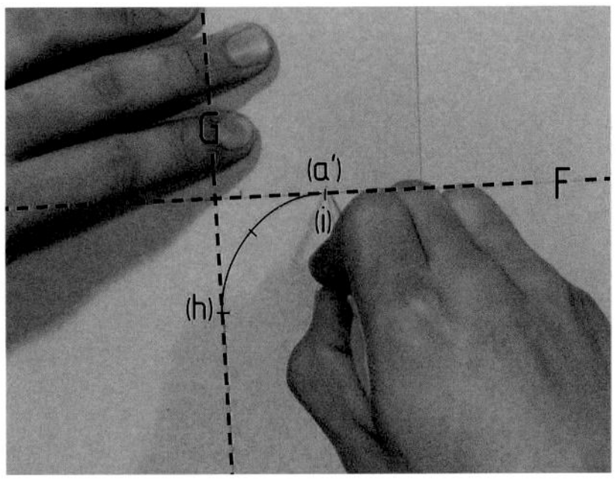

12. Remove the curved template. We are going to transfer the length of arc D onto line F using the straight template. Place this template onto line F aligning point (i) with point (a') of the straight template.

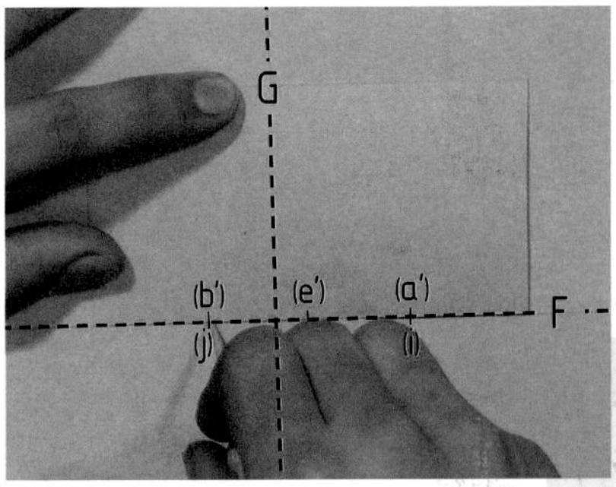

13. Use an awl to mark points (e') and (b') of the template onto line F. Call this last point (j).

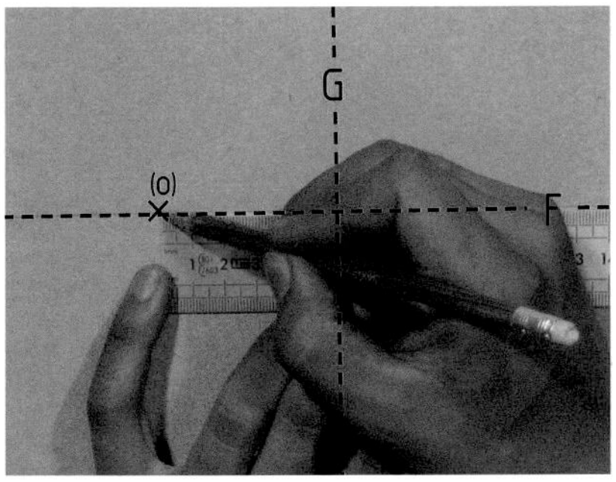

14. Place a point (o) onto line F, 5.5 cm to the left of the G axis.

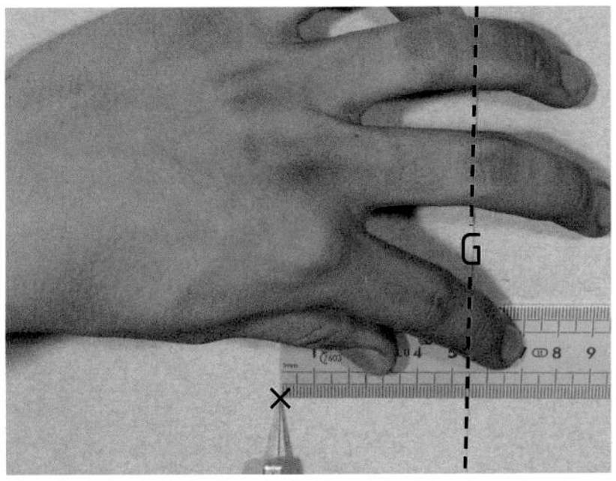

15. Transfer this measurement to the top left of the G axis.

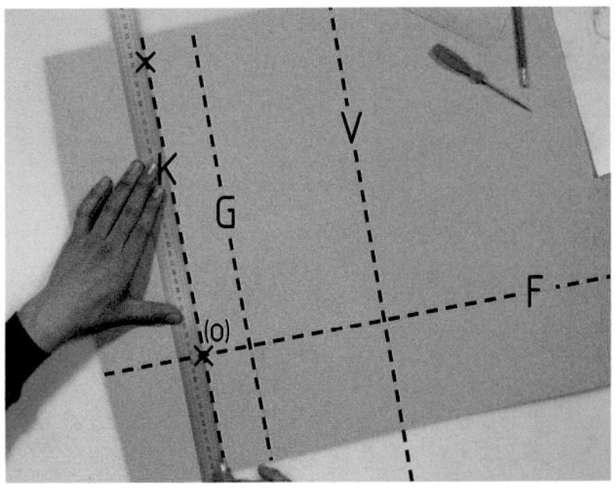

16 Join these two marks with a cutter in order to score the K axis. This is the vertical axis of the pattern's side section.

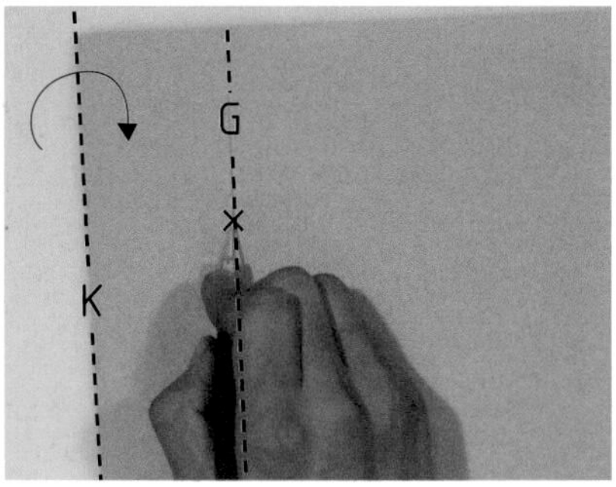

17. Fold the card along the K axis. Use the cutter to mark the ends of line G so that the half-width of the side on the half-folded card can be transferred.

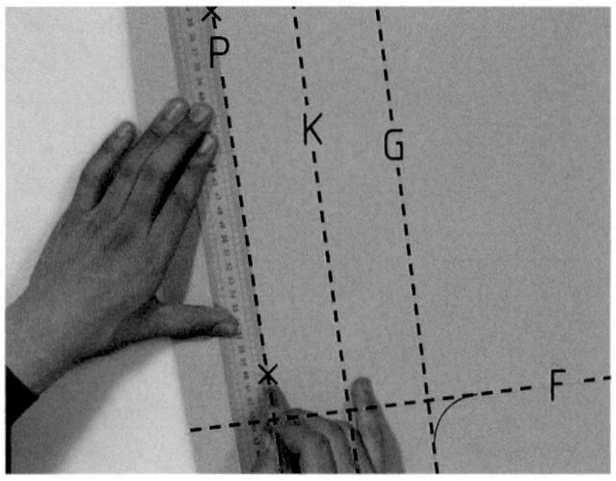

18. Unfold and join the two marks up with the pencil. We have just traced line P of the pattern's side section.

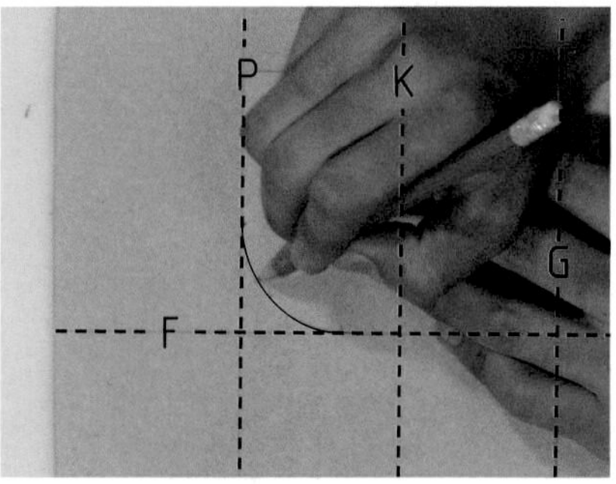

19. Draw the curve of the side section of the bag. Place the curved template to the right of line P and above line F.

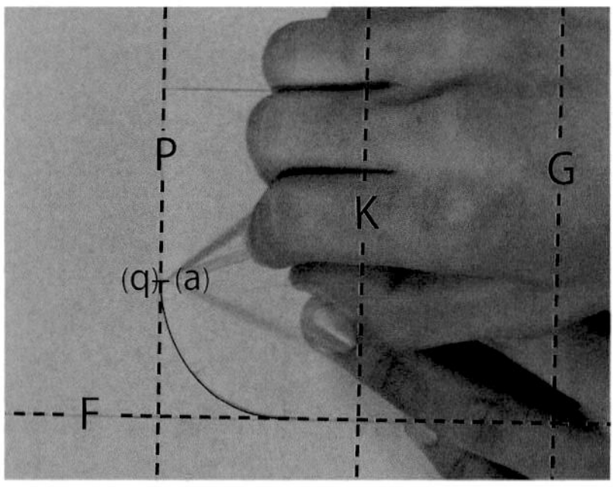

20. Use the awl to mark point (a) of the template onto line P of the pattern. Name this point (q).

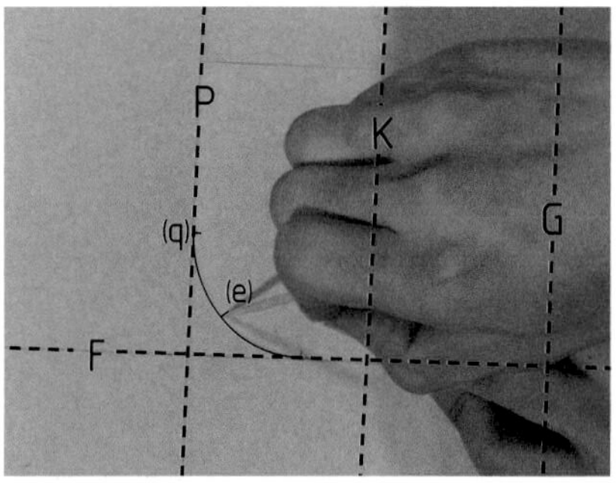

21. Use the awl to mark point (e) of the template onto the pattern.

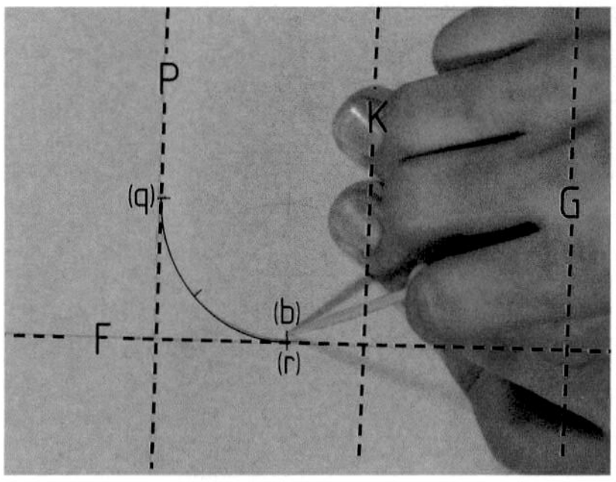

22. Mark point (b) of the template onto the F line of the pattern. Call this point (r). The curve of the side section of the bag is now drawn.

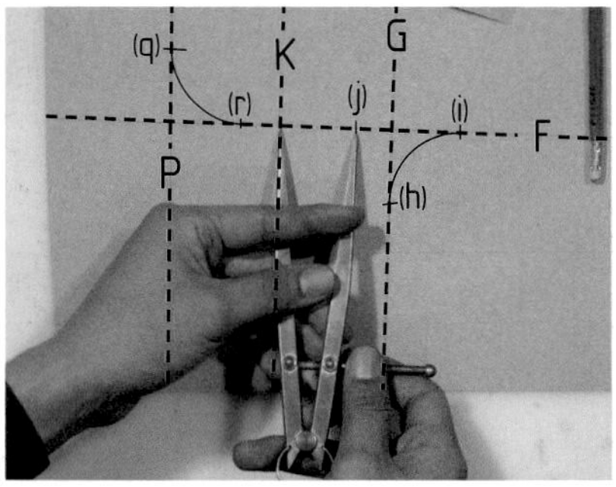

23. The two sections of the bag are assembled diagonally. On the pattern, one side of the underneath section must be drawn longer than the other. Draw the larger side of the underneath section. On line F, use the compass to set the measurement between the side's K axis and point (j).

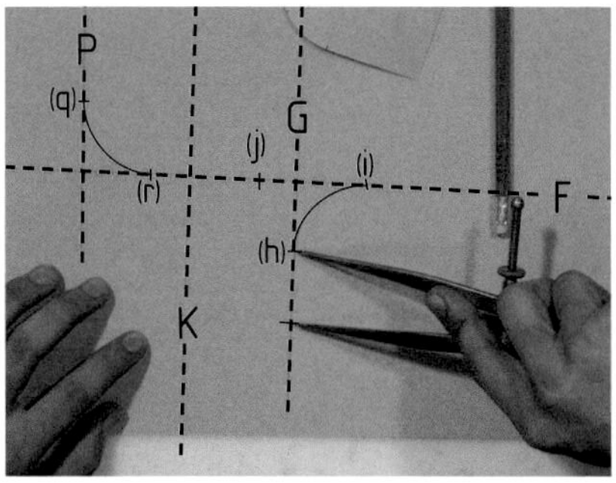

24. Then transfer this measurement onto line G starting at point (h).

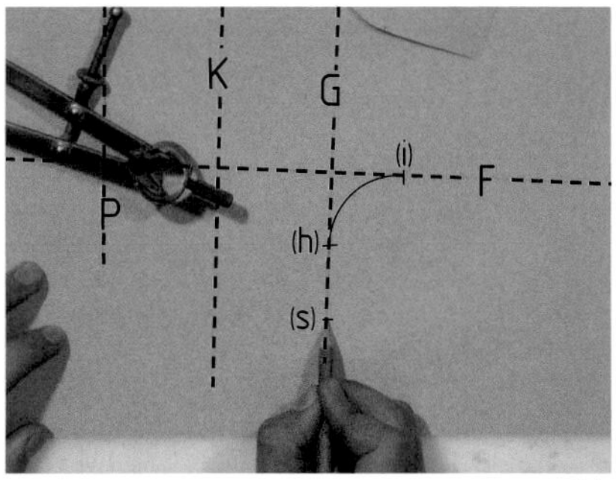

25. Mark this point with a pencil and call it (s). The measurement between line F and point (s) is equal to the width of the larger side of the underneath of the bag.

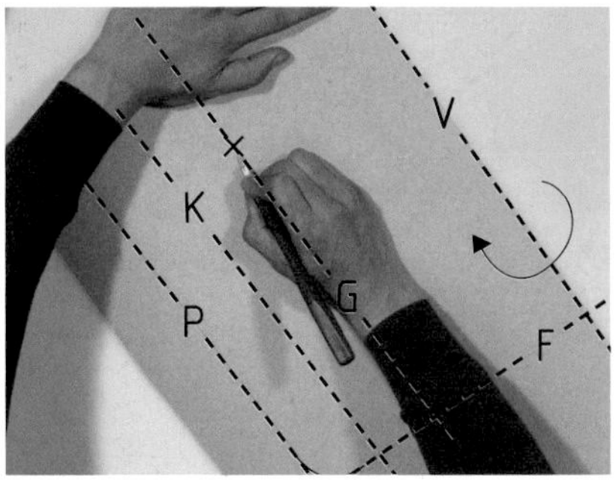

26. Fold the card along the V axis. Mark with a cutter the ends of line G so that the half-width of the front can be transferred symmetrically onto the folded half of the card.

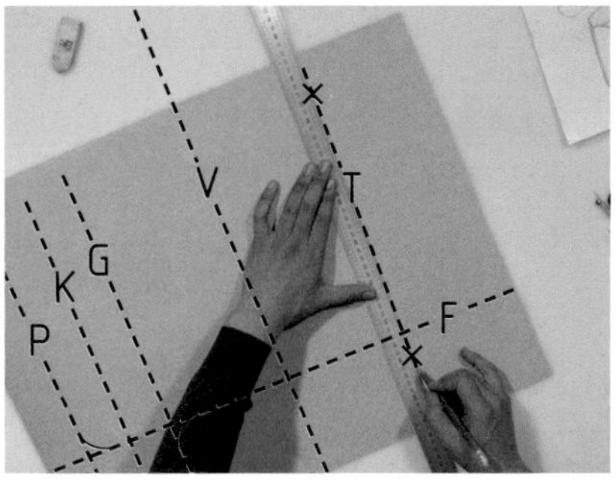

27. Unfold and join the two marks up with a pencil. We have just drawn line T of the right side of the pattern's front section.

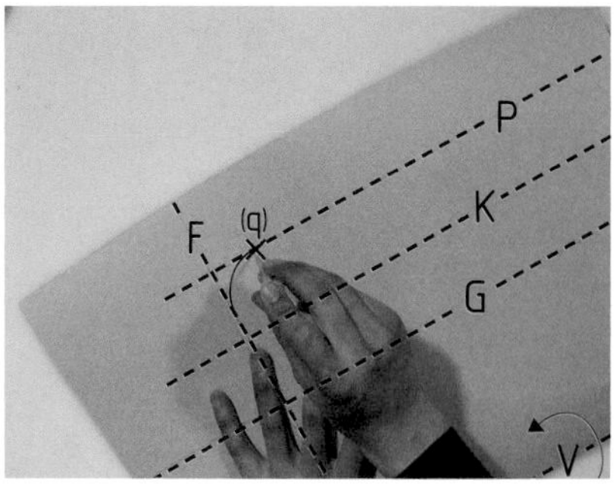

28. To trace the length of the smaller side of the underside section, fold the pattern in two along its V axis. Use the awl to mark through the two layers of card transferring point (q) on line P onto the half-folded card. Unfold and call this point (q').

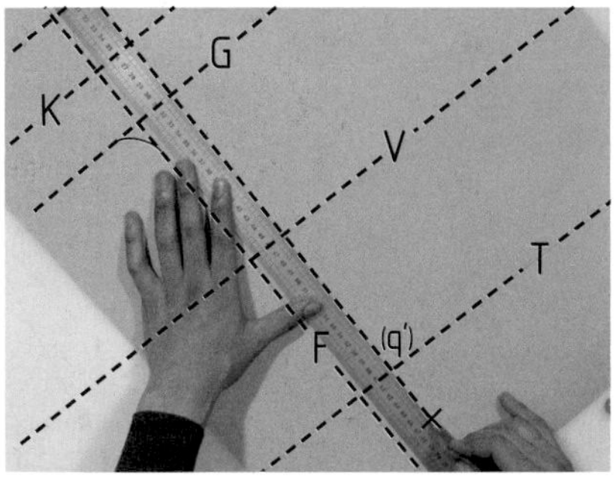

29. Use a pencil to join up points (q) and (q') drawing a line parallel to line F.

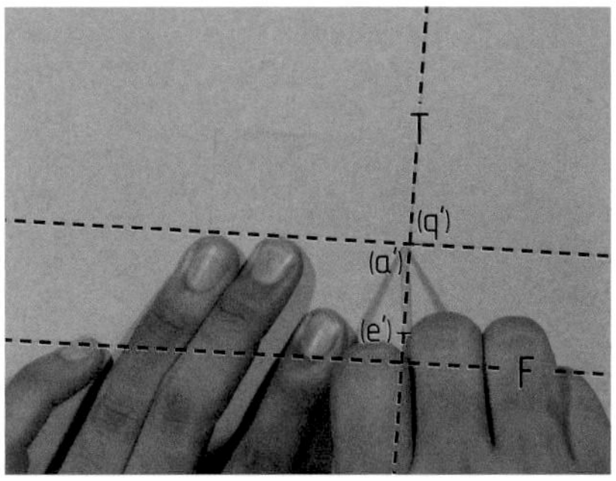

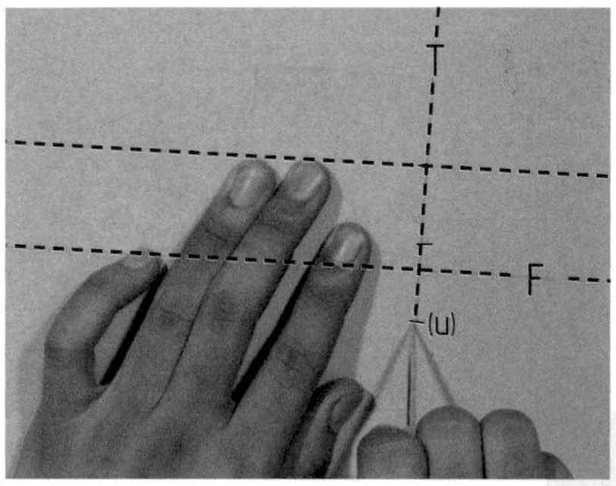

30 & 31. Place the straight template against line T, lining up point (a') of the template on the intersection of line (qq') with line T. Draw points (a') ,(e') and (b') of the template onto line T. Call this last point (u).

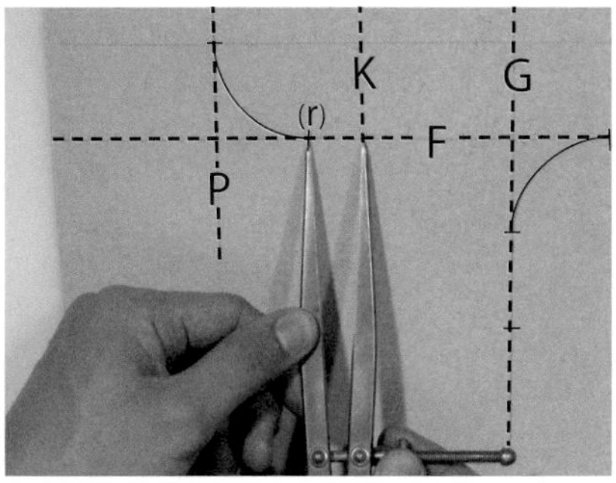

32. Set the compass to measure the distance between point (r) and K axis on line F.

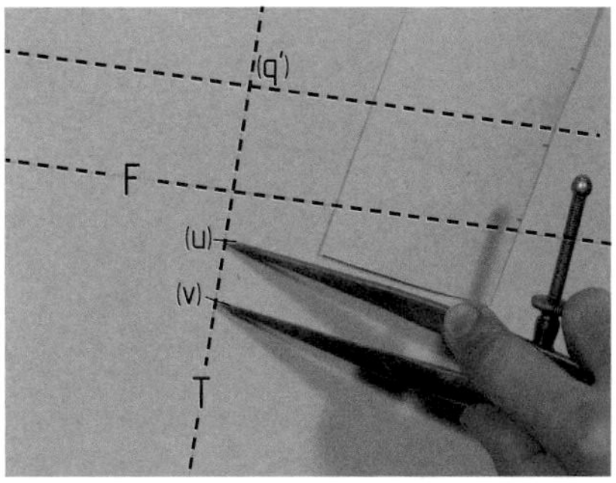

33. Transfer this measurement onto line T, starting at point (u). Mark point (v). The measurement between line F and point (v) is equal to the width of the small section of the underside of the bag.

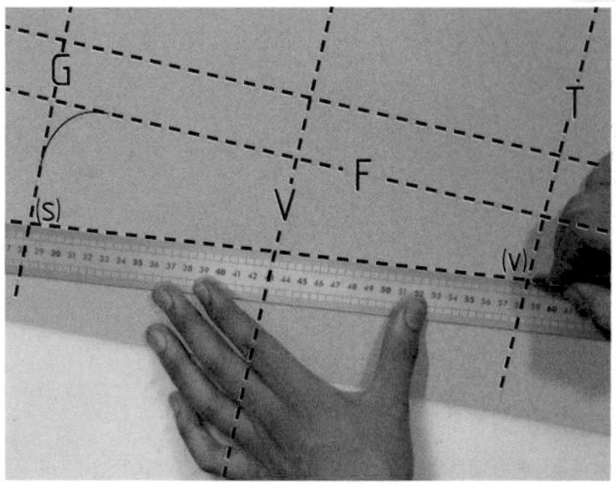

34. Join points (s) and (v) to draw up the shape of half the bag's underside.

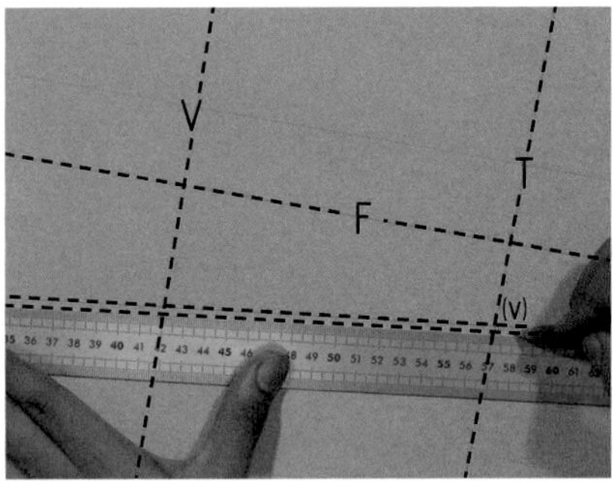

35. Add a 1 cm seam allowance under this line (sv).

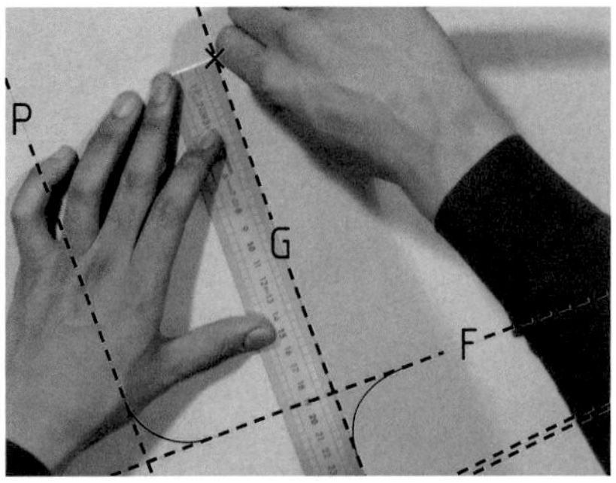

36. Mark with a cutter the measurement of the height of the front, on line G , 19 cm above line F.

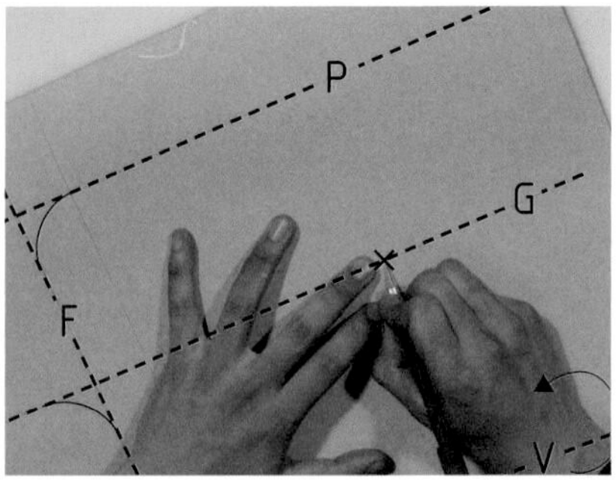

37. Fold the front section on its V axis. With a cutter, transfer this measurement symmetrically onto the other half, making sure to mark through the two layers.

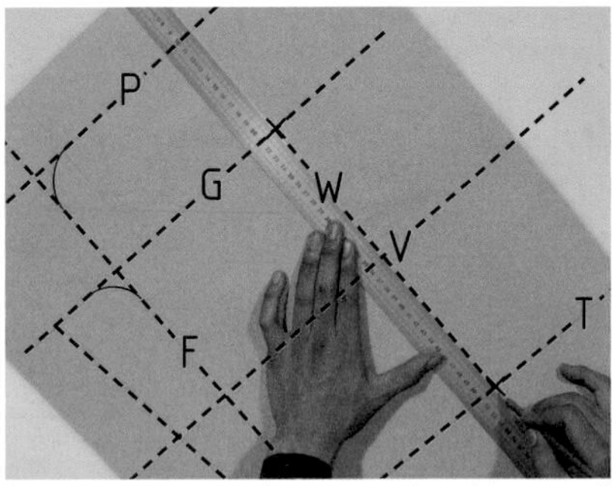

38. Unfold and join the two marks with a pencil to draw line W at the top of the front.

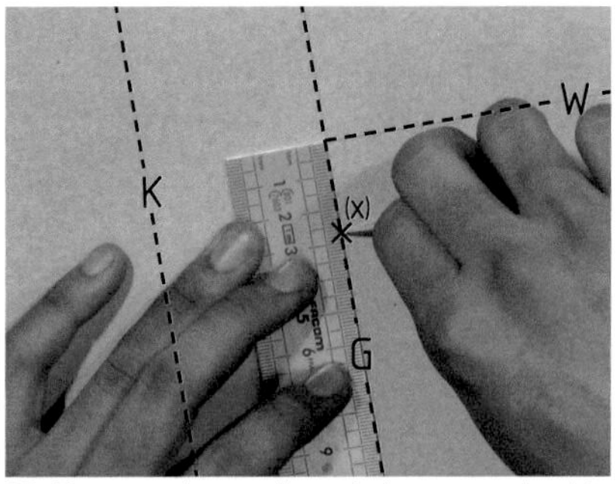

39. To trace the top line of the pattern's side section, use a cutter to mark a point on line G, 2.7 cm under this line. Call this point (x).

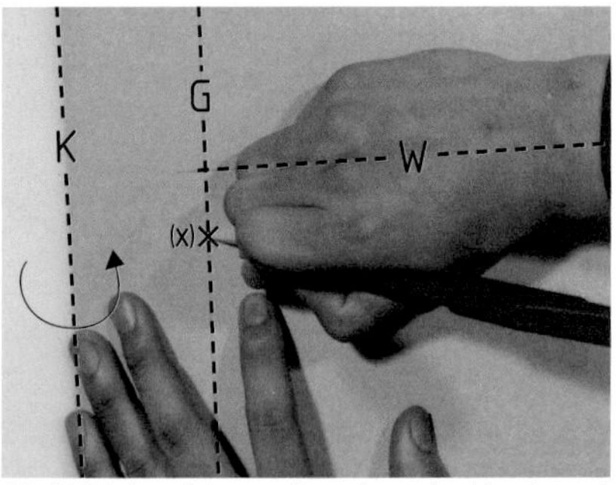

40. Fold the side section along its K axis and transfer point (x) symmetrically onto the folded section, marking through the two card thicknesses.

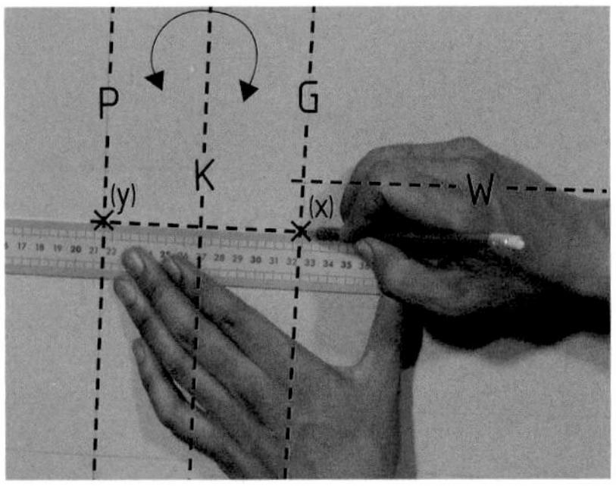

41. Unfold and use a pencil to join the two marks drawing a line Y, which corresponds to the top of the bag's side.

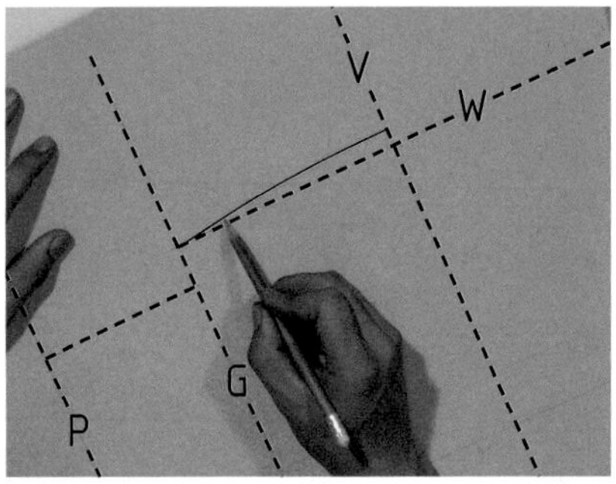

42. Draw a slight curve onto half of the top front, between line G and the V axis. This curve cuts the V axis 1 cm above line W.

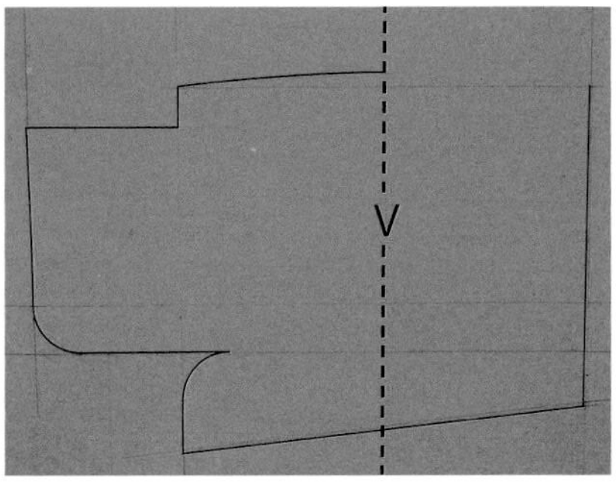

43. The pattern has now been achieved. All that is left is to cut it out.

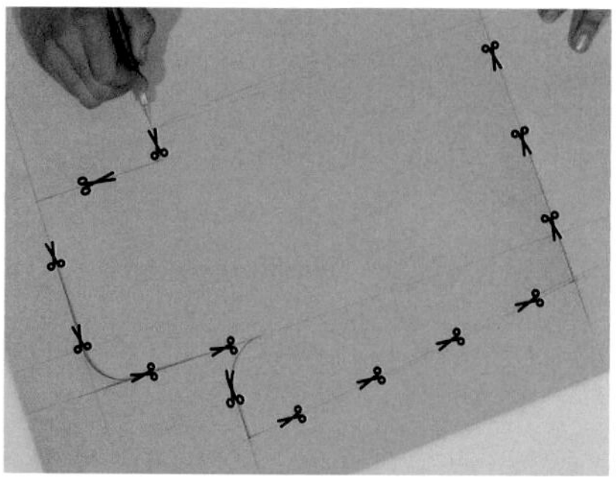

44. Begin by cutting the straight side of the front along line T, starting at the top and working towards the bottom. After this, cut the underneath section followed by the side section.

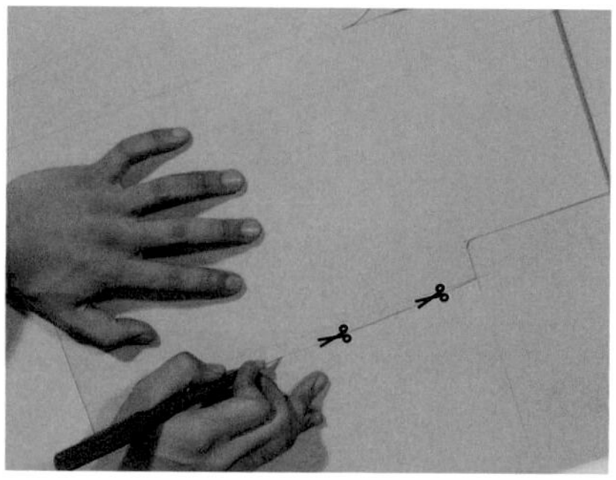

45. Cut half the top of the front, stopping at the V axis.

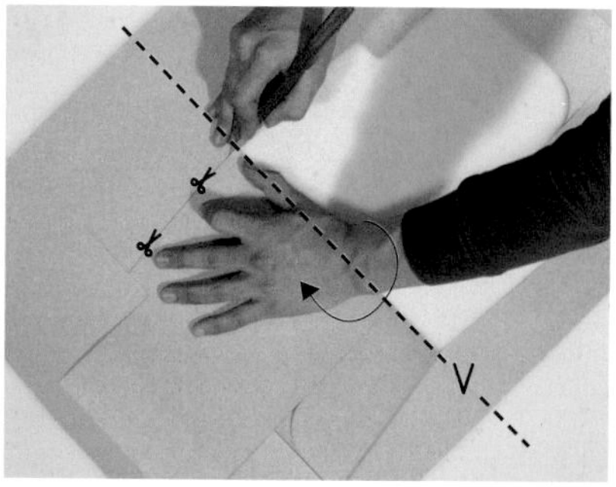

46. Fold the front along its V axis and cut the second half of the top of the front symmetrically.

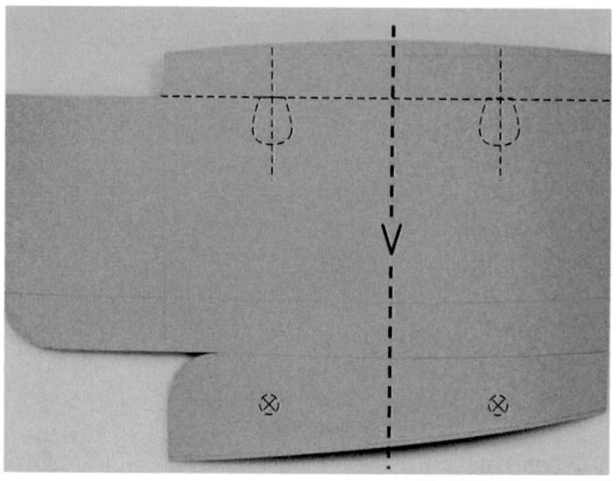

47. The pattern of this piece has now been achieved. Draw on the position for the handles, buckles and feet (protection).

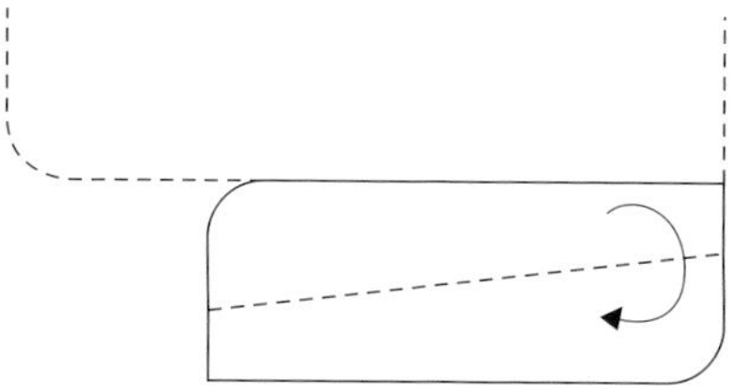

48. Construct the lining pattern of the bag's base.

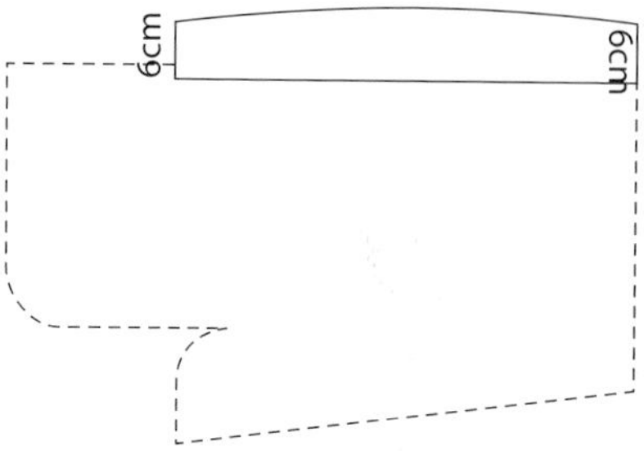

49. Construct the front and back shapes transferring the measurement of the top front.

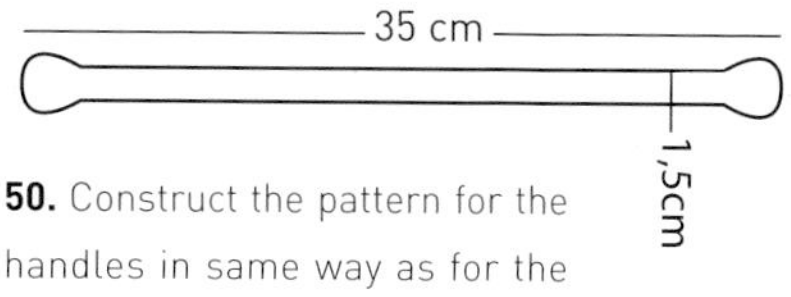

50. Construct the pattern for the handles in same way as for the cylindrical bag.

Cutting and assembling the bag

The bag will be made from calfskin.

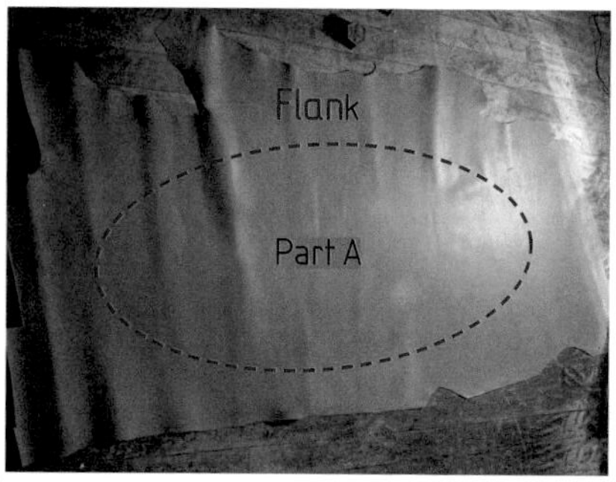

1. The centre of the skin (part A) is the best quality leather. Place the front and back in this area so that the bag is fault free and uniform.

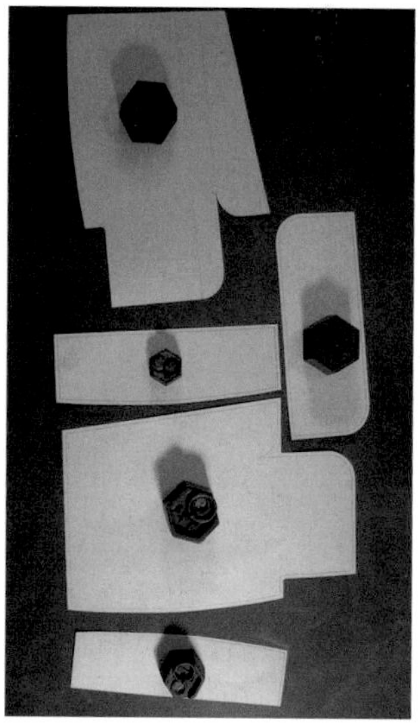

2. The cutting plan is made up of two main pieces, a lining for the base and two shapes for the top front/back.

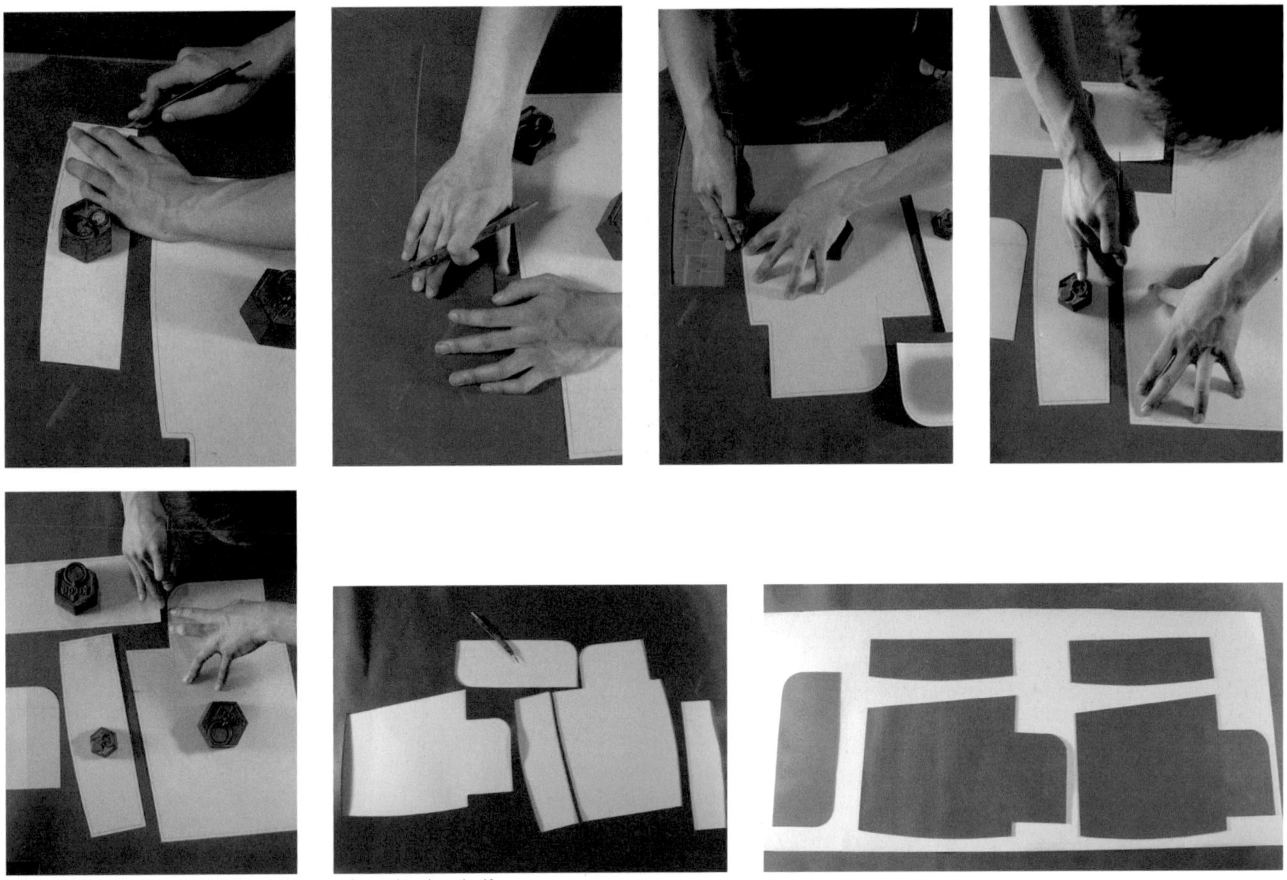

3. Roughly cut out around the pattern using a leather knife.

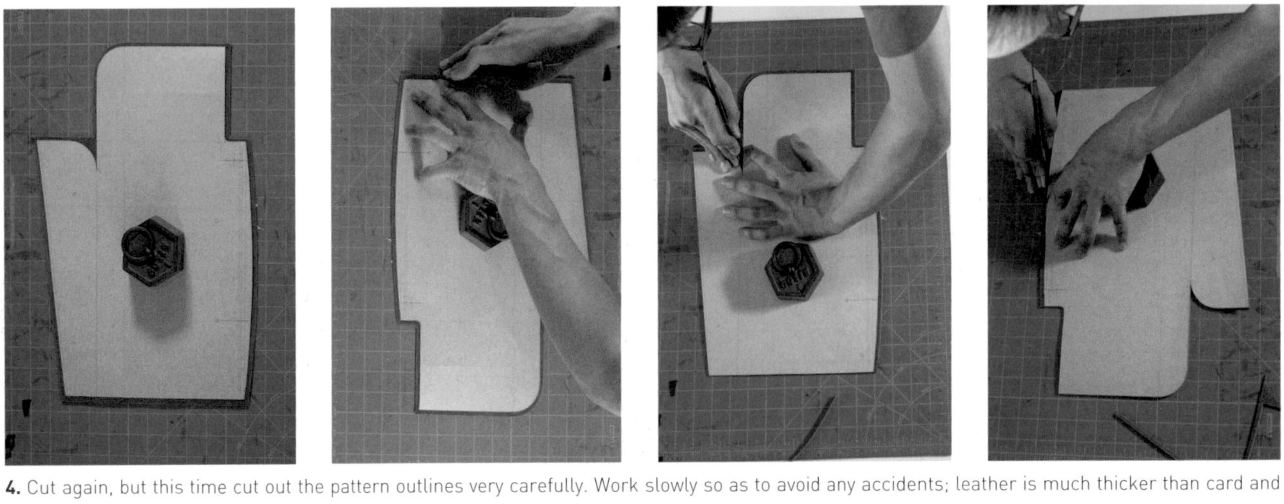

4. Cut again, but this time cut out the pattern outlines very carefully. Work slowly so as to avoid any accidents; leather is much thicker than card and therefore more difficult to cut.

5. With the awl, mark the position of pieces such as handles and feet (for protection).

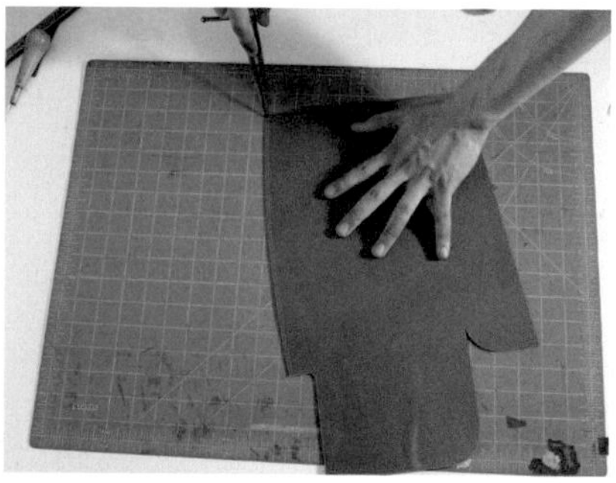

6. With the compass, mark the seams using the edges of the pieces as a guide.

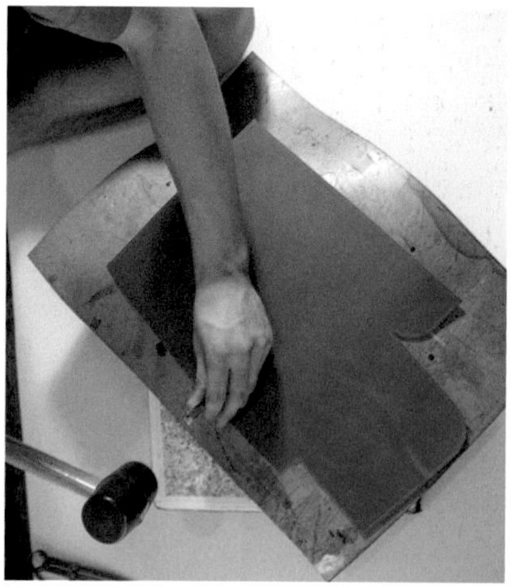

7. On the compass mark, use the claw knife to make holes for the seam positions. A roulette can also be used to mark the seam holes at regular intervals.

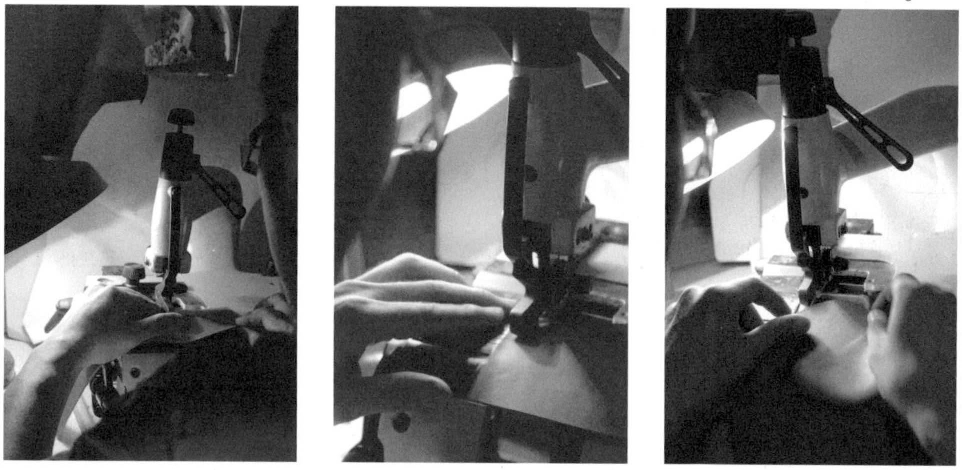

8. A paring machine is used to thread the edges of the piece. This tool means the leather can be thinned out near the seams making it easier to assemble.

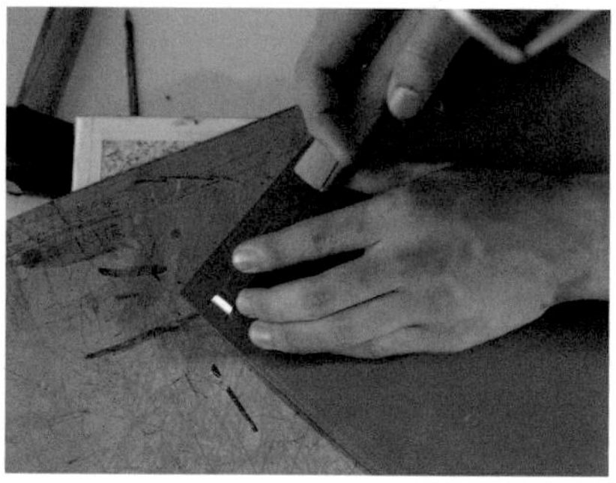

9. It is also possible to thin the leather with a paring knife.

10. Threading a needle with a linen thread in preparation for hand sewing.

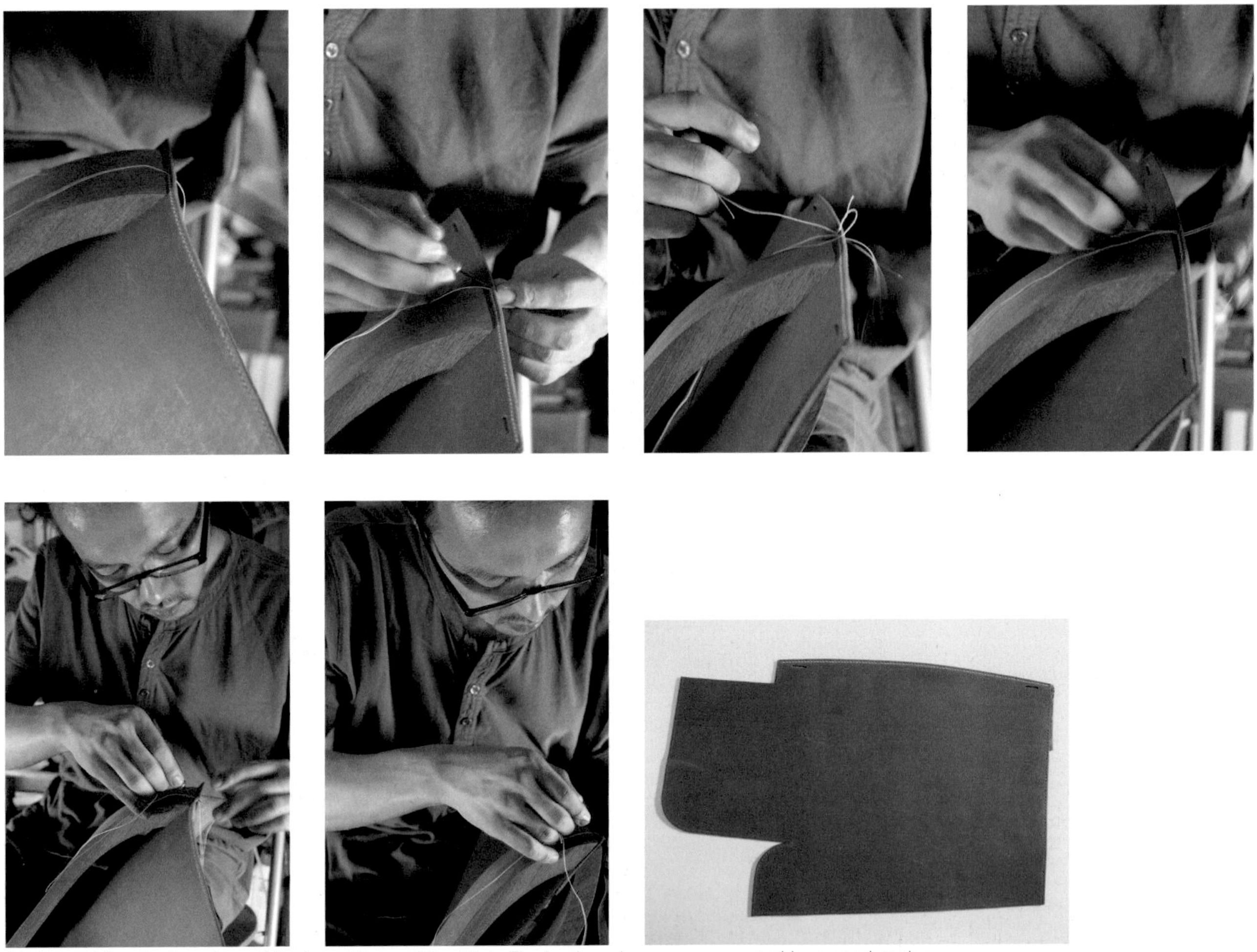

11. Assembling the top piece of the bag with a saddle stitch. The leather pieces are supported by a wooden vice.

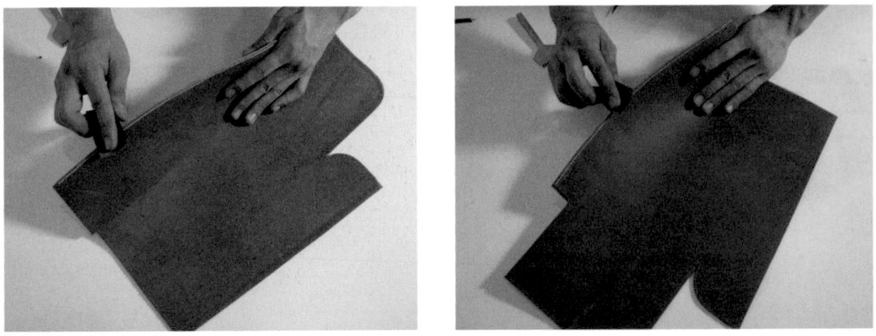

12. Sanding the edges to make them rounder.

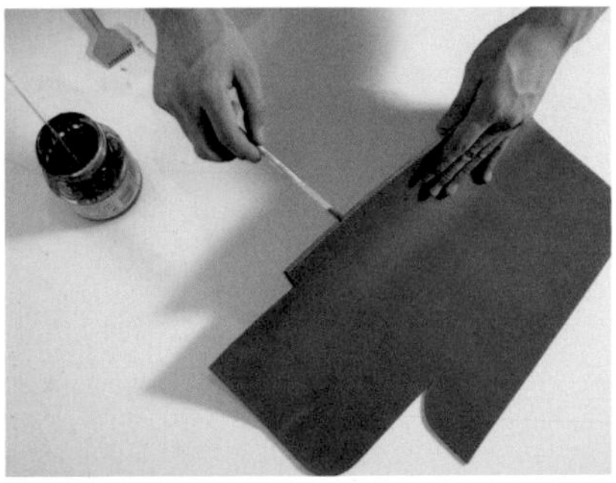

13. Dyeing the cut edges.

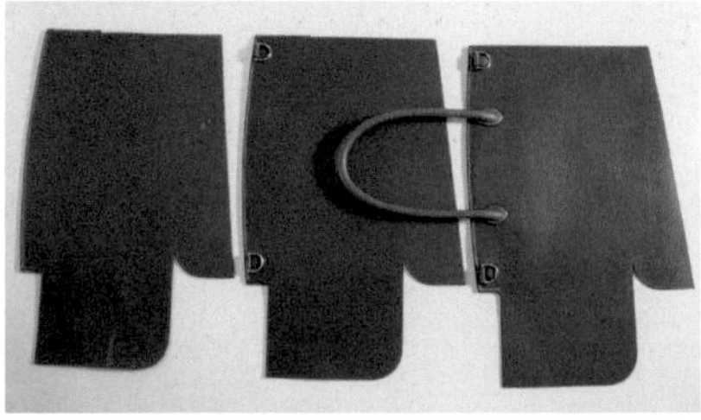

14. We have just positioned the buckles. Stick the edges of the handle together. Fold back with the wrong-sides together and flatten the seam with a mallet. Assemble with a saddle stitch stopping 5 cm from each end. Sand, then dye the edges of the handles. Stick the handles in place on the bag and secure them with a saddle stitch.

15. Stick the front and the back overlapping each other, seam on seam, and flatten them with a mallet. If the sewing holes have become blocked with glue, or aren't big enough, use an awl to slightly open them up (the leather, being rigid, is difficult to pierce with a needle).

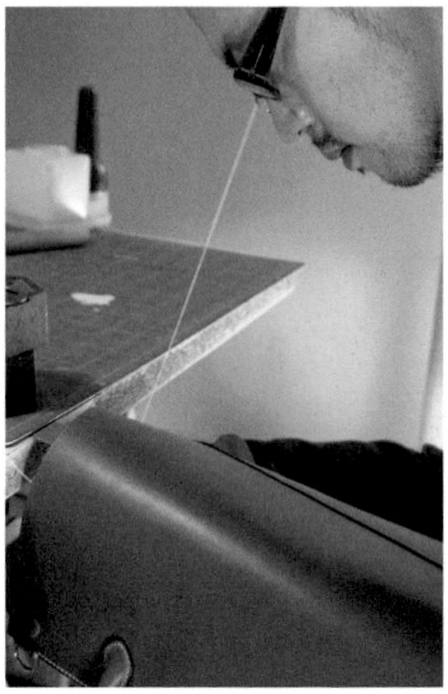

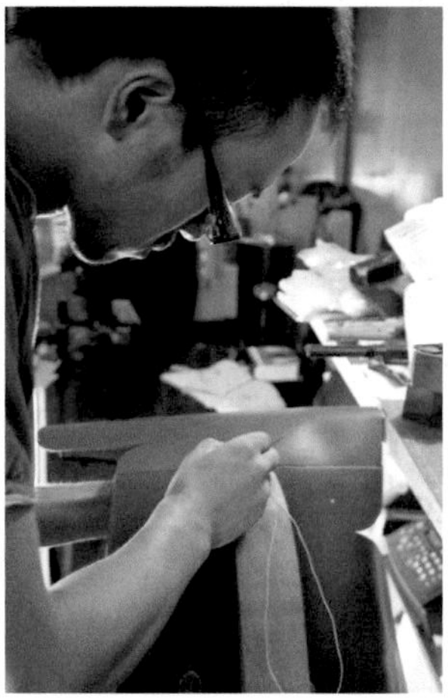

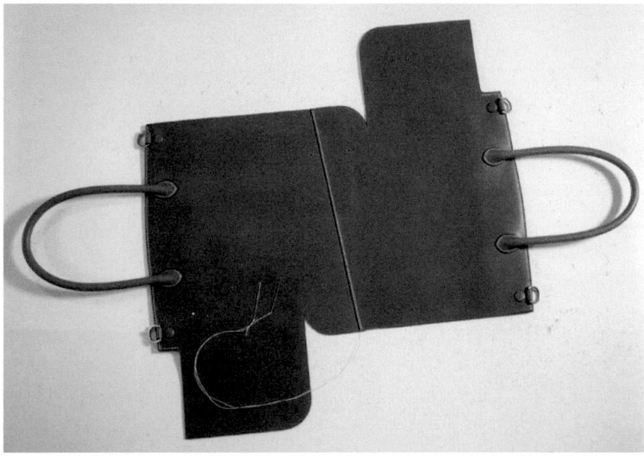

16. Sewing the underside.

17. Sticking and fixing the feet onto the base of the bag. Pierce their positions with a hole-puncher and fix the feet into these holes.

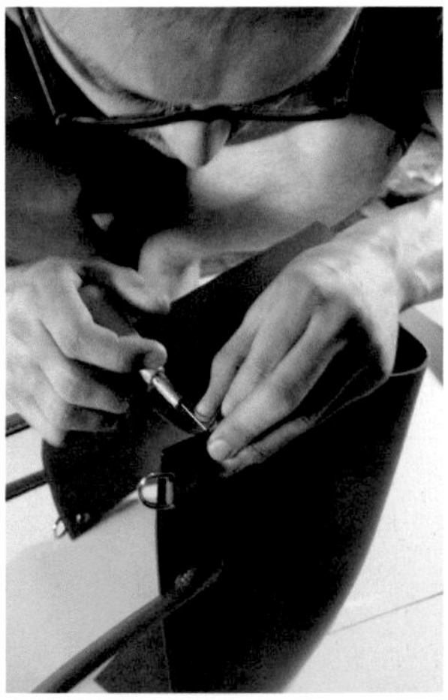
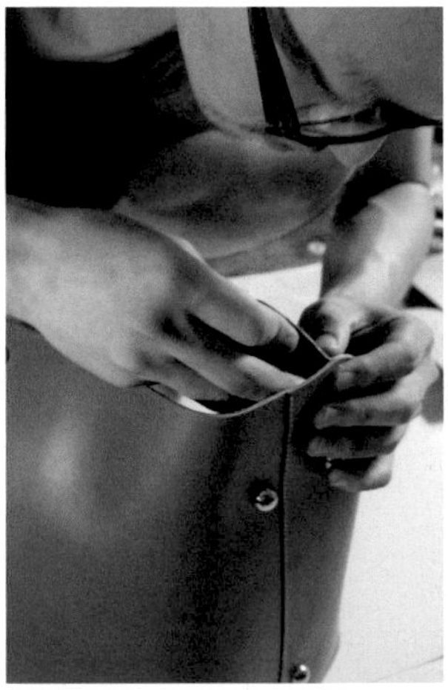
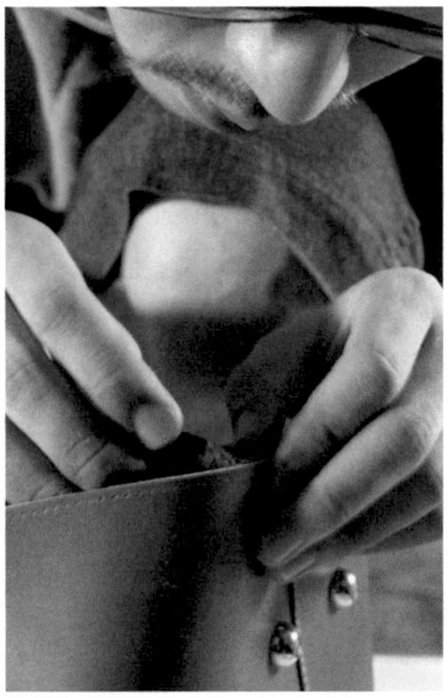

18. Sticking the front and back sides to the gussets. Use a pair of pliers to flatten the seams.

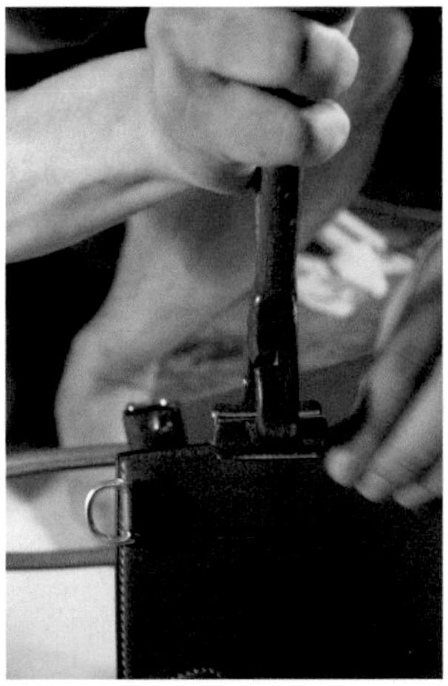
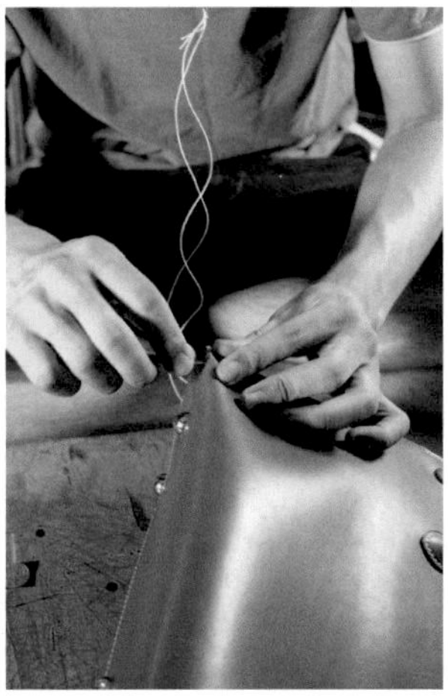
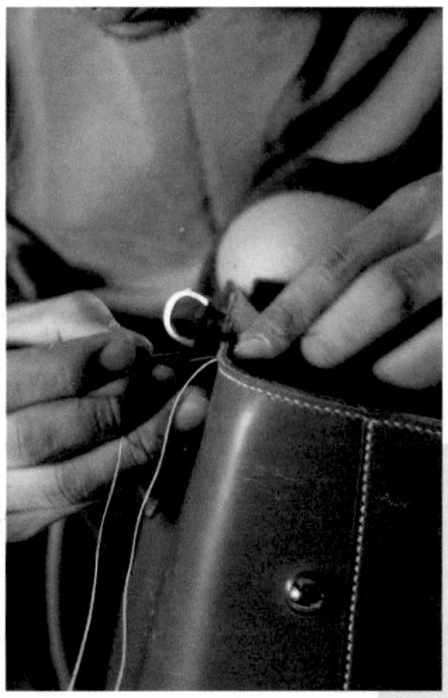

19. Sewing the gussets to the side seams using saddle stitching.

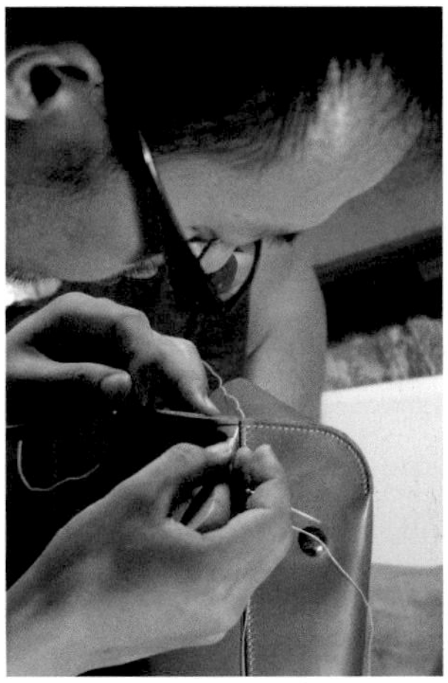
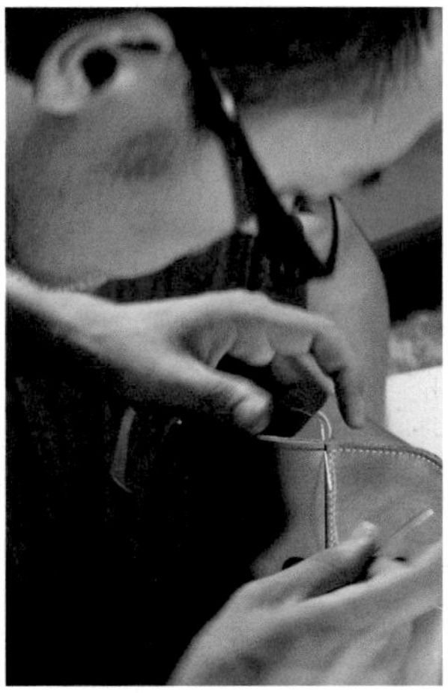
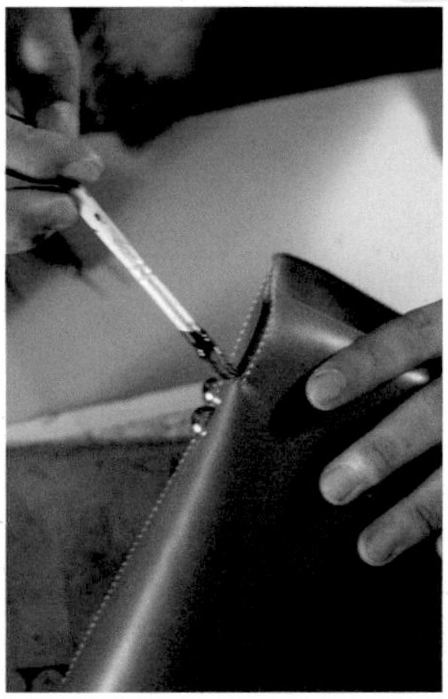

20. Dyeing the seams.

The commercial promotion of a product is essential and, of course, it follows that this rule applies to fashion accessories, as well. A brand's reputation needs to be well-represented. So, in this chapter, we will touch on the principal methods and stages of promotion for brands and their accessories.

The logo is the first sign of a brand's recognition: Ralph Lauren's polo player, Louis Vuitton's LV monogram, Chanel's CC and even Martine Boutron's M&B are all famous symbols which could be likened to a brand's coat-of-arms for the brands.

The same can be said for young, up-and-coming designers and their effect on brands. These young rising stars bring a breath of fresh air and direction to the fashion houses with John Galliano for Dior, Alber Elbaz for Lanvin, Marc Jacobs for Louis Vuitton to name but a few. They have a heavy responsibility to the brands they represent and act as a sort of 'headliner' for the label. Their role is also closely linked to the promotion of the fashion house they represent.

In addition, advertising campaigns are a vital tool in the brand's promotion. Fashion houses employ a host of photographers, illustrators and video makers with some collaborations between famous photographers and prestigious brands becoming legendary. These all contribute to reinforcing these luxury brand names, i.e. Charles Jourdan and Guy Bourdin, Yves Saint Laurent and Helmut Newton, Marc Jacobs and Jurgen Teller.

These type of brands often choose cinema stars to represent them. For example, Carole Bouquet and Chanel's jewellery; Vanessa Paradis, Diane Kruger and Anna Mouglalis have all advertised Chanel's leather goods and Scarlett Johansson with the 2007 Vuitton campaign.

International groups such as LVMH (Louis Vuitton, Moet Hennessy) and PPR (Pinault, Printemps, Redoute) also collaborate with artists of great repute. They act as patrons on many levels: for example, they employ artists to design their promotional spaces from time to time – Louis Vuitton being a case in point when he called on Bob Wilson to dress his shop window. Louis Vuitton's *concept shop* on the Champs Elysées in Paris regularly showcases contemporary artists' exhibitions. There are a number of luxury groups who have established contemporary art foundations – The Pinault Foundation, for example, set itself up in Venice and opened a second contemporary art museum. LVMH has invited Frank Gehry, the architect of the Guggenheim Museum in Bilbao, to design his private museum on the Seguin island at Boulogne-Billancourt in the Hauts-de-Seine region of France which is due to open in 2012. These museums have impressive showcases presenting the brands' products to their best. Louis Vuitton's Travel museum at Asnières (Hauts-de-Seine) is a fine example of its brand's image and prestigious past housed in the family home (see Chapter 1, p.14). Equally, the Goyard fashion house fuses antique suitcases with its latest creations to remind us that the brand has existed for decades and figures amongst the most illustrious names in luxury travel goods.

Brands will regularly participate at art shows in order to

Chapter 6 - Sales and promotion

have their image associated with the major cultural events. This type of communication campaign is essential and vital to a brand's success. The festival of *La Mode d'Hyères* in the Var, France, which rewards young designers, invited Christian Lacroix to decorate the roads in the town during the time of the festival.

Window displays are equally important for reaching the greater public and great rivalry ensues in order to achieve original displays which show the merchandise off to its best advantage. Certain designers, such as Alber Elbaz, can construct veritable stage sets. When a designer integrates his work with the décor, as both Karl Lagerfield and Paul Smith have done in the window displays at the Printemps Haussmann store in Paris, the displays can become pure theatre. The presence of live models in window displays have become the norm. To celebrate spring in 2007, the designer Isabelle Marant lit up a window display with effervescent spermatozoa. This unusual use of the display reinforces the idea of collusion between art and fashion. At Hermes, Hilton McConnico, who began by staging temporary exhibitions, has created the whole concept of the brand's latest boutique to be opened in Japan.

Certain brands are very minimal. Dirk Birkenstock and his eco-shoes for example. The concept here is so strong that the message is driven home with a recurring theme (leitmotiv). The same is true with the name of the brand No Name – this is also original and effective, for it radically sets itself apart from other brands. The slogan takes a footmark super-imposed on the brand name and this becomes the principal driving force for its promotional strategy. Mystery arouses curiosity. This is evident with the designer Martin Margiela who refuses to be photographed for the promotion of his brand. This attitude intrigues and attracts the press. Faced with the media over-exposure of top models, he obscures his catwalk models' faces by making them wear masks so that there is more attention placed on the products. This created a powerful media message in itself!

Specialised trade fairs such as Première Classe, le Tranoi and professional showrooms contribute in their own way to a brand's promotion. Today, fashion shows are broadcast simultaneously on the television, as well as over the Internet, which, in turn, helps to advertise the brands worldwide.

We should mention the Comité Colbert. This is an association which represents 68 large, luxury French fashion houses. The committee was created in 1954 by J.-J. Guerlain , the objective of this collective being to promote the members' shared cultural values and highlight the French concept of luxury on a worldwide scale.

In this chapter we look in detail into the necessary means and tools needed for the promotion of a product. We see at what point the role of the agent, and that of the distribution channels, cannot be ignored in the commercialisation process, before analysing the staging of the collections in every visual aspect contributing towards their promotion.

Distribution

1

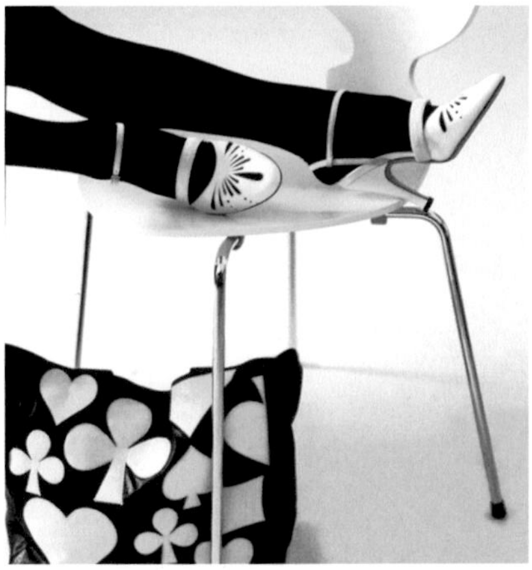
2

3

4

5

6

The predominance of the accessory according to the designer Jean-Philippe Bouyer

'Today, the accessory is an essential and undeniable product in terms of turnover for every level of the range. For the majority of the time, the accessory's turnover is much larger than for *prêt-à-porter*, in particular for the large luxury brands. (For the more accessible brands such as Zara, Mango and H&M, the development of accessories is still a bit behind.) Fashion trends have propelled the accessory to the status of an indispensable product. Each season new brands are born specialising in jewellery, leather goods, shoes etc.

These accessories are sold on different circuits: boutiques, chain stores, large distribution, without forgetting, of course, mail order and over the Internet. The channels of distribution will depend on the brand itself. This may involve a global brand with accessory collections or purely an accessory brand. In both cases, depending on the price point, we have the opportunity of using one, or several methods, of distribution. Large brands such as Chanel, Dior, Hermès, Vuitton etc. present the accessory benefiting from their already existing image. These lines have several avenues of distribution available to them : flagship boutiques and large department stores with their specialist counters, generally dedicated around the accessory but also the duty free shops. On the other hand, some brands propose only accessories - Goyard with its suitcases and leather goods; Charles Jourdan, Longchamps and his hand bags; Christian Louboutin with his shoes and bags etc. are just a few examples of this. These brands are also promoted in flagship boutiques and counters of department stores.

Accessory sales are becoming more and more specialised. The design studios study the collections very closely and this is particularly important within the brands. There is also particular attention paid to the price point. An accessory can now be likened to perfume as a commodity – a product which is within the grasp of a greater number of clients, which can be considered as a part of a dream which someone can buy.

The potential client's profile will determine the means of distribution. For example, with a shoe, the flagship store will be the most favoured option. As the market is very competitive, a good deal of planning and rigorous organisation will be necessary. Rules of sale are conditioned by the brands' and distributors' respective financial power; the power struggle can therefore vary considerably. One or other's margins of manoeuvre are directly linked to their financial capacity and investment.'

7

Accessory counters

Large department stores place more and more emphasis on their accessory counters. These spaces are dedicated to a brand or a designer revealing that this is a particularly efficient method of distribution. Nowadays, these counters are generally found on the ground floor of these stores and, more often then not, are entirely reserved to accessories and are the most visited areas.

The promotion of visual supports are also taken care of by the large stores. For example, the *look books* are a sort of synopsis of the visuals representative of the collections. The accessory lends itself perfectly to a still-life style, which has been represented on this page by colour combinations. Luxury labels can be shown together on the same photo.

It should be note that department stores will often take advantage of these counters to introduce their own accessory collections within the world of the big brands.

1. *Cut-away back with hand bag.* Mint dress, Babe bag and Maliparmi ring.

2. *Black and white.* Robert Normand sandals and Delphine Pariente bag.

3. *Flamingos.* Lulu Guinness hat, shoes and bag, Le Bon Marche scarf, Mademoiselle de la Brindille necklace.

4. *Balloons and Shoes.* Shoes by Rupert Sanderson, Le Bon Marche, Lulu Guinness, jewellery by Zuwa, Rada and Exquisites.

5. *Mosaic Chairs.* Bags by Rows, Patch and Omnia., Irregular Choice mules and Omnia hat.

6. *White-Blue Gloves.* Le Bon Marche tank top and tee-shirt, Jean Yanuk, Agnelle fingerless gloves.

7. *Yellow Fingernails.* Hybris tee-shirt, Le Bon Marche shorts, Medecine Douce belt, Fischer fingerless-gloves, Marc Jacobs' ballet pumps, Medecine Douce key rings, Francesco Biasia bag, Le Bon Marche scarf.

1 to 7. Photos by Stephan Schopferer, extracts from Bon Marché's 2005-06 press releases.

The agent

The ideal agent

An agent is the brand's contractual ambassador in one, or several, countries. If there is an exclusivity clause in the contract, every transaction which is made in these countries' domestic markets must pass by the agent's office.

Foreign distribution implies two choices which are of equal importance: the choice of accessory, in relation to a particular country, and the choice of agent, depending on the accessory to be promoted. The agent, who must be well-integrated into the country and possess a perfect working knowledge of the market, needs to make his network of contacts available to the brands he represents. The quality of his office, showrooms, database and financial and marketing means are a determining factor. It is also important to check the legal status of the company and to find out about the human resources the agent has at his disposal and on the solvency of his clients.

It is essential that the agent possesses a good understanding of the brands he will be representing, as well as their objectives and outcomes.

According to Charles Raith, an accessory agent in Japan, to be able to work in this world, the agent must, first of all, love women and naturally accessories. He must possess a good understanding of fashion culture and be a convincing story-teller: i.e. know how to explain the origins of a product, the materials, manufacturing processes etc.

The agent's jobs

The agent must be in tune with current fashion and be in close contact with the key decision-makers and the buyers. This work demands great rigour: it is recommended, for example, that the agent keeps a client's dossier which includes all the relevant information concerning his or her profile. In conjunction with this, regular client visits are necessary where new trends, and even samples, are bought to their attention. These repeated points of contact help establish links between the agent and the client, building up a good working relationship. This way, the agent can gain quick and efficient access to distribution channels. He must be the first to present his products onto the market, offering a faultless service and always remain at the client's disposition.

The agent can work in a variety of ways: he can be exclusive, or not, importing and distributing the products himself or, on the other hand, not import the goods but find clients who are willing to import the products themselves.

The remuneration is therefore very different depending on what kind of contract is established. If the agent imports the goods himself, he can then control the brand's image and the retail price, which in turn will ensure a harmonious relationship. In Japan, the professional clientele are very sensitive to retail prices which must remain the same across the national market. It is therefore recommended for a brand to confine itself to an agent who is experienced and able to control the image and retail prices. Numerous cosmetic brands have to deal with imports that are in strong competition with their own internal circuit which undercut them and destabilise the official distribution channels.

The agent's networks

The agent works with a multitude of professionals and essential partners.

In the case of large department stores, the counters are dedicated to various brands, with any potential financial risk being their own responsibility. It is the profitability of these spaces (per square metre) which will determine whether the counter is viable or not. These stands will also include a designer's showcase.

Wholesalers are rapidly disappearing due to modern communication means - principally to the Internet - and are no longer an essential cog in the distribution wheel.

Multi-brand boutiques or 'select shops' - such as *Maria Luisa, L'Éclaireur, Montaigne Market* - have a reputation for breaking new ground with interesting products and showcasing fashion accessories.

Flagship stores - or single-brand boutiques - are nowadays the surest way of distributing a product.

The duty free shops are the most difficult means for relatively unknown brands. Nevertheless, they provide an important distribution network for accessories and cosmetics for the better known brands.

The market for company presents - which is very big in Japan - represent more than 25 % of the accessory market with competitive prices in large quantities.

Big holding companies which already possess fashion labels such as Kashiyama, Itokin, Itochu, are always looking for new ideas and help other brands to establish themselves by signing contracts which include manufacturing and distribution licences, in particular in Japan and the United States.

Marketing

Let us take a look at the essential point that is marketing. It is important to define a product in view of its creation and place in the market. Market research needs to be professionally carried out in order to analyse whether a market, in fact, exists for a particular product. Another study is then necessary to define the product's target audience and potential clientele. It is at this point that the agent puts his knowledge of the market into practice. He instigates and drives the market research which is led by his staff, or by an independent market research company.

It is vital that an agent knows his product well. Part of the brand's marketing budget is reserved for the agents so that they can promote it through their own markets. It is important that the agent and the brand work together on these points so as to develop the best promotion for the brand. It is also imperative that the results of this advertising are regularly monitored in relation to the objectives which have already been fixed by the brand.

Presentation

1

2

Window concepts

Brands pay particular attention to the design and creation of their boutiques' windows. The creative directors are very involved in researching ideas for this and more often than not, they follow their creation very closely. This is very much the case with Alber Elbaz at Lanvin.

Whatever the price level, the window displays represent the brand's image. H&M and Zara, for example, make the most out of their image with the product settings for their windows. Accessories occupy a large part of their external window display area but are also evident with their inside displays, i.e. on podiums etc. Every label dedicates entire window spaces for accessories and visual communication, specifically for advertising campaigns and it is proven that the strength of a brand's window display has a real impact on customers and turnover.

Certain window displays have acquired a great reputation and deserve a special visit, such as those of the Hermès store on rue du Faubourg-Saint-Honoré which have been styled by Leila Menchari for many years now. This stylist uses opulence and originality to make each setting a real event whilst at the same time endorsing the quality and luxury of this great fashion house.

A brand's window displays are designed in relation to the visuals used for their advertising campaigns. They are often all working on the same theme together in order to increase the impact and coherence of the brand. To keep things fresh, they are changed very regularly and are unveiled as soon as new products hit the store. Several times a year, the large stores make special window displays specifically for accessories.

Displays

Each type of accessory requires research for original props and display cases. These elements are chosen in relation to the particular look of a boutique, seasonal themes and, of course, the product which is to be presented. A *totem* can be used to display a necklace, like in the adjacent photo of Loulou de la Falaise's jewellery (fig. 3).

Martine Boutron wanted to create a special atmosphere with her products (figs 1 and 2). The stylist made a display which recreated the feel of a workshop, where a blow torch and the different tools necessary for jewellery manufacture are used as props for the presentation.

3

1 and 2. Display recreating a jeweller's workbench by Martine Boutron.

3. Loulou de la Falaise window display of jewellery items in wood, shells, mother of pearl, with brooches in *pate de verre* and crystal glass presented on Chinese lacquered red support.

Advertising campaign visuals

1

2

3

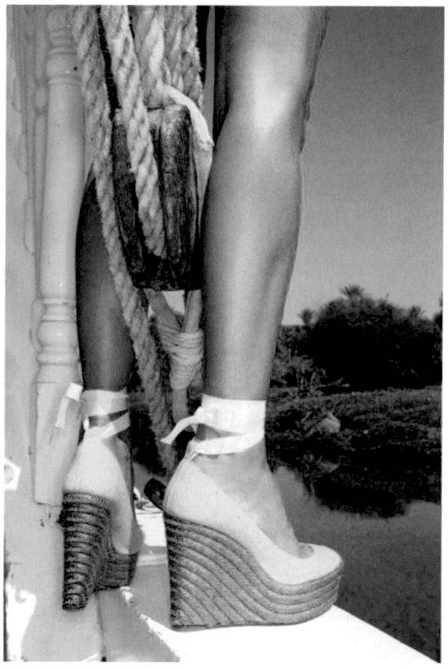

4

Everyday brands invest more and more in publicity to make their image more noticeable. The sector reserved for accessories is also constantly growing. Accessory visuals are considered and developed in relation to the type of object to be promoted i.e. spectacles, handbags, shoes etc. and they also make up an integral part of a brand's press book or catalogue. Fashion magazines such as *Vogue, L'Officiel, Elle, Marie Claire* etc. now possess special editions which are dedicated to accessories, as well as out-of-series seasonal editions. In these publications accessories are presented as snapshots, as close-ups at fashion shows, or as 'still lives'.

Each season, press books are produced for the new collections. These

5

6

are primarily destined for the journalists. In order to set themselves apart from other stylists and to attract the attention of editors, the designers call on top photographers to style their products their best advantage. In Figures 5 and 6, Helena Zubeldia's jewellery is presented on a model. The choice of obscured lighting and zoom photography on the jewellery helps to accentuate the product.

Photographers and creative directors intensify their efforts to try and come up with original and unusual ideas. Nowadays, celebrities are frequently used to promote a particular brand from which they will receive a large remuneration. Examples of this include Longchamp with Kate Moss and Chanel with Vanessa Paradis, who were engaged to solely promote their handbag lines.

If, globally, the accessory photo appeals to easily understood stereotypes, important names in photography will remain forever associated with the big brands such as Guy Bourdin and Charles Jourdan, for example. Peter Lindbergh has also worked on several publicity campaigns, most notably with David Yurman's jewellery. This photographer is internationally known for his artistic fashion and accessory photography which emulates realism and lacks pretension. We should also mention photographers such as, Mario Testino, with the renaissance of the Gucci label in the 1990s, Jean Lariviere for Louis Vuitton and Bruce Weber for Calvin Klein.

Lady Rouge shoes by Christian Louboutin, Summer 2006.

Miss Marple Red shoes by Christian Louboutin, summer 2006.

Gwenissima shoes in golden and natural leather by Christian Louboutin, Summer 2006.

Formetera Rose shoe by Christain Louboutin. Summer 2006.

5 and 6. Visuals from Helene Zubeldia's internet site.

Fashion illustrations

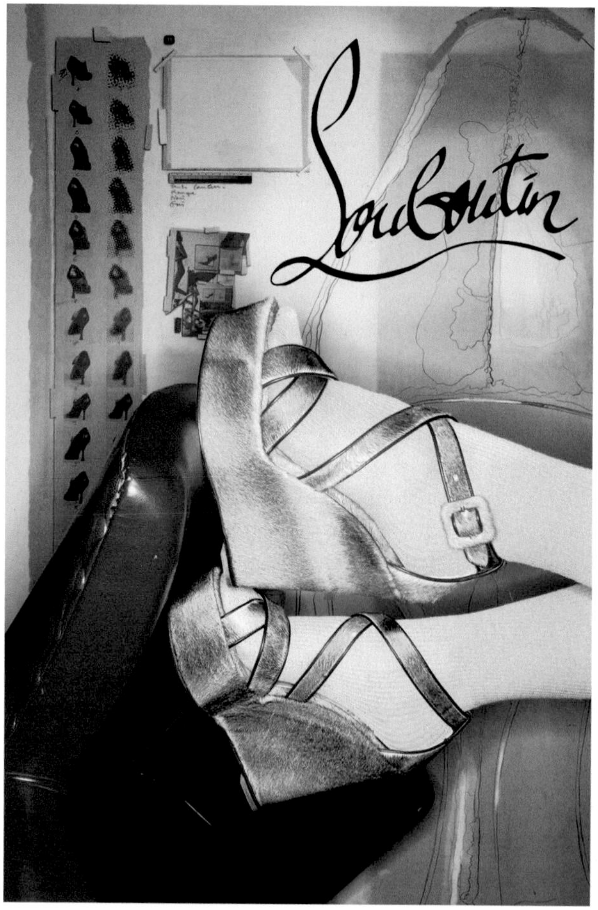

1

Although photography remains the most used means of communication for advertising, illustration, nevertheless, constitutes a choice of expression favoured for the presentation of the products. The association between illustration and photography generally reinforces the identity and original impact of a brand, as we can see with Christian Louboutin's publicity in Figure 1 where the shoe is reworked by drawing (behind the photo). The singularity of a drawing is sometimes more effective in communicating the spirit of a name. Andy Warhol started his career as a fashion illustrator and his accessories drawings bear witness to this.

Manolo Blahnik uses illustrations to promote his shoes to press magazines. The designer Alexandra Neel has also used illustrations on some of her styles (see fig. 3).

René Gruau, who was associated with the house of Christian Dior in the 1950s, became well-known for his illustrations for the brand's communication campaigns. Still with Dior, John Galliano uses his personal collages as publicity visuals.

The amount invested by a brand for an illustration however is very often lower than that which is spent on a photographic visual. Some designers prefer to gamble on using illustrators to promote their product. An example being Loulou de la Falaise who invited the illustrator Elie Top to portray her jewellery range for the 2003-2004 Aautumn-Winter press release, using herself as the muse (fig. 5).

Fashion journalists will sometimes use illustrators to liven up their articles. In the 1980s Nicole Pibault collaborated with the magazine *Marie-Claire* for a long time and Antoine Kruk, whose illustrations are shown in Figures 2 and 4, has notably worked with the *Stiletto* magazine.

4

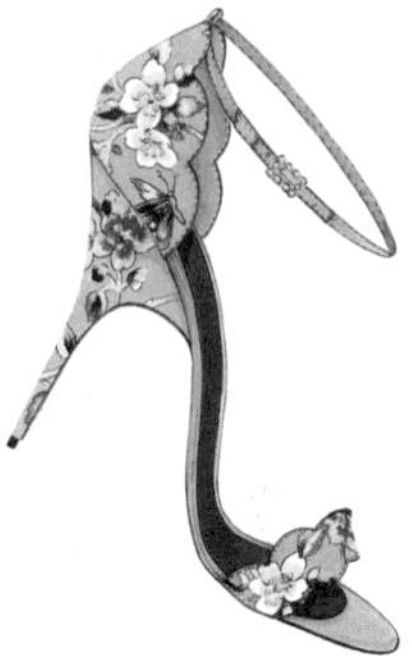

3

2

Nacre et perles
de Tahiti, Poteries
d'Afrique, Laque
de Chine, Pierres
du Rajasthan
tous les
Soleils
du
monde
!!!!

5

1. *VIVA ZEPPA* SHOES BY CHRISTIAN LOUBOUTIN, AUTUMN-WINTER 2005-6.

2. HANDBAG ILLUSTRATION BY ANTOINE DE KRUK MADE ESPECIALLY FOR THIS BOOK.

3. ALEXANDRA NEEL, ILLUSTRATION FOR A PRESS PRESENTATION INVITATION CARD, SPRING-SUMMER 2005.

4. COORDINATED HANDBAG AND ACCESSORIES ILLUSTRATED BY ANTOINE DE KRUK FOR THIS BOOK.

5.ILLUSTRATION REPRESENTING LOULOU DE LA FALAISE BY ELIE TOP.

Appendices

Accessory directory

Shops and suppliers

Button Queen (buttons etc.)
19 Marylebone Lane
London W1U 2NF
020 7435 1505
www.thebuttonqueen.co.uk

Cyril Leathergoods (leather products)
127 Regent Street
London W1B 4HU
020 7734 3181

Cyril Leathergoods (leather products)
The Ritz Arcade
Piccadilly
London W1J 9BT
020 7629 5015

Electrum (jewellery)
21 South Molton Street
London W1K 5QZ
020 7629 6325
www.electrumgallery.co.uk

Lesley Craze Gallery (jewellery)
34 Clerkenwell Green
London EC1R 0DU
020 7608 0393
www.lesleycrazegallery.co.uk

Liberty (ribbons, trimmings etc.)
Great Marlborough Street
London W1B 5AH
020 7734 1234
www.liberty.co.uk

London Bead Shop (beads)
24 Earlham Street
London WC2H 9LN
020 7279 9214
www.beadshop.co.uk

Swarovski (gems and crystals)
411 Oxford Street
London W1
020 7499 4221
www.swarovski.com

Drawing suppliers

Cass Art
13 Charing Cross Road
London WC2H 0EP
020 7930 9940
www.cass-arts.co.uk

L. Cornelissen & Son
105 Great Russell Street
London WC1B 3RY
020 7636 1045
www.cornelissen.com

Cowling & Wilcox
26-28 Broadwick Street
London W1F 8HX
020 7734 9556
www.cowlingandwilcox.com

London Graphic Centre
16-18 Shelton Street
London WC2H 9JL
020 7759 4500
www.londongraphics.co.uk

Studio and boutique equipment

MacCulloch & Wallis
25-26 Dering Street
London W1S 1AT
020 7629 0311
www.macculloch-wallis.co.uk

Morplan
56 Great Titchfield Street
London W1W 7DF
020 7636 1887
www.morplan.com

Sundries

Button Queen
47 Berwick Street
London W1F 8SJ
020 7437 5155
www.thebuttonqueen.co.uk

McCulloch & Wallis
25-26 Dering Street
London W1S 1AT
020 7629 0311
www.macculloch-wallis.co.uk

V.V. Rouleaux
54 Sloane Street
London SW1W 8AX
020 7730 3125
www.vvrouleaux.com

V.V. Rouleaux
94 Miller Street
Glasgow G1 1DT
0141 221 2277
www.vvrouleaux.com

Useful addresses

British Fashion Council
5 Portland Place
London W1B 1PW
020 7636 7788

Fashhion schools

France

Atelier Chardon Savard
BTS Stylisme de mode
15, rue Gambey
75011 Paris

Chambre syndicale de la couture parisienne
Formations aux métiers artistiques (École)
45, rue Saint-Roch
75001 Paris

École Camondo (design et décoration d'intérieur)
266, boulevard Raspail
75014 Paris

École C-SIX-DOUZE
École supérieure privée art et design
44 bis, rue Lucien-Sampaix
75010 Paris

École Duperré
BTS Mode-Textile, DMA Arts textiles
11, rue Dupetit-Thouars
75003 Paris

École Grégoire-Ferrandi
28, rue de l'Abbé-Grégoire
75006 Paris
Tél. : 01 49 54 28 00
www.egf.ccip.fr

ENSAAMA Olivier de Serres
BTS Art textile et Impression
63-65, rue Olivier-de-Serres
75015 Paris

ESMOD
École supérieure privée de création de mode
12, rue La Rochefoucauld
75009 Paris

LISAA
13, rue Vaucquelin
75005 Paris

Lycée Auguste Renoir
Arts appliqués (spécialisation Industrie de l'habillement, prépa BT)
24, rue Ganneron
75018 Paris

Lycée Choiseul
BTS Arts appliqués - Stylisme de mode
78, rue des Douets
39095 Tours

Lycée de la mode
BTS Stylisme de mode
20, rue du Carteron
49321 Cholet

Studio Berçot
29, rue des Petites-Écuries
75010 Paris

Belgium

Académie royale des beaux-arts d'Anvers
Blindestraat 9
2000 Anvers
Flanders Fashion Institute

Mode Natie
Nationale Straat
Drukkerijstraat
Anvers

Hogeschool Antwerp
Fashion Departement
Nationalestraat 28/3
2000 Antwerp (Anvers)

La Cambre
École supérieure d'arts visuels
21, Abbaye de la Cambre
1000 Bruxelles

UK

Central Saint Martin's College of Art and Design
School of Fashion and Textiles
107-109 Charing Cross Road
Londres WC2H 0DU

Edinburgh College of Art
Lauriston Place
Edinburgh EH3 9DF

Kingston University
School of Fashion
Knights Park
Kingston upon Thames
Surrey KT1 2 QJ

London College of Fashion
20 John Princes Street
London W1M 0BJ

Manchester Metropolitan University
Faculty of Art & Design
Ormond Building
Ormond Street
Manchester M15 6BH

Middlesex University
School of Fashion and Textiles
Cat Hill
Barnet
Hertfordshire EN4 8HT

Royal College of Art
School of Fashion and Textiles
Kensington Gore
London SW7 2EU

University of Brighton
School of Design - Fashion Textiles
Grand Parade, Brighton
East Sussex BN2 2U

University of Newcastle-upon-Tyne
Department of Fine Art
5 Kensington Terrace
Newcastle-upon-Tyne NE4 7SA

USA

Parsons School of Design
560 Fashion Avenue
New York, NY 10018

Japan

Bunka Fashion College
3-22-1 Yoyogi Shibuya-Ku Tokyo

Doreme Sugino Gakuen
4-6-19 Oosaki Shibuya-Ku Tokyo

ESMOD Japon
3-29-6 Ebisu Shibuya-Ku Tokyo

Mode Gakuen
1-6-2 Nishishinjuku Shibuya-Ku Tokyo

Vantan Design Institute
3-9-4 Ebisu-Minami Shibuya-Ku Tokyo

Recruitment sites for fashion professional

www.abc-luxe.com
www.bethe1.com
www.fashionjob.fr
www.ks-interim.com
www.lejournaldutextile.com
www.modefashion.com
www.modemonline.com
www.profilmode.com

Recruitment agencies

Chantal Baudron
61, boulevard Haussman
75008 Paris
www.chantal-baudron.fr

Fashion Expert
54, rue du Faubourg-Montmartre
75009 Paris
Tél. : 01 44 63 13 52

Floriane de Saint-Pierre
134, rue du Faubourg-Saint-Honoré
75008 Paris

Kate Sasson conseil
21, rue Cambon
75001 Paris
www.katesansson.com

Janou Pakter
4, rue du Faubourg-Saint-Honoré
75008 Paris
Tél. : 01 45 23 18 54

Interim Nation
75, boulevard de Picpus
75012 Paris
Tél. : 01 43 45 50 00
www.interim-nation.fr

Intouch (Caroline Pavaux)
400, rue Saint-Honoré
75001 Paris

Manpower Couture
42, rue Washington
75008 Paris
Tél. : 01 56 59 32 70

Modelor
18-20, rue Daunou
75002 PARIS
www.modelor.fr

Proman Paris Saint-Lazare
2, rue de l'Isly
75008 Paris
Tél. : 01 53 42 18 30
www-poman-interim.com

Sterling (Michael Boroian)
1, rue François-Ier
75008 Paris
Tél. : 01 55 73 30 00

Vedior bis couture
120, boulevard Diderot
72012 Paris
Tél. : 01 43 44 32 00

Libraries

Libraries in Paris

Les Archives de la presse
51, rue des Archives
75003 Paris
Tél. : 01 42 72 93 72

Les Arts décoratifs
63, rue Monceau
75008 Paris
Tél. : 01 53 89 06 40

Bibliothèque des Arts décoratifs
107, rue de Rivoli
75001 Paris
Tél. : 01 44 55 57 50

Bibliothèque municipale de la Ville de Paris
Bibliothèque Forney et arts graphiques
Hôtel de sens
1, rue du Figuier
75004 Paris
Tél. : 01 42 78 14 60

French national libraries

Bibliothèque François-Mitterrand
11, quai François-Mauriac
75013 Paris

Bibliothèque Publique d'information – Centre Georges-Pompidou
19, rue Beaubourg
75004 Paris
Tél. : 01 44 78 12 33

Musée Galliera - Musée de la mode de la Ville de Paris
Centre de documentation - bibliothèque
10, avenue Pierre-Ier-de-Serbie
75115 Paris
Tél. : 01 56 52 86 00

Libraries in UK

British Library
96 Euston Road
London NW1 2DB
0870 4441500

Bodleian Library
Cattle Street
Oxford OX1 3BG
01865 277000

Museums

UK

Design Museum
Shad Thames
London SE1 2YD
London SE1 2YD
020 7403 6933

Fashion Museum
Assembly Rooms
Bennett Street
Bath
BA1 2QH
01225 477173

Fashion and Textile Museum
83 Bermondsey Street
London SE1 3XF

National Museum of Costume
Shambellie House
New Abbey
Dumfriesshire
Scotland DG2 8HQ
01387 85037

National Wool Museum
Dre-Fach Felindre
Near Newcastle Emlyn
Llandysul
Carmarthenshire
Wales SA44 5UP
01559 370929

Victoria & Albert Museum
Cromwell Road
London SW7 2RL
020 7942 2000

France and Spain

Centre Pompidou
19, rue Beaubourg
75004 Paris

Fondation Cartier
261, boulevard Raspail
75014 Paris

Musée des Arts décoratifs de Paris
107, rue de Rivoli
75001 Paris

Musée du Costume de la Ville de Paris
14, avenue de New-York
75016 Paris

Musée Galliera
10, avenue Pierre-Ier-de-Serbie
75016 Paris

Musée de l'Impression sur étoffes
14, rue Jean-Jacques-Henner
BP1468
68072 Mulhouse Cedex

Musée international de la Chaussure
2, rue Sainte-Marie
26100 Romans-sur-Isère
Tél. : 04 75 05 51 81
Courriel : musee@ville-romans26.fr

Musée de la Mode de Marseille
11, La Canebière
13001 Marseille

Musée de la Mode et du Textile
107, rue de Rivoli
75001 Paris

Musée des Tissus et des Arts décoratifs
34, rue de la Charité
69002 Lyon

Museu d'Història del Calçat
Plaça San Felip Neri
Barcelone (Espagne)

Palais de Tokyo
2, rue de la Manutention
75116 Paris

Principal trade fairs

Accessories

Mod'amont
(fournitures pour accessoires) (Paris)
Première classe
(tous les accessoires) (Paris)
Midec (chaussures et maroquinerie)
Mido (lunettes)
Silmo (lunettes)
Bijorca (bijoux)

Leather

Anteprima (Milan)
Le Cuir à Paris
Linea Pelle (accessoires et prêt-à-porter)
(Bologne)
Salon du cuir

Luxury goods

Salon de la Haute Joaillerie (Genève, Suisse)
Salon de l'Horlogerie (Bâle, Suisse)

Knitwear

Expofil (Paris)
Moda In (Milan)
Pitti Filatil (Florence)

Prêt-à-porter

Atmosphère (Hôtel Saint-James, Paris)
Paris sur mode (Paris)
Première classe (Paris)
Ritz (place Vendôme, Paris)
Tranoï (Paris)
Who's next (Paris)
Workshop (Paris)
19 Vendôme (Paris)

Fabrics

Indigo (Lille)
Moda In (Milan)
Première Vision Paris : septembre et mars
Texworld (Paris)
Tissu Premier (Lille) : janvier

Bibliography

Books

Maggy Baum, Chantal Boyeldieu, *Dictionnaire des textiles*, Paris, Éditions de l'industrie textile, 2003.

George Beylerian, Andrew Dent, *Material Connexion - The Global Resource of New and Innovative Materials for Architects, Artists and Designers*, New York, John Wiley & Sons, 2005.

François Boucher, *Histoire du costume en Occident de l'Antiquité à nos jours*, Paris, Flammarion, 1983.

David Bowie, Karl Lagerfeld, Mario Testino, *Dreaming in Print: A decade of Visionnaire*, New York, Éditions 7L (Steidl) 2002.

Farid Chenoune (dir.), *Le cas du sac : histoires d'une utopie portative*, Paris, Le Passage, 2004.

Collectif, *Artenergie*. New York, Ed. Charta, 1998.

Collectif, *Belgian Fashion Design*, New York, Ludion, 1999.

Collectif, *Dictionnaire international de la mode*, Paris, Éditions du Regard, 1994-2004.

Collectif, *Embroidery*, New York, Damiani, 2006.

Collectif, *Fabrica 10 - From chaos to order and back*, Milan, Electa s.p.a., 2004.

Collectif, *Head, Heart & Hips - The Seductive World of Big Active, Verlag*, Berlin, 2004.

Collectif, *Modemuseum. The Fashion Museum*, New York, Ludion, 2003.

Collectif, *Shopping*, New York, Hatje Cantz, 2003.

Collectif, *Technologie du vêtement*, Québec, Guérin, 1999.

Collectif, *The Fashion Generation*, New York, Hatje Cantz, 2006.

Collectif, *Total Living*, New York, Charta, 2002.

Collectif, *Uniform: Order and Disorder*, New York, Charta, 2001.

Maria Luisa Frisa, Stefano Tonchi, *Excess: Fashion and the Underground in the 80's*, New York, Charta / Fondazione Pitti Immagine Discovery, 2004.

Christine Garaud, Bernadette Sautreuil, *Technologie des tissus*, Paris, André Casteilla, 1984.

Pierre Hirsch, *Lexique textile français-anglais*, Metz, Librairie de l'industrie textile, 1994.

Sue Jenkyn Jones, *Le stylisme, guide des métiers*, Paris, Pyramyd, 2005.

Dorling Kindersley, *Le Grand Livre de la couture*, Paris, Hachette, 1997.

Antoine Kruk, *Shibuya Soul*, Archimbaud, 2006.

Didier Ludot, *La Petite Robe noire*, Paris, Assouline, 2001.

Stéphane Marais, *Beauty Flash*, Paris, 7L (Steidl) éditions, 2001.

Pierre Marly, Jean-Claude Margolin, Paul Biérent, *Lunettes et lorgnettes*, Paris, Hoëbeke, 2e éd. 1999.

Isaac Mizrahi, *The Adventures of Sandee the Supermodel*, S&S Editions Comic Book Series, New York, 1997.

Paul-Gérard Pasols, *Louis Vuitton*, La Martinière, 2005.

András Szunyoghy, György Fehér, *Grand Cours d'anatomie artistique*, Cologne, H. F. Ullmann, 2007.

Françoise Tellier-Loumagne, *Mailles, les mouvements du fil*, Genève, Minerva, 2003.

Heidemaria Tengler-Stadelmaier, *La Couture pratique*, Hoenheim, V. A. Burda 2002.

Walter Van Beirendonck, *Mode 2001: Landed-Geland Part I*, New York, Merz, 2002.

Walter Van Beirendonck, *Mode 2001: Landed-Geland Part II*, New York, Merz, 2002

Nadine Vasseur, *Les Plis*, Paris, Le Seuil, 2002.

Veerle Windels, Young Belgian *Fashion Design*, New York, Ludion, 2001.

Fashion trade publications

Bloom
California Apparel News
Daily News Record (DNR)
Fashion Daily News
Fashion Reporter
Journal du textile
Selvedge
Texnews (www.texnews.fr)
Textile View
Tobe Report
View textile
Womens Wear Daily (WWD)

Fashion magazines

20 ans (français)
Another Magazine (anglais)
Another Man (mode homme – anglais)
Arena homme (mode homme – anglais)
Biba (français)
Citizen K (français)
Collezioni (italien)
Crash (français)
Deutsch (Allemagne)
Doingbird (australien)
Elle (international)
Glamour (international)
GQ (mode homme – international)
Harper's Bazaar (international)
ID (anglais)
Jalouse (français)
L'Officiel (français)
L'uomo Vogue (mode homme – italien)
Le Figaro Madame (français)
Marie-Claire (international)
Milk (mode enfant – français)
Muteen (français)
Neo2 (espagnol)
Numéro (français)
Nylon (americain)
Oyster (australien)
Pop (anglais)
Purple (français)
Quest (Allemagne)
Self-Service (français)
Sleek (Allemagne)
Stiletto (français)
Tank (anglais)
Ten (anglais)
Ten Men (version homme – anglais)
V (americain)
V men (version homme – americain)
Visionaire (americain)
Vogue (international)
W (americain)
Wad (français)
Zoo (Allemagne)

Acknowledgements

I would like to thank :

The team at school C-6-12 and the students.

Vincent Le Coz, freelance editor.

Benoît Bonté, Victoria Cahouet, Tomoe Kamiya, Masaya Ito, Steve-Régis N'Sondé, Martine Adrien, Marie-Thérèse Coudert.

External contributor : The designer Sak (unic13sak@gmail.com), Antoine Kruk for his illustrations. David Courtin, Fréderic Cabrera, Stephan Schopferer for his photos.

Textile proffesionals :

Alber Elbaz for his preface, and the following companies : Jeanne Lanvin, Louis Vuitton, Loulou de la Falaise, Yazbukey, Sonia Rykiel, Didier Ludot, Christian Louboutin, Eléna Cantacuzène, Hélène Zubeldia, Philippe Roucou, Kazu Huggler, Martine Boutron, Alexandra Neel, Alexis Mabille, Pierre Marly, Jacques Le Corre, Bethony Vernon, Céline Robert, Charles Jourdan, Sak, Marc Rozier, The Charles Jourdan Shoe museum at Romans and Louis Vuitton's Travel museum at Asnières ;

Didier Ludot for his information on vintage and fashion history, Edouard Schneider, Françoise Plaud for her competition and presentation on the House of Jeanne Lanvin, Loulou de la Falaise for being there, Élisabeth Guers and Jean Philippe Bouyer for their information and text on professional shoe designers and advertising. Satoru Hosoi for making handbag prototypes, Odile Gilbert and Rebecca Leach ;

Le Bon Marché for their visuals.

And, in particular, Anne le Bras, for the interest she has shown in my work, for her collaboration, advice and time dedicated in the making of this book.

Credits

Illustrations

Morgan Cahouet : p. 43

Antoine Kruk : p. 213

Photos

Cover : Stephan Schopferer

Other copyright images in the text :

© Alexandra Neel : photos 11-13, p. 49 ; 15 and 21, p. 50

© Alexis Mabille : photos 9-14, p. 52

© Bethony Vernon : photos 1, 2 and 5, p. 60

© Christian Laboutin : photos on pp. 36-37 ; photos 7-8, p. 44 ; 16, p. 45 ; 6 and 8, p. 49 ; 17, 23 and 24, p. 50 ; 3 and 5, p. 72

© Didier Ludot : photos 3-8, p. 52

© Jacques Le Corre : photos 1-4, p. 56 ; 6, p. 57

© Kazu Huggler : photo 15, p. 45

© Lanvin : photos on pp. 26-27 ; 2, p. 44 ; 2, 3 and 7, p. 48 ; 9 and 10, p. 49 ; 7, 8 and 10, p. 61 ; 1, 2, 6 and 7, p. 72

© Loulou de la Falaise : photos on pp 30-31 ; 24-29, p. 63 ; photo on p. 209

© Martine Boutron : photos 12, p. 45 ; 1 and 2, p. 208

© Odille Gilbert : photo 5, p. 57

© Philippe Roucou : photos 1, 3, 4 and 9, p. 44

© Pierre Marly : photos 5 and 6, p. 54

© Sak : photos on pp. 98-99

© Sonia Rykiel : photos on pp. 34-35 ; 4, 5 and 8, p. 44 ; 11, 13, 14, 17-19, p. 45 ; 1 and 4, p. 48 ; 15, 18-20, 22, p. 50 ; 3, 4 and 6, p. 60 ; 9 and 11, p. 61, photos on p. 81 and 83.

© Ninjin Puntjag, photos on pp. 100-109

© Stehpan Schopferer : photos on pp. 22-23, 38-39 ; 1-4 and 7, p. 55 ; photos on pp. 94-97 and 110-111

© Stephanie : photos on pp. 195-201